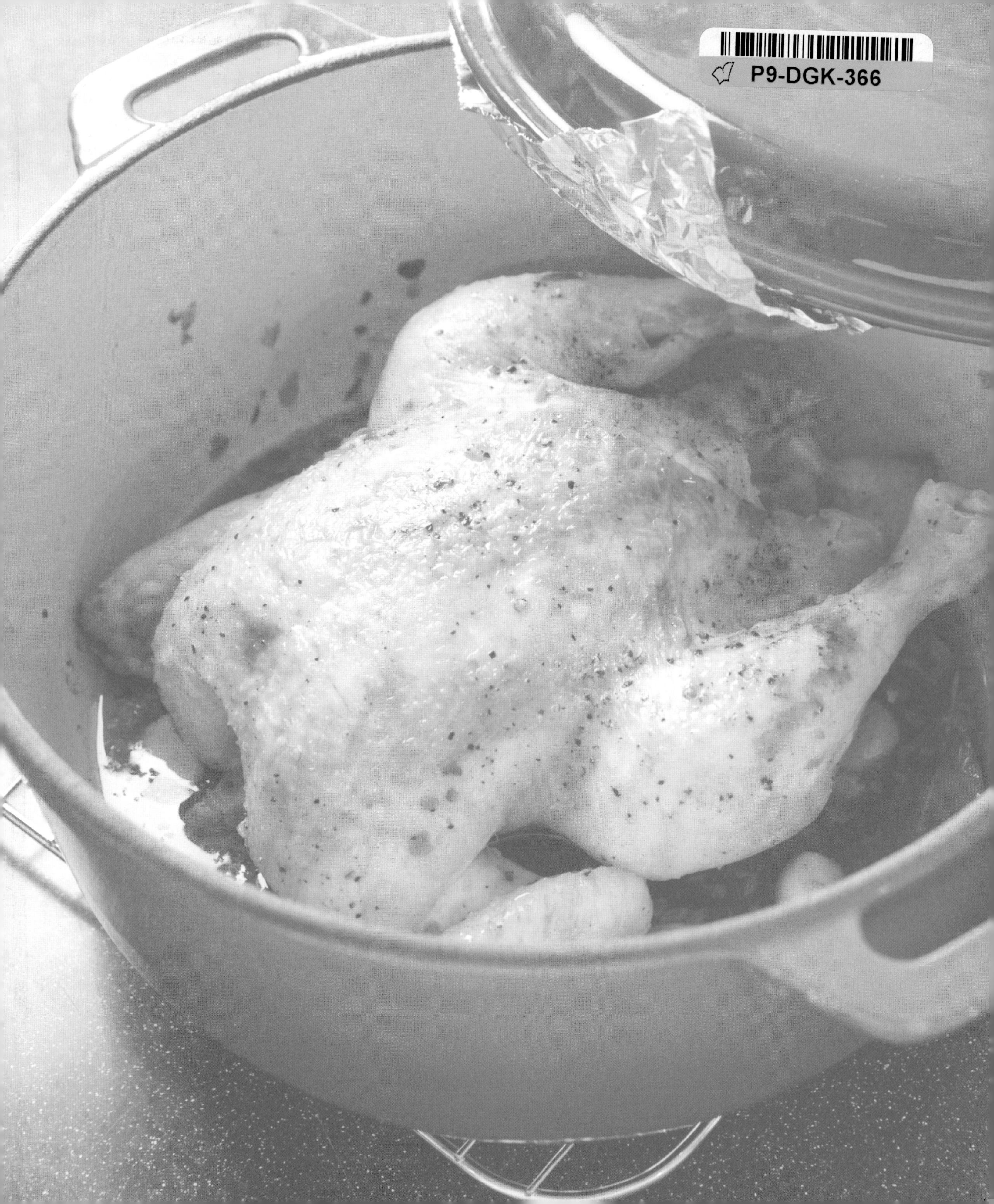

Also by the Editors at America's Test Kitchen

The America's Test Kitchen New Family Cookbook
The Complete Cooking for Two Cookbook
The Cook's Illustrated Baking Book
The Cook's Illustrated Cookbook
The Science of Good Cooking
The America's Test Kitchen Cooking School Cookbook
The America's Test Kitchen Menu Cookbook
The America's Test Kitchen Quick Family Cookbook
The America's Test Kitchen Healthy Family Cookbook
The America's Test Kitchen Family Baking Book

THE AMERICA'S TEST KITCHEN LIBRARY SERIES

The Make-Ahead Cook
The How Can It Be Gluten-Free Cookbook
Slow Cooker Revolution Volume 2: The Easy-Prep Edition
Slow Cooker Revolution
The 6-Ingredient Solution
Pressure Cooker Perfection
Comfort Food Makeovers
The America's Test Kitchen D.I.Y. Cookbook
Pasta Revolution
Simple Weeknight Favorites
The Best Simple Recipes

THE TV COMPANION SERIES

The Complete Cook's Country TV Show Cookbook
The Complete America's Test Kitchen TV Show
Cookbook 2001–2015
America's Test Kitchen: The TV Companion Cookbook
(2002–2009 and 2011–2015 Editions)

AMERICA'S TEST KITCHEN ANNUALS

The Best of America's Test Kitchen
(2007–2015 Editions)
Cooking for Two (2010–2013 Editions)
Light & Healthy (2010–2012 Editions)

THE COOK'S COUNTRY SERIES

From Our Grandmothers' Kitchens
Cook's Country Blue Ribbon Desserts
Cook's Country Best Potluck Recipes
Cook's Country Best Lost Suppers
Cook's Country Best Grilling Recipes
The Cook's Country Cookbook
America's Best Lost Recipes

THE BEST RECIPE SERIES

The New Best Recipe
More Best Recipes
The Best One-Dish Suppers
Soups, Stews & Chilis
The Best Skillet Recipes
The Best Slow & Easy Recipes
The Best Chicken Recipes
The Best International Recipe
The Best Make-Ahead Recipe
The Best 30-Minute Recipe
The Best Light Recipe
The Cook's Illustrated Guide to Grilling and Barbecue
Best American Side Dishes
Cover & Bake
Steaks, Chops, Roasts & Ribs
Italian Classics
American Classics

**FOR A FULL LISTING OF ALL OUR BOOKS OR
TO ORDER TITLES**
CooksIllustrated.com
AmericasTestKitchen.com
or call 800-611-0759

THE COOK'S ILLUSTRATED MEAT BOOK

THE COOK'S ILLUSTRATED

MEAT BOOK

THE GAME-CHANGING GUIDE THAT TEACHES YOU
HOW TO COOK MEAT AND POULTRY WITH 425 BULLETPROOF RECIPES

THE EDITORS AT AMERICA'S TEST KITCHEN

America's
TEST KITCHEN

BROOKLINE, MASSACHUSETTS

America's Test Kitchen
17 Station Street, Brookline, MA 02445

Library of Congress Cataloging-in-Publication Data

The cook's illustrated meat book : the game-changing guide that teaches you how to cook meat and poultry with 425 bulletproof recipes / the editors of America's Test Kitchen.
     pages cm
Includes index.
ISBN 978-1-936493-86-9
1. Cooking (Meat) I. America's Test Kitchen (Firm)
TX749.C66 2014
641.6'6--dc23
                                        2014016170

Hardcover: $40 US

Manufactured in the United States of America
10 9 8 7 6 5 4 3 2 1

Distributed by America's Test Kitchen
17 STATION STREET, BROOKLINE, MA 02445

EDITORIAL DIRECTOR: Jack Bishop
EDITORIAL DIRECTOR, BOOKS: Elizabeth Carduff
EXECUTIVE EDITOR: Lori Galvin
ASSISTANT EDITOR: Melissa Herrick
EDITORIAL ASSISTANTS: Rachel Greenhaus, Samantha Ronan
CONTRIBUTING EDITOR: Elizabeth Emery
DESIGN DIRECTOR: Amy Klee
ART DIRECTOR: Greg Galvan
ASSOCIATE ART DIRECTOR: Taylor Argenzio
DESIGNER: Allison Boales
ILLUSTRATION: John Burgoyne
PHOTOGRAPHY DIRECTOR: Julie Cote
PHOTOGRAPHY: Keller + Keller, Carl Tremblay
STAFF PHOTOGRAPHER: Daniel J. van Ackere
FOOD STYLING: Catrine Kelty, Marie Piraino
PRODUCTION DIRECTOR: Guy Rochford
SENIOR PRODUCTION MANAGER: Jessica Quirk
DIRECTOR, PROJECT MANAGEMENT: Alice Carpenter
PROJECT MANAGER: Britt Dresser
WORKFLOW AND DIGITAL ASSET MANAGER: Andrew Mannone
SENIOR COLOR AND IMAGING SPECIALIST: Lauren Pettapiece
PRODUCTION AND IMAGING SPECIALISTS: Heather Dube, Lauren Robbins
COPYEDITOR: Cheryl Redmond
PROOFREADER: Jane Tunks Demel
INDEXER: Elizabeth Parson

PICTURED ON FRONT OF JACKET: Pepper-Crusted Beef Tenderloin (page 99)

Contents

Welcome to America's Test Kitchen

This book has been tested, written, and edited by the folks at America's Test Kitchen, a very real 2,500-square-foot kitchen located just outside of Boston. It is the home of *Cook's Illustrated* magazine and *Cook's Country* magazine and is the Monday-through-Friday destination for more than four dozen test cooks, editors, food scientists, tasters, and cookware specialists. Our mission is to test recipes over and over again until we understand how and why they work and until we arrive at the "best" version.

We start the process of testing a recipe with a complete lack of preconceptions, which means that we accept no claim, no theory, no technique, and no recipe at face value. We simply assemble as many variations as possible, test a half-dozen of the most promising, and taste the results blind. We then construct our own hybrid recipe and continue to test it, varying ingredients, techniques, and cooking times until we reach a consensus. The result, we hope, is the best version of a particular recipe, but we realize that only you can be the final judge of our success (or failure). As we like to say in the test kitchen, "We make the mistakes, so you don't have to."

All of this would not be possible without a belief that good cooking, much like good music, is indeed based on a foundation of objective technique. Some people like spicy foods and others don't, but there is a right way to sauté, there is a best way to cook a pot roast, and there are measurable scientific principles involved in producing perfectly beaten, stable egg whites. This is our ultimate goal: to investigate the fundamental principles of cooking so that you become a better cook. It is as simple as that.

If you're curious to see what goes on behind the scenes at America's Test Kitchen, check out our daily blog, *The Feed*, at AmericasTestKitchenFeed.com, which features kitchen snapshots, exclusive recipes, video tips, and much more. You can watch us work (in our actual test kitchen) by tuning in to *America's Test Kitchen* (AmericasTestKitchen.com) or *Cook's Country from America's Test Kitchen*

(CooksCountryTV.com) on public television. Tune in to *America's Test Kitchen Radio* (ATKradio.com) on public radio to listen to insights, tips, and techniques that illuminate the truth about real home cooking. Want to hone your cooking skills or finally learn how to bake—from an America's Test Kitchen test cook? Enroll in a cooking class at our online cooking school at OnlineCookingSchool.com. And find information about subscribing to *Cook's Illustrated* magazine at CooksIllustrated.com or *Cook's Country* magazine at CooksCountry.com. Both magazines are published every other month. However you choose to visit us, we welcome you into our kitchen, where you can stand by our side as we test our way to the best recipes in America.

facebook.com/AmericasTestKitchen
twitter.com/TestKitchen
youtube.com/AmericasTestKitchen
instagram.com/TestKitchen
pinterest.com/TestKitchen
americastestkitchen.tumblr.com
google.com/+AmericasTestKitchen

If I told you that we had just published *The Cook's Illustrated Meat Book*, you might be surprised. For one, haven't all the meat recipes you might want (we include chicken here as well) already been published? And isn't everyone turning away from meat toward "healthier" food choices, including fruits and vegetables?

Well, here at America's Test Kitchen, we don't concern ourselves with trends. In fact, we take our cues from our readers, whom we survey almost every day to find out what they want and how they want it. There is no question that meat is still an important part of almost everyone's diet but home cooks are looking for new and better ways to cook it.

So with that in mind, we set out to rethink meat cookery. For extra-crisp chicken skin, we use a rub of salt and baking powder. To poach chicken breasts, we created a soy sauce brine that we also use to poach the breasts. Turkey burgers are made juicy by using dark meat and then incorporating a paste using some of the meat, gelatin, soy sauce, and baking soda. We then mix in chopped raw white mushrooms to improve texture. Thick-cut steaks start in a low oven to get their internal temperature up to 95 degrees and then we finish them with a quick sear—this provides a turbo-charged aging process that increases flavor and tenderness. A third-rate cut, eye round, is transformed into a delicious roast by salting it and letting it rest for 24 hours before roasting at a low oven temperature. We then finish it in the oven after turning off the heat completely. A maple-glazed pork tenderloin is started in a skillet after being coated with cornstarch to hold the glaze and then finished in a moderate oven. And don't get us started on burgers—the best are made with meat ground in a food processor. It takes just a little extra work but they are a whole lot better.

In terms of cooking techniques, we invented the brinerade, which is a marinade that contains salt or a salty ingredient such as soy sauce. You get the flavor benefits of a marinade with the juiciness produced by a brine. Dry salting is now standard practice for many recipes, especially when chicken or turkey skin needs to be crisp or when one is dealing with beef.

We also debunked many meat myths, including the following:

• Searing meat seals in juices: No truth in this whatsoever; it just makes the outside more flavorful.

• Bottled Italian salad dressing makes a good marinade: Nope—it has a strange artificial flavor and the outside of the meat just turns to mush.

• Poultry should be rinsed before cooking: Nope again. This is likely to spread any potential bacteria around your sink. Besides, rinsing will not kill all the bacteria.

• Thaw meat in the fridge: Yes, this works just fine for large roasts but for smaller cuts, like steaks, chops, or chicken breasts, place them in a zipper-lock bag and submerge in 140-degree water. Chicken will thaw in 8 minutes and the other cuts in 12.

I love music and play the guitar. I have found over many years that the more I know, the less I know. At the outset, meat cookery seems easy enough but after 40 years of experience, I know that a better recipe or technique is just around the corner. Hopefully this volume delivers more than a few recipes that fit that bill.

That reminds me of the story of the city feller who was visiting our small Vermont town. He stopped at the Wayside Country Store and asked whether someone could direct him to the old covered bridge across the Battenkill River. The proprietor replied, "Yup, I could. But I don't know if you would ever make it!"

So, yes, I could just go on and on about our technique and recipes but perhaps the best way to enjoy this book is for me to stop talking and for you to start cooking. I am confident, unlike that old-time Vermonter, that you will "make it!"

Cordially,
Christopher Kimball
Founder and Editor
America's Test Kitchen

Meat Essentials

Shopping

You can buy meat from a butcher, a supermarket, a big box store, and even from some farmers' markets. Here's what to look for no matter where you shop for meat.

Pay Attention to Temperature

Cleanliness is essential, but temperature is important, too. Is the packaging cool to the touch? Even at the farmers' market, meat should be stored under 40 degrees. On especially hot days, take advantage of your market's insulated shopping bags (or pack an insulated cooler bag—the type used to keep lunches cool). Of course, you can also keep a cooler in the trunk of your car. If you have a lot of items on your grocery list, make the meat counter one of your last stops, so the meat stays cooler until you can get it home.

Looks Matter

Meat should look moist but not sodden. For example, an excessive amount of juices inside a meat package, also called purge, can be an indication that the meat has been on the shelf too long. As for color, red meat will appear mahogany or purplish when butchered but the flesh will turn bright red or pink once exposed to oxygen. Meat that has turned brown all the way through is on its way to spoiling. Avoid meat that has green spots—this is an indication of spoilage and bacteria. Additionally, examine a meat's texture when shopping: It should have a tight, even grain. A broken grain can indicate poor handling. Likewise, note that packaged parts, whether pork chops, chicken breasts, or steaks, may be of varying sizes and thicknesses, which will have an adverse effect on cooking times. If possible, buy parts individually so you can make sure they're of similar size and thus will cook through at the same rate.

Fat Is Flavor

Streaks of white throughout meat, especially beef, are an indication of marbling. The marbling is fat and adds flavor to meat. Don't confuse marbling with gristle. Gristle, which is often translucent rather than white, is connective tissue and does not break down upon cooking. Note that some exterior fat is desirable, especially when selecting roasts. In the oven or on the grill, this fat will melt and flavor the meat. This is especially important when selecting relatively lean cuts like pork loin or beef brisket. However, excessive exterior fat will need to be trimmed from roasts, steaks, and chops, and since you're buying meat by the pound, more than ½ inch of exterior fat is generally less than ideal.

Use Your Nose

You know how fresh fish shouldn't smell overtly fishy? The same goes for meat. Truly fresh meat should have little aroma. Any strong off-odors or sour odors indicate spoilage.

MEAT LABELS DECODED

Does "pasture-raised" mean that the beef you're buying came from a cow that spent its days roaming a bucolic field? That may not exactly be the case. Here are just a few terms that we think require a bit more explanation. (See individual chapters for more information on meat labeling.)

Pasture-Raised

The term "pasture-raised" is not regulated by the U.S. Department of Agriculture (USDA) and is not clearly defined in the industry. As with the term "free-range" (used for poultry and eggs), the animals' access to a pasture may be extremely limited. (Read more about poultry labeling on page 345.) Note also that geography may affect the duration of pasture-raising; animals in colder climates might spend less time in the pasture than those in more temperate areas. A "pasture-raised" label can be an indication of quality, but to be sure, you should ask the producer how they define the term.

No Hormones and No Antibiotics

While beef may be labeled "no hormones administered" if the producer can provide documentation proving that the animal wasn't raised with hormones, the USDA prohibits the use of hormones (and steroids) with both poultry and pork. The agency requires that if a "no hormones" label is used, it must be followed by the statement, "Federal regulations prohibit the use of hormones." In short, the label is an empty reassurance since the practice is prohibited for pork and poultry.

Like the "no hormones" label, the term "no antibiotics" can be applied if the producer provides documentation that the animal was not raised with antibiotics.

Natural

"Natural" simply means that the meat was minimally processed and contains no artificial ingredients. The USDA defines minimally processed meat as meat "processed in a manner that does not fundamentally alter the product." Our advice is to stick to buying your meat fresh if possible and skip the frozen food aisle, where there's probably not much natural about frozen sliced sandwich "steak," chicken nuggets and patties, and bags of frozen meatballs.

Organic

In contrast to "natural," the USDA's definition of "organic" is a bit more involved: Organic food is produced by farmers who emphasize the use of renewable resources and the conservation of soil and water to enhance environmental quality for future generations. Organic meat, poultry, eggs, and dairy products come from animals that are given no antibiotics or growth hormones. Organic food is produced without using most conventional pesticides; fertilizers made with synthetic ingredients or sewage sludge; bioengineering; or ionizing radiation. Before a product can be labeled "organic," a government-approved certifier inspects the farm where the food is grown to make sure the farmer is following all the rules necessary to meet USDA organic standards. A farm must use organic processes for three years before it can become accredited.

Storage

Keep It Cold

Meat should be refrigerated promptly after purchase. A refrigerator thermometer will tell you if your fridge and freezer are working properly. Check the temperature of your refrigerator regularly to ensure that it is between 35 and 40 degrees; your freezer should be below zero degrees.

Keep in mind that the back of a refrigerator is the coldest, while the door is the least cold. Make sure that raw meat is stored well wrapped and never on shelves that are above other food, especially when thawing.

As for freezing meat, in general, meat tastes best when it hasn't been frozen. The slow process of freezing that occurs in a home freezer (as compared with a commercial freezer) causes large ice crystals to form. The crystals rupture the cell walls of the meat, permitting the release of juices during cooking. That said, if you're going to freeze meat, we've found that the best method is to remove it from its packaging, vacuum-seal it or simply wrap it well in plastic, and then place the meat in a zipper-lock bag and squeeze out excess air.

REFRIGERATING AND FREEZING MEAT AND POULTRY

	STORAGE TIME: REFRIGERATOR	STORAGE TIME: FREEZER
Beef, Pork, Lamb, Veal	Fresh cuts and roasts: 3 days Smoked ham and bacon: 2 weeks once opened Ground meat: 2 days Defrosted cuts: 2 days Cooked meat: 2–3 days	About 1 month
Chicken, Turkey	Fresh whole birds or parts: 2 days Ground chicken and turkey: 2 days Defrosted: 2 days Cooked chicken and turkey: 2–3 days	About 1 month

Tips for Vacuum Sealing

Vacuum sealing food for storage can greatly improve shelf life and help maintain quality—but only when done properly. Poorly sealed bags allow oxygen to contact food, speeding spoilage and freezer burn. Here are two tricks to make it more foolproof.

COVER BONES Protruding bones can easily puncture the bag during vacuuming or storage. To prevent this, use plastic wrap to secure a layer of parchment paper to the bones, effectively blunting them.

FOLD BAGS When loading food into vacuum bags, it can be difficult to keep the cut end of the bag free of grease and moisture, two enemies of a proper seal. To guarantee a clean sealing edge, fold back the last 2 to 3 inches of the bag into a cuff. Fill bag, unfold the cuff and seal.

Quick Chilling Tip

When freezing cuts like steaks, pork chops, chicken parts, or small roasts like tenderloins for long-term storage, we like to quick-chill the meat before it goes into the freezer. Why? The faster the meat freezes the smaller the ice crystals. Smaller ice crystals translate into less cellular damage and less loss of juices during cooking. We quick-chill through an ice bath with added salt. Adding salt to an ice bath lowers the freezing point of water and turns the bath into a superfast freezer. How is this possible? When ice and water are combined, the exteriors of the ice cubes immediately start to melt. Dissolving salt in the ice water causes individual salt ions to form. These particles disperse throughout the ice water and physically reduce the tendency of water molecules to form ordered crystals of ice at 32 degrees. In other words, the salt depresses the freezing point of the mixture so that more of the ice cubes turn to liquid. Since ice cubes out of most home freezers can be as cold as zero degrees (the temperature that most home freezers are set to), this process introduces very cold water to the ice bath. In the test kitchen we were able to achieve slushy ice baths with temperatures as low as 17 degrees.

To make an ice bath for quick chilling, combine 1 cup ice, 1 pound salt, and ⅓ cup water, which is enough to quick chill 4 steaks, chops, or chicken parts. Wrap the meat in plastic wrap, place the pieces in a zipper-lock bag, and submerge the bag in the ice, salt, and water. Once the meat is frozen solid (thick cuts will take longer than thin ones), remove the bag from the ice bath and transfer it to the freezer.

Thawing Small Cuts

To prevent the growth of harmful bacteria when thawing frozen meat, we defrost thicker (1 inch or greater) cuts in the refrigerator and place thinner cuts on a heavy cast-iron or steel pan at room temperature; the metal's rapid heat transfer safely thaws the meat in about an hour. But an article by food scientist Harold McGee in the *New York Times* alerted us to an even faster way: Soak cuts such as chops, steaks, and cutlets in hot water. Simply seal chicken breasts, steaks, and chops in zipper-lock bags and submerge the packages in very hot (140-degree) water. Chicken will take less than 8 minutes and the other cuts roughly 12 minutes, both fast enough that the rate of bacterial growth falls into the "safe" category, and the meat doesn't start to cook. (Large roasts or whole birds are not suitable for hot thawing.)

Thawing Large Cuts or Whole Birds

Large roasts or whole birds are best defrosted in the refrigerator. Allow one day for every 4 pounds. A 12-pound turkey requires three days to thaw in the refrigerator. If you need to thaw a large frozen roast or whole bird quickly, leave it wrapped in the original packaging, place it in a large bucket of cold water, and set it in the refrigerator. Plan on 30 minutes of defrosting for every 1 pound; a 12-pound turkey will take about 6 hours.

Food Safety

No one likes to think about getting sick from eating a meal, but cleanliness in the kitchen and taking care when handling food are important steps to preventing foodborne illness.

KEEPING A CLEAN KITCHEN

Wash Your Hands

Washing your hands is one of the best ways to stop the spread of foodborne pathogens. Wash before and during cooking, especially after touching raw meat or poultry. The U.S. Food and Drug Administration recommends at least 20 seconds in hot, soapy water. How long is that? Try singing "Happy Birthday."

Sanitize Your Sink

Studies have found that the kitchen sink contains even more bacteria than the garbage bin (the drain alone typically harbors 18,000 bacteria per square inch). The faucet handle, which can reintroduce bacteria to your hands after you've washed them, is a close second. Depending on factors such as moisture, temperature, and the particular strain of bacteria, microbes can live as long as 60 hours in your kitchen.

We've found that hot, soapy water is amazingly effective at eliminating bacteria. For added insurance, clean the sink and faucet handles frequently with a solution of 1 tablespoon bleach per quart of water (the bleach will also kill off some of those microbes in the drain).

Clean Your Sponges

Whenever possible, use a paper towel or a clean dishcloth instead of a sponge to wipe up. If you do use a sponge, disinfect it. To find the best method, we tried microwaving, freezing, bleaching, and boiling sponges that had seen a hard month of use in the test kitchen, as well as running them through the dishwasher and simply washing them in soap and water. Lab results showed that microwaving and boiling were most effective, but sponges can burn in a high-powered microwave, so we recommend boiling them for 5 minutes.

Clean Your Cutting Boards

Keeping cutting boards clean is a major part of preventing cross-contamination and killing harmful bacteria. We've conducted a number of tests to see if any particular cutting board material is better than another in resisting bacteria growth. While bamboo boards do have natural antimicrobial properties that help kill off bacteria (providing a head start on cleaning), all of the materials we tested came perfectly clean when scrubbed thoroughly with hot, soapy water. If your board is dishwasher-safe, you can put it through the dishwasher, but keep in mind that wooden boards should never go through the dishwasher.

TIPS FOR AVOIDING CROSS-CONTAMINATION

Don't Rinse Meat

Avoid rinsing raw meat and poultry. Contrary to what some cookbooks (or your grandmother) advise, rinsing is more likely to spread contaminants around the sink (and perhaps onto nearby foods like lettuce sitting on the counter) than to send them down the drain. And our kitchen tests failed to demonstrate any flavor benefit to rinsing meat or poultry before cooking.

Put Up a Barrier

Items that come in contact with both raw and cooked food, like scales and platters, should be covered with plastic wrap or aluminum foil to create a protective barrier. Once the item has been used, the wrap—and any bacteria—can be discarded. Similarly, wrapping your cutting board with plastic wrap before pounding meat and poultry will limit the spread of bacteria.

Season Safely

Though bacteria can't live for more than a few minutes in direct contact with salt (which quickly dehydrates bacteria, leading to cell death), it can live on the edges of a box or shaker. To avoid contamination, we grind pepper into a small bowl and then mix it with salt. This way, we can reach into the bowl for seasoning without having to wash our hands every time we touch raw meat or fish. Afterward, the bowl goes right into the dishwasher.

Don't Recycle Used Marinade

Used marinade is contaminated with raw meat juice and is therefore unsafe to consume. If you want a sauce to serve with cooked meat, make a little extra marinade and set it aside before adding the rest to the raw meat.

Seasoning Meat

No matter how well cooked meat is, if it's not properly seasoned it won't taste very good. Contrary to what many people think, seasoning meat is as important before cooking as it is after (see "The Basics of Seasoning: Salt and Pepper" on page 6). You can also use salt (and time) in advance of cooking to improve the texture of many cuts of meat. There are two ways to do this: salting and brining. While salting can be used with a wide variety of meat, brining is preferable for lean poultry and pork.

SALTING

Salting is more convenient than brining (no need to cram a large container of salt water in the fridge), and it won't thwart the goal of crispy skin on poultry or a well-browned crust on steak, chops, and roasts since no moisture is added to their exteriors. When salt is applied to raw meat, juices inside the meat are drawn to the surface. The salt then dissolves in the exuded liquid, forming a brine that is eventually reabsorbed by the meat. The salt changes the structure of the muscle proteins, allowing them to hold on to more of their own natural juices. Salting is the best choice for meats that are already relatively juicy and/or well marbled.

We prefer to use kosher salt for salting because it's easier to distribute the salt evenly. The chart lists the meat items that we typically salt, along with notes on timing and method. If using Morton kosher salt, reduce the amounts listed by 33 percent. (See the shaded box below for more details.)

SALTING MEAT AND POULTRY

CUTS	TIME	KOSHER SALT	METHOD
Steaks, Lamb Chops, Pork Chops	1 hour	¾ teaspoon per 8-ounce chop or steak	Apply salt evenly over surface and let rest at room temperature, uncovered, on wire rack set in rimmed baking sheet.
Beef, Lamb, and Pork Roasts	At least 6 hours or up to 24 hours	1 teaspoon per pound	Apply salt evenly over surface, wrap tightly with plastic wrap, and let rest in refrigerator.
Whole Chicken	At least 6 hours or up to 24 hours	1 teaspoon per pound	Apply salt evenly inside cavity and under skin of breasts and legs and let rest in refrigerator on wire rack set in rimmed baking sheet. (Wrap with plastic wrap if salting for longer than 12 hours.)
Bone-In Chicken Pieces; Boneless or Bone-In Turkey Breast	At least 6 hours or up to 24 hours	¾ teaspoon per pound	If poultry is skin-on, apply salt evenly between skin and meat, leaving skin attached, and let rest in refrigerator on wire rack set in rimmed baking sheet. (Wrap with plastic wrap if salting for longer than 12 hours.)
Whole Turkey	24 to 48 hours	1 teaspoon per pound	Apply salt evenly inside cavity and under skin of breasts and legs, wrap tightly with plastic wrap, and let rest in refrigerator.

Salt Varieties

Whether mined from underground salt deposits or obtained by evaporating seawater, salt in its most basic form is the same: sodium chloride. What distinguishes one salt from another is texture, shape, and mineral content. These qualities can affect how a salt tastes.

TABLE SALT Table salt, also known as common salt, consists of tiny, uniformly shaped crystals created during rapid vacuum evaporation. It usually includes anti-caking agents that help it pour smoothly.
• How We Use It: Fine-grain table salt dissolves easily, making it our go-to for most applications, both sweet and savory.
• Shopping Tip: Avoid iodized salt, which can impart a chemical flavor.

KOSHER SALT Coarse-grain kosher salt is raked during the evaporation process to yield flaky crystals originally used for koshering meat. Unlike table salt, kosher salt doesn't contain any additives.
• How We Use It: Kosher salt is our top choice for seasoning meat. The large grains distribute easily and cling well to the meat's surfaces.
• Shopping Tip: The two major brands of kosher salt—Morton and Diamond Crystal—work equally well; however, their crystal sizes differ considerably (see right), and this makes a difference when measuring by volume.

SEA SALT Sea salt is the product of seawater evaporation—a time-consuming, expensive process that yields irregularly shaped, mineral-rich flakes that vary in color but only slightly in flavor.
• How We Use It: Don't bother cooking with pricey sea salt; we've found that mixed into food, it doesn't taste any different than table salt. Instead, we use it as a "finishing salt," where its delicate crunch stands out.
• Shopping Tip: Texture—not exotic provenance—is the main consideration. Look for brands boasting large, flaky crystals, such as Maldon Sea Salt.

HOW MUCH SALT IS IN THAT TEASPOON?

Given its coarser crystal structure, kosher salt packs a lot less into each teaspoon when compared with table salt. In fact, even the volume measurements between the two major brands of kosher salt—Morton and Diamond Crystal—very significantly. Here's how they measure up:

1 teaspoon table salt	=	1½ teaspoons Morton kosher salt	=	2 teaspoons Diamond Crystal kosher salt

Seasoning Meat

BRINING

Brining works pretty much the same way as salting. Salt in the brine seasons the meat and promotes a change in its protein structure, reducing its overall toughness and creating gaps that fill up with water and keep the meat juicy and flavorful. Brining works faster than salting and can also result in juicier lean cuts since it adds, rather than merely retains, moisture—which is why we prefer brining to salting in poultry and lean cuts of pork such as pork tenderloin. Note that brining inhibits browning, and it entails fitting a brining container in the fridge.

We prefer to use table salt for brining since it dissolves quickly in the water. The chart lists the meat items that we typically brine, along with notes on timing and the amount of water needed.

BRINING MEAT AND POULTRY

PORK	TIME	COLD WATER	TABLE SALT
4 (12-ounce) bone-in pork rib chops, 1½ inches thick	1 hour	1½ quarts	3 tablespoons
1 (3- to 6-pound) pork roast	1½ to 2 hours	2 quarts	¼ cup
CHICKEN			
1 whole chicken (3½ to 4 pounds)	½ to 1 hour	2 quarts	½ cup
2 whole chickens (3½ to 4 pounds each)	½ to 1 hour	3 quarts	¾ cup
4 pounds bone-in chicken pieces (whole breasts, split breasts, leg quarters, thighs, and/or drumsticks)	½ to 1 hour	2 quarts	½ cup
4 boneless, skinless chicken breasts	½ to 1 hour	2 quarts	¼ cup
TURKEY			
1 whole turkey (12 to 17 pounds)	6 to 12 hours	2 gallons	1 cup
1 whole turkey (18 to 24 pounds)	6 to 12 hours	3 gallons	1½ cups
1 bone-in turkey breast (6 to 8 pounds)	3 to 6 hours	1 gallon	½ cup

THE BASICS OF SEASONING: SALT AND PEPPER

If you've seen chefs season meat, you know that they often sprinkle salt and pepper high above the food. This isn't just kitchen theatrics—this technique distributes the seasoning more evenly than if sprinkled close to the meat, where it will clump in spots. And remember, it's crucial to taste a dish for seasoning before serving it. When adjusting seasonings after cooking, keep in mind that unlike salt, pepper has more punch when unheated, so after cooking, use pepper sparingly.

The Difference Between Curing and Brining

A cure is introduced into meat by way of a brine—a solution of salt, sugar, spices, nitrites, and water—by soaking, injection, or both. This technique is known as brine curing. The goal of brine curing is to have maximum penetration and distribution of the cure to the center of the meat before it spoils. (Thereafter, the meat is cooked.) Nitrites serve not only as a preservative (protecting against botulism, for example) but also produce changes in the flavor, color, and texture of the meat.

Our brines, used to enhance flavor and provide a cushion of moisture, are, properly speaking, flavor brines. Flavor brining promotes changes in the flavor, color, and texture of meats in a manner similar to curing. The difference is largely one of degree: Flavor brining is less concentrated, contains no nitrites, and thus has no preservative effects.

DOES FATTIER MEAT NEED MORE SALT?

Throughout years of cooking in the test kitchen, we've noticed that we tend to season fatty meat more generously than lean meat. To bolster our anecdotal evidence with real data, we set up the following experiment.

Experiment We rounded up five meats with various levels of fat: turkey breast, pork loin, strip steak, and both 80 percent and 90 percent lean ground beef. We cooked the meat and chopped it into pieces. We then tossed 10-gram portions of each meat with increasing amounts of salt (0.1 percent, 0.25 percent, 0.5 percent, 0.75 percent, 1 percent, and 1.5 percent by weight of each sample). We had tasters try the samples in order, starting with an unsalted control, and had them record at what percentage the meat tasted properly seasoned. We also sent cooked samples of each type of meat to a lab to determine fat content.

Results Sure enough, the fattier the meat the more salt it needed to taste properly seasoned. Tasters preferred the lean turkey breast (0.7 percent fat) and pork loin (2.6 percent fat) seasoned with 0.5 percent salt by weight. The strip steak (6 percent fat) and 90 percent lean ground beef (10 percent fat) required about 0.75 percent salt by weight to taste seasoned. And finally, the 80 percent lean ground beef (20 percent fat) tasted seasoned to a majority of tasters only when it reached 1 percent salt by weight.

Takeaway Our experiment adds credence to the conclusion of several recent published studies that fat has a dulling effect on taste. So when you season meat, remember to use a heavier hand on fatty burgers than you would on moderately fatty meats like strip steak and 90 percent ground beef. Use a lighter hand on lean meats like turkey breast and pork loin.

Seasoning Meat

DRY AGING

Meat, typically beef, is aged to develop its flavor and improve its texture. In commercial dry aging, butchers hold large primal cuts of beef (typically the rib or short loin sections) for at least 30 days in humid refrigerators ranging between 32 and 40 degrees. This effort comes at a premium—dry-aged steaks can cost twice as much as their fresh counterparts. To see if we could save money by dry-aging steak on a smaller scale, we bought strip steaks and stored them in the back of the refrigerator, where the temperature is coldest. Since home refrigerators are less humid than the commercial units used for dry aging, we wrapped the steaks in cheesecloth to allow air to pass through while also preventing excessive dehydration and checked them after four days (the longest length of time we felt comfortable storing raw beef in a home fridge). The results? Our home dry-aged steaks simply didn't have the nutty, almost cheese-like flavor or ultratender texture of commercially dry-aged steak. In our opinion, leave dry aging to the pros who have access to primal cuts and specially designed refrigerators. And take comfort; whether dry-aged or not, a great steak is still a great steak.

MARINATING

Marinating is often regarded as a cure-all for bland, chewy meat. Years of testing have taught us that while it can bump up flavor, a marinade will never turn a tough cut tender. But with the right ingredients in the mix, marinating can enhance juiciness and add complexity to steak, chicken, and pork. Successful marinating is all about getting as much of the soaking liquid flavors into (and on) the meat as possible. Brining in a saltwater solution is a way to create more juiciness. To pump up flavor as well as juiciness, our marinades combine both approaches, with soaking liquids that not only contain lots of seasonings and flavorings but so much salt that you might even call them "brinerades." (In fact, our marinades typically have two to three times more salt than our brines.) As in a brine, salt in a marinade affects meat in three ways. Through osmotic pressure, it pulls moisture from a place of higher water concentration (the marinade) into a place with a lower one (the meat). In addition, it restructures the protein molecules in the meat, creating gaps that fill with water to further increase juiciness. It also seasons the meat, enhancing its inherent flavors.

Marinade Must-Haves

Both salt and oil are critical to a successful marinade; soy, sugar, and honey are great flavor boosters.

SALT: NOT JUST SEASONING To increase the meat's juiciness, our marinades usually include a high concentration of salt (typically about 1½ teaspoons per 3 tablespoons of liquid), and thus serve as "brinerades" that combine the benefits of marinating and brining.

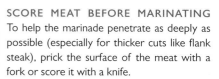

OIL: FLAVOR FACILITATOR Most of the herbs and spices we add to marinades are oil-soluble, which means they only release their full flavor when mixed in oil. So, to get the most out of a marinade, always include oil. But note: These flavors will merely coat, not penetrate, the meat. Meat proteins are saturated with water, so they won't absorb the oil or its flavors.

SOY: FLAVOR ENHANCER For more complex flavor, use soy sauce instead of salt—besides being salty, it contains glutamic acid, which boosts meaty flavor.

SUGAR/HONEY: BROWNING BOOSTERS Sweeteners like sugar and honey not only add complexity, they also help foods brown during cooking, further developing flavor.

Marinating Tips for Success

USE LOTS OF FLAVORINGS AND SEASONINGS In tests, we've found that a high concentration of salt in a marinade (and we use plenty) can inhibit meat from absorbing the flavors of other ingredients, unless they're included in copious quantities (e.g., three or four cloves of garlic and at least a tablespoon of chopped herbs).

SCORE MEAT BEFORE MARINATING To help the marinade penetrate as deeply as possible (especially for thicker cuts like flank steak), prick the surface of the meat with a fork or score it with a knife.

FLIP OR STIR Place meat in a zipper-lock bag with the air squeezed out or use a large baking dish covered with plastic wrap. Flip the bag or stir the meat halfway through the soaking time to ensure that the meat is thoroughly coated.

REFRIGERATE WHILE MARINATING To eliminate the risk of microorganisms spreading in raw meat, don't leave meat on the counter—refrigerate it. This keeps it out of the temperature danger zone of 40 to 140 degrees, within which bacteria spread rapidly.

DON'T RECYCLE USED MARINADE Used marinade is contaminated with raw meat juice and is therefore unsafe. If you want sauce to serve with the cooked meat, just make a little extra marinade and set it aside before marinating the meat.

Principles of Meat Cookery

Meat can be prepared by numerous cooking methods—everything from roasting to grilling. However, there are five basic principles that apply to the vast majority of these recipes, as well as to most poultry recipes.

High Heat Develops Flavor

Browning creates a tremendous amount of flavor and is a key step when cooking meat. This happens through a process called the Maillard reaction, named after the French chemist who first described it in the early 1900s. The Maillard reaction occurs when the amino acids and sugars in the food are subjected to heat, which causes them to combine. In turn, hundreds of different flavor compounds are created. These compounds break down to form yet more new flavor compounds, and so on, and so on. When browning meat, you want a deep brown sear and a discernibly thick crust on all sides—best obtained by quick cooking over high heat. To ensure that meat browns properly, first make sure the meat is dry before it goes into the pan; pat it thoroughly with paper towels. This is especially important with previously frozen meat, which often releases a great deal of water. Second, make sure the pan is hot by preheating it over high heat until the fat added to the pan is shimmering or almost smoking. Finally, make sure not to overcrowd the pan; there should be at least ¼ inch of space between the pieces of meat. If there isn't, the meat is likely to steam instead of brown. If need be, cook the meat in two or three batches.

Low Heat Preserves Moisture

For large cuts of meat or poultry, we often advocate a low-and-slow cooking method. We find that this approach allows the center to come up to the desired internal temperature with less risk of overcooking the outer layers.

An experiment we recently conducted proves that even cooking isn't the only benefit of slow roasting: It also helps minimize the loss of flavorful juices (and fat). We took two 6-pound rib roasts and roasted one at 450 degrees and the other at 250 degrees until each was medium-rare. We then weighed the cooked roasts. The slow-cooked roast had lost about 9.25 percent of its starting weight, while the high-temperature roast had lost nearly 25 percent of its original weight. Why the difference? Proteins shrink less and express less moisture and fat when cooked at moderate temperatures than when roasted at high heat.

Match the Cut to the Cooking Method

Tough cuts, which generally come from the heavily exercised parts of the animal, such as the shoulder or rump, respond best to slow-cooking methods, such as pot roasting, stewing, or barbecuing. The primary goal of slow cooking is to melt collagen in the connective tissue, thereby transforming a tough piece of meat into a tender one. These cuts are always served well done.

Tender cuts with little connective tissue generally come from parts of the animal that receive little exercise (like the loin, the area along the back of the cow or pig). These cuts respond best to quicker, dry-heat cooking methods, such as grilling or roasting. These cuts are cooked to a specific doneness. Prolonged cooking increases moisture loss and can turn these tender cuts tough. See individual chapters for our retail cuts charts and recommended recipes.

Don't Forget About Carryover Cooking

Since the temperature of meat will continue to rise as it rests, an effect called carryover cooking, meat should be removed from the oven, grill, or pan when it's 5 to 10 degrees below the desired serving temperature. Carryover cooking doesn't apply to poultry and fish (they don't retain heat as well as the dense muscle structure in meat). The following temperatures should be used to determine when to stop the cooking process.

DONENESS TEMPERATURES FOR MEAT AND POULTRY*

BEEF/LAMB/VEAL	TEMPERATURE
Rare	115 to 120 degrees (120 to 125 degrees after resting)
Medium-Rare	120 to 125 degrees (125 to 130 degrees after resting)
Medium	130 to 135 degrees (135 to 140 degrees after resting)
Medium-Well	140 to 145 degrees (145 to 150 degrees after resting)
Well-Done	150 to 155 degrees (155 to 160 degrees after resting)
PORK	
Medium	140 to 145 degrees (150 degrees after resting)
Well-Done	150 to 155 degrees (160 degrees after resting)
CHICKEN AND TURKEY	
White Meat	160 degrees
Dark Meat	175 degrees

*The doneness temperatures in this book represent the test kitchen's assessment of palatability weighed against safety. The basics from the USDA differ somewhat: Cook whole cuts of meat, including pork, to an internal temperature of at least 145 degrees and let rest for at least 3 minutes. Cook all ground meats to an internal temperature of at least 160 degrees. Cook all poultry, including ground poultry, to an internal temperature of at least 165 degrees. For more information on food safety from the USDA, visit www.fsis.usda.gov/factsheets.

Why Resting Meat Is Essential

The purpose of resting meat is to allow the juices, which are driven to the center during cooking, to redistribute themselves throughout the meat. As a result, meat that has rested will shed much less juice than meat sliced straight after cooking. To test this theory, we grilled four steaks and let two rest while slicing into the other two immediately. The steaks that had rested for 10 minutes shed 40 percent less juice than the steaks sliced right after cooking. The meat on the unrested steaks also looked grayer and was not as tender. A thin steak or chop should rest for 5 to 10 minutes, a thicker roast for 15 to 20 minutes. And when cooking a large roast like a turkey, the meat should rest for about 40 minutes before it is carved.

How to Cook Meat—Cut by Cut

No matter how you choose to cook meat, there are specific steps you can take to ensure your dish turns out great every time. But first, it's imperative to match the cut with the cooking method. A chuck-eye roast takes well to braising (as for pot roast) because the method turns all the fat and connective tissue into gelatin, and the result is flavorful and tender. Take that same cut and try roasting it, and the results are fatty and tough.

The following cooking methods (and the cuts we think are best for each) should be seen as a jumping-off point to understanding the best ways to cook meat—there may be slight departures depending on particular recipes.

SAUTÉING

• **Best for:** Thin cutlets and medallions

Thin, lean cuts of meat like chicken or veal cutlets are typically sautéed, a method that relies on cooking food in a small amount of fat over moderately high heat, usually with the goal of browning the food. Getting browning to develop with these quick-cooking cuts is a challenge. We found flouring the cutlets and cooking them over moderately high heat for longer on the first side than the second was the answer. This method will also work with turkey cutlets; however, since they are bigger you will need to cook them in batches.

1. SKIP PACKAGED CUTLETS Chances are, the cutlets you purchase in a package will be of uneven thickness. Either try to buy your cutlets at the meat counter where you can choose each cutlet, or buy chicken breasts and slice them into cutlets yourself. Freezing the breasts for 20 minutes firms them up and makes slicing easier.

2. DRY AND DREDGE Flouring cutlets prior to sautéing protects the meat from drying out and helps to keep it from sticking to the skillet. The flour also encourages browning and helps pan sauces cling to the cutlets. Mixing the seasoning into the flouring keeps the process streamlined.

3. SAUTÉ QUICKLY Vegetable oil has a high smoke point and neutral flavor, which makes it the best choice here. Cutlets are so thin that to avoid overcooking it's best to deeply brown one side and cook the second side for only a few seconds. This is sufficient to develop flavor, lend visual appeal, and leave some fond in the pan to make a sauce, all without overcooking the meat.

4. KEEP WARM IN THE OVEN Thin cutlets cool off quickly, so remove them to a platter, tent them with foil, and keep them warm in a low oven while making a pan sauce or cooking a second batch.

Cutting your own cutlets is a snap—just slice horizontally.

Drying the cutlets before coating with flour ensures that the flour won't turn gummy in the hot skillet.

Stay close to the stove when cooking cutlets—they take just a few minutes.

Cutlets cool off quickly. Keep them warm in the oven while you cook a second batch or make a pan sauce.

KEY STEPS TO MAKING A PAN SAUCE

Pan sauces are the easiest way to dress up pan-seared steaks, chops, boneless, skinless chicken breasts, and chicken parts. These sauces start in the empty pan used to cook the meat. There are browned bits (called fond) sticking to that pan from the searing process, and that fond is packed with flavor. The goal is to build on that flavor, then loosen and dissolve the fond to create a simple sauce. (The process of loosening and dissolving fond with liquid is called deglazing.) Although the ingredients and amounts change depending on the sauce, the steps are the same—sauté aromatics, add liquid and scrape the pan, simmer to reduce and concentrate flavors, then finish with butter.

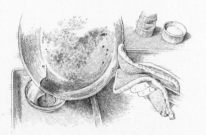

1. POUR OFF EXCESS FAT If there's more than 2 teaspoons of fat in the pan, you want to pour off the excess—otherwise, the sauce will be greasy. If there's very little fat in the pan, add a little vegetable oil (up to 2 teaspoons) as needed. But don't wash that skillet—it's packed with flavorful fond.

2. ADD AROMATICS Aromatics like shallot, garlic, onion, or a leek will enhance the flavor of a quick pan sauce and give it depth. Don't let the aromatics burn—garlic will cook very quickly, while onions and leeks will require a bit more time.

3. DEGLAZE THE PAN Add liquid to the pan and use a wooden spoon to scrape up the browned bits on the pan bottom. Choose potent liquids (wine, brandy, vermouth, broth, cider). With the liquid in the pan, you can now loosen the fond on the pan bottom. It will dissolve as the liquid simmers, enriching the sauce with meaty flavors.

4. SIMMER AND MEASURE Once the liquid is in the pan, it should simmer briskly. (If necessary, increase the heat.) You want to reduce the liquid to both concentrate flavors and change its consistency. If in doubt, pour the liquid into a measuring cup to check your progress. Don't shortcut this process, or your sauce will be too watery.

5. ADD MEAT JUICES As the meat rests, it will exude juices on the plate. Add these meat juices to the skillet and stir to combine. These juices are potent and shouldn't go to waste. If you end up adding more than 1 tablespoon of meat juices, simmer the sauce to slightly reduce it.

6. WHISK IN BUTTER Off heat, whisk in chilled unsalted butter, 1 tablespoon at a time, to emulsify the sauce and make it thick and glossy. To finish, add fresh herbs or other potent ingredients such as mustard or lemon juice to preserve their flavor. Adjust seasonings with salt and pepper.

PAN SAUCES AND NONSTICK SKILLETS

Pan sauces typically rely on fond (the browned bits that get stuck to the bottom of the pan) for added flavor. Nonstick skillets are undeniably convenient, but the fact that the nonstick surface doesn't allow much fond to develop made us suspect that sauces made in them would have less flavor. To find out, we cooked chicken breasts in nonstick and stainless-steel skillets, then made a vermouth pan sauce in each. Sure enough, the sauces made in nonstick skillets were pale compared to those made in stainless steel. Also, we noticed a striking difference in the flavor of the sauces. The sauce made in stainless steel had robust chicken flavor, while the sauce made in a nonstick skillet was watery and weak. The bottom line? For best flavor and color, stick with stainless steel.

How to Cook Meat–Cut by Cut

PAN SEARING

• **Best for:** Boneless steaks and chops

Cooking a steak or chop in a skillet is a basic technique that should be in every cook's repertoire. When the steak or chop is thicker than 1 inch you need to use a combination method that starts in the oven and finishes in the skillet (see next page). But for your average supermarket steaks or chops, the operation can take place entirely on top of the stove. While the meat rests, make a quick pan sauce (see "Key Steps to Making a Pan Sauce").

1. TRIM THE FAT When searing meat on the stovetop, keep the splattering to a minimum by trimming excess fat. You can also place a splatter screen over the skillet as the meat cooks.

2. PAT THE MEAT DRY Browning equals flavor, and browning occurs only once all surface moisture has evaporated. Do pat the meat dry or the meat will steam.

3. SEASON LIBERALLY For individual steaks and chops, use kosher salt. Freshly ground pepper is a must; use as much as you like (a 4:1 ratio of salt to pepper generally works well).

4. GET THE PAN HOT We use the temperature of the oil to gauge the temperature of the pan. When vegetable oil begins to smoke, the pan is about 450 degrees, the perfect temperature for searing.

5. DON'T CROWD THE SKILLET Use a pan large enough to accommodate the pieces of meat in a single layer, with about ¼ inch between them. If the meat is crowded into the pan, it will steam instead of brown.

6. LEAVE THEM ALONE Leaving the pieces of meat in place helps build a better crust. Also, meat will tend to stick when first added to the pan. If you leave it alone until the crust forms the meat will free itself naturally from the pan.

7. TAKE THEIR TEMPERATURE Don't attempt to gauge doneness by cutting into the meat. Use a good thermometer and you will never overcook another steak or chop. See page 8 for doneness temperatures for meat.

8. REST BEFORE SERVING A short rest allows the muscle fibers in the meat to relax and reabsorb their natural juices. Use this time to make a quick sauce in the pan.

Less fat means less splatter, so trimming the fat is recommended.

Seasoning is important for flavor. We like kosher salt here. Don't be shy with the pepper—the heat will tame its kick.

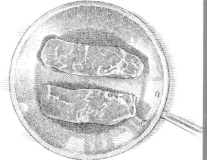

Make sure the oil is hot for a proper sear and don't move the steaks or chops until a crust has formed.

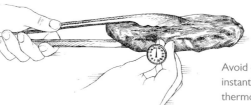

Avoid overcooking by using an instant-read thermometer—insert the thermometer from the side to get an accurate reading.

How to Cook Meat—Cut by Cut

REVERSE PAN SEARING

- **Best for:** Thick steaks and chops

If you attempt to cook thicker steaks (1½ to 1¾ inches thick) such as filets mignons and pork chops entirely on the stovetop, you end up with a burnt exterior and a raw center. Even if you can manage to avoid burning the exterior, the meat around the perimeter is overcooked by the time the center comes up to temperature. The secret to getting a great crust on extra-thick chops and steaks without making them tough is to cook them in a very low oven, then quickly sear them. The gentle oven heat minimizes moisture loss and promotes a natural enzymatic reaction that breaks down connective tissue in the meat and makes it especially tender. The stint in the oven also dries the surface of the meat. The steaks and chops brown in record time, and since the meat is in the pan for just a few minutes, there isn't time for it to lose much moisture.

1. BAKE YOUR CHOP This technique starts like traditional pan-searing recipes—by drying and seasoning the meat—but it starts in the oven, not the stovetop. Thus, the meat needs to be set on a wire rack nestled into a rimmed baking sheet. The rack is essential since it allows the gentle heat of the oven to circulate evenly around the meat. The low oven temperature accomplishes two things: It ensures that the exterior part of the steaks or chops doesn't race ahead of the interior. And it prolongs the period during which a natural enzymatic reaction in the meat breaks down muscle fibers.

2. TEMP IT Since these chops or steaks are going to be seared just before serving, you don't want to overcook them in the oven. Once the internal temperature is 25 to 30 degrees shy of the desired final internal temperature, take the meat out of the oven.

3. CREATE A CRUST The searing part of this process should happen quickly. Get the pan very hot so you can put a crust on the meat swiftly. If you slow down this process, the meat can overcook. Other than lifting meat once to let the fat redistribute itself, leave the meat alone so that a crust can form. You may need to turn down the heat when cooking in batches to prevent the fond from burning.

4. SEAR THE SIDES The sides on a thick steak or chop are so tall that it seems like a mistake not to brown them as well. Once the tops and bottoms are browned, we brown the sides, holding two at a time with tongs, in the pan. Don't worry about getting a perfect crust here—the idea is to put some color on the sides and boost overall flavor.

5. MAKE A PAN SAUCE Thick chops or steaks should rest for 10 minutes before serving so the meat fibers have time to reabsorb their juices. That skillet is filled with flavorful fond, and you might as well turn it into a quick sauce (see "Key Steps to Making a Pan Sauce," page 10).

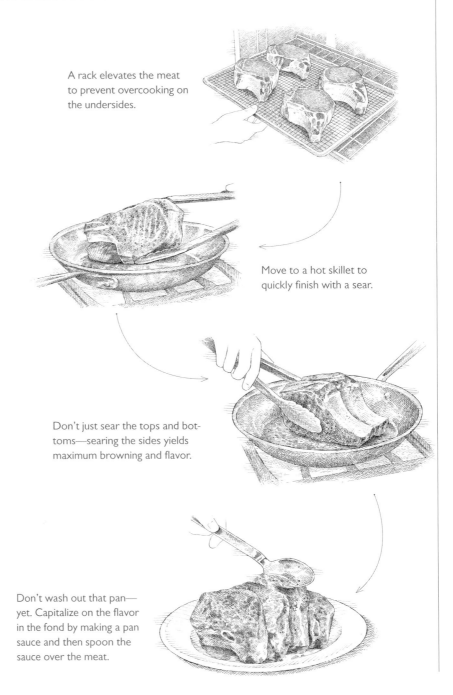

A rack elevates the meat to prevent overcooking on the undersides.

Move to a hot skillet to quickly finish with a sear.

Don't just sear the tops and bottoms—searing the sides yields maximum browning and flavor.

Don't wash out that pan—yet. Capitalize on the flavor in the fond by making a pan sauce and then spoon the sauce over the meat.

How to Cook Meat—Cut by Cut

PAN ROASTING
• **Best for:** Chicken parts

Like roasting a whole chicken, pan roasting chicken pieces delivers crisp skin, tender meat, and flavorful drippings, but on a weeknight time frame. In addition to the obvious fact that smaller pieces of chicken cook more quickly than a whole bird, pan roasting speeds up the cooking time by browning the chicken on the stovetop, then moving it to the oven to finish. White and dark meat cook at different rates, but by cutting each split breast in half, the breasts will be done at the same time as the thinner thighs and slim drumsticks, which require a higher doneness temperature. While a pan sauce isn't required, the chicken needs to rest regardless, so it makes sense to utilize that time—and the flavorful drippings in the skillet—to make a quick sauce (see "Key Steps to Making a Pan Sauce," page 10).

1. CUT THE CHICKEN INTO PIECES We cut our chicken into 8 pieces: Cutting the large breasts in half ensures they will cook through in about the same amount of time as the thighs and drumsticks. Brining the chicken isn't required, but it makes for juicier meat and also adds some insurance against overcooking the more delicate breast meat. However, note that brined meat won't brown as well.

2. HEAT THE OIL IN A LARGE OVENSAFE SKILLET Since the chicken will go into the oven, skillet and all, after browning, make sure your skillet is ovensafe.

3. BROWN THE CHICKEN Browning the chicken lends visual appeal, builds flavor, and creates fond that can be use to build a pan sauce. Browning also jump-starts the cooking process.

4. FINISH IN THE OVEN Finishing in the oven ensures even cooking: A moderately hot oven finishes cooking the chicken before it dries out. Keeping the chicken skin side down ensures perfectly crisp, dark russet–colored skin.

5. MAKE A PAN SAUCE It takes only about 5 minutes to make a pan sauce, which can be conveniently prepared while the chicken rests (see "Key Steps to Making a Pan Sauce," page 10). Just make sure you are careful of the hot handle on the skillet during this step; in the test kitchen we usually leave a potholder on the handle as a reminder.

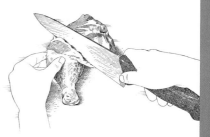

Cutting up a bird yourself ensures similar-size pieces. And cutting breasts in half ensures they cook through at the same rate as the thighs and drumsticks.

Jump-starting the chicken on the stovetop browns the skin and moving it to the oven cooks the meat through without drying it out.

While making the pan sauce, slip a folded kitchen towel or potholder over the hot skillet handle—otherwise you might forget that the handle is hot and burn yourself.

How to Cook Meat—Cut by Cut

STIR-FRYING

• **Best for:** Boneless poultry and meat

Stir-frying is a great way to turn quick-cooking meat (or other protein) and vegetables into a complete dinner. However, the classic restaurant method doesn't work at home. Conical woks rest in cutouts in the stovetop, and intense flames heat the entire pan. At home, on a flat burner, the results are usually underwhelming, with poor browning and not nearly enough evaporation and concentration of flavors.

Our advice is to skip a wok in favor of a large nonstick skillet. The diameter of a large skillet provides a wide, broad cooking surface that promotes good browning, which translates to great flavor. We like a nonstick pan (to reduce the amount of oil needed). It is essential to use a skillet that heats evenly and quickly recovers heat each time food is added to the pan.

I. FREEZE AND SLICE We find it helpful to freeze the meat briefly to make it firmer for slicing. Make sure the final cut is against the grain of the meat. If you look closely at a piece of meat, you'll notice little bundles of closely packed muscle fibers that run parallel to one another. This pattern of fibers is known as the grain. Recipes recommend slicing against the grain—perpendicular to the fibers—to shorten them and thereby make the meat easier to chew.

2. MARINATE THE MEAT A quick marinade that includes salt or a salty ingredient such as soy sauce guarantees that the meat will taste well seasoned. Be sure to drain off any moisture from the marinade before stir-frying so that the meat will brown in the skillet.

3. CUT THE VEGETABLES EVENLY Cutting the vegetables to the right size will help ensure that they cook evenly.

4. COOK IN BATCHES Meat and vegetables usually cook at different rates, so it's key to stir-fry them separately and bring them together at the end. And despite the name of this technique, don't stir the food as it cooks; leave it alone so it can brown.

5. ADD THE AROMATICS LATER Many stir-fry recipes add aromatics early in the process. We add them near the end so that they don't scorch. Mashing the aromatics into the skillet ensures they cook through and won't taste harsh or raw in the finished stir-fry—before integrating them into the vegetables.

6. GO EASY ON THE CORNSTARCH We use just enough to thicken the sauce so that it lightly coats the ingredients.

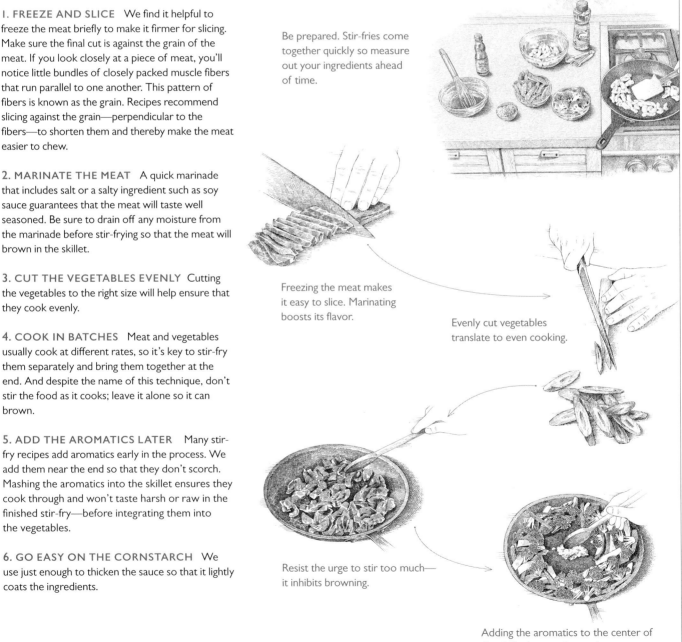

Be prepared. Stir-fries come together quickly so measure out your ingredients ahead of time.

Freezing the meat makes it easy to slice. Marinating boosts its flavor.

Evenly cut vegetables translate to even cooking.

Resist the urge to stir too much—it inhibits browning.

Adding the aromatics to the center of the skillet later in the cooking process ensures that they don't burn.

How to Cook Meat–Cut by Cut

ROASTING MEAT
• **Best for:** Big cuts

Roasting involves cooking food in a hot oven. As you will see in the roast recipes throughout this book, the oven temperature can vary considerably. In general, tender cuts such as pork tenderloin can be roasted in a moderately hot oven: 300 to 375 degrees. Tougher cuts such as eye round benefit from long, slow cooking, with oven temperatures below 300 degrees.

While we generally brown before roasting, there are recipes where we roast first and brown last. (This method works especially with roast beef tenderloin; see recipe on page 98.) The important thing is to brown the meat at some point in the process. Make sure to refer to the doneness chart on page 8. And don't forget to let all roasts rest for at least 15 minutes before slicing; during this time the meat fibers will relax and reabsorb juices so that they end up in the meat, not on the carving board.

1. SEASON THE ROAST Sprinkle the exterior of the roast with salt (preferably kosher) and let it stand at room temperature for at least an hour (in most cases). As the roast sits, the salt draws out its juices, which then combine with the salt before being reabsorbed into the meat. The result: a roast that is flavorful both inside and out.

2. TIE THE ROAST Most roasts are unevenly shaped, which leads to uneven cooking. For cylindrical cuts, such as beef tenderloin or pork loin, we even out the thickness with kitchen twine tied down the length. You can also fold the thin end under the roast and tie it in place. For squat roasts such as the eye round, wrap longer pieces of twine around the perimeter to cinch in the sides and give the roast a neater shape.

3. BROWN THE ROAST IN A SKILLET The sloped sides of a traditional skillet allow for quick evaporation of moisture, and the stainless-steel finish encourages the development of a flavorful crust. Avoid nonstick pans when roasting.

4. ELEVATE, THEN ROAST SLOWLY A roasting rack ensures even heating and means you don't have to turn the roast. Also, elevating the roast keeps the bottom crust intact. For most cuts of beef, we roast low and slow to keep the internal temperature of the meat below 122 degrees. This allows the enzymes in the meat to break down the muscle fibers, effectively tenderizing the meat. Low heat also reduces the temperature differential between the exterior and the interior of the meat, so you end up with a roast that is more uniformly cooked.

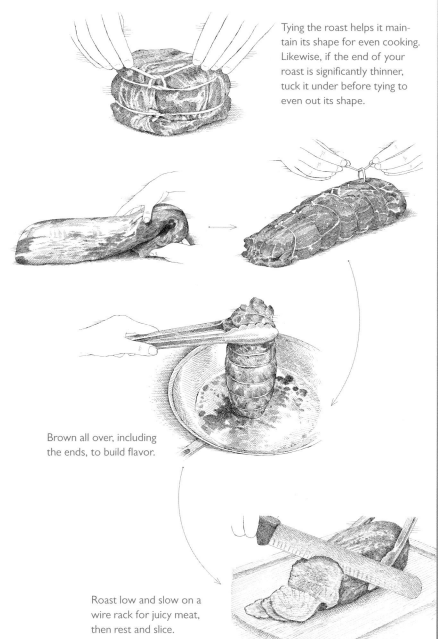

Tying the roast helps it maintain its shape for even cooking. Likewise, if the end of your roast is significantly thinner, tuck it under before tying to even out its shape.

Brown all over, including the ends, to build flavor.

Roast low and slow on a wire rack for juicy meat, then rest and slice.

How to Cook Meat–Cut by Cut

ROASTING POULTRY

• **Best for:** Whole birds

Roasting poultry is different than roasting a beef or pork roast. The biggest challenge is getting the white and dark meat to finish cooking at the same time. The bird is thicker and thinner in spots, and the breast meat dries out at an internal temperature above 160 degrees, while the dark meat isn't even done until it reaches at least 175 degrees. In addition, the challenge of achieving crispy skin is often elusive. (And note that while there are some similarities between roasting a chicken and a turkey, such as brining, the size of a turkey poses other challenges and thus requires a different roasting technique—see page 439.)

1. BRINE THE BIRD Brining—soaking the chicken in a saltwater solution—seasons the bird and helps to keep the white meat from drying out. However, don't brine kosher chickens; they will be far too salty if brined.

2. LOOSEN THE SKIN Loosening the skin makes it easier for the fat in the skin to render and drain. Make sure to be gentle so as not to tear it. We also apply butter under the skin to further ensure moist meat.

3. RUB AND SEASON SKIN Oil rubbed on the skin helps it crisp in the oven. Since the bird has been brined, there's no need to season with salt; just use pepper. Tuck the wings behind the back so it maintains its shape.

4. ROAST ON EACH SIDE For even cooking, we start by laying the chicken with one wing facing up and roast for about 15 minutes. Then we flip it to the other side and roast another 15 minutes. Spraying the rack keeps the skin from sticking, and preheating the pan ensures the thighs and breast cook at the same rate. For a good grip, hold a wad of paper towels in each hand when you flip the chicken.

5. FINISH COOKING BREAST SIDE UP Remove the roasting pan from the oven and, using two large wads of paper towels, flip the chicken so that the breast side is facing up. Roast until the breast registers 160 degrees and the thighs register 175 degrees, 20 to 25 minutes longer.

6. REST BEFORE CARVING The heat of the oven forces the juices of the meat toward the center of the bird. Letting the chicken rest for 15 to 20 minutes gives the juices time to redistribute, ensuring that every bite of chicken is moist and flavorful.

Brine for a juicy, well-seasoned bird.

Butter spread under the skin flavors the meat and keeps it moist. Oil and pepper over the skin encourages browning and adds flavor.

Roasting on one side and then the other and finishing the bird breast side up delivers an evenly cooked roast.

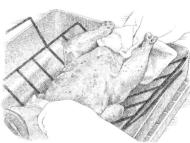

Resting before carving ensures every slice is moist and flavorful.

How to Cook Meat–Cut by Cut

STEWING OR BRAISING
• **Best for:** Tough cuts

Stewing and braising (also known as pot roasting) are moist-heat cooking methods that transform tough, sinewy cuts such as chuck-eye roast into tender, yielding meat in a rich sauce. Braising is the umbrella term used to describe the combination cooking method that involves browning food and then gently simmering it in liquid. Stewing is a subset of braising, and the term applies to dishes with small chunks of boneless meat such as pork butt. The steps that follow demonstrate stewing, but the technique for braising a large cut is similar.

I. CUT THE STEW MEAT Skip packaged stew meat at the supermarket because it is cut so small that it overcooks and becomes tough. For the best results, buy a roast and cut it yourself. Start by pulling the roast apart and trimming away the big pieces of fat. Cut the meat into big chunks. Simply put, bigger chunks make a better stew. They are less likely to overcook, and they give the dish heft.

2. DRY, SEASON, AND BROWN The pieces of meat should be patted dry with paper towels so they can brown (rather than steam). Also, the meat should be seasoned lightly (if at all) with salt and pepper since, depending on the stew, other salty ingredients will be going into the pot. Don't let the fond at the bottom of the pot burn. If you notice the fond starting to get dark between batches, add a little water or broth to the pot, scrape up the fond, and then add this liquid to the bowl where you're holding the browned meat.

3. SAUTÉ THE AROMATICS After browning the meat, add aromatics (such as onion, carrot, celery, leek, and garlic) and sauté. If flour is being used to thicken the stew, it should be stirred into the sautéed vegetables. The flour mixed with the fat already in the pot creates a roux, a fat-and-flour paste for thickening sauces.

4. DEGLAZE THE PAN Before the meat and vegetables go into the pot, it's important to loosen the fond so it can dissolve into the liquid ingredients. Use wine good enough to drink and avoid so-called cooking wine. Also, use broth with a moderate sodium content of 400 to 700 milligrams per serving—the liquid will be reducing and can become very salty if the broth is salty.

5. SIMMER IN THE OVEN Most stew recipes stay on the stovetop, but this means you have to stir it often. By moving the action to the oven, you eliminate the risk of scorching the bottom of the pot and you get much more even cooking.

Cutting the meat yourself into big chunks means a heartier stew and less chance of overcooking. For chuck-eye roasts, pull apart at the seams before cutting into chunks.

Cook the meat in batches if necessary— you want to allow plenty of room so the meat browns and creates a flavorful fond.

Adding flour to the sautéed aromatics helps thicken the stew.

Wine or broth loosens the fond for complex flavor.

Oven heat gently finishes cooking the stew—no stirring required.

How to Cook Meat–Cut by Cut

GRILLING

• **Best for:** Steaks, burgers, chops, and chicken parts

Build a hot fire and cook the meat directly over the coals—nothing could be simpler. When grilling, the temperature will be in excess of 400 degrees, if not 500 degrees. As a result, meat cooks very quickly. By the time the exterior is nicely browned, the interior will be cooked through. This method works best with moderately thin steaks and chops. For thicker steaks, chops, or chicken parts, you may need to grill over a two-level fire, which is a fire with two heat levels—a hotter zone for searing and a cooler zone to cook meat through more gently. Here's how to set up and cook over both types of fires.

IA. SETTING UP A SINGLE-LEVEL FIRE

For a charcoal grill, open the bottom vent and distribute the coals in an even layer across the bottom of the grill (see page 20). For a gas grill, preheat the grill, then turn all burners to the heat setting directed in the recipe. A single-level fire delivers a uniform level of heat across the entire cooking surface and is often used for small, quick-cooking pieces of food, such as hamburgers and sausages.

IB. GRILLING ON A SINGLE LEVEL-FIRE

Place the meat evenly across the grill, open the bottom vent, and cook uncovered. Opening the vents provides the fire with more oxygen so that it burns hotter and faster. In general, we open the bottom vent and don't use the lid when grilling something that takes a short period of time.

2A. SETTING UP A TWO-LEVEL FIRE

For a charcoal grill, evenly distribute two-thirds of the lit coals over half of the grill, then distribute the remainder in an even layer over the other half of the grill. For a gas grill, preheat the grill, then leave the primary burner on high and turn the other burner(s) to medium. This setup creates two cooking zones; a hotter area for searing and a slightly cooler area to cook food more gently.

2B. GRILLING ON A TWO-LEVEL FIRE

Brown the meat over the hot side and finish over the cooler side. For recipes calling for this setup, such as bone-in chicken breasts, we start the pieces on the hotter side until lightly browned on one side, then we move the chicken to the cooler side of the grill, browned side up, to cook the interior. Because chicken breasts have a thin end and a thicker end, we position the breasts with the thicker ends facing the hotter side. Finally, we move them back to the hotter side to brown more deeply.

To make a single-level fire on a charcoal grill, pour the hot coals evenly over the bottom of the grill.

With quick-cooking pieces of food, simply arrange evenly across the cooking grate and cook uncovered.

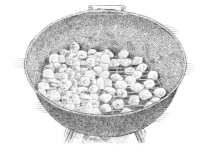

To make a two-level fire, pour two-thirds of the hot coals over half of the grill, and the remaining coals over the other half of the grill.

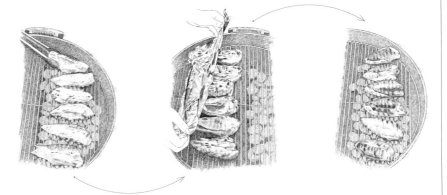

Two levels of fire means we can brown food over the hotter level and finish cooking gently over the cooler level. With chicken breasts, after browning on one side, we cover with foil over the cool side, and then move them back to the hotter side to finish browning. This way the interior has time to cook through without the risk of burning the exterior.

THE BASICS OF OUTDOOR COOKING

Grilling is much less precise than stovetop cooking because of the differences among various grills, the vagaries of live flames, and environmental conditions (weather has an impact). Understanding how to heat your grill and build the right fire will reduce these variables and ensure success. See page 27 for information on our top-rated charcoal and gas grills.

Lighting a Charcoal Grill—Use a Chimney Starter

We find that a chimney starter (also called a flue starter) is the best way to light charcoal (see the illustration below). A chimney starter is foolproof, and it also eliminates the need for lighter fluid, which can impart harsh, acrid flavors to food. We strongly recommend that you visit a hardware store (or another shop that sells grilling equipment) and purchase this indispensable device. We like a large chimney (one that holds about 6 quarts of charcoal and measures about 7½ inches across by 12 inches high) because it holds just the right amount for grilling most foods over medium-hot heat in a kettle grill. Expect to pay between $15 and $26 for a chimney starter—a very modest investment for such a useful tool.

To use a chimney starter, place several sheets of crumpled newspaper in the lower chamber and set the starter on the bottom grate of a kettle grill (where the charcoal will eventually go); the top cooking grate should not be in place. Fill the upper chamber with as much charcoal as directed. Light the newspaper through the holes in the side of the chimney starter and wait until the coals at the top of the pile are covered with fine, gray ash. (This will take about 20 minutes.) Dump the lit charcoal in the bottom of the grill and arrange as directed. (For more firepower, add more unlit charcoal and wait until it has caught fire before grilling.) You can then set the cooking grate in place, allow it to heat up, and clean it. After that, you are ready to grill. Note that after you empty the lit charcoal into the grill, the starter will still be very hot. Don't put it down on the lawn—it will burn the grass. Instead, set the starter on a concrete or stone surface away from any flammable objects and allow it to cool off for at least a half-hour. Make sure you choose a spot away from children and pets.

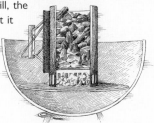

Lighting a Fire Without a Chimney Starter

If you don't have access to a chimney starter, use this method:

1. Open bottom vent and place 8 sheets of balled newspaper beneath bottom grate.

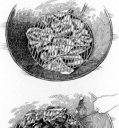

2. Pile charcoal in even pile in center of rack and light paper. After about 20 minutes, coals will be covered with gray ash and ready to be rearranged for cooking. (Don't use instant-light charcoal, which can impart nasty flavors to food.)

Lighting a Gas Grill

Follow the directions in your owner's manual regarding the order in which the burners must be lit. And always keep the lid up when lighting any gas grill. An electric igniter lights the burners on most grills, but these can fail; most models have a hole for lighting the burners with a match. Be sure to wait several minutes (or as directed) between lighting attempts to allow excess gas to dissipate. Make sure to check the propane level in your tank before starting. For tanks without a gauge, we do this by bringing a cup or so of water to a boil in a small saucepan or kettle and pouring the water over the side of the tank. Where the water has succeeded in warming the tank, the tank is empty; where the tank remains cool to the touch, there is propane inside.

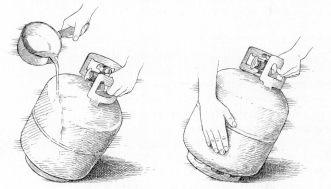

Cleaning and Oiling the Grate

You wouldn't cook in a dirty pan, would you? Why cook on a dirty grate? Cleaning the grill grate and swiping it with oil are essential steps to successful grilling.

1. Just before placing food on grill, scrape cooking grate clean with grill brush (or improvise with tongs and aluminum foil) to remove any residue.

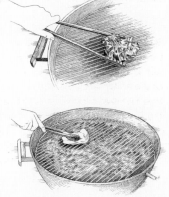

2. After scraping cooking grate, dip large wad of paper towels in vegetable oil, grab it with tongs, and wipe grate thoroughly to lubricate it and prevent food from sticking.

HOW TO CREATE A CUSTOM FIRE

While cooking with a conventional oven is akin to driving an automatic automobile, charcoal grilling is a lot like driving a standard shift—a little more work but a lot more fun. Instead of just turning dials and pressing buttons to manipulate heat as you would with an oven, you must arrange lit coals according to what types of food you are grilling. For a gas grill, it's quite simple to regulate the heat—just adjust the burners.

	CUSTOM FIRE	CHARCOAL	GAS EQUIVALENT
	SINGLE-LEVEL FIRE Delivers direct, moderate heat. Use with fairly thin foods that cook quickly, such as fruits, vegetables, fish and shellfish, kebabs, and hamburgers.	Arrange all the lit coals in an even layer.	Adjust the burners to high for a hot fire or turn the burners to medium after heating the cooking grate.
	TWO-LEVEL FIRE Allows the cook to sear foods over a very hot section of the grill and to finish cooking them over a cooler section so that the exterior doesn't burn. Use for chops, steaks, turkey burgers, bone-in chicken legs and thighs, and thick fish fillets.	Arrange two-thirds of the lit coals in a single layer on half of the grill. Leave the remaining coals in a pile on the other side of the grill.	Leave one burner on high and turn the other(s) to medium.
	HALF-GRILL FIRE Ideal for foods that are susceptible to burning but require a long cooking time. A half-grill fire can also be used to create an especially hot fire when grilling small, thin cuts of meat. Use for bone-in chicken breasts, boneless chicken breasts and thighs, sausages, flank steak, pork tenderloin, rack of lamb, and butterflied leg of lamb.	Pile all the lit coals onto one side of the grill, leaving the other side empty. We often cover foods on the cooler side of the grill with a disposable aluminum pan to trap the heat and create an ovenlike cooking environment.	Leave one burner on high and turn off the other burner(s).
	BANKED FIRE Similar to a half-grill fire, except the heat is concentrated in an even smaller part of the grill. The large heat-free area can accommodate a pan of water and large cuts. This setup is often used for large foods that require hours on the grill, such as brisket or pulled pork.	Bank all the lit coals steeply against one side of the grill, leaving the rest of the grill free of coals.	After preheating the grill, adjust the primary burner as directed in the recipe, and turn off the other burner(s).
	DOUBLE-BANKED FIRE Sets up a cool area in the middle so that the food cooks evenly without the need for rotating it. Since the flame-free area is quite narrow and the heat output of this type of fire is not steady over an extended time, a double-banked fire is good for relatively small, quick-cooking foods such as a whole chicken. We sometimes place a disposable pan in the empty center area of the grill to catch drips and prevent flare-ups. The pan also keeps the piles of coals banked against the sides of the grill. This type of fire can be created in a gas grill only if the grill has at least three burners—and burners that ideally run from front to back on the grill.	Divide lit coals into two steeply banked piles on opposite sides of the grill, leaving the center free of coals.	After preheating the grill, leave the primary burner and the burner at the opposite end of the grill on medium-high, medium, or as directed in the recipe, and turn off the center burner(s).

How to Cook Meat—Cut by Cut

GRILL ROASTING

• **Best for:** Whole birds and tender roasts

Grill roasting is best for relatively large foods that are already tender and don't require prolonged cooking. Grill-roasting temperatures typically range from 300 to 400 degrees, and cooking times are relatively short, usually less than 1 or 2 hours. (Whole turkeys, which can take up to 3 hours, are an exception.) Grill-roasted meats and poultry can be seasoned a number of ways. You can simply let the smokiness from the grill be the primary flavoring, or add wood chips or chunks during cooking to bump up the smoke factor. Meat and poultry can also be dusted with a spice rub or seasoned with herbs and/or garlic before grill roasting. Or, during the final minutes of cooking, the food can be basted with a glaze.

1. SET UP AN INDIRECT FIRE Grill roasting relies on indirect cooking; the food isn't placed directly over the coals or lit burner, so the fire must be fashioned accordingly as a half-grill fire or double-banked fire so that part of the grill has no fire. Depending on how long you're cooking your food, the top and bottom vents will be open either completely or halfway. For a half-grill fire on a gas grill, leave one burner on high and the other burners off. For a double-banked fire on a gas grill, after preheating the grill, leave the primary burner and the burner at the opposite end of the grill on medium-high, medium, or as directed in the recipe, and turn off the center burner(s). Barbecuing requires the same setup except less coals are used.

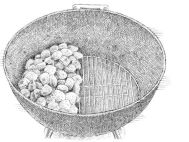

Customize your fire by setting up a Half-Grill Fire (left) or a Double-Banked Fire (right).

2. ADD WOOD CHIPS, IF DESIRED Grill-roasted foods can be given a boost of smoky flavor by adding wood chips to the fire during cooking, but they are not always used. If using wood chips or chunks, the lid vent is positioned over the food to envelop it with heat and smoke.

Wood chips (soaked and wrapped in foil) or soaked wood chunk(s) are sometimes used with grill roasting to impart smoky flavor to meat.

3. START BY SEARING Clean and oil the cooking grate. Place the food over a hot side of the grill and cook, turning as infrequently as possible, until well browned. In most cases (but not when cooking whole birds), a hot side of the grill is used to sear the exterior of the food to develop color and flavor.

4. MOVE TO THE COOL SIDE After searing, the food is moved to the cooler side to finish cooking (in the case of a whole bird, it is set over the cool side from the get-go). The grill is always covered when grill-roasting so that heat stays trapped inside. Most of the foods that are grill-roasted (beef roast, pork roast, whole birds) are cooked to a specific internal temperature. If using a modified two-level fire, make sure to rotate the food at the midway point in the projected cooking time so that the side that had been facing the fire is now turned away from the fire. In some cases, you might need replenish a charcoal fire with additional hot coals (see page 22).

Searing your food over a hot side of the grill browns the exterior of the meat and develops flavor.

Finishing over the cooler side allows the meat to cook through without the exterior overcooking. Keeping the cover on prevents heat from escaping.

How to Cook Meat–Cut by Cut

BARBECUING

• **Best for:** Tough cuts

In barbecuing, the goal is to impart a deep, intense smokiness while transforming chewy, tough, fatty cuts into tender, succulent meats. This means a long cooking time (usually several hours) over low heat—hence the barbecue adage: "Low-and-slow is the way to go." Although there is some debate among experts as to the proper heat level for barbecuing, we find a cooking temperature between 250 and 300 degrees to be optimal for most types of meats.

Some barbecue purists would call it heretical to barbecue on a gas grill; we admit that, in comparison with a charcoal grill, a gas grill results in a milder, less-pervasive smoky flavor, but it still yields good results. Either way, you will need to use wood—without smoke you're not barbecuing. Remember, you should use wood chunks only with a charcoal grill. Also see "How to Create a Custom Fire" (page 20).

1. BUILD A VERY SMALL FIRE The fire for barbecuing is built in much the same way as it is for grill roasting (using a half-grill fire or banked fire), with one side of the grill hotter than the other, but often with fewer coals or with the primary burner at a lower setting. The top and bottom vents should be open partway.

2. ADD WOOD CHIPS OR CHUNKS Wood chips or chunks are added to the hot side of the grill to generate smoke that envelops and flavors the food. (Positioning the lid vent over the food will help the smoke and heat draw in the right direction.) Before being wrapped in foil, wood chips should be soaked in water to cover for 15 minutes. Wood chunks should be soaked in water for 1 hour; they do not need to be wrapped in foil.

3. COVER AND COOK ON THE COOLER SIDE Clean and oil the cooking grate. Place the food on the grill as far from the fire as possible. Cover, positioning the lid vent over the food and cook, turning as infrequently as possible. The grill is always covered when barbecuing so that heat, smoke, and moisture are trapped inside. Make sure to rotate the food at the midway point of the projected cooking time so that the side that has been facing the fire is now turned away from the fire.

4. ADD HOT COALS AS NEEDED Barbecued foods that cook for more than a couple of hours often require a fuel replenishment to keep the fire sufficiently hot. On a charcoal grill, this means adding a few fresh coals to the fire. (On a gas grill, just make sure you have plenty of gas.)

5. FINISH IN THE OVEN Depending on the cut of meat, barbecuing can take the better part of a day on the grill and require monitoring and multiple fuel replenishments. For a simpler way that yields equally great results, we cook the food just long enough on the grill for it to pick up plenty of smoke. Then we move indoors and finish it in a low oven.

Because of the lengthy cooking time when barbecuing, we start with a small fire.

Sometimes we place a small pan of water under the cooking grate to provide just a little moisture that prevents the surface of the meat from drying out.

When barbecuing, it's important to keep the cover on the grill to prevent the fire from dying out. The lid vent, which is opened partway, is set over the food to envelop it with heat and smoke.

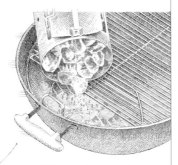

Add hot coals as needed to maintain the fire during the long barbecuing time. A grill with a hinged grate will make this easier to do.

Finishing the meat in the oven makes barbecue doable and more convenient.

A Meat Cookery Manifesto–Our Checklist

Shop Carefully
Buy the recommended size and thickness specified in recipes whether you're cooking stew, steak, or a whole turkey to ensure that the meat cooks through evenly and on time.

Pay Attention to Pan Size
Make sure your skillet is large enough; meat will be overcrowded in a too-small skillet, which inhibits browning. And invest in a roomy roasting pan. Improvising with a smaller pan, such as a 13 by 9-inch baking pan (we've all done it), doesn't allow for air circulation around the roast. Even worse, once the roast gets cooking, its rendered fat can splatter all over your oven. Look for a pan that measures 18 by 13 inches, a size large enough to accommodate any size roast.

Pat the Meat Dry Before Cooking
Wet meat will steam and not sear in a hot skillet. Likewise, excess moisture on a roast will need to evaporate in the oven before browning can begin. The result? A less flavorful crust or not-so-crispy skin.

Temperature Counts
Use an oven thermometer to calibrate your oven. And preheat your oven or get that pan hot on the stovetop. When frying, be sure the oil is at the right temperature by using a candy thermometer or thermometer that registers high temperatures.

Grill Meat on a Clean Grate
When grilling, be sure to clean the cooking grate before placing any food on it. There is nothing appetizing about tonight's grilled steak picking up charred bits of last week's barbecued chicken.

Choose the Right Setup When Grilling
You wouldn't cook a soufflé on the stovetop, right? So don't grill a large roast over a single-level fire unless you want unevenly cooked meat.

Gauge Doneness with a Meat Thermometer
Roasts and thick cuts may need to be temped in a few places (be sure to avoid bones) to ensure doneness. Thin cuts like boneless chicken breasts and thin steaks should be temped from the side to gauge an accurate reading.

Rest Meat Before Slicing
While smaller cuts should rest for 5 to 10 minutes, large roasts such as turkey may rest for about 40 minutes. Resting meat allows the juices, which are driven to the surface of the meat during cooking, to redistribute evenly throughout.

When Carving Roasts, Slice the Meat as Directed
Most roasts should be carved into thin slices, ideally no thicker than ¼ inch. Slicing meat thin cuts the muscle fibers into short lengths, resulting in a texture that's perceived as more tender than if the meat is cut into thick slices with longer sections.

Meat Myths Debunked

In our research, we found no shortage of misinformation about cooking meat. Here are some common fallacies and why they're untrue.

MYTH Searing meat seals in juices.
FACT Searing does not lock in flavor, but it does provide great benefit. We sear meat to develop a browned crust and a flavorful fond in which to build a pan sauce. (For more information about the benefits of searing meat, see page 57.)

MYTH Marinating meat in bottled Italian salad dressing makes it juicy and tender.
FACT Due to high levels of acidity, salad dressings don't add complex flavor and only make meat mushy. Plus, they are laden with sweeteners, stabilizers, and gums, which add a gelatinous consistency and unnatural flavor. (For more information about marinating, see page 7.)

MYTH Pink pork will make you sick.
FACT The pork of yesteryear was always cooked till gray, but that pork was a lot fattier than what's on the market today. Selective breeding has made today's pork much leaner, and if you cook it till gray, the meat will be dry and tough. We think the leanest cuts—like tenderloin—are best cooked to 145 degrees. At this point, the meat will still have a tinge of pink in the center. (For more information about modern pork, see page 177.)

MYTH Poultry should be rinsed before cooking.
FACT Both the USDA and the FDA advise against washing poultry. According to their research, while rinsing may remove some bacteria, the only way to ensure that all bacteria are killed is through proper cooking. Moreover, splashing bacteria around the sink can be dangerous, especially if water lands on food that is ready to be served.

MYTH A pop-up timer is the best way to gauge the doneness of a turkey.
FACT A pop-up timer goes off when your turkey is overcooked, so skip it. Instead, use an instant-read thermometer. Insert the thermometer into both the breast and thigh. The breast should register 165 degrees and the thigh should register 175 degrees.

MYTH Salt is salt—it doesn't matter which salt you use when seasoning or cooking meat.
FACT It depends. For everyday cooking, we use table salt, which dissolves easily and is inexpensive. We save kosher and sea salt for seasoning dishes just before we eat them, where their larger texture can be appreciated. Furthermore, because of the size of their grains, these salts can't be substituted for one another without making adjustments.

Recommended Tools of the Trade

Here are the pots, pans, tools, and equipment we turn to most often when preparing meat, whether it's a simple burger or an impressive holiday roast.

CHEF'S KNIFE A good chef's knife is an invaluable tool in the kitchen. We use it for chopping vegetables and herbs, slicing chicken breasts into cutlets, cutting tenderloins into medallions, and countless other tasks. In the test kitchen, we use our favorite **Victorinox Swiss Army 8-Inch Fibrox Chef's Knife** daily. Because a chef's knife is used so often, it is important to have one that fits comfortably in your hand, with a nonslip grip. It should be lightweight to allow for easy maneuvering on a variety of tasks. Thin, high-carbon stainless-steel blades are best for their long-lasting, super-sharp edges.

PARING KNIFE In the test kitchen, we like to use a paring knife for detailed work like trimming silverskin from meat or removing ribs from a chile pepper. We like the balance of a lightweight handle with a comfortable grip. Blade sizes run the gamut from a stumpy 2¾ inches to as long as 5 inches. We prefer 3- to 3½-inch blades, like the one on our favorite paring knife, the **Wüsthof Classic with PEtec, 3½-Inch**, since longer blades compromise precision and agility. Slightly curved blades with sharply pointed tips are best for the widest number of tasks.

BONING KNIFE Often, buying larger cuts of meat or whole birds and butchering them yourself is more economical than buying precut meat; plus, it will turn out more evenly sized pieces. If you choose to do this, a boning knife like the **Victorinox Swiss Army 6-Inch Fibrox Flexible Boning Knife** can be a useful tool. A good boning knife should be at least 6 inches long, very sharp, and allow you to easily maneuver around joints and bones. Look for a narrow, straight blade with good overall balance and a nonslip handle.

SLICING KNIFE The right knife can mean the difference between ragged, lopsided slices and professional, even ones. The heft, sharpness, length, and shape of a slicing knife all affect its cutting ability. We prefer an extra-long tapered blade that can cut through large roasts in one easy glide. It is also good to look for a rounded tip, which won't get caught on the way down. A Granton edge (which has small oval scallops carved out on both sides of the blade) makes for effortless slicing. In the test kitchen, we use the **Victorinox Swiss Army 12-Inch Fibrox Granton Edge Slicing Knife**.

STEAK KNIVES When it comes to steak knives, we want sturdy blades that won't wobble, even when cutting through thick pieces of meat. We find that serrated blades create jagged tears and don't make cutting any easier. We recommend buying steak knives with very sharp straight edges, like the **Victorinox Swiss Army Rosewood Straight Edge Steak Knife Set**. Look for comfortable, smooth handles.

CARVING FORK Carving forks may seem like a basic tool, but differences between models can either help or hinder the meat-slicing process. Carving forks come in two styles: curved, with prongs that follow the shape of a roast, and bayonet style, with long, straight prongs. We prefer curved forks, like the **Mercer Cutlery Genesis 6-Inch High-Carbon Carving Fork**, for their better sight lines and ability to hold roasts firmly while staying out of the knife's way. We also find that they can more easily transfer meat to a platter. Look for a carving fork that won't bend when lifting or turning heavy roasts, with a comfortable, nonslip handle.

MEAT CLEAVERS Meat cleavers can look intimidating, but we find that they are an important addition to the home kitchen, particularly when chopping meat and bones for stock. A good meat cleaver should do most of the chopping work for you, so look for one with a razor-sharp blade balanced by a comfortable handle. Our favorite is the **Global 6-Inch Meat Cleaver**.

MEAT POUNDERS Since we often prefer to pound our own cutlets rather than buy uneven precut cutlets from the store, a meat pounder is an important piece of equipment. There are two styles of meat pounders: those with vertical handles and those with offset handles (i.e., horizontally oriented). We prefer vertical handles, which offer better leverage and control. In the test kitchen, we use the **Norpro GRIP-EZ Meat Pounder**. Look for a meat pounder that weighs at least 1½ pounds.

DO HANDHELD MEAT TENDERIZERS WORK?

Handheld meat tenderizers are used to physically break down tough protein strands in meat, presumably resulting in more tender meat. Is it worth adding one to your kitchen arsenal? We put the two most common manual tenderizers to the test: a mallet with a jagged-toothed surface and a Jaccard meat tenderizer, which presses multiple sharp spikes into the meat. We used each tenderizer on a batch of pork cutlets and then compared them to cutlets that were lightly pounded with a smooth-surfaced pounder. Neither manual tenderizer improved the tenderness of the cutlets and each caused other problems. The toothed mallet gave the cutlets an unappealing pocked appearance that was especially bad around the edges. The sharp spikes on the Jaccard gave the meat a torn, "Salisbury steak" texture that we didn't like. If you want cutlets, we suggest buying tender boneless rib or loin chops and using a meat pounder or a smooth mallet to pound them into thin cutlets.

CUTTING/CARVING BOARDS Cutting boards are useful when breaking down a chicken, dicing vegetables, or performing other prep tasks. The best ones have ample work space—at least 15 by 20 inches is best—and enough heft to keep them from slipping and sliding around. Our preferred cutting board is the **Proteak Edge Grain Teak Cutting Board**. And when it comes time to carve a finished roast, we reach for a spacious carving board. We value heavy, sturdy boards that won't move while we're carving. Look for a deep, wide trench to prevent juices from running over the sides. We prefer models with some kind of meat-anchoring mechanism—our favorite, the **Williams-Sonoma Medium Reversible Carving Board**, has an oval-shaped central well where the meat can rest snugly.

TWINE In the test kitchen, we use kitchen twine for a variety of tasks, from trussing whole chickens to tying rolled stuffed meats to making bundles of herbs for flavoring stews. Good twine should stay tied without burning, fraying, or breaking. We prefer a center-fed cotton or linen twine, like **Librett Cotton Butcher's Twine**, for its neat ties and ability to withstand all conditions without slipping. Make sure that your twine is labeled "food-safe" or "kitchen twine."

FAT SEPARATOR A fat separator is an essential tool when performing tasks such as making gravy from the drippings of a roast or making a homemade stock into soup. There are three basic designs for fat separators: pitcher-type measuring cups with a pouring spout set into the base of the cup; ladles with slots around the perimeter; and brushes with long, soft bristles made from plastic fibers, called "fat mops." We prefer a pitcher-type, like the **Trudeau Gravy Separator with Integrated Strainer**, for its versatility and ease of use. Since fat separators are often used with hot liquids, shock-resistant plastic is more suited to this task than glass. We like models with large mouths, which make pouring liquid into the separator easier. An integrated strainer is a beneficial add-on for times when the liquid contains aromatic vegetables or herbs.

KITCHEN SHEARS In the test kitchen, we pick up our kitchen shears regularly. A good pair should be powerful enough to cut through chicken bones and tough herb stems, but also maneuverable enough to trim pie dough. We find comfortable handles to be key; models that sacrifice comfort for style are often more difficult to use. Although pull-apart handles make for easy cleaning, make sure to look for a pair that separates at a wide angle and won't separate spontaneously while cutting. Of course, supersharp blades are important, and our favorite, the **Kershaw 1120M TaskMaster Kitchen Shears**, have microserrations on the blades to help grip objects while cutting. We also prefer shears with adjustable tension settings. If you or someone you cook with is left-handed, be sure to look for shears that have symmetrical handles.

FOOD PROCESSOR You can use a food processor to chop meat for burgers or whip together salsas, pestos, and even soup bases in no time. Fitted with different blades, this appliance can fulfill a wide array of functions. Still, pick the wrong processor and suddenly this great convenience leaves you worse off than when you started. It seems like it should be a given, but not all food processors come with sharp blades. Blades with deep serrations tend to mangle food like bad steak knives. We prefer blades that are smooth or have miniserrations. Just as important is the blade's location in the workbowl. The gap between the blade and the workbowl should be as small as possible, preferably less than ⅛ inch. Look for a workbowl that has a capacity of at least 11 cups, with a wide, rather than narrow, feed tube. A heavy base keeps the food processor in place, rather than wobbling across the counter. Our favorite is the **Cuisinart Custom 14-Cup Food Processor**.

DIGITAL THERMOMETER Sight, touch, and experience are age-old ways to gauge when food is done, but for consistent results, nothing is as reliable as taking the food's internal temperature. We use our favorite **Splash-Proof Super-Fast Thermapen** every day. An instant-read thermometer makes it easier to tell if your roast is fully cooked or still raw on the inside without having to cut into it, draining valuable juices. There are two types of commonly sold handheld thermometers: digital and dial face. They both take accurate readings, but while pocket-size dial-face thermometers are less expensive than digital models, they are much less legible, and most have narrower effective temperature ranges than digitals (look for a thermometer with a wide temperature range, at least -10 to 425 degrees). We also prefer digital models because they register temperatures faster and are easier to read. The size of the thermometer stem can make a big difference. A long stem (one that measures at least 4 inches) is necessary to reach the center of whole birds and large roasts. Water-resistant thermometers are helpful as they're easier to clean and less likely to be damaged by spills.

REMOTE THERMOMETER A remote thermometer allows you to monitor the temperature of your food from a distance. A temperature probe inserted into the meat connects to a base that rests outside the grill or oven, which communicates with a pager you carry with you. Almost all models will work from a distance of more than 100 feet, even behind walls. As with any thermometer, we value accuracy above all else, but we also prefer models that are intuitive and easy to use, like the **Taylor Gourmet Wireless Thermometer**.

OVEN THERMOMETER Unless you have your oven routinely calibrated, there is a good chance that its temperature readings may be off. We tested 16 home ovens of friends and colleagues and found many that varied as much as 50 degrees in either direction. Inaccurate temperatures will dramatically impact your food, leaving it underdone on the inside or overbrowned and tough. To avoid such problems, we recommend purchasing an inexpensive oven thermometer, like the **Cooper-Atkins Oven Thermometer**, and checking it once the oven is preheated. Look for a thermometer that mounts securely in the oven and has clearly marked numbers that make it easy to read quickly.

TONGS During testing, we found that nonstick versus regular materials made less difference than the shape of the pincers. We prefer slightly concave pincers with wide, shallow scallops around the edges. Soft cushioning on the handles makes gripping easier and keeps them from overheating. We prefer a length of 12 inches, which keeps our hands far from the heat but is still easily maneuverable. Tongs should open and close easily and fit comfortably in your hand. In the test kitchen, we use **OXO Good Grips 12-Inch Locking Tongs**.

RIMMED BAKING SHEET In the test kitchen, we use baking sheets for more than just baking. They also come in handy for everything from oven-barbecued spareribs to roasted Cornish game hens. When buying baking sheets, look for ones that are light-colored and thick. A light-colored surface will heat and brown evenly. And a pan that isn't thick enough can buckle or transfer heat too intensely, burning the food. We prefer pans that are 18 by 13 inches with a 1-inch rim all around. And because they have so many different uses, we recommend having more than one. Our recommended rimmed baking sheet is the **Wear-Ever Half Size Heavy Duty Sheet Pan (13 Gauge) by Vollrath, model 5314**.

DRY MEASURING CUPS As a kitchen staple, a set of measuring cups must be durable. Look for heavy, well-constructed, evenly weighted stainless-steel models—plastic cups can warp in the dishwasher or melt easily. The measurement markings should be easy to read even when the cup is full; cups with measurement markings on the handles are the most common and most practical. Dry ingredients like flour or cornmeal should always be measured in dry measuring cups; in a liquid measuring cup, it is impossible to level the surface of the contents to obtain an exact measurement. An extra-long 4-inch handle is helpful when dipping into a bin of flour; a short, awkward handle can make dipping difficult, and a shoddy, thin handle will bend under pressure. Also avoid cups with heavy handles that tilt when set down. Handles that are straight and flush with the rim of the measuring cups make it easy to scrape off any excess ingredient for a level, accurate measure. We prefer the **Amco Houseworks Professional Performance 4-Piece Measuring Cup Set** for measuring dry ingredients.

LIQUID MEASURING CUPS The simple **Pyrex 2-Cup Measuring Cup** with red lines and a pour spout is the industry standard, with good reason. It is easy to use, accurate, and durable. We prefer glass models to plastic because the lines tend to wear off on the latter. The measurement markings should be clear and easy to read from the outside of the cup, even when full of a dark-colored ingredient, and should cover a range of gradations, including in-between sizes. To read the cup properly, make sure the cup is on a flat surface and you're at eye level with the meniscus (the concave surface of the liquid); otherwise, you may measure too little or too much. Since liquid measuring cups cost just a few dollars, it makes sense to own at least two; we find the 2-cup and 4-cup sizes most useful, but a 1-cup measure is worth having on hand for measuring small amounts. The very best cups are just an inch or two wider than a spatula, with rounded bottoms instead of sharp corners. This design will trap less honey or other sticky ingredients and allow you to swipe away what's left behind with a rubber spatula.

MEASURING SPOONS When we need to measure ingredients like salt, baking soda, and spices as well as herbs and small amounts of many other ingredients, we reach for our **Cuisipro Stainless Steel Measuring Spoons Set**. We prefer heavy, well-constructed stainless-steel models with long, sturdy, well-designed handles. Plastic models, no matter how thick, feel flimsy and are more likely to break, bend, crack, warp, or melt. Long, slim spoons have an easier time reaching into tall, narrow jars, and their slim metal handles make for compact storage. As with dry measuring cups, these spoons should have a flat rim and handle so that dry ingredients can be easily leveled. We prefer spoons with deeper bowls as opposed to those with narrow and elongated or wide and shallow bowls. Shallow bowls can allow more liquid to spill as the result of a slight misstep or unsteady hand. Also, the spoons should be comfortable to use on their ring and easy to remove from it.

SKILLETS Skillets are simply frying pans with low, flared sides. Their shape encourages evaporation, which is why skillets excel at searing, browning, and sauce reduction. We can cook almost anything in a 12-inch skillet, whether we want to sear, sauté, shallow-fry, pan-roast, or even stir-fry. In the test kitchen, we like to have three types of skillets on hand: traditional, cast-iron, and nonstick. Our favorite traditional skillet, the **All-Clad Stainless 12-Inch Fry Pan**, is what we reach for when we want to create caramelized, browned bits called fond that are the foundation for great flavor in sautéed or pan-seared dishes. Cast-iron skillets are also useful for their excellent heat retention for high-heat cooking techniques such as frying and searing. And unlike most consumer products, cast-iron pans actually improve with time and heavy use. Our favorite is the **Lodge 12-Inch Skillet**. Well-made traditional or cast-iron skillets should last a lifetime (or two). For cooking delicate foods like breaded chicken cutlets, however, a nonstick skillet is ideal. We also use them in stir-frying or other batch-cooked foods, where we don't want fond to build up and scorch. Our favorite nonstick skillet is the **T-fal Professional Non-Stick Fry Pan, 12.5 inches**.

SAUCEPANS In the short list of indispensable home kitchen equipment, a good 4-quart saucepan with a lid occupies a secure place near the top, somewhere just below a sharp chef's knife and a 12-inch skillet. We can't picture doing without a saucepan with a hefty frame, deep bowl, long arm, and tight-fitting lid, which make it the go-to vessel for steamed rice, soups, and sauces—and we've gladly paid dearly for a model that can take a daily dose of shuffling around the stovetop. We like "fully clad" models, meaning they have a layered construction to evenly disperse heat. We also prefer slightly rounded corners—as opposed to sharply angled ones—because thick sauces are less likely to get stuck. The best saucepans, such as our top-rated **All-Clad Stainless 4-Quart Saucepan**, are relatively lightweight and easy to maneuver, and their handles are comfortable and sturdy.

DUTCH OVEN A good Dutch oven (variously called a stockpot, round oven, French oven, or casserole) is a kitchen essential. They're heavier and thicker than stockpots, allowing them to retain and conduct heat more effectively, and deeper than a skillet, so they can handle large cuts of meat and cooking liquid. These qualities make Dutch ovens the best choice for braises, pot roasts, and stews, especially as they can go on the stovetop to sear foods and then into the oven to finish cooking. Their tall sides make them useful for deep frying, and many cooks press Dutch ovens into service for jobs like boiling pasta. Our favorite pots are wide enough (at least 8 inches) to brown 3½ pounds of beef in three or four batches. We like the **Le Creuset 7¼-Quart Round French Oven**; or, for a lighter-weight Dutch oven, we prefer the **All-Clad Stainless 8-Quart Stockpot**.

ROASTING PAN/V-RACK A good roasting pan should be a sturdy, large workhorse, able to brown food evenly and withstand high-heat searing on the stovetop. We prefer durable tri-ply stainless-steel pans with a lighter finish, which allows monitoring of browning. Look for roomy, secure handles, which make maneuvering easier and safer. Most models come with a rack, which should fit snugly in the pan and not move or slide around. Our favorite roasting pan is the **Calphalon Contemporary Stainless Roasting Pan with Rack**.

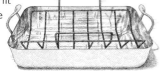

GARLIC PRESS Over the years, we've learned that for the average home cook, a garlic press is faster, easier, and more effective than trying to get a fine, even mince with a chef's knife. More important, garlic's flavor and aroma emerge only as its cell walls are ruptured, so a finely processed clove gives you a better distribution of garlic and fuller garlic flavor throughout the dish. Even our test cooks, trained to mince with a knife, generally grab our favorite **Kuhn Rikon Stainless Steel Epicurean Garlic Press** when cooking. We recommend choosing a garlic press that produces a fine, uniform mince. It should be simple and comfortable to use, as well as easy to clean.

PEPPER MILL Freshly ground pepper adds spice and crunch to many of our favorite recipes, and the right pepper mill makes achieving equal-size pieces a cinch and efficient. We like pepper mills with easily adjustable and well-marked grind sizes. The best ones are straightforward to use and don't produce a lot of pepper dust along with the crushed peppercorns. Look for a mill that fits comfortably in your hand, with smooth, padded handles or a rounded top. We prefer the **Cole & Mason Derwent Gourmet Precision Pepper Mill**.

GRILLS In summer, there's nothing better than cooking outdoors. Grilling and barbecue enthusiasts insist that charcoal grills are the gold standard for outdoor cooking, but gas grills have strong merits too: Turn on the gas, hit the ignition switch, and *voilà*—an instant fire of whatever intensity you need for tonight's recipe. Whichever type of grill you choose to use, make sure it has ample space for cooking large roasts or burgers for a crowd. When it comes to charcoal grills, we prefer one that can accommodate a full 6-quart chimney starter's worth of charcoal. Most importantly, we look for a charcoal grill that maintains heat levels and has well-placed vents that allow us to control temperature. Side trays, wheels, and ease of storage are also pluses. Our favorite charcoal grill is the **Weber Performer Platinum 22.5-Inch Charcoal Grill with Touch-n-Go Gas Ignition**. Gas grills, on the other hand, deliver what 21st-century Americans prize most: ease. Because gas grills allow precise heat control, they are especially well suited to barbecuing and grill roasting. These techniques require low, indirect heat (in the range of 250 to 350 degrees) for a long time to cook through large cuts of meat or whole birds. We find that it is important that a gas grill have an effective design for fat drainage to limit the problem of flare-ups. Our go-to gas grill is the **Weber Spirit E210**.

Beef

(CONTINUED)

Beef Basics

Buying a steak or a roast or even a package of ground beef isn't as easy as it used to be. First, there are many cuts of beef in the market, many of which are sold under a variety of alternate names. Beef labels can also be confusing. On page 2, we address general meat labeling terms and here, we explain more about labels specific to beef. In addition, our retail cuts chart on page 33 will help you understand shopping for beef, cut by cut.

GRADING

The U.S. Department of Agriculture (USDA) assigns different quality grades to beef, but most meat available to consumers is confined to three of the quality grades assigned by the USDA: prime, choice, and select. Grading is voluntary on the part of the meat-packer. If meat is graded, it should bear a USDA stamp indicating the grade, though it may not be visible to the consumer. To grade meat, inspectors evaluate color, grain, surface texture, and fat content and distribution.

Prime meat is heavily marbled with intramuscular fat, which makes for a tender, flavorful steak. About 2 percent of graded beef is considered prime. Prime meats are most often served in restaurants or sold in high-end butcher shops. The majority of graded beef is choice. While the levels of marbling in choice beef can vary, it is generally moderately marbled with intramuscular fat. Select beef has little marbling.

Our blind tasting of all three grades of rib-eye steaks produced predictable results: Prime ranked first for its tender, buttery texture and rich flavor. Next came choice, with good meaty flavor and more chew. The tough and stringy select steak followed, with flavor that was barely acceptable. Our advice: When you're willing to splurge, go for prime steak, but a choice steak that exhibits a moderate amount of marbling is a fine, affordable option. Just stay clear of select-grade steak.

PRIME
Heavily marbled,
tender, and flavorful

CHOICE
Moderately marbled,
good flavor and value

SELECT
Lightly marbled, tough,
poor flavor

LABELING

Grain-Fed Versus Grass-Fed Beef

Most U.S. beef is raised on grain but grass-fed beef is becoming an increasingly popular option. Grain-fed beef is generally considered to be richer and fattier, while grass-fed beef is leaner, chewy, and more gamy—or at least that's the conventional wisdom. In our taste tests, we pitted grain-fed and grass-fed rib-eye steaks and strip steaks against each other. We found differences among the various strip steaks to be quite small. The grain-fed rib eyes had a milder flavor compared with the nutty, complex flavor of the grass-fed beef, but our tasters' preferences were evenly split. The texture of all samples was similar.

Organic Versus Natural

The government regulates the use of the term "organic" on beef labels, but producers set their own guidelines when it comes to the term "natural." If you want to ensure that you're buying meat raised without antibiotics or hormones and fed an organic diet (and no mammalian or aviary products), then look for the USDA's organic seal. (For more information about the organic label, see page 2.)

Mechanically Tenderized Beef

Blade tenderized (also known as "mechanically tenderized," or "needled") meat has been passed through a machine that punctures it with small, sharp blades or needles to break up the connective tissue and muscle fibers with the aim of making a potentially chewy cut more palatable (or an already tender cut even more so). Because the blades can potentially transfer illness-causing bacteria such as *E. coli* from the surface of the meat to the interior, the meat should be cooked to 160 degrees (well-done) to ensure that any potential bacteria is no longer viable. While the USDA has published guidelines suggesting that all mechanically tenderized meat be labeled and accompanied by a reminder to cook the meat to 160 degrees, it does not become a mandatory rule until January 2016. A handful of retailers, including Costco, already label their tenderized beef, but if you're concerned, you can always ask your supermarket butcher.

As for the effectiveness of blade tenderizing, we compared tenderized top sirloin steaks and rib-eye steaks from Costco with traditional steaks, and found that the blade-tenderized steaks were indeed more tender when all the steaks were cooked to a safe 160 degrees. But we prefer our steaks cooked to medium-rare, and since that isn't advisable with blade-tenderized beef, we'll stick with traditional meat.

Primal Cuts of Beef

Before you choose a particular cut of beef, it helps to understand something about the anatomy of a cow. Eight different cuts of beef are sold at the wholesale level. From this first series of cuts, known in the trade as primal cuts, a butcher (usually at a meatpacking plant in the Midwest but sometimes on-site at your local market) will make the retail cuts that you bring home from the market. How you choose to cook a particular piece of beef depends on where the meat comes from on the cow and how it was butchered.

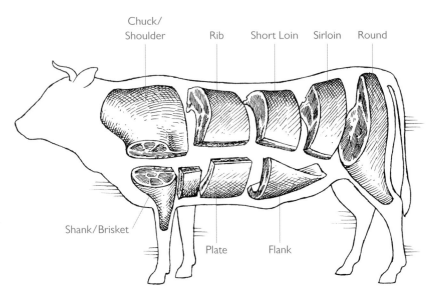

Chuck/
Shoulder   Rib   Short Loin   Sirloin   Round

Shank/Brisket

Plate   Flank

Chuck/Shoulder

The chuck (also called the shoulder) runs from the neck down to the fifth rib. There are four major muscles in this region, and meat from the chuck tends to be flavorful and fairly fatty, which is why ground chuck makes the best hamburgers. Chuck also contains a fair amount of connective tissue, so when the meat is not ground it generally requires a long cooking time to become tender.

Rib

The rib section extends along the back of the animal from the sixth to the 12th rib. The prime rib comes from this area, as do rib-eye steaks. Rib cuts have excellent beefy flavor and are quite tender.

Short Loin

The short loin (also called the loin) extends from the last rib back through the midsection of the animal to the hip area. It contains two major muscles—the tenderloin and the shell. The tenderloin is extremely tender (it is positioned right under the spine) and has quite a mild flavor. This muscle may be sold whole as a roast or sliced crosswise into steaks, called filets mignons. The shell is a much larger muscle and has a more robust beef flavor as well as more fat. Strip steaks (also called shell steaks) come from this muscle and are a test kitchen favorite. Two steaks from the short loin area contain portions of both the tenderloin and shell muscles. These steaks are called the T-bone and porterhouse, and both are excellent.

Sirloin

The sirloin contains relatively inexpensive cuts that are sold as both steaks and roasts. We find that sirloin cuts are fairly lean and tough. In general, we prefer other parts of the animal, although top sirloin makes a decent roast.

Round

Roasts and steaks cut from the round are usually sold boneless. They are quite lean and can be tough. We generally prefer cuts from other parts of the cow, although top round can be roasted with some success.

Brisket/Shank, Plate, and Flank

Moderately thick boneless cuts are removed from the three primal cuts that run along the underside of the animal. The brisket (also called shank) is rather tough and contains a lot of connective tissue. The plate is rarely sold at the retail level (it is used to make pastrami). The flank is a leaner cut that makes an excellent steak when grilled.

Shopping for Beef–Cut by Cut

We've rated the following cuts on flavor (★★★★ being the most flavorful) and cost ($$$$ being the most expensive). Additionally, steaks are rated on tenderness (★★★★ being the most tender). This characteristic is less important for roasts, since long cooking methods like braising or barbecuing can transform tough cuts into very tender meat.

PRIMAL CUT: CHUCK/SHOULDER

SHOULDER STEAK
This 1½- to 2-pound boneless steak is a great value for cost-conscious cooks. Although cut from the shoulder, it is relatively lean, with a moderately beefy flavor. Since this steak can be a bit tough, it should be sliced thin on the bias after cooking.

Flavor: ★★ **Tenderness:** ★★
Cost: $

Alternate Name: Chuck steak

Best Cooking Method: Grilling

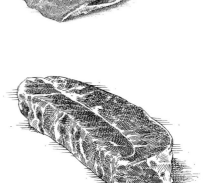

Recommended Recipe: Grilled Chuck Steaks (page 81)

BLADE STEAK
Blade steak is a small shoulder cut. It is an all-purpose steak. While it is very tender and richly flavored, a line of gristle that runs through the center of the meat makes this steak a poor option for serving whole. Remove the gristle and slice the steak thinly for stir-fries, or cut into cubes for kebabs or stews.

Flavor: ★★★ **Tenderness:** ★★★
Cost: $

Alternate Names: Top blade steak, flat-iron steak

Best Cooking Methods: Stir-frying, broiling, grilling, stewing, braising

Recommended Recipes: Stir-Fried Thai-Style Beef with Chiles and Shallots (page 72), Carbonnade à la Flamande (page 142), Ultimate Beef Chili (page 145)

TOP BLADE ROAST
This broad, flat cut is quite flavorful, and because it is boneless it's the best substitute for a chuck-eye roast. Even after cooking, this cut retains a distinctive strip of connective tissue, which is not unpleasant to eat.

Flavor: ★★★ Cost: $ $

Alternate Names: Chuck roast, first cut, blade roast, top chuck roast

Best Cooking Methods: Roasting, stewing, braising

CHUCK 7-BONE ROAST
A bone shaped like the number seven gives this cut its name. The deep flavor of this thin cut needs less liquid to braise and less time to cook than other cuts from the chuck.

Flavor: ★★★ Cost: $ $

Alternate Names: Center-cut pot roast, center-cut chuck roast

Best Cooking Methods: Roasting, stewing, braising

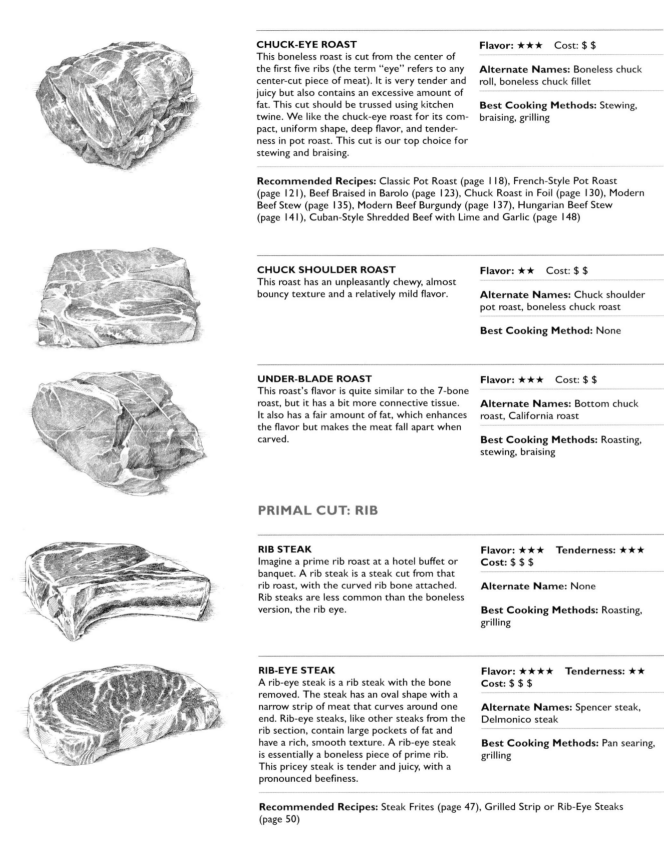

CHUCK-EYE ROAST

This boneless roast is cut from the center of the first five ribs (the term "eye" refers to any center-cut piece of meat). It is very tender and juicy but also contains an excessive amount of fat. This cut should be trussed using kitchen twine. We like the chuck-eye roast for its compact, uniform shape, deep flavor, and tenderness in pot roast. This cut is our top choice for stewing and braising.

Flavor: ★★★   **Cost:** $ $

Alternate Names: Boneless chuck roll, boneless chuck fillet

Best Cooking Methods: Stewing, braising, grilling

Recommended Recipes: Classic Pot Roast (page 118), French-Style Pot Roast (page 121), Beef Braised in Barolo (page 123), Chuck Roast in Foil (page 130), Modern Beef Stew (page 135), Modern Beef Burgundy (page 137), Hungarian Beef Stew (page 141), Cuban-Style Shredded Beef with Lime and Garlic (page 148)

CHUCK SHOULDER ROAST

This roast has an unpleasantly chewy, almost bouncy texture and a relatively mild flavor.

Flavor: ★★   **Cost:** $ $

Alternate Names: Chuck shoulder pot roast, boneless chuck roast

Best Cooking Method: None

UNDER-BLADE ROAST

This roast's flavor is quite similar to the 7-bone roast, but it has a bit more connective tissue. It also has a fair amount of fat, which enhances the flavor but makes the meat fall apart when carved.

Flavor: ★★★   **Cost:** $ $

Alternate Names: Bottom chuck roast, California roast

Best Cooking Methods: Roasting, stewing, braising

PRIMAL CUT: RIB

RIB STEAK

Imagine a prime rib roast at a hotel buffet or banquet. A rib steak is a steak cut from that rib roast, with the curved rib bone attached. Rib steaks are less common than the boneless version, the rib eye.

Flavor: ★★★   **Tenderness:** ★★★
Cost: $ $ $

Alternate Name: None

Best Cooking Methods: Roasting, grilling

RIB-EYE STEAK

A rib-eye steak is a rib steak with the bone removed. The steak has an oval shape with a narrow strip of meat that curves around one end. Rib-eye steaks, like other steaks from the rib section, contain large pockets of fat and have a rich, smooth texture. A rib-eye steak is essentially a boneless piece of prime rib. This pricey steak is tender and juicy, with a pronounced beefiness.

Flavor: ★★★★   **Tenderness:** ★★
Cost: $ $ $

Alternate Names: Spencer steak, Delmonico steak

Best Cooking Methods: Pan searing, grilling

Recommended Recipes: Steak Frites (page 47), Grilled Strip or Rib-Eye Steaks (page 50)

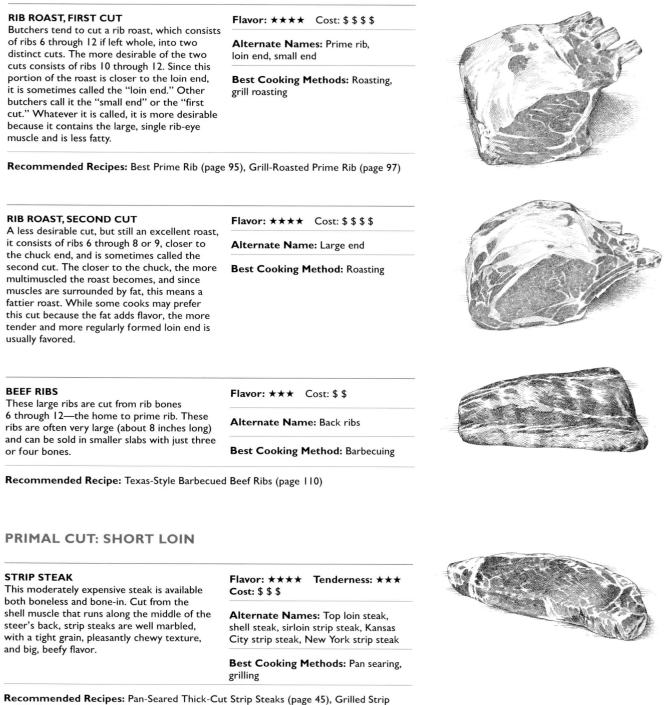

RIB ROAST, FIRST CUT
Butchers tend to cut a rib roast, which consists of ribs 6 through 12 if left whole, into two distinct cuts. The more desirable of the two cuts consists of ribs 10 through 12. Since this portion of the roast is closer to the loin end, it is sometimes called the "loin end." Other butchers call it the "small end" or the "first cut." Whatever it is called, it is more desirable because it contains the large, single rib-eye muscle and is less fatty.

Flavor: ★★★★   **Cost:** $ $ $ $

Alternate Names: Prime rib, loin end, small end

Best Cooking Methods: Roasting, grill roasting

Recommended Recipes: Best Prime Rib (page 95), Grill-Roasted Prime Rib (page 97)

RIB ROAST, SECOND CUT
A less desirable cut, but still an excellent roast, it consists of ribs 6 through 8 or 9, closer to the chuck end, and is sometimes called the second cut. The closer to the chuck, the more multimuscled the roast becomes, and since muscles are surrounded by fat, this means a fattier roast. While some cooks may prefer this cut because the fat adds flavor, the more tender and more regularly formed loin end is usually favored.

Flavor: ★★★★   **Cost:** $ $ $ $

Alternate Name: Large end

Best Cooking Method: Roasting

BEEF RIBS
These large ribs are cut from rib bones 6 through 12—the home to prime rib. These ribs are often very large (about 8 inches long) and can be sold in smaller slabs with just three or four bones.

Flavor: ★★★   **Cost:** $ $

Alternate Name: Back ribs

Best Cooking Method: Barbecuing

Recommended Recipe: Texas-Style Barbecued Beef Ribs (page 110)

PRIMAL CUT: SHORT LOIN

STRIP STEAK
This moderately expensive steak is available both boneless and bone-in. Cut from the shell muscle that runs along the middle of the steer's back, strip steaks are well marbled, with a tight grain, pleasantly chewy texture, and big, beefy flavor.

Flavor: ★★★★   **Tenderness:** ★★★
Cost: $ $ $

Alternate Names: Top loin steak, shell steak, sirloin strip steak, Kansas City strip steak, New York strip steak

Best Cooking Methods: Pan searing, grilling

Recommended Recipes: Pan-Seared Thick-Cut Strip Steaks (page 45), Grilled Strip or Rib-Eye Steaks (page 50), Grilled Argentine Steaks with Chimichurri Sauce (page 55)

FILET MIGNON
The tenderloin, a long, cylindrical muscle that is the most tender meat on the cow, may be cut into a number of different steaks, each of which has its own name but all of which are very expensive, since Americans prize tenderness in their steaks above all else. Châteaubriand is a 3-inch-thick steak cut from the thickest part of the tenderloin, usually large enough to serve two. Filet, filet mignon, or tenderloin steak is typically 1 to 2 inches thick, cut from the narrow end of the tenderloin. Tournedos are the smallest tenderloin steaks, about an inch thick, cut toward the tip end. Tenderloin steaks are buttery smooth and very tender, with very mild beef flavor.

Flavor: ★   **Tenderness:** ★★★★
Cost: $ $ $ $

Alternate Names: Châteaubriand, tenderloin steak, tournedo

Best Cooking Methods: Pan searing, grilling

Recommended Recipe: Pepper-Crusted Filets Mignons (page 49)

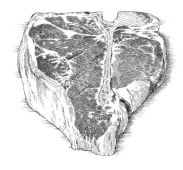

T-BONE STEAK
A classic grilling steak, this cut is named for the T-shaped bone that runs through the meat. This bone separates two muscles, the flavorful strip (or shell, left) and the buttery tenderloin (right). Because the tenderloin is small and will cook more quickly than the strip, this steak should be positioned over the cooler side of the fire when grilling.

Flavor: ★★★★   **Tenderness:** ★★★
Cost: $ $ $

Alternate Name: None

Best Cooking Methods: Pan searing, grilling

Recommended Recipes: Grilled Porterhouse or T-Bone Steaks (page 51), Grilled Tuscan Steak with Olive Oil and Lemon (page 52)

PORTERHOUSE STEAK
The porterhouse is really just a huge T-bone steak with a larger tenderloin section, which accounts for its higher price. It is cut farther back on the animal than the T-bone. Like the T-bone steak, the porterhouse steak, with both strip and tenderloin sections, has well-balanced flavor and texture. Most porterhouse steaks are big enough to serve two.

Flavor: ★★★★   **Tenderness:** ★★★
Cost: $ $ $

Alternate Name: None

Best Cooking Methods: Pan searing, grilling

Recommended Recipes: Grilled Porterhouse or T-Bone Steaks (page 51), Grilled Tuscan Steak with Olive Oil and Lemon (page 52)

TENDERLOIN
The tenderloin is the most tender piece of beef you can buy. A center-cut tenderloin roast is sometimes labeled Châteaubriand. Its flavor is pleasantly mild, almost nonbeefy. Unpeeled tenderloins come with an incredibly thick layer of exterior fat still attached, which should be removed. Peeled roasts have scattered patches of fat that need not be removed. This roast can be cut into individual steaks to make filets mignons.

Flavor: ★   **Cost:** $ $ $ $

Alternate Names: Whole filet, Châteaubriand

Best Cooking Methods: Roasting, grill roasting

Recommended Recipes: Pepper-Crusted Beef Tenderloin Roast (page 99), Grill-Roasted Beef Tenderloin (page 103)

PRIMAL CUT: SIRLOIN

SHELL SIRLOIN STEAK

Several steaks are cut from the sirloin, or hip, section; moving from the front to the rear of the steer, they are pin- or hip-bone steak, flat-bone steak, round-bone steak, and wedge-bone steak. Of these, the round bone is best; the others are rarely found in supermarkets. Shell sirloin steak is simply a round-bone sirloin steak that has had the small piece of tenderloin removed. It is most commonly found in the Northeast. Do not confuse sirloin steaks with the superior top loin steak, which is sometimes called sirloin strip steak or New York strip steak.

Flavor: ★★   **Tenderness:** ★★
Cost: $

Alternate Names: New York sirloin steak, round-bone steak

Best Cooking Methods: Pan searing, grilling

Recommended Recipes: Pan-Seared Inexpensive Steaks (page 56), Inexpensive Grilled Steaks with Spice Rubs (page 77)

TOP SIRLOIN STEAK

Cut from the hip, this steak is the boneless version of round-bone steak. Top sirloin steak is a large, inexpensive steak with decent tenderness and flavor, but do not confuse it with the superior New York strip steak. Slice thin against the grain after cooking.

Flavor: ★★   **Tenderness:** ★★★
Cost: $

Alternate Names: New York sirloin steak, sirloin butt steak

Best Cooking Methods: Pan searing, grilling

SIRLOIN STEAK TIP

Cut from the area just before the hip, this large (upward of 2½ pounds), rectangular steak is most often sold in strips or cubes. To ensure that you are buying the real thing, buy the whole steak and cut it yourself. Though not particularly tender, this steak has a distinct grain and a robust beefiness. Slice thin against the grain after cooking.

Flavor: ★★★   **Tenderness:** ★★
Cost: $ $

Alternate Name: Flap meat

Best Cooking Methods: Pan searing, grilling

Recommended Recipes: Chicken-Fried Steak (page 58), Steak Tips with Mushroom-Onion Gravy (page 60), Beef Stroganoff (page 61), Crispy Orange Beef (page 75), Grilled Steak Tips (page 87), Grilled Beef Kebabs (page 92), Best Old-Fashioned Burgers (page 153), Juicy Pub-Style Burgers (page 155)

TOP SIRLOIN ROAST

This cut from the hip area tastes incredibly meaty and has plenty of marbling, which makes for a succulent roast. Aside from the vein of gristle that runs through it, which is slightly unpleasant to eat, the roast is tender and juicy, with big, beefy flavor. Other parts of the sirloin are lean and tough, but top sirloin roast is one of our favorite inexpensive roasts.

Flavor: ★★★   **Cost:** $ $

Alternate Names: Top butt, center-cut roast

Best Cooking Methods: Grill roasting, roasting

Recommended Recipes: Inexpensive Grill-Roasted Beef (page 107), Baltimore Pit Beef (page 109)

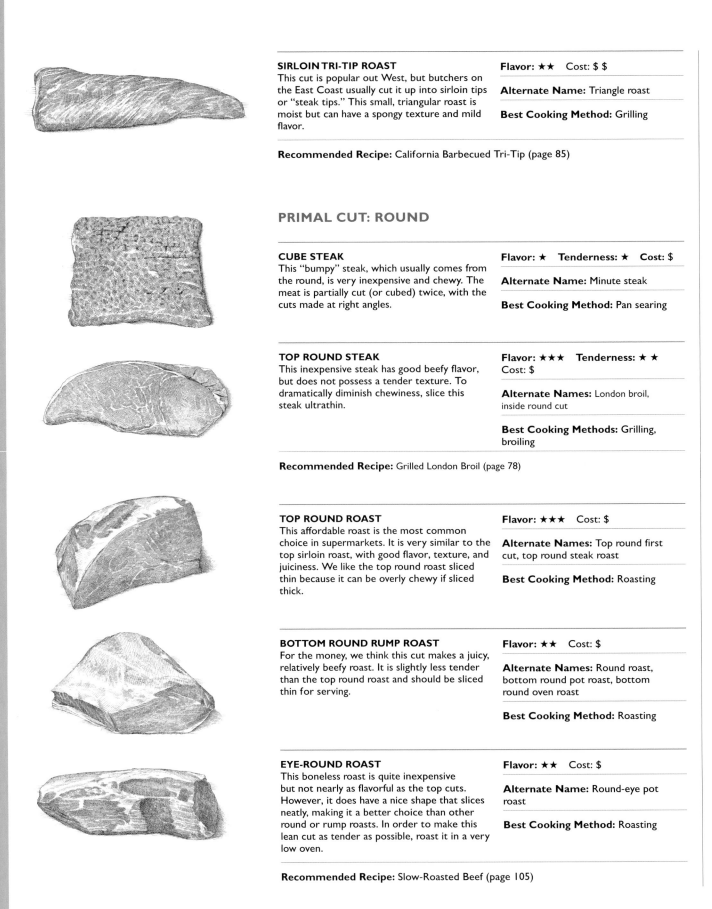

SIRLOIN TRI-TIP ROAST

This cut is popular out West, but butchers on the East Coast usually cut it up into sirloin tips or "steak tips." This small, triangular roast is moist but can have a spongy texture and mild flavor.

Flavor: ★★ **Cost:** $ $

Alternate Name: Triangle roast

Best Cooking Method: Grilling

Recommended Recipe: California Barbecued Tri-Tip (page 85)

PRIMAL CUT: ROUND

CUBE STEAK

This "bumpy" steak, which usually comes from the round, is very inexpensive and chewy. The meat is partially cut (or cubed) twice, with the cuts made at right angles.

Flavor: ★ **Tenderness:** ★ **Cost:** $

Alternate Name: Minute steak

Best Cooking Method: Pan searing

TOP ROUND STEAK

This inexpensive steak has good beefy flavor, but does not possess a tender texture. To dramatically diminish chewiness, slice this steak ultrathin.

Flavor: ★★★ **Tenderness:** ★★ **Cost:** $

Alternate Names: London broil, inside round cut

Best Cooking Methods: Grilling, broiling

Recommended Recipe: Grilled London Broil (page 78)

TOP ROUND ROAST

This affordable roast is the most common choice in supermarkets. It is very similar to the top sirloin roast, with good flavor, texture, and juiciness. We like the top round roast sliced thin because it can be overly chewy if sliced thick.

Flavor: ★★★ **Cost:** $

Alternate Names: Top round first cut, top round steak roast

Best Cooking Method: Roasting

BOTTOM ROUND RUMP ROAST

For the money, we think this cut makes a juicy, relatively beefy roast. It is slightly less tender than the top round roast and should be sliced thin for serving.

Flavor: ★★ **Cost:** $

Alternate Names: Round roast, bottom round pot roast, bottom round oven roast

Best Cooking Method: Roasting

EYE-ROUND ROAST

This boneless roast is quite inexpensive but not nearly as flavorful as the top cuts. However, it does have a nice shape that slices neatly, making it a better choice than other round or rump roasts. In order to make this lean cut as tender as possible, roast it in a very low oven.

Flavor: ★★ **Cost:** $

Alternate Name: Round-eye pot roast

Best Cooking Method: Roasting

Recommended Recipe: Slow-Roasted Beef (page 105)

BOTTOM ROUND ROAST
This cut is our least favorite. It is essentially devoid of flavor and has a rubbery, chewy texture. This roast is not worth even the little that it costs.

Flavor: no stars   **Cost:** $

Alternate Name: None

Best Cooking Method: None

PRIMAL CUTS: BRISKET/SHANK, PLATE, AND FLANK

SKIRT STEAK
This thin steak from the underside of the animal has an especially beefy flavor. It was the original choice for fajitas, although most cooks now use easier-to-find flank steak. Although it can be cooked like flank steak, skirt steak is fattier and juicier. Look for it at better markets and butcher shops.

Flavor: ★★★   **Tenderness:** ★★
Cost: $ $ $

Alternate Names: Fajita steak, Philadelphia steak

Best Cooking Methods: Pan searing, grilling, stir-frying

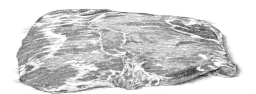

Recommended Recipe: Philly Cheesesteaks (page 64)

FLANK STEAK
Flank steak is a large, flat cut from the underside of the cow, with a distinct longitudinal grain. Flank steak is thin and cooks quickly, making it ideal for the grill. Although very flavorful, flank steak is slightly chewy. It should not be cooked past medium and should always be sliced thin against the grain.

Flavor: ★★★   **Tenderness:** ★★
Cost: $ $ $

Alternate Name: Jiffy steak

Best Cooking Methods: Grilling, pan searing, stir-frying

Recommended Recipes: Steak Tacos (page 65), Teriyaki Stir-Fried Beef (page 69), Grilled Marinated Flank Steak (page 82), Classic Grilled Beef Fajitas (page 88), Grilled Beef Satay (page 89), Thai Grilled Beef Salad (page 94)

HANGER STEAK
This bistro favorite is actually a thick muscle attached to the diaphragm on the underside of the cow. When a cow is butchered, this steak hangs down into the center of the carcass, thus its name. Hanger steak is much tougher than flank steak and not nearly as flavorful.

Flavor: ★★   **Tenderness:** ★
Cost: $ $ $

Alternate Names: Hanging tenderloin, butcher's steak, hanging tender

Best Cooking Methods: Pan searing, grilling

BRISKET
This large, rectangular cut weighs about 13 pounds, so it is often divided into two subcuts, the flat cut (on the left side in this brisket) and the point cut (on the right side). The flat cut is leaner, thinner, and more widely available. When shopping for flat-cut brisket, look for a roast with a decent fat cap on top. The point cut is well marbled and thicker. If you can find it, you can use it in place of the flat-cut brisket in most recipes; however, the cooking time might need to be extended.

Flavor: ★★★   **Cost:** $ $

Alternate Name: None

Best Cooking Methods: Barbecuing, braising

Recommended Recipes: Barbecued Beef Brisket (page 116), Onion-Braised Beef Brisket (page 127), Corned Beef and Cabbage (page 131)

SHANK

This round cut is a cross-section of the front leg and can be sold with or without the bone. The meat is fatty but flavorful and is especially good when used in soup or simmered in a boiled dinner such as pot-au-feu. This cut is the same as osso buco, but from a cow rather than a calf.

Flavor: ★★ **Cost:** $

Alternate Name: Center beef shank

Best Cooking Method: Braising

Recommended Recipe: Pot-au-Feu (page 132)

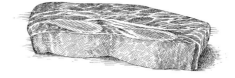

SHORT RIBS

These meaty ribs can be cut from various locations on the cow, although they commonly come from the underside of the animal. In most markets, each rib bone has been separated and cut crosswise so that a large chunk of meat is attached to one side of the bone. You can also buy short ribs boneless, which we use in some of our recipes.

Flavor: ★★★ **Cost:** $

Alternate Name: English-style short ribs

Best Cooking Methods: Grilling, grill roasting, stewing, braising

Recommended Recipes: Grill-Roasted Beef Short Ribs (page 112), Korean Grilled Short Ribs (page 115), Braised Boneless Beef Short Ribs (page 125), Pot-au-Feu (page 132), Catalan-Style Beef Stew with Mushrooms (page 138), Best Old-Fashioned Burgers (page 153), Juicy Pub-Style Burgers (page 155)

FLANKEN-STYLE SHORT RIBS

Like English-style short ribs, these short ribs can be cut from various parts of the animal, although mostly commonly they come from the plate. In this case, the ribs are cut into thin cross-sections that contain two or three pieces of bone surrounded by pieces of meat. Flanken-style short ribs can be hard to find compared with commonly available English-style short ribs and are generally available only at butcher shops.

Flavor: ★★★ **Cost:** $ $

Alternate Name: Flanken

Best Cooking Methods: Braising, barbecuing

Ground Beef

Supermarkets label ground beef either by fat content (for example, "90 percent lean" or "80 percent lean") or by cut (for example, "ground chuck"). Ideally, we like to buy meat that is labeled both ways, but you may not always have that option.

Shopping by Cut

Ground chuck generally has quite a lot of fat, which translates to rich flavor and tender texture—it's the best choice for burgers. Ground sirloin has good flavor but is a bit less tender (because it's leaner). Ground sirloin is great in meatloaf and Bolognese sauce but can be a bit dry in burgers. Ground round is often gristly and lacking in beef flavor; we don't recommend it.

Shopping by Fat

For burgers, we recommend buying beef labeled 80 percent lean (or 85 percent lean). Ideally, the label will indicate that the meat is from the chuck, but round can have a similar content. For recipes with additional sources of fat and moisture (such as meatloaf), 85 percent lean or even 90 percent lean ground beef is best. Ground sirloin usually is 90 percent to 93 percent lean and is a good choice here.

Does Color Matter?

Have you ever noticed that the ground meat you just brought home from the supermarket is red on the outside but dark purple or brown on the inside? Is this an indication of meat past its prime? Fortunately, no.

The color in meat comes from a muscle protein called myoglobin. When the meat is freshly cut, this protein is deep purple. As the meat sits in its packaging (or in the butcher's display case), the myoglobin will convert to bright red oxymyoglobin on the meat's exterior, where it is exposed to more oxygen. Inside the meat, where less oxygen can penetrate, it will slowly convert to brown metmyoglobin. Color changes of this nature are typical and should not cause alarm. But once the meat turns brown on the exterior, it's on its way to spoiling.

Food Safety and Ground Beef

Regardless of where the meat is processed, ground beef (as well as other ground meats like pork and poultry) is safe to eat as long as it is cooked to a temperature at which potential pathogens are inactivated (160 degrees). But since ground beef is frequently served at temperatures lower than 160 degrees, foodborne illness can be an issue. Meat-processing plants have stringent guidelines intended to prevent cross-contamination, but anyone who reads the news knows that outbreaks of salmonella and the harmful 0157:H7 strain of *E. coli* routinely occur.

Ground beef poses a greater risk of foodborne illness than whole cuts because contaminants do not penetrate the surface of a steak or a roast, and any that may be present on the surface will be killed during cooking, making the meat safe even if the interior is served rare. The risk occurs during grinding, when the exterior of the meat is distributed into the interior, taking any potential pathogens along with it.

As long as you follow safe food-handling guidelines—including frequent and thorough hand washing, thorough cleaning of surfaces, and storing meat below 40 degrees—we believe that grinding beef at home is safer than buying ground beef at the store. Here's why: The chance of a single cut of beef (that you then grind at home) being contaminated is relatively slim. Conversely, a single portion of preground beef can

be an amalgam of various grades of meat from different parts of many different cattle. In fact, when we consulted Robert V. Tauxe, deputy director of the Division of Foodborne, Waterborne, and Environmental Diseases at the National Center for Emerging and Zoonotic Infectious Diseases, he estimated that a typical hamburger may contain meat from hundreds of different animals. And obviously, the more cattle that go into your burger the greater the odds of contamination.

What's the bottom line? The only way to be absolutely certain that ground beef is free from harmful bacteria is to cook it to 160 degrees. Alternatively, grinding beef at home isn't hard to do. You just need a food processor. Here's how:

Grinding Beef at Home

We use this method with our Best Old-Fashioned Burgers (page 153) and Juicy Pub-Style Burgers (page 155).

1. Cut meat into 1-inch chunks and freeze on rimmed baking sheet until it is very firm and starting to harden around edges but still pliable, 15 to 25 minutes.

2. Working with 8 ounces of meat at a time, pulse chunks in food processor until they are coarsely ground, 10 to 15 pulses (longer for finer grind), stopping and redistributing meat around bowl as necessary to ensure even grinding.

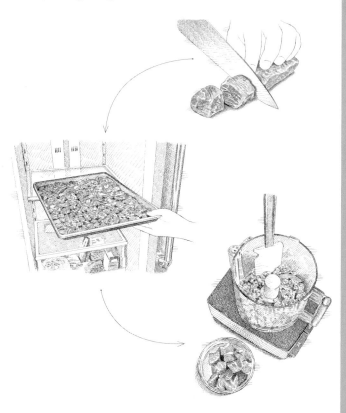

Common (and Key) Prep Tips for Beef

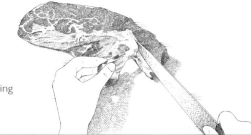

Trimming Fat from Steaks

Skip this step when pan searing and you'll have fat all over your stovetop and a greasy pan sauce.

Use sharp paring knife to trim hard, white fat from perimeter of steaks, leaving no more than ⅛ inch fat. We trim fat to keep splattering to a minimum if we're pan searing.

Fat adds flavor, but too much can cause splattering on the stovetop.

Trimming a Beef Tenderloin

Trimmed (or peeled) beef tenderloins are sold with the outer layer of fat and silverskin already removed. Although trimmed tenderloins are convenient and can save the cook about 20 minutes of trimming time, at roughly $25 per pound, compared with about $14 per pound for untrimmed roasts (which often sell for as little as $9 per pound at warehouse clubs), we prefer to do the work ourselves. For more illustrations detailing trimming a beef tenderloin, see page 102.

1. Pull away outer layer of fat to expose fatty chain of meat and discard fatty chain.

2. Remove sinewy silverskin (and any other large pieces of fat) by inserting tip of knife under it and slicing outward at slight angle. Continue to trim all over roast.

Tenderloin is pricey but you can make it more affordable by purchasing an unpeeled roast and doing the trimming yourself.

Two Ways to Tie a Roast

Most roasts are unevenly shaped, which leads to uneven cooking. For cylindrical cuts, such as beef tenderloin, we even out thickness with a series of ties down the length. You can also fold the thin end under the roast and tie it in place. For squat roasts such as the eye round, wrap longer pieces of kitchen twine around the perimeter to cinch in the sides and give the roast a neater shape.

1A. For Long Roasts: Fold thin end, if needed, under roast. Wrap piece of kitchen twine around roast and fasten with double knot, repeating along length of roast, spacing ties about 1½ inches apart.

1B. For Squat Roasts: Wrap piece of kitchen twine around roast about 1 inch from bottom and tie with double knot. Repeat with second piece of twine, wrapping it about 1 inch from top.

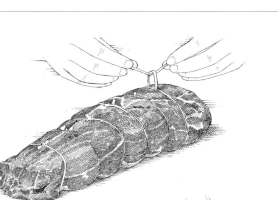

Roasts are tied to maintain their shape and ensure even cooking.

Cutting a Chuck Roast into Stew Meat

Packaged stew meat sold in most supermarkets is cut much too small, so it overcooks and becomes tough. And who knows what cut you're getting? For the best results, buy a roast and cut it yourself.

1. Pull apart roast at its major seams (delineated by lines of fat). Cut away all exposed fat.

2. Cut meat into 1½- to 2-inch chunks (depending on recipe), trimming additional fat.

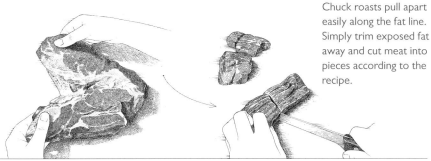

Chuck roasts pull apart easily along the fat line. Simply trim exposed fat away and cut meat into pieces according to the recipe.

Cutting Beef for Stir-Fries

Slicing the meat thin is the key to ensuring maximum surface area and thus maximum browning. A sharp knife is essential. We also find it helpful to freeze the meat briefly to make it firmer for slicing. If you look closely at a piece of meat, you'll notice little bundles of closely packed muscle fibers that run parallel to one another. This pattern of fibers is known as the grain. Recipes recommend slicing against the grain—perpendicular to the fibers—to shorten them and thereby make the meat easier to chew.

Place meat in freezer until just firm, about 15 minutes. With a very sharp knife, cut meat against grain into thin pieces, ⅛ to ¼ inch thick.

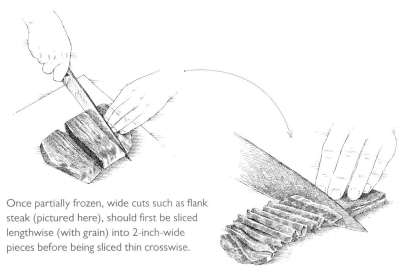

Once partially frozen, wide cuts such as flank steak (pictured here), should first be sliced lengthwise (with grain) into 2-inch-wide pieces before being sliced thin crosswise.

BEEF DONENESS CHART

The chart below lists optimum internal temperatures based on maximum juiciness and flavor. For optimum safety, follow USDA guidelines: Cook whole cuts of meat to an internal temperature of at least 145 degrees and let rest for at least 3 minutes. Cook ground beef to an internal temperature of at least 160 degrees. For more information on carryover cooking and resting meat, see page 8.

To determine internal temperature, insert an instant-read thermometer deep into the meat away from any bone. For small cuts, like steaks, take the temperature of the meat from the side (see illustration on page 11), so you can easily reach the center. For large cuts of beef, take two or three readings to make sure the entire piece of meat has reached the proper temperature.

STEAKS AND ROASTS	TEMPERATURE
Rare	115 to 120 degrees (120 to 125 degrees after resting)
Medium-Rare	120 to 125 degrees (125 to 130 degrees after resting)
Medium	130 to 135 degrees (135 to 140 degrees after resting)
Medium–Well	140 to 145 degrees (145 to 150 degrees after resting)
Well-Done	150 to 155 degrees (155 to 160 degrees after resting)
GROUND BEEF	
Medium-Rare	125 to 130 degrees
Medium	135 to 140 degrees
Medium-Well	145 to 160 degrees
Well-Done	160 degrees and up

Pan-Seared Thick-Cut Strip Steaks

✔ WHY THIS RECIPE WORKS

Pan searing a thick-cut steak (a steak almost as thick as it is wide) presents a unique challenge: how to keep the perimeter from overcooking while the very center of the steak reaches the desired temperature. We wanted our steak to have a good crust and a medium-rare center, without a wide band of dry, gray meat between the two.

SIZE MATTERS Be sure to check the thickness of your steak. One that is thinner than specified in our recipe will overcook.

REVERSE ENGINEER We found that it was essential to sear the steaks quickly to keep the meat directly under the crust from turning gray. In order to do that we needed to start with dry meat and reverse the order of our cooking method. To that end, we started by moving the steaks straight from the fridge into a 275-degree oven, which warmed them to 95 degrees and dried the outside of the meat thoroughly before searing.

FINISH BY SEARING—ALL OVER While most recipes instruct the cook to sear steaks on both flat sides, we found it beneficial to sear these thick steaks on their edges as well. We used a pair of tongs to hold two steaks at a time on their edges in the pan. The extra browning adds flavor and doesn't overheat the steaks because the steaks are being rotated in the pan and don't spend very long in any one place.

🔖 AT THE MEAT COUNTER

PREFERRED CUT Boneless Strip Steak

Boneless strip steak is also called top loin, shell, sirloin strip, Kansas City strip, or New York strip (see page 35 for more information).

ALTERNATE CUT Rib Eye or Filet Mignon

Rib eyes or filets mignons of similar thickness can be substituted for the strip steaks. Rib eyes are also called Spencer steak or Delmonico steak; filets mignons are also called Châteaubriand, tenderloin steak, or tournedo (see pages 34 and 36 for more information). When cooking the filets mignons, increase the oven time by about 5 minutes.

PAN-SEARED THICK-CUT STRIP STEAKS

SERVES 4

When cooking lean strip steaks without an external fat cap (or filets mignons), add an extra tablespoon of oil to the pan. If desired, serve with a pan sauce or relish (recipes follow). Prepare the sauce or relish ingredients while the steaks are in the oven and then make the recipe itself while the steaks rest.

- 2 (1-pound) boneless strip steaks, 1½ to 1¾ inches thick, trimmed
  Salt and pepper
- 1 tablespoon vegetable oil

1. Adjust oven rack to middle position and heat oven to 275 degrees. Pat steaks dry with paper towels. Cut each steak in half vertically to create four 8-ounce steaks. Season steaks with salt and pepper; gently press sides of steaks until uniform 1½ inches thick. Place steaks on wire rack set in rimmed baking sheet. Cook until meat registers 90 to 95 degrees (for rare to medium-rare), 20 to 25 minutes, or 100 to 105 degrees (for medium), 25 to 30 minutes.

2. Heat oil in 12-inch skillet over high heat until just smoking. Place steaks in skillet and

ON THE SIDE

BLENDER BÉARNAISE SAUCE

This classic French sauce is buttery and decadent and not just great with steak—try it with other type of meats, poultry, fish, or steamed vegetables. It's important to make sure the butter is still hot so the béarnaise thickens properly.

1. Bring ½ cup white wine vinegar, 2 tarragon sprigs, and 1 thinly sliced shallot to simmer in 8-inch skillet over medium heat. Cook until vinegar has reduced to about 1 tablespoon, 6 to 8 minutes. Using fork, remove and discard shallot slices and tarragon sprigs.

2. Process 3 large yolks, 1½ teaspoons lemon juice, ¼ teaspoon salt, pinch cayenne, and reduced vinegar mixture in blender until frothy, about 10 seconds. With blender running, very slowly drizzle in 16 tablespoons unsalted butter, melted but still hot (about 180 degrees), until fully incorporated and thick, about 2 minutes.

3. Stir in 1½ tablespoons minced fresh tarragon. Adjust consistency with hot water 1 teaspoon at a time as necessary (sauce should slowly drip from spoon). Season with salt and cayenne to taste. Serve with steak. (Serves 8.)

SEARING TWO STEAKS AT ONCE

We like to sear our thick-cut steaks all around for maximum flavor.

Use tongs to hold two steaks (filets mignons pictured above) at once and sear.

PAT YOUR STEAKS DRY

With regard to searing meat, we have long recommended patting the exterior dry with paper towels before adding it to the hot pan; this ensures rapid, flawless browning. We recently retested this assumption, cooking two sets of steaks in a hot skillet: one set patted dry, the other left untouched. The dry steaks achieved a crisp, dark, even sear and left behind flavorful golden bits (or fond)—the perfect base for a pan sauce. After initially steaming, the moist steaks achieved a reasonably dark sear, but it was much softer than that on the dried steaks, showing clearly that the excess moisture did not cook off but remained trapped between the meat and the surface of the hot pan. In addition, excess moisture allowed soluble proteins to migrate out from under the steaks (where it's cooler) to exposed areas of the pan, producing a fond that quickly burned and turned bitter by the time the meat had cooked, making it unusable for pan sauce. This is yet one more reason to pat meat dry before searing.

sear until well browned and crusty, 1½ to 2 minutes, lifting once halfway through cooking to redistribute fat underneath each steak. (Reduce heat if fond begins to burn.) Using tongs, turn steaks and cook until well browned on second side, 2 to 2½ minutes. Transfer all steaks to clean wire rack and reduce heat under pan to medium. Use tongs to stand 2 steaks on their edges. Holding steaks together, return to skillet and sear on all sides until browned, about 1½ minutes. Repeat with remaining 2 steaks.

3. Transfer steaks to wire rack and let rest, tented loosely with aluminum foil, for 10 minutes. Arrange steaks on individual plates and serve.

RED WINE–MUSHROOM PAN SAUCE
MAKES ABOUT 1 CUP

Prepare all the ingredients for this sauce while the steaks are in the oven.

1	tablespoon vegetable oil
8	ounces white mushrooms, trimmed and sliced thin
1	small shallot, minced
1	cup dry red wine
½	cup chicken broth
1	tablespoon balsamic vinegar
1	teaspoon Dijon mustard
2	tablespoons unsalted butter, cut into 4 pieces and chilled
1	teaspoon minced fresh thyme
	Salt and pepper

After transferring steaks to wire rack, pour off fat from skillet. Heat oil in now-empty skillet over medium-high heat until just smoking. Add mushrooms and cook, stirring occasionally, until beginning to brown and liquid has evaporated, about 5 minutes. Add shallot and cook, stirring frequently, until beginning to soften, about 1 minute. Increase heat to high; add red wine and broth, scraping

bottom of skillet with wooden spoon to loosen any browned bits. Simmer rapidly until liquid and mushrooms are reduced to 1 cup, about 6 minutes. Add vinegar, mustard, and any meat juices; cook until thickened, about 1 minute. Off heat, whisk in butter and thyme; season with salt and pepper to taste. Spoon sauce over steaks and serve.

SUN-DRIED TOMATO RELISH
MAKES ½ CUP

This relish also pairs well with grilled chicken.

½	cup chicken broth
	Pinch red pepper flakes
2	tablespoons oil-packed sun-dried tomatoes, rinsed and chopped
1	tablespoon capers, rinsed and chopped
1	tablespoon extra-virgin olive oil
2	teaspoons lemon juice
1	teaspoon honey
2	tablespoons chopped fresh parsley
1	tablespoon minced fresh mint
	Salt and pepper

After transferring steaks to wire rack, pour off fat from skillet and return to high heat. Add broth to now-empty skillet and scrape bottom of pan with wooden spoon to loosen any browned bits. Add pepper flakes and boil until liquid is reduced to 2 tablespoons, about 5 minutes. Add any meat juices to pan. Add tomatoes, capers, oil, lemon juice, and honey to pan and swirl vigorously to emulsify. Off heat, add parsley and mint. Season with salt and pepper to taste. Spoon relish over steaks and serve.

TEQUILA-POBLANO PAN SAUCE
MAKES ⅔ CUP

Before flambéing, be sure to roll up long shirtsleeves, tie back long hair, and turn off the exhaust fan and any lit burners.

1 small shallot, minced

1 poblano chile, stemmed, seeded, and chopped fine

½ teaspoon ground cumin

½ cup white tequila

½ cup chicken broth

1 tablespoon lime juice

3 tablespoons unsalted butter, cut into 3 pieces and chilled

1 tablespoon chopped fresh cilantro
Salt and pepper

After transferring steaks to wire rack, pour off all but 1 tablespoon fat from skillet. Return pan to high heat and add shallot and poblano; cook, stirring frequently, until lightly browned and fragrant, 1 to 2 minutes. Add cumin and continue to cook for 30 seconds. Transfer pan contents to bowl. Off heat, add all but 2 teaspoons tequila to now-empty skillet, and let warm through, about 5 seconds. Wave lit match over pan until tequila ignites, then shake pan to distribute flames. When flames subside, add broth and 2 teaspoons lime juice. Reduce to ⅓ cup, about 6 minutes. Add remaining 2 teaspoons tequila, remaining 1 teaspoon lime juice, and any meat juices to pan. Remove from heat and whisk in butter, cilantro, and poblano and shallot; season with salt and pepper to taste. Spoon sauce over steaks and serve.

Steak Frites

✔ WHY THIS RECIPE WORKS

Too often, steak frites in American restaurants misses the mark. The fries are usually too soggy and the steak just isn't as flavorful as it should be. We wanted to re-create the steak frites of our Parisian dreams, with perfectly cooked steak and fries that were fluffy on the inside and crisp on the outside, even when bathed in juices from the meat.

FRY TWICE For ultracrispy fries, we had first determined that we'd cook them in batches, which minimizes the drop in oil temperature when the potatoes are added to the oil (see "Crispy Tricks"). We also found that peanut oil gave the fries the best flavor and texture.

TOSS IN CORNSTARCH To absorb some of the potatoes' surface moisture, we tossed the raw potatoes with cornstarch before frying. This coating made a superprotective sheath around each fry, helping to create the shatteringly crisp crust we wanted.

CHOOSE THICK STRIP OR RIB EYE We found that thick strip steaks or rib eyes gave us more time to get a nice sear without overcooking the middle. A little herb butter added a final flavor boost to the dish.

STEAK FRITES
SERVES 4

Strip steak is also called top loin, shell steak, sirloin strip, Kansas City strip, or New York Strip; rib eye is also known as Spencer steak or Delmonico steak (see pages 35 and 34 for more information). In order to have four steaks that fit in a skillet at the same time, it is necessary to buy two 1-pound steaks and cut them in half according to their thickness. If your steaks are 1¼ to 1¾ inches thick, cut them in half vertically into small, thick steaks. If your steaks are thicker than 1¾ inches, cut them in half horizontally into two thinner steaks. Make sure to dry the potatoes well before tossing them with the cornstarch. For safety, use a Dutch oven with a capacity of at least 7 quarts. A 12-inch skillet is essential for cooking four steaks at once. The ingredients can be halved to serve two—keep the oil amount the same and forgo blanching and frying the potatoes in batches.

CUTTING POTATOES FOR FRENCH FRIES

Cutting potatoes into even pieces is the first step to a perfect batch.

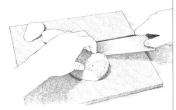

1. Square off potato by cutting ¼-inch-thick slice from each of its 4 long sides.

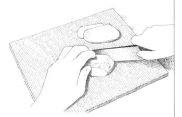

2. Cut potato lengthwise into ¼-inch planks.

3. Stack 3 or 4 planks and cut into ¼-inch batons. Repeat with remaining planks.

2½ pounds russet potatoes, sides squared and cut lengthwise into ¼-inch-thick fries
2 tablespoons cornstarch
3 quarts peanut oil
1 tablespoon vegetable oil
2 (1-pound) boneless strip or rib-eye steaks, trimmed and cut in half
  Kosher salt and pepper
1 recipe Herb Butter (recipe follows)

1. Rinse cut potatoes in bowl under cold running water until water turns clear. Cover with cold water and refrigerate for 30 minutes or up to 12 hours.

2. Pour off water, spread potatoes onto dish towels, and dry thoroughly. Transfer potatoes to bowl and toss with cornstarch until evenly coated. Transfer potatoes to wire rack set in rimmed baking sheet and let rest until fine white coating forms, about 20 minutes.

3. Meanwhile, heat peanut oil in large Dutch oven over medium heat to 325 degrees. Line baking sheet with brown paper bag or triple layer of paper towels.

4. Add half of potatoes, a handful at a time, to hot oil and increase heat to high. Fry, stirring with wire skimmer or slotted spoon, until potatoes start to turn from white to blond, 4 to 5 minutes. (Oil temperature will drop about 75 degrees during this frying.) Transfer fries to prepared sheet. Return oil to 325 degrees and repeat with remaining potatoes. Reduce heat to medium and let fries cool while cooking steaks, at least 10 minutes. (Recipe can be prepared through step 4 up to 2 hours in advance; turn off heat under oil, turning heat back to medium when you start step 6.)

5. Heat vegetable oil in 12-inch skillet over medium-high heat until just smoking. Meanwhile, pat steaks dry with paper towels and season with salt and pepper. Lay steaks in pan, leaving ¼ inch between them. Cook, without moving steaks, until well browned, about 4 minutes. Using tongs, flip steaks and continue to cook until meat registers 115 to 120 degrees (for rare) or 120 to 125 degrees (for medium-rare), 3 to 7 minutes. Transfer steaks to large plate, top with herb butter, and tent loosely with aluminum foil; let rest while finishing fries.

6. Increase heat under Dutch oven to high and heat oil to 375 degrees. Add half of fries, a handful at a time, and fry until golden brown and puffed, 2 to 3 minutes. Transfer to clean brown paper bag or paper towels. Return oil to 375 degrees and repeat with remaining fries. Season fries with salt to taste, and serve with steaks.

HERB BUTTER
MAKES ¼ CUP

---

4 tablespoons unsalted butter, softened
½ shallot, minced
1 tablespoon minced fresh parsley
1 tablespoon minced fresh chives
1 garlic clove, minced
¼ teaspoon salt
¼ teaspoon pepper

Combine all ingredients in bowl.

Pepper-Crusted Filets Mignons

✓ WHY THIS RECIPE WORKS

Black peppercorns can give mild-tasting filet mignon a welcome flavor boost, but they can also create a punishing blast of heat. We wanted pepper-crusted filets mignons with a flavorful crust that wouldn't overwhelm the beef.

TEMPER THE HEAT WITH OIL Peppercorns contain a natural irritant called piperine, which mellows over time. In your cupboard, this compound can take months to convert into more complex, less harsh flavor molecules. Hot oil serves as a catalyst, driving the conversion at hundreds of times its natural speed, as well as vaporizing some of the piperine, quickly tempering the pepper's pungency.

COAT AND PRESS We used a two-step process to create a well-browned and attractive pepper crust: First, we rubbed the raw steaks with a paste of the cooked cracked peppercorns, oil, and salt; then we pressed the paste into each steak using a sheet of plastic wrap to ensure it stayed put. The paste not only added flavor to the meat but also coaxed out the meat's own beefy flavor. Adding salt to the rub made it easy to season the steaks at the same time the crust was applied.

SEAR, THEN ROAST We seared the steaks in order to get them to brown and become flavorful and then let them finish cooking in the oven on a preheated baking sheet. This ensured even cooking of the steaks and also limited the searing time, which prevented the pepper crust from burning.

PEPPER-CRUSTED FILETS MIGNONS
SERVES 4

Filet mignon is also known as Châteaubriand, tenderloin steak, or tournedo (see page 36 for more information). While heating the peppercorns in oil tempers much of their pungent heat, this recipe is still pretty spicy. If you prefer a very mild pepper flavor, drain the cooled peppercorns in a fine-mesh strainer in step 1, toss them with 5 tablespoons of fresh oil, add the salt, and proceed. If desired, serve with either Blue Cheese–Chive Butter or Port Cherry Reduction (recipes follow); note that both need to be prepared before the steak is cooked.

> 5   tablespoons black peppercorns, crushed
> 5   tablespoons plus 2 teaspoons olive oil
> 1   tablespoon kosher salt
> 4   (7- to 8-ounce) center-cut filets mignons, 1½ to 2 inches thick, trimmed

1. Heat peppercorns and 5 tablespoons oil in small saucepan over low heat until faint bubbles appear. Continue to cook at bare simmer, swirling pan occasionally, until pepper is fragrant, 7 to 10 minutes. Remove from heat and set aside to cool. When mixture is room temperature, add salt and stir to combine. Rub steaks with oil and pepper mixture, thoroughly coating top and bottom of each steak with peppercorns. Cover steaks with plastic wrap and press gently to make sure peppercorns adhere; let stand at room temperature for 1 hour.

2. Meanwhile, adjust oven rack to middle position, place baking sheet on oven rack, and heat oven to 450 degrees. When oven reaches 450 degrees, heat remaining 2 teaspoons oil in 12-inch skillet over medium-high heat until just smoking. Place steaks in skillet and cook, without moving, until dark brown crust has formed, 3 to 4 minutes. Using tongs, turn steaks and cook until well browned on second side, about 3 minutes. Off heat, transfer steaks to hot baking sheet in oven. Roast until meat registers 115 to 120 degrees (for rare),

You can crush peppercorns with the bottom of a skillet, but a Pyrex measuring cup also works—and it has an extra advantage. The cup is not only heavy enough to crush the peppercorns, but its clear glass bottom allows you to gauge progress as you crush.

HOW TO REHEAT A STEAK

One of the best methods we have found for cooking steaks is to slowly warm them in the oven and then sear them in a hot skillet. This produces medium-rare meat from edge to edge, with a well-browned crust. Could this same method work for leftovers?

The answer is yes. When we rewarmed leftover cooked steaks in a low oven and then briefly seared them, the results were remarkably good. The reheated steaks were only slightly less juicy than freshly cooked ones, and their crusts were actually more crisp.

Here's the method: Place leftover steaks on a wire rack set in a rimmed baking sheet and warm them on the middle rack of a 250-degree oven until the steaks register 110 degrees (roughly 30 minutes for 1½-inch-thick steaks, but timing will vary according to thickness and size). Pat the steaks dry with a paper towel and heat 1 tablespoon of vegetable oil in a 12-inch skillet over high heat until smoking. Sear the steaks on both sides until crisp, 60 to 90 seconds per side. Let the steaks rest for 5 minutes before serving. After resting, the centers should be at medium-rare temperature (125 to 130 degrees).

120 to 125 degrees (for medium-rare), or 130 to 135 degrees (for medium), 3 to 7 minutes. Transfer steaks to wire rack and let rest, tented loosely with aluminum foil, for 5 minutes before serving.

BLUE CHEESE–CHIVE BUTTER
MAKES ABOUT ½ CUP

1½   ounces mild blue cheese, room temperature
3   tablespoons unsalted butter, softened
⅛   teaspoon salt
2   tablespoons minced fresh chives

Combine blue cheese, butter, and salt in medium bowl and mix with stiff rubber spatula until smooth. Fold in chives. While steaks are resting, spoon 1 to 2 tablespoons butter onto each one.

PORT-CHERRY REDUCTION
MAKES ABOUT 1 CUP

1½   cups port
½   cup balsamic vinegar
½   cup dried tart cherries
1   shallot, minced
2   sprigs fresh thyme
1   tablespoon unsalted butter
    Salt

1. Combine port, vinegar, cherries, shallot, and thyme in medium saucepan; simmer over medium-low heat until liquid has reduced to about ⅓ cup, about 30 minutes. Set aside, covered.

2. While steaks are resting, reheat sauce. Off heat, remove thyme sprigs, then whisk in butter until melted. Season with salt to taste; spoon over steak and serve.

Grilled Premium Steaks

✔ WHY THIS RECIPE WORKS

When you're splurging on premium steaks, getting them just right is especially important. We wanted nicely charred exteriors with perfectly tender interiors.

SEASON MINIMALLY To let the big, beefy flavor shine through, we seasoned our steaks with just a sprinkle of salt and pepper.

USE TWO LEVELS OF HEAT To get a flavorful, charred crust, we started by searing the steaks over high heat, then moved them to the cooler side of the grill to finish cooking through.

LET IT REST Even though it's tempting to dig right in, giving these steaks time to rest is key. If sliced too soon, the meat will exude its flavorful juices and be dry.

GRILLED STRIP OR RIB-EYE STEAKS
SERVES 6

Strip steak is also called top loin, shell steak, sirloin strip, Kansas City strip, or New York Strip; rib eye is also known as Spencer steak or Delmonico steak (see pages 35 and 34 for more information). Try to buy steaks of even thickness so they cook at the same rate.

4   (12- to 16-ounce) strip or rib-eye steaks, with or without bone, 1¼ to 1½ inches thick, trimmed
    Salt and pepper

1A. FOR A CHARCOAL GRILL: Open bottom vent completely. Light large chimney starter filled with charcoal briquettes (6 quarts). When top coals are partially covered with ash, pour two-thirds evenly over grill, then pour remaining coals over half of grill. Set cooking grate in place, cover, and heat grill until hot, about 5 minutes.

1B. FOR A GAS GRILL: Turn all burners to high, cover, and heat grill until hot, about 15 minutes. Leave primary burner on high and turn other burner(s) to medium.

2. Clean and oil cooking grate. Pat steaks dry with paper towels and season with salt and pepper. Place steaks on hotter side of grill and cook, uncovered, until well browned on both sides, 4 to 6 minutes, flipping steaks halfway through cooking. Move steaks to cooler side of grill (if using charcoal) or turn all burners to medium (if using gas) and continue to cook until meat registers 115 to 120 degrees (for rare) or 120 to 125 degrees (for medium-rare) 5 to 8 minutes longer.

3. Transfer steaks to serving platter, tent loosely with aluminum foil, and let rest for 10 minutes before serving.

Grilled Porterhouse or T-Bone Steaks

✔ WHY THIS RECIPE WORKS

T-bone steaks are really two steaks—a tender New York strip steak on one side of the bone and a buttery, quicker-cooking tenderloin on the other. We wanted both parts to cook evenly and sport a dark (but not blackened) crust, smoky aroma, and deep grilled flavor.

PICK YOUR T-BONE Both T-bone and porterhouse steaks contain a strip steak and a tenderloin steak connected by a T-shaped bone. The strip steak section is a bit chewy, with a noticeable grain, while the tenderloin, a long, cylindrical muscle, is the most tender meat on the cow but has a less beefy flavor. The porterhouse is really just a huge T-bone steak with a larger tenderloin section and is cut farther back in the animal than the T-bone steak.

TIME TO SEASON We like to salt the meat an hour before cooking. This enables the salt to penetrate the meat's interior, boosting the flavor from crust to bone. Be sure to remove any moisture on the surface of the steaks with paper towels before grilling, though. If left in place, this moisture can cause the steaks to steam rather than develop a crust.

SHIELD THE TENDERLOIN We'd found in prior testing that cooking steaks over two levels of heat delivered rosy meat and a flavorful crust, but we still encountered one problem with our tenderloin. Though tasters were impressed with the crust and the steaks' grilled flavor, they found the coveted tenderloin section to be somewhat tough and dry. The solution: We positioned the meat so that the tenderloin faced the cooler side of the grill, with the bone between the tenderloin and the fire. This allowed the delicate tenderloin to cook at a slightly slower rate and stay tender and juicy.

GRILLED PORTERHOUSE OR T-BONE STEAKS

SERVES 4 TO 6

See page 36 for more information on these steaks. Be sure to buy steaks that are at least 1 inch thick.

2 (1¾-pound) porterhouse or T-bone steaks, 1 to ½ inches thick, trimmed

2 teaspoons salt

2 teaspoons pepper

1 recipe Chive Butter (recipe follows)

TWO TYPES OF T-BONES

Both T-bone and porterhouse steaks contain a strip steak (left) and a tenderloin steak (right) connected by a T-shaped bone. Technically, a T-bone must have a tenderloin portion at least ½ inch across, and a porterhouse's tenderloin must measure at least 1¼ inches across.

T-Bone

Porterhouse

1. Cut along bone to remove large strip section.

2. Turn steak around and cut tenderloin section off bone.

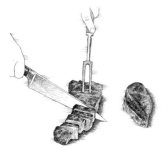

3. Cut each piece crosswise into ¼-inch-thick slices.

1. Season entire surface of each steak with 1 teaspoon salt and let sit at room temperature for 1 hour. Pat steaks dry with paper towels and season each with 1 teaspoon pepper.

2A. FOR A CHARCOAL GRILL: Open bottom vent completely. Light large chimney starter three-quarters filled with charcoal briquettes (4½ quarts). When top coals are partially covered with ash, pour evenly over half of grill. Set cooking grate in place, cover, and open lid vent completely. Heat grill until hot, about 5 minutes.

2B. FOR A GAS GRILL: Turn all burners to high, cover, and heat grill until hot, about 15 minutes. Leave primary burner on high and turn other burner(s) to low.

3. Clean and oil cooking grate. Place steaks on hotter side of grill with tenderloin sides (smaller side of T-bone) facing cooler side of grill. Cook (covered if using gas) until dark crust forms, 6 to 8 minutes. (If steaks start to flame, move them to cooler side of grill and/or extinguish flames with squirt bottle.) Flip steaks and turn so that tenderloin sides are facing cooler side of grill. Continue to cook (covered if using gas) until dark brown crust forms on second side, 6 to 8 minutes longer.

4. Brush with chive butter, if using, and transfer steaks to cooler side of grill with bone side facing hotter side of grill. Cover grill and continue to cook until meat registers 115 to 120 degrees (for rare) or 120 to 125 degrees (for medium-rare), 2 to 4 minutes longer, flipping halfway through cooking.

5. Transfer steaks to carving board, tent loosely with aluminum foil, and let rest for 10 minutes. Cut strip and tenderloin pieces off bones, then slice each piece crosswise into ¼-inch-thick slices. Serve.

CHIVE BUTTER
MAKES ABOUT 6 TABLESPOONS

4 tablespoons unsalted butter, melted
2 tablespoons minced shallot
1 garlic clove, minced
1 tablespoon minced fresh chives
   Salt and pepper

Combine all ingredients in bowl and season with salt and pepper to taste.

Grilled Tuscan Steak with Olive Oil and Lemon

✔ WHY THIS RECIPE WORKS

This Italian-style preparation is deceivingly simple: a thick, juicy steak, grilled rare and drizzled with high-quality olive oil and a squeeze of lemon. We wanted the flavor of the steak to be complemented by the lemon and oil, without these delicate flavors getting lost in the process.

COOK IT RIGHT T-Bone and porterhouse steaks were the most commonly called for steaks in the recipes we tried, and we found no reason to veer from this tradition. For these hefty, expensive steaks, we used our go-to grilling method: a two-level fire. We achieved a browned crust over the hot side of the grill, then moved the steaks to the cooler side to evenly cook them through.

CHOOSE GOOD OIL Since the oil is an essential component of this dish, we recommend using extra-virgin olive oil, which has a more distinctive character and bolder flavor

EXTRA-VIRGIN OLIVE OIL

Extra-virgin olive oil has a uniquely fruity flavor that makes it a great choice for marinades, vinaigrettes, and pestos. Many things can impact the quality and flavor of olive oil, but the type of olives, the harvest (earlier means greener and more peppery; later, more golden and mild), and processing are the most important factors. The best-quality oil comes from olives picked at their peak and processed as soon as possible, without heat or chemicals (which can coax more oil from the olives but at the expense of flavor). In a tasting, our favorite oils were produced from a blend of olives and, thus, were well rounded. Our favorite brand is **Columela Extra Virgin Olive Oil** from Spain. This oil took top honors for its fruity flavor and excellent balance.

than pure olive oil. We also discovered differences among brands, and found that we preferred a fuller-bodied oil for this recipe. See "Extra-Virgin Olive Oil" for information on our top-rated olive oil.

REST, SLICE, AND GARNISH Drizzling the steaks with the olive oil after slicing and serving the steaks with wedges of lemon ensured that the flavor nuances of the oil remained intact and the lemon stayed bright and fresh.

GRILLED TUSCAN STEAKS WITH OLIVE OIL AND LEMON

SERVES 4 TO 6

See page 36 for more information on these steaks. Be sure to buy steaks that are at least 1 inch thick.

2   (1¾-pound) porterhouse or T-bone steaks, 1 to 1½ inches thick, trimmed
    Salt and pepper
3   tablespoons extra-virgin olive oil
    Lemon wedges

1A. FOR A CHARCOAL GRILL: Open bottom vent completely. Light large chimney starter three-quarters filled with charcoal briquettes (4½ quarts). When top coals are partially covered with ash, pour evenly over half of grill. Set cooking grate in place, cover, and open lid vent completely. Heat grill until hot, about 5 minutes.

1B. FOR A GAS GRILL: Turn all burners to high, cover, and heat grill until hot, about 15 minutes. Leave primary burner on high and turn other burner(s) to low.

2. Clean and oil cooking grate. Pat steaks dry with paper towels and season with salt and pepper. Place steaks on hotter side of grill with tenderloin sides (smaller side of T-bone) facing cooler side of grill. Cook (covered if using gas) until dark crust forms, 6 to 8 minutes. (If steaks start to flame, move them to cooler side of grill and/or extinguish flames with squirt bottle.) Flip steaks and turn so that tenderloin sides are facing cooler side of grill. Continue to cook (covered if using gas) until dark brown crust forms on second side, 6 to 8 minutes longer.

3. Transfer steaks to cooler side of grill with bone side facing hotter side of grill. Cover grill and continue to cook until meat registers 115 to 120 degrees (for rare) or 120 to 125 degrees (for medium-rare), 2 to 4 minutes longer, flipping halfway through cooking.

4. Transfer steaks to carving board, tent loosely with aluminum foil, and let rest for 10 minutes. Cut strip and tenderloin pieces off bones, then slice each piece crosswise into ¼-inch-thick slices. Transfer to serving platter, drizzle with oil, and serve with lemon wedges.

GRILLED TUSCAN STEAKS WITH GARLIC ESSENCE

Rub halved garlic cloves over bone and meat on each side of steaks before seasoning with salt and pepper.

Grilled Argentine Steaks with Chimichurri Sauce

☑ WHY THIS RECIPE WORKS

In Argentina, 2-pound steaks are grilled over a hard-wood fire so they pick up a lot of smoke flavor. Because these steaks are so big, they spend plenty of time on the grill and emerge with a thick, flavorful browned crust. When translated to smaller American steaks, the method falters. Our goal was to devise a technique that would prolong the grill time (so the steaks could pick up more wood flavor) and maximize browning.

USE THE FREEZER AS A DEHYDRATOR The freezer is a harsh environment for meat. Even when well wrapped, steaks can lose moisture and become covered with freezer burn. But in this recipe we used this effect to our advantage. We found that steaks placed in the freezer for a short period of time emerged firmer and drier thanks to the evaporation of surface moisture. Rubbing the steaks with salt helped draw extra moisture to the surface, where it could evaporate. Adding some cornstarch to the rub absorbed moisture and promoted the development of an especially crisp crust on the grilled steaks. The starches in the cornstarch also enhanced the browning by adding more "fuel" for the Maillard reaction (read more about the Maillard reaction on page 251).

MAKE SMOKE We used a lot of wood to produce sufficient smoke to flavor the steaks during the quick cooking time. Oak is the traditional choice for this recipe, but any wood will do. Placing the lid on the grill for the first few minutes of cooking time trapped the smoke and helped jump-start the flavoring process. A charcoal grill does a much better job of producing smoke, although we did develop a work-around for a gas grill by placing the packets with the wood chips directly on the cooking grate.

BIG STEAKS NEED BIG SAUCE Steaks in Argentina are traditionally served with a tart herb-based sauce called *chimichurri*. The sharp, grassy flavors of the sauce are the perfect complement to the fatty, smoky beef. We made a traditional version of this sauce with parsley, cilantro, oregano, garlic, red wine vinegar, red pepper flakes, and salt—all emulsified with a fruity extra-virgin olive oil.

🔖 AT THE MEAT COUNTER

PREFERRED CUT Strip Steak
Strip steak is also called top loin, shell, sirloin strip, Kansas City strip, or New York strip (see page 35 for more information).

ALTERNATE CUT Boneless Shell Sirloin
Boneless shell sirloin steak is also called round-bone or New York sirloin steak (see page 37 for more information).

GRILLED ARGENTINE STEAKS WITH CHIMICHURRI SAUCE

SERVES 6 TO 8

If you'd like to use wood chunks instead of wood chips when using a charcoal grill, substitute four medium wood chunks, soaked in water for 1 hour, for the wood chip packets. The chimichurri sauce can be made up to three days in advance.

SAUCE
- ¼ cup hot water
- 2 teaspoons dried oregano
- 1 teaspoon salt
- 1⅓ cups fresh parsley leaves
- ⅔ cup fresh cilantro leaves
- 6 garlic cloves, minced
- ½ teaspoon red pepper flakes
- ¼ cup red wine vinegar
- ½ cup extra-virgin olive oil

WAGYU AND KOBE

Wagyu is a breed of cattle originally raised in Kobe, the capital city of Japan's Hyogo prefecture. Wagyu have been bred for centuries for their rich intramuscular fat, the source of the buttery-tasting, supremely tender meat. Wagyu cattle boast extra fat since they spend an average of one year longer in the feedlot than regular cattle, and end up weighing between 200 and 400 pounds more at slaughter. What's more, the fat in Wagyu beef is genetically predisposed to be about 70 percent desirable unsaturated fat and about 30 percent saturated fat, while the reverse is true for conventional American cattle.

The "American Wagyu" or "American-Style Kobe Beef" that appears on some menus is usually a cross between Wagyu and Angus, but the USDA requires that the animal be at least 50 percent Wagyu and remain in the feedlot for at least 350 days to receive these designations.

Snake River Farms, located in Idaho, has one of the largest herds of American Wagyu. When we tasted its beef ($18 to $50 per pound, depending on the cut) against regular prime beef ($13 to $30/pound), the Wagyu proved itself a delicacy worthy of an occasional splurge: It was strikingly rich, juicy, and tender. The prime beef was also very good, but its texture and taste weren't quite as luxuriant.

To measure the thickness of a steak at the market, hold it up to your thumb. The distance between the tip and your knuckle is about 1 inch.

RED WINE VINEGAR

Red wine vinegar has a sharp but clean flavor, making it the most versatile choice in salad dressings. While acidity is the obvious key factor in vinegar, it is actually the inherent sweetness of the grapes used to make the vinegar that makes its flavor appealing to the palate.

After tasters sampled 10 red wine vinegars plain, in vinaigrette, and in pickled onions, it was clear that they found highly acidic vinegars too harsh; brands with moderate amounts of acidity scored higher. Tasters also preferred those brands that were blends—either blends of different grapes or blends of different vinegars—as they offered more complex flavor. In the end, tasters ranked French import **Laurent du Clos Red Wine Vinegar** first. Made from a mix of red and white grapes, this vinegar won the day with its "good red wine flavor."

STEAKS

1 tablespoon cornstarch
1½ teaspoons salt
4 (1-pound) boneless strip steaks, 1½ inches thick, trimmed
4 cups wood chips, soaked in water for 15 minutes and drained
Pepper

1. FOR THE SAUCE: Combine water, oregano, and salt in small bowl and let sit until oregano is softened, about 15 minutes. Pulse parsley, cilantro, garlic, and pepper flakes in food processor until coarsely chopped, about 10 pulses. Add water mixture and vinegar and pulse to combine. Transfer mixture to bowl and slowly whisk in oil until emulsified. Cover with plastic wrap and let sit at room temperature for 1 hour.

2. FOR THE STEAKS: Meanwhile, combine cornstarch and salt in bowl. Pat steaks dry with paper towels and place on wire rack set in rimmed baking sheet. Rub entire surface of steaks with cornstarch mixture and place steaks, uncovered, in freezer until very firm, about 30 minutes.

3. Using 2 large pieces of heavy-duty aluminum foil, wrap soaked chips in 2 foil packets and cut several vent holes in tops.

4A. FOR A CHARCOAL GRILL: Open bottom vent halfway. Light large chimney starter filled with charcoal briquettes (6 quarts). When top coals are partially covered with ash, pour evenly over grill. Place wood chip packets on coals. Set cooking grate in place, cover, and open lid vent halfway. Heat grill until hot and wood chips are smoking, about 5 minutes.

4B. FOR A GAS GRILL: Place wood chip packets on cooking grate. Turn all burners to high, cover, and heat grill until hot, about 15 minutes. Leave all burners on high.

5. Clean and oil cooking grate. Season steaks with pepper. Place steaks on grill, cover, and cook until beginning to brown on both sides, 4 to 6 minutes, flipping halfway through cooking.

6. Flip steaks and cook, uncovered, until well browned on first side, 2 to 4 minutes. Flip steaks and continue to cook until meat registers 115 to 120 degrees (for rare) or 120 to 125 degrees (for medium-rare), 2 to 6 minutes longer.

7. Transfer steaks to carving board, tent loosely with aluminum foil, and let rest for 10 minutes. Slice each steak ¼ inch thick. Transfer to serving platter and serve, passing sauce separately.

Pan-Seared Inexpensive Steaks

✔ WHY THIS RECIPE WORKS

For this recipe, we set out to prove that a great steak dinner doesn't have to be an expensive affair. But many inexpensive steaks lacked the beefy depth we wanted, or worse, had an unappealing liver-y flavor. We wanted a flavorful, affordable steak that could compete with any porterhouse.

CHOOSE THE RIGHT STEAK Our favorite inexpensive steaks differ, depending on the cooking method. For pan searing, we prefer the boneless shell sirloin, a cut from the hip muscle of the cow. Finding a piece with uniform thickness helped ensure even cooking.

KEEP PREP SIMPLE We wanted straight-on beefy flavor, so we decided to eschew enhancements such as marinades and rubs. Instead, we focused on perfecting the cooking technique.

GO BEYOND RARE Even tasters who usually preferred rare steaks found medium-rare or medium more appealing here. Cooking the steaks for slightly longer improved their texture and reduced chewiness. Slicing the steaks against the grain also improved texture.

✒ AT THE MEAT COUNTER
PREFERRED CUT Shell Sirloin Steaks
Shell sirloin steak is also known as round-bone steak or New York sirloin steak (see page 37 for more information).

ALTERNATE CUT Sirloin Steak Tips
Sirloin steak tips, also known as flap meat, are sold as whole steaks, cubes, and strips (see page 37 for more information). For this dish, we prefer to purchase a 2-pound whole steak. Avoid small strips of meat or large steaks that taper drastically at one end.

PAN-SEARED INEXPENSIVE STEAKS
SERVES 4

If desired, make Classic Red Wine Pan Sauce, Mustard-Cream Pan Sauce, or Tomato-Caper Pan Sauce (recipes follow) while the steaks rest after cooking; be sure to prepare all of the sauce ingredients before cooking the steaks. To serve two instead of four, use a 10-inch skillet to cook a 1-pound steak and halve the sauce ingredients. Keep in mind that even those tasters who usually prefer rare beef preferred these steaks cooked medium-rare or medium because the texture is firmer and not quite so chewy.

2 tablespoons vegetable oil
   Salt and pepper
2 (1-pound) whole boneless shell sirloin steaks, 1¼ inches thick, trimmed

I. Heat oil in 12-inch skillet over medium-high heat until just smoking. Meanwhile, pat steaks dry with paper towels and season both sides with salt and pepper. Place steaks in skillet; cook, without moving, until well browned, about 2 minutes. Using tongs, flip steaks; reduce heat to medium. Cook until well browned on second side and meat registers 120 to 125 degrees (for medium-rare) or 130 to 135 degrees (for medium), 5 to 6 minutes.

2. Transfer steaks to large plate and tent loosely with aluminum foil; let rest 12 to 15 minutes.

3. Slice each steak about ¼ inch thick against grain on bias, arrange on platter or on individual plates; serve.

CLASSIC RED WINE PAN SAUCE
MAKES ½ CUP

4 tablespoons unsalted butter, cut into 4 pieces and chilled
I shallot, minced
½ cup red wine
I teaspoon packed brown sugar
½ cup beef broth
¼ teaspoon minced fresh thyme
   Salt and pepper

After transferring steaks to large plate, pour off fat from skillet. Return skillet to medium-low heat and melt 1 tablespoon butter. Add shallot; cook, stirring frequently, until beginning to brown, 2 to 3 minutes. Add wine and sugar to skillet and increase heat to medium-high; simmer rapidly, scraping up any browned bits, until liquid is reduced to glaze, about 30 seconds; add broth and simmer until reduced to ⅓ cup, about 3 minutes. Stir in thyme and remaining 3 tablespoons butter; season with salt and pepper to taste. Spoon sauce over sliced steak and serve.

MUSTARD-CREAM PAN SAUCE
MAKES ¾ CUP

I shallot, minced
2 tablespoons dry white wine
½ cup chicken broth
6 tablespoons heavy cream
3 tablespoons whole-grain mustard
   Salt and pepper

Since the crunchy texture
of a finishing salt is just as
important as the seasoning it
provides, we were disap-
pointed when the flaky sea
salt we sprinkled on fish fillets,
steaks, and chicken breasts
dissolved almost instantly in
the food's juices.

In search of a way to
maintain the crunch, we
tried tossing Maldon Sea Salt
Flakes (our favorite finishing
salt) in a spoonful of oil to
create a moisture barrier.
While the oil-coated crystals
indeed stayed intact on food
(after 10 minutes they were
unchanged), the oil caused
the salt to clump, making even
sprinkling virtually impossible.

Next, we turned to
vegetable oil spray, which
produced a gossamer coating
that precluded clumping—and
dissolving. Simply discharge a
⅓-second spray into a small
bowl (say "one," and you're
done), add 1½ teaspoons
of flaky sea salt, and stir to
coat. (Be sure to spritz first
and then add the salt, lest the
flakes fly everywhere.)

After transferring steaks to large plate, pour off all but 1 tablespoon fat from skillet. Return skillet to low heat and add shallot; cook, stirring frequently, until beginning to brown, 2 to 3 minutes. Add wine and increase heat to medium-high; simmer rapidly, scraping up any browned bits, until liquid is reduced to glaze, about 30 seconds; add broth and simmer until reduced to ¼ cup, about 3 minutes. Add cream and any meat juices; cook until heated through, about 1 minute. Stir in mustard; season with salt and pepper to taste. Spoon sauce over sliced steak and serve.

TOMATO-CAPER PAN SAUCE
MAKES ¾ CUP

If ripe fresh tomatoes are not available, substitute two or three whole canned tomatoes.

- 1   shallot, minced
- 1   teaspoon all-purpose flour
- 2   tablespoons dry white wine
- 1   cup chicken broth
- 2   tablespoons capers, rinsed
- 1   ripe tomato, cored, seeded, and cut into ¼-inch dice
- ¼   cup minced fresh parsley
    Salt and pepper

After transferring steaks to large plate, pour off all but 1 tablespoon fat from skillet. Return skillet to low heat and add shallot; cook, stirring frequently, until beginning to brown, 2 to 3 minutes. Sprinkle flour over shallot; cook, stirring constantly, until combined, about 1 minute. Add wine and increase heat to medium-high; simmer rapidly, scraping up any browned bits, until liquid is reduced to glaze, about 30 seconds; add broth and simmer until reduced to ⅔ cup, about 4 minutes. Reduce heat to medium; add capers, tomato, and any meat juices and cook until flavors are blended, about 1 minute. Stir in parsley; season with salt and pepper to taste. Spoon sauce over sliced steak and serve.

Chicken-Fried Steak

✔ WHY THIS RECIPE WORKS
Chicken-fried steak traditionally consists of a cheap steak pounded to tenderness, coated, fried, and served with a peppery cream gravy. Most recipes we found called for cube steak—steak cut from the round and put through a tenderizing machine that makes cubelike indentations. Unfortunately, most butchers mangle the job, and the steak starts to resemble coarse hamburger. We wanted a cheap cut that would fry up tender and still resemble steak, and a coating that would be crisp and crunchy.

TAKE A CUE FROM CUBE STEAK Even though we weren't satisfied with the flavor and texture of cube steak, we used a similar technique to prepare a more flavorful cut. We decided to use sirloin tips and scored the meat at ¼-inch intervals to imitate cube steak. Scoring shortened the fibers and made the meat easy to pound out for maximum tenderness.

POUND, DON'T JUST COAT When we lightly coated the steak with flour (à la fried chicken), the coating quickly became soggy and peeled off the meat. We discovered that pounding flour into the steaks created a sticky surface layer by damaging the meat's cell structure and releasing moisture from the surface. Dipping the steaks in egg and another layer of flour created a crisp crust that clung to the meat.

CHILL FOR A THICKER COATING Briefly refrigerating the steaks after coating them in the egg and flour helped the initial coating dry out and stick to the meat. We then dipped the steaks in flour again before frying them, which gave us the extra-thick, supercrunchy coating we wanted.

SHALLOW-FRY Submerging the coated meat in deep fat trapped in moisture and prevented it from evaporating, resulting in a soggy crust. We cut down on the amount of oil, using only enough so that the steaks would float in the pan. When we saw steam wisping up from the steaks as they cooked, we knew we'd gotten it right.

AT THE MEAT COUNTER

PREFERRED CUT Sirloin Steak Tips
Sirloin steak tips, also known as flap meat, are sold as whole steaks, cubes, and strips (see page 37 for more information). To ensure uniform pieces that cook evenly, we prefer to purchase whole steaks and cut them ourselves.

ALTERNATE CUT Boneless Shell Sirloin Steak
Shell sirloin steak is also called round-bone steak or New York sirloin steak (see page 37 for more information).

CHICKEN-FRIED STEAK
SERVES 4

Serve with mashed potatoes and Cream Gravy.

3½	cups all-purpose flour
½	cup cornstarch
1	tablespoon garlic powder
1	tablespoon onion powder
2	teaspoons baking powder
	Salt and pepper
½	teaspoon cayenne pepper
4	large eggs
¼	cup whole milk
1	pound sirloin steak tips, trimmed and cut into four 4-ounce pieces
1½	cups peanut or vegetable oil

1. Whisk flour, cornstarch, garlic powder, onion powder, baking powder, 1 teaspoon salt, 2 teaspoons pepper, and cayenne in large bowl. Transfer 1 cup seasoned flour mixture to shallow dish. Beat eggs in second shallow dish. Add milk to bowl with remaining flour mixture and rub with fingers until mixture resembles coarse meal.

2. Pat steaks dry with paper towels and season with salt and pepper. Score meat lightly at ¼-inch intervals in crosshatch pattern, and then dredge meat in seasoned flour. Using a meat pounder, pound steaks to between ⅛ and ¼ inch thick. One at a time, coat steaks lightly with seasoned flour again, dip in egg mixture, and then transfer to bowl with milk and flour mixture, pressing to adhere. Arrange steaks on wire rack set in rimmed baking sheet and refrigerate for at least 15 minutes or up to 4 hours; do not discard milk and flour mixture.

3. Adjust oven rack to middle position and heat oven to 200 degrees. Heat oil in large Dutch oven over medium-high heat until just smoking. Return 2 steaks to bowl with milk and flour mixture and turn to coat. Fry 2 steaks until deep golden brown and crisp, 2 to 3 minutes per side. Transfer to clean wire rack set in rimmed baking sheet and keep warm in oven. Repeat with remaining steaks. Serve.

CREAM GRAVY
MAKES ABOUT 3 CUPS

Avoid low-fat or skim milk in this recipe.

3	tablespoons unsalted butter
3	tablespoons all-purpose flour
½	teaspoon garlic powder
1½	cups chicken broth
1½	cups whole milk
¾	teaspoon salt
½	teaspoon pepper

Melt butter in 12-inch skillet over medium heat. Stir in flour and garlic powder and cook until golden, about 2 minutes. Slowly whisk in broth, milk, salt, and pepper and simmer until thickened, about 5 minutes. Spoon over steaks. (Gravy can be refrigerated for 2 days.)

GARLIC PRODUCTS

Garlic powder and granulated garlic are both made from garlic cloves that are dehydrated and then ground (garlic powder has a negligibly finer texture); dehydrated minced garlic is minced while fresh and then dehydrated and packaged; and garlic salt is typically 3 parts salt to 1 part garlic powder. Are any of these ever an acceptable substitute for fresh garlic?

To find out, we compared each product with fresh minced garlic in a Caesar salad (with garlic in both the dressing and the croutons) and garlic bread. We were surprised that the differences were minimal in the Caesar dressing, where the assertive flavor of the anchovies, Dijon mustard, and Worcestershire sauce masked any processed garlic flavor. On the other hand, the results were glaringly different for the crouton and garlic bread tests.

Without any other flavors to hide behind, the "sweet and strong" flavor of the fresh garlic stood out among the other "muted," "artificial" contenders. Tasters gave the garlic salt exceptionally low scores, objecting to its "chemical," "supersalty" taste.

When garlic is a predominant flavor in a recipe, nothing comes close to fresh. That said, in recipes where garlic is a background flavor, in a pinch you can use any dried garlic product except garlic salt. We like garlic powder best because of its "natural," "sweet" flavor. Substitute ¼ teaspoon of garlic powder for each clove of fresh garlic.

Steak Tips with Mushroom-Onion Gravy

✔ WHY THIS RECIPE WORKS

Steak tips smothered in mushroom and onion gravy is a classic combination, appearing on menus at pubs and family-style restaurants across the country. But this dish is too often plagued by chewy, overcooked beef, bland gravy, and prefab ingredients like canned cream of mushroom soup. We wanted tender, meaty steak and full-flavored gravy, enriched by the essence of fresh mushrooms and onions—and we wanted to do it with as few pans as possible.

TIPS ARE THE RIGHT TYPE Why drown premium steak in sauce? We determined that relatively inexpensive steak tips were the ideal choice for this recipe, since their wealth of marbling melted into the muscle fibers and made for tender meat. Cutting the pieces to the right size—in this case, 1½-inch chunks—proved to be key for creating enough surface area to brown without risking overcooking.

BOOST MEATINESS WITH MUSHROOMS During testing, we found that even a full pound of white mushrooms simply wasn't giving us the deep mushroom flavor we were after. Adding a few dried porcini mushrooms was an easy way to intensify the mushroom flavor without a perceptible change in the texture of the gravy.

ONE PAN IS ALL YOU NEED Giving the meat an initial sear in a hot skillet left a flavorful fond, which provided a meaty base for the gravy. We also found that allowing the meat to finish cooking in the gravy blended the flavors and built depth.

🔪 AT THE MEAT COUNTER
PREFERRED CUT Sirloin Steak Tips

Sirloin steak tips, also known as flap meat, are sold as whole steaks, cubes, and strips (see page 37 for more information). To ensure uniform pieces that cook evenly, we prefer to purchase whole steaks and cut them ourselves.

ALTERNATE CUT Boneless Shell Sirloin

Shell sirloin steak is also known as round-bone steak or New York sirloin steak (see page 37 for more information).

STEAK TIPS WITH MUSHROOM-ONION GRAVY

SERVES 4 TO 6

If you can find only cubes or strips rather than whole steak tips, reduce the cooking time slightly to avoid overcooking any smaller or thinner pieces. Cremini mushrooms can be used in place of the white mushrooms. This dish can be served over rice or egg noodles.

1	tablespoon soy sauce
1	teaspoon sugar
1½	pounds sirloin steak tips, trimmed and cut into 1½-inch chunks
1¾	cups beef broth
¼	ounce dried porcini mushrooms, rinsed
	Salt and pepper
2	tablespoons vegetable oil
1	pound white mushrooms, trimmed and sliced ¼ inch thick
1	large onion, halved and sliced thin
4	teaspoons all-purpose flour
1	garlic clove, minced
½	teaspoon minced fresh thyme
1	tablespoon chopped fresh parsley

1. Combine soy sauce and sugar in medium bowl. Add steak, toss well, and marinate for at least 30 minutes or up to 1 hour, tossing once more.

2. Meanwhile, microwave ¼ cup broth and porcini mushrooms in covered bowl until steaming, about 1 minute. Let stand until softened, about 5 minutes. Place fine-mesh strainer over bowl and line with coffee filter. Drain porcini mushrooms in strainer, then mince. Set aside porcini mushrooms and liquid.

3. Pat steak dry with paper towels and sprinkle with ½ teaspoon pepper. Heat 1 tablespoon oil in 12-inch skillet over medium-high heat until smoking. Add steak and cook until well browned on all sides, 6 to 8 minutes. Transfer to large plate and set aside.

4. Add remaining 1 tablespoon oil to now-empty skillet and heat over medium-high heat. Add white mushrooms, minced porcini mushrooms, and ¼ teaspoon salt; cook, stirring frequently, until all liquid has evaporated and mushrooms start to brown, 7 to 9 minutes. Scrape bottom of pan with wooden spoon to loosen any browned bits. Add onion and ¼ teaspoon salt; cook, stirring frequently, until onion begins to brown and dark bits form on pan bottom, 6 to 8 minutes longer. Add flour, garlic, and thyme; cook, stirring constantly, until vegetables are coated with flour mixture, about 1 minute. Stir in remaining 1½ cups broth and porcini soaking liquid, scraping bottom of skillet with wooden spoon to loosen any browned bits, and bring to boil.

5. Nestle steak into mushroom-onion mixture and add any accumulated juices to skillet. Reduce heat to medium-low and simmer until steak registers 125 to 130 degrees, 3 to 5 minutes, turning steak over several times. Season with salt and pepper to taste, sprinkle with parsley, and serve.

Beef Stroganoff

✓ WHY THIS RECIPE WORKS

Traditional beef stroganoff recipes call for tenderloin, which has a tender texture but lacks beefy flavor. We wanted both, so we set out to develop a recipe that would amp up the meaty flavor without sacrificing the texture.

USE A FLAVORFUL CUT We decided to forgo the tenderloin altogether and replaced it with sirloin steak tips (also known as flap meat), which have an intensely beefy taste. While not tough, their texture is a far cry from tenderloin, so we knew we would need a marinade, too.

MAKE A SIMPLE MARINADE We marinated the sirloin steak tips in soy sauce, which is so salty it works just like a brine. This helped the meat retain more juice and worked to break down proteins in the meat and loosen the bundles of muscle fibers, making them easier to bite through and chew. Soy sauce also contains glutamates, which boost meaty flavor. Poking the meat prior to marinating allowed for faster absorption.

SEAR BIG PIECES, THEN SLICE We pan-seared large pieces of meat and cut them into strips only after they browned and left their flavorful fond in the pan. This allowed enough time for the meat to develop rich, dark fond without overcooking. Moreover, we let it rest before slicing, further improving juiciness.

MICROWAVE THE MUSHROOMS We packed a pound of white mushrooms into our recipe. Cooked on the stovetop, it took up to 20 minutes for all their moisture to evaporate before they could brown in the pan. Microwaving the mushrooms before putting

---

PURCHASING AND STORING PORCINI

When purchasing dried porcini mushrooms (or any dried mushroom), avoid packages filled with small, dusty pieces marred by pinholes (a sign of worms) or those labeled "wild mushroom mix"—they are often older and of lesser quality. Dried mushrooms should have an earthy (not musty or stale) aroma. Store dried mushrooms in an airtight container in a cool, dry place for up to one year.

EGG NOODLES

Egg noodles are the starchy soul of many of our favorite comfort foods. The best versions should taste lightly wheaty, like traditional pasta, but have a richer flavor that comes from eggs in the pasta dough. We sampled seven brands of egg noodles, both plain and in soup. Rich, eggy flavor was a huge plus, but tasters also favored noodles made with semolina flour, which gave the noodles a firm yet tender bite. Our winning egg noodles, **Pennsylvania Dutch Wide Egg Noodles**, used the most yolks of any of the products, which gave the noodles a gentle egg flavor that was just rich enough. Their wide corkscrew shape worked well in both soup and pasta.

them in the pan reduced the process to a mere 6 to 8 minutes.

BUILD FLAVOR While many contemporary recipes call for ketchup, we chose tomato paste; just a bit stirred in after the onions and mushrooms browned brought subtle depth to the sauce. In addition, we used a paste made of dry mustard bloomed in warm water and seasoned with sugar and black pepper to give a little kick and bring the other flavors into focus. White wine added brightness, allowing the beef and mushrooms to shine through.

TEMPER THE SOUR CREAM The acidity of sour cream causes its casein proteins to become so unstable that exposure to even a little heat makes them clump. For this reason, we tempered the sour cream by adding it when the sauce was off the heat.

AT THE MEAT COUNTER

PREFERRED CUT Sirloin Steak Tips
Sirloin steak tips, also known as flap meat, are sold as whole steaks, cubes, and strips (see page 37 for more information). To ensure uniform pieces, we prefer to purchase whole steaks and cut them ourselves.

ALTERNATE CUT Blade Steak
Blade steak is also called top blade steak or flat-iron steak (see page 33 for more information). You can substitute 1½ pounds of blade steak for the sirloin steak tips; if using, cut each steak in half lengthwise and remove the gristle that runs down the center before cooking. Since blade steak yields smaller strips of meat, reduce the cooking time in step 3 by several minutes.

BEEF STROGANOFF
SERVES 4

If the mushrooms are larger than 1 inch, cut them into six even wedges. Serve the stroganoff over buttered egg noodles.

1¼   pounds sirloin steak tips, trimmed and cut lengthwise with grain into 4 equal pieces
2   teaspoons soy sauce
1   pound white mushrooms, trimmed and quartered
1   tablespoon dry mustard
2   teaspoons hot water
1   teaspoon sugar
    Salt and pepper
1   tablespoon vegetable oil
1   onion, chopped fine
4   teaspoons all-purpose flour
2   teaspoons tomato paste
1½   cups beef broth
⅓   cup plus 1 tablespoon white wine or dry vermouth
½   cup sour cream
1   tablespoon chopped fresh parsley or dill

1. Using fork, poke each piece of steak 10 to 12 times. Place in baking dish; rub both sides evenly with soy sauce. Cover with plastic wrap and refrigerate at least 15 minutes or up to 1 hour.

2. While meat marinates, place mushrooms in medium bowl, cover, and microwave until mushrooms have decreased in volume by half, 4 to 5 minutes (there should be as much as ¼ cup liquid in bowl). Drain mushrooms and set aside; discard liquid. Combine mustard, water, sugar, and ½ teaspoon pepper in small bowl until smooth paste forms; set aside.

3. Pat steak pieces dry with paper towels and season with pepper. Heat oil in 12-inch skillet over medium-high heat until just smoking. Place steak pieces in skillet and cook until browned on all sides and meat registers 125 to 130 degrees, 6 to 9 minutes. Transfer meat to large plate and set aside while cooking sauce.

4. Add mushrooms, onion, and ½ teaspoon salt to skillet and cook until vegetables begin to brown and dark bits form on bottom of pan, 6 to 8 minutes. Add flour and tomato paste and cook, stirring constantly, until onions and mushrooms are coated, about 1 minute. Stir in broth, ⅓ cup wine, and mustard paste and bring to simmer, scraping bottom of pan to

CURDLE-FREE DAIRY
Dishes like Beef Stroganoff and Chicken Paprikash (page 397) wouldn't be complete without a little sour cream or yogurt stirred in at the end. However, these cultured dairy products are sensitive to heat and can easily curdle if the stew is too hot or reheated. We wondered if another dairy product would provide a more stable tang.

To find out, we stirred dollops of whole-milk yogurt, full-fat sour cream, and crème fraîche (which boasts much more fat) into water that we brought to just a simmer (185 degrees). After letting the samples sit for 10 seconds, we found that both the yogurt and the sour cream mixtures quickly curdled, while the crème fraîche mixture remained perfectly creamy.

Why? Curdling occurs when excessive heat causes the whey proteins in dairy to denature (unfold) and bind with casein proteins, forming clumps of larger proteins. The greater amount of butterfat in crème fraîche (30 to 40 percent, versus 18 to 20 percent and roughly 4 percent in sour cream and yogurt, respectively) protects against this process by more thoroughly coating the proteins and preventing them from binding together. Plus, with more fat, crème fraîche has far fewer proteins to bind together in the first place—it's so resistant to curdling that it can withstand reheating. If you're looking for a curdle-free dairy for hot dishes, consider crème fraîche.

Our recipe for Beef Stroganoff calls for a pound of white mushrooms, which can take as long as 20 minutes to cook before all their moisture evaporates and they finally brown. Microwaving the mushrooms before putting them in the pan reduced the process to a mere 6 to 8 minutes in the skillet.

loosen browned bits. Reduce heat to medium and cook until sauce has reduced slightly and begun to thicken, 4 to 6 minutes.

5. While sauce is reducing, slice steak pieces against grain into ¼-inch-thick slices. Stir meat and any accumulated juices into

thickened sauce and cook until beef has warmed through, 1 to 2 minutes. Remove pan from heat and let any bubbles subside. Stir in sour cream and remaining 1 tablespoon wine; season with salt and pepper to taste. Sprinkle with parsley and serve.

Philly Cheesesteaks

✔ WHY THIS RECIPE WORKS

You can only get a real Philly cheesesteak in Philadelphia. Or can you? In restaurants, these sandwiches are made using a meat slicer, a flattop griddle, and pricey rib eye—all three of which, as far as we were concerned, were out of the question for a sandwich made at home. To that end, we set out to tailor Philly cheesesteaks to the home kitchen.

SKIRT THE ISSUE We were not enthusiastic at the prospect of spending $15 to $20 a pound on rib eyes for sandwich meat. Instead, we tested cheaper cuts and decided that skirt steak was a satisfying alternative.

FREEZE THEN SLICE To re-create the thin-sliced meat that is essential to the classic sandwich, we tried a number of shortcut methods (including buying presliced deli roast beef and using a food processor to slice the meat) but slicing by hand gave us the best results by far. A quick stint in the freezer made the meat easier to slice thinly and cleanly. Then we coarsely chopped the steak before cooking it to imitate the restaurant method of hashing the steak with metal spatulas.

BROWN IN BATCHES On a restaurant's flattop griddle, moisture evaporates almost instantly, allowing the meat to crisp up nicely. Using a 12-inch nonstick skillet and cooking the meat in batches proved to be a reasonable alternative. We let each batch drain in a colander before returning it to the pan to mix with the cheese, further cutting down on extra moisture—and greasiness.

GO ALL-AMERICAN Melting, gooey American cheese is the typical crowning touch to classic Philly cheesesteak and we saw no reason to change course. We did, however, amp up the complexity of the cheese flavor with a little bit of nutty Parmesan cheese.

🔪 AT THE MEAT COUNTER

PREFERRED CUT Skirt Steak

Skirt steak is also known as fajita steak or Philadelphia steak (see page 39 for more information).

ALTERNATE CUT Sirloin Steak Tips

Sirloin steak tips, also known as flap meat, are sold as whole steaks, cubes, and strips (see page 37 for more information). To ensure uniform pieces, we prefer to purchase whole steaks and cut them ourselves.

PHILLY CHEESESTEAKS
SERVES 4

Top these sandwiches with chopped pickled hot peppers, sautéed onions or bell peppers, sweet relish, or hot sauce.

2	pounds skirt steak, trimmed and sliced with grain into 3-inch-wide strips
4	(8-inch) Italian sub rolls, split lengthwise
2	tablespoons vegetable oil
½	teaspoon salt

⅛ teaspoon pepper

¼ cup grated Parmesan cheese

8 slices white American cheese (8 ounces)

1. Place steak pieces on large plate or baking sheet and freeze until very firm, about 1 hour.

2. Meanwhile, adjust oven rack to middle position and heat oven to 400 degrees. Spread split rolls on baking sheet and toast until lightly browned, 5 to 10 minutes.

3. Using sharp knife, shave steak pieces as thin as possible against grain. Mound meat on cutting board and chop coarsely with knife 10 to 20 times.

4. Heat 1 tablespoon oil in 12-inch nonstick skillet over high heat until smoking. Add half of meat in even layer and cook without stirring until well browned on 1 side, 4 to 5 minutes. Stir and continue to cook until meat is no longer pink, 1 to 2 minutes. Transfer meat to colander set in large bowl. Wipe out skillet with paper towel. Repeat with remaining 1 tablespoon oil and remaining sliced meat.

5. Return now-empty skillet to medium heat. Drain excess moisture from meat. Return meat to skillet (discard any liquid in bowl) and add salt and pepper. Heat, stirring constantly, until meat is warmed through, 1 to 2 minutes. Reduce heat to low, sprinkle with Parmesan, and shingle slices of American cheese over meat. Allow cheeses to melt, about 2 minutes. Using heatproof spatula or wooden spoon, fold melted cheese into meat thoroughly. Divide mixture evenly among toasted rolls. Serve immediately.

PREVENTING A STICKY SITUATION

Steak sticks during cooking when the sulfur atoms in the protein react with the metal atoms in the pan, forming a strong chemical bond and fusing the meat to the skillet. Once the pan becomes hot enough, the link between the protein and the metal will loosen, and the bond will eventually break.

To prevent steak from sticking, follow these steps: Heat oil in a heavy-bottomed skillet over high heat until it is just smoking (on most stovetops, this takes 2 to 3 minutes). Sear the meat without moving it, using tongs to flip it only when a substantial browned crust forms around the edges. If the meat doesn't lift easily, continue searing until it does.

Steak Tacos

✔ WHY THIS RECIPE WORKS

Steak tacos are great on the grill, but we wanted to bring them indoors for those times when grilling outside isn't an option.

STAKE OUT THE STEAK Traditional Mexican recipes typically call for skirt or flank steak for taco meat, both of which come from the belly of the cow. We also tried blade steak, which comes from the shoulder, and steak tips, from the sirloin of the animal. Flank steak, however, turned out to be the best choice; it has a nice beefy flavor and, when sliced thin against the grain, is quite tender.

QUARTER AND SEAR In order to maximize flavor, we cut the steak lengthwise with the grain into four long strips, about 2½ inches wide and 1 inch thick. Because the strips were relatively thick, we were able to brown them on four sides rather than just two, which gave us even more exposed edges to cook until crisp and flavorful.

SALT AND MARINADE We slathered our steak with a wet, pesto-like paste made of vegetable oil, cilantro, scallions, garlic, and jalapeños. When coupled with salt, this oil-based marinade provided plenty of fat-soluble cumin-chile flavor on the surface as well as penetrating water-soluble flavors from the garlic, flavoring it throughout. We reserved some of the fresh marinade to toss with the steak after it was sliced for a bright finish of flavor.

🔪 AT THE MEAT COUNTER

PREFERRED CUT Flank Steak

Flank steak is also known as jiffy steak (see page 39 for more information).

ALTERNATE CUT Sirloin Steak Tips

Sirloin steak tips, also known as flap meat, are sold as whole steaks, cubes, and strips (see page 37 for more information). To ensure uniform pieces, we prefer to purchase whole steaks and cut them ourselves.

CORN TORTILLAS FOR TACOS

The rule of thumb when buying tortillas is to buy a brand made with nothing more than ground corn treated with lime (an alkali that removes the germ and hull) and water. Look for brands sold in the refrigerator case of the supermarket, as these have few, if any, preservatives and tend to be more moist and flavorful.

HOW TO WARM TORTILLAS

Our preferred method for warming tortillas is to place each one over the medium flame of a gas burner until slightly charred, about 30 seconds per side. We also like toasting them in a dry skillet over medium-high heat until softened and speckled with brown spots, 20 to 30 seconds per side.

You can also use the oven: Divide tortillas into 2 stacks and wrap each stack in aluminum foil. Heat tortillas on middle rack of 350-degree oven for 5 minutes.

Keep warmed tortillas wrapped in foil or dish towel until ready to use or they will dry out. (If tortillas are very dry, pat each with a little water before warming.)

STEAK TACOS
SERVES 4 TO 6

For a more spicy dish, add the seeds from the chiles. In addition to the toppings suggested below, try serving the tacos with Sweet and Spicy Pickled Onions (recipe follows), thinly sliced radishes or cucumber, or salsa.

HERB PASTE
- ½ cup fresh cilantro leaves
- 3 scallions, chopped coarse
- 1 jalapeño chile, stemmed, seeds reserved, and chopped coarse
- 3 garlic cloves, chopped coarse
- ½ teaspoon ground cumin
- ¼ cup vegetable oil
- 1 tablespoon lime juice

STEAK
- 1 (1½- to 1¾-pound) flank steak, trimmed and sliced lengthwise (with grain) into 4 equal pieces
- 1 tablespoon kosher salt
- ½ teaspoon sugar
- ½ teaspoon pepper
- 2 tablespoons vegetable oil

TACOS
- 12 (6-inch) corn tortillas, warmed
  Fresh cilantro
  Minced white or red onion
  Lime wedges

1. FOR THE HERB PASTE: Pulse cilantro, scallions, jalapeño, garlic, and cumin in food processor until finely chopped, 10 to 12 pulses, scraping down sides of bowl as necessary. Add oil and process until mixture is smooth and resembles pesto, about 15 seconds, scraping down sides of bowl as necessary. Transfer 2 tablespoons herb paste to medium bowl; whisk in lime juice and set aside.

2. FOR THE STEAK: Using dinner fork, poke each piece of steak 10 to 12 times on each side. Place in large baking dish; rub all sides of steak pieces evenly with salt and then coat with remaining herb paste. Cover with plastic wrap and refrigerate at least 30 minutes or up to 1 hour.

3. Scrape herb paste off steak and sprinkle all sides of pieces evenly with sugar and pepper. Heat oil in 12-inch nonstick skillet over medium-high heat until just smoking. Place steak in skillet and cook until well browned, about 3 minutes. Flip steak and sear until second side is well browned, 2 to 3 minutes. Using tongs, stand each piece on a cut side and cook, turning as necessary, until all cut sides are well browned and meat registers 125 to 130 degrees, 2 to 7 minutes. Transfer steak to carving board and let rest for 5 minutes.

4. FOR THE TACOS: Slice steak pieces thin against grain. Transfer sliced steak to bowl with herb paste–lime juice mixture and toss to coat. Season with salt to taste. Spoon small amount of sliced steak into center of each warm tortilla and serve, passing toppings separately.

SWEET AND SPICY PICKLED ONIONS
MAKES ABOUT 2 CUPS

To make this dish spicier, add the reserved chile seeds with the vinegar.

- 1 red onion, sliced thin
- 1 cup red wine vinegar
- ⅓ cup sugar
- 2 jalapeño chiles, stemmed, seeds reserved, and cut into thin rings
- ¼ teaspoon salt

Place onion in medium heatproof bowl. Bring vinegar, sugar, jalapeños, and salt to simmer in small saucepan over medium-high heat, stirring occasionally, until sugar dissolves. Pour vinegar mixture over onion, cover loosely, and let cool to room temperature, about 30 minutes. Once cool, drain and discard liquid. (Pickled onions can be refrigerated in airtight container for up to 1 week.)

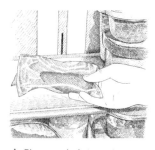

Teriyaki Stir-Fried Beef with Vegetables

✔ WHY THIS RECIPE WORKS

Stir-fries suffer from a number of common problems—including burnt garlic and ginger and watery sauces—but the biggest problem is the meat, which is often steamed, bland, and tough. We knew we could fix this dish with some tried-and-true test kitchen techniques.

START WITH THE RIGHT CUT Flank steak is the classic choice because it's relatively affordable, quick-cooking, and flavorful.

SLICE THIN, AGAINST THE GRAIN Cutting the meat against the grain into thin strips ensured that it would be tender and easy to eat. Why? Cutting the meat against the grain shortens long, tough muscle fibers (most of which run from end to end on this oblong cut), dramatically diminishing chewiness. Freeze the meat for 15 minutes before slicing it and make sure to use a sharp knife.

USE A BIG PAN Piling food up in the skillet hampers browning. For maximum browning and flavor we used a 12-inch skillet. We preferred a nonstick pan, which required very little oil and kept the stir-fry from becoming greasy.

COOK EVERYTHING IN BATCHES The goal when stir-frying is to keep the temperature in the pan very hot. On a professional restaurant stove, this might not be much of a challenge, but at home it is. We cooked the meat in two batches so that each piece was in direct contact with the pan. Likewise, we also cooked the vegetables in batches, with the slow-cooking vegetables (like mushrooms) going into the pan before faster-cooking vegetables (like green beans).

ADD THE GARLIC AND GINGER LAST Many stir-fry recipes start by cooking the garlic and ginger. The idea, we think, is to flavor everything that subsequently goes into the pan. Sounds good, but the result is that the garlic and ginger often burn, imparting a scorched, bitter flavor to the dish. Instead, we added the garlic and ginger at the end of the cooking time, pushing the vegetables to the side of the pan and making a clearing in the center for the garlic, ginger, and a little oil (which prevented the aromatics from burning). Once the aromatics were fragrant, we stirred them back into the vegetables to finish the stir-fry.

DON'T FORGET CORNSTARCH A good stir-fry sauce starts with very potent ingredients. Some restaurants thicken their stir-fry sauces with so much cornstarch that the result is a pasty, gloppy stir-fry. Many home cooks don't bother with any cornstarch and their sauces are so watery they pool on the plate, rather than clinging to the food. We found that a little cornstarch (usually about 1 teaspoon for a typical stir-fry sauce) struck just the right balance. Make sure to add the cornstarch to the sauce before it hits the pan. Cornstarch must be dispersed in cold or room-temperature liquids. If added to hot liquids or directly to the pan, the granules will swell quickly and form lumps.

🔪 AT THE MEAT COUNTER

PREFERRED CUT Flank Steak

Flank steak is also known as jiffy steak (see page 39 for more information).

ALTERNATE CUT Blade Steak

Blade steak is also called top blade steak or flat-iron steak (see page 33 for more information). If using blade steaks, you will need to remove excess fat and gristle, especially the line that runs lengthwise down the center of the steak, so start with 1 pound to compensate for the trimmings.

TERIYAKI STIR-FRIED BEEF WITH GREEN BEANS AND SHIITAKES

SERVES 4

To make slicing the flank steak easier, freeze it for 15 minutes. You can substitute 1 tablespoon white wine or sake mixed with 1 teaspoon sugar for the mirin. Serve with Sticky Rice (page 114).

SAUCE

½ cup chicken broth

2 tablespoons soy sauce

2 tablespoons sugar

1 tablespoon mirin

1 teaspoon cornstarch

¼ teaspoon red pepper flakes

STIR-FRY

2 tablespoons soy sauce

1 teaspoon sugar

1 (12-ounce) flank steak, trimmed and sliced thin against grain on slight bias

2 tablespoons vegetable oil

3 garlic cloves, minced

1 tablespoon grated fresh ginger

8 ounces shiitake mushrooms, stemmed and cut into 1-inch pieces

12 ounces green beans, trimmed and halved

¼ cup water

3 scallions, cut into 1½-inch pieces, white and light green parts quartered lengthwise

1. FOR THE SAUCE: Whisk all ingredients together in small bowl and set aside.

2. FOR THE STIR-FRY: Combine soy sauce and sugar in medium bowl. Add beef, toss well, and marinate for at least 10 minutes or up to 1 hour, stirring once. Meanwhile, combine 1 teaspoon oil, garlic, and ginger in small bowl.

3. Drain beef and discard liquid. Heat 1 teaspoon oil in 12-inch nonstick skillet over high heat until just smoking. Add half of beef in single layer, break up any clumps, and cook, without stirring, for 1 minute. Stir beef and continue to cook until browned, 1 to 2 minutes. Transfer beef to clean bowl. Repeat with 1 teaspoon oil and remaining beef. Rinse skillet clean and dry with paper towels.

4. Add remaining 1 tablespoon oil to clean, dry skillet and heat until just smoking. Add mushrooms and cook until beginning to brown, about 2 minutes. Add green beans and cook, stirring frequently, until spotty brown, 3 to 4 minutes. Add water, cover, and continue to cook until green beans are crisp-tender, 2 to 3 minutes longer. Uncover, clear center of skillet, and add garlic mixture. Cook, mashing mixture into pan, until fragrant, 15 to 20 seconds. Stir mixture into vegetables. Return beef and any accumulated juices to skillet, add scallions, and stir to combine. Whisk sauce to recombine, add to skillet, and cook, stirring constantly, until thickened, about 30 seconds. Serve.

STIR-FRIED BEEF WITH SUGAR SNAP PEAS AND RED PEPPERS

SERVES 4

To make slicing the flank steak easier, freeze it for 15 minutes. Serve with Sticky Rice (page 114).

SAUCE

½ cup chicken broth

¼ cup oyster sauce

2 tablespoons dry sherry

1 tablespoon sugar

1 teaspoon cornstarch

STIR-FRY

2 tablespoons soy sauce

1 teaspoon sugar

1 (12-ounce) flank steak, trimmed and sliced thin against grain on slight bias

2 tablespoons vegetable oil

3 garlic cloves, minced

1 tablespoon grated fresh ginger

12 ounces sugar snap peas, strings removed

1 red bell pepper, stemmed, seeded, and cut into ¼-inch-wide strips

2 tablespoons water

PREPEELED GARLIC

We've never met a garlic product we like better than a fresh clove. Recently, we've noticed many supermarkets carrying jars or deli containers of prepeeled garlic cloves and wondered how they compare to fresh garlic bought by the head. We tasted both kinds of garlic raw in aïoli, sautéed in spaghetti with garlic and olive oil, and lightly cooked in stuffed rolled flank steak. In all cases, results were mixed, with neither freshly peeled nor prepeeled garlic claiming victory.

However, we did notice a difference in shelf life: A whole head of garlic stored in a cool, dry place will last for at least a few weeks, while prepeeled garlic in a jar (which must be kept refrigerated) lasts for only about two weeks before turning yellowish and developing an overly pungent aroma, even if kept unopened in its original packaging. (In fact, in several instances we found containers of garlic that had started to develop this odor and color on the supermarket shelf.) But if you go through a lot of garlic, prepeeled cloves can be an acceptable alternative. Just make sure they look firm and white with a matte finish when you purchase them.

Snap off tip of snow pea or sugar snap pea while pulling down along flat side of pod to remove string.

I. FOR THE SAUCE: Whisk all ingredients together in small bowl and set aside.

2. FOR THE STIR-FRY: Combine soy sauce and sugar in medium bowl. Add beef, toss well, and marinate for at least 10 minutes or up to 1 hour, stirring once. Meanwhile, combine 1 teaspoon oil, garlic, and ginger in small bowl.

3. Drain beef and discard liquid. Heat 1 teaspoon oil in 12-inch nonstick skillet over high heat until just smoking. Add half of beef in single layer, break up any clumps, and cook, without stirring, for 1 minute. Stir beef and continue to cook until browned, 1 to 2 minutes. Transfer beef to clean bowl. Repeat with 1 teaspoon oil and remaining beef. Rinse skillet clean and dry with paper towels.

4. Add remaining 1 tablespoon oil to clean, dry skillet and heat until just smoking. Add snap peas and bell pepper and cook, stirring frequently, until beginning to brown, 3 to 5 minutes. Add water and continue to cook until vegetables are crisp-tender, 1 to 2 minutes longer. Clear center of skillet, add garlic mixture, and cook, mashing mixture into pan, until fragrant, 15 to 20 seconds. Stir mixture into vegetables. Return beef and any accumulated juices to skillet and stir to combine. Whisk sauce to recombine, add to skillet, and cook, stirring constantly, until thickened, about 30 seconds. Serve.

TANGERINE STIR-FRIED BEEF WITH ONION AND SNOW PEAS

SERVES 4

To make slicing the flank steak easier, freeze it for 15 minutes. Make sure to zest the tangerine for the beef and vegetables before juicing them for the sauce (you should need to zest only one of the tangerines). Two or three oranges can be substituted for the tangerines. If available, substitute 1 teaspoon toasted and ground Sichuan peppercorns for the red pepper flakes. Serve with Sticky Rice (page 114).

SAUCE

¾	cup tangerine juice (4 tangerines)
2	tablespoons soy sauce
I	tablespoon packed light brown sugar
I	teaspoon toasted sesame oil
I	teaspoon cornstarch

STIR-FRY

2	tablespoons soy sauce
I	teaspoon packed light brown sugar
I	(12-ounce) flank steak, trimmed and sliced thin against grain on slight bias
2	tablespoons vegetable oil
3	garlic cloves, minced
I	tablespoon grated fresh ginger
I	tablespoon black bean garlic sauce
I	teaspoon grated tangerine zest
¼–½	teaspoon red pepper flakes
I	large onion, halved through root end and cut into ½-inch wedges
10	ounces snow peas, strings removed
2	tablespoons water

I. FOR THE SAUCE: Whisk all ingredients together in small bowl and set aside.

2. FOR THE STIR-FRY: Combine soy sauce and sugar in medium bowl. Add beef, toss well, and marinate for at least 10 minutes or up to 1 hour, stirring once. Meanwhile, combine 1 teaspoon oil, garlic, ginger, black bean sauce, tangerine zest, and pepper flakes in small bowl.

3. Drain beef and discard liquid. Heat 1 teaspoon oil in 12-inch nonstick skillet over high heat until just smoking. Add half of beef in single layer, break up any clumps, and cook, without stirring, for 1 minute. Stir beef and continue to cook until browned, 1 to 2 minutes. Transfer beef to clean bowl. Repeat with 1 teaspoon oil and remaining beef. Rinse skillet clean and dry with paper towels.

4. Add remaining 1 tablespoon oil to clean, dry skillet and heat until just smoking. Add onion and cook, stirring frequently, until beginning to brown, 3 to 5 minutes. Add snow peas and cook until spotty brown, about

2 minutes longer. Add water and continue to cook until vegetables are crisp-tender, about 1 minute longer. Clear center of skillet, add garlic mixture, and cook, mashing mixture into pan, until fragrant, 15 to 20 seconds. Stir mixture into vegetables. Return beef and any accumulated juices to skillet and stir to combine. Whisk sauce to recombine, add to skillet, and cook, stirring constantly, until thickened, about 30 seconds. Serve.

KOREAN STIR-FRIED BEEF WITH KIMCHI

SERVES 4

To make slicing the flank steak easier, freeze it for 15 minutes. You can find kimchi, a spicy Korean pickled vegetable condiment, in the refrigerated section of Asian markets and some well-stocked supermarkets. Cut large pieces of kimchi into bite-size pieces before stir-frying. If the kimchi is made from green cabbage rather than napa cabbage, extend the cooking time by 1 to 2 minutes. Serve with Sticky Rice (page 114).

SAUCE

½   cup chicken broth
2   tablespoons soy sauce
1   tablespoon sugar
1   teaspoon toasted sesame oil
1   teaspoon cornstarch

STIR-FRY

2   tablespoons soy sauce
1   teaspoon sugar
1   (12-ounce) flank steak, trimmed and sliced thin against grain on slight bias
2   tablespoons vegetable oil
3   garlic cloves, minced
1   tablespoon grated fresh ginger
1   cup kimchi, chopped into 1-inch pieces
4   ounces bean sprouts (2 cups)
5   scallions, cut into 1½-inch pieces, white and light green pieces quartered lengthwise

1. FOR THE SAUCE: Whisk all ingredients together in small bowl and set aside.

2. FOR THE STIR-FRY: Combine soy sauce and sugar in medium bowl. Add beef, toss well, and marinate for at least 10 minutes or up to 1 hour, stirring once. Meanwhile, combine 1 teaspoon oil, garlic, and ginger in small bowl.

3. Drain beef and discard liquid. Heat 1 teaspoon oil in 12-inch nonstick skillet over high heat until just smoking. Add half of beef in single layer, break up any clumps, and cook, without stirring, for 1 minute. Stir beef and continue to cook until browned, 1 to 2 minutes. Transfer beef to clean bowl. Repeat with 1 teaspoon oil and remaining beef. Rinse skillet clean and dry with paper towels.

4. Add remaining 1 tablespoon oil to clean, dry skillet and heat until just smoking. Add kimchi and cook, stirring frequently, until aromatic, 1 to 2 minutes. Add bean sprouts and stir to combine. Clear center of skillet, add garlic mixture, and cook, mashing mixture into pan, until fragrant, 15 to 20 seconds. Stir mixture into vegetables. Return beef and any accumulated juices to skillet, add scallions, and stir to combine. Whisk sauce to recombine, add to skillet, and cook, stirring constantly, until thickened, about 30 seconds. Serve.

STIR-FRIED RED CURRY BEEF WITH EGGPLANT

SERVES 4

To make slicing the flank steak easier, freeze it for 15 minutes. Serve with Sticky Rice (page 114).

SAUCE

½   cup chicken broth
3   tablespoons canned coconut milk
2   tablespoons packed light brown sugar
1   tablespoon lime juice
1   tablespoon fish sauce
1   teaspoon cornstarch

STIR-FRYING IN CAST IRON?

For stir-frying, our go-to pan is a 12-inch nonstick skillet. But given that a well-seasoned cast-iron pan also has excellent nonstick properties and that it could potentially do a better job at searing (thus more closely imitating restaurant-quality stir-fries cooked in a ripping hot wok), we wondered whether this style of pan could work for stir-frying. We compared results using two recipes: a stir-fried beef dish and a stir-fried noodle dish.

The beef cooked more or less similarly in both pans, though cast iron came with pros and cons. On the one hand, it gave the meat a deeper sear. On the other, the beef's marinade (which contained sugar) caused a good bit of fond to develop—and the meat to sometimes stick slightly, despite this vessel's seasoning. Stir-frying noodles in cast iron was a disaster: Both the noodles and the eggs in the dish stuck relentlessly to its surface.

Why the difference? Nonstick pan surfaces, whether cast iron or manufactured nonstick, rely on polymers for their slickness. When seasoning cast iron, we create the polymer ourselves by heating oil above its smoke point, at which time it forms a hard film on the pan surface. Most manufactured nonstick pans rely on polytetrafluoroethylene (PTFE), a polymer that creates a very slick surface. While both polymers repel water and fat, PTFE is more effective than is the homemade version on cast iron.

We'll be sticking, so to speak, with nonstick skillets for stir-fries.

It can be tricky to remove the sticky ribs and seeds from chiles. Here's a simple method that allows you to do so effortlessly. (The same technique can be used to seed sweet peppers.)

1. Slice lengthwise along 1 side of chile, keeping stem and seedpod intact.

2. Turn chile flat side down and slice off another side. Repeat twice, leaving seeds behind.

3. Discard stem, seeds, and ribs (or add minced ribs and seeds judiciously to your recipe).

STIR-FRY

2 tablespoons soy sauce

1 teaspoon packed light brown sugar

1 (12-ounce) flank steak, trimmed and sliced thin against grain on slight bias

2 tablespoons vegetable oil

3 garlic cloves, minced

1½ teaspoons red curry paste

1 pound eggplant, peeled and cut into ¾-inch cubes

2 cups fresh basil leaves
   Lime wedges

1. FOR THE SAUCE: Whisk all ingredients together in small bowl and set aside.

2. FOR THE STIR-FRY: Combine soy sauce and sugar in medium bowl. Add beef, toss well, and marinate for at least 10 minutes or up to 1 hour, stirring once. Meanwhile, combine 1 teaspoon oil, garlic, and curry paste in small bowl.

3. Drain beef and discard liquid. Heat 1 teaspoon oil in 12-inch nonstick skillet over high heat until just smoking. Add half of beef in single layer, break up any clumps, and cook, without stirring, for 1 minute. Stir beef and continue to cook until browned, 1 to 2 minutes. Transfer beef to clean bowl. Repeat with 1 teaspoon oil and remaining beef. Rinse skillet clean and dry with paper towels.

4. Add remaining 1 tablespoon oil to clean, dry skillet and heat until just smoking. Add eggplant and cook, stirring frequently, until browned and no longer spongy, 5 to 7 minutes. Clear center of skillet, add garlic-curry mixture, and cook, mashing mixture into pan, until fragrant, 15 to 20 seconds. Stir mixture into eggplant. Return beef and any accumulated juices to skillet and stir to combine. Whisk sauce to recombine, add to skillet along with basil, and cook, stirring constantly, until thickened, about 30 seconds. Serve, passing lime wedges separately.

Stir-Fried Thai-Style Beef with Chiles and Shallots

✓ WHY THIS RECIPE WORKS

Traditional Thai-style beef relies on obscure ingredients like galangal, palm sugar, and dried prawns, and requires hours of prep plus deep-frying. We wanted to spend minimal time cooking to achieve the same unique flavor profile using easily available ingredients.

USE A SALTY MARINADE We replaced our usual stir-fry marinade base—soy sauce—with the equally salty fermented fish sauce that is traditional in Thai chile beef. The fish sauce simulated the briny flavors of the dried shrimp and shrimp paste listed in many original recipes. To this, we added a little light brown sugar, coriander, and white pepper, which is a key ingredient in traditional recipes.

STIR-FRY WELL As with all our stir-fries, we cooked our ingredients in a predictable order. First, we cooked the beef in batches to maximize browning, then we added the vegetables (in this case the chiles and shallots), and finished with the garlic (to keep it from scorching). For a Thai dish like this one, we wanted our sauce to contain salty, sweet, spicy, and sour notes. To that end, we used salty fish sauce and sweet brown sugar. Rice vinegar gave us a sour note and the spice came from the chiles. Thai stir-fries are often finished with fresh herbs (we used cilantro and mint here) and something crunchy (we used peanuts).

CONTROL THE HEAT We removed the seeds and ribs from the chiles in order to control the level of heat, and then cut the chiles into strips. We added another layer of heat to the mix with Asian chili-garlic sauce, which provided a complex mix of spicy, toasty, and garlicky flavors. Using two types of heat gave us the opportunity to control the spice level even more.

✒ AT THE MEAT COUNTER
PREFERRED CUT Blade Steak

Blade steak is also known as top blade steak or flat-iron steak (see page 33 for more information). Note that you will need to remove excess fat and gristle, especially the line that runs lengthwise down the center of the steak.

ALTERNATE CUT Flank Steak

Flank steak is also known as jiffy steak (see page 39 for more information). Because flank steak requires less trimming, you will need only about 1¾ pounds. To prepare flank steak, first cut the steak with the grain into 1½-inch-wide strips, then cut the strips against the grain into ¼-inch-thick slices.

STIR-FRIED THAI-STYLE BEEF WITH CHILES AND SHALLOTS
SERVES 4

White pepper lends this stir-fry a unique penetrating flavor; black pepper is not a good substitute. Serve the stir-fry with steamed jasmine rice.

BEEF AND MARINADE
- 1   tablespoon fish sauce
- 1   teaspoon packed light brown sugar
- ¾   teaspoon ground coriander
- ⅛   teaspoon ground white pepper
- 2   pounds beef blade steak, trimmed and sliced crosswise into ¼-inch-thick strips

STIR-FRY
- 2   tablespoons fish sauce
- 2   tablespoons rice vinegar
- 2   tablespoons water
- 1   tablespoon packed light brown sugar
- 1   tablespoon Sriracha sauce
- 3   tablespoons vegetable oil
- 3   garlic cloves, minced
- 3   serrano or jalapeño chiles, stemmed, seeded, and sliced thin
- 3   shallots, peeled, quartered, and layers separated
- ½   cup fresh mint leaves, large leaves torn into bite-size pieces
- ½   cup fresh cilantro leaves
- ⅓   cup dry-roasted peanuts, chopped
       Lime wedges

1. FOR THE BEEF AND MARINADE: Whisk fish sauce, sugar, coriander, and pepper together in large bowl. Add beef, toss well, and marinate for 15 minutes.

2. FOR THE STIR-FRY: Combine fish sauce, vinegar, water, sugar, and Sriracha in small bowl. In second small bowl, combine 1 teaspoon oil and garlic. Heat 2 teaspoons oil in 12-inch nonstick skillet over high heat until smoking. Add one-third of beef to skillet in single layer. Cook, without stirring, until well browned, about 2 minutes, then stir and continue cooking until beef is browned around edges and no longer pink in center, about 30 seconds. Transfer beef to clean bowl. Repeat with 4 teaspoons oil and remaining beef in 2 more batches.

3. Reduce heat to medium, add remaining 2 teaspoons oil to now-empty skillet, and swirl to coat. Add serranos and shallots and cook, stirring frequently, until beginning to soften, 3 to 4 minutes. Clear center of skillet, add garlic mixture, and cook, mashing mixture into pan, until fragrant, 15 to 20 seconds. Stir mixture into vegetables. Whisk sauce to recombine and add to skillet; increase heat to high and cook until slightly reduced and thickened, about 30 seconds. Return beef and any accumulated juices to skillet and stir to combine. Stir in half of mint and half of cilantro. Sprinkle with peanuts and remaining mint and cilantro. Serve, passing lime wedges separately.

SIZING UP CHILE HEAT

In the test kitchen, we've noticed that some jalapeños are searingly hot, while others are as mild as bell peppers. We tracked down a number of theories to explain this great variation—and size kept popping up. According to this theory, a small chile will be hotter than a larger one.

But when we arranged a tasting of jalapeños of various sizes, there seemed to be no correlation between size and heat. To investigate the matter further, we sent five similarly size jalapeños to the lab, requesting levels of capsaicin and dihydrocapsaicin (the compounds responsible for the majority of the perception of "heat"). Sure enough, some chiles were nearly 10 times hotter than others—even though they all looked alike. One burning question remained: Are there any visual indicators of pungency? No, says Danise Coon of the Chile Pepper Institute, who explained that capsaicin production is tied to the environment. Chiles grown in sunny, arid weather undergo a lot of stress, and stressed chiles produce more capsaicin than chiles grown in temperate climates. (Hot, dry New Mexico is known for producing very hot chiles.)

Until someone comes up with a procedure for diagnosing stressed-out chiles, the only surefire way to judge the heat level of a chile is to taste it. If you want more control over the heat when you're cooking with chiles, start with an easy-to-measure heat source such as cayenne, red pepper flakes, or chili-garlic sauce, then layer on modest amounts of fresh chiles, removing the ribs and seeds if you want less heat.

Crispy Orange Beef

✓ WHY THIS RECIPE WORKS

Most versions of this Chinese restaurant standard are better dubbed "Soggy Orange Beef." We wanted truly crispy strips of beef doused in a sweet, savory, tangy citrus sauce.

DRY YOUR MEAT In order to achieve a perfectly crisp coating, we needed to dry the surface of the meat as much as possible. To start, we simplified the coating, replacing the traditional multi-ingredient batter with only a dredge in cornstarch. The flavorless cornstarch absorbed the excess surface moisture. To supplement the drying effect of the cornstarch, we put the coated pieces of meat in the freezer for 45 minutes to remove even more surface moisture, guaranteeing that the crisp coating wouldn't have any competition.

CUT BACK ON OIL While frying beef in vats of oil may work for restaurants, it's not practical for the home cook. We made our recipe work with only 3 cups of oil by cooking the beef in three batches. To prevent the pieces of meat from folding over and sticking together in the oil, we cut them into matchsticks.

BROWN THE ORANGE Traditionally, this dish gets its pungent depth from dried tangerine peels, a difficult ingredient to find in most grocery stores. To imitate the flavor profile, we used pieces of more readily available orange peels. Keeping some of the pith on the peels added a subtle bitterness, and browning them in oil introduced deeper, caramelized notes to the sauce. We further enhanced the orange flavor with freshly squeezed orange juice.

🔪 AT THE MEAT COUNTER
PREFERRED CUT Sirloin Steak Tips

Sirloin steak tips, also known as flap meat, are sold as whole steaks, cubes, and strips (see page 37 for more information). To ensure uniform pieces that cook evenly, we prefer to purchase whole steaks and cut them ourselves.

ALTERNATE CUT Flank Steak

Flank steak is also known as jiffy steak (see page 39 for more information). Because flank steak requires less trimming, you will need only about 1¼ pounds. To prepare flank steak, first cut the steak with the grain into 2½- to 3-inch-wide strips, then cut the strips against the grain into ½-inch-thick slices, and each slice into ½-inch-wide strips.

CRISPY ORANGE BEEF
SERVES 4

Use a vegetable peeler on the oranges and make sure that your strips contain some pith. Do not use low-sodium soy sauce. Serve this dish with Sticky Rice (page 114).

1½	pounds sirloin steak tips, trimmed
3	tablespoons soy sauce
6	tablespoons cornstarch
10	(3-inch) strips orange peel, sliced thin lengthwise (¼ cup), plus ¼ cup juice (2 oranges)
3	tablespoons molasses
2	tablespoons dry sherry
1	tablespoon rice vinegar
1½	teaspoons toasted sesame oil
3	cups vegetable oil
1	jalapeño chile, stemmed, seeded, and sliced thin lengthwise
2	tablespoons grated fresh ginger
3	garlic cloves, minced
½	teaspoon red pepper flakes
2	scallions, sliced thin on bias

1. Cut beef with grain into 2½- to 3-inch-wide lengths. Slice each piece against grain into ½-inch-thick slices. Cut each slice lengthwise into ½-inch-wide strips. Toss beef with 1 tablespoon soy sauce in bowl. Add cornstarch and toss until evenly coated. Spread beef in single layer on wire rack set in rimmed

DEEP-FRIED DOESN'T HAVE TO MEAN GREASY

The most common belief about deep-frying battered foods is that the results are always greasy. But this doesn't have to be the case at all. When battered foods are deep-fried in hot oil, water in the batter and near the exterior of the food turns to vapor and exits. Once the water exits, there is space for a small amount of oil to take its place. The amount of oil absorbed is directly proportional to the amount of water lost. The more water out the more oil in.

But our Crispy Orange Beef seemed to take in even less oil than we expected: When we weighed the fry oil before and after cooking, we found that the entire 1½ pounds of beef absorbed only ⅞ ounce, or 2 tablespoons, of oil. How was this possible? It all comes down to the meat's coating. Instead of dipping the beef in the traditional batter for this recipe—a moist mixture of egg white and cornstarch—we simply dredged it in dry cornstarch. Since cornstarch has virtually no moisture to lose on its own, this meant that all the moisture lost during frying was coming from the beef alone. (With battered beef, both the coating and the meat lose moisture.) The upshot: Less moisture was lost, so less oil was absorbed.

The key to using a mortar and pestle effectively is circular grinding, not up-and-down pounding. (Pounding is less efficient and scatters ingredients.) Here's how to effectively grind spices to a fine powder.

Place spices in mortar. Steady mortar with your hand and firmly press pestle's rounded base against inside of mortar with your other hand. Rotate pestle, without lifting head and maintaining downward pressure at all times, until spices are ground to desired consistency.

baking sheet. Transfer sheet to freezer until meat is very firm but not completely frozen, about 45 minutes.

2. Whisk orange juice, molasses, sherry, vinegar, sesame oil, and remaining 2 tablespoons soy sauce together in bowl.

3. Line second rimmed baking sheet with triple layer of paper towels. Heat vegetable oil in large Dutch oven over medium heat until oil registers 375 degrees. Carefully add one-third of beef and fry, stirring occasionally to keep beef from sticking together, until golden brown, about 1½ minutes. Using wire-mesh skimmer, transfer meat to paper towel–lined

sheet. Return oil to 375 degrees and repeat twice more with remaining beef. After frying, reserve 2 tablespoons frying oil.

4. Heat reserved oil in 12-inch skillet over medium-high heat until shimmering. Add orange peel and jalapeño and cook, stirring occasionally, until about half of orange peel is golden brown, 1½ to 2 minutes. Add ginger, garlic, and pepper flakes; cook, stirring frequently, until garlic is beginning to brown, about 45 seconds. Add soy sauce mixture and cook, scraping up any browned bits, until slightly thickened, about 45 seconds. Add beef and scallions and toss. Serve immediately.

Inexpensive Grilled Steak with Spice Rubs

✔ WHY THIS RECIPE WORKS

Spice rubs can sometimes counteract flavor and texture deficiencies in less expensive steaks, but only when done right. Too often, if they manage to cling to the meat at all, they turn out dry, dusty, and flat-tasting. We wanted a rub that would not only impart good flavor, but would also aid in the creation of a crispy, crunchy crust.

PUT GLUTAMATES TO WORK We know from past test kitchen experience that certain ingredients high in glutamates can amp up savory, meaty flavors without imparting their own distinguishing flavors. Tomato paste and fish sauce are two of the most potent carriers of glutamates, and they did their job well here as a wet rub for the steak: The flavor of the meat was noticeably deeper, without tasting like fish or tomatoes. We then built on that base by adding a couple of basic spices. Since the flavor compounds in garlic powder and

onion powder are water-soluble, we were able to completely infuse the steak with flavor even before we added the rub.

CHOOSE SPICES WISELY FOR DRY RUB Dried herbs and other delicate spices can lose their flavor in the intense heat of the grill, but spices containing capsaicin, such as paprika, chiles, and peppers, fare well. We preferred the taste and texture of whole spices that we toasted and ground ourselves, and we eliminated the raw spice flavors by spritzing the steaks with vegetable oil, allowing the spices to bloom right on the steaks.

MAKE SLITS FOR STICKING POWER Making a series of very small slits on both sides of the steaks proved to be doubly advantageous: It increased the flavor-imparting surface area for our initial rub, and it helped the second spice rub to stick to the meat (instead of the grill grates).

GRILLED STEAK WITH
NEW MEXICAN CHILE RUB

SERVES 6 TO 8

Shell sirloin steak is also known as round-bone steak or New York sirloin steak (see page 37 for more information). Spraying the rubbed steaks with oil helps the spices bloom, preventing a raw flavor.

STEAK

- 2 teaspoons tomato paste
- 2 teaspoons fish sauce
- 1½ teaspoons kosher salt
- ½ teaspoon onion powder
- ½ teaspoon garlic powder
- 2 (1½- to 1¾-pound) whole boneless shell sirloin steaks, 1 to 1¼ inches thick, trimmed

SPICE RUB

- 2 dried New Mexican chiles, stemmed, seeded, and torn into ½-inch pieces
- 4 teaspoons cumin seeds
- 4 teaspoons coriander seeds
- ½ teaspoon red pepper flakes
- ½ teaspoon black peppercorns
- 1 tablespoon sugar
- 1 tablespoon paprika
- ¼ teaspoon ground cloves
  Vegetable oil spray

1. FOR THE STEAK: Combine tomato paste, fish sauce, salt, onion powder, and garlic powder in bowl. Pat steaks dry with paper towels. With sharp knife, cut ⅟₁₆-inch-deep slits on both sides of steaks, spaced ½ inch apart, in crosshatch pattern. Rub salt mixture evenly on both sides of steaks. Place steaks on wire rack set in rimmed baking sheet; let stand at room temperature for at least 1 hour. (After 30 minutes, prepare grill.)

2. FOR THE SPICE RUB: Toast chiles, cumin, coriander, pepper flakes, and peppercorns in 10-inch skillet over medium-low heat, stirring frequently, until just beginning to smoke, 3 to 4 minutes. Transfer to plate to cool, about 5 minutes. Grind spices in spice grinder or in mortar with pestle until coarsely ground. Transfer spices to bowl and stir in sugar, paprika, and cloves.

3A. FOR A CHARCOAL GRILL: Open bottom vent completely. Light large chimney starter mounded with charcoal briquettes (7 quarts). When top coals are partially covered with ash, pour two-thirds evenly over grill, then pour remaining coals over half of grill. Set cooking grate in place, cover, and open lid vent completely. Heat grill until hot, about 5 minutes.

3B. FOR A GAS GRILL: Turn all burners to high, cover, and heat grill until hot, about 15 minutes. Leave primary burner on high and turn other burner(s) to medium.

4. Clean and oil cooking grate. Sprinkle half of spice rub evenly over 1 side of steaks and press to adhere until spice rub is fully moistened. Lightly spray rubbed side of steak with oil spray, about 3 seconds. Flip steaks and repeat process of sprinkling with spice rub and coating with oil spray on second side.

5. Place steaks over hotter part of grill and cook until browned and charred on both sides and center registers 125 degrees (for medium-rare) or 130 degrees (for medium), 3 to 4 minutes per side. If steaks have not reached desired temperature, move to cooler side of grill and continue to cook. Transfer steaks to clean wire rack set in rimmed baking sheet, tent loosely with aluminum foil, and let rest for 10 minutes. Slice meat thin against grain and serve.

GRILLED STEAK WITH SPICY
CHIPOTLE CHILE RUB

Substitute 2 dried chipotle chiles for New Mexican chiles, 1 teaspoon dried oregano for paprika, and ½ teaspoon ground cinnamon for ground cloves.

GRILLED STEAK WITH
ANCHO CHILE-COFFEE RUB

Substitute 1 dried ancho chile for New Mexican chiles, 2 teaspoons ground coffee for paprika, and 1 teaspoon unsweetened cocoa powder for ground cloves.

KEEPING CHILES
FRESHER LONGER

Fresh chiles like jalapeños and serranos have a relatively brief shelf life in the refrigerator. We tried four different refrigerator storage methods to see if any would help these chiles keep their crisp texture and fresh flavor longer. We sealed whole chiles in a plastic bag; left them loose in the crisper drawer; sliced them in half (to allow liquid to penetrate) and stored them in plain white vinegar; and sliced them in half and submerged them in a brine solution (1 tablespoon salt per cup of water). In both the bag and the crisper, the chiles began to soften and turn brown within a week. Storing in vinegar was also not ideal; after about a week, the chiles began tasting more pickled than fresh. The brine-covered chiles, however, retained their crispness, color, and bright heat for several weeks and, after a quick rinse to remove excess brine, were indistinguishable from chiles when we sampled them raw and in salsa. After a month they began to soften, but they remained perfectly usable in cooked applications for several weeks.

CROSSHATCHING
CREATES A CRISPY
CRUST

Cut ½-inch crosshatch
pattern, ¼ inch deep, on
both sides of steak.

Grilled London Broil

✓ WHY THIS RECIPE WORKS

London broil used to be a catchall term for inexpensive cuts of meat. Today, it's usually a top round steak that's marinated and quickly grilled. But recipes that produce a nice char on the outside produce overcooked gray bands of meat inside. We wanted to perfect the grilling method for this robustly flavored cut.

START WITH SOY SAUCE We stuck with top round for the meat and for our marinade we found that soy sauce was a perfect base. The salty liquid encouraged moisture retention by plumping the meat's muscle fibers. Plus, the abundance of savory glutamates found in soy sauce boosted the already-beefy flavor of the steak. By adding Italian-style flavorings and whirring them together in a blender, we came up with a potent marinade that provided deep flavor.

FLIP FREQUENTLY Many of the recipes we tried left an unappealing, gray, overcooked band around the rosy pink center of the meat. Flipping the steak every minute for the duration of the cooking time eliminated this problem. And, since the cooking time is less than 10 minutes, we weren't bothered by having to babysit the grill.

CROSSHATCH FOR MAXIMUM BROWNING Since we were flipping the steak so often, the meat did not have time to develop a nicely charred crust. To remedy this without sacrificing our perfectly pink interior, we crosshatched both sides of the steak to expose additional surface area and create thin ridges that would crisp up quickly. We also patted the steak dry when we removed it from the marinade and added a simple spice rub of sweet paprika and black pepper. Not only did the spices crust nicely on the grill, they also provided a peppery kick to counter the meat's richness.

GRILLED LONDON BROIL
SERVES 4

Top round steak is also known as London broil (see page 38 for more information). Because it's so lean, it is best served medium-rare to medium and sliced very thin (it will be tough and dry if cooked to well or beyond). You can use thyme in place of the rosemary and either sweet or hot paprika. Serve with Sweet and Smoky Grilled Tomato Salsa (recipe follows), if desired, but note that it will need to be prepared ahead.

1	(1½- to 2-pound) top round steak, 1½ inches thick, trimmed
½	cup soy sauce
2	tablespoons balsamic vinegar
2	tablespoons ketchup
2	tablespoons chopped fresh sage
5	garlic cloves, minced
1½	tablespoons vegetable oil
1	teaspoon chopped fresh rosemary
1½	teaspoons coarsely ground pepper
1	teaspoon paprika

1. Cut ½-inch crosshatch pattern, ¼ inch deep, on both sides of steak. Place steak in 1-gallon zipper-lock bag. Combine soy sauce, vinegar, ketchup, sage, garlic, oil, and rosemary in blender and process until garlic and herbs are finely chopped, about 30 seconds. Add marinade to bag with steak, seal, and turn to coat. Let sit at room temperature for 2 hours or refrigerate for up to 8 hours. (If refrigerated, bring steak to room temperature before grilling.)

2A. **FOR A CHARCOAL GRILL:** Open bottom vent completely. Light large chimney starter filled with charcoal briquettes (6 quarts). When top coals are partially covered with ash, pour evenly over half of grill.

Set cooking grate in place, cover, and open lid vent completely. Heat grill until hot, about 5 minutes.

2B. FOR A GAS GRILL: Turn all burners to high, cover, and heat grill until hot, about 15 minutes. Leave all burners on high.

3. Combine pepper and paprika in bowl. Remove steak from marinade, pat dry with paper towels, and season with pepper mixture.

4. Clean and oil cooking grate. Grill steak (hotter side of grill if using charcoal) for 1 minute. Flip and grill on second side for 1 minute. Repeat, flipping every minute, until steak registers 125 degrees (for medium-rare), 5 to 7 minutes, or 130 degrees (for medium), about 9 minutes. Transfer to carving board, tent loosely with aluminum foil, and let rest for 10 minutes. Slice steak thin against grain and serve.

SWEET AND SMOKY GRILLED TOMATO SALSA

MAKES ABOUT 3 CUPS

Sugar and lime juice should be added at the end to taste, depending on the ripeness of the tomatoes. To make this salsa spicier, add the chile seeds. The salsa can be refrigerated in an airtight container for up to two days; bring back to room temperature before serving. Wood chunks are not recommended for this recipe.

1	cup wood chips, soaked in water for 15 minutes and drained
2	pounds plum tomatoes, cored and halved lengthwise
2	large jalapeño chiles
2	teaspoons vegetable oil
3	tablespoons finely chopped red onion
2	tablespoons chopped fresh cilantro
2	tablespoons extra-virgin olive oil
	Salt and pepper
1–2	tablespoons lime juice
½–1	teaspoon sugar

1. Using large piece of heavy-duty aluminum foil, wrap soaked chips in foil packet and cut several vent holes in top.

2A. FOR A CHARCOAL GRILL: Open bottom vent halfway. Light large chimney starter filled with charcoal briquettes (6 quarts). When top coals are partially covered with ash, pour evenly over half of grill. Set cooking grate in place, cover, and open lid vent halfway. Heat grill until hot, about 5 minutes.

2B. FOR A GAS GRILL: Turn all burners to high, cover, and heat grill until hot, about 15 minutes. Leave all burners on high.

3. Toss tomatoes, jalapeños, and vegetable oil together in bowl. Place tomatoes cut side down on hot side of grill, cover, and cook until evenly charred on both sides and juices bubble, 8 to 12 minutes, flipping halfway through cooking.

4. Meanwhile, cook jalapeños on hot side of grill until skins are blackened on all sides, 8 to 10 minutes, turning as needed.

5. Transfer tomatoes and jalapeños to baking dish. If using charcoal, remove cooking grate and place wood chip packet on coals; set cooking grate in place. If using gas, remove cooking grate and place wood chip packet over primary burner; leave primary burner on high and turn other burner(s) to medium-low.

6. Place tomatoes and jalapeños on cool side of grill, cover (position lid vent over tomatoes if using charcoal), and cook for 2 minutes. Transfer tomatoes and jalapeños to cutting board and let sit until cool enough to handle.

7. Stem, peel, seed, and finely chop jalapeños. Pulse tomatoes in food processor until broken down but still chunky, about 6 pulses. Transfer tomatoes to clean bowl and stir in jalapeños, onion, cilantro, olive oil, 1 teaspoon salt, and ¼ teaspoon pepper. Season with lime juice, sugar, salt, and pepper to taste. Let sit for 10 minutes before serving.

Grilled Chuck Steaks

✔ WHY THIS RECIPE WORKS

Treated like their pricey counterparts, inexpensive chuck steaks can turn tough and chewy. We wanted to develop a recipe that would produce tender steaks, while capitalizing on chuck's beefy flavor and moderate price.

EYE ON THE PRIZE The chuck contains several different cuts, but during testing, we found that not all chuck steaks are created equal. We found chuck-eye steaks to have the best texture and good, beefy flavor.

BE YOUR OWN BUTCHER Despite their wide availability, the chuck-eye steaks we were getting from the store were inconsistent in size and shape, so they cooked at very different rates. We decided to avoid this problem by buying a boneless chuck-eye roast and cutting the steaks ourselves. This bit of extra (and easy) work resulted in four thick steaks that were a snap to cook evenly.

SPICE IT UP While chipotle chile powder and salt made an assertive base for our spice rub, we needed something more. Granulated garlic and ground coriander provided complementary flavors, but we found that a surprising ingredient—cocoa powder—added great depth. Brown sugar helped smooth out the bitter edges. Letting the spice-rubbed steaks sit in the refrigerator for at least 6 hours allowed the flavors to really sink in to the meat before they hit the grill.

GRILLED CHUCK STEAKS
SERVES 4

Chuck-eye roast is also known as boneless chuck roll or boneless chuck fillet (see page 34 for more information). We prefer to cut a whole roast and slice the steaks ourselves to ensure even thickness and even cooking. Choose a roast without too much fat at the natural seam.

I	tablespoon kosher salt
I	tablespoon chipotle chile powder
I	teaspoon unsweetened cocoa powder
I	teaspoon packed brown sugar
½	teaspoon ground coriander
½	teaspoon granulated garlic
I	(2½- to 3-pound) boneless beef chuck-eye roast
2	tablespoons vegetable oil

I. Combine salt, chile powder, cocoa, sugar, coriander, and garlic in bowl. Separate roast into 2 pieces along natural seam. Turn each piece on its side and cut in half lengthwise against grain. Remove silverskin and trim fat to ¼-inch thickness. Pat steaks dry with paper towels and rub with spice mixture. Transfer steaks to zipper-lock bag and refrigerate for at least 6 hours or up to 24 hours.

2A. FOR A CHARCOAL GRILL: Open bottom vent halfway. Light large chimney starter filled with charcoal briquettes (6 quarts). When top coals are partially covered with ash, pour evenly over half of grill. Set cooking grate in place, cover, and open lid vent halfway. Heat grill until hot, about 5 minutes.

2B. FOR A GAS GRILL: Turn all burners to high, cover, and heat grill until hot, about 15 minutes. Turn primary burner to medium-high and other burner(s) to medium-low.

3. Clean and oil cooking grate. Brush steaks all over with oil. Place steaks over hotter side of grill and cook (covered if using gas) until well charred on both sides, about 5 minutes per side. Move steaks to cooler side of grill and continue to cook (covered if using gas) until steaks register 125 degrees (for medium-rare), 5 to 8 minutes.

4. Transfer steaks to carving board, tent loosely with aluminum foil, and let rest for 10 minutes. Slice steaks thin against grain and serve.

TURNING CHUCK-EYE ROASTS INTO STEAKS

1. After separating roast at its natural seam, turn each piece on its side and cut it in half lengthwise, against grain.

2. Remove and discard chewy silverskin and any excess fat.

A widespread belief holds that piercing meat with a fork during cooking should be avoided since it allegedly allows precious juices to escape. To put this theory to the test, we cooked two sets of five steaks to medium-rare. We gently turned one set with a pair of tongs; we jabbed the other steaks with a sharp fork to turn them. We then compared the raw and cooked weights of each steak. Both sets of steaks lost exactly the same amount of moisture during cooking—an average of 19.6 percent of their weight. The reason: Virtually all moisture that is lost when meat is cooked is a result of muscle fibers contracting in the heat and squeezing out their juices. Piercing does not damage the fibers enough to cause additional juices to leak out (any more than poking a wet sponge with a fork would expel its moisture).

When it comes to the moisture level and tenderness of meat, cooking time and temperature are the most important factors.

Grilled Marinated Flank Steak

✔ WHY THIS RECIPE WORKS

Often, flank steak is marinated in bottled salad dressing—a method that doesn't save enough time to make it worth the significant sacrifice in texture. We wanted to come up with a simple homemade marinade that would pack a flavorful punch without making the meat mushy.

LOSE THE ACID The acidic vinegar in bottled salad dressing was destroying the texture of our flank steak, making the outside mushy instead of tender. We decided to do away with the acidic element altogether and turned instead to oil, which carries flavor well. But using too much oil would make the steak greasy, so we used just enough to act as a binder for our flavorings. Quickly mincing a few ingredients by hand, especially potent garlic and herbs, and then giving everything a whir in the blender gave us a cohesive paste that flavored the steak in just 1 hour.

GET FLAVOR THROUGHOUT To ensure that our flavorful marinade penetrated the meat, we poked holes on both sides with a fork before applying salt and our paste. This gave the steak pronounced flavor all the way through.

HIGH HEAT WORKS BEST Since flank steak is a relatively thin cut of meat, it doesn't need long to cook. Grilling over high heat gave us a nice sear and crisp crust, and by the time it had seared on both sides, it was done to a perfect medium-rare.

🔪 AT THE MEAT COUNTER
PREFERRED CUT Flank Steak
Flank steak is also known as jiffy steak (see page 39 for more information).

ALTERNATE CUT Skirt Steak or Sirloin
Steak Tips
Skirt steak is also known as fajita steak or Philadelphia steak; sirloin steak tips are also known as flap meat (see pages 39 and 37 for more information). Note that cooking times may vary.

GRILLED MARINATED FLANK STEAK
SERVES 4 TO 6

Don't forget to prick the steak with a fork before applying the marinade.

- I   (2- to 2½-pound) flank steak, trimmed
- I   teaspoon salt
- I   recipe wet paste marinade (recipes follow)
    Pepper

1. Pat steak dry with paper towels and place in large baking dish. Using dinner fork, prick steak about 20 times on each side. Rub both sides of steak evenly with salt, then with paste. Cover with plastic wrap and refrigerate for at least 1 hour or up to 24 hours.

2A. FOR A CHARCOAL GRILL: Open bottom vent completely. Light large chimney starter filled with charcoal briquettes (6 quarts). When top coals are partially covered with ash, pour two-thirds evenly over grill, then pour remaining coals over half of grill. Set cooking grate in place, cover, and open lid vent completely. Heat grill until hot, about 5 minutes.

2B. FOR A GAS GRILL: Turn all burners to high, cover, and heat grill until hot, about 15 minutes. Leave all burners on high.

3. Clean and oil cooking grate. Using paper towels, wipe paste off steak and season with pepper. Place steak on grill (hotter side if using charcoal) and cook (covered if using gas) until well browned on first side, 4 to 6 minutes. Flip steak and cook (covered if using gas) until meat registers 120 to 125 degrees (for medium-rare) or 130 to 135 degrees (for medium), 3 to 6 minutes. If exterior of meat is browned but steak is not yet cooked through, move to cooler side of grill (if using charcoal) or turn down burners (if using gas) and continue to cook to desired doneness.

4. Transfer steak to carving board, tent loosely with aluminum foil, and let rest for 10 minutes. Slice steak ¼ inch thick against grain on bias and serve.

GARLIC-SHALLOT-ROSEMARY WET PASTE MARINADE

MAKES ABOUT ⅔ CUP

Fresh rosemary is a must in this marinade.

6 tablespoons olive oil
1 shallot, minced
6 garlic cloves, minced
2 tablespoons minced fresh rosemary

Process all ingredients in blender until smooth, about 30 seconds, scraping down sides of blender jar as needed.

GARLIC-CHILE WET PASTE MARINADE

MAKES ABOUT ⅔ CUP

This recipe only uses a small amount of chipotle, but the remainder can be stored in the refrigerator for up to 2 weeks or frozen for long-term storage (see page 77).

6 tablespoons vegetable oil
6 garlic cloves, minced
2 scallions, minced
1 tablespoon minced canned chipotle chile in adobo sauce
1 jalapeño chile, stemmed, seeded, and minced

Process all ingredients in blender until smooth, about 30 seconds, scraping down sides of blender jar as needed.

GARLIC-GINGER-SESAME WET PASTE MARINADE

MAKES ABOUT ⅔ CUP

Toasted sesame oil is crucial to the flavor of this marinade.

¼ cup toasted sesame oil
3 tablespoons grated fresh ginger
2 tablespoons vegetable oil
2 scallions, minced
3 garlic cloves, minced

Process all ingredients in blender until smooth, about 30 seconds, scraping down sides of blender jar as needed.

GETTING TO KNOW YOUR THERMOMETER

Do you know how your thermometer works? You should. Understanding how a thermometer works will help you take an accurate reading of your steak's temperature. Location is key. You might assume that the sensor on your thermometer is right at the tip, but on some models it is in fact an inch or two up.

To find out where the sensor is on your thermometer, bring a pot of water to a boil and slowly lower your thermometer into the pot until it registers 212 degrees (adjusting, of course, for high altitudes). Knowing the location of the sensor is only half the battle, however. Now you have to insert the thermometer into the steak so that the sensor is right in the middle.

We have found that the easiest way to do this for a steak (no matter where the sensor is located) is to use tongs to lift the steak off the grill (or out of the pan) and insert the thermometer through the side of the steak. Make sure the thermometer is not touching any bone, which will throw off the reading. And make sure to check each steak, if cooking more than one—some will cook faster than others depending on their thickness and their location on the grill (or in the pan).

California Barbecued Tri-Tip

✔ WHY THIS RECIPE WORKS

Tri-tip is a large, boomerang-shaped cut of beef from the bottom sirloin, and in California, it is the subject of a unique barbecue tradition. Unlike other styles of barbecue, in which the meat is often slow-cooked and slathered with sauce, California barbecued tri-tip recipes call for cooking the meat over high heat and seasoning it only with salt, pepper, garlic, and the sweet smoke of the grill. The recipes we tried consistently produced charred exteriors with very rare centers, and tasted overly smoky. We wanted the outside cooked less, the inside cooked more, and a better balance of flavor.

LOW HEAT HELPS Our go-to grilling technique in the test kitchen is to create two heat zones on the grill: one high, one low. We start the meat over high heat to achieve a sear, then move it to the lower heat to cook through. Since the traditional California barbecue high-heat-only technique wasn't producing the results we wanted, we went back to our old standby—and, as always, it worked perfectly.

DON'T OVERSMOKE When we tried adding a handful of wood chips at the beginning of cooking, the smoke flavor became overwhelming. To lessen the impact, we waited to add the wood chips until after we had moved the meat to the cooler side of the grill. This allowed the smoke to dissipate slightly before contacting the meat, perfuming it with subtle, smoky flavor.

USE TWO FORMS OF GARLIC Since California tri-tip relies on only a few flavors (smoke, salt, pepper, and garlic) it was important for those flavors to be noticeable. We decided to amp up the garlic flavor of the meat by marinating it first. We made a simple paste using fresh minced garlic, and pricked the meat with a fork to allow the paste

to penetrate the thick cut of meat. Then, just before grilling, we sprinkled the meat with garlic salt (and pepper), giving us a double layer of garlic flavor.

CALIFORNIA BARBECUED TRI-TIP
SERVES 4 TO 6

Tri-tip roast is also known as triangle roast (see page 38 for more information). If you'd like to use wood chunks instead of wood chips when using a charcoal grill, substitute two medium wood chunks, soaked in water for 1 hour, for the wood chip packet. Serve with Santa Maria Salsa (recipe follows). We prefer this roast cooked medium-rare.

- 6 garlic cloves, minced
- 2 tablespoons olive oil
- ¾ teaspoon salt
- 1 (2-pound) sirloin tri-tip roast, trimmed
- 1 teaspoon pepper
- ¾ teaspoon garlic salt
- 2 cups wood chips

1. Combine garlic, oil, and salt in bowl. Pat meat dry with paper towels, poke it about 20 times on each side with fork, and rub it evenly with garlic mixture. Wrap meat in plastic wrap and let sit at room temperature for at least 1 hour or refrigerate for up to 24 hours. (If refrigerated, let sit at room temperature for 1 hour before grilling.) Before cooking, unwrap meat, wipe off garlic paste using paper towels, and rub it evenly with pepper and garlic salt. Just before grilling, soak wood chips in water for 15 minutes, then drain. Using large piece of heavy-duty aluminum foil, wrap soaked chips in foil packet and cut several vent holes in top.

CALIFORNIA TRI-TIP—FROM THE GRINDER TO THE GRILL

One day in the late 1950s, Bob Shutz and Larry Viegas, butchers at a Safeway supermarket in Santa Maria, California, were busy grinding pounds of bottom sirloin butt into hamburger. On a whim—perhaps motivated by hunger—they seasoned a 2-pound piece with salt, pepper, and garlic salt and placed it on a rotisserie to cook. Forty-five minutes later, they shared it with coworkers, who raved about its tenderness and pronounced beefy flavor. Shutz dubbed the triangular-shaped roast "tri-tip" and began selling this relatively inexpensive cut to his customers. Word soon spread across California's Central Coast, where tri-tip remains a favorite among grillers.

CUTTING TOMATOES FOR SALSA

1. Cut each cored tomato in half through equator.

2. Cut each half into ½-inch-thick slices.

3. Stack 2 slices; cut them into ½-inch strips, then into ½-inch dice.

2A. FOR A CHARCOAL GRILL: Open bottom vent completely. Light large chimney starter filled with charcoal briquettes (6 quarts). When top coals are partially covered with ash, pour evenly over half of grill. Set cooking grate in place, cover, and open lid vent completely. Heat grill until hot, about 5 minutes.

2B. FOR A GAS GRILL: Turn all burners to high, cover, and heat grill until hot, about 15 minutes. Leave all burners on high.

3. Clean and oil cooking grate. Grill meat on hotter side of grill until well browned on both sides, about 10 minutes. Transfer meat to plate.

4. Remove cooking grate and place wood chip packet directly on coals or primary burner. If using gas, leave primary burner on high and turn off other burner(s).

5. Place meat on cooler side of grill. Cover (positioning lid vent over meat if using charcoal) and cook until meat registers 120 to 125 degrees (for medium-rare), about 20 minutes.

6. Transfer meat to carving board, tent loosely with aluminum foil, and let rest for 20 minutes. Slice meat thin against grain and serve.

SANTA MARIA SALSA
MAKES ABOUT 4 CUPS

The distinct texture of each ingredient is part of this salsa's identity and appeal, so we don't recommend using a food processor.

2	pounds tomatoes, cored and chopped
2	teaspoons salt
2	jalapeño chiles, stemmed, seeded, and chopped fine
1	small red onion, chopped fine
1	celery rib, chopped fine
¼	cup lime juice (2 limes)
¼	cup chopped fresh cilantro
1	garlic clove, minced
⅛	teaspoon dried oregano
⅛	teaspoon Worcestershire sauce

1. Place tomatoes in strainer set over bowl and sprinkle with salt; drain for 30 minutes. Discard liquid. Meanwhile, combine jalapeños, onion, celery, lime juice, cilantro, garlic, oregano, and Worcestershire in large bowl.

2. Add drained tomatoes to jalapeño mixture and toss to combine. Cover with plastic wrap and let stand at room temperature for 1 hour before serving. (Salsa can be refrigerated for up to 2 days.)

Grilled Steak Tips

✓ WHY THIS RECIPE WORKS

Steak tips are a restaurant-chain staple, but are often tough, dry, or even mushy. In addition, steak tips can come from multiple parts of the cow and are packaged in a variety of shapes and sizes. We wanted to clear up the confusion and come up with a recipe that would be worth making at home.

GO FOR THE GRILL Steak tips are generally cooked in one of two styles: sautéed and served with a sauce (often called pub-style) or marinated and grilled (call tailgate tips).

We found grilling an appealing way to highlight the beefy flavor of the tips and keep the hands-on work to a minimum.

FALL FOR FLAP After testing more than 50 pounds of tips, we determined that the only one worth grilling was what butchers referred to as "flap meat," also known as sirloin steak tips. It had good flavor, and although it was a bit chewy when we grilled it on its own, we knew that it had potential.

MARINATE WITH SOY SAUCE The soy sauce in the marinades acted like a brine, giving the meat a tender texture. Even when we cooked the steak to well-done, it stayed juicy and tender. The high glutamate content of soy sauce also helped boost the savory flavor of the meat and promoted browning. We also liked that it could act as a base for a variety of flavor profiles.

GRILLED STEAK TIPS
SERVES 4 TO 6

Sirloin steak tips, also known as flap meat, are sold as whole steaks, strips, and cubes (see page 37 for more information). We prefer to buy whole steaks for this dish. A two-level fire allows you to brown the steak over the hot side of the grill, then move it to the cooler side if it is not yet cooked through. If your steak is thin, however, you may not need to use the cooler side of the grill. Serve lime wedges with the Southwestern-marinated tips, orange wedges with the tips marinated in garlic, ginger, and soy sauce.

1   recipe marinade (recipes follow)
2   pounds sirloin steak tips, trimmed
    Lime wedges

1. Combine marinade and beef in 1-gallon zipper-lock bag and toss to coat; press out as much air as possible and seal bag. Refrigerate for 1 hour, flipping bag halfway through marinating.

2A. FOR A CHARCOAL GRILL: Open bottom vent completely. Light large chimney starter filled with charcoal briquettes (6 quarts). When top coals are partially covered with ash, pour two-thirds evenly over grill, then pour remaining coals over half of grill. Set cooking grate in place, cover, and open lid vent completely. Heat grill until hot, about 5 minutes.

2B. FOR A GAS GRILL: Turn all burners to high, cover, and heat grill until hot, about 15 minutes. Leave all burners on high.

3. Clean and oil cooking grate. Remove beef from bag and pat dry with paper towels.

Place steak tips on grill (hotter side if using charcoal) and cook (covered if using gas) until well browned on first side, about 4 minutes. Flip steak tips and continue to cook (covered if using gas) until meat registers 120 to 125 degrees (for medium-rare) or 130 to 135 degrees (for medium), 6 to 10 minutes longer. If exterior of meat is browned but steak is not yet cooked through, move to cooler side of grill (if using charcoal) or turn down burners to medium (if using gas) and continue to cook to desired doneness.

4. Transfer steak tips to carving board, tent loosely with aluminum foil, and let rest for 5 to 10 minutes. Slice steak tips very thin against grain on bias and serve with lime wedges.

SOUTHWESTERN MARINADE
MAKES ABOUT ¾ CUP

⅓   cup soy sauce
⅓   cup vegetable oil
3   garlic cloves, minced
1   tablespoon packed dark brown sugar
1   tablespoon tomato paste
1   tablespoon chili powder
2   teaspoons ground cumin
¼   teaspoon cayenne pepper

Combine all ingredients in bowl.

GARLIC, GINGER, AND SOY MARINADE
MAKES ABOUT ⅔ CUP

⅓   cup soy sauce
3   tablespoons vegetable oil
3   tablespoons toasted sesame oil
2   tablespoons packed dark brown sugar
1   tablespoon grated fresh ginger
2   teaspoons grated orange zest
1   scallion, sliced thin
3   garlic cloves, minced
½   teaspoon red pepper flakes

Combine all ingredients in bowl.

Classic Grilled Beef Fajitas

✔ WHY THIS RECIPE WORKS

Fajitas are everywhere these days, but the classic, simple Southwestern version has been lost in a sea of overdressed, topping-heavy preparations. We wanted to bring char-grilled beef, sweet peppers and onions, and perfect, chewy tortillas back to the table.

CHOOSE FLANK We landed on flank steak for its beefy flavor. It also made an excellent candidate for grilling, since it is usually a thin cut that cooks quickly and picks up a nice sear over a hot fire.

GO BACK TO BASICS Many recipes call for marinated or spice-rubbed steak, but we found that marinades often turned the steak mushy if it sat for too long, while spice rubs were overpowering. We cut back on the flavorings in favor of simple salt, pepper, and a squeeze of lime juice just before the steak hit the grill.

GRILL EVERYTHING For a traditional accompaniment for our fajitas, we grilled bell peppers and a red onion. To avoid losing thin strips of veggies through the grill grate, we sliced the onions into thick rings and cut the peppers into slabs. After we took them off the grill, it was easy to separate the onions into individual rings and slice the peppers into thin strips. For a finishing touch, we gave the tortillas a brief stint on the grill to warm them.

🔪 AT THE MEAT COUNTER

PREFERRED CUT Flank Steak

Flank steak is also known as jiffy steak (see page 39 for more information).

ALTERNATE CUT Skirt Steak or Sirloin Steak Tips

Skirt steak is also known as fajita steak or Philadelphia steak; sirloin steak tips are also known as flap meat (see pages 39 and 37 for more information). Note that cooking times may vary.

CLASSIC GRILLED BEEF FAJITAS

SERVES 4 TO 6

You can use red, yellow, orange, or green bell peppers in this recipe. When you head outside to grill, bring a clean kitchen towel in which to wrap the tortillas and keep them warm. Guacamole and tomato salsa make good accompaniments.

1	(2- to 2½-pound) flank steak, trimmed
¼	cup lime juice (2 limes)
	Salt and pepper
1	large red onion, peeled and cut into ½-inch-thick rounds (do not separate rings)
2	large red bell peppers, quartered, stemmed, and seeded
8–12	(6-inch) flour tortillas

1A. FOR A CHARCOAL GRILL: Open bottom vent completely. Light large chimney starter mounded with charcoal briquettes (7 quarts). When top coals are partially covered with ash, pour evenly over half of grill. Set cooking grate in place, cover, and open lid vent completely. Heat grill until hot, about 5 minutes.

1B. FOR A GAS GRILL: Turn all burners to high, cover, and heat grill until hot, about 15 minutes. Leave all burners on high.

2. Clean and oil cooking grate. Pat steak dry with paper towels and sprinkle with lime juice, salt, and pepper. Place steak on grill (hotter side if using charcoal) and cook (covered if using gas) until well browned on first side, 4 to 7 minutes. Flip steak and continue to cook until meat registers 120 to 125 degrees (for medium-rare) or 130 to 135 degrees (for medium), 3 to 8 minutes. Transfer steak to carving board, tent loosely with aluminum foil, and let rest for 10 minutes.

3. While steak rests, place onion rounds and bell peppers (skin side down) on hotter side of grill (if using charcoal) or turn all burners to medium (if using gas). Cook until tender and charred on both sides, 8 to 12 minutes, flipping every 3 minutes. Transfer onions and bell peppers to carving board with beef.

4. Place tortillas in single layer on hotter side of grill (if using charcoal) or turn all burners to low (if using gas). Cook until warm and lightly browned, about 20 seconds per side (do not grill too long or tortillas will become brittle). As tortillas are done, wrap in dish towel or large sheet of aluminum foil.

5. Separate onions into rings and slice bell peppers into ¼-inch strips. Slice steak ¼ inch thick against grain. Transfer beef and vegetables to serving platter and serve with warmed tortillas.

Grilled Beef Satay

✔ WHY THIS RECIPE WORKS

Beef satay, a well-known Thai street food, should consist of tender strips of assertively flavored meat grilled to lightly burnished perfection. But at some point in its journey from the streets of Bangkok to American restaurants, satay lost something—and we wanted it back.

MORE THAN MEAT ON A STICK To determine the best type of meat for this recipe, we tested several inexpensive cuts and found flank steak to be the best choice. Thanks to its evenly distributed fat, it had good flavor. As an added benefit, its symmetrical shape made for easy slicing.

COOK THAI STYLE Flipping individual skewers over a very hot flame was a difficult task. Instead, we created a setup that mimicked those of the Thai street vendors. The vendors use trough-shaped grills, which suspend the meat inches above the hot coals. For our version, we filled a disposable aluminum roasting pan with charcoal and lined up the skewers over the pan.

MARINATE AND BASTE For maximum flavor, we kept the marinade simple, using only fish sauce (for a savory flavor boost), oil, and sugar (to aid with browning). During grilling, we basted the meat heavily with a sauce made of coconut milk redolent with ginger, lemon grass, and spices. This provided a boost of flavor but didn't make the meat mushy.

GET SAUCY The peanut sauce is a key element of satay. Using chunky peanut butter as a base, we spiced things up with Thai red curry paste and garlic. Coconut milk contributed body, and chopped roasted peanuts offered additional texture. A final hit of lime juice, coupled with soy and fish sauce, lent brightness.

🔪 AT THE MEAT COUNTER
PREFERRED CUT Flank Steak

Flank steak is also known as jiffy steak (see page 39 for more information).

ALTERNATE CUT Skirt Steak

Skirt steak is also known as fajita steak or Philadelphia steak (see page 39 for more information). Note that cooking time may vary.

GRILLED BEEF SATAY
SERVES 6

You will need ten to twelve 12-inch metal skewers for this recipe, or you can substitute bamboo skewers, soaked in water for 30 minutes. The disposable aluminum roasting pan used for charcoal grilling should be at least 2¾ inches deep; you will not need the pan for a gas grill. Kitchen shears work well for punching the holes in the pan. Unless you have a very high-powered gas grill, these skewers will not be as well seared as they would be with charcoal. Serve with Peanut Sauce (recipe follows). To make it a meal, serve this dish with white rice.

GRILL SETUP FOR SATAY: EAST MEETS WEST

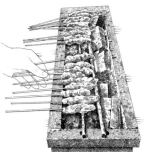

Thai Way
The trough-shaped grills used by Thai street-food vendors concentrate the firepower but require flipping the skewered meat constantly so it doesn't burn.

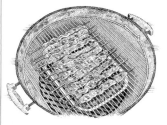

Our Way
We corralled the coals in an aluminum pan in the center of the grill to bring them closer to the meat—but not so close that we needed to flip it more than once.

HOW TO PREP LEMON GRASS

The tender heart of the lemon grass stalk is used to flavor many Southeast Asian dishes, including our Grilled Beef Satay. When buying lemon grass, look for green (not brown) stalks that are firm and fragrant. To mince lemon grass follow the steps below.

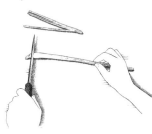

1. Trim dry leafy top (this part is usually green) and tough bottom of each stalk.

2. Peel and discard dry outer layer until moist, tender inner stalk is exposed.

3. Smash peeled stalk with bottom of heavy saucepan to release maximum flavor from fibrous stalk.

4. Cut smashed stalk into long, thin strips; cut crosswise to mince.

BASTING SAUCE

- ¾ cup canned regular or light coconut milk
- 3 tablespoons packed dark brown sugar
- 3 tablespoons fish sauce
- 2 tablespoons vegetable oil
- 3 shallots, minced
- 2 lemon grass stalks, trimmed to bottom 6 inches and minced
- 2 tablespoons grated fresh ginger
- 1½ teaspoons ground coriander
- ¾ teaspoon red pepper flakes
- ½ teaspoon ground cumin
- ½ teaspoon salt

BEEF

- 2 tablespoons vegetable oil
- 2 tablespoons packed dark brown sugar
- 1 tablespoon fish sauce
- 1 (1½- to 1¾-pound) flank steak, trimmed, halved lengthwise, and sliced on slight bias against grain into ¼-inch-thick slices
- 1 disposable aluminum roasting pan

1. FOR THE BASTING SAUCE: Whisk all ingredients together in bowl. Reserve one-third of sauce in separate bowl.

2. FOR THE BEEF: Whisk oil, sugar, and fish sauce together in medium bowl. Toss beef with marinade and let stand at room temperature for 30 minutes. Weave beef onto 12-inch metal skewers, 2 to 4 pieces per skewer, leaving 1½ inches at top and bottom of skewer exposed. You should have 10 to 12 skewers.

3A. FOR A CHARCOAL GRILL: Punch twelve ½-inch holes in bottom of disposable roasting pan. Open bottom vent completely and place roasting pan in center of grill. Light large chimney starter mounded with charcoal briquettes (7 quarts). When top coals are partially covered with ash, pour into roasting pan. Set cooking grate over coals with bars parallel to long side of roasting pan, cover, and open lid vent completely. Heat grill until hot, about 5 minutes.

3B. FOR A GAS GRILL: Turn all burners to high, cover, and heat grill until hot, about 15 minutes. Leave all burners on high.

4. Clean and oil cooking grate. Place beef skewers on grill (directly over coals if using charcoal) perpendicular to grate bars. Brush meat with reserved basting sauce and cook (covered if using gas) until browned, about 3 minutes. Flip skewers, brush with half of remaining basting sauce, and cook until browned on second side, about 3 minutes. Brush meat with remaining basting sauce and cook 1 minute longer. Transfer to large platter and serve.

PEANUT SAUCE
MAKES ABOUT 1½ CUPS

- 1 tablespoon vegetable oil
- 1 tablespoon Thai red curry paste
- 1 tablespoon packed dark brown sugar
- 2 garlic cloves, minced
- 1 cup canned regular or light coconut milk
- ⅓ cup chunky peanut butter
- ¼ cup unsalted dry-roasted peanuts, chopped
- 1 tablespoon lime juice
- 1 tablespoon fish sauce
- 1 teaspoon soy sauce

Heat oil in small saucepan over medium heat until shimmering. Add curry paste, sugar, and garlic; cook, stirring constantly, until fragrant, about 1 minute. Add coconut milk and bring to simmer. Whisk in peanut butter until smooth. Remove from heat and stir in peanuts, lime juice, fish sauce, and soy sauce. Let cool to room temperature.

The flavorful oil that is found in the outer layer, or zest, of lemon skin protects the fruit from drying out. Once you remove that layer, you remove its primary defense against dehydration.

We stripped the zest (but not the white pith) from four lemons and stored them in the fridge in three different ways: wrapped in plastic, enclosed in a zipper-lock bag, and rubbed with a thin layer of vegetable oil. As a control, we refrigerated a fourth zested lemon that we left alone. To measure moisture loss, we weighed the lemons before and after three weeks of refrigeration. The plastic-wrapped and bagged lemons lost only 2.5 percent and 6 percent of their weight, respectively, yielding plenty of juice. By contrast, the oil-coated lemon suffered a 40 percent loss in weight and was almost indistinguishable from the shriveled control sample, in both its firmness and the miserly portion of bitter juice it released. (Without skin or other protection, the juice in a lemon oxidizes, changing its flavor profile.)

The upshot? If you're not going to be juicing a zested lemon for a while, wrap it in plastic before refrigerating it.

Marinated Grilled Beef Kebabs

✓ WHY THIS RECIPE WORKS

Although stringing meat and colorful vegetables together onto skewers looks appealing, the dish often results in burnt vegetables or lackluster chunks of meat. We wanted to have it all—juicy, flavorful meat and crisp-tender vegetables.

POWER UP THE MARINADE We created a turbocharged marinade with three key ingredients: salt, tomato paste, and beef broth. Tomato paste is full of glutamates, which enhanced the meaty flavor. And when we used beef broth instead of only water, tasters raved about the depth of flavor. This is because many commercial broths contain yeast extract, which boasts powerful flavor enhancers.

PICK THE RIGHT CUT We tried five different cuts of meat for this recipe, from pricey tenderloin to bottom round. After cutting them all into big, 2-inch pieces and cooking them on the grill, we discovered that the tenderloin was a waste of money, as tasters found it bland, and the bottom round was too chewy. The more marbled cuts—skirt steak, blade steak, and steak tips—all boasted respectable flavor, but the looser-grained steak tips outdid the others in both beefiness and tender texture.

PUREE THE SAUCE We mixed our marinade up in a blender so that the flavors are optimally combined. No blender? Don't worry. A food processor will work too.

SEPARATE THE MEAT AND VEG Often, all the ingredients for kebabs are threaded onto a single skewer. This method doesn't work well, since the meat and vegetables cook at different rates. Putting the beef and vegetables on separate skewers allowed us to cook them over different levels of heat and for different amounts of time, ensuring that all of the elements of this dish were perfectly cooked.

🔪 AT THE MEAT COUNTER
PREFERRED CUT Sirloin Steak Tips

Sirloin steak tips, also known as flap meat, are sold as whole steaks, cubes, and strips. (See page 37 for more information.) To ensure uniform pieces that cook evenly, we prefer to purchase whole steaks and cut them ourselves.

ALTERNATE CUT Blade Steak

Blade steak is also called top blade steak or flat-iron steak (see page 33 for more information). You can substitute 1½ pounds of blade steak for the steak tips; if using, cut each steak in half lengthwise and remove the gristle that runs down the center before cooking.

GRILLED BEEF KEBABS WITH LEMON AND ROSEMARY MARINADE
SERVES 4 TO 6

You will need four 12-inch metal skewers for this recipe. If you have long, thin pieces of meat, roll or fold them into approximate 2-inch cubes before skewering.

MARINADE

1	onion, chopped
⅓	cup beef broth
⅓	cup vegetable oil
3	tablespoons tomato paste
6	garlic cloves, chopped
2	tablespoons chopped fresh rosemary
2	teaspoons grated lemon zest
2	teaspoons salt
1½	teaspoons sugar
¾	teaspoon pepper

BEEF AND VEGETABLES

2   pounds sirloin steak tips, trimmed and
    cut into 2-inch chunks

1   large zucchini or summer squash,
    halved lengthwise and sliced 1 inch thick

1   large red or green bell pepper,
    stemmed, seeded, and cut into
    1½-inch pieces

1   large red or sweet onion, halved
    through the root end, each half cut
    into 4 wedges, and each wedge cut
    crosswise into thirds

1. FOR THE MARINADE: Process all ingredients in blender until smooth, about 45 seconds. Transfer ¾ cup marinade to large bowl and set aside.

2. FOR THE BEEF AND VEGETABLES: Place remaining marinade and beef in 1-gallon zipper-lock bag and toss to coat; press out as much air as possible and seal bag. Refrigerate for at least 1 or up to 2 hours, flipping bag every 30 minutes.

3. Meanwhile, add zucchini, bell pepper, and onion to bowl with reserved marinade and toss to coat. Cover and let sit at room temperature for at least 30 minutes.

4. Remove beef from bag and pat dry with paper towels. Thread beef tightly onto two 12-inch metal skewers. Alternating pattern of zucchini, bell pepper, and onion, thread vegetables onto two 12-inch metal skewers.

5A. FOR A CHARCOAL GRILL: Open bottom vent completely. Light large chimney starter mounded with charcoal briquettes (7 quarts). When top coals are partially covered with ash, pour evenly over center of grill, leaving 2-inch gap between grill wall and charcoal. Set cooking grate in place, cover, and open lid vent completely. Heat grill until hot, about 5 minutes.

5B. FOR A GAS GRILL: Turn all burners to high, cover, and heat grill until hot, about 15 minutes. Leave primary burner on high and turn other burner(s) to medium-low.

6. Clean and oil cooking grate. Place beef skewers on grill (directly over coals if using charcoal or over hotter part of grill if using gas). Place vegetable skewers on grill (near edge of coals but still over coals if using charcoal or over cooler part of grill if using gas). Cook (covered if using gas), turning skewers every 3 to 4 minutes, until beef is well browned and registers 120 to 125 degrees (for medium-rare) or 130 to 135 degrees (for medium), 12 to 16 minutes. Transfer beef skewers to platter and tent loosely with aluminum foil. Continue to cook vegetable skewers until tender and lightly charred, about 5 minutes; serve with beef skewers.

GRILLED BEEF KEBABS WITH NORTH AFRICAN MARINADE

Substitute 20 cilantro sprigs, 2 teaspoons paprika, 1½ teaspoons ground cumin, and ½ teaspoon cayenne pepper for rosemary and lemon zest.

GRILLED BEEF KEBABS WITH RED CURRY MARINADE

Substitute ½ cup fresh basil leaves, 3 tablespoons Thai red curry paste, 2 teaspoons lime zest, and 2 teaspoons grated fresh ginger for rosemary and lemon zest.

MARINADE MAGIC

Contrary to popular opinion, almost none of the flavors in a marinade penetrate to the center of the meat. But studies published in the *Journal of Food Science* indicate that salts—ordinary table salt as well as sodium glutamates, the naturally occurring flavor enhancers found in many foods—actually travel far into meat and beef up taste as they go. With this in mind, we created a turbocharged marinade with three key ingredients for our kebabs.

Salt
Not only does it penetrate meat to thoroughly season it, salt also swells and dissolves some of the proteins, allowing them to retain juices.

Tomato Paste
This condiment is a potent source of naturally occurring glutamates.

Beef Broth
Many commercial beef broths contain yeast extract, a rich source of two flavor-enhancing molecules: glutamates and nucleotides. The latter amplify flavor 20-fold, so that even ⅓ cup of broth in the marinade has a big impact.

This salad's Thai name, *nam tok* (literally "water falling"), refers to the beads of moisture that form on the surface of the steak as it cooks—an age-old Thai cookery clue that the meat is ready to be flipped. While this method sounded imprecise, during testing we found it to be a surprisingly accurate gauge of when the flank steak is halfway done. Here's why: As this steak's interior gets hotter, its tightly packed fibers contract and release some of their interior moisture, which the fire's heat then pushes to the meat's surface. When turned at this point and cooked for an equal amount of time on the second side, the steak emerged deeply charred on the outside and medium-rare within. (Note: We do not recommend this technique across the board for steaks; since the thickness and density of the meat fibers vary from cut to cut, the time it takes for heat to penetrate and for beads of moisture to be pushed to the meat's surface differs.)

Thai Grilled Beef Salad

✔ WHY THIS RECIPE WORKS

In the best versions of Thai grilled beef salad, known as nam tok, *the cuisine's five signature flavor elements—hot, sour, salty, sweet, and bitter—come into balance, making for a light but satisfying dish that's traditionally served with steamed jasmine rice. We set out to re-create the version we found at the best Thai restaurants.*

HIGH-STEAKS DECISIONS The recipes we found were all over the map in terms of the beef they called for and the method of preparing it. We tested a wide variety of cuts at a range of price points, from lean tenderloin to heavily marbled New York strip steaks. We landed on flank steak as our winner for its uniform shape, moderate price, and decent tenderness. We determined that marinating the steak was unnecessary, since the dressing provided plenty of flavor and a marinade only thwarted browning.

OLD GRILL, NEW TRICKS We used the test kitchen's standard two-level fire for grilling the meat: We started the meat over high heat to sear the crust and then moved it to the cooler side of the grill to finish cooking. The recipes we tested were generally vague about grill setup, but some did offer a useful new trick: when beads of moisture appear on the surface of the meat, it's ready to flip. This technique worked perfectly in concert with our method, producing medium-rare steak with a nicely charred crust.

BALANCING ACT The dressing for this dish should have a good balance between hot, sour, salty, and sweet to provide a counterpoint to the subtle bitter char of the meat. Fish sauce, lime juice, and sugar provided three of these elements—but the fourth, spicy element needed some extra attention. A fresh Thai chile added a fruity, fiery hit to each bite, but on its own it lacked depth. To remedy this, we toasted a bit of cayenne pepper and sweet paprika for a deeper, more complex spicy flavor. The final element of the dressing—toasted rice powder—was called for in most of the recipes we found, and was simple to make with a spice grinder. We found it added extra body to the dressing, and could work as a slightly crunchy element when sprinkled on at the table.

🔪 AT THE MEAT COUNTER
PREFERRED CUT Flank Steak

Flank steak is also known as jiffy steak (see page 39 for more information).

ALTERNATE CUT Skirt Steak

Skirt steak is also known as fajita steak or Philadelphia steak (see page 39 for more information). Note that cooking time may vary.

THAI GRILLED BEEF SALAD
SERVES 4 TO 6

Serve with rice, if desired. If fresh Thai chiles are unavailable, substitute ½ serrano chile. Don't skip the toasted rice; it's integral to the texture and flavor of the dish. Any variety of white rice can be used. Toasted rice powder (kao kua) can also be found in many Asian markets; substitute 1 tablespoon rice powder for the white rice.

1	teaspoon paprika
1	teaspoon cayenne pepper
1	tablespoon white rice
3	tablespoons lime juice (2 limes)
2	tablespoons fish sauce
2	tablespoons water
½	teaspoon sugar
1	(1½-pound) flank steak, trimmed
	Salt and coarsely ground white pepper
1	seedless English cucumber, sliced ¼ inch thick on bias
4	shallots, sliced thin
1½	cups fresh mint leaves, torn
1½	cups fresh cilantro leaves
1	Thai chile, stemmed, seeded, and sliced thin into rounds

1. Heat paprika and cayenne in 8-inch skillet over medium heat; cook, shaking pan, until fragrant, about 1 minute. Transfer to small bowl. Return skillet to medium-high heat, add rice and toast, stirring constantly, until deep golden brown, about 5 minutes. Transfer to small bowl and let cool for 5 minutes. Grind rice with spice grinder, mini food processor, or mortar and pestle until it resembles fine meal, 10 to 30 seconds (you should have about 1 tablespoon rice powder).

2. Whisk lime juice, fish sauce, water, sugar, and ¼ teaspoon toasted paprika mixture in large bowl and set aside.

3A. FOR A CHARCOAL GRILL: Open bottom vent completely. Light large chimney starter filled with charcoal briquettes (6 quarts). When top coals are partially covered with ash, pour in even layer over half of grill. Set cooking grate in place, cover, and open lid vent completely. Heat grill until hot, about 5 minutes.

3B. FOR A GAS GRILL: Turn all burners to high, cover, and heat grill until hot, about 15 minutes. Leave primary burner on high and turn off other burner(s).

4. Clean and oil cooking grate. Season steak with salt and white pepper. Place steak on grate over hotter part of grill and cook until beginning to char and beads of moisture appear on outer edges of meat, 5 to 6 minutes. Flip steak, continue to cook on second side until meat registers 125 degrees, about 5 minutes longer. Transfer to carving board, tent loosely with aluminum foil, and let rest for 10 minutes (or allow to cool to room temperature, about 1 hour).

5. Line large platter with cucumber slices. Slice steak ¼ inch thick against grain on bias. Transfer sliced steak to bowl with fish sauce mixture. Add shallots, mint, cilantro, chile, and half of rice powder, and toss to combine. Arrange steak over cucumber-lined platter. Serve, passing remaining rice powder and remaining toasted paprika mixture separately.

Best Prime Rib

✔ **WHY THIS RECIPE WORKS**
Prime rib is a hefty, expensive, but extraordinarily flavorful cut. If we were going to bother shelling out the extra money for this premium roast, we wanted to make sure it was the best it could be.

BROWN FIRST Low-temperature roasting will ensure a juicy roast but it does little for the exterior. That's why we started our recipe by browning the roast (a first-cut rib roast) on the stovetop. If you have a heavy-duty roasting pan, you can brown the roast right in the roasting pan. This step also renders fat.

ELEVATE THE ROAST To ensure even heating, we moved the browned roast to a rack set inside a baking sheet. This step also ensured that the roast was elevated above any additional fat that was rendered during the long cooking time.

LET IT REST Don't be impatient and slice into the roast too soon. The meat needs time for the muscle fibers to relax. If you cut into the roast too soon, the muscle fibers won't be able to hold on to those juices, which will flood onto the carving board and result in a drier roast.

BEST PRIME RIB
SERVES 6 TO 8

First-cut beef rib roast is also known as prime rib, loin end, or small end (see page 35 for more information). Look for a roast with an untrimmed fat cap (ideally ½ inch thick). We prefer the flavor and texture of prime-grade beef, but choice grade will work as well. To remove the bones from the roast, use a sharp knife and run it down the length of the bones,

CHOOSING THE RIGHT ROAST

While testing our Best Prime Rib recipe, we discovered that choosing the right roast was almost as important as deciding how to cook it. Butchers tend to cut a whole rib roast (which contains seven ribs) into two rib roasts, known most commonly as first-cut and second-cut roasts. Our recipe calls for a three-bone first-cut roast, which sits closer to the loin end of the cow and consists of ribs 10 through 12. First-cut roasts feature more of the flavorful, tender rib-eye muscle than do second-cut roasts (ribs 6 through 8 or 9), which are comprised of a mix of smaller muscles and more pockets of fat.

We also found prime-grade prime rib, the darling of steakhouses, to be consistently more tender and flavorful than choice-grade prime rib because of its higher level of intramuscular fat (or "marbling"). It's true that these upgrades add to the sticker price (prime costs roughly 25 percent more than choice), but we think they're well worth the extra money.

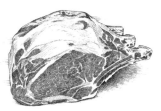

Prime-grade first-cut roast is our top choice for Best Prime Rib.

After removing twine and bones, carve meat against grain into ¾-inch-thick slices.

following the contours as closely as possible until the meat is separated (see the illustrations on page 98). Monitoring the roast with a meat-probe thermometer is best. If you use an instant-read thermometer, open the oven door as little as possible and remove the roast from the oven while taking its temperature. If the roast has not reached the correct temperature in the time range specified in step 3, heat the oven to 200 degrees, wait for 5 minutes, then shut it off, and continue to cook the roast until it reaches the desired temperature. Serve with Mustard Cream Sauce (recipe follows), if desired.

1   **(7-pound) first-cut beef standing rib roast (3 bones), meat removed from bones, bones reserved**
    Kosher salt and pepper
2   **teaspoons vegetable oil**
    Coarse salt

1. Using sharp knife, cut slits in surface layer of fat, spaced 1 inch apart, in crosshatch pattern, being careful to not cut into meat. Rub 2 tablespoons kosher salt over entire roast and into slits. Place meat back on bones (to save space in refrigerator), transfer to large plate, and refrigerate, uncovered, at least 24 hours and up to 96 hours.

2. Adjust oven rack to middle position and heat oven to 200 degrees. Heat oil in 12-inch skillet over high heat until just smoking. Sear sides and top of roast (reserving bone) until browned, 6 to 8 minutes total (do not sear side where roast was cut from bone). Place meat back on ribs, so bones fit where they were cut, and let cool for 10 minutes; tie meat to bones with 2 lengths of kitchen twine between ribs. Transfer roast, fat side up, to wire rack set in rimmed baking sheet and season with pepper. Roast until meat registers 110 degrees, 3 to 4 hours.

3. Turn off oven; leave roast in oven, opening door as little as possible, until meat registers about 120 degrees (for rare) or about 125 degrees (for medium-rare), 30 minutes to 1¼ hours longer.

4. Remove roast from oven (leave roast on baking sheet), tent loosely with aluminum foil, and let rest for at least 30 minutes or up to 1¼ hours.

5. Adjust oven rack about 8 inches from broiler element and heat broiler. Remove foil from roast, form into 3-inch ball, and place under ribs to elevate fat cap. Broil until top of roast is well browned and crisp, 2 to 8 minutes.

6. Transfer roast to carving board. Slice meat into ¾-inch-thick slices. Season with coarse salt to taste, and serve.

MUSTARD CREAM SAUCE
MAKES ABOUT 1 CUP

½   **cup sour cream**
½   **cup heavy cream**
2   **large egg yolks**
5   **teaspoons Dijon mustard**
1   **tablespoon white wine vinegar**
    Salt and pepper
⅛   **teaspoon sugar**
1   **tablespoon minced fresh chives**

Whisk sour cream, heavy cream, yolks, mustard, vinegar, ¼ teaspoon salt, and sugar together in small saucepan. Cook over medium heat, whisking constantly, until sauce thickens and coats back of spoon, 4 to 5 minutes. Immediately transfer to serving bowl, stir in chives, and season with salt and pepper to taste. Serve warm or at room temperature.

Grill-Roasted Prime Rib

✔ WHY THIS RECIPE WORKS

Usually, when we think of grilling, we think of steaks and ribs. In this recipe, we wanted to harness the smoky environment of the grill for a different purpose: to cook prime rib. But to ensure that this premium cut got the treatment it deserved, we needed to perfect the method.

GRILL IT RIGHT If you're going to grill a prime rib, the last thing you want is an overcooked gray ring surrounding the rosy interior. We decided to forgo searing the flat cut sides, which meant the roast spent less time over high heat. The reduced amount of searing time was enough to create a browned crust, but not enough to start overcooking the meat. The other problem we encountered was persistent flare-ups from the fat that dripped down through the grate. To minimize this, we had the butcher trim the fat to a mere ⅛-inch thickness.

DON'T THROW OUT THE BONES Although we liked the idea of a boneless roast for easy carving, we knew that the bones would protect the underside of the meat from overbrowning. We bought our prime rib bone-in, removed the bones ourselves and then secured the detached bones onto the roast just for the grill.

CREATE LAYERS OF FLAVOR AND TEXTURE Using a grill to roast a prime rib gave us the advantage of being able to create both flavor and texture contrast between the exterior and interior. A garlic-rosemary paste, brushed on after browning, gave the crunchy crust extra flavor. Wood chips, though a nontraditional addition, gave the outer ½ inch of the roast a subtly smoky flavor, further heightening the contrast between layers.

GRILL-ROASTED PRIME RIB
SERVES 6 TO 8

First-cut beef rib roast is also known as prime rib, loin end, or small end (see page 35 for more information). If your butcher doesn't trim excess fat from the roast and remove the bones (which you need for this recipe), see page 98 for information on removing the bones. If all you have is a boneless roast, see our tip at right for making a false bone. If you'd like to use wood chunks instead of wood chips when using a charcoal grill, substitute 2 medium wood chunks, soaked in water for 1 hour, for the wood chip packet.

- 1 (7-pound) first-cut beef standing rib roast (3 or 4 bones), meat removed from bones, bones reserved, exterior fat trimmed to ⅛ inch
- 1 tablespoon vegetable oil
  Kosher salt and pepper
- 2 cups wood chips
- 1 (16 by 12-inch) disposable aluminum roasting pan (if using charcoal)

1. Pat roast dry with paper towels, rub with oil, and season with pepper. Spread ¼ cup salt on rimmed baking sheet and press roast into salt to coat evenly on all sides. Place meat back on ribs so bones fit exactly where they were cut; tie meat to bones with 2 lengths of kitchen twine. Refrigerate roast, uncovered, for 1 hour, then let sit at room temperature for 2 hours.

2. Just before grilling, soak wood chips in water for 15 minutes, then drain. Using large piece of heavy-duty aluminum foil, wrap soaked chips in foil packet and cut several vent holes in top.

3A. FOR A CHARCOAL GRILL: Open bottom vent halfway and place disposable pan on 1 side of grill. Light large chimney starter two-thirds filled with charcoal briquettes (4 quarts). When top coals are partially covered with ash, pour evenly over

NO BONE? NO PROBLEM.

If all you can find is boneless prime rib, here's how to mimic the protective bones with aluminum foil.

1. Fold a 12- to 14-foot sheet of aluminum foil in half lengthwise and then in half lengthwise again; gently roll and scrunch it into a narrow tube. Coil the foil tube into a tight disk about 6 inches across. Flatten to form a rectangle.

2. Tie the foil "bone" to the roast (where the real bones were removed) and proceed with the recipe.

If your butcher doesn't
remove the bones from the
prime rib for you, here's how
you can do it yourself.

1. Holding meaty lobe in
one hand and sharp boning
or chef's knife in your other
hand, run knife down length
of first bone, following contours as closely as possible, to
separate it from meat.

2. Flip roast so uncut portion
faces you. Holding bones
back with your hand, cut
meat from remaining ribs.
Once meat is removed, proceed with seasoning and tying
as directed in recipe.

**TAMING THE GRILL'S
HEAT**

After searing roast's
fat-covered perimeter
directly over coals, transfer
it to cooler side, with tips of
bones facing away from fire.

other half of grill (opposite disposable pan).
Set cooking grate in place, cover, and open
lid vent halfway. Heat grill until hot, about
5 minutes.

3B. FOR A GAS GRILL: Turn all burners
to high, cover, and heat grill until hot, about
15 minutes. Turn primary burner to medium
and turn off other burner(s). (Adjust primary
burner as needed to maintain grill temperature
of about 325 degrees.)

4. Clean and oil cooking grate. Place roast
on hotter side of grill and cook (covered if
using gas) until well browned on all sides,
10 to 15 minutes, turning as needed. (If flare-
ups occur, move roast to cooler side of grill
until flames die down.)

5. Transfer roast to second rimmed baking
sheet. If using charcoal, remove cooking grate
and place wood chip packet on pile of coals;
set cooking grate in place. If using gas, place

wood chip packet directly on primary burner.
Place roast on cooler side of grill, bone side
down, with tips of bones pointed away from
fire. Cover (position lid vent over meat if using
charcoal) and cook until meat registers 115 to
120 degrees (for rare) or 120 to 125 degrees
(for medium-rare), 2 to 2½ hours.

6. Transfer roast to carving board, tent
loosely with aluminum foil, and let rest for
20 minutes. Remove twine and bones, slice
meat into ½-inch-thick slices, and serve.

GRILL-ROASTED PRIME RIB WITH GARLIC-ROSEMARY CRUST

Combine ½ cup extra-virgin olive oil,
12 minced garlic cloves (¼ cup), and ¼ cup
minced fresh rosemary in bowl. Brush paste
onto roast after browning.

Roast Beef Tenderloin

✓ WHY THIS RECIPE WORKS

*Many recipes sear, then roast, beef tenderloin. But
it takes a long time to sear a tenderloin straight from
the refrigerator because a lot of surface moisture
has to evaporate before any browning can occur.
During this time, too much heat is transferred to the
roast and you end up with a band of overcooked
gray meat below the surface. We wanted to remedy
this problem and make the recipe foolproof.*

BUY A CENTER-CUT ROAST A whole
tenderloin is hard to handle. It's usually covered with a lot of fat and sinew and the meat
varies widely in girth. For indoor cooking, we
much preferred to buy a center-cut tenderloin, also called a Châteaubriand, because it's
already trimmed and the thickness is the same
from end to end. This 2-pound roast fits in a
skillet and doesn't break the bank either.

TIE THE ROAST Tying the roast ensures
it maintains its shape and cooks evenly.

USE SALT AND BUTTER To add flavor
to this relatively bland cut, we applied salt an
hour before cooking. The salt pulled juices
out of the meat, then reversed the flow, drawing flavor deep into the meat. For richness, we
slathered the roast with softened butter before
cooking, then covered it with a compound
butter as it rested.

ROAST BEEF TENDERLOIN
SERVES 4 TO 6

---

*Center-cut beef tenderloin roast is also known as
Châteaubriand (see page 36 for more information).
Ask your butcher to prepare a trimmed center-cut
Châteaubriand, as this cut is not usually available
without special ordering. If you are cooking for a
crowd, this recipe can be doubled to make two
roasts. Sear the roasts one after the other, wiping
out the pan and adding new oil after searing the first*

roast. Both pieces of meat can be roasted on the same rack.

- 1 (2-pound) center-cut beef tenderloin roast, trimmed
- 2 teaspoons kosher salt
- 1 teaspoon coarsely ground pepper
- 2 tablespoons unsalted butter, softened
- 1 tablespoon vegetable oil
- 1 recipe Shallot and Parsley Butter (recipe follows)

1. Using 12-inch lengths of kitchen twine, tie roast crosswise at 1½-inch intervals. Sprinkle roast evenly with salt, cover loosely with plastic wrap, and let stand at room temperature for 1 hour. Meanwhile, adjust oven rack to middle position and heat oven to 300 degrees.

2. Pat roast dry with paper towels. Sprinkle roast evenly with pepper and spread unsalted butter evenly over surface. Transfer roast to wire rack set in rimmed baking sheet. Roast until meat registers 125 degrees (for medium-rare), 40 to 55 minutes, or 135 degrees (for medium), 55 minutes to 1 hour, 10 minutes, flipping roast halfway through cooking.

3. Heat oil in 12-inch skillet over medium-high heat until just smoking. Place roast in skillet and sear until well browned on all sides, 4 to 8 minutes. Transfer roast to carving board and spread 2 tablespoons flavored butter evenly over top of roast; let rest for 15 minutes. Remove twine and cut roast crosswise into ½-inch-thick slices. Serve, passing remaining flavored butter separately.

SHALLOT AND PARSLEY BUTTER
MAKES ABOUT ½ CUP

- 4 tablespoons unsalted butter, softened
- ½ shallot, minced
- 1 tablespoon minced fresh parsley
- 1 garlic clove, minced
- ¼ teaspoon salt
- ¼ teaspoon pepper

Combine all ingredients in bowl.

ON THE SIDE
CLASSIC MASHED POTATOES

Boiling potatoes in their skins gives the mash a more pronounced potato flavor.

1. Place 2 pounds unpeeled russet potatoes in large saucepan and cover with 1 inch cold water. Bring to boil over high heat, reduce heat to medium-low, and simmer until potatoes are just tender (paring knife can be slipped in and out of potatoes with little resistance), 30 to 45 minutes. Drain.

2. Using potholder or folded dish towel to hold potatoes, peel skins from potatoes with paring knife. For slightly chunky texture, return peeled potatoes to now-empty pot and mash smooth using potato masher. For creamy texture, set ricer or food mill over now-empty pot; cut peeled potatoes into large chunks and press or mill into saucepan in batches.

3. Stir in 8 tablespoons unsalted melted butter until incorporated. Gently whisk in 1 cup warmed half-and-half and season with salt and pepper to taste. Serve. (Serves 4.)

Pepper-Crusted Beef Tenderloin Roast

✓ WHY THIS RECIPE WORKS

When it comes to special-occasion entrées, it's hard to beat beef tenderloin. It's easy to make—just oven-roast it until it's done—and, as the absolute most tender cut of beef, it's luxurious to eat. But that tenderness comes at a cost (beyond the hefty price tag): Tenderloin is not known for its beefy flavor. To give it a boost, we wanted to give our tenderloin a crunchy peppercorn crust that would stick to the roast without being punishingly spicy.

GLUE ON THE PEPPERCORNS To make sure we ended up with a full pepper crust and not a scant scattering of pepper, we rubbed the roast with a mixture of coarse kosher salt and baking soda, which roughed up the surface and made it slightly tacky. We then pressed the cracked peppercorns onto the sticky surface. We also sprayed the twine with vegetable oil, so that it wouldn't stick to the roast when we removed it and take our peppercorn crust with it.

TURN DOWN THE HEAT We took two approaches to ensure our pepper crust wasn't overly spicy. First, we added sugar to the salt and baking soda rub. Sucrose, which is found in sugar, has been proven to temper

the spiciness of black pepper. Second, we simmered the cracked peppercorns in oil, which mellowed out some of the heat compounds in the pepper.

AMP UP THE PEPPERY CHARACTER Unfortunately, less heat came at a cost. Simmering the peppercorns in oil had drawn out not only their spiciness but also the nuanced piney and floral flavors that contributed much to making this dish so good. We learned that the compounds found in pepper are also found in high concentrations in orange zest and nutmeg. Adding both of these elements to the simmered peppercorns amped up the pepper flavor for a balanced finish.

FINISH WITH A SAUCE To give an extra boost of flavor, we created a sauce that mirrored and enhanced the flavors we had used to prepare the beef.

PEPPER-CRUSTED BEEF TENDERLOIN ROAST

SERVES 10 TO 12

Whole beef tenderloin is also known as whole filet (see page 36 for more information). Not all pepper mills produce a coarse enough grind for this recipe. For more information on our top-rated pepper mill, see "Pepper Grinder Testing." For an alternative method for cracking peppercorns, see page 49. Serve with Red Wine–Orange Sauce (recipe follows), if desired.

1½	tablespoons kosher salt
1½	teaspoons sugar
¼	teaspoon baking soda
9	tablespoons olive oil
½	cup coarsely cracked black peppercorns
1	tablespoon grated orange zest
½	teaspoon ground nutmeg
1	(6-pound) whole beef tenderloin, trimmed, tail end tucked and tied at 2-inch intervals

1. Adjust oven rack to middle position and heat oven to 300 degrees. Combine salt, sugar, and baking soda in bowl; set aside. Heat

6 tablespoons oil and peppercorns in small saucepan over low heat until faint bubbles appear. Continue to cook at bare simmer, swirling pan occasionally, until pepper is fragrant, 7 to 10 minutes. Using fine-mesh strainer, drain cooking oil from peppercorns. Discard cooking oil and mix peppercorns with remaining 3 tablespoons oil, orange zest, and nutmeg.

2. Set tenderloin on sheet of plastic wrap. Sprinkle salt mixture evenly over surface of tenderloin and rub into tenderloin until surface is tacky. Tuck tail end of tenderloin under about 6 inches to create more even shape. Rub top and side of tenderloin with peppercorn mixture, pressing to make sure peppercorns adhere. Transfer prepared tenderloin to wire rack set in rimmed baking sheet, keeping tail end tucked under.

3. Roast until thickest part of meat registers about 120 degrees (for rare) or about 125 degrees (for medium-rare) (thinner parts of tenderloin will be slightly more done), 1 hour to 1 hour 10 minutes. Transfer to carving board and let rest for 30 minutes.

4. Remove twine and slice meat into ½-inch-thick slices. Serve.

RED WINE–ORANGE SAUCE

MAKES 1 CUP

2	tablespoons unsalted butter, plus 4 tablespoons cut into 4 pieces and chilled
2	shallots, minced
1	tablespoon tomato paste
2	teaspoons sugar
3	garlic cloves, minced
2	cups beef broth
1	cup red wine
¼	cup orange juice
2	tablespoons balsamic vinegar
1	tablespoon Worcestershire sauce
1	sprig fresh thyme
	Salt and pepper

1. Pull away outer layer of fat to expose fatty chain of meat.

2. Pull chain of fat away from roast, cut it off, and discard chain.

3. Scrape silverskin at creases in thick end to expose lobes.

4. Trim silverskin by slicing under it and cutting upward.

5. Remove remaining silverskin in creases at thick end. Turn tenderloin over and remove fat from underside.

1. Melt 2 tablespoons butter in medium saucepan over medium-high heat. Add shallots, tomato paste, and sugar; cook, stirring frequently, until deep brown, about 5 minutes. Add garlic and cook until fragrant, about 1 minute. Add broth, wine, orange juice, vinegar, Worcestershire, and thyme sprig, scraping up any browned bits. Bring to simmer and cook until reduced to 1 cup, 35 to 40 minutes.

2. Strain sauce through fine-mesh strainer and return to saucepan. Return saucepan to medium heat and whisk in remaining 4 tablespoons butter, 1 piece at a time. Season with salt and pepper to taste.

Grill-Roasted Beef Tenderloin

✔ WHY THIS RECIPE WORKS

At high-end butcher shops, whole beef tenderloins can run more than $30 a pound—no small investment, even for a special-occasion dinner. But when cooked right, the ultratender, buttery texture of tenderloin has undeniable appeal. We wanted to find a way to enjoy this roast without breaking the bank.

PUT IN THE EXTRA TIME On our hunt for more reasonably priced beef tenderloins, we discovered that wholesale clubs often sell them for about a third of the price of butcher shops. The catch: These roasts come "unpeeled," meaning they have a thick layer of fat and silverskin that must be removed before cooking. We were able to peel away most of the fat by hand without losing much of the valuable meat. We removed the silverskin (a muscle sheath that would cause the roast to curl up on the grill if left on) with a flexible boning knife. Finally, we tucked the narrow tip end of the roast under and secured it with twine to ensure that every part cooked evenly. The prepwork took about 20 extra minutes— but it saved a significant chunk of change. (Be aware that the tenderloin trimmings can weigh more than 1½ pounds, so plan accordingly.)

WORTH YOUR SALT To give our mild-flavored tenderloin a boost, we tested salting the roast for different amounts of time: 1 hour, 4 hours, or overnight. The roast salted overnight turned gray and had a webby texture. We found that this roast turned out best when salted for just an hour at room temperature, which flavored the meat throughout and gave it time to lose some of its chill so that it would cook more evenly.

PULL IT EARLY Because of carryover cooking, when we cooked the roast on the grill to medium-rare, it had reached medium-well by the time we sliced it. We removed the roast from the grill when it was still rare in order to achieve a perfectly pink, juicy interior.

GRILL-ROASTED BEEF TENDERLOIN
SERVES 10 TO 12

Whole beef tenderloin is also known as whole filet (see page 36 for more information). Beef tenderloins purchased from wholesale clubs require a good amount of trimming before cooking. At the grocery store, however, you may have the option of having the butcher trim it for you. Once trimmed, and with the butt tenderloin still attached (the butt tenderloin is the lobe attached to the large end of the roast), the roast should weigh 4½ to 5 pounds. If you purchase an already-trimmed tenderloin without the butt tenderloin attached, begin checking for doneness about 5 minutes early. If you'd like to use wood chunks instead of wood chips when using a charcoal grill, substitute 2 medium wood chunks, soaked in water for 1 hour, for the wood chip packet (if using). Serve with Cilantro-Parsley Sauce with Pickled Jalapeños, Romesco Sauce, or Salsa Verde (recipes follow), if desired.

1 **(6-pound) whole beef tenderloin, trimmed, tail end tucked and tied with kitchen twine at 2-inch intervals**
1½ **tablespoons kosher salt**
2 **cups wood chips (optional)**
2 **tablespoons olive oil**
1 **tablespoon pepper**

1. Pat tenderloin dry with paper towels and rub with salt. Cover loosely with plastic wrap and let sit at room temperature for 1 hour.

2. Just before grilling, soak wood chips, if using, in water for 15 minutes, then drain. Using large piece of heavy-duty aluminum foil, wrap soaked wood chips in foil packet and cut several vent holes in top.

3A. FOR A CHARCOAL GRILL: Open bottom vent halfway. Light large chimney starter filled with charcoal briquettes (6 quarts). When top coals are partially covered with ash, pour evenly over half of grill. Place wood chip packet, if using, on coals. Set cooking grate in place, cover, and open lid vent halfway. Heat grill until hot and wood chips are smoking, about 5 minutes.

3B. FOR A GAS GRILL: Place wood chip packet, if using, directly on primary burner. Turn all burners to high, cover, and heat grill until hot and wood chips are smoking, about 15 minutes. Leave all burners on high.

4. Clean and oil cooking grate. Rub tenderloin with oil and season with pepper. Place roast on hotter side of grill if using charcoal or opposite primary burner if using gas and cook (covered if using gas) until well browned on all sides, 8 to 10 minutes, turning as needed.

5. For gas grill, leave primary burner on, turning off other burner(s). (Adjust primary burner as needed to maintain grill temperature of 350 degrees.) Move roast to cooler side of grill, cover (position lid vent over meat if using

charcoal), and cook until meat registers 115 to 120 degrees (for rare) or 120 to 125 degrees (for medium-rare), 15 to 30 minutes.

6. Transfer roast to carving board, tent loosely with aluminum foil, and let rest for 10 to 15 minutes. Remove twine, slice meat into ½-inch-thick slices, and serve.

CILANTRO-PARSLEY SAUCE WITH PICKLED JALAPEÑOS

MAKES ABOUT 1½ CUPS

This sauce will discolor if left to sit for too long; it's best served within 4 hours of making it.

2–3 **slices hearty white sandwich bread, crusts removed, bread lightly toasted and cut into ½-inch pieces (1 cup)**
1 **cup extra-virgin olive oil**
¼ **cup lemon juice (2 lemons)**
2 **cups fresh cilantro leaves**
2 **cups fresh parsley leaves**
3 **tablespoons chopped jarred jalapeño slices**
1 **garlic clove, minced**
Salt

Process bread, oil, and lemon juice in food processor until smooth, 10 to 15 seconds. Add cilantro, parsley, jalapeños, garlic, and

---

SIZING UP HERBS

Herbs come in all shapes, sizes, and weights. If a recipe calls for ½ cup chopped basil, how many ounces should you buy? Here's a chart to help you gauge.

TYPE OF HERB	WHOLE LEAVES PER ½ OUNCE	FINELY MINCED LEAVES PER ½ OUNCE
Woody: Thyme, Rosemary	½ cup	2–2½ tablespoons
Leafy: Parsley, Cilantro, Dill, Tarragon, Mint, Basil	¾ cup	3 tablespoons
Other: Chives	No whole leaves	4 tablespoons
Delicate (Fluffy): Oregano, Marjoram, Sage	¾ cup	5 tablespoons

ROASTED RED PEPPERS

You can certainly roast your own peppers at home, but jarred peppers are especially convenient. Since not all are created equal, we tasted eight supermarket brands, both straight out of the jar and in a soup. When they sampled the peppers plain, our tasters preferred firmer, smokier, sweeter-tasting peppers in strong yet simple brines of salt and water. Peppers packed in brines that contained garlic, vinegar, olive oil, and grape must—characteristic of most of the European peppers—rated second. The extra ingredients provided "interesting" and "lively" flavor profiles, but the vinegar often masked the authentic red pepper flavor and smoky notes that tasters preferred. The blandest peppers were also the slimiest ones, both of which rated dead last. Our winner? Tasters preferred the domestically produced **Dunbars Sweet Roasted Peppers**, which lists only red bell peppers, water, salt, and citric acid in its ingredient list.

¼ teaspoon salt and pulse until finely chopped (mixture should not be smooth), about 10 pulses. Season with salt to taste, and transfer to serving bowl.

ROMESCO SAUCE
MAKES ABOUT 2 CUPS

In addition to being an excellent accompaniment to beef, fish, and poultry, this sauce is also terrific spread on toasted bread or used as a dip for crudités.

1–2   slices hearty white sandwich bread, crusts removed, bread lightly toasted and cut into ½-inch pieces (½ cup)
3   tablespoons slivered almonds, toasted
1¾   cups jarred roasted red peppers
1   small ripe tomato, cored, seeded, and chopped
2   tablespoons extra-virgin olive oil
1½   tablespoons sherry vinegar
1   large garlic clove, minced
¼   teaspoon cayenne pepper
  Salt

Process bread and almonds in food processor until almonds are finely ground, 10 to 15 seconds. Add red peppers, tomato, oil, vinegar, garlic, cayenne, and ½ teaspoon salt. Process until mixture has texture similar to mayonnaise, 20 to 30 seconds. Season with salt to taste, and transfer to serving bowl. (Sauce can be refrigerated for up to 2 days.)

SALSA VERDE
MAKES 1½ CUPS

While an excellent accompaniment to beef, fish, and poultry, this sauce can also be served with steamed potatoes, fresh sliced tomatoes, or spread on sandwiches.

2–3   slices hearty white sandwich bread, lightly toasted and cut into ½-inch pieces (about 1½ cups)
1   cup extra-virgin olive oil
¼   cup lemon juice (2 lemons)
4   cups fresh parsley leaves
¼   cup capers, rinsed
4   anchovy fillets, rinsed
1   garlic clove, minced
¼   teaspoon salt

Process bread, oil, and lemon juice in food processor until smooth, about 10 seconds. Add parsley, capers, anchovies, garlic, and salt and pulse until finely chopped (mixture should not be smooth), about 5 pulses. Transfer to serving bowl. (Sauce can be refrigerated for up to 2 days.)

LEMON-BASIL SALSA VERDE

Substitute 2 cups fresh basil leaves for 2 cups parsley, increase garlic to 2 cloves, and add 1 teaspoon grated lemon zest.

SALSA VERDE WITH ARUGULA

Arugula gives this variation a peppery kick that's a nice match for grilled foods.

Substitute 2 cups chopped arugula for 2 cups parsley and increase garlic to 2 cloves.

Slow-Roasted Beef

✔ WHY THIS RECIPE WORKS

We wanted to transform a bargain cut into a tender, juicy roast—perfect for an old-fashioned Sunday dinner.

CHOOSE FROM A LOW-COST LINEUP Not all bargain cuts have the potential to taste like a million bucks—or look like it when carved and served on a plate. We tried the eye-round roast, chuck-eye roast, top round, and bottom round rump. While the chuck eye was too fatty, the top round an odd, uneven shape, and the bottom round rump too tough to carve, we loved the eye-round roast for its good flavor, relative tenderness, and uniform shape, which meant even cooking and good looks when sliced into rosy slabs.

SALT EARLY We tried salting the roast for 4, 12, and 24 hours and discovered that a full 24 hours gave it the most time to penetrate deep into the meat and season the roast evenly (though as few as 18 hours was effective). The salt dissolved some of the proteins, too, making it easier for the enzymes to break them down.

SEAR, THEN ELEVATE A roast cooked entirely in a cool oven will have a soft, pallid exterior. A quick sear in a hot skillet developed a flavorful crust on the meat and was an essential first step in this recipe. Rather than placing the roast directly in a roasting pan, we elevated the roast on a rack set in a rimmed baking sheet. The rack allowed the oven heat to circulate evenly around the meat and prevented the bottom crust from steaming in the oven.

UTILIZE CARRYOVER COOKING It's important to shut the oven off before the internal temperature of the roast reaches 122 degrees; in this recipe we stopped at 115 degrees. This allowed the oven to cool while the roast continued to cook, just more slowly. The roast took another 30 to 50 minutes to slowly climb from 115 to a final temperature of 130 degrees for medium-rare.

SLOW-ROASTED BEEF
SERVES 6 TO 8

Eye-round roast is also known as round-eye pot roast (see page 38 for more information). We don't recommend cooking this roast past medium. Open the oven door as little as possible and remove the roast from the oven while taking its temperature. If the roast has not reached the desired temperature in the time specified in step 3, heat the oven to 225 degrees for 5 minutes, shut it off, and continue to cook the roast to the desired temperature. For a smaller (2½- to 3½-pound) roast, reduce the amount of salt to 1 tablespoon and pepper to 1½ teaspoons. For a 4½- to 6-pound roast, cut in half crosswise before cooking to create 2 smaller roasts. Slice the roast as thin as possible and serve with Horseradish Cream Sauce (recipe follows), if desired.

1	(3½- to 4½-pound) boneless eye-round roast
4	teaspoons kosher salt
2	teaspoons plus 1 tablespoon vegetable oil
2	teaspoons pepper

1. Season all sides of roast evenly with salt. Wrap with plastic wrap and refrigerate for 18 to 24 hours.

2. Adjust oven rack to middle position and heat oven to 225 degrees. Pat roast dry with paper towels; rub with 2 teaspoons oil and season all sides evenly with pepper. Heat remaining 1 tablespoon oil in 12-inch skillet

Buyer beware: "Prepared horseradish" can vary astonishingly from brand to brand, and much depends on where you buy it. Refrigerated products are simply grated horseradish, vinegar, and salt. Shelf-stable ones add a laundry list of other ingredients, including sugar, eggs, citric acid, high-fructose corn syrup, soybean oil, artificial flavorings, and preservatives. These filler-packed horseradishes are rife with chemical tastes. Equally problematic: Many have a slimy texture and are overwhelmingly hot. The refrigerated ones deliver more natural flavor with less mushiness and are hot without being overpowering.

Our advice: Avoid shelf-stable brands with fillers and go straight to the refrigerator aisle, making sure the label reads simply "grated horseradish, vinegar, and salt."

And what about brand? To choose our favorite, we narrowed our focus to four refrigerated brands, which we tasted both plain from the jar and in creamy horseradish sauce. Our favorite, **Boar's Head Pure Horseradish**, won by a landslide for its "intense," "wasabi-like" heat and "great, lingering bite." Finely grated, it left "no unpleasant shreds" or chewy bits when mixed into cream sauce. Its "peppery," "complex," "fresh" flavor put it beyond its rivals.

over medium-high heat until just smoking. Sear roast until browned on all sides, about 12 minutes. Transfer roast to wire rack set in rimmed baking sheet. Roast until meat registers 115 degrees (for medium-rare) or 125 degrees (for medium), 1¼ to 2¼ hours.

3. Turn oven off; leave roast in oven, without opening door, until meat registers 130 degrees (for medium-rare) or 140 degrees (for medium), 30 to 50 minutes longer. Transfer roast to carving board and let rest for 15 minutes. Slice meat as thin as possible and serve.

HORSERADISH CREAM SAUCE
MAKES ABOUT I CUP

½ cup heavy cream
½ cup prepared horseradish, drained
I teaspoon salt
⅛ teaspoon pepper

Whisk cream in bowl until thickened but not yet holding soft peaks, 1 to 2 minutes. Gently fold in horseradish, salt, and pepper. Transfer to serving bowl and refrigerate at least 30 minutes or up to 1 hour before serving.

Inexpensive Grill-Roasted Beef

✔ WHY THIS RECIPE WORKS

Grill roasting has produced delicious results in the test kitchen, but for less expensive roasts, our previous grill-roasting methods fell short. We set out to develop a method that would produce tender meat, even when we didn't spend a lot.

CHOOSE TOP SIRLOIN Top sirloin has good beefy flavor, an affordable price tag, and holds up on the grill.

SEASON AND CHILL OUT We rubbed the roast all over with a generous amount of garlic, rosemary, and salt, wrapped the roast in plastic wrap, and refrigerated it for at least 18 hours to season the meat.

KEEP THE HEAT DOWN Traditional recipes for grill roasting sear the meat over the hot side of the grill, then move it to the cooler side, where it cooks at a gentler pace. To ensure an evenly cooked, pink, tender interior, we adjusted that approach in two ways: First, we minimized the heat output by using only half a chimney's worth of coals—just enough to give the meat a good sear. (To replicate this effect on a gas grill, we turned one burner to medium and the other burners off.) Second, we shielded the seared roast from excess heat by placing it in a disposable aluminum pan when we moved it to the grill's cooler side. Both methods helped to tenderize the roast by keeping the temperature low.

PUNCH HOLES It's important to punch holes in the disposable aluminum roasting pan. Without them, the juices that exude from the meat as it cooks on the grill will pool around the roast and turn its underside boiled and gray, ruining any crust achieved from searing. The addition of a dozen or so small escape channels in the bottom of the pan allows the liquid to drain away and leaves the meat perfectly pink with a crisp, flavorful crust.

THINK THIN When slicing this roast beef to serve, use a slicing knife to cut wafer-thin slices of the rosy meat. Cutting extra-thin slices will make the meat seem even more tender.

AT THE MEAT COUNTER
PREFERRED CUT Top Sirloin Roast

Top sirloin roast is also known as top butt or center-cut roast (see page 37 for more information).

ALTERNATE CUT Top Round Roast

Top round roast is also known as top round first cut and top round steak roast (see page 38 for more information).

INEXPENSIVE GRILL-ROASTED BEEF WITH GARLIC AND ROSEMARY
SERVES 6 TO 8

A pair of kitchen shears works well for punching the holes in the aluminum pan. Start this recipe the day before you plan to grill so the salt rub has time to flavor and tenderize the meat.

- 6 garlic cloves, minced
- 2 tablespoons minced fresh rosemary
- 4 teaspoons kosher salt
- I tablespoon pepper
- I (3- to 4-pound) top sirloin roast, trimmed
- I (13 by 9-inch) disposable aluminum roasting pan

1. Combine garlic, rosemary, salt, and pepper in bowl. Sprinkle all sides of roast evenly with garlic mixture, wrap tightly in plastic wrap, and refrigerate for 18 to 24 hours.

2A. FOR A CHARCOAL GRILL: Open bottom vent halfway. Light large chimney starter half filled with charcoal briquettes (3 quarts). When top coals are partially covered with ash, pour evenly over one-third of grill. Set cooking grate in place, cover, and open lid vent halfway. Heat grill until hot, about 5 minutes.

2B. FOR A GAS GRILL: Turn all burners to high, cover, and heat grill until hot, about 15 minutes. Leave all burners on high.

3. Clean and oil cooking grate. Place roast on grill (hotter side if using charcoal) and cook (covered if using gas) until well browned on all sides, 10 to 12 minutes, turning as needed. (If flare-ups occur, move roast to cooler side of grill until flames die down.)

4. Meanwhile, punch fifteen ¼-inch holes in center of disposable pan in area roughly same size as roast. Once browned, place beef in pan over holes and set pan over cooler side of grill (if using charcoal) or turn primary burner to medium and turn off other burner(s) (if using gas). (Adjust primary burner as needed to maintain grill temperature of 250 to 300 degrees.) Cover and cook until meat registers 120 to 125 degrees (for medium-rare) or 130 to 135 degrees (for medium), 40 minutes to 1 hour, rotating pan halfway through cooking.

5. Transfer roast to wire rack set in rimmed baking sheet, tent loosely with aluminum foil, and let rest for 20 minutes. Transfer roast to carving board, slice very thin against grain, and serve.

INEXPENSIVE GRILL-ROASTED BEEF WITH SHALLOT AND TARRAGON

Substitute 1 minced shallot for garlic and 2 tablespoons minced fresh tarragon for rosemary.

Baltimore Pit Beef

✔ WHY THIS RECIPE WORKS

Baltimore's "barbecue" tradition involves cooking a mammoth cut of beef against the direct heat of the grill. Superthin slices of beef are piled on a soft bun with "tiger sauce," a simple sauce of mayonnaise and horseradish. We set out to unlock the secrets of this beloved sandwich for the home kitchen.

START WITH THE RIGHT BEEF To figure out which cut of beef to use in this recipe, we went right to the source, and found out that many of Baltimore's pit beef joints use whole top or bottom rounds. Although flavorful, these cuts are huge and require a meat slicer to cut them thin enough to be tender. Instead, we turned to top sirloin roast: Its affordability, tenderness, and flavor make it a test kitchen favorite for grill-roasted beef and a perfect candidate for this recipe.

DOUBLE THE FLAVOR What sets pit beef apart is the salty, spicy, nearly blackened crust. Most recipes called for a paprika-based spice rub containing black pepper, cayenne, garlic powder, dried oregano, and salt. Since the ingredients are simple, getting the ratio right was important—but even more important was making sure that the flavor penetrated beyond just the surface of the meat. While some restaurants "marinate" the meat with the spices for several days, we wanted to speed up the process. To get the most flavor in less time, we cut the roast in half to maximize surface area and then let the flavors permeate the roast for at least 6 hours. The bonus: twice the smoky, spicy crust.

COOK FROM THE INSIDE OUT To protect our roasts from developing an overcooked, gray ring around the edges, we wrapped them in aluminum foil and started them over an indirect flame. Later, we removed the foil and cranked up the grill to achieve the signature dark crust with a perfectly rosy interior.

BALTIMORE PIT BEEF
SERVES 10

Top sirloin roast is also known as top butt or center-cut roast (see page 107 for more information). Buy refrigerated prepared horseradish, not the shelf-stable kind, which contains preservatives and additives.

TIGER SAUCE
- ½ cup mayonnaise
- ½ cup hot prepared horseradish
- 1 teaspoon lemon juice
- 1 garlic clove, minced
  Salt and pepper

PIT BEEF
- 4 teaspoons kosher salt
- 1 tablespoon paprika
- 1 tablespoon pepper
- 1 teaspoon garlic powder
- 1 teaspoon dried oregano
- ¼ teaspoon cayenne pepper
- 1 (4- to 5-pound) top sirloin roast, trimmed and halved crosswise
- 10 kaiser rolls, split
- 1 onion, sliced thin

1. FOR THE TIGER SAUCE: Whisk mayonnaise, horseradish, lemon juice, and garlic together in bowl. Season with salt and pepper to taste. (Sauce can be refrigerated for up to 2 days.)

2. FOR THE PIT BEEF: Combine salt, paprika, pepper, garlic powder, oregano, and cayenne in bowl. Pat roasts dry with paper towels and rub with 2 tablespoons seasoning mixture. Wrap meat tightly with plastic wrap and refrigerate for 6 to 24 hours.

3A. FOR A CHARCOAL GRILL: Open bottom vent halfway. Light large chimney starter filled with charcoal briquettes (6 quarts). When top coals are partially covered with ash, pour evenly over half of grill. Set cooking grate in place, cover, and open lid vent halfway. Heat grill until hot, about 5 minutes.

3B. FOR A GAS GRILL: Turn all burners to high, cover, and heat grill until hot, about 15 minutes. Leave primary burner on high and turn off other burner(s).

4. Clean and oil cooking grate. Unwrap roasts and place end to end on long side of 18 by 12-inch sheet of aluminum foil. Loosely fold opposite long side of foil around top of roasts. Place meat on cooler part of grill with foil-covered side closest to heat source. Cover (positioning lid vent over meat if using charcoal) and cook until meat registers 100 degrees, 45 minutes to 1 hour.

5. Transfer roasts to plate and discard foil. Turn all burners to high if using gas. If using charcoal, carefully remove cooking grate and light large chimney starter three-quarters filled with charcoal briquettes (4½ quarts). When top coals are partially covered with ash, pour evenly over spent coals. Set cooking grate in place and cover. Heat grill until hot, about 5 minutes.

6. Pat roasts dry with paper towels and rub with remaining spice mixture. Place meat on hotter part of grill. Cook (covered if using gas), turning occasionally, until charred on all sides and meat registers 120 to 125 degrees (for medium-rare), 10 to 20 minutes. Transfer meat to carving board, tent loosely with foil, and let rest for 15 minutes. Slice meat thin against grain. Transfer sliced beef to rolls, top with onion slices, and drizzle with sauce. Serve.

Texas-Style Barbecued Beef Ribs

✔ WHY THIS RECIPE WORKS

In true Texas style, Texas barbecued beef ribs are big, unapologetically beefy slabs of meat. Unlike their pork-rib cousins, the meat is not fall-off-the-bone tender, but instead retains some chew and heft. The challenge of replicating these ribs at home is twofold: not having a specialized smoke pit to constantly infuse smoky flavor into the ribs, and not wanting to spend 10 hours babysitting the grill. We wanted to adjust the process to make these ribs achievable for the home cook.

STEAM POWER To speed up the cooking process, some recipes call for parboiling ribs. But we have found that the tenderness gained by boiling meat is canceled out by the washed-out flavor. Instead, we gave the ribs a head start by steaming them in the oven. This method

started to break down the connective tissue in the ribs much sooner than grilling alone.

BARK AND BITE To create a flavorful charred crust—called "bark" by barbecue enthusiasts—we started with a basic spice rub to flavor the meat. We grilled the ribs over the cooler side of the grill to imitate the low-and-slow heat environment of professional smoke pits, and used a wood chip packet to infuse them with smoky flavor. Grilling the ribs after steaming them gave us just the right amount of chew and plenty of crunch.

SAUCE ON THE SIDE Beef ribs don't get a slathering of sauce on the grill; instead they are usually served with a thinner sauce on the side. We came up with a simple one-pot solution for Texas barbecue sauce.

TEXAS-STYLE BARBECUED BEEF RIBS
SERVES 4

Beef ribs are also known as back ribs (see page 35 for more information). They are sold in slabs with up to seven bones, but slabs with three to four bones are easier to manage on the grill. If you cannot find ribs with a substantial amount of meat on the bones, don't bother making this recipe. If you'd like to use wood chunks instead of wood chips when using a charcoal grill, substitute one medium wood chunk, soaked in water for 1 hour, for the wood chip packet.

TEXAS BARBECUE SAUCE

2	tablespoons unsalted butter
½	small onion, chopped fine
2	garlic cloves, minced
1½	teaspoons chili powder
1½	teaspoons pepper
½	teaspoon dry mustard
2	cups tomato juice
6	tablespoons distilled white vinegar
2	tablespoons Worcestershire sauce
2	tablespoons packed brown sugar
2	tablespoons molasses
	Salt

RIBS

3	tablespoons packed brown sugar
4	teaspoons chili powder
1	tablespoon salt
2	teaspoons pepper
½	teaspoon cayenne pepper
3–4	beef rib slabs (3 or 4 ribs per slab, about 5 pounds total), trimmed
1	cup wood chips, soaked in water for 15 minutes and drained

1. FOR THE SAUCE: Melt butter in medium saucepan over medium heat. Add onion and cook until softened, about 5 minutes. Stir in garlic, chili powder, pepper, and dry mustard and cook until fragrant, about 30 seconds. Stir in tomato juice, vinegar, Worcestershire, sugar, and molasses and simmer until sauce is reduced to 2 cups, about 20 minutes. Season with salt to taste. (Sauce can be refrigerated in airtight container for 1 week.)

2. FOR THE RIBS: Combine sugar, chili powder, salt, pepper, and cayenne in bowl. Pat ribs dry with paper towels and rub them evenly with spice mixture. Cover ribs with plastic wrap and let sit at room temperature for 1 hour.

3. Adjust oven rack to middle position and heat oven to 300 degrees. Set wire rack in rimmed baking sheet and add just enough water to cover sheet bottom. Arrange ribs on rack and cover tightly with aluminum foil. Cook until fat has rendered and meat begins to pull away from bones, about 2 hours. Using large piece of heavy-duty foil, wrap soaked chips in foil packet and cut several vent holes in top.

4A. FOR A CHARCOAL GRILL: Open bottom vent halfway. Light large chimney starter filled with charcoal briquettes (6 quarts). When top coals are partially covered with ash, pour into steeply banked pile against side of grill. Place wood chip packet on coals. Set cooking grate in place, cover, and open lid vent halfway. Heat grill until hot and wood chips are smoking, about 5 minutes.

4B. FOR A GAS GRILL: Place wood chip packet directly on primary burner. Turn all burners to high, cover, and heat grill until hot and wood chips are smoking, about 15 minutes. Leave primary burner on high and turn off other burner(s). (Adjust primary burner as needed to maintain grill temperature of 250 to 300 degrees.)

5. Clean and oil cooking grate. Place ribs meat side down on cooler side of grill; ribs may overlap slightly. Cover (positioning lid vent over meat if using charcoal) and cook until ribs are lightly charred and smoky, about 1½ hours, flipping and rotating racks halfway through grilling. Transfer to cutting board, tent with foil, and let rest for 10 minutes and cut ribs into portions. Serve with barbecue sauce.

BUYING TEXAS-STYLE BEEF RIBS

Texas-style barbecued beef ribs are all about the meat. Because beef ribs are located on the cow next to expensive cuts such as rib eye and prime rib, butchers often overtrim the ribs so they can maximize the bulk (and their profits) on the pricier cuts. Be sure to buy slabs with a thick layer of meat that covers the bones. Also, steer clear of the gargantuan seven-rib slabs, which won't fit on the kettle grill. A three- or four-rib slab works best.

Grill-Roasted Beef Short Ribs

✓ WHY THIS RECIPE WORKS

Flavorful, well-marbled short ribs seem like the perfect candidate for grilling, but getting the texture just right can be a challenge. We wanted meltingly tender meat with the nicely browned exterior that the grill provides—without having to constantly fiddle with the fire.

RUB YOUR RIBS To distinguish our short ribs from a typical slab of barbecued ribs, we opted for a flavorful spice rub and a sweet-tart glaze. We borrowed two ingredients from common pork-rib rubs: garlic powder and brown sugar. Ground fennel and cumin added more complex layers to the rub. For the glaze, we used tangy, bright flavors like mustard to help temper the richness of the meat.

GO BONE-IN Short ribs are full of collagen, which convert to gelatin during cooking and produce a tender texture. But during testing, boneless ribs shriveled and blackened by the time the collagen had enough time to break down. Bone-in ribs were the clear choice for their ability to stand up to the heat of the grill.

DON'T JUST GRILL Even a carefully monitored grill inevitably produces hot and cold spots, and the spotty heat was causing our short ribs to cook unevenly. We decided that starting the ribs in the more even-heat environment of the oven was the optimal solution. When the ribs reached 165 degrees, we moved them to the grill to finish cooking and get a smoky, crunchy crust.

GRILL-ROASTED BEEF SHORT RIBS
SERVES 4 TO 6

Meaty English-style short ribs are preferred in this recipe over thinner-cut flanken-style ribs (see page 40 for more information). Make sure to choose ribs that are 4 to 6 inches in length and have at least 1 inch of meat on top of the bone.

SPICE RUB
2	tablespoons kosher salt
1	tablespoon packed brown sugar
2	teaspoons pepper
2	teaspoons ground cumin
2	teaspoons garlic powder
1¼	teaspoons paprika
¾	teaspoon ground fennel
⅛	teaspoon cayenne pepper

SHORT RIBS
5	pounds bone-in English-style beef short ribs, trimmed
2	tablespoons red wine vinegar
1	recipe glaze (recipes follow)

1. FOR THE SPICE RUB: Combine all ingredients in bowl. Measure out 1 teaspoon rub and set aside for glaze.

2. FOR THE SHORT RIBS: Adjust oven rack to middle position and heat oven to 300 degrees. Sprinkle ribs with spice rub, pressing into all sides of ribs. Arrange ribs, bone side down, in 13 by 9-inch baking dish, placing thicker ribs around perimeter of baking

THE PERFECT SHORT RIB FOR GRILL ROASTING

Bone-in English-style short ribs (those with long, continuous pieces of meat and a single bone) are a must, but we found that they can vary widely from package to package. Here's what to look for in order for this recipe to work.

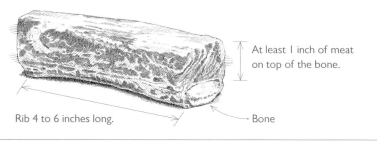

At least 1 inch of meat on top of the bone.

Rib 4 to 6 inches long.

Bone

STICKY RICE

This rice is just soft enough to soak up the sauce in a stir-fry and just sticky enough to be easily eaten with chopsticks.

Bring 3 cups water, 2 cups long-grain white rice, and ½ teaspoon salt to boil in large saucepan. Cook over medium-high heat until water level drops below surface of rice and small holes form in rice, about 10 minutes. Reduce heat to low, cover, and continue to cook until rice is tender, about 15 minutes. (Serves 4 to 6)

dish and thinner ribs in center. Sprinkle vinegar evenly over ribs. Cover baking dish tightly with aluminum foil. Bake until thickest ribs register 165 to 170 degrees, 1½ to 2 hours.

3A. FOR A CHARCOAL GRILL: Open bottom vent halfway. Arrange 2 quarts unlit charcoal into steeply banked pile against side of grill. Light large chimney starter half filled with charcoal (3 quarts). When top coals are partially covered with ash, pour on top of unlit charcoal to cover one-third of grill with coals steeply banked against side of grill. Set cooking grate in place, cover, and open lid vent halfway. Heat grill until hot, about 5 minutes.

3B. FOR A GAS GRILL: Turn all burners to high, cover, and heat grill until hot, about 15 minutes. Leave primary burner on medium and turn off other burner(s). Adjust primary burner as needed to maintain grill temperature of 275 to 300 degrees.

4. Clean and oil cooking grate. Place short ribs, bone side down, on cooler side of grill about 2 inches from flames. Brush with ¼ cup glaze. Cover and cook until ribs register 195 degrees, 1¾ to 2¼ hours, rotating and brushing ribs with ¼ cup glaze every 30 minutes. Transfer ribs to large platter, tent loosely with foil, and let rest for 5 to 10 minutes before serving.

MUSTARD GLAZE
MAKES ABOUT 1 CUP

½	cup Dijon mustard
½	cup red wine vinegar
¼	cup packed brown sugar
1	teaspoon reserved spice rub
⅛	teaspoon cayenne pepper

Whisk all ingredients together in bowl.

BLACKBERRY GLAZE
MAKES ABOUT 1 CUP

10	ounces (2 cups) fresh or frozen blackberries
½	cup ketchup
¼	cup bourbon
2	tablespoons packed brown sugar
1½	tablespoons soy sauce
1	teaspoon reserved spice rub
⅛	teaspoon cayenne pepper

Bring all ingredients to simmer in small saucepan over medium-high heat. Simmer, stirring frequently to break up blackberries, until reduced to 1¼ cups, about 10 minutes. Strain through fine-mesh strainer, pressing on solids to extract as much liquid as possible. Discard solids.

HOISIN-TAMARIND GLAZE
MAKES ABOUT 1 CUP

Tamarind paste can be found in some well-stocked supermarkets or Asian markets.

1	cup water
⅓	cup hoisin sauce
¼	cup tamarind paste
1	(2-inch) piece ginger, peeled and sliced into ½-inch-thick rounds
1	teaspoon reserved spice rub
⅛	teaspoon cayenne pepper

Bring all ingredients to simmer in small saucepan over medium-high heat. Simmer, stirring frequently, until reduced to 1¼ cups, about 10 minutes. Strain through fine-mesh strainer, pressing on solids to extract as much liquid as possible. Discard solids.

Korean Grilled Short Ribs (Kalbi)

✔ **WHY THIS RECIPE WORKS**

Koreans know how to take tough short ribs and transform them into tender barbecued beef in just minutes. We wanted to learn from their example and modify the recipe to work with readily available equipment and ingredients.

MAKE ENGLISH-STYLE RIBS WORK Most Korean barbecue recipes use flanken-style short ribs, which are short ribs that are cut across the bones. But we rarely found them in stores, and when we did, they were far too big for the quick-cooking method. We decided to go with English-style short ribs, which consist of a single bone with a thick piece of meat attached. We removed the bones, cut the ribs into four pieces, and pounded the pieces into thin, even slabs.

PEAR UP Many recipes we found called for pureed pear as a marinade ingredient. We discovered that the acidity in the pear worked in concert with the soy sauce and rice vinegar to tenderize the tough meat. Plus, the pear added a pleasantly sweet, fruity layer of flavor.

A HOT GRILL WORKS BEST To re-create the traditional Korean barbecue setup, we created a two-level grill fire and cooked the short ribs over high heat, moving them to the cooler side when flare-ups occurred. The intense heat gave a quick char without making the meat tough.

KOREAN GRILLED SHORT RIBS (KALBI)

SERVES 4 TO 6

For more information on short ribs, see page 40. Make sure to buy English-style ribs that have at least 1 inch of meat on top of the bone, avoiding ones that have little meat and large bones. Two pounds of boneless short ribs at least 4 inches long and 1 inch thick can be used instead of bone-in ribs. Alternatively, 2½ pounds of thinly sliced Korean-style ribs can be used (no butchering is required), but if using charcoal, reduce to 3 quarts. Serve with Sticky Rice (page 114), kimchi, and, if available, a spicy bean paste called gochujang. Traditionally, all these ingredients are wrapped in a lettuce leaf with the meat and eaten like a taco.

1	ripe pear, peeled, halved, cored, and chopped coarse
½	cup soy sauce
6	tablespoons sugar
2	tablespoons toasted sesame oil
6	garlic cloves, peeled
4	teaspoons grated fresh ginger
1	tablespoon rice vinegar
3	scallions, sliced thin
½	teaspoon red pepper flakes (optional)
5	pounds bone-in English-style short ribs, meat removed from bone, trimmed, sliced widthwise at angle into ½- to ¾-inch-thick pieces, and pounded ¼ inch thick

1. Process pear, soy sauce, sugar, oil, garlic, ginger, and vinegar in food processor until smooth, 20 to 30 seconds. Transfer to medium bowl and stir in scallions and pepper flakes, if using.

2. Spread one-third of marinade in 13 by 9-inch baking pan. Place half of meat in single layer over marinade. Pour half of remaining marinade over meat, followed by remaining meat and remaining marinade. Cover tightly with plastic wrap and refrigerate for at least 4 hours or up to 12 hours, turning meat once or twice.

3A. FOR A CHARCOAL GRILL: Open bottom vent completely. Light large chimney

1. Remove meat from bone, positioning chef's knife as close as possible to bone.

2. Trim excess hard fat and silverskin from both sides of meat.

3. Slice meat at angle into 4 or 5 pieces ranging from ½ to ¾ inch thick.

4. Place plastic wrap over meat and pound into even ¼-inch-thick pieces.

TURNING YOUR GRILL INTO A SMOKER

The massive smokers used in Texas employ indirect-heat cooking to turn tough cuts like brisket tender. We did the same thing in a kettle grill by pushing the lit coals as far to one side as possible. Pouring the lit coals onto a pile of unlit coals keeps the fire going strong for hours. To ensure a slow release of smoke, we placed soaked wood chunks on the coals. We also put a disposable pan filled with water below the brisket to encourage the pink smoke ring under the crust.

WHY IS BRISKET PINK?

Championship barbecue brisket always contains a thick smoke ring—the pink layer just beneath the meat's surface. Smoke doesn't play much of a role—it's actually caused by reactions that occur when meat is cooked for a long time at a low temperature in a closed chamber. The fire emits gasses that dissolve in the moisture on the surface of the meat to create new compounds similar to the nitrates that keep deli meats pink. We found that placing a pan of water in the grill added enough moisture for a proper smoke ring.

starter two-thirds filled with charcoal briquettes (4 quarts). When top coals are partially covered with ash, pour into even layer over half of grill. Set cooking grate in place, cover, and open lid vent completely. Heat grill until hot, about 5 minutes.

3B. FOR A GAS GRILL: Turn all burners to high, cover, and heat grill until hot, about 15 minutes. Leave primary burner on high and turn off other burner(s).

4. Clean and oil cooking grate. Place half of meat on hotter side of grill and cook (covered if using gas), turning every 2 to 3 minutes, until well browned on both sides, 8 to 13 minutes. Move first batch of meat to cooler side of grill and repeat browning with second batch.

5. Transfer second batch of meat to serving platter. Return first batch of meat to hotter side of grill and warm for 30 seconds; transfer to serving platter and serve.

Barbecued Beef Brisket

✔ WHY THIS RECIPE WORKS

In researching recipes for barbecued brisket, we found that cooks could agree on one thing: slow-cooking (for up to 12 hours) for the purpose of tenderizing. That seemed like a lot of time, though. We wanted to figure out a way to make cooking this potentially delicious cut of meat less daunting and less time-consuming, and we wanted to trade in a professional smoker for a backyard grill.

PICK ONE CUT OF BRISKET Cut from the cow's breast section, a whole brisket is a boneless, coarse-grained cut composed of two smaller roasts: the flat (or first) cut and the point (or second) cut. We chose the widely available flat cut. The flat cut's meat is lean and topped with a thick fat cap, which we trimmed to ⅓ to ½ inch thick. We brined the brisket to season it throughout and to allow the meat to remain juicy even after hours on the grill.

CHOOSE THE RIGHT WOOD We liked hickory wood chunks to smoke our brisket. Pecan, maple, oak, or fruitwoods such as apple, cherry, and peach also worked well. We suggest you avoid mesquite, which turns bitter during the long process of barbecuing. Use wood chunks that are about the size of a tennis ball.

BURN IT DOWN In our tests, we had trouble figuring out how to maintain a low temperature in the grill without frequently refueling. But then we realized that fire can burn down as well as up. We layered unlit briquettes on the bottom of our grill and added 4 quarts of hot coals on top. The result? A fire that burned consistently in the optimal 300-degree range for about 3 hours. We then transferred the brisket to the oven to finish cooking.

USE A FOIL SHIELD If your brisket is smaller than 5 pounds or the fat cap has been removed, or if you are using a small charcoal grill, it may be necessary to build an aluminum foil shield in order to keep the brisket from becoming too dark. To do this, make two ½-inch folds on the long side of an 18 by 20-inch piece of heavy-duty aluminum foil to form a reinforced edge. Place the foil on the center of the cooking grate, with the reinforced edge over the hot side of the grill. Position the brisket fat side down over the cool side of the grill so that it covers about half of the foil. Pull the foil over the brisket to loosely tent it.

BARBECUED BEEF BRISKET

SERVES 8 TO 10

For more information on brisket, see page 39. If you'd like to use wood chunks instead of wood chips when using a charcoal grill, substitute two medium wood chunks, soaked in water for 1 hour, for the wood chip packet. Some of the traditional accompaniments to barbecued brisket include barbecue sauce (see Barbecue Sauce for Texas-Style Barbecued Beef Ribs on page 111), sliced white bread or saltines, pickle chips, and thinly sliced onion.

- 1   (5- to 6-pound) beef brisket, flat cut
- 2/3   cup salt
- 1/2   cup plus 2 tablespoons sugar
- 2   cups wood chips, soaked in water for 15 minutes and drained
- 3   tablespoons kosher salt
- 2   tablespoons pepper
- 1   (13 by 9-inch) disposable aluminum roasting pan (if using charcoal) or 1 disposable aluminum pie plate (if using gas)

1. Using sharp knife, cut slits in fat cap, spaced 1 inch apart, in crosshatch pattern, being careful to not cut into meat. Dissolve salt and 1/2 cup sugar in 4 quarts cold water in large container. Submerge brisket in brine, cover, and refrigerate for 2 hours.

2. Using large piece of heavy-duty aluminum foil, wrap soaked chips in foil packet and cut several vent holes in top.

3. Combine remaining 2 tablespoons sugar, kosher salt, and pepper in bowl. Remove brisket from brine and pat dry with paper towels. Transfer to rimmed baking sheet and rub salt mixture over entire brisket and into slits.

4A. FOR A CHARCOAL GRILL: Open bottom vent halfway. Arrange 3 quarts unlit charcoal banked against side of grill and disposable pan filled with 2 cups water on empty side of grill. Light large chimney starter two-thirds filled with charcoal (4 quarts). When top coals are partially covered with ash, pour on top of unlit charcoal to cover one-third of grill with coals steeply banked against side of grill. Place wood chip packet on top of coals. Set cooking grate in place, cover, and open lid vent halfway. Heat grill until hot and wood chips are smoking, about 5 minutes.

4B. FOR A GAS GRILL: Place wood chip packet directly on primary burner. Place disposable aluminum pie plate filled with 2 cups water on other burner(s). Turn all burners to high, cover, and heat grill until hot and wood chips are smoking, about 15 minutes. Turn primary burner to medium and turn off other burner(s). (Adjust primary burner as needed to maintain grill temperature of 250 to 300 degrees.)

5. Line rimmed baking sheet with foil and set wire rack in sheet. Clean and oil cooking grate. Place brisket on cooler side of grill, fat side down, as far away from coals and flames as possible with thickest side facing coals and flames. Loosely tent meat with aluminum foil. Cover (position lid vent over meat if using charcoal) and cook for 3 hours. Transfer brisket to prepared baking sheet.

6. Adjust oven rack to middle position and heat oven to 325 degrees. Roast brisket until tender and meat registers 195 degrees, about 2 hours.

7. Transfer brisket to carving board, tent loosely with foil, and let rest for 30 minutes. Slice brisket against grain into long, thin slices and serve.

A FOIL SHIELD FOR SMALLER GRILLS

When using a charcoal grill less than 22 inches in diameter or a gas grill with only two burners, or when barbecuing a small brisket without a fat cap, we found it necessary to make a foil shield to protect the brisket from getting too dark and leathery on the side closest to the heat. The shield is only needed for the first half of cooking.

Make two 1/2-inch folds on long side of 18 by 20-inch piece of heavy-duty aluminum foil to form reinforced edge. Place foil on center of cooking grate, with reinforced edge over hot side of grill. Position brisket, fat side down, over cool side of grill so that it covers about one-third of foil. Pull foil over brisket to loosely tent it; remove foil before transferring brisket to oven.

1. Pull roast apart at its major seams (delineated by lines of fat) into 2 halves. Use knife as necessary.

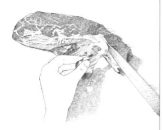

2. With knife, remove large knobs of fat from each piece, leaving thin layer of fat on meat.

3. Tie 3 pieces of kitchen twine around each piece of meat to keep it from falling apart.

Classic Pot Roast

✔ WHY THIS RECIPE WORKS

For classic pot roast, we wanted perfectly tender meat that wasn't dried out after spending a long time in the oven.

CHOOSE A CHUCK EYE For this pot roast, we chose to use chuck-eye roast. This boneless roast is cut from the center of the first five ribs. It is very tender and juicy, though it does contain a healthy amount of fat.

COOK UNTIL DONE, AND THEN SOME To create a tight seal and prevent liquid from escaping, we covered the pot first with foil, and then with the lid. We cooked the roast until it was very well-done—to an internal temperature of about 210 degrees, the point at which the fat and connective tissue are really melting well. But simply bringing the meat to this temperature did not achieve the desired fall-apart-tender pot roast. We found that leaving the pot roast to cook at that same internal temperature for a full hour longer made it so tender that a fork poked into its center was met with no resistance, nearly disappearing into the flesh.

COOK AT A LOW BUT NOT TOO LOW TEMPERATURE We began pot—roasting in an oven set to 250 degrees, and then tested roasts at higher temperatures to see if it would be possible to reduce the cooking time. Heat levels above 350 degrees boiled the meat to a stringy, dry texture because the exterior overcooked before the interior was cooked and tender. The right oven temperature turned out to be 300 degrees—just enough heat to keep the meat at a low simmer while high enough to shave a few minutes off the cooking time.

REDUCE, REDUCE, REDUCE Some recipes thicken the pot roast sauce with a mixture of butter and flour or a slurry of cornstarch mixed with a little braising liquid. Both techniques make the sauce more gravylike than we prefer, as well as diluting the flavor.

We like to remove the roast from the pot and reduce the liquid until the flavors are well concentrated and the texture is more substantial.

🔪 AT THE MEAT COUNTER

PREFERRED CUT Chuck-Eye Roast
Chuck-eye roast is also called boneless chuck roll or boneless chuck fillet (see page 34 for more information).

ALTERNATE CUT Top Blade Roast
Top blade roast is also known as chuck roast, first cut, blade roast, or top chuck roast (see page 33 for more information). Note that blade roast will take slightly longer to cook. Do not separate the roast into 2 pieces. Top blade should tied with kitchen twine before cooking so that it maintains an even shape and cooks evenly.

CLASSIC POT ROAST
SERVES 6 TO 8

Chilling the whole cooked pot roast overnight improves its flavor and makes it moister and easier to slice.

1	(3½- to 4-pound) boneless beef chuck-eye roast, pulled apart at seams and trimmed
	Kosher salt and pepper
2	tablespoons unsalted butter
2	onions, halved and sliced thin
1	large carrot, peeled and chopped
1	celery rib, chopped
2	garlic cloves, minced
2–3	cups beef broth
¾	cup dry red wine
1	tablespoon tomato paste
1	bay leaf
1	sprig fresh thyme, plus ¼ teaspoon chopped
1	tablespoon balsamic vinegar

1. Season pieces of meat with 1 tablespoon salt, place on wire rack set in rimmed baking sheet, and let stand at room temperature for 1 hour.

2. Adjust oven rack to lower-middle position and heat oven to 300 degrees. Melt butter in Dutch oven over medium heat. Add onions and cook, stirring occasionally, until softened and beginning to brown, 8 to 10 minutes. Add carrot and celery; continue to cook, stirring occasionally, for about 5 minutes. Add garlic and cook until fragrant, about 30 seconds. Stir in 1 cup broth, ½ cup wine, tomato paste, bay leaf, and thyme sprig; bring to simmer.

3. Pat meat dry with paper towels and season with pepper. Tie 3 pieces of kitchen twine around each piece of meat to create 2 evenly shaped roasts.

4. Nestle meat on top of vegetables. Cover pot tightly with large piece of aluminum foil and cover with lid; transfer pot to oven. Cook meat until fully tender and fork slips easily in and out of meat, 3½ to 4 hours, turning meat halfway through cooking.

5. Transfer roasts to carving board and tent loosely with foil. Strain liquid through fine-mesh strainer into 4-cup liquid measuring cup. Discard bay leaf and thyme sprig. Transfer vegetables to blender. Let liquid settle for 5 minutes, then skim fat; add broth to bring liquid amount to 3 cups. Add liquid to blender and process until smooth, about 2 minutes. Transfer sauce to medium saucepan and bring to simmer over medium heat.

6. Meanwhile, remove twine from roasts and slice against grain into ½-inch-thick slices. Transfer meat to serving platter. Stir remaining ¼ cup wine, chopped thyme, and vinegar into gravy and season with salt and pepper to taste. Spoon half of gravy over meat. Serve, passing remaining gravy separately.

TO MAKE AHEAD: Follow recipe through step 4, then transfer cooked roasts to large bowl. Strain and defat liquid and add broth to bring liquid amount to 3 cups; transfer liquid and vegetables to bowl with roasts, let cool for 1 hour, cover with plastic wrap, cut vents in plastic with paring knife, and refrigerate up to 2 days. One hour before serving, adjust oven rack to middle position and heat oven to 325 degrees. Slice roasts as directed, place in 13 by 9-inch baking dish, cover tightly with foil, and bake until heated through, about 45 minutes. Process liquid and vegetables in blender, bring gravy to simmer, and finish as directed.

CLASSIC POT ROAST WITH ROOT VEGETABLES

Add 1 pound carrots, peeled and cut into 2-inch pieces; 1 pound parsnips, peeled and cut into 2-inch pieces; and 1½ pounds russet potatoes, peeled and halved lengthwise, each half quartered, to Dutch oven after cooking beef for 3 hours. Continue to cook until meat is fully tender, 30 minutes to 1 hour longer. Transfer large pieces of carrot, parsnip, and potato to serving platter using slotted spoon, cover tightly with aluminum foil, and proceed with recipe as directed.

CLASSIC POT ROAST WITH MUSHROOM AND PRUNE GRAVY

Substitute ½ cup dark beer (porter or stout) for red wine in step 2. Add 1 ounce dried porcini mushrooms, rinsed, soaked for 1 hour, and drained, and ½ cup pitted prunes with broth and beer. While roast is resting, sauté 1 pound thinly sliced cremini mushrooms in 2 tablespoons butter until softened and lightly browned and add to finished gravy, along with ¼ cup dark beer instead of balsamic vinegar in step 6.

French-Style Pot Roast

✔ WHY THIS RECIPE WORKS

French-style pot roast is richer than its American cousin. With a recipe calling for an entire bottle of wine, we set out to make sure our French-style pot roast was flavorful—not boozy.

USE A NEW METHOD *Boeuf à la mode*— "beef in the latest fashion"—is a classic French recipe that dates to a time when a multiday recipe was the rule rather than the exception. Although boeuf à la mode bears some similarity to American pot roast, this elegant French dish relies heavily on wine for flavor, adds collagen-rich veal and pork parts for body, and has a separately prepared mushroom-onion garnish. Today's grain-fed beef gets little exercise and has much more marbling than the leaner, grass-fed beef eaten in France when this recipe was created. Therefore, we were able to simplify this dish and skip the traditional larding and marinating of the beef, yet still produce a tender pot roast in a suave, rich wine sauce with great body.

SALT THE BEEF We took our favorite pot roast cut, chuck-eye roast, and split it in half to expose (and remove) excess fat so we could guarantee an especially refined final product. We then salted the meat for an hour to ramp up the meaty flavor by drawing moisture out of the meat and forming a shallow brine.

REDUCE THE WINE In all of the classic recipes, the meat is marinated in a mixture of red wine and large-cut *mirepoix* (carrots, onions, and celery) for a significant period of time, up to three days in some cases. Testing various lengths of time, we found that the effect was superficial unless we were willing to invest at least two full days. Even then, the wine flavor penetrated only the outer part of the meat, and the vegetables didn't really add much. Frankly, the meat picked up so much wine flavor during the hours-long braising time that marinating didn't seem worth the effort. In fact, we felt that the meat picked up too much wine flavor as it cooked and ended up tasting sour and harsh. We fixed this problem by cooking the wine before braising the beef. When we combined the reduced wine with the beef broth and used this mixture as the braising liquid, we knew we'd got it right. The wine tasted complex and fruity, not sour and astringent. Reducing the wine before using it in this recipe also cut the alcohol content in the final dish.

PUT IT IN THE OVEN We cooked this pot roast, covered, in the oven and used aluminum foil to maintain a good seal. The steam that collected in the pot helped to cook the meat slowly and evenly.

MAKE IT THICK AND GLOSSY Compared with regular pot roast braising liquid, which is flavorful but relatively thin and brothy, the sauce that accompanies boeuf à la mode is richer and more akin to a sauce that might be found on a steak at a fine restaurant. Adding some flour to the sautéed onion and garlic helped with the overall consistency, but the sauce still needed body. Instead of adding pork rind, split calves' feet, or veal bones, which were called for in some recipes, we went straight to the source: powdered gelatin. Adding powdered gelatin after the sauce finished reducing gave us the results we wanted: a rich and velvety sauce, on par with the best classic recipes out there.

🔪 AT THE MEAT COUNTER

PREFERRED CUT Chuck-Eye Roast

Chuck-eye roast is also called boneless chuck roll or boneless chuck fillet (see page 34 for more information).

ALTERNATE CUT Top Blade Roast

Top blade roast is also known as chuck roast, first cut, blade roast, or top chuck roast (see page 33 for more information). Note that blade roast will take slightly longer to cook.

see page 34; see page 33

RED WINE FOR COOKING

What's the best type of red wine to use for cooking? To find out, we tested more than 30 bottles—from $5 jug wines to a $30 Bordeaux—using each to make a hearty tomato sauce, a quick-cooking pan sauce, and a slow-simmered beef stew.

When the dust settled, we were able to divine a few general guidelines. First, save the expensive wine for drinking. Although one or two tasters perceived "greater complexity" in the pan sauces made with the $30 bottles, the differences were minimal at best; wines that cost $10 and under are usually fine for cooking. Second, stick with blends like Côtes du Rhône or generically labeled "table" wines that use a combination of grapes to yield a balanced, fruity finish. If you prefer single grape varietals, choose medium-bodied wines, such as Pinot Noir and Merlot. Steer clear of oaky wines like Cabernet Sauvignon, which turn bitter when cooked. Finally, whatever you do, avoid the "cooking wines" sold in supermarkets. These low-alcohol concoctions have little flavor, a high-pitched acidity, and enormous amounts of salt, all of which combine to produce inedible dishes.

Do not separate the roast into 2 pieces. Top blade should tied with kitchen twine before cooking so that it maintains an even shape and cooks evenly.

FRENCH-STYLE POT ROAST
SERVES 6 TO 8

A medium-bodied, fruity red wine, such as a Côtes du Rhône or Pinot Noir, is best for this recipe. The gelatin lends richness and body to the finished sauce; don't omit it. Serve this dish with boiled potatoes, buttered noodles, or steamed rice.

1	(4- to 5-pound) boneless beef chuck-eye roast, pulled apart at seams and trimmed
	Kosher salt and pepper
1	(750-ml) bottle red wine
10	sprigs fresh parsley, plus 2 tablespoons minced
2	sprigs fresh thyme
2	bay leaves
3	slices thick-cut bacon, cut into ¼-inch pieces
1	onion, chopped fine
3	garlic cloves, minced
1	tablespoon all-purpose flour
2	cups beef broth
4	carrots, peeled and cut on bias into 1½-inch pieces
2	cups frozen pearl onions, thawed
¾	cup water
3	tablespoons unsalted butter
2	teaspoons sugar
10	ounces white mushrooms, trimmed and halved if small and quartered if large
1	tablespoon unflavored gelatin

1. Season pieces of meat with 2 teaspoons salt, place on wire rack set in rimmed baking sheet, and let rest at room temperature for 1 hour.

2. Meanwhile, bring wine to simmer in large saucepan over medium-high heat. Cook until reduced to 2 cups, about 15 minutes. Using kitchen twine, tie parsley sprigs, thyme sprigs, and bay leaves into bundle.

3. Pat beef dry with paper towels and season generously with pepper. Tie 3 pieces of kitchen twine around each piece of meat to keep it from falling apart.

4. Adjust oven rack to lower-middle position and heat oven to 300 degrees. Cook bacon in Dutch oven over medium-high heat, stirring occasionally, until crisp, 6 to 8 minutes. Using slotted spoon, transfer bacon to paper towel–lined plate and reserve. Pour off all but 2 tablespoons fat; return Dutch oven to medium-high heat and heat until fat begins to smoke. Add beef to pot and brown on all sides, 8 to 10 minutes total. Transfer beef to large plate and set aside.

5. Reduce heat to medium; add onion and cook, stirring occasionally, until beginning to soften, 2 to 4 minutes. Add garlic, flour, and reserved bacon; cook, stirring constantly, until fragrant, about 30 seconds. Add reduced wine, broth, and herb bundle, scraping bottom of pot to loosen browned bits. Return and any accumulated juices to pot; increase heat to high and bring liquid to simmer, then place large sheet of aluminum foil over pot and cover tightly with lid. Transfer pot to oven and cook, using tongs to turn beef every hour, until fork slips easily in and out of meat, 2½ to 3 hours, adding carrots to pot after 2 hours.

6. While meat cooks, bring pearl onions, ½ cup water, butter, and sugar to boil in 12-inch skillet over medium-high heat. Reduce heat to medium, cover, and cook until onions are tender, 5 to 8 minutes. Uncover, increase heat to medium-high, and cook until all liquid evaporates, 3 to 4 minutes. Add mushrooms and ¼ teaspoon salt; cook, stirring occasionally, until vegetables are browned and glazed, 8 to 12 minutes. Remove from heat and set aside. Place remaining ¼ cup water in small bowl and sprinkle gelatin on top.

7. Transfer beef to carving board; tent with foil to keep warm. Let braising liquid settle, about 5 minutes; using large spoon, skim fat from surface. Remove herb bundle and stir in onion-mushroom mixture. Bring liquid to simmer over medium-high heat and cook until

mixture is slightly thickened and reduced to 3¼ cups, 20 to 30 minutes. Season sauce with salt and pepper to taste. Add softened gelatin and stir until completely dissolved.

8. Remove twine from roasts and slice meat against grain into ½-inch-thick slices. Divide beef among warmed bowls or transfer to platter; arrange vegetables around meat, pour sauce over top, and sprinkle with minced parsley. Serve immediately.

TO MAKE AHEAD: Follow recipe through step 7, skipping step of softening and adding gelatin. Place meat back in pot, cool to room temperature, cover, and refrigerate for up to 2 days. To serve, slice beef and arrange in 13 by 9-inch baking dish with vegetables around meat. Bring sauce to simmer and stir in gelatin until completely dissolved. Pour warm sauce over meat, cover with foil, and bake in 350-degree oven until heated through, about 30 minutes.

Beef Braised in Barolo

✓ **WHY THIS RECIPE WORKS**

Beef in Barolo can be the ultimate pot roast—or it can be a very expensive mistake. We wanted a foolproof recipe that would be well worth the $30 bottle of wine.

CHOOSE CHUCK The traditional Italian method for braising beef in Barolo calls for a tough cut that is slowly braised in the famed Piedmontese wine. We had our doubts about pairing an inexpensive pot roast with expensive wine, but when we tried other cuts in initial tests, none measured up to our favorite cut for pot roast, the chuck-eye roast. In order to rid the roast of excess pockets of unsightly fat and connective tissue, we split the roast in two and trimmed some of the fat from the center seam. For added flavor, we browned the roast in rendered pancetta fat.

BRAVO, BAROLO Made from Nebbiolo grapes in the Northern Italian region of Piedmont, Barolo is unapologetically bold, full-bodied, and tannic. But the robust flavor was challenging to work with; we needed to temper the wine without muddying it or dulling its flavor. Drained diced tomatoes provided the balance of sweet, salty, hearty flavor that the dish needed.

REDUCE YOUR SAUCE We took advantage of the resting time of the meat to elevate our sauce to a level worthy of this dish. By straining out the vegetables and reducing the sauce to 1½ cups, we were able to achieve a dark, lustrous sauce reminiscent of something you might serve over a good steak.

🔪 **AT THE MEAT COUNTER**

PREFERRED CUT Chuck-Eye Roast

Chuck-eye roast is also called boneless chuck roll or boneless chuck fillet (see page 34 for more information).

ALTERNATE CUT Top Blade Roast

Top blade roast is also known as chuck roast, first cut, blade roast, or top chuck roast (see page 33 for more information). Note that blade roast will take slightly longer to cook. Do not separate the roast into 2 pieces. Top blade should tied with kitchen twine before cooking so that it maintains an even shape and cooks evenly.

BEEF BRAISED IN BAROLO
SERVES 6

Purchase pancetta that is cut to order, about ¼ inch thick. If pancetta is not available, substitute an equal amount of meaty salt pork, cut it into ¼-inch cubes, and boil it in 3 cups of water for about

2 minutes to remove excess salt. After draining, use it as you would the pancetta. Use a Dutch oven or large pot that holds at least 8 quarts for this recipe.

1	(3½-pound) boneless beef chuck-eye roast, pulled apart at seams and trimmed
	Salt and pepper
4	ounces pancetta, cut into ¼-inch cubes
2	onions, chopped
2	carrots, peeled and chopped
2	celery ribs, chopped
1	tablespoon tomato paste
3	garlic cloves, minced
1	tablespoon all-purpose flour
½	teaspoon sugar
1	(750-ml) bottle Barolo wine
1	(14.5-ounce) can diced tomatoes, drained
10	sprigs fresh parsley
1	sprig fresh rosemary
1	sprig fresh thyme, plus 1 teaspoon minced

1. Adjust oven rack to middle position heat oven to 300 degrees. Pat beef dry with paper towels, season with salt and pepper. Tie 3 pieces of kitchen twine around each piece of meat to keep from falling apart. Place pancetta in 8-quart Dutch oven; cook over medium heat, stirring occasionally, until browned and crisp, about 8 minutes. Using slotted spoon, transfer pancetta to paper towel–lined plate and set aside. Pour off all but 2 tablespoons fat; set Dutch oven over medium-high heat and heat until beginning to smoke. Add beef to pot and cook until well browned on all sides, about 8 minutes. Transfer beef to large plate and set aside.

2. Reduce heat to medium, add onions, carrots, celery, and tomato paste to now-empty pot and cook, stirring occasionally, until vegetables begin to soften and brown, about 6 minutes. Add garlic, flour, sugar, and reserved pancetta; cook, stirring constantly, until fragrant, about 30 seconds. Add wine and tomatoes, scraping bottom of pan to loosen browned bits; add parsley, rosemary, and thyme sprigs. Return roast and any accumulated juices to pot; increase heat to high and bring liquid to boil, then place large sheet of aluminum foil over pot and cover tightly with lid. Set pot in oven and cook, using tongs to turn beef every 45 minutes, until fork slips easily in and out of meat, about 3 hours.

3. Transfer beef to carving board; tent with foil to keep warm. Let braising liquid settle, about 5 minutes; using large spoon, skim fat from surface. Add minced thyme, bring liquid to boil over high heat, and cook, whisking vigorously to help vegetables break down, until mixture is thickened and reduced to about 3½ cups, about 18 minutes. Strain liquid through large fine-mesh strainer, pressing on solids to extract as much liquid as possible; you should have 1½ cups strained sauce (if necessary, return strained sauce to Dutch oven and reduce to 1½ cups). Discard solids in strainer. Season sauce with salt and pepper to taste.

4. Remove twine from roasts and discard. Slice meat against grain into ½-inch-thick slices. Divide meat among warmed bowls or plates; pour about ¼ cup sauce over top and serve immediately.

TO MAKE AHEAD: Follow recipe through step 2. Let cool to room temperature, cover, and refrigerate for up to 2 days. To serve, skim fat from surface and gently warm until meat is heated through. Proceed with recipe from step 3.

Braised Boneless Beef Short Ribs

✓ WHY THIS RECIPE WORKS

Braised short ribs are a warm, hearty dinner on a cold day. We wanted to cut the usual long cooking time to only a few hours, and get a silky, grease-free sauce to accompany our ribs.

SIZE DOES MATTER To eliminate hours of cooking, we started with boneless short ribs. Butchers typically divide short ribs into sections about 10 inches square and 3 to 5 inches thick. Cutting the ribs between the bones and into lengths between 2 and 6 inches yields what butchers call "English"-style short ribs, a cut typically found in European braises. Cutting the meat across the bone yields the "flanken" cut, more typically found in Asian cuisines. We focused on the widely available English-style short ribs but found that the smallest (about 2 inches) were too short; once braised, they shrunk into pieces resembling stew meat. At the other extreme, the 6- to 8-inchers were fairly unwieldy to brown in the pan. We split the difference and settled on 4-inch-long ribs.

BROWN WELL The first step in most braises is browning the meat, since searing adds color and flavor. But here, searing also rid the ribs of some of their excess fat by rendering. The boneless ribs made less fat than bone-in ribs would, which allowed us to simply skim the sauce at the end of cooking. To make up for the viscosity usually provided by the bones, we added gelatin.

FLAVOR ACTION To jump-start the flavor of our sauce, we reduced the wine right over the browned aromatics, which added an intensity and depth. Still in need of more liquid for the braise, however, we found that beef broth offered a nice flavor balance to the wine.

BRAISED BONELESS BEEF SHORT RIBS
SERVES 6

Meaty English-style short ribs are preferred in this recipe over thinner-cut flanken-style ribs (see page 40 for more information). Make sure that the ribs are at least 4 inches long and 1 inch thick. If boneless ribs are unavailable, substitute 7 pounds of bone-in beef short ribs at least 4 inches long with 1 inch of meat above the bone. We recommend a bold red wine such as a Cabernet Sauvignon. Serve with buttered egg noodles, mashed potatoes, or roasted potatoes.

3½	pounds English-style boneless beef short ribs, trimmed
	Kosher salt and pepper
2	tablespoons vegetable oil
2	large onions, sliced thin
1	tablespoon tomato paste
6	garlic cloves, peeled
2	cups red wine
1	cup beef broth
4	large carrots, peeled and cut into 2-inch pieces
4	sprigs fresh thyme
1	bay leaf
¼	cup water
½	teaspoon unflavored gelatin

1. Adjust oven rack to lower-middle position and heat oven to 300 degrees. Pat beef dry with paper towels and season with 2 teaspoons salt and 1 teaspoon pepper. Heat 1 tablespoon oil in Dutch oven over medium-high heat until smoking. Add half of beef and cook, without moving, until well browned, 4 to 6 minutes. Turn beef and continue to cook on second side until well browned, 4 to

6 minutes longer, reducing heat if fat begins to smoke. Transfer beef to medium bowl. Repeat with remaining 1 tablespoon oil and remaining meat.

2. Reduce heat to medium, add onions, and cook, stirring occasionally, until softened and beginning to brown, 12 to 15 minutes. (If onions begin to darken too quickly, add 1 to 2 tablespoons water to pan.) Add tomato paste and cook, stirring constantly, until it browns on sides and bottom of pan, about 2 minutes. Add garlic and cook until fragrant, about 30 seconds. Increase heat to medium-high, add wine and simmer, scraping bottom of pan to loosen browned bits, until reduced by half, 8 to 10 minutes. Add broth, carrots, thyme sprigs, and bay leaf. Add beef and any accumulated juices to pot; cover and bring to simmer. Transfer pot to oven and cook, turning meat twice during cooking, until fork slips easily in and out of meat, 2 to 2½ hours.

3. Place water in small bowl and sprinkle gelatin on top; let stand at least 5 minutes. Using tongs, transfer meat and carrots to serving platter and tent with aluminum foil. Strain cooking liquid through fine-mesh strainer into fat separator or bowl, pressing on solids to extract as much liquid as possible; discard solids. Let liquid settle for 5 minutes and skim fat. Return cooking liquid to pot and cook over medium heat until reduced to 1 cup, 5 to 10 minutes. Remove from heat and stir in gelatin mixture; season with salt and pepper to taste. Pour sauce over meat and serve.

BRAISED BONELESS BEEF SHORT RIBS WITH GUINNESS AND PRUNES

Substitute 1 cup Guinness (or other full-flavored porter or stout) for red wine and omit wine reduction time in step 2. Add ⅓ cup pitted prunes to pot along with broth.

FOUR STEPS TO BRAISED BRISKET

1. Use Dutch oven or cast-iron skillet to weight meat as it browns.

2. Carefully pour sauce and onions into foil-lined baking dish.

3. Place brisket on top of sauce, fat side up, nestling meat into liquid and onions.

4. Fold flaps of foil to wrap brisket securely, but do not wrap too tightly.

Onion-Braised Beef Brisket

✓ WHY THIS RECIPE WORKS

When this notoriously tough cut finally turns tender, it's often dried out, and cuts in shreds rather than slices. We wanted tender, moist meat that we could slice neatly, even after hours of unattended cooking.

BUY THE RIGHT CUT Beef brisket is usually sold in two pieces, the flat (or first) cut and the point cut. The flat cut is leaner and thinner, with a rectangular shape and an exterior fat cap. It is more commonly available at supermarkets than the point cut, which has an oblong, irregular shape and contains large interior pockets of fat. We found the point cut to be marginally more flavorful but, more important, much less prone to drying out, thanks to all that extra fat. Unfortunately, more than a few tasters found the point cut too fatty to enjoy, and it was next to impossible to carve it into neat slices. The flat cut is easier to sear and to slice, provided it has cooled. Butchers usually trim away some or all of the fat cap, but try to find one with at least ¼ inch of fat in place, as it will help to keep the meat moist during cooking. If the fat cap is very thick and untrimmed in places, cut it down to a thickness of about ¼ inch. A flat-cut brisket roast usually weighs between 4 and 5 pounds, though butchers occasionally cut them into smaller 2- to 3-pound roasts. You can substitute two of these smaller cuts if that is all that is available, although the cooking time may vary.

USE HEAVY-DUTY FOIL For this braise, we used 18-inch-wide heavy-duty aluminum

THE TRUTH ABOUT BRAISING

It's a common misconception that braising—cooking food half-submerged in liquid in a covered pot at low heat—results in moister meat than dry cooking methods do. The reality is that despite the wet conditions, braising does not add moisture to meat. To see the dynamic at work for ourselves, we set up a test designed to simulate braising. We placed samples of beef chuck, along with measured amounts of broth, in individual vacuum-sealed bags to eliminate the possibility of evaporation. We then submerged the bags in water held at 190 degrees (the temperature of a typical braise) for 1½ hours. We found that the weight of the meat decreased an average of 12.5 percent during cooking while the volume of liquid increased, demonstrating that moisture had been pulled from the meat into the surrounding liquid, not the other way around.

So why, then, does braised meat seem so moist? Gentle cooking helps break down the meat's connective tissue and collagen, which lubricate and tenderize its fibers. The resulting soft, tender texture is (mistakenly) perceived as moist.

foil to seal in the brisket as it cooks. It was essential to create a tight seal around the meat so that it could cook in the even heat of the simmering liquid, but also in the heat of the steam collecting in the closed container. The steam generated in the foil package helped the meat reach a higher temperature relatively quickly. This melted the collagen and kept the meat moist, despite its lack of fat. Be careful not to crimp the foil too tightly when you enclose the brisket—you will need to open it later when checking for doneness.

CHICKEN OR BEEF? Though many recipes call for the use of beef broth in the braising liquid of brisket, we've found most canned beef broths to taste salty and artificial. In testing this recipe, we found that testers preferred chicken to beef broth for its cleaner flavor. To boost the flavor of the sauce, we added red wine.

REST OVERNIGHT We find it's preferable to leave the brisket in the refrigerator overnight. Not only does it produce a juicier, more tender brisket, but it also allows you to slice the meat without it falling apart or shredding. This is perfect if you're cooking brisket for a crowd: Making this dish a day ahead reduces the stress of timing in the kitchen and the neatly sliced brisket creates a much more elegant spread on the serving platter.

FINISH THE SAUCE While we were testing this recipe, a debate sprang up in the test kitchen over the proper thickness of the finished sauce. "Gravy" enthusiasts wanted a thick sauce that would cling to the meat, while their opponents backed a thinner, more natural jus. But everyone agreed that too much flour, stirred into the skillet while building the sauce, resulted in a sauce that was overly pasty; just 2 tablespoons was enough to give it the proper body. To further thicken the sauce, we put it back on the stove to simmer while slicing the finished brisket. Just before serving, we added a couple of teaspoons of cider vinegar to brighten the flavor.

ONION-BRAISED BEEF BRISKET
SERVES 6 TO 8

For more information on brisket, see page 39. This recipe requires a few hours of unattended cooking as well as advance preparation. After cooking, the brisket must stand overnight in the braising liquid that later becomes the sauce; this helps to keep the brisket moist and flavorful. Defatting the sauce is essential. If you prefer a spicy sauce, increase the amount of cayenne pepper to ¼ teaspoon. You will need 18-inch-wide heavy-duty aluminum foil for this recipe. Good accompaniments to braised brisket include mashed potatoes and buttered egg noodles. Matzo meal or potato starch can be substituted for the flour.

1	(4- to 5- pound) beef brisket, flat cut, fat trimmed to ¼ inch
	Salt and pepper
	Vegetable oil
2½	pounds onions, halved and sliced ½ inch thick
1	tablespoon packed brown sugar
3	garlic cloves, minced
1	tablespoon tomato paste
1	tablespoon paprika
⅛	teaspoon cayenne pepper
2	tablespoons all-purpose flour
1	cup chicken broth
1	cup dry red wine
3	bay leaves
3	sprigs fresh thyme
2	teaspoons cider vinegar

1. Adjust oven rack to lower-middle position and heat oven to 300 degrees. Line 13 by 9-inch baking dish with two 24-inch-long sheets of 18-inch-wide heavy-duty aluminum foil, positioning sheets perpendicular to each other and allowing excess foil to extend beyond edges of pan. Pat brisket dry with paper towels. Place brisket, fat side up, on cutting board; using dinner fork, poke holes

in meat through fat layer about 1 inch apart. Season both sides of brisket with salt and pepper.

2. Heat 1 teaspoon oil in 12-inch skillet over medium-high heat until oil just begins to smoke. Place brisket, fat side up, in skillet (brisket may climb up sides of pan); weight brisket with heavy Dutch oven or cast-iron skillet and cook until well browned, about 7 minutes. Remove Dutch oven; using tongs, flip brisket and cook on second side without weight until well browned, about 7 minutes longer. Transfer brisket to platter.

3. Pour off all but 1 tablespoon fat from pan (or, if brisket was lean, add enough oil to fat in skillet to equal 1 tablespoon); stir in onions, sugar, and ¼ teaspoon salt and cook over medium-high heat, stirring occasionally, until onions are softened, 10 to 12 minutes. Add garlic and cook, stirring frequently, until fragrant, about 1 minute; add tomato paste and cook, stirring to combine, until paste darkens, about 2 minutes. Add paprika and cayenne and cook, stirring constantly, until fragrant, about 1 minute. Add flour and cook, stirring constantly, until well combined, about 2 minutes. Add broth, wine, bay leaves, and thyme sprigs, stirring to scrape up browned bits from pan; bring to simmer and simmer for 5 minutes to fully thicken.

4. Pour sauce and onions into foil-lined baking dish. Nestle brisket, fat side up, in sauce and onions. Fold foil extensions over and seal (do not tightly crimp foil because foil must later be opened to test for doneness). Place in oven and cook until fork slips easily in and out of meat, 3½ to 4 hours (when testing for doneness, open foil with caution as contents will be steaming). Carefully open foil and let brisket cool at room temperature, 20 to 30 minutes.

5. Transfer brisket to large bowl; set fine-mesh strainer over bowl and strain sauce over brisket. Discard bay leaves and thyme sprigs from onions and transfer onions to small bowl. Cover both bowls with plastic wrap, cut vents in plastic, and refrigerate overnight.

6. About 45 minutes before serving, adjust oven rack to lower-middle position; heat oven to 350 degrees. While oven heats, transfer cold brisket to carving board. Scrape off and discard any fat from surface of sauce, then heat sauce in medium saucepan over medium heat until warm, skimming any fat on surface with wide shallow spoon (you should have about 2 cups sauce without onions; if necessary, simmer sauce over medium-high heat until reduced to 2 cups). Slice brisket against grain into ¼-inch-thick slices and place slices in 13 by 9-inch baking dish. Stir reserved onions and vinegar into warmed sauce and season with salt and pepper to taste. Pour sauce over brisket slices, cover baking dish with foil, and bake until heated through, 25 to 30 minutes. Serve immediately.

SAME-DAY ONION-BRAISED BEEF BRISKET

After removing brisket from oven in step 4, reseal foil and let brisket sit at room temperature for 1 hour. Transfer brisket to carving board and continue with straining, defatting, and reheating sauce and slicing meat; omit step of returning brisket to oven once reheated sauce is poured over it.

Chuck Roast in Foil

✔ WHY THIS RECIPE WORKS

Traditionally, this lazy cook's pot roast involves rubbing a chuck roast with onion soup mix, wrapping it in foil, and cooking it in the oven until tender. While we liked the ease of this dish, we weren't fans of its artificial, salty taste. We wanted a more complex flavor with all the simplicity of the original.

DITCH THE ONION SOUP MIX In the recipes we tried, the prefab onion soup packets made our pot roast stringy, greasy, and very salty. We traded out the artificial-tasting packet for a homemade rub. We started with onion powder, salt, and sugar—like the packet—but gave our rub a flavor boost with dried thyme and celery seeds. For extra depth, we switched the white sugar for brown sugar, and added a bit of espresso powder for a deep, toasty note.

ADD TWO SECRET INGREDIENTS We added cornstarch to the rub as well, which helped our roast brown. The monosodium glutamate found in the soup mix packet had to go, but we needed a replacement for its glutamates, which gave the roast a savory, meaty flavor. We found one in soy sauce, which improved the flavor of the jus tremendously.

LOWER THE HEAT Following the conventional "wisdom" of roasting at 350 degrees produced stringy, dry roasts. We lowered the temperature to 300 degrees and, to shorten the cooking time, we cut the roast in half. The two smaller roasts needed only about 4½ hours to cook, and the added surface area allowed us to apply even more of our flavorful rub.

ADD VEGETABLES In addition to adding flavor and volume to our jus, roasting vegetables along with the meat made for a convenient side dish. Choosing sturdy vegetables and cutting them into large chunks was essential for getting veggies that were tender but firm, not mushy, after hours of cooking.

🔪 AT THE MEAT COUNTER

PREFERRED CUT Chuck-Eye Roast
Chuck-eye roast is also called boneless chuck roll or boneless chuck fillet (see page 34 for more information).

ALTERNATE CUT Top Blade Roast
Top blade roast is also known as chuck roast, first cut, blade roast, or top chuck roast (see page 33 for more information). Note that blade roast will take slightly longer to cook. Do not separate the roast into 2 pieces. Top blade should tied with kitchen twine before cooking so that it maintains an even shape and cooks evenly.

CHUCK ROAST IN FOIL
SERVES 4 TO 6

You will need 18-inch-wide heavy-duty aluminum foil for wrapping the roast. We prefer to use small red potatoes, measuring 1 to 2 inches in diameter, in this recipe.

RUB
- 3   tablespoons cornstarch
- 4   teaspoons onion powder
- 2   teaspoons packed light brown sugar
- 2   teaspoons salt
- 1   teaspoon pepper
- 1   teaspoon garlic powder
- 1   teaspoon instant espresso powder
- 1   teaspoon dried thyme
- ½   teaspoon celery seeds

CHUCK ROAST
- 1   (4-pound) boneless beef chuck-eye roast, pulled apart at seams, fat trimmed to ¼ inch, and tied at 1-inch intervals
- 2   onions, quartered
- 1   pound small red potatoes, quartered

4   carrots, peeled and cut into 1½-inch
    pieces
2   bay leaves
2   tablespoons soy sauce

1. FOR THE RUB: Adjust oven rack to lower-middle position and heat oven to 300 degrees. Combine all ingredients in small bowl.

2. FOR THE CHUCK ROAST: Pat roast dry with paper towels. Place two 30 by 18-inch sheets of heavy-duty aluminum foil perpendicular to each other inside large roasting pan. Place onions, potatoes, carrots, and bay leaves in center of foil and drizzle with soy sauce. Set roasts on top of vegetables. Rub roasts all over with rub. Fold opposite corners of foil toward each other and crimp edges tightly to seal. Transfer pan to oven and cook until meat is completely tender, about 4½ hours.

3. Remove roasts from foil pouch and place on carving board. Tent meat with foil and let rest for 20 minutes. Remove onions and bay leaves. Using slotted spoon, place carrots and potatoes on serving platter. Strain contents of roasting pan through fine-mesh strainer into fat separator. Let liquid settle, then pour defatted pan juices into serving bowl.

4. Remove kitchen twine from roasts. Slice roasts thin against grain and transfer to platter with vegetables. Pour ½ cup pan juices over meat. Serve with remaining pan juices.

Corned Beef and Cabbage

✓ WHY THIS RECIPE WORKS

We wanted to take an ordinary supermarket corned beef, throw away the seasoning packet, and figure out a better way to add flavor. To go with it, we wanted tender, well-seasoned vegetables.

GIVE IT A RINSE Corned beef can be punishingly salty. While some recipes recommend removing some of the salt by bringing the beef to a boil in water, then setting it off heat to soak for an hour or so, we found a simpler method—just rinse the beef under cold running water before cooking.

SWAP OUT THE SEASONING PACKET The seasoning packets that are packaged with supermarket corned beef are listless at best. For a braising liquid with fresh, clean, bright flavor we used equal parts water and chicken broth (all broth turned the liquid too salty), then added carrots, celery, onion, bay leaves, peppercorns, thyme, and allspice to the braising liquid.

BAKE, DON'T BOIL Most recipes we'd come across for corned beef boiled the meat on the stovetop (and boiled and boiled). But in the test kitchen, we often prefer the gentle heat of the oven for braises, so we ditched the burner for the low, even temperature of a 300-degree oven.

MOISTEN THE MEAT Once the meat was out of the oven, we poured some of the defatted cooking liquid over it, covered the dish with foil, and let the meat rest and soak up more flavor while we turned to the vegetables.

SIMMER AND SERVE Cooking the vegetables along with the meat was a nonstarter. We wanted to retain the vegetables' flavor as much as possible, so while the meat rested, we added the vegetables (and a little butter) to the cooking liquid—small red potatoes went in first, followed by carrots and cabbage wedges—and simmered them until just tender.

CORNED BEEF AND CABBAGE
SERVES 6 TO 8

Use flat-cut corned beef brisket, not point-cut; it's more uniform in shape and thus will cook more evenly (see page 39 for more information).

When slicing the cabbage, leave the core intact or the cabbage will fall apart during cooking.

- 1 (4- to 5-pound) corned beef brisket roast, rinsed, fat trimmed to ¼ inch thick
- 4 cups chicken broth
- 4 cups water
- 12 carrots, peeled (3 chopped, 9 halved crosswise)
- 2 celery ribs, chopped
- 1 onion, quartered
- 3 bay leaves
- 1 tablespoon black peppercorns
- 1 tablespoon minced fresh thyme
- 1 teaspoon allspice berries
- 3 tablespoons unsalted butter
- 1½ pounds small red potatoes
- 1 head green cabbage (2 pounds), cut into 8 (2-inch) wedges
  Pepper

1. Adjust oven rack to middle position and heat oven to 300 degrees. Combine beef, broth, water, chopped carrots, celery, onion, bay leaves, peppercorns, thyme, and allspice in Dutch oven. Cover and bake until fork slips easily in and out of meat, 4½ to 5 hours.

2. Transfer meat to 13 by 9-inch baking dish. Strain cooking liquid through fine-mesh strainer into large bowl, discard solids, and skim fat from liquid. Pour 1 cup cooking liquid over meat. Cover dish tightly with aluminum foil and let rest for 30 minutes.

3. Meanwhile, return remaining cooking liquid to Dutch oven, add butter, and bring to simmer over medium-high heat. Add potatoes and simmer until they begin to soften, about 10 minutes. Add carrot halves and cabbage, cover, and cook until tender, 10 to 15 minutes. With slotted spoon, transfer vegetables to serving platter and season with pepper to taste. (Discard cooking liquid.)

4. Transfer beef to carving board and slice against grain into ¼-inch-thick slices. Serve with vegetables.

TO MAKE AHEAD: Prepare corned beef through step 2. Refrigerate moistened beef and cooking liquid separately for up to 24 hours. To serve, adjust oven rack to middle position and heat oven to 350 degrees. Transfer meat to carving board and slice against grain into ¼-inch-thick slices and return to baking dish. Cover dish tightly with foil and bake until meat is heated through, about 25 minutes. While meat is heating, proceed with step 3.

Pot-au-Feu

✓ WHY THIS RECIPE WORKS

With the proliferation of exotic, chef-inspired recipes available to home cooks, classic dishes like the French boiled dinner have fallen by the wayside. We wanted to put this appealingly simple meal back on the menu.

THE RIGHT STUFF The simplicity of pot-au-feu means that there are no potent ingredients or flavorful sauces to mask mistakes, so every ingredient must be carefully chosen. Traditionally, this dish utilizes multiple cuts of beef—usually a boneless roast and a bone-in cut. We chose our favorite pot-roast meat, chuck-eye roast, to serve as the boneless roast. For the bone-in element, we decided to use both short ribs (for their rich, decadent meat) and beef shanks (for their flavorful marrow which melted into the broth). Traditional vegetables like potatoes, carrots, parsnips, and green beans were our favorites.

FLAVOR THE BROTH While bay leaves, garlic and peppercorns provided some flavor for our broth, we found that sweating the traditional French *mirepoix* elements (carrots, celery, and onions) gave our broth even

TYING THE MEAT FOR POT-AU-FEU

SHANKS: Cut four 1-foot pieces of kitchen twine for each shank. Wrap each piece of twine around shank and tie in center.

CHUCK ROAST: Cut two 2-foot pieces of kitchen twine. Wrap 1 piece around roast about 1 inch from bottom and tie with double knot. Snip off excess and repeat with second piece about 1 inch from top.

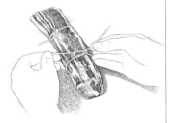

SHORT RIBS: Cut two 1-foot pieces of kitchen twine for each rib. Wrap 1 piece about 1 inch from top and tie with double knot. Snip off excess and repeat with second piece about 1 inch from bottom.

more depth and complexity. Parsley and thyme added freshness, and reducing the amount of water concentrated the flavor of the broth.

COOK THE VEGGIES SEPARATELY Adding pounds of veggies to our broth made it taste too much like vegetable soup—not what we were after. Instead, we cooked the vegetables separately in a pot of salted water, which made their flavors cleaner and brighter. Adding the vegetables to the water in batches, according to how long they took to cook through, gave us perfect tender veggies.

POT-AU-FEU
SERVES 8 TO 10

For more information on the cuts used in this recipe, see pages 34 and 40. A stockpot with at least a 12-quart capacity is necessary for this recipe. Cheesecloth is ideal for straining the broth, although a quadruple layer of paper towels will do in a pinch. Once the beef braise reaches a boil, reduce the heat to maintain a steady simmer; if left to boil, the resulting broth will be murky. We prefer to use small red potatoes, measuring 1 to 2 inches in diameter, in this recipe. Buy refrigerated prepared horseradish, not the shelf-stable kind, which contains preservatives and additives. For serving, arrange the meat and vegetables on a large warmed platter and give diners individual shallow soup bowls to serve themselves.

BEEF BRAISE
- 2 teaspoons vegetable oil
- 2 onions, chopped
- 2 carrots, peeled and chopped
- 1 celery rib, chopped
- 1 (3-pound) boneless beef chuck-eye roast, trimmed and tied
- 3 pounds beef short ribs (about 5 large ribs), trimmed and tied
- 2 pounds beef shanks, 1½ inches thick, trimmed and tied
- 3 bay leaves
- 1 teaspoon black peppercorns
- 5 cloves
- 1 large garlic head, outer papery skins removed and top third of head cut off and discarded
- 10 sprigs fresh parsley
- 8 sprigs fresh thyme
- 1 tablespoon salt

VEGETABLES
- 2 pounds small red potatoes, halved if larger than 1½ inches
- 2 tablespoons salt
- 1½ pounds carrots, peeled, halved crosswise, thicker half quartered lengthwise, thinner half halved lengthwise
- 1½ pounds parsnips, peeled, halved crosswise, thicker half quartered lengthwise, thinner half halved lengthwise
- 1 pound green beans, trimmed

GARNISHES AND CONDIMENTS
- ¼ cup chopped fresh parsley
- 1 (12-inch) baguette, sliced thick
  Dijon mustard or whole-grain mustard
  Sea salt
  Cornichons
  Prepared horseradish

1. FOR THE BEEF BRAISE: Combine oil, onions, carrots, and celery in large stockpot; cook, covered, over low heat, stirring frequently, until vegetables are softened but not browned, 8 to 10 minutes. (If vegetables begin to brown before softening, add 1 tablespoon water and continue to cook.) Add 5 quarts water, roast, ribs, shanks, bay leaves, peppercorns, and cloves; increase heat to medium-high and bring to boil, using large spoon to skim any fat. Reduce heat to low and simmer, uncovered, for 2½ hours, skimming surface of fat every 30 minutes.

2. Add garlic, parsley sprigs, thyme sprigs, and salt. Simmer until tip of paring knife inserted into meats meets little resistance, 1 to 1½ hours.

3. Using tongs, transfer roast, ribs, shanks, and garlic to large carving board and tent with aluminum foil. Strain broth through fine-mesh strainer lined with double layer of cheesecloth into large container (you should have about 12 cups liquid). Let broth settle for at least 5 minutes; using large spoon, skim fat from surface.

4. FOR THE VEGETABLES: While broth settles, rinse out stockpot and add 4 quarts water, potatoes, and salt; bring to boil over high heat and cook for 7 minutes. Add carrots and parsnips and cook for 3 minutes. Add green beans and cook for 4 minutes. Using slotted spoon, transfer vegetables to large serving platter and tent with foil.

5. Using tongs, squeeze garlic cloves out of skins and into small serving bowl. Remove kitchen twine from roast and separate roast at its seams; slice roast against grain into ½-inch-thick slices and transfer to platter with vegetables. Remove twine from shanks and ribs and arrange on platter. Ladle about 1 cup broth over meat and vegetables and sprinkle with chopped parsley. Serve, ladling broth over individual servings and passing garlic, baguette, and condiments separately.

Modern Beef Stew

✔ WHY THIS RECIPE WORKS

Even with hours of simmering, beef stew often falls flat. We wanted to amp up the flavor for a rich but approachable beef stew with tender meat, flavorful vegetables, and a luscious gravy that would justify the long cooking time.

CHUCK IS BEST Packaged "stew meat" from the supermarket usually consists of scraggly, uneven bits and pieces of meat—impossible to cook evenly. Chuck-eye roast is one of our favorite cuts for recipes that require a long cooking time, since it has good beefy flavor, turns meltingly tender when properly cooked, and is inexpensive, to boot. It doesn't take long to trim and cut a chuck-eye roast, and the results are well worth the small amount of extra time.

SEAR IN BATCHES If you crowd the pan, the meat steams in its own juices and never develops a flavorful browned exterior. Since we wanted to maximize beefy flavor, we cooked the meat in two batches and also added a variety of savory, glutamate-rich ingredients like tomato paste, salt pork, and anchovies.

USE GELATIN In long-cooked beef stews, the collagen in beef bones is transformed into gelatin, giving the stew a silky-smooth finish. Since we wanted to cut down on the amount of time needed to produce our stew, we mimicked the luxurious texture by adding gelatin.

🔪 AT THE MEAT COUNTER

PREFERRED CUT Chuck-Eye Roast

Chuck-eye roast is also called boneless chuck roll or boneless chuck fillet (see page 134 for more information).

ALTERNATE CUT Blade Steak

Blade steak is also known as top blade steak or flat-iron steak (see page 133 for more information). You can use 4 pounds of blade steaks, trimmed, instead of the chuck-eye roast. While the blade steak will yield slightly thinner pieces after trimming, it should still be cut into 1½-inch pieces. Note that the cooking time may vary.

MODERN BEEF STEW
SERVES 6 TO 8

Use a good-quality, medium-bodied wine, such as a Côtes du Rhône or Pinot Noir, for this stew. Try to find beef that is well marbled with white veins of fat. Meat that is too lean will come out slightly dry. Look for salt pork that is roughly 75 percent lean. If the pearl onions have a papery outer coating, remove it by rinsing them in warm water and gently squeezing individual onions between your fingertips.

FROZEN PEAS

In our years of recipe testing, we have come to depend on frozen peas. Not only are they more convenient than their fresh comrades, but they taste better. Test after test, we found frozen peas to be tender and sweet while fresh peas tasted starchy and bland. Trying to understand why, we looked to the frozen food industry for some answers.

Green peas are one of the oldest vegetables known to humankind. Yet despite this long history, they are relatively delicate; fresh peas have little stamina. Green peas lose a substantial portion of their nutrients within 24 hours of being picked. This rapid deterioration is the reason for the starchy, bland flavor of most "fresh" peas found at the grocery store. These not-so-fresh peas might be several days old, depending on where they came from and how long they were kept in the cooler.

Frozen peas, on the other hand, are picked, cleaned, sorted, and frozen within several hours of harvest, which helps to preserve their delicate sugars and flavors. When commercially frozen vegetables began to appear in the 1920s and 1930s, green peas were one of the first among them.

Finding good frozen peas is not hard. After tasting peas from the two major national frozen food purveyors along with some from a smaller organic company our panel of tasters found little difference among them. All of the peas were sweet and fresh, with a bright green color. So unless you grow your own or can stop by your local farm stand for fresh picked, you're better off cruising up the frozen food aisle for a bag of frozen peas.

2	garlic cloves, minced
4	anchovy fillets, rinsed and minced
I	tablespoon tomato paste
I	(4-pound) boneless beef chuck-eye roast, pulled apart at seams, trimmed, and cut into 1½-inch pieces
2	tablespoons vegetable oil
I	large onion, halved and sliced ⅛ inch thick
4	carrots, peeled and cut into 1-inch pieces
¼	cup all-purpose flour
2	cups red wine
2	cups chicken broth
4	ounces salt pork, rinsed
2	bay leaves
4	sprigs fresh thyme
I	pound Yukon Gold potatoes, cut into 1-inch pieces
1½	cups frozen pearl onions, thawed
2	teaspoons unflavored gelatin
½	cup water
I	cup frozen peas, thawed
	Salt and pepper

I. Adjust oven rack to lower-middle position and heat oven to 300 degrees. Combine garlic and anchovies in small bowl; press with back of fork to form paste. Stir in tomato paste and set aside.

2. Pat meat dry with paper towels. Do not season. Heat 1 tablespoon oil in Dutch oven over high heat until just starting to smoke. Add half of beef and cook until well browned on all sides, about 8 minutes. Transfer beef to large plate. Repeat with remaining beef and remaining 1 tablespoon oil, leaving second batch of meat in pot after browning.

3. Reduce heat to medium and return first batch of beef to pot. Stir in onion and carrots and cook, scraping bottom of pan to loosen browned bits, until onion is softened, 1 to 2 minutes. Add garlic mixture and cook, stirring constantly, until fragrant, about 30 seconds. Add flour and cook, stirring constantly, until no dry flour remains, about 30 seconds.

4. Slowly add wine, scraping bottom of pan to loosen browned bits. Increase heat to high and simmer until wine is thickened and slightly reduced, about 2 minutes. Stir in broth, pork, bay leaves, and thyme sprigs. Bring to simmer, cover, transfer to oven, and cook for 1½ hours.

5. Remove pot from oven; discard bay leaves, thyme sprigs, and salt pork. Stir in potatoes, cover, return to oven, and cook until potatoes are almost tender, about 45 minutes.

6. Using large spoon, skim fat from surface of stew. Stir in pearl onions; cook over medium heat until potatoes and onions are cooked through and fork slips easily in and out of beef (meat should not be falling apart), about 15 minutes. Meanwhile, sprinkle gelatin over water in small bowl and allow to soften for 5 minutes.

7. Increase heat to high, stir in softened gelatin mixture and peas; simmer until gelatin is fully dissolved and stew is thickened, about 3 minutes. Season with salt and pepper to taste; serve. (Stew can be refrigerated for up to 2 days.)

THREE WAYS TO SEPARATE AND SKIM FAT

A pitcher-style fat separator can be an indispensable tool. Our favorite, the Trudeau Gravy Separator with Integrated Strainer, has a sharply angled spout that allows the liquid portion of a stock or gravy to flow through, leaving behind the less-dense fat. But what if you don't have one, or need to defat a chunky stew? Forget about mopping up the surface with a lettuce leaf or paper towel. Both techniques are messy and require fresh replacements every few strokes. Here are three far more effective methods, in order of preference.

TOOLS	METHOD	BEST FOR
Cooking Spoon	Allow liquid to settle for about 10 minutes and use wide, shallow (1- to 2-ounce) spoon to skim fat from surface and deposit in another container. A tedious method, but it works very well.	Stock, gravy, stew
Zipper-Lock Bag	Fill heavy-duty zipper-lock bag with cooled liquid; allow fat to rise. Snip small hole in corner of bag and allow liquid to flow into another container. Pinch bag before fat flows out. Don't use this method with chunky stew or chili.	Stock
Bulb Baster	Plunge tip of baster into liquid beneath fat; draw liquid into baster. Deposit defatted liquid in another container.	Stock, gravy

Modern Beef Burgundy

✔ WHY THIS RECIPE WORKS

We wanted our boeuf bourguignon recipe to have tender braised beef and a silky, rich sauce with bold red wine flavor, but without all the work that the classic recipe requires.

ROASTING PAN TO THE RESCUE
Much of the time-consuming hands-on work in traditional beef burgundy recipes comes from the time spent searing the salt pork and beef over the stove before the stew goes into the oven. We wanted to figure out a way to skip this initial 40 minutes of work. From previous recipes, we knew that we could brown and braise meat at the same time by not submerging the meat fully in the braising liquid. When we tried this trick, it worked like a charm. To get even more flavorful browning on the meat, we decided to use a roasting pan. To further reduce hands-on time, we cranked the heat of the oven to brown the salt pork before adding the beef.

MAKE THE MOST OF YOUR OVEN
Rather than taking out two more pans and spending an hour babysitting the mushrooms and onions, we spread them out on a baking sheet with some butter and let the even heat of the oven do the work. A little bit of sugar aided caramelization.

ADD THE WINE IN BATCHES To punch up the flavor of the wine, we opted to add part of the bottle at the beginning, saving some to add to the final reduction of the sauce at the end. This brightened the wine's flavor without having to open a second bottle.

◥ AT THE MEAT COUNTER

PREFERRED CUT Chuck-Eye Roast
Chuck-eye roast is also called boneless chuck roll or boneless chuck fillet (see page 34 for more information).

ALTERNATE CUT Blade Steak
Blade steak is also known as top blade steak or flat-iron steak (see page 33 for more information). You can use 4 pounds of blade steaks,

trimmed, instead of the chuck-eye roast. While the blade steak will yield slightly thinner pieces after trimming, it should still be cut into 1½- to 2-inch pieces. Note that cooking time may vary.

MODERN BEEF BURGUNDY
SERVES 6 TO 8

If the pearl onions have a papery outer coating, remove it by rinsing them in warm water and gently squeezing individual onions between your fingertips. Two minced anchovy fillets can be used in place of the anchovy paste. To save time, salt the meat and let it stand while you prep the remaining ingredients. Serve with mashed potatoes or buttered noodles.

1	(4-pound) boneless beef chuck-eye roast, trimmed and cut into 1½- to 2-inch pieces, scraps reserved
	Salt and pepper
6	ounces salt pork, cut into ¼-inch pieces
3	tablespoons unsalted butter
1	pound cremini mushrooms, trimmed, halved if medium or quartered if large
1½	cups frozen pearl onions, thawed
1	tablespoon sugar
⅓	cup all-purpose flour
4	cups beef broth
1	(750-ml) bottle red Burgundy or Pinot Noir
5	teaspoons unflavored gelatin
1	tablespoon tomato paste
1	teaspoon anchovy paste
2	onions, chopped coarse
2	carrots, peeled and cut into 2-inch lengths
1	garlic head, cloves separated, unpeeled, and crushed
2	bay leaves
½	teaspoon black peppercorns
½	ounce dried porcini mushrooms, rinsed
10	sprigs fresh parsley, plus 3 tablespoons minced
6	sprigs fresh thyme

1. Toss beef and 1½ teaspoons salt together in bowl and let stand at room temperature for 30 minutes.

2. Adjust oven racks to lower-middle and lowest positions and heat oven to 500 degrees. Place salt pork, beef scraps, and 2 tablespoons butter in large roasting pan. Roast on upper rack until well browned and fat has rendered, 15 to 20 minutes.

3. While salt pork and beef scraps roast, toss cremini mushrooms, pearl onions, remaining 1 tablespoon butter, and sugar together on rimmed baking sheet. Roast on lower rack, stirring occasionally, until moisture released by mushrooms evaporates and vegetables are lightly glazed, 15 to 20 minutes. Transfer vegetables to large bowl, cover, and refrigerate.

4. Remove roasting pan from oven and reduce temperature to 325 degrees. Sprinkle flour over rendered fat and whisk until no dry flour remains. Whisk in broth, 2 cups wine, gelatin, tomato paste, and anchovy paste until combined. Add onions, carrots, garlic, bay leaves, peppercorns, porcini mushrooms, parsley sprigs, and thyme sprigs to pan. Arrange beef in single layer on top of vegetables. Add water as needed to come three-quarters up side of beef (beef should not be submerged). Return roasting pan to oven and cook until meat is tender, 3 to 3½ hours, stirring after 1½ hours and adding water to keep meat at least halfway submerged.

5. Using slotted spoon, transfer beef to bowl with cremini mushrooms and pearl onions; cover and set aside. Strain braising liquid through fine-mesh strainer set over large bowl, pressing on solids to extract as much liquid as possible; discard solids. Stir in remaining wine and let cooking liquid settle, 10 minutes. Using large spoon, skim fat.

6. Transfer liquid to Dutch oven and bring mixture to boil over medium-high heat. Simmer briskly, stirring occasionally, until sauce is thickened to consistency of heavy cream, 15 to 20 minutes. Reduce heat to medium-low, stir in beef and mushroom-onion garnish, cover, and cook until just heated through, 5 to 8 minutes. Season with salt and pepper to taste. Stir in minced parsley and serve. (Stew can be refrigerated for up to 3 days.)

Catalan-Style Beef Stew

✔ WHY THIS RECIPE WORKS

Catalan-style stews generally start with a slow-cooked tomato-onion jam known as sofrito *and end with a pesto-like paste of fried bread, herbs, and nuts known as* picada. *We wanted to build a recipe that would utilize the multilayered flavors and textures of this regional specialty.*

SHORT RIBS FOR LONG COOKING Although we generally use chuck-eye roast in beef stew recipes, we chose short ribs for this one. Short ribs are a more traditional choice for this dish, and become very tender with the long, slow simmer that this recipe requires. Additionally, their excellent beef flavor made them the perfect candidate for this stew.

GRATE YOUR TOMATOES Traditional sofritos consist of finely chopped onions, browned slowly over low heat until caramelized, and tomatoes. Adding a sprinkle of salt and sugar to the onions aided in caramelization, and we liked the brightness and acidity of fresh tomatoes. We didn't want to spend a lot of time blanching and peeling tomatoes, so we simplified the process by grating the pulpy flesh with a box grater and then simply discarding the leathery skins.

SKIP THE SHERRY Tasters found that sherry, a traditional addition, made the sauce too cloying. We decided instead to use a dry Spanish white wine called *Albariño*.

BRIGHTEN IT UP For a jolt of bright flavor, we used parsley, blanched almonds, and raw garlic to make a pungent picada. We found that chopping the parsley by hand provided better flavor than running it through the food processor. A splash of sherry vinegar at the end made for an extra-bright finish and complemented the warm spices of the stew.

CATALAN-STYLE BEEF STEW WITH MUSHROOMS

SERVES 4 TO 6

For more information on short ribs, see page 40. Remove the woody base of the oyster mushroom stems before cooking. An equal amount of quartered white mushrooms may be substituted for the oyster mushrooms. Serve the stew with boiled or mashed potatoes or rice.

STEW

- 2 tablespoons olive oil
- 2 large onions, chopped fine
- ½ teaspoon sugar
  Kosher salt and pepper
- 2 plum tomatoes, halved lengthwise, pulp grated on large holes of box grater, and skins discarded
- 1 teaspoon smoked paprika
- 1 bay leaf
- 1½ cups dry white wine
- 1½ cups water
- 1 large sprig fresh thyme
- ¼ teaspoon ground cinnamon
- 2½ pounds boneless beef short ribs, trimmed and cut into 2-inch cubes

PICADA

- 2 tablespoons olive oil
- ¼ cup whole blanched almonds
- 1 slice hearty white sandwich bread, crust removed, torn into 1-inch pieces
- 2 garlic cloves, peeled
- 3 tablespoons minced fresh parsley

- 8 ounces oyster mushrooms, trimmed
- 1 teaspoon sherry vinegar

1. FOR THE STEW: Adjust oven rack to middle position and heat oven to 300 degrees. Heat oil in Dutch oven over medium-low heat until shimmering. Add onions, sugar, and ½ teaspoon salt; cook, stirring often, until onions are deeply caramelized, 30 to 40 minutes. Add tomato, paprika, and bay leaf; cook, stirring often, until darkened and thick, 5 to 10 minutes.

2. Add wine, water, thyme sprig, and cinnamon to pot, scraping up any browned bits. Season beef with 1½ teaspoons salt and ½ teaspoon pepper and add to pot. Increase heat to high and bring to simmer. Transfer to oven and cook, uncovered. After 1 hour stir stew to redistribute meat, return to oven, and continue to cook until meat is tender, 1½ to 2 hours longer.

3. FOR THE PICADA: While stew is in oven, heat 1 tablespoon oil and almonds in 10-inch skillet over medium heat; cook, stirring often, until almonds are golden brown, 3 to 6 minutes. Using slotted spoon, transfer almonds to food processor. Return now-empty skillet to medium heat, add bread, and cook, stirring often, until toasted, 2 to 4 minutes; transfer to food processor with almonds. Add garlic to almonds and bread and process until mixture is finely ground, about 20 seconds, scraping down bowl as needed. Transfer mixture to separate bowl, stir in parsley, and set aside.

4. Return again-empty skillet to medium heat. Heat remaining 1 tablespoon oil until shimmering. Add mushrooms and ½ teaspoon salt; cook, stirring often, until tender, 5 to 7 minutes. Transfer to bowl and set aside.

5. Discard bay leaf and thyme sprig. Stir picada, mushrooms, and vinegar into stew. Season with salt and pepper to taste. Serve.

TO MAKE AHEAD: Follow recipe through step 3 and refrigerate for up to 3 days. To serve, add 1 cup water and reheat over medium heat. Proceed with step 4.

Hungarian Beef Stew

✔ WHY THIS RECIPE WORKS

The Americanized versions of Hungarian goulash bear little resemblance to the traditional dish. Mushrooms, green peppers, and most herbs have no place in the pot and sour cream is not authentic to the dish. We wanted the real deal—a simple dish of tender braised beef packed with paprika flavor.

MAKE PAPRIKA CREAM To achieve the desired level of spicy intensity, we create our own version of paprika cream, a condiment common in Hungarian cooking but hard to find in the United States. Pureeing the paprika with roasted red peppers, tomato paste, and vinegar imparted vibrant paprika flavor without any grittiness.

SKIP THE SEAR, NOT THE FLAVOR Most stews begin by browning meat on the stovetop to boost flavor. They also call for lots of added liquid. We decided to skip the extra step of searing since, over time, the dry top layer of meat will begin to brown in the oven. We stirred the meat every 30 minutes to expose new surfaces and promote as much slow browning as possible.

BE JUDICIOUS WITH THE BROTH For this stew, you'll notice that only one cup of broth is added to the stew. That's not a mistake—the meat cooks mostly in its own juices and liquid from the onions for a stew packed with concentrated meaty flavor.

🔪 AT THE MEAT COUNTER

PREFERRED CUT Chuck-Eye Roast

Chuck-eye roast is also called boneless chuck roll or boneless chuck fillet (see page 34 for more information).

ALTERNATE CUT Blade Steak

Blade steak is also known as top blade steak or flat-iron steak (see page 33 for more information). You can use 4 pounds of blade steaks, trimmed, instead of the chuck-eye roast. While the blade steak will yield slightly thinner pieces after trimming, it should still be cut

into 1½-inch pieces. Note that the cooking time may vary.

HUNGARIAN BEEF STEW
SERVES 6

Do not substitute hot, half-sharp, or smoked Spanish paprika for the sweet paprika in the stew, as they will compromise the flavor of the dish. Since paprika is vital to this recipe, it is best to use a fresh container. Cook the stew in a Dutch oven with a tight-fitting lid. (Alternatively, to ensure a tight seal, place a sheet of aluminum foil over the pot before adding the lid.) Serve the stew over boiled potatoes or buttered egg noodles.

1	(3½- to 4-pound) boneless beef chuck-eye roast, pulled apart at seams, trimmed, and cut into 1½-inch pieces
	Salt and pepper
⅓	cup paprika
1	cup jarred roasted red peppers, rinsed and patted dry
2	tablespoons tomato paste
1	tablespoon distilled white vinegar
2	tablespoons vegetable oil
4	large onions, chopped fine
4	large carrots, peeled and cut into 1-inch pieces
1	bay leaf
1	cup beef broth, warmed
¼	cup sour cream (optional)

1. Adjust oven rack to lower-middle position and heat oven to 325 degrees. Season meat evenly with 1 teaspoon salt and let stand for 15 minutes. Process paprika, roasted peppers, tomato paste, and 2 teaspoons vinegar in food processor until smooth, 1 to 2 minutes, scraping down sides of bowl as needed.

2. Combine oil, onions, and 1 teaspoon salt in Dutch oven; cover and set over medium heat. Cook, stirring occasionally, until onions soften but have not yet begun to

PAPRIKA PRIMER

"Paprika" is a generic term for a spice made from ground dried red peppers. Whether paprika is labeled sweet, smoked, or hot is determined by the variety (or varieties) of pepper used and how the pepper is manipulated.

Sweet paprika (sometimes called "Hungarian paprika" or simply "paprika") is the most common. Typically made from a combination of mild red peppers, sweet paprika is prized more for its deep scarlet hue than for its very subtle flavor.

Smoked paprika, a Spanish favorite, is produced by drying peppers (either sweet or hot) over smoldering oak embers. Since smoked paprika has a deep, musky flavor all its own, we do not recommend using it for all paprika applications; it is best used to season grilled meats or to add a smoky aroma to boldly flavored dishes.

Hot paprika, most often used in chilis, curries, or stews, can be made from any number of hot peppers. It can range from slightly spicy to punishingly assertive, and it shouldn't be substituted for sweet paprika in cooking. On the other hand, sweet paprika can be substituted for hot by simply adding cayenne pepper to boost the burn.

When making carbonnade,
purists will settle for nothing
less than a traditional copper-
colored Belgian ale with fruity,
spicy aromas and a pleasant
hoppy bitterness—our favorite is Chimay Pères Trappistes
Ale Première. But is it the
only choice? To find out, we
pulled together nine different
styles of beer, ranging from
a dark, full-bodied stout to a
nonalcoholic brew. We even
included Bud Light (after all, it
was already in the fridge).

After a few hours in the
oven, the flavors you taste
straight from the bottle are
concentrated and easily recognized in this stew. Our tasters preferred beers that pos-
sessed plenty of sweetness
matched with moderate bitterness. Light-bodied beers,
like Bud Light, were noted for
a mild sweetness but lacked
the contrasting bitterness to
make a balanced, full-flavored
stew. On the other hand,
brews with a high degree of
bitterness often did not have
enough sweetness. This was
the case with Sierra Nevada's
Pale Ale, which came across
as singularly bitter.

brown, 8 to 10 minutes. (If onions begin to brown, reduce heat to medium-low and stir in 1 tablespoon water.)

3. Stir in paprika mixture; cook, stirring occasionally, until onions stick to bottom of pan, about 2 minutes. Add carrots, bay leaf, and beef; stir until beef is well coated. Using rubber spatula, scrape down sides of pot. Cover pot and transfer to oven. Cook until meat is almost tender and surface of liquid is ½ inch below top of meat, 2 to 2½ hours, stirring every 30 minutes. Remove pot from oven and add enough broth so that surface of liquid is ¼ inch from top of meat (beef should not be fully submerged). Return covered pot to oven and continue to cook until fork slips easily in and out of beef, about 30 minutes longer.

4. Using large spoon, skim fat from surface of stew; stir in remaining 1 teaspoon vinegar and sour cream, if using. Discard bay leaf, season with salt and pepper to taste, and serve. (Stew, minus optional sour cream, can be refrigerated for up to 2 days. Stir sour cream into reheated stew just before serving.)

Carbonnade à la Flamande

✔ WHY THIS RECIPE WORKS

In a carbonnade, the heartiness of beef melds with the soft sweetness of onions and the malty flavor of beer in a lightly thickened broth that is rich, deep, and satisfying. But making an excellent carbonnade can be tricky. We wanted a foolproof method of highlighting our three main ingredients.

BLADE IS BEST Blade steak has a decent amount of fat and marbling, which gives it a buttery flavor that is well suited to carbonnade. We browned the beef in the pot and then set it aside so the onions could cook and pick up flavorful fond left by the meat.

MELLOW YELLOW Although we tested this recipe with red, white, and yellow onions, white and red proved to be cloyingly sweet. Thinly sliced yellow onions worked best. We lightly browned the onions with tomato paste and some minced garlic to heighten the flavor.

DO AS THE BELGIANS DO The type of beer we chose was essential to the success of this dish. In Belgium, beer is used in recipes as much as wine as used in other cuisines. Light lagers, not traditional to carbonnade, made for watery, pale stew. Darker beers worked much better, such as dark Belgian ales and stouts. We found that beer alone did not have enough body, so we supplemented with a combination of beef and chicken broth. This mix provided depth and complexity. A dash of cider vinegar brightened the flavor and added sweet-and-sour notes.

🔪 AT THE MEAT COUNTER
PREFERRED CUT Blade Steak

Blade steak is also known as top blade steak or flat-iron steak (see page 33 for more information). Be sure to remove the line of gristle that runs lengthwise down the center of the steak before cutting into pieces.

ALTERNATE CUT Chuck-Eye Roast

Chuck-eye roast is also known as boneless chuck roll or boneless chuck fillet (see page 34 for more information). You can use 4 pounds of boneless beef chuck-eye roast, well trimmed of fat, instead of the blade steak.

CARBONNADE À LA FLAMANDE (BELGIAN BEEF, BEER, AND ONION STEW)

SERVES 6

Buttered egg noodles or mashed potatoes make excellent accompaniments to carbonnade. The traditional copper-colored Belgian ale works best in this stew. If you can't find one, choose another dark or amber-colored ale of your liking.

3½	pounds beef blade steaks, 1 inch thick, trimmed and cut into 1-inch pieces
	Salt and pepper
3	tablespoons vegetable oil
2	pounds onions, halved and sliced ¼ inch thick
1	tablespoon tomato paste
2	garlic cloves, minced
3	tablespoons all-purpose flour
¾	cup chicken broth
¾	cup beef broth
1½	cups beer
4	sprigs fresh thyme, tied with kitchen twine
2	bay leaves
1	tablespoon cider vinegar

1. Adjust oven rack to lower-middle position and heat oven to 300 degrees. Pat beef dry with paper towels and season with salt and pepper. Heat 2 teaspoons oil in Dutch oven over medium-high heat until beginning to smoke; add about one-third of beef to pot. Cook without moving until well browned, 2 to 3 minutes; using tongs, turn each piece and continue cooking until second side is well browned, about 5 minutes longer. Transfer browned beef to medium bowl. Repeat with 2 teaspoons oil and half of remaining beef. (If drippings in bottom of pot are very dark, add about ½ cup of chicken or beef broth and scrape pan bottom with wooden spoon to loosen browned bits; pour liquid into bowl with browned beef, then proceed.) Repeat once more with 2 teaspoons oil and remaining beef.

2. Add remaining 1 tablespoon oil to now-empty Dutch oven; reduce heat to medium-low. Add onions, ½ teaspoon salt, and tomato paste; cook, scraping bottom of pot to loosen browned bits, until onions have released some moisture, about 5 minutes. Increase heat to medium and continue to cook, stirring occasionally, until onions are lightly browned, 12 to 14 minutes. Stir in garlic and cook until fragrant, about 30 seconds. Add flour and stir until onions are evenly coated and flour is lightly browned, about 2 minutes. Stir in chicken and beef broths, scraping pan bottom to loosen browned bits; stir in beer, thyme sprigs, bay leaves, vinegar, browned beef with any accumulated juices, and salt and pepper to taste. Increase heat to medium-high and bring to simmer, stirring occasionally; cover partially, then place pot in oven. Cook until fork slips easily in and out of beef, about 2 hours.

3. Discard thyme sprigs and bay leaves. Season with salt and pepper to taste, and serve. (Stew can be refrigerated for up to 2 days.)

TRIMMING BLADE STEAKS

Blade steaks contain a distinct line of gristle that should be removed before cooking. Here's how.

1. Cut each steak in half lengthwise, leaving gristle attached to one half.

2. Cut away gristle from half to which it is still attached.

Simple Beef Chili

✓ WHY THIS RECIPE WORKS

Chili doesn't have to be a big to-do. A simple chili made with ground beef, tomatoes, and chili powder should be spiced but not spicy, easy but not boring. We wanted to use basic supermarket ingredients to create a no-fuss chili that tasted better than the sum of its parts.

SPICE IT UP We knew from past test kitchen experience that ground spices taste best when they are toasted in hot oil, so we added them along with the aromatics to fully develop and bloom their flavors. We upped the chili powder and supplemented with cumin, coriander, and oregano. This mix worked to give the chili depth, and cayenne added heat.

ALL BEEF ALL THE WAY We tried supplementing the beef with other types of meat, such as ground pork or crumbled sausage, but we preferred the hearty flavor of all-beef chili. Our top choice was 85 percent lean beef for full-flavored but not greasy results.

CONSISTENCY MATTERS We found that using a combination of diced tomatoes and tomato puree was key for creating the thick consistency we were after. Removing the cover halfway through cooking ensured that our chili had time to reduce and thicken.

SIMPLE BEEF CHILI WITH KIDNEY BEANS

SERVES 8 TO 10

Good choices for condiments include diced fresh tomatoes, diced avocado, sliced scallions, finely chopped red onion, minced fresh cilantro, sour cream, and/or shredded Monterey Jack or cheddar cheese. The flavor of the chili improves with age; if possible, make it the day before you plan to serve it.

2	tablespoons vegetable oil
2	onions, chopped fine
1	red bell pepper, stemmed, seeded, and cut into ½-inch pieces
6	garlic cloves, minced
¼	cup chili powder
1	tablespoon ground cumin
2	teaspoons ground coriander
1	teaspoon red pepper flakes
1	teaspoon dried oregano
½	teaspoon cayenne pepper
2	pounds 85 percent lean ground beef
2	(15-ounce) cans red kidney beans, rinsed
1	(28-ounce) can diced tomatoes
1	(28-ounce) can tomato puree
	Salt
	Lime wedges

1. Heat oil in Dutch oven over medium heat until shimmering but not smoking. Add onions, bell pepper, garlic, chili powder, cumin, coriander, pepper flakes, oregano, and cayenne and cook, stirring occasionally, until vegetables are softened and beginning to brown, about 10 minutes. Increase heat to medium-high and add half of beef. Cook, breaking up pieces with spoon, until no longer pink and just beginning to brown, 3 to 4 minutes. Add remaining beef and cook, breaking up pieces with spoon, until no longer pink, 3 to 4 minutes.

2. Add beans, tomatoes and their juice, tomato puree, and ½ teaspoon salt; bring to

boil, then reduce heat to low and simmer, covered, stirring occasionally, for 1 hour. Remove cover and continue to simmer 1 hour longer, stirring occasionally (if chili begins to stick to bottom of pot, stir in ½ cup water and continue to simmer), until beef is tender and chili is dark, rich, and slightly thickened. Season with salt to taste. Serve with lime wedges. (Chili can be refrigerated for up to 2 days.)

SIMPLE BEEF CHILI WITH BACON
AND BLACK BEANS

Cook 8 slices bacon, cut into ½-inch pieces, in Dutch oven over medium heat, stirring frequently, until browned, about 8 minutes. Pour off all but 2 tablespoons fat, leaving bacon in pot. Substitute bacon fat in Dutch oven for vegetable oil and canned black beans for canned kidney beans.

Ultimate Beef Chili

✔ WHY THIS RECIPE WORKS

Our goal in creating an "ultimate" beef chili was to determine which of the "secret ingredients" recommended by chili experts around the world were spot-on—and which were expendable.

CHOOSE YOUR MEAT After deciding to use diced—not ground—beef, we began by testing six different cuts of beef for our chili: flap meat, brisket, chuck-eye roast, skirt steak, blade steak, and short ribs. Though the short ribs were extremely tender, some tasters felt that they tasted too much like pot roast. The brisket was wonderfully beefy but lean and a bit tough. The clear winner was blade steak, favored for its tenderness and rich flavor. Chuck-eye roast is a good second option.

BRINE THE BEANS It's important to brine your beans in order to get them to cook quickly, with a lasting tender and creamy texture. We used a quick brine because beans were not the central focus and, after all, the rest of the recipe took a fair amount of work. The timing worked out perfectly: By the time the beans were done brining (1 hour), the rest of the work was done.

SEED, TOAST, AND PUREE For complex chile flavor, we traded in commercial chili powder in favor of ground dried ancho and arbol chiles; for a grassy heat, we added fresh jalapeños. We toasted the anchos to develop their flavor and seeded all our chiles to control the heat. We also included oregano, cumin, cocoa, and salt.

ADD FLAVOR AND TEXTURE A combination of beer and chicken broth outperformed red wine, coffee, and beef broth as the liquid component. To balance the sweetness of our pot, mild molasses beat out other off-beat ingredients (including prunes and Coca-Cola). For the right level of thickness, flour and peanut butter didn't perform as promised; instead, a small amount of ordinary cornmeal (which we processed with the chiles and spices) sealed the deal, providing just the right consistency in our ultimate beef chili.

🔪 AT THE MEAT COUNTER

PREFERRED CUT Blade Steak
Blade steak is also known as top blade steak or flat-iron steak (see page 33 for more information). Be sure to remove the line of gristle that runs lengthwise down the center of the steak before cutting into pieces.

ALTERNATE CUT Chuck-Eye Roast
Chuck-eye roast is also known as boneless chuck roll or boneless chuck fillet (see page 34 for more information). You can use 4 pounds boneless chuck-eye roast, well trimmed of fat, instead of the blade steak.

ULTIMATE BEEF CHILI

SERVES 6 TO 8

Because much of the chili flavor is held in the fat of this dish, refrain from skimming fat from the surface. Dried New Mexican or guajillo chiles make a good substitute for the anchos; each dried arbol may be replaced with ⅛ teaspoon cayenne pepper. If you prefer not to work with any whole dried chiles, the anchos and arbols can be replaced with ½ cup commercial chili powder and ¼ to ½ teaspoon cayenne pepper, though the texture of the chili will be slightly compromised. Good choices for condiments include diced avocado, finely chopped red onion, chopped cilantro, lime wedges, sour cream, and shredded Monterey Jack or cheddar cheese.

- 8 ounces (1¼ cups) dried pinto beans, picked over and rinsed
  Salt
- 6 dried ancho chiles, stemmed, seeded, and torn into 1-inch pieces
- 2–4 dried arbol chiles, stemmed, seeded, and split into 2 pieces
- 3 tablespoons cornmeal
- 2 teaspoons dried oregano
- 2 teaspoons ground cumin
- 2 teaspoons unsweetened cocoa powder
- 2½ cups chicken broth
- 2 onions, cut into ¾-inch pieces
- 3 small jalapeño chiles, stemmed, seeded, and cut into ½-inch pieces
- 3 tablespoons vegetable oil
- 4 garlic cloves, minced
- 1 (14.5-ounce) can diced tomatoes
- 2 teaspoons molasses
- 3½ pounds beef blade steak, ¾ inch thick, trimmed and cut into ¾-inch pieces
- 1½ cups mild lager, such as Budweiser

1. Combine 4 quarts water, beans, and 3 tablespoons salt in Dutch oven and bring to boil over high heat. Remove pot from heat, cover, and let stand for 1 hour. Drain and rinse well.

2. Adjust oven rack to lower-middle position and heat oven to 300 degrees. Place ancho chiles in 12-inch skillet set over medium-high heat; toast, stirring frequently, until flesh is fragrant, 4 to 6 minutes, reducing heat if chiles

KEY STEPS TO ULTIMATE BEEF CHILI

1. Quick-brine beans by bringing to boil in salt solution and letting stand 1 hour.

2. Toast ancho chiles in skillet to enhance flavor.

3. Make paste by grinding toasted anchos, dried árbols, spices, cornmeal, and broth.

4. Sauté onions, jalapeños, and garlic in Dutch oven.

5. Add chile paste, tomatoes, molasses, broth, and beans to Dutch oven. Stir to combine.

6. Sear beef in batches in skillet until well browned; transfer to Dutch oven.

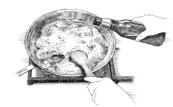

7. Deglaze skillet with lager between batches and scrape up fond; add to Dutch oven.

8. Transfer chili to oven and cook until meat and beans are fully tender, 1½ to 2 hours.

begin to smoke. Transfer to food processor and let cool. Do not wash out skillet.

3. Add arbol chiles, cornmeal, oregano, cumin, cocoa, and ½ teaspoon salt to food processor with toasted ancho chiles; process until finely ground, about 2 minutes. With processor running, slowly add ½ cup broth until smooth paste forms, about 45 seconds, scraping down sides of bowl as necessary. Transfer paste to small bowl. Place onions in now-empty processor and pulse until roughly chopped, about 4 pulses. Add jalapeños and pulse until consistency of chunky salsa, about 4 pulses, scraping down bowl as necessary.

4. Heat 1 tablespoon oil in Dutch oven over medium-high heat. Add onion mixture and cook, stirring occasionally, until moisture has evaporated and vegetables are softened, 7 to 9 minutes. Add garlic and cook until fragrant, about 1 minute. Add chile paste, tomatoes and their juice, and molasses; stir until chile paste is thoroughly combined. Add remaining 2 cups broth and drained beans; bring to boil, then reduce heat to simmer.

5. Meanwhile, heat 1 tablespoon oil in now-empty 12-inch skillet over medium-high heat until shimmering. Pat beef dry with paper towels and sprinkle with 1 teaspoon salt. Add half of beef and cook until browned on all sides, about 10 minutes. Transfer meat to Dutch oven. Add half of beer to skillet, scraping up browned bits from bottom of pan, and bring to simmer. Transfer beer to Dutch oven. Repeat with remaining 1 tablespoon oil, remaining beef, and remaining beer. Stir to combine and return mixture to simmer.

6. Cover pot and transfer to oven. Cook until meat and beans are fully tender, 1½ to 2 hours. Let chili stand, uncovered, for 10 minutes. Stir well, season with salt to taste, and serve. (Chili can be refrigerated for up to 3 days.)

Cuban-Style Shredded Beef with Lime and Garlic

✔ WHY THIS RECIPE WORKS

When we heard about vaca frita (literally translated as "fried cow"), we loved the idea of garlicky beef with a crispy crust, but many recipes produced meat with a dry, stringy interior. We wanted to transform this Cuban classic to achieve moist, tender meat with perfectly crisped edges.

CUT CHUNKS OF CHUCK We tested several cuts for this recipe, but chuck won out with its big beef flavor. Simmering the whole roast took close to 3 hours, so to cut down on cooking time, we cut the meat into small cubes. This extra step shaved an hour off the cooking time, making it well worth the extra knife work. Cutting the meat up also allowed us to remove large pockets of fat and connective tissue.

POUND IT To keep some (but not all) of the moisture in some (but not all) of the meat, we needed different-size pieces. We came across a technique that called for hitting the cooked meat with a mallet in order to generate flattened but irregular pieces. The fine threads fried up perfectly crispy, and the larger chunks stayed moist and tender inside while still getting a crispy crust outside.

PUNCH IT UP To brighten the lime flavor, we tried adding zest and more lime juice, but ended up overpowering the beef with too much acidity. Instead, we added 2 tablespoons of orange juice, which rounded out the fruity taste nicely and more subtly. To curb the harsh flavor of raw garlic, we browned it briefly in oil, and bloomed the cumin at the same time.

CUBAN SHREDDED BEEF WITH LIME AND GARLIC

SERVES 4 TO 6

Use a well-marbled chuck-eye roast in this recipe. Chuck-eye roast is also known as boneless chuck roll or boneless chuck fillet (see page 34 for more information). When trimming the beef, don't remove all visible fat—some of it will be used in lieu of oil later in the recipe. If you don't have enough reserved fat in step 3, use vegetable oil.

2   pounds boneless beef chuck-eye roast, pulled apart at seams, trimmed, and cut into 1½-inch pieces
    Kosher salt and pepper
3   garlic cloves, minced
1   teaspoon vegetable oil
¼   teaspoon ground cumin
2   tablespoons orange juice
1½   teaspoons grated lime zest plus 1 tablespoon juice, plus lime wedges for serving
1   onion, halved and sliced thin
2   tablespoons dry sherry

1. Bring beef, 2 cups water, and 1¼ teaspoons salt to boil in 12-inch nonstick skillet over medium-high heat. Reduce heat to low, cover, and gently simmer until beef is very tender, about 1 hour 45 minutes. (Check beef every 30 minutes, adding water so that bottom third of beef is submerged.) While beef simmers, combine garlic, oil, and cumin in bowl. Combine orange juice and lime zest and juice in second bowl.

2. Remove lid from skillet, increase heat to medium, and simmer until water evaporates and beef starts to sizzle, 3 to 8 minutes. Using slotted spoon, transfer beef to rimmed baking sheet. Pour off and reserve fat from skillet. Place sheet of aluminum foil over beef and, using meat pounder or heavy sauté pan, pound to flatten beef into ⅛-inch-thick pieces, discarding any large pieces of fat or connective tissue. (Some beef should separate into shreds. Larger pieces that do not separate can be torn in half.)

3. Heat 1½ teaspoons reserved fat in clean, dry skillet over high heat. When fat begins to sizzle, add onion and ¼ teaspoon salt. Cook, stirring occasionally, until onion is golden brown and charred in spots, 5 to 8 minutes. Add sherry and ¼ cup water and cook until liquid evaporates, about 2 minutes. Transfer onion to bowl. Return skillet to high heat, add 1½ teaspoons reserved fat, and heat until it begins to sizzle. Add beef and cook, stirring frequently, until dark golden brown and crusty, 2 to 4 minutes.

4. Reduce heat to low and push beef to sides of skillet. Add garlic mixture to center and cook, stirring frequently, until fragrant and golden brown, about 30 seconds. Off heat, add orange juice mixture and onion, and toss to combine. Season with pepper to taste. Serve immediately with lime wedges.

Ground Beef Tacos

✓ **WHY THIS RECIPE WORKS**

Beef tacos have undeniable appeal—spicy ground beef, shredded cheese, crispy taco shells. But prefab supermarket ingredients simply weren't living up to our expectations. We wanted a homemade version that would please kids and adults alike.

DITCH THE SEASONING PACKET To build a flavorful filling for our tacos, we immediately ditched the premade seasoning packets, which tasted stale and dusty. We started by sautéing an onion until it was softened and sweet. We added fresh minced garlic along with our spices, which allowed their flavors to fully bloom. This gave us a flavor-packed base on which to build our filling.

MAKE A SAUCE We preferred to use 90 percent lean ground beef in these tacos so that our filling wouldn't be greasy, but the lean meat didn't create much liquid on its own. A combination of chicken broth and plain tomato sauce improved the taste and texture of the filling. Brown sugar expanded and enriched the flavor of the spices, while a splash of cider vinegar added just enough acidity to balance out the warm flavors.

SKIP STORE-BOUGHT SHELLS Although store-bought shells are convenient, they seemed to us more like unhealthy snack food than dinner fare. We decided to turn flat tortillas into shells by frying them at home. We fried half of each tortilla until it was stiff, then submerged the other half in oil while we held open the "mouth" with tongs. Although frying our own shells took some time, we found the extra steps to be well worth it, since the results were significantly better.

GROUND BEEF TACOS

SERVES 4

Tomato sauce is sold in cans in the same aisle that carries canned whole tomatoes. Do not use jarred pasta sauce in its place. There's no need to prepare all the toppings listed below, but cheese, lettuce, and tomatoes are, in our opinion, essential.

BEEF FILLING

- 2 teaspoons vegetable oil or corn oil
- 1 small onion, chopped fine
- 3 garlic cloves, minced
- 2 tablespoons chili powder
- 1 teaspoon ground cumin
- 1 teaspoon ground coriander
- ½ teaspoon dried oregano
- ¼ teaspoon cayenne pepper
  Salt and pepper
- 1 pound 90 percent lean ground beef
- ½ cup canned tomato sauce
- ½ cup chicken broth
- 2 teaspoons cider vinegar
- 1 teaspoon packed brown sugar

SHELLS AND TOPPINGS

- 8 Home-Fried Taco Shells (recipe follows)
- 4 ounces cheddar or Monterey Jack cheese, shredded (1 cup)
- 2 cups shredded iceberg lettuce
- 2 small tomatoes, cored and chopped fine
- ½ cup sour cream
- 1 avocado, halved, pitted, and chopped fine
- 1 small onion, chopped fine
- 2 tablespoons minced fresh cilantro
  Hot sauce

1. FOR THE FILLING: Heat oil in 12-inch skillet over medium heat until shimmering, about 2 minutes; add onion and cook, stirring occasionally, until softened, about 4 minutes. Add garlic, chili powder, cumin, coriander, oregano, cayenne, and ½ teaspoon salt; cook, stirring constantly, until fragrant, about 1 minute. Add ground beef and cook, breaking meat up with wooden spoon and scraping pan bottom to prevent scorching, until beef is no longer pink, about 5 minutes. Add tomato sauce, broth, vinegar, and sugar; bring to simmer. Reduce heat to medium-low and simmer, uncovered, stirring frequently and breaking meat up so that no chunks remain, until liquid has reduced and thickened (mixture should not be completely dry), about 10 minutes. Season with salt and pepper to taste.

2. Using wide, shallow spoon, divide filling evenly among taco shells; place 2 tacos on individual plates. Serve, passing toppings separately.

HOME-FRIED TACO SHELLS
MAKES 8 TACO SHELLS

Be sure to use a heavy-bottomed skillet for this recipe. The taco shells can be fried before you make the filling and rewarmed in a 200-degree oven for about 10 minutes before serving.

¾   cup vegetable oil
8   (6-inch) corn tortillas

1. Heat oil in 8-inch skillet over medium heat to 350 degrees, about 5 minutes (oil should bubble when small piece of tortilla is dropped in; tortilla piece should rise to surface in 2 seconds and be light golden brown in about 1½ minutes). Meanwhile, line rimmed baking sheet with double layer of paper towels.

2. Using tongs to hold tortilla, slip half of tortilla into hot oil. With metal spatula in other hand, keep half of tortilla submerged in oil. Fry until just set, but not brown, about 30 seconds.

3. Flip tortilla; hold tortilla open about 2 inches while keeping bottom submerged in oil. Fry until golden brown, about 1½ minutes. Flip again and fry other side until golden brown, about 30 seconds.

4. Transfer shell upside down to prepared baking sheet to drain. Repeat with remaining tortillas, adjusting heat as necessary to keep oil between 350 and 375 degrees.

FRYING TACO SHELLS

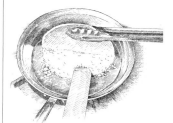

1. Using tongs to hold tortilla, slip half of it into hot oil. With metal spatula in your other hand, submerge half in oil. Fry until just set, but not brown, about 30 seconds.

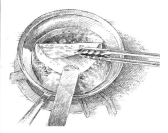

2. Flip tortilla; using tongs, hold tortilla open about 2 inches while keeping bottom submerged in oil. Fry until golden brown, about 1½ minutes. Flip again and fry other side until golden brown, about 30 seconds.

3. Transfer shell, upside down, to paper towel–lined baking sheet to drain. Repeat with remaining tortillas, adjusting heat as necessary to keep oil between 350 and 375 degrees.

Cuban-Style Picadillo

✔ WHY THIS RECIPE WORKS
This Latin staple is a homey one-pot dish with a balance of sweet, sour, and savory flavors. Traditional recipes involved chopping an entire roast into very small pieces. We wanted to make this dish work with simpler ground beef to make it an easy weeknight option.

ADD PORK When we used ground beef alone, it turned out chalky and dull. Adding a full pound of ground pork made the *picadillo* juicier, more supple, and slightly sweeter. To imitate the tender texture of a hand-chopped roast, we briefly treated the raw meat with baking soda. Just ½ teaspoon was enough to prevent the meat from toughening during cooking. Skipping the sear and adding the meat directly to the sauce in larger chunks rendered tender, juicy meat. And in order to compensate for the lost savoriness normally provided by searing, we added beef broth to the mix.

BOOST THE ACIDITY Along with sweet raisins, the warm spice flavors of picadillo come from cumin and cinnamon. To balance out the warmth of the cumin and cinnamon, we turned to the classic additions of tomatoes and dry white wine. Although the tomatoes are an important element, we didn't want the picadillo to taste tomato-based, so we opted for one small can of tomatoes. We weren't fond of the traditional *vino seco*, which was salty and overly acidic, so we used a dry white wine in its place. The wine provided just the punch we were looking for.

RAISIN THE BAR When we added the raisins at the end of cooking, their sweet jammy flavor appeared only sporadically. We decided to add them along with the broth and the bay leaves to let them simmer and diffuse their flavor through the sauce.

CUBAN-STYLE PICADILLO
SERVES 6

We prefer this dish prepared with raisins, but they can be replaced with 2 tablespoons of brown sugar added with the broth in step 2. Picadillo is traditionally served with rice and black beans. It can also be topped with chopped parsley, toasted almonds, and/or chopped hard-cooked egg.

1	pound 85 percent lean ground beef
1	pound ground pork
2	tablespoons water
½	teaspoon baking soda
	Salt and pepper
1	green bell pepper, stemmed, seeded, and cut into 2-inch pieces
1	onion, halved and cut into 2-inch pieces
2	tablespoons vegetable oil
1	tablespoon dried oregano
1	tablespoon ground cumin
½	teaspoon ground cinnamon
6	garlic cloves, minced
1	(14.5-ounce) can whole peeled tomatoes, drained and chopped coarse
¾	cup dry white wine
½	cup beef broth
½	cup raisins
3	bay leaves
½	cup pimento-stuffed green olives, chopped coarse
2	tablespoons capers, rinsed
1	tablespoon red wine vinegar, plus extra for seasoning

1. Toss beef and pork with water, baking soda, ½ teaspoon salt, and ¼ teaspoon pepper in bowl until thoroughly combined. Set aside for 20 minutes. Meanwhile, pulse bell pepper and onion in food processor until chopped into ¼-inch pieces, about 12 pulses.

2. Heat oil in large Dutch oven over medium-high heat until shimmering. Add oregano, cumin, cinnamon, ¼ teaspoon salt, and chopped vegetables; cook, stirring frequently, until vegetables are softened and beginning to brown, 6 to 8 minutes. Add garlic and cook, stirring constantly, until fragrant, about 30 seconds. Add tomatoes and wine and cook, scraping up any browned bits, until pot is almost dry, 3 to 5 minutes. Stir in broth, raisins, and bay leaves and bring to simmer.

3. Reduce heat to medium-low, add meat mixture in 2-inch chunks to pot, and bring to gentle simmer. Cover and cook, stirring occasionally with 2 forks to break meat chunks into ¼- to ½-inch pieces, until meat is cooked through, about 10 minutes.

4. Discard bay leaves. Stir in olives and capers. Increase heat to medium-high and cook, stirring occasionally, until sauce is thickened and coats meat, about 5 minutes. Stir in vinegar and season with salt, pepper, and extra vinegar to taste. Serve.

CUBAN-STYLE PICADILLO WITH FRIED POTATOES

After pulsing vegetables in food processor, toss 1 pound russet potatoes, peeled and cut into ½-inch pieces, with 1 tablespoon vegetable oil in medium bowl. Cover and microwave until potatoes are just tender, 4 to 7 minutes, tossing halfway through microwaving. Line surface of large plate with double layer of coffee filters and lightly spray with vegetable oil spray. Drain potatoes well, transfer to coffee filters, and spread in even layer. Let cool for 10 minutes; proceed with step 2. After step 3, heat 1 cup vegetable oil in large saucepan over medium-high heat until shimmering. Add cooled potatoes and cook, stirring constantly until deep golden brown, 3 to 5 minutes. Using slotted spoon, transfer potatoes to paper towel–lined plate and set aside. Add potatoes to pot with vinegar in step 4.

Best Old-Fashioned Burgers

✔ WHY THIS RECIPE WORKS

Classic drive-in burgers used to mean freshly ground high-quality beef, but today fast-food burgers are nothing more than tasteless, mass-produced patties. We wanted to bring back the original—an ultracrisp, ultrabrowned, ultrabeefy burger perfect with melted cheese and a tangy sauce.

DOUBLE UP ON THE BEEF We used a combination of sirloin steak tips and boneless beef short ribs for this burger. Though this made our technique a bit more complicated, it was worth it. We chose sirloin steak tips for their beefy flavor, and the short ribs added an element of fat and provided some much-needed juiciness.

FREEZE FIRST Most home cooks don't own a meat grinder, but don't worry: A food processor will work. When meat gets too warm, however, it can end up being smeared in the processor instead of evenly chopped. We found it important to cut the meat into chunks and chill them in the freezer before processing. That way they were chopped, not pulverized, and the patties cooked up just as perfectly tender (with as crisp a crust) as those ground in a meat grinder.

HANDS OFF We struggled with rubbery meat when developing this recipe and discovered that collagen was the culprit. As the collagen proteins are heated past 140 degrees, they begin to squeeze the meat, causing it to become dense and rubbery. The key to a tender burger was to keep it as loosely packed as possible. In fact, we hardly touched the meat at all. After letting it fall directly onto a baking sheet after grinding, we separated the ground meat and gently pressed it into four patties.

KEEP NOOKS AND CRANNIES Because our burgers are so loosely packed with home-ground meat, there are many nooks and crannies on their surfaces as they cook. This allows juices to bubble up through their porous surface and drip back down, basting the burgers as they cook. The finished result is juicy with a substantial, crisp crust.

TOP IT OFF This style of burger is often served with a tangy and sweet Thousand Island–style dressing. We replicated this by adding relish, sugar, and white vinegar to a mayo and ketchup base: a great foil for the juicy, salty burger. We liked American cheese, a classic choice that filled the cracks and crevices in the patty with gooey cheese and didn't compete against the other flavors. Garnishing simply with onions—in lieu of "the works"—kept the flavor of the beef at center stage.

BEST OLD-FASHIONED BURGERS
SERVES 4

This recipe yields juicy medium to medium-well burgers. Sirloin steak tips are also called flap meat (see page 37 for more information). It's important to use very soft buns. If doubling the recipe, process the meat in three batches in step 2. Because the cooked burgers do not hold well, fry four burgers and serve them immediately before frying more, or cook them in two pans. Extra patties can be frozen for up to two weeks (see "Freezing Burgers"). Thaw burgers in a single layer on a baking sheet at room temperature for 30 minutes before cooking.

- 10 ounces sirloin steak tips, trimmed and cut into 1-inch chunks
- 6 ounces boneless beef short ribs, trimmed and cut into 1-inch chunks
  Salt and pepper
- 4 hamburger buns, toasted and buttered
- ½ teaspoon vegetable oil
- 4 slices deli American cheese
  Thinly sliced onion
- 1 recipe Classic Burger Sauce (recipe follows)

FREEZING BURGERS

If you'd like the convenience of pulling out burgers as you need them, follow this easy method, which also works for steaks and chops.

Separate burgers with sheets of parchment paper, cover the stack(s) in plastic wrap, place the meat in zipper-lock freezer bags, and freeze. The parchment paper makes it much easier to pull individual pieces from the frozen package.

1. Place beef chunks on baking sheet in single layer, leaving ½ inch of space around each chunk. Freeze meat until very firm and starting to harden around edges but still pliable, 15 to 25 minutes.

2. Pulse half of meat in food processor until coarsely ground, 10 to 15 pulses, stopping and redistributing meat around bowl as necessary to ensure beef is evenly ground. Transfer meat to baking sheet, overturning workbowl and without directly touching meat. Repeat grinding with remaining meat. Spread meat over sheet and inspect carefully, discarding any long strands of gristle or large chunks of hard meat or fat.

3. Gently separate ground meat into 4 equal mounds. Without picking meat up, use your fingers to gently shape each mound into loose patty ½ inch thick and 4 inches in diameter, leaving edges and surface ragged. Season top of each patty with salt and pepper. Using spatula, flip patties and season other side. Refrigerate while toasting buns.

4. Refrigerate patties until ready to cook. (Patties can be refrigerated for up to 24 hours.)

5. Return clean, dry skillet to high heat; add oil and heat until just smoking. Using spatula, transfer burgers to skillet and cook without moving for 3 minutes. Using spatula, flip burgers over and cook for 1 minute. Top each patty with slice of cheese and continue to cook until cheese is melted, about 1 minute longer.

6. Transfer patties to bun bottoms and top with onion. Spread about 1 tablespoon of burger sauce on each bun top. Cover burgers and serve immediately.

CLASSIC BURGER SAUCE
MAKES ABOUT ¼ CUP

2	tablespoons mayonnaise
1	tablespoon ketchup
½	teaspoon sweet pickle relish
½	teaspoon sugar
½	teaspoon distilled white vinegar
¼	teaspoon pepper

Whisk all ingredients together in bowl.

Juicy Pub-Style Burgers

✓ WHY THIS RECIPE WORKS

Few things are as satisfying as a thick, juicy pub-style burger. But avoiding the usual gray band of overcooked meat is a challenge. We wanted a patty that was well seared, juicy, and evenly rosy from center to edge.

CUT INTO SMALL PIECES Cutting the meat into small ½-inch chunks before grinding and lightly packing the meat to form patties gave the burgers just enough structure to hold their shape in the skillet. If we cut the pieces any larger, we found that these hefty, pub-size patties broke apart when flipped in the pan.

ADD STRAIGHT FAT A little melted butter, which solidified as it hit the cold meat, created pinhead-size particles of fat strewn throughout the patties. The butter acted as lubrication and added a little more moisture, improving the burgers' flavor and juiciness. Also, and even better, the dairy proteins and sugar (lactose) in the butter boosted the browning on the burgers' exteriors.

USE TWO COOKING METHODS Using a standard cooking method for these burgers—preheating a skillet over high heat and then cooking the patties to medium-rare for about 4 minutes on each side—doesn't work. The meat is marred by a thick band of gray meat that no extra fat can help. Instead we used a two-method cooking technique, first searing the burgers over the high heat of a skillet to produce a great crust and then sticking them in the gentle, ambient heat of the oven to finish.

TRANSFER TO A COLD PAN While the two-method cooking technique is important, it makes only a small change in the finished product without an important element: a cold baking sheet. When we simply transferred the burgers in the hot skillet to the oven to finish, the bottom of the burgers cooked too quickly. But if placed on a cold sheet pan in a 300-degree oven, the burgers emerged after 3 to 5 minutes with perfect interiors—juicy and rosy throughout.

JUICY PUB-STYLE BURGERS
SERVES 4

Sirloin steak tips are also known as flap meat (see page 37 for more information). When stirring the butter and pepper into the ground meat and shaping the patties, take care not to overwork the meat or the burgers will become dense. For the best flavor, season the burgers aggressively just before cooking. The burgers can be topped as desired or with Pub-Style Burger Sauce or one of the test kitchen's favorite combinations (recipes follow).

- 2   pounds sirloin steak tips, trimmed and cut into ½-inch chunks
- 4   tablespoons unsalted butter, melted and cooled slightly
      Salt and pepper
- 1   teaspoon vegetable oil
- 4   large hamburger buns, toasted and buttered

1. Place beef chunks on baking sheet in single layer, leaving ½ inch of space around each chunk. Freeze meat until very firm and starting to harden around edges but still pliable, 15 to 25 minutes.

2. Pulse one-quarter of meat in food processor until finely ground into ⅟₁₆-inch pieces, about 35 pulses, stopping and redistributing meat around bowl as necessary to ensure beef is evenly ground. Transfer meat to baking sheet, overturning workbowl and without directly touching meat. Repeat grinding in 3 batches with remaining meat. Spread meat over baking sheet and inspect carefully, discarding any long strands of gristle or large chunks of hard meat or fat.

3. Adjust oven rack to middle position and heat oven to 300 degrees. Drizzle melted butter over ground meat and add 1 teaspoon pepper. Gently toss with fork to combine. Divide meat into 4 lightly packed balls. Gently flatten into patties ¾ inch thick and about 4½ inches in diameter. Refrigerate patties until ready to cook. (Patties can be refrigerated for up to 24 hours.)

4. Season 1 side of patties with salt and pepper. Using spatula, flip patties and season other side. Heat oil in 12-inch skillet over high heat until just smoking. Using spatula, transfer burgers to skillet and cook without moving for 2 minutes. Using spatula, flip burgers over and cook for 2 minutes longer. Transfer patties to rimmed baking sheet and bake until burgers register 125 degrees (for medium-rare), 3 to 5 minutes.

5. Transfer burgers to plate and let rest for 5 minutes. Transfer to buns and serve.

JUICY PUB-STYLE BURGERS WITH CRISPY SHALLOTS AND BLUE CHEESE

Heat ½ cup vegetable oil and 3 thinly sliced shallots in medium saucepan over high heat; cook, stirring frequently, until shallots are golden, about 8 minutes. Using slotted spoon, transfer shallots to paper towel–lined plate, season with salt, and let drain until crisp, about 5 minutes. (Cooled shallots can be stored at room temperature for up to 3 days.) Top each burger with 1 ounce crumbled blue cheese before transferring to oven. Top with crispy shallots just before serving.

JUICY PUB-STYLE BURGERS WITH SAUTÉED ONIONS AND SMOKED CHEDDAR

Heat 2 tablespoons vegetable oil in 12-inch skillet over medium-high heat until just smoking. Add 1 thinly sliced onion and ¼ teaspoon salt; cook, stirring frequently, until softened and lightly browned, 5 to 7 minutes. Top each burger with 1 ounce grated smoked cheddar cheese before transferring to oven. Top with onions just before serving.

PUB-STYLE BURGER SAUCE
MAKES ABOUT 1 CUP

¾ cup mayonnaise
2 tablespoons soy sauce
1 tablespoon packed dark brown sugar
1 tablespoon Worcestershire sauce
1 tablespoon minced fresh chives
1 garlic clove, minced
¾ teaspoon pepper

Whisk all ingredients together in bowl.

Grilled Well-Done Hamburgers

WHY THIS RECIPE WORKS

Not everyone wants their burger cooked to medium, but well-done burgers often turn out more like hockey pucks than burgers. We wanted a well-done burger that would be as juicy as any other burger.

PICK YOUR GROUND CHUCK We worked with supermarket ground beef here—nothing fancy. Our testers preferred the fattier 80 percent lean: The well-done chuck burgers were noticeably moister than the inedible versions we tried with the leaner sirloin.

USE A PANADE We packed our burger patties with a panade, a basic paste made from bread and milk. Panades are often used in meatballs and meatloaf to keep them moist, and the same principles applied here.

SEASON AGGRESSIVELY To punch up the flavor in our well-done hamburger recipe, we added minced garlic and tangy steak sauce. This contributed to a deep, meaty flavor.

DON'T OVERWORK It's important not to overwork these burger patties—too much handling can result in a rubbery burger.

Aggressively grinding meat, as they do in the supermarket (often multiple times), releases too many soluble proteins that act as a glue, causing the meat to stick together in a dense, rubbery mass.

USE HIGH HEAT While grilling our burgers over a medium fire would ensure a juicier, more tender burger, it would be a burger without that flavorful sear. We cooked these burgers over high heat to create great flavor. The panade helped to stem the moisture loss along the way. And the burgers turned out just as well when we cooked them indoors. We used a little oil and a hot skillet for well-seared, well-done burgers that were still juicy and full of flavor.

GRILLED WELL-DONE HAMBURGERS
SERVES 4

Adding bread and milk to the beef creates burgers that are juicy and tender even when well-done. For cheeseburgers, follow the optional instructions below.

DIMPLING BURGERS

To prevent hamburgers from puffing up during cooking, many sources recommend making a slight depression in the center of the raw patty before placing it on the heat.

But we find the need for a dimple depends entirely on how the burger is cooked. Meat inflates upon cooking when its connective tissue, or collagen, shrinks at temperatures higher than 140 degrees. If burgers are cooked on a grill or under a broiler, a dimple is in order. Cooked with these methods, the meat is exposed to direct heat not only from below or above but also on its sides; as a result, the edges of the patty shrink, cinching the hamburger like a belt, compressing its interior up and out.

But when the patty is cooked in a skillet, as in our recipe for Juicy Pub-Style Burgers, only the part of the patty in direct contact with the pan gets hot enough to shrink the collagen. Because the edges of the burger never directly touch the heat, the collagen it contains doesn't shrink much at all, and the burger doesn't puff.

Not all burgers require dimpling—it depends on how you cook them.

PANKO AND PANADE

A panade is a milk-and-bread paste that's folded into ground meat before shaping it into meatloaf and meatballs or even burgers; the bread starches absorb milk to form a gel that coats and lubricates the meat, keeping it moist and tender.

We found that when we kept the milk at 2 tablespoons and did a straight swap of ½ cup of panko for ½ cup of fresh bread crumbs in a panade that we mixed into burgers, the panko crumbs swelled to twice their volume and resembled fresh crumbs. They didn't form a paste, though, so we increased the amount of milk to help the panko break down and disperse evenly in our patties. Bottom line? Panko can be thought of as a sort of fresh bread-crumb concentrate. Here's the substitution formula: For every slice of bread (or ½ cup of fresh crumbs) and 2 tablespoons of milk called for, use ¼ cup of panko and 3 tablespoons of milk.

1 slice hearty white sandwich bread, crust removed, cut into ¼-inch pieces
2 tablespoons whole milk
2 teaspoons steak sauce
1 garlic clove, minced
¾ teaspoon salt
¾ teaspoon pepper
1½ pounds 80 percent lean ground chuck
6 ounces sliced cheese (optional)
4 hamburger buns, toasted

1. Mash bread and milk in large bowl with fork until homogeneous. Stir in steak sauce, garlic, salt, and pepper. Using your hands, gently break up meat over bread mixture and toss lightly to distribute. Divide meat into 4 portions and lightly toss 1 portion from hand to hand to form ball, then lightly flatten ball with your fingertips into ¾-inch-thick patty. Press center of patty down with your fingertips until it is about ½ inch thick, creating slight depression. Repeat with remaining portions.

2A. FOR A CHARCOAL GRILL: Open bottom vent completely. Light large chimney starter filled with charcoal briquettes (6 quarts). When top coals are partially covered with ash, pour two-thirds evenly over grill, then pour remaining coals over half of grill. Set cooking grate in place, cover, and open lid vent completely. Heat grill until hot, about 5 minutes.

2B. FOR A GAS GRILL: Turn all burners to high, cover, and heat grill until hot, about 15 minutes. Leave all burners on high.

3. Clean and oil cooking grate. Place burgers on grill (on hot side if using charcoal) and cook, without pressing on them, until well browned on first side, 2 to 4 minutes. Flip burgers and cook 3 to 4 minutes for medium-well or 4 to 5 minutes for well-done, adding cheese, if using, about 2 minutes before reaching desired doneness, covering grill to melt cheese.

4. Transfer burgers to serving platter, tent loosely with aluminum foil, and let rest for 5 to 10 minutes before serving on buns.

WELL-DONE BACON-CHEESEBURGERS

Most bacon burgers simply top the burgers with bacon. We also add bacon fat to the ground beef, which adds juiciness and unmistakable bacon flavor throughout the burger.

Cook 8 slices bacon in 12-inch skillet over medium heat until crisp, 7 to 9 minutes. Transfer bacon to paper towel–lined plate and set aside. Reserve 2 tablespoons fat and refrigerate until just warm. Add reserved bacon fat to bread and milk with seasonings mixture in step 1. Include optional cheese in step 3. Top each burger with 2 slices bacon before serving.

STOVETOP WELL-DONE HAMBURGERS

Heat 2 teaspoons vegetable oil in 12-inch nonstick skillet over medium heat until just beginning to smoke. Add meat patties, indentation side up, and cook until well browned, about 5 minutes. Using wide spatula, flip burgers and continue cooking, about 4 minutes for medium-well or 5 minutes for well-done. Distribute equal portion of cheese, if using, on burgers about 2 minutes before they reach desired doneness, covering skillet with lid to melt cheese. Serve on buns.

Pasta with Simple Italian-Style Meat Sauce

✔ WHY THIS RECIPE WORKS

Simmering a meat sauce all day does two things: It concentrates flavors as the liquid reduces slowly over the 3- to 4-hour cooking time; and it breaks down the meat, giving it a soft, lush texture. We wanted a quick version that would taste as though it had simmered all day.

TEACH AN OLD PANADE NEW TRICKS We used a basic panade in this sauce (white bread, whole milk). Even though it's for a sauce and not a compact construction like a burger, meatball, or meatloaf, the goal is the same: producing tender, juicy meat. We mixed the beef and panade in a food processor in order to help ensure that the starch was well dispersed so that all of the meat reaped its benefits. The food processor also broke down the meat into tiny pieces that cooked up supple and tender. When we skipped this step, the meat was chunkier—more like chili than a good sauce.

USE FLAVOR ENHANCERS We ramped up flavor in this quick sauce in a few ways. First: mushrooms. Basic white ones (browned in the pan with an onion) were enough to impart a real beefy taste. We also added tomato paste and Parmesan cheese, which are rich in glutamates and add a savory taste, along with liberal amounts of red pepper flakes and fresh oregano.

GRIND THE MUSHROOMS, TOO We processed the mushrooms in a food processor until finely chopped before browning them in a pan. After all, we wanted the beefy flavor that the mushrooms added to the sauce but were not interested in their squishy texture. This way, the mushrooms blended right in with the ground beef.

DEGLAZE WITH JUICE We saved some tomato juice from the drained diced tomatoes to deglaze the pan after browning the mushrooms. This (plus a bit of tomato paste) gave the sauce's tomato flavor a boost.

PASTA WITH SIMPLE ITALIAN-STYLE MEAT SAUCE

SERVES 8 TO 10

High-quality canned tomatoes will make a big difference in this sauce. If using dried oregano, add the entire amount with the canned tomato liquid in step 2.

- 4 ounces white mushrooms, trimmed and halved if small or quartered if large
- 1 slice hearty white sandwich bread, torn into quarters
- 2 tablespoons whole milk
  Salt and pepper
- 1 pound 85 percent lean ground beef
- 1 tablespoon olive oil
- 1 large onion, chopped fine
- 6 garlic cloves, minced
- 1 tablespoon tomato paste
- ¼ teaspoon red pepper flakes
- 1 (14.5-ounce) can diced tomatoes, drained with ¼ cup juice reserved
- 1 tablespoon minced fresh oregano or 1 teaspoon dried
- 1 (28-ounce) can crushed tomatoes
- ¼ cup grated Parmesan cheese, plus extra for serving
- 2 pounds spaghetti or linguine

1. Pulse mushrooms in food processor until finely chopped, about 8 pulses, scraping down sides of processor as needed; transfer to separate bowl. Add bread, milk, ½ teaspoon salt, and ½ teaspoon pepper to now-empty food processor and pulse until paste forms,

PANADE TO THE RESCUE

A paste of milk and bread, called a panade, is responsible for keeping the ground beef in our simple Italian-style meat sauce moist and tender. Because panades are typically used to help foods like meatballs and meatloaf hold their shape (and moisture), adding a panade to a meat sauce in which the beef is crumbled seemed like an odd idea. Wouldn't the mashed-up milk and bread just dissolve into the sauce? We were left scratching our heads when the panade worked.

Our science editor explained what was happening: Starches from the bread absorb liquid from the milk to form a gel that coats and lubricates the protein molecules in the meat, much in the same way as fat, keeping them moist and preventing them from linking together to form a tough matrix. Mixing the beef and panade in a food processor helps to ensure that the starch is well dispersed so that all the meat reaps its benefits.

Instead of tossing out scraps of cured meat such as dry sausage and prosciutto, place leftovers in a zipper-lock freezer bag and store them in the freezer. When making tomato sauce, soups, or stews, add the meat to the simmering pot for extra flavor.

about 8 pulses. Add ground beef and pulse until mixture is well combined, about 6 pulses.

2. Heat oil in large saucepan over medium-high heat until just smoking. Add onion and mushrooms and cook until vegetables are softened and well browned, 6 to 12 minutes. Stir in garlic, tomato paste, and pepper flakes and cook until fragrant and tomato paste starts to brown, about 1 minute. Stir in reserved tomato juice and 2 teaspoons fresh oregano, scraping up any browned bits. Stir in meat mixture and cook, breaking up any large pieces with wooden spoon, until no longer pink, about 3 minutes, making sure that meat does not brown.

3. Stir in crushed tomatoes and diced tomatoes, bring to gentle simmer, and cook until sauce has thickened and flavors meld, about 30 minutes. Stir in Parmesan and remaining 1 teaspoon fresh oregano and season with salt and pepper to taste. (Sauce can be refrigerated for up to 2 days or frozen for up to 1 month.)

4. Meanwhile, bring 8 quarts water to boil in 12-quart pot. Add pasta and 2 tablespoons salt and cook, stirring often, until al dente. Reserve ½ cup cooking water, then drain pasta and return it to pot. Add 1 cup sauce and reserved cooking water to pasta and toss to combine. Serve, topping individual portions with more sauce and passing Parmesan separately.

Ragu Alla Bolognese

✔ WHY THIS RECIPE WORKS

Ragu alla bolognese *comes in many forms, and the recipe varies from household to household. Our goal was to figure out the richest, most savory interpretation of this famous meat sauce.*

MIX MEATS Most Bolognese recipes use multiple types of meat for maximum flavor. We settled on a 1:1 ratio of ground beef, pork, and veal, plus 4 ounces each of mortadella and pancetta. Browning the meats gave our sauce a savory backbone, and cooking the vegetables in the rendered fat amped up the savoriness even further.

TOMATO PASTE RULES Though the recipes we found called for every type of canned tomato product (and some called for none at all), we preferred the unobtrusive texture and deep savory flavor of tomato paste.

USE GELATIN FOR SILKINESS We didn't want to add the extra time-consuming step of making our own beef broth since our ragu recipe was already time-consuming. But store-brought broth wasn't giving our sauce the silky texture of homemade broth, which contains gelatin from the simmered bones. Luckily, there was an easy solution: Add the gelatin back in. We decided that a fairly hefty amount of gelatin (8 teaspoons) dissolved in store-bought chicken and beef broths gave the ragu a texture that most closely resembled that from homemade broth.

LIVERS DELIVER While gelatin gave our sauce a silky texture, the canned broth still lacked depth and complexity. We found one recipe that called for chicken livers, and these proved to be the key ingredient in providing the complex savory flavor we wanted. Pureeing the livers ensured that they didn't overpower the other flavors and incorporated seamlessly into the sauce.

PASTA WITH RAGU ALLA BOLOGNESE

SERVES 4 TO 6

Eight teaspoons of gelatin is equivalent to 1 ounce. If you can't find ground veal, use an additional 12 ounces of ground beef. This recipe makes enough for 2 pounds of pasta.

1	cup chicken broth
1	cup beef broth
8	teaspoons unflavored gelatin
1	onion, chopped coarse
1	large carrot, peeled and chopped coarse
1	celery rib, chopped coarse
4	ounces mortadella, chopped
4	ounces pancetta, chopped
6	ounces chicken livers, trimmed
3	tablespoons extra-virgin olive oil
12	ounces 85 percent lean ground beef
12	ounces ground pork
12	ounces ground veal
3	tablespoons minced fresh sage
1	(6-ounce) can tomato paste
2	cups dry red wine
	Salt and pepper
1	pound pappardelle or tagliatelle Grated Parmesan cheese

1. Combine chicken broth and beef broth in bowl; sprinkle gelatin over top and set aside. Pulse onion, carrot, and celery together in food processor until finely chopped, about 10 pulses, scraping down sides of bowl as needed; transfer to separate bowl. Pulse mortadella and pancetta together in now-empty food processor until finely chopped, about 25 pulses, scraping down sides of bowl as needed; transfer to second bowl. Process chicken livers in again-empty food processor until pureed, about 5 seconds; transfer to third bowl.

2. Heat oil in Dutch oven over medium-high heat until shimmering. Add beef, pork, and veal; cook, breaking up pieces with wooden spoon, until all liquid has evaporated and meat begins to sizzle, 10 to 15 minutes. Add pancetta mixture and sage; cook, stirring frequently, until pancetta is translucent, 5 to 7 minutes, adjusting heat as needed to keep fond from burning. Add chopped vegetables and cook, stirring frequently, until softened, 5 to 7 minutes. Add tomato paste and cook, stirring constantly, until rust-colored and fragrant, about 3 minutes.

3. Stir in wine, scraping up any browned bits. Simmer until sauce has thickened, about 5 minutes. Stir in broth mixture and return to simmer. Reduce heat to low and cook at bare simmer until thickened (wooden spoon should leave trail when dragged through sauce), about 1½ hours.

4. Stir in pureed chicken livers, bring to boil, and remove from heat. Season with salt and pepper to taste.

5. Meanwhile, bring 4 quarts water to boil in large pot. Add pasta and 1 tablespoon salt and cook, stirring often, until al dente. Reserve ¾ cup cooking water, then drain pasta and return it to pot. Add half of sauce and cooking water to pasta and toss to combine. Serve, passing Parmesan separately. (Leftover sauce can be refrigerated for up to 3 days or frozen for up to 1 month.)

TOMATO PASTE

Tomato paste is basically tomato puree with most of the moisture cooked out. It adds body, color, and intensity to many dishes, including pastas, stews, and soups. To find out which brand is best, we gathered 10 brands for a tasting: nine in small cans and one in a toothpaste-like tube. We had tasters sample the paste straight from the container, cooked by itself, and cooked in marinara sauce.

When the brands were sampled uncooked, tasters downgraded some for "dried herb" notes, including oregano. Because tomato paste is usually cooked, we sautéed each brand in a skillet and tasted again. Some pastes became dull; others sprang to life. In the marinara sauce, tasters leaned toward those pastes that provided long-simmered flavor and depth. But ultimately, we found that while better tomato pastes improved the taste of the marinara, no brand ruined the dish.

Overall scores were relatively close, but one paste came in slightly ahead of the pack. **Goya Tomato Paste** was praised for its "bright, robust tomato flavor." Tasters liked its sweetness (this brand had one of the highest levels of natural sugars in the lineup) yet found it well balanced.

It's all too easy to forget to
save a bit of pasta cooking
water to thin a sauce when
the recipe recommends it.
Here's a surefire reminder:
Before cooking the pasta,
place a measuring cup inside
the colander you'll use to
drain it.

SPAGHETTI

Spaghetti makes a versa-
tile partner for just about
any type of sauce. Plus, it
promises a cheap dinner—or
at least it used to. When we
recently checked out brands
at the supermarket, we saw
a few boxes priced around a
dollar, while others cost four
times that. We sampled eight
brands of spaghetti to find
out if we had to spend more
money for great pasta.

After cooking and tasting
six Italian imports and two
domestic brands dressed
simply with olive oil and
tossed with tomato sauce,
we found our winner. Our
favorite spaghetti—and also
one of the two cheapest
brands we tasted (less than
$2 a pound)—was an Italian
import. Tasters preferred
**DeCecco Spaghetti
no. 12** for its "clean wheat
flavor" and "firm" strands
with "good chew."

Classic Spaghetti and Meatballs for a Crowd

✔ WHY THIS RECIPE WORKS

Making spaghetti and meatballs to serve a crowd can try the patience of even the toughest Italian grandmother. We sought an easier way to put this homey favorite on the table.

MIX YOUR MEATS We first tried making these meatballs with beef alone, using 85 per-cent lean ground beef (anything less fatty would almost certainly produce a dry, bland meatball). However, we found that replacing some of the beef with ground pork (we like a 2:1 ratio best) made for a markedly richer, meatier taste.

PICK PANKO For this panade we used panko, supercrunchy Japanese bread crumbs that hold on to meat juices and keep the meatballs from getting tough, along with but-termilk, which adds more flavor to meatballs than regular milk.

GRATE THE ONION TO REDUCE CRUNCH We grated the onion for this sauce on the large holes of a box grater. This allowed us to have the onion taste without the big crunch. We didn't even have to sauté it first.

BUILD FLAVOR We chopped up some prosciutto, which is packed with gluta-mates that enhance savory flavor, and mixed it in with the meat for an extra-meaty flavor. A generous amount of Parmesan added more glutamates to the meatballs.

ADD GELATIN We pondered adding veal to these meatballs because veal has lots of gela-tin and could add suppleness to the dish. While the veal did add suppleness, another problem arose: Ultralean veal is usually ground very fine, and these meatballs lacked the pleasantly coarse texture of the beef-and-pork batch. Instead, we added 1½ teaspoons of powdered gelatin moistened in a little water to the meatballs.

FLAVOR THE SAUCE Because we roasted our meatballs in the oven, there were no pan drippings to add flavor to the sauce. So we dropped the roasted meatballs into the simple marinara sauce and braised them together in the oven for an hour. With time, the rich flavor of the browned meat infiltrated the sauce. One problem we found with this technique, how-ever, was that as the meatballs absorbed the liq-uid around them, the sauce overreduced in the oven. To combat this, we swapped almost half of the crushed tomatoes in our marinara recipe for an equal portion of tomato juice, leaving us with a full-bodied, but not sludgy, sauce.

CLASSIC SPAGHETTI AND MEATBALLS FOR A CROWD

SERVES 12

You can substitute 1 cup of plain yogurt thinned with ½ cup of milk for the buttermilk. Grate the onion on the large holes of a box grater. You can cook the spaghetti in two pots if you don't have a pot that's large enough to cook all the pasta together.

MEATBALLS
2¼ cups panko bread crumbs
1½ cups buttermilk
1½ teaspoons unflavored gelatin
3 tablespoons water
2 pounds 85 percent lean ground beef
1 pound ground pork
6 ounces thinly sliced prosciutto, chopped fine
3 large eggs
3 ounces Parmesan cheese, grated (1½ cups), plus extra for serving
6 tablespoons minced fresh parsley
3 garlic cloves, minced
1½ teaspoons salt
½ teaspoon pepper

SAUCE

- 3 tablespoons extra-virgin olive oil
- 1 large onion, grated
- 6 garlic cloves, minced
- 1 teaspoon dried oregano
- ½ teaspoon red pepper flakes
- 3 (28-ounce) cans crushed tomatoes
- 6 cups tomato juice
- 6 tablespoons dry white wine
  Salt and pepper
- ½ cup chopped fresh basil
- 3 tablespoons minced fresh parsley
  Sugar

- 3 pounds spaghetti

1. FOR THE MEATBALLS: Adjust oven racks to upper-middle and lower-middle positions and heat oven to 450 degrees. Line 2 rimmed baking sheets with aluminum foil. Set wire racks in sheets and spray wire racks with vegetable oil spray.

2. Combine panko and buttermilk in large bowl and let sit, mashing occasionally with fork, until smooth paste forms, about 10 minutes. Meanwhile, sprinkle gelatin over water in bowl and let sit until gelatin softens, about 5 minutes.

3. Mix beef, pork, prosciutto, eggs, Parmesan, parsley, garlic, salt, pepper, and gelatin mixture into panko mixture using your hands. Pinch off and roll mixture into 2-inch meatballs (about 40 meatballs total) and arrange on prepared sheets. Bake until well browned, about 30 minutes, switching and rotating sheets halfway through baking.

4. FOR THE SAUCE: While meatballs bake, heat oil in Dutch oven over medium heat until shimmering. Add onion and cook until softened and lightly browned, 5 to 7 minutes. Stir in garlic, oregano, and pepper flakes and cook until fragrant, about 30 seconds. Stir in tomatoes, tomato juice, wine, 1½ teaspoons salt, and ¼ teaspoon pepper. Bring to simmer and cook until thickened slightly, about 15 minutes.

5. Remove meatballs from oven and reduce oven temperature to 300 degrees. Gently nestle meatballs into sauce. Cover, transfer to oven, and cook until meatballs are firm and sauce has thickened, about 1 hour. (Sauce and meatballs can be cooled and refrigerated for up to 2 days. To reheat, drizzle ½ cup water over sauce, without stirring, and reheat on lower-middle rack of 325-degree oven for 1 hour.)

6. Meanwhile, bring 10 quarts water to boil in 12-quart pot. Add pasta and 2 tablespoons salt and cook, stirring often, until al dente. Reserve ½ cup cooking water, then drain pasta and return it to pot.

7. Gently stir basil and parsley into sauce and season with sugar, salt, and pepper to taste. Add 2 cups sauce (without meatballs) to pasta and toss to combine. Add reserved cooking water as needed to adjust consistency. Serve, topping individual portions with more tomato sauce and several meatballs and passing extra Parmesan separately.

Classic Bacon-Wrapped Glazed Meatloaf

WHY THIS RECIPE WORKS

Nearly all aspects of meatloaf recipes can vary, from meat to flavorings to cooking method. Although we know there is no absolute right or wrong way to make meatloaf, we decided to sift through the myriad of options to come up with an outstanding version of our own.

MEATLOAF MIX IS BEST We tested a variety of combinations of meat for this recipe, and found that a ratio of 2 parts ground chuck to 1 part ground pork and 1 part ground veal gave us the best flavor and texture. The extra ground chuck gave the meatloaf a distinct but not overpowering beefy flavor, and kept the loaf firm enough to slice neatly. The pork provided depth of flavor, and the veal kept our meatloaf moist and tender.

THE FILLER SHOULD BE FLAVORLESS We wanted our filler to aid with texture but not add its own distinct flavor. After testing a veritable cornucopia of grains, cereals, and starches, we landed on three that achieved perfect results: crushed saltines, quick oats, and fresh bread crumbs. This gave our recipe a bit of flexibility, since you can use whichever binder you have on hand.

GO FREE-FORM Loaf pans can be problematic when making meatloaf: The meat stews in its own juices, and those juices can bubble up the sides and dilute the glaze. We prefer to bake our meatloaf free-form on an aluminum foil–lined wire rack. Free from excess liquid, the sides and top of our meatloaf browned nicely, and the bacon crisped up perfectly. Eliminating the loaf pan also allowed us to glaze the entire meatloaf, rather than just the top.

BACON-WRAPPED MEATLOAF WITH BROWN SUGAR–KETCHUP GLAZE

SERVES 6 TO 8

If you like, you can omit the bacon topping from the loaf. In this case, brush on half the glaze before baking and the other half during the last 15 minutes of baking. If it's available at your supermarket in the meat case or by special order, you can use 2 pounds meatloaf mix in place of the ground beef, pork, and veal.

BROWN SUGAR–KETCHUP GLAZE

- ½   cup ketchup or chili sauce
- ¼   cup packed brown sugar
- 4   teaspoons cider vinegar or distilled white vinegar

MEATLOAF

- 2   teaspoons vegetable oil
- 1   onion, chopped
- 2   garlic cloves, minced
- ½   cup whole milk or plain yogurt, plus extra if needed
- 2   large eggs
- 2   teaspoons Dijon mustard
- 2   teaspoons Worcestershire sauce
- 1   teaspoon salt
- ½   teaspoon pepper
- ½   teaspoon dried thyme
- ¼   teaspoon hot sauce
- 1   pound 80 percent lean ground chuck
- ½   pound ground pork
- ½   pound ground veal
- ⅔   cup crushed saltines (about 16) or ⅔ cup quick oats or 1⅓ cups fresh bread crumbs
- ⅓   cup minced fresh parsley
- 8–12   slices bacon

Many meatloaf recipes call for three different meats (beef, pork, and veal), and each one has a core function. Beef contributes assertive beefiness, while pork adds dimension with flavor and extra fattiness. With veal, it's mostly about the gelatin—a viscous substance with natural water-retaining qualities that help keep a meatloaf moist and unctuous. Gelatin is formed when collagen, the protein in a cow's connective tissue, breaks down during cooking. Collagen is naturally present in cows of all ages, but the collagen in calves (the source of veal) is more loosely structured—and therefore converts to gelatin more easily—than the collagen in an adult cow. In our all-beef meatloaf, we successfully replicated the gelatinous qualities of veal by adding powdered gelatin.

So how does it work? Gelatin is a pure protein that suspends water in a meshlike, semisolid matrix. By slowing down the movement of liquids, gelatin has a stabilizing effect, making it harder for water and other liquids to be forced out, essentially fencing them in. In meatloaf, then, gelatin helps by (1) decreasing the amount of liquid leaking from the meat as the other proteins coagulate and (2) improving the texture by making the liquids more viscous even when very hot—sort of a transitional state between liquid and solid. That viscosity translates to a luxuriant texture in the mouth—much like reduced stock, or demi-glace—and the perception of greater richness, as if we had added more fat.

1. FOR THE GLAZE: Combine all ingredients in small saucepan; set aside.

2. FOR THE MEATLOAF: Line 13 by 9-inch baking pan with aluminum foil. Adjust oven rack to middle position and heat oven to 350 degrees. Heat oil in 10-inch skillet over medium heat. Add onion and garlic, stirring until softened, about 5 minutes. Let cool while preparing remaining ingredients.

3. In large bowl, combine milk, eggs, mustard, Worcestershire, salt, pepper, thyme, and hot sauce. Add beef, pork, veal, saltines, parsley, and sautéed onion mixture; mix with fork until evenly blended and meat mixture does not stick to bowl. (If mixture sticks, add additional milk, 2 tablespoons at a time, until mixture no longer sticks.)

4. Turn meat mixture onto counter. With wet hands, pat mixture into approximately 9 by 5-inch loaf shape. Place in prepared baking pan. Brush with half of glaze, then arrange bacon slices, crosswise, over loaf, overlapping slightly and tucking only bacon tip ends under loaf.

5. Bake loaf until bacon is crisp and loaf registers 160 degrees, about 1 hour. Let cool at least 20 minutes. Simmer remaining glaze over medium heat until thickened slightly. Slice meatloaf and serve with extra glaze.

LOAF-PAN MEATLOAF

Omit bacon. Turn meat mixture into meatloaf pan with perforated bottom, fitted with drip pan. Use fork to pull mixture from pan sides to prevent glaze from dripping into oven. Brush with one-quarter of glaze. Bake until glaze is set, about 45 minutes. Top with another one-quarter of glaze; continue to bake until second coat has set and loaf registers 160 degrees, about 15 minutes longer. Let cool at least 20 minutes. Simmer remaining glaze over medium heat until thickened slightly. Slice meatloaf and serve with extra glaze.

Glazed All-Beef Meatloaf

✔ WHY THIS RECIPE WORKS

For a tender, moist, and light meatloaf, a combination of ground beef, pork, and veal (known as meatloaf mix) is usually the way to go. But sometimes we can't find meatloaf mix or don't have it on hand. We wanted to develop a recipe for an all-beef meatloaf that would be just as good as one made with meatloaf mix.

USE TWO KINDS OF BEEF We recommend using equal parts ground chuck and ground sirloin, which provide just the right balance of juicy, tender meat and assertive beefy flavor. (Simply using 85 percent lean ground beef works, too.)

ADD A PANADE We used saltines as the bread for our panade, delivering a well-seasoned, tender loaf with good moisture. Instead of milk, which does little to tone down beef's naturally liver-y flavor, we used chicken broth, which added savory notes to the loaf. Powdered gelatin rounded out the panade, replacing what was lost in the ground veal of a meatloaf mix, and giving our version a luxurious smoothness.

FREEZE YOUR CHEESE We added cheese to this meatloaf for its flavor, moisture, and binding quality, but we didn't want little pockets of cheese that oozed unappealing liquid when the loaf was cut. Dicing and shredding left those undesirable hot pockets of cheese. Grated cheese proved superior, and freezing the shredded cheese kept it crumbly.

BIND WITH EGGS While the additions of frozen, grated cheese and the saltine panade were important steps toward binding the meatloaf together, more was required. We also added two large eggs to the mix. The eggs, which solidified as they cooked, held in moisture and added body to the meatloaf.

BAKE FREE-FORM Allowing meatloaf baked in a loaf pan to stew in its own juices makes for a greasy mess. We ditched the loaf pan and baked the meatloaf "free-form" on a raised surface we made from aluminum foil set atop a wire cooling rack. This setup not only allowed the fat to drain away, preventing the meatloaf from tasting greasy, it also encouraged allover browning, which added a layer of flavor.

GLAZE LATE The almost-finished meatloaf needs its crowning glory—a glaze. But applied at the beginning of cooking, the glaze mixes unappealingly with the liquids seeping out of the loaf. Finishing with the glaze produced better results, especially when placing the loaf briefly under the broiler.

GLAZED ALL-BEEF MEATLOAF
SERVES 6 TO 8

If you can't find chuck and/or sirloin, substitute any 85 percent lean ground beef. Handle the meat gently; it should be thoroughly combined but not pastelike. To avoid using the broiler, glaze the loaf in a 500-degree oven; increase cooking time for each interval by 2 to 3 minutes.

MEATLOAF

- 3 ounces Monterey Jack cheese, shredded (¾ cup)
- 1 tablespoon unsalted butter
- 1 onion, chopped fine
- 1 celery rib, chopped fine
- 2 teaspoons minced fresh thyme
- 1 garlic clove, minced
- 1 teaspoon paprika
- ¼ cup tomato juice
- ½ cup chicken broth
- 2 large eggs
- ½ teaspoon unflavored gelatin
- ⅔ cup crushed saltines (about 16)
- 2 tablespoons minced fresh parsley
- 1 tablespoon soy sauce
- 1 teaspoon Dijon mustard
- ¾ teaspoon salt
- ½ teaspoon pepper
- 1 pound ground sirloin
- 1 pound ground beef chuck

GLAZE

- ½ cup ketchup
- ¼ cup cider vinegar
- 3 tablespoons packed light brown sugar
- 1 teaspoon hot sauce
- ½ teaspoon ground coriander

1. FOR THE MEATLOAF: Adjust oven rack to middle position; heat oven to 375 degrees. Spread Monterey Jack on plate and place in freezer until ready to use. Fold piece of heavy-duty aluminum foil to form 10 by 6-inch rectangle. Center foil on wire rack and place rack in rimmed baking sheet. Poke holes in foil with skewer about ½ inch apart. Spray foil with vegetable oil spray and set aside.

2. Melt butter in 10-inch skillet over medium-high heat; add onion and celery and cook, stirring occasionally, until beginning to brown, 6 to 8 minutes. Add thyme, garlic, and paprika and cook, stirring constantly, until fragrant, about 1 minute. Reduce heat to low and add tomato juice. Cook, scraping bottom of skillet with wooden spoon to loosen any browned bits, until thickened, about 1 minute. Transfer mixture to bowl and set aside to cool.

3. Whisk broth and eggs in large bowl until combined. Sprinkle gelatin over liquid and let stand for 5 minutes. Stir in saltines, parsley, soy sauce, mustard, salt, pepper, and onion mixture. Crumble frozen cheese into coarse powder and sprinkle over mixture. Add ground sirloin and ground chuck; mix gently with hands until thoroughly combined, about 1 minute. Transfer meat to aluminum foil rectangle and shape into 10 by 6-inch oval about 2 inches high. Smooth top and edges of meatloaf with moistened spatula. Bake until meatloaf registers 135 to 140 degrees, 55 minutes to 1 hour 5 minutes. Remove meatloaf from oven and turn on broiler.

4. FOR THE GLAZE: While meatloaf cooks, combine all ingredients in small saucepan. Bring to simmer over medium heat and cook, stirring, until thick and syrupy, about 5 minutes. Spread half of glaze evenly over cooked meatloaf with rubber spatula; place under broiler and cook until glaze bubbles and begins to brown at edges, about 5 minutes. Remove meatloaf from oven and spread evenly with remaining glaze; place back under broiler and cook until glaze is again bubbling and beginning to brown, about 5 minutes more. Let meatloaf cool about 20 minutes before slicing.

Shepherd's Pie

✔ WHY THIS RECIPE WORKS

Shepherd's pie can be the ultimate comfort food: The classic combination of meat, potatoes, and gravy is undeniably appealing on cold winter nights. But recipes for shepherd's pie often produce overly heavy pies that take the better part of a day to make. We wanted a recipe that would be lighter and simpler with all the comforting elements of the original.

TENDERIZE WITH BAKING SODA An easy shortcut for our shepherd's pie was trading out chunks of meat, which needed to be cut, trimmed, and browned, for preground beef. We skipped browning, since ground beef has so much surface area that browning leaches the moisture out of the meat and makes dry, nubbly crumbles. But this was not enough to produce the tender texture we wanted, so we tossed the raw beef with baking soda to make it soft and tender.

GOOD GRAVY Since we didn't have browned meat flavors on which to build our gravy, we looked to other sources for deep savory flavor. Browning onions and mushrooms started to create a fond in the pan; adding tomato paste bolstered the savory flavor and gave the fond a dark, rich color. We deglazed the pan with fortified wine, since regular wine left the sauce too boozy. A couple of sprigs of fresh thyme lent freshness, and beef broth and Worcestershire sauce rounded out the savory flavors to produce a rich gravy.

LIGHTEN THE POTATOES For a mashed potato topping that wouldn't weigh down our shepherd's pie, we reduced the amount of butter and traded out half-and-half for milk. We also added chopped scallions to freshen up the flavor. Although we tried simply spreading the potatoes over the filling with a spatula, this proved messy. Piping the potatoes out of a zipper-lock bag with one corner cut off was simple and effective, and making ridges in the potatoes with a fork created extra surface area for a crisp, browned topping.

SHEPHERD'S PIE
SERVES 4 TO 6

Don't use ground beef that's fattier than 93 percent or the dish will be greasy.

1½	pounds 93 percent lean ground beef
2	tablespoons plus 2 teaspoons water
	Salt and pepper
½	teaspoon baking soda
2½	pounds russet potatoes, peeled and cut into 1-inch chunks
4	tablespoons unsalted butter, melted
½	cup milk
1	large egg yolk
8	scallions, green parts only, sliced thin
2	teaspoons vegetable oil
1	onion, chopped
4	ounces white mushrooms, trimmed and chopped
1	tablespoon tomato paste
2	garlic cloves, minced
2	tablespoons Madeira or ruby port
2	tablespoons all-purpose flour
2	carrots, peeled and chopped

1¼ cups beef broth

2 teaspoons Worcestershire sauce

2 sprigs fresh thyme

1 bay leaf

2 teaspoons cornstarch

1. Toss beef with 2 tablespoons water, 1 teaspoon salt, ¼ teaspoon pepper, and baking soda in bowl until thoroughly combined. Set aside for 20 minutes.

2. Meanwhile, place potatoes in medium saucepan; add water to just cover and 1 tablespoon salt. Bring to boil over high heat. Reduce heat to medium-low and simmer until potatoes are soft and tip of paring knife inserted into potato meets no resistance, 8 to 10 minutes. Drain potatoes and return to saucepan. Return saucepan to low heat and cook, shaking pot occasionally, until any surface moisture on potatoes has evaporated, about 1 minute. Remove pan from heat and mash potatoes well. Stir in melted butter. Whisk together milk and egg yolk in small bowl, then stir into potatoes. Stir in scallions and season with salt and pepper to taste. Cover and set aside.

3. Heat oil in broiler-safe 10-inch skillet over medium heat until shimmering. Add onion, mushrooms, ½ teaspoon salt, and ¼ teaspoon pepper; cook, stirring occasionally, until vegetables are just starting to soften and dark bits form on bottom of skillet, 4 to 6 minutes. Stir in tomato paste and garlic; cook until bottom of skillet is dark brown, about 2 minutes. Add Madeira and cook, scraping up any browned bits, until evaporated, about 1 minute. Stir in flour and cook for 1 minute. Add carrots, broth, Worcestershire, thyme sprigs, and bay leaf; bring to boil, scraping up any browned bits. Reduce heat to medium-low, add beef in 2-inch chunks to broth, and bring to gentle simmer. Cover and cook until beef is cooked through, 10 to 12 minutes, stirring and breaking up meat chunks with 2 forks halfway through. Stir cornstarch and remaining 2 teaspoons water together in bowl. Stir cornstarch mixture into filling and continue to simmer for 30 seconds. Discard thyme sprigs and bay leaf. Season with salt and pepper to taste.

4. Adjust oven rack 5 inches from broiler element and heat broiler. Place mashed potatoes in large zipper-lock bag and snip off 1 corner to create 1-inch opening. Pipe potatoes in even layer over filling, making sure to cover entire surface. Smooth potatoes with back of spoon, then use tines of fork to make ridges over surface. Place skillet on rimmed baking sheet and broil until potatoes are golden brown and crusty and filling is bubbly, 10 to 15 minutes. Let cool for 10 minutes before serving.

Beef Empanadas

✔ WHY THIS RECIPE WORKS

These Latin American pastry pockets stuffed with briny, spiced beef make a savory, transportable meal. We wanted to streamline the recipe to make it work for a weeknight dinner.

LAYER YOUR FLAVORS For a sweet-savory filling, we turned to a Chilean-inspired combination of ground beef, sautéed garlic and onions, hard-cooked eggs, raisins, and olives. To keep the meat tender, we used a panade made with chicken broth instead of milk, which intensified the meat's flavor. We bloomed our warm spices—cumin, cayenne, and cloves—to bring out their flavor, and a handful of cilantro leaves and a splash of vinegar brightened the base sauce. The traditional chopped eggs, raisins, and green olives provided freshness, sweetness, and acidity, as well as adding interest to the texture and flavor of the filling.

ASSEMBLING EMPANADAS

1. Divide dough in half, then divide each half into 6 equal pieces. Refrigerate until firm, about 45 minutes or up to 2 days.

2. Roll each piece into 6-inch round about ⅛ inch thick.

3. Place ⅓ cup filling on each round. Brush edges with water.

4. Fold dough over filling, then crimp edges using fork.

ADJUST THE CRUST Our favorite recipe for pie dough produces a buttery, flaky crust (and relies on a secret ingredient, vodka, to make it easy to roll), but tasters found it out of place in this recipe. To introduce more Latin flavors, we turned to masa harina, which gave our pastry a nutty richness and rough-hewn texture well suited to our filling. To make sure our crust crisped up nicely in the oven, we preheated the baking sheet and brushed it with oil, and brushed the tops of the empanadas with oil as well. Baked this way, the crusts turned out so shatteringly crispy, they could almost pass for fried.

BEEF EMPANADAS
SERVES 4 TO 6

The alcohol in the dough is essential to the texture of the crust and imparts no flavor—do not substitute. Masa harina can be found in the international foods aisle with other Latin American foods. If you cannot find masa harina, replace it with additional all-purpose flour (for a total of 4 cups).

FILLING

I	slice hearty white sandwich bread, torn into quarters
2	tablespoons plus ½ cup chicken broth
I	pound 85 percent lean ground beef
	Salt and pepper
I	tablespoon olive oil
2	onions, chopped fine
4	garlic cloves, minced
I	teaspoon ground cumin
¼	teaspoon cayenne pepper
⅛	teaspoon ground cloves
½	cup chopped fresh cilantro
2	large hard-cooked eggs, chopped coarse
⅓	cup raisins, chopped coarse
¼	cup pitted green olives, chopped coarse
4	teaspoons cider vinegar

DOUGH

3	cups (15 ounces) all-purpose flour
I	cup (5 ounces) masa harina
I	tablespoon sugar
2	teaspoons salt
12	tablespoons unsalted butter, cut into ½-inch pieces and chilled
½	cup cold vodka or tequila
½	cup cold water
5	tablespoons olive oil

1. FOR THE FILLING: Process bread and 2 tablespoons broth in food processor until paste forms, about 5 seconds, scraping down sides of bowl as necessary. Add beef, ¾ teaspoon salt, and ½ teaspoon pepper and pulse until mixture is well combined, 6 to 8 pulses.

2. Heat oil in 12-inch nonstick skillet over medium-high heat until shimmering. Add onions and cook, stirring frequently, until beginning to brown, about 5 minutes. Stir in garlic, cumin, cayenne, and cloves; cook until fragrant, about 1 minute. Add beef mixture and cook, breaking meat into 1-inch pieces with wooden spoon, until browned, about 7 minutes. Add remaining ½ cup broth and simmer until mixture is moist but not wet, 3 to 5 minutes. Transfer mixture to bowl and let cool for 10 minutes. Stir in cilantro, eggs, raisins, olives, and vinegar. Season with salt and pepper to taste, and refrigerate until cool, about 1 hour. (Filling can be refrigerated for up to 2 days.)

3. FOR THE DOUGH: Process 1 cup flour, masa harina, sugar, and salt in food processor until combined, about 2 pulses. Add butter and process until homogeneous and dough resembles wet sand, about 10 seconds. Add remaining 2 cups flour and pulse until mixture is evenly distributed around bowl, 4 to 6 quick pulses. Empty mixture into large bowl.

4. Sprinkle vodka and water over mixture. Using your hands, mix dough until it forms tacky mass that sticks together. Divide dough in half, then divide each half into 6 equal pieces. Transfer dough pieces to plate, cover with plastic wrap, and refrigerate until firm, about 45 minutes or up to 2 days.

5. TO ASSEMBLE: Adjust oven racks to upper-middle and lower-middle positions, place 1 rimmed baking sheet on each rack, and

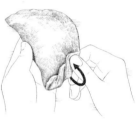

Use Wet Hands
Dip your fingers in bowl
of water after every 2 or
3 meatballs to prevent meat
from sticking as you form
meatballs.

heat oven to 425 degrees. While sheets are preheating, remove dough from refrigerator. Roll out each dough piece on lightly floured counter into 6-inch circle about ⅛ inch thick, covering each dough round with plastic wrap while rolling remaining dough. Place about ⅓ cup filling in center of each dough round. Brush edges of dough with water and fold dough over filling. Trim any ragged edges. Press edges to seal. Crimp edges of empanadas using fork. (Empanadas can be made through

step 5, covered tightly with plastic wrap, and refrigerated for up to 2 days.)

6. TO BAKE: Drizzle 2 tablespoons oil over surface of each hot baking sheet, then return to oven for 2 minutes. Brush empanadas with remaining 1 tablespoon oil. Carefully place 6 empanadas on each sheet and cook until well browned and crisp, 25 to 30 minutes, switching and rotating sheets halfway through baking. Let empanadas cool on wire rack for 10 minutes and serve.

Swedish Meatballs

✔ WHY THIS RECIPE WORKS

Traditional Swedish meatballs are light, springy, and flavorful, but many recipes produce flavorless lumps of beef covered in a heavy, grainy gravy. We wanted to develop a recipe that would give us standout Swedish meatballs that could serve as the center-piece of a meal.

POWDER POWER Panades are used in meatballs to keep them moist and tender, but while Italian-style meatballs are meant to be nearly fall-apart tender, we wanted our Swedish-style meatballs to hold together. But simply reducing the amount of panade made our meatballs dry and tough. We lightened the meatballs using baking powder in addition to the panade.

BORROW FROM SAUSAGE We wanted our Swedish meatballs to have some spring—think of the snap when you bite into a sausage. So we borrowed a technique used in sausage making, which requires whipping the meat, fat, salt, and flavorings into a homogenous paste. But whipping the ground beef made our meatballs more like bite-size hot dogs. An easy fix turned out to be replacing some of the beef with pork. We found that whipping the pork into an emulsified paste and then folding in the beef provided both the springy texture and hearty flavor we were after.

SUGAR AND SPICE Invariably, Swedish meatball recipes call for sweetener. The depth and complexity of brown sugar was per-fect; it lent sweetness without being cloying. A pinch of nutmeg and allspice added a touch of warmth.

USE LESS CREAM Most recipes call for a flour-thickened blend of broth and cream in roughly equal proportions, but this gravy turned out far too rich and heavy. We made our gravy using mostly broth with some cream. A splash of lemon juice just before serving contributed brightness.

SWEDISH MEATBALLS
SERVES 4 TO 6

For a slightly less sweet dish, omit the brown sugar in the meatballs and reduce the brown sugar in the sauce to 2 teaspoons. A 12-inch slope-sided skil-let can be used in place of the sauté pan—use 1½ cups of oil to fry instead of 1¼ cups. Serve the meatballs with mashed potatoes, boiled red pota-toes, or egg noodles.

MEATBALLS
1   large egg
¼   cup heavy cream

1 slice hearty white sandwich bread, crusts removed, torn into 1-inch pieces
8 ounces ground pork
¼ cup grated onion
1½ teaspoons salt
1 teaspoon packed brown sugar
1 teaspoon baking powder
⅛ teaspoon ground nutmeg
⅛ teaspoon ground allspice
⅛ teaspoon pepper
8 ounces 85 percent lean ground beef
1¼ cups vegetable oil

SAUCE

1 tablespoon unsalted butter
1 tablespoon all-purpose flour
1½ cups chicken broth
1 tablespoon packed brown sugar
½ cup heavy cream
2 teaspoons lemon juice
Salt and pepper

1. FOR THE MEATBALLS: Whisk egg and cream together in bowl. Stir in bread and set aside. Meanwhile, using stand mixer fitted with paddle attachment, beat pork, onion, salt, sugar, baking powder, nutmeg, allspice, and pepper on high speed until smooth and pale, about 2 minutes, scraping down bowl as needed. Using fork, mash bread mixture until no large dry bread chunks remain; add mixture to mixer bowl and beat on high speed until smooth and homogeneous, about 1 minute, scraping down bowl as needed. Add beef and mix on medium-low speed until just incorporated, about 30 seconds, scraping down bowl as needed. Using moistened hands, form generous tablespoon of meat mixture into 1-inch round meatball; repeat with remaining mixture to form 25 to 30 meatballs.

2. Heat oil in 10-inch straight-sided sauté pan over medium-high heat until edge of meatball dipped in oil sizzles (oil should register 350 degrees on instant-read thermometer), 3 to 5 minutes. Add meatballs in single layer and fry, flipping once halfway through cooking, until lightly browned all over and cooked through, 7 to 10 minutes. (Adjust heat as needed to keep oil sizzling but not smoking.)

Using slotted spoon, transfer browned meatballs to paper towel–lined plate.

3. FOR THE SAUCE: Pour off and discard oil in pan, leaving any browned bits behind. Return pan to medium-high heat and melt butter. Add flour and cook, whisking constantly, until flour is light brown, about 30 seconds. Slowly whisk in broth, scraping bottom of pan with wooden spoon to loosen any browned bits. Add sugar and bring to simmer. Reduce heat to medium and cook until sauce is reduced to about 1 cup, about 5 minutes. Stir in cream and return to simmer.

4. Add meatballs to sauce and simmer, turning occasionally, until heated through, about 5 minutes. Stir in lemon juice, season with salt and pepper to taste, and serve.

TO MAKE AHEAD: Meatballs can be fried and then frozen for up to 2 weeks. To continue with recipe, thaw meatballs in refrigerator overnight and proceed from step 3.

SWEDISH PICKLED CUCUMBERS
MAKES 3 CUPS

Pickling cucumbers are also called Kirby cucumbers. If these small cucumbers are unavailable, substitute 1 large American cucumber. Serve the pickles chilled or at room temperature.

1 pound pickling cucumbers, sliced into ⅛- to ¼-inch-thick rounds
1½ cups distilled white vinegar
1½ cups sugar
1 teaspoon salt
12 allspice berries

Place cucumber slices in medium heatproof bowl. Bring vinegar, sugar, salt, and allspice to simmer in small saucepan over high heat, stirring occasionally to dissolve sugar. Pour vinegar mixture over cucumbers and stir to separate slices. Cover bowl with plastic wrap and let sit for 15 minutes. Uncover and let cool to room temperature, about 15 minutes.

TO MAKE AHEAD: Pickles can be refrigerated in their liquid in airtight container for up to 2 weeks.

PANADE VARIATIONS

A panade is a paste, typically made of milk and bread. It is often used in recipes calling for ground meat, such as hamburgers and meatballs, to help the formed meat hold its shape and retain moisture during cooking. We usually call for white sandwich bread in our panades because many cooks keep it on hand; plus, its neutral flavor incorporates easily into the meat mixture and doesn't interfere with other flavors in a recipe.

To find out if we could substitute whole-wheat sandwich bread or store-bought bread crumbs for the white bread, we tested each in our recipes for Swedish meatballs and hamburgers. Tasters immediately picked up on a distracting wheat flavor from the whole-wheat panade in both the meatballs and the burgers; plus, its high fiber content turned out dry meat. Meatballs and burgers made with the packaged bread crumbs tasted fine but lacked the tenderness of those made with white bread. Our conclusion? When it comes to panade, stick with white sandwich bread (unless the recipe says otherwise).

Pork

(CONTINUED)

Pork Basics

Before you shop for pork, it's helpful to understand some basic information as well as the primal cuts from which the retail cuts are butchered. Buying and cooking today's lean pork chops or tenderloins can be a challenge. And in addition, there are many cuts of pork in the market, many of which are sold under a variety of alternate names. Pork labels can also be confusing. On page 2, we address general meat labeling terms and here, we explain more about labels specific to pork. In addition, our retail cuts chart will help you understand shopping for pork, cut by cut.

THE OTHER WHITE MEAT

The majority of pork sold in today's supermarkets bears little resemblance to the pork our grandparents consumed. New breeding techniques and feeding systems have slimmed down the modern pig, which contains a third less fat than it did 30 years ago. As you might imagine, leaner pork is not as flavorful and is prone to drying out as it cooks. We find that lean cuts of pork are best cooked to an internal temperature of 140 to 145 degrees. After the meat rests, the internal temperature will rise to 150 degrees. The pork will have a slight tinge of pink, and it will be juicy. If you cook lean pork just 10 degrees higher (as recommended in many older books), the meat will be tough and dry.

LABELING

Heritage Breeds

After years of advertising pork as "the other white meat," pork producers have started to change their tune. Nowadays, fat, flavor, and even deeper color are making a comeback, with chefs and consumers paying top dollar for specialty breeds touted as being fattier, juicier, and far more flavorful. But we were skeptical: Are those pedigreed labels like Berkshire (known as Kurobuta in Japan) and Duroc a true indication of quality—or just a premium price tag? (Once mail-order shipping is factored in, specialty pork can cost at least twice as much as supermarket meat.)

If color was any indication of better quality, we were certainly on the right track. Three of the five bone-in chops we mail-ordered were cut from 100 percent Berkshire pigs, and their pigments were strikingly crimson-colored compared with the supermarket chops we bought.

The other two mail-order samples, both blends of Berkshire and other "heritage" breeds like Duroc, were less dark, though not as ghostly pale as the supermarket meat. But it wasn't until we'd pan-seared all six samples that we were won over by the pricey pork. While the supermarket chops were comparatively bland and chewy, and the heritage samples weren't markedly better, the Berkshire pork was juicy, smoky, and intensely porky—even bacon-like. (Just to be sure we'd taken cooking variations out of the equation as much as possible, we repeated the test by bringing the chops to exactly 135 degrees in a *sous vide* machine before briefly searing them. The results were nearly identical.)

We were sold on the Berkshire pork, and we wondered if its better flavor and juiciness were related to anything more than just the specific breed. As it turned out, the meat's deep pink tint was more significant that we thought. According to Kenneth Prusa, professor of food science at Iowa State University, that color really is an indication of quality. It reflects the meat's pH, which Prusa pinpoints as the "overall driver of quality" in pork. In mammals, normal pH is around 7. But Prusa told us even small differences in pH can have a significant impact on pork's flavor and texture. Berkshire pigs are bred to have a slightly higher pH than normal, which in turn makes their meat darker, firmer, and more flavorful. In fact, a high pH can be even more important than fat in determining flavor. Conversely, pork with low pH is paler, softer, and relatively bland.

In addition to genetics, pH is influenced by husbandry, along with slaughtering and processing methods. Berkshire pigs are raised in low-stress environments that keep them calm. And the calmer the animal, the more evenly blood flows through its system, distributing flavorful juices throughout. Berkshire pigs are also slaughtered with methods that minimize stress, which causes a buildup of lactic acid in the muscles and lowers pH. Chilling the meat very rapidly after slaughter is yet another factor that affects pH, which begins to decline immediately once blood flow stops. Increasingly, commercial producers are adopting similar measures in slaughtering and processing in an effort to keep the pH of their pork as high as possible. The bottom line? Berkshire pork won't become a regular purchase for most of us, but we think our favorite sample is worth the occasional splurge. In the meantime, we'll be picking out the pinkest pork at the supermarket.

Enhanced or Not?

Because modern supermarket pork is so lean and therefore somewhat bland and prone to dryness if overcooked, many producers now inject their fresh pork products with a sodium solution. So-called enhanced pork is now the only option at many supermarkets, especially when buying lean cuts like the tenderloin. (To be sure, read the label; if the pork has been enhanced it will have an ingredient label, while natural pork will not have an ingredient label.)

Enhanced pork is injected with a solution of water, salt, sodium phosphates, sodium lactate, potassium lactate, sodium diacetate, and varying flavor agents, generally adding 7 to 15 percent extra weight. While enhanced pork does cook up juicier (it has been pumped full of water!), we find the texture almost spongy, and the flavor is often unpleasantly salty. We prefer the genuine pork flavor of natural pork and we brine lean cuts to keep them juicy (see page 6 for information on brining). Note that enhanced pork loses six times more moisture when frozen and thawed compared to natural pork—yet another reason to avoid enhanced pork.

Nitrites versus Nitrates

Cured pork products, such as bacon, often contain nitrites and/or nitrates. Nitrites have been shown to form carcinogenic compounds called nitrosamines when heated in the presence of proteins, like those in pork. While nitrites and nitrates are virtually identical, only nitrites have been shown to form potentially harmful nitrosamines.

So should you buy "nitrate-free" or "nitrite-free" bacon? These products are generally brined with salt, a bacterial lactic-acid starter culture, and celery juice (which is sometimes listed as "natural flavor"). The problem is that celery juice contains a high level of nitrate, which is converted to the problematic nitrite by the bacteria in the starter culture. While technically these products can be labeled "no nitrates or nitrites added," the compounds are naturally formed during production.

When we analyzed various brands of bacon, we found that regular bacon actually contained lower levels of nitrites and nitrates than some brands labeled "no nitrites or nitrates added." All bacons tested fell well within federal standards for these compounds, but if you want to avoid nitrites and nitrates you need to avoid bacon and other processed pork products altogether.

Bacon, Pancetta, Salt Pork, and Fatback

Various pork products appear in recipes throughout this book, including bacon, pancetta, salt pork, and fatback. The location on the pig and processing methods define these pork products, which are commonly used as flavoring ingredients. Pancetta, American bacon, and salt pork all come from the belly, while fatback comes, as its name implies, from the back of the pig. Pancetta, bacon, and salt pork are all cured (pancetta's cure includes salt and spices; the others just salt), but bacon is also smoked. Fatback, on the other hand, is not cured, salted, or smoked; it's simply fresh pork fat.

Primal Cuts of Pork

Four different cuts of pork are sold at the wholesale level. From this first series of cuts, known in the trade as primal cuts, a butcher (usually at a meatpacking plant in the Midwest but sometimes on-site at your market) will make the retail cuts that you bring home from the market.

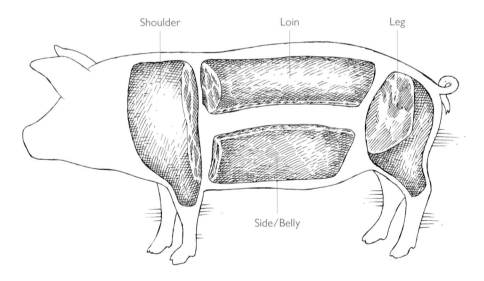

Shoulder

Cuts from the upper portion of the shoulder (called the blade shoulder) are well marbled with fat and contain a lot of connective tissue, making them ideal candidates for slow-cooking methods like braising, stewing, or barbecuing. Cuts from the arm, or picnic shoulder, are a bit more economical than those from the blade area but are otherwise quite similar.

Loin

The area between the shoulder and back legs is the leanest, most tender part of the animal. Rib and loin chops are cut from this area, as are pork loin roasts and tenderloin roasts. These cuts will be dry if overcooked.

Leg

The rear legs are often referred to as "ham." This primal cut is sold as large roasts and is available fresh or cured.

Side/Belly

The underside is the fattiest part of the animal and is the source of bacon and spareribs.

Shopping for Pork–Cut by Cut

Not all roasts, chops, and ribs are created alike. We've rated the following cuts on flavor (★★★★ being the most flavorful) and cost ($$$$ being the most expensive).

PRIMAL CUT: SHOULDER

PORK BUTT ROAST

This large, flavorful cut (often labeled Boston butt or pork shoulder at markets) can weigh as much as 8 pounds when sold with the bone in. Many markets take out the bone and sell this cut in smaller chunks, often wrapped in netting to hold the roast together.

Flavor: ★★★★   Cost: $ $

Alternate Names: Boston shoulder, pork butt, Boston butt

Best Cooking Methods: Slow roasting, barbecuing, stewing, braising

Recommended Recipes: Chinese Barbecued Pork (page 243), Indoor Pulled Pork with Sweet and Tangy Barbecue Sauce (page 245), Barbecued Pulled Pork (page 246), Lexington-Style Pulled Pork (page 249), Mexican Pulled Pork (Carnitas) (page 251), Spicy Mexican Shredded Pork (Tinga) Tostadas (page 253), French-Style Pork Stew (page 255), Slow-Roasted Pork Shoulder with Peach Sauce (page 258)

PORK SHOULDER

This affordable cut can be sold bone-in or boneless. It is rich in fat and connective tissue.

Flavor: ★★★★   Cost: $

Alternate Names: Shoulder arm picnic, picnic shoulder, fresh picnic, picnic roast

Best Cooking Methods: Grill roasting, barbecuing, roasting, braising

Recommended Recipes: French Pork and White Bean Casserole (Cassoulet) (page 256), Cuban-Style Grill-Roasted Pork (page 261), Glazed Picnic Ham (Smoked Shoulder) (page 278)

PRIMAL CUT: LOIN

BLADE CHOP

Cut from the shoulder end of the loin, these chops can be difficult to find at the market. They are fatty and tough, despite good flavor and juiciness.

Flavor: ★★★   Cost: $ $ $

Alternate Name: Pork chop end cut

Best Cooking Methods: Braising, barbecuing

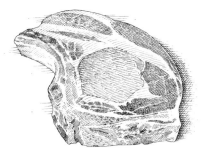

Recommended Recipes: Red Wine–Braised Pork Chops (page 200), Smothered Pork Chops (page 203)

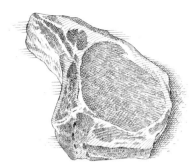

RIB CHOP

Cut from the rib section of the loin, these chops have a relatively high fat content, rendering them flavorful and unlikely to dry out during cooking. They are a favorite in the test kitchen. These chops are easily identified by the bone that runs along one side and the one large eye of loin muscle. Note that rib chops are also sold boneless. In fact, most boneless pork chops you'll find are cut from the rib chop.

Flavor: ★★★ **Cost:** $ $ $

Alternate Names: Rib cut chops, pork chops end cut

Best Cooking Methods: Grilling, pan searing, braising

Recommended Recipes (Bone-In): Easy Pork Chops (page 186), Pan-Seared Thick-Cut Pork Chops (page 189), Stuffed Thick-Cut Pork Chops (page 194), Pork Chops with Vinegar and Sweet Peppers (page 198), Grilled Bone-In Pork Chops (page 205), Grill-Smoked Pork Chops (page 207)
Recommended Recipes (Boneless): Crispy Pan-Fried Pork Chops (page 187), Glazed Pork Chops (page 192), Crunchy Baked Pork Chops (page 196), Easy Grilled Boneless Pork Chops (page 204)

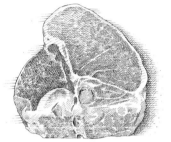

CENTER-CUT CHOP

These chops can be identified by the bone that divides the loin meat from the tenderloin muscle. The lean tenderloin section cooks more quickly than the loin section, making these chops a challenge. They have good flavor, but since they contain less fat than the rib chops, they are not quite as moist.

Flavor: ★★ **Cost:** $ $ $ $

Alternate Names: Top loin chops, loin chops

Best Cooking Methods: Searing, grilling

Recommended Recipes: Easy Pork Chops (page 186), Pork Chops with Vinegar and Sweet Peppers (page 198), Grilled Bone-In Pork Chops (page 205)

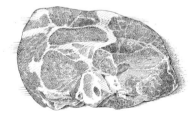

SIRLOIN CHOPS

These chops, cut from the sirloin, or hip, end of the pig, are tough, dry, and tasteless. The chops contain tenderloin and loin meat, plus a slice of hipbone. We do not recommend this cut.

Flavor: **Cost:** $ $ $

Alternate Name: Sirloin steaks

Best Cooking Method: None

BABY BACK RIBS

Baby back ribs are cut from the section of the rib cage closest to the backbone. Loin center-cut roasts and chops come from the same part of the pig, which explains why baby back ribs can be expensive. This location also explains why baby back ribs are much leaner than spareribs—and why they need special attention to keep from drying out on the grill.

Flavor: ★★★ **Cost:** $ $ $ $

Alternate Names: Loin back ribs, riblets

Best Cooking Methods: Grilling, barbecuing

Recommended Recipes: Barbecued Baby Back Ribs (page 272), Grilled Glazed Baby Back Ribs (page 274)

COUNTRY-STYLE RIBS

These meaty, tender, boneless ribs are cut from the upper side of the rib cage from the fatty blade end of the loin. Butchers usually cut them into individual ribs and package several ribs together. These ribs can be braised and shredded for pasta sauce, or pounded flat and grilled or pan-seared as cutlets.

Flavor: ★★★   **Cost:** $ $ $

Alternate Name: Country ribs

Best Cooking Methods: Braising, grilling, pan searing

Recommended Recipes: Sichuan Stir-Fried Pork in Garlic Sauce (page 227), Pork Stir-Fry with Noodles (Lo Mein) (page 229)

BLADE-END ROAST

The part of the loin closest to the shoulder, the bone-in blade roast can be chewy. It can also be difficult to carve because of its many separate muscles and fatty pockets. Also sold boneless (see below).

Flavor: ★★★   **Cost:** $ $

Alternate Names: Pork seven-rib roast, pork five-rib roast, pork loin rib end, rib-end roast

Best Cooking Method: Roasting

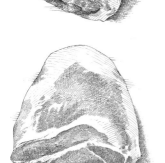

BONELESS BLADE-END ROAST

This is our favorite boneless roast for roasting. It is cut from the shoulder end of the loin and has more fat (and flavor) than the boneless center-cut loin roast. Unfortunately, this cut can be hard to find in many markets. This roast is also sold with the bone in, although that cut is even harder to locate.

Flavor: ★★★   **Cost:** $ $

Alternate Names: Blade roast, blade loin roast

Best Cooking Methods: Roasting, grill roasting

Recommended Recipes: Grill-Roasted Pork Loin (page 234), Grill-Roasted Bone-In Pork Rib Roast (page 238)

CENTER-CUT LOIN ROAST

This popular boneless roast is juicy, tender, and evenly shaped with somewhat less fat than the center-cut rib roast. We prefer the more flavorful boneless blade-end roast, but the two cuts can be used interchangeably. Make sure to buy a center-cut roast with a decent fat cap on top.

Flavor: ★★   **Cost:** $ $ $

Alternate Name: Center-cut pork roast

Best Cooking Methods: Roasting, grill roasting

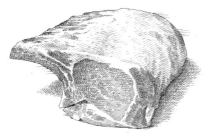

Recommended Recipes: Herb-Crusted Pork Roast (page 233), Grilled Pork Loin with Apple-Cranberry Filling (page 236)

CENTER-CUT RIB ROAST

Often referred to as the pork equivalent of prime rib or rack of lamb, this mild, fairly lean roast consists of a single muscle with a protective fat cap. It may be cut with anywhere from five to eight ribs. Because the bones (and nearby fat) are still attached, we find this roast a better option than the center-cut loin roast, which is cut from the same muscle but is minus the bones and fat.

Flavor: ★★★   **Cost:** $ $ $

Alternate Names: Rack of pork, pork loin rib half, center-cut pork roast

Best Cooking Methods: Roasting, grill roasting

Recommended Recipes: Tuscan-Style Garlic-Rosemary Roast Pork Loin (page 230), Grill-Roasted Bone-In Pork Rib Roast (page 238), Slow-Roasted Bone-In Pork Rib Roast (page 240)

TENDERLOIN ROAST

This lean, delicate, boneless roast cooks very quickly because it's so small, usually weighing just about 1 pound. Since there is very little marbling, this roast (which is equivalent to beef tenderloin) cannot be overcooked without ruining its texture. Tenderloins are often sold two to a package. Many tenderloins sold in the supermarket are enhanced; look for one that has no ingredients other than pork on the label.

Flavor: ★ **Cost:** $ $ $

Alternate Name: None

Best Cooking Methods: Roasting, pan searing, sautéing, stir-frying

Recommended Recipes: Pork Schnitzel (page 208), Maple-Glazed Pork Tenderloins (page 211), Thick-Cut Pork Tenderloin Medallions (page 212), Pan-Seared Oven-Roasted Pork Tenderloins (page 215), Grilled Pork Tenderloins (page 218), Grilled Glazed Pork Tenderloin Roast (page 220), Spicy Stir-Fried Pork, Asparagus, and Onions with Lemon Grass (page 223), Thai Pork Lettuce Wraps (page 224)

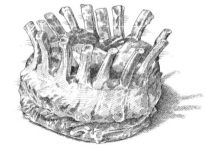

SIRLOIN ROAST

This sinuous cut with a good amount of connective tissue is difficult to cook evenly and to carve.

Flavor: **Cost:** $ $ $

Alternate Name: None

Best Cooking Method: None

CROWN ROAST

Butchers tie two bone-in center-cut rib or center-cut loin roasts together to create this impressive-looking roast. We find that a crown roast with 16 to 20 ribs is the best choice, as smaller and larger roasts are harder to cook evenly. Because of its shape and size, this roast is prone to overcooking.

Flavor: ★★ **Cost:** $ $ $

Alternate Name: Crown rib roast

Best Cooking Method: Roasting

Recommended Recipe: Crown Roast of Pork (page 263)

PRIMAL CUT: SIDE/BELLY

ST. LOUIS–STYLE SPARERIBS

Regular spareribs are cut close to the belly of the pig (which is also where bacon comes from). Because whole spareribs contain the brisket bone and surrounding meat, each rack can weigh upward of 5 pounds. Some racks of spareribs are so big they barely fit on the grill. We prefer this more manageable cut because the brisket bone and surrounding meat are trimmed off to produce a narrower, rectangular rack that usually weighs in at a relatively svelte 3 pounds.

Flavor: ★★★★ **Cost:** $ $ $

Alternate Name: Spareribs

Best Cooking Methods: Roasting, barbecuing

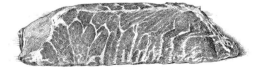

Recommended Recipes: Oven-Barbecued Spareribs (page 264), Barbecued Pork Spareribs (page 266), Memphis-Style Barbecued Spareribs (page 269), Chinese-Style Barbecued Spareribs (page 270)

PRIMAL CUT: LEG

FRESH HAM, SHANK END

The leg is divided into two cuts—the tapered shank end and the more rounded sirloin end. The sirloin end has a lot of bones that make carving tricky. We prefer the shank end. This cut is usually covered in a thick layer of fat and skin, which should be scored before roasting. This cut is not as fatty as you might think and benefits from brining.

Flavor: ★★★   **Cost:** $ $

Alternate Name: Shank end fresh ham

Best Cooking Methods: Roasting, grill roasting

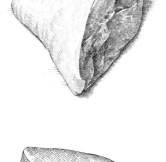

Recommended Recipes: Slow-Roasted Fresh Ham (page 277), Grill-Roasted Ham (page 282)

FRESH HAM, SIRLOIN HALF

Because of its bone structure, the rounded sirloin is more difficult to carve than the shank end and is our second choice. Its flavor, however, is quite good.

Flavor: ★★★   **Cost:** $ $

Alternate Name: None

Best Cooking Method: Roasting

SPIRAL-SLICED BONE-IN HALF HAM

This is our favorite wet-cured ham because the meat is not pumped up with water (the label should read "ham with natural juices") and because it is so easy to carve. Make sure to buy a bone-in ham; it will taste better than a boneless ham. Although packages are not labeled as such, look for a ham from the shank rather than from the sirloin end. You can pick out the shank ham by its tapered, more pointed end opposite the flat cut side of the ham. The sirloin ham has more rounded or blunt ends.

Flavor: ★★★★   **Cost:** $

Alternate Name: Spiral-cut ham

Best Cooking Method: Roasting

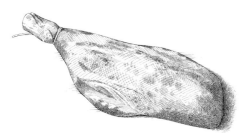

Recommended Recipe: Glazed Spiral-Sliced Ham (page 275)

COUNTRY HAM

This Southern favorite starts with the whole leg and is dry-cured like prosciutto or serrano ham. This ham has a complex, meaty, and nutty flavor. The meat is very salty and dry (even after soaking). Serve it in small pieces with biscuits or use in recipes with greens, rice, or pasta.

Flavor: ★★★   **Cost:** $ $ $

Alternate Name: None

Best Cooking Method: Roasting

Recommended Recipe: Roast Country Ham (page 279)

Sausages

Sausage can be made from almost any type of meat (or combination of meats), although you'll find that many of the world's most popular sausages are made from pork. Here are some of our favorites.

Knackwurst

Knackwurst (often incorrectly spelled "knockwurst") is named for the characteristic pop you hear when you take a bite; *knack* is German for "crack." Like the familiar hot dog or frankfurter, knackwurst is pre-cooked and can be made entirely from beef or a combination of beef and pork. Eat it with traditional sausage toppings such as mustard and sauerkraut.

Bratwurst

At Midwestern backyard barbecues and tailgates, these sweet, herbal sausages are more common than hot dogs. They are made from ground pork and veal gently seasoned with caraway, coriander, ginger, and nutmeg. We prefer the coarse, pebbly texture of fresh, uncooked bratwurst to the mealiness of partially cooked versions. Simmer bratwurst on the grill in a pan of water or, preferably, beer, and finish them by crisping the skin over a medium-hot fire.

Genoa Salami

Popular in the deli case and key for Italian sandwiches and antipasto platters, Genoa salami is cured pork sausage with visibly chunky pockets of fat. Its slightly sour, fermented flavor may stem from a measure of wine added before it's salted and air-dried (no smoking here), while whole black peppercorns contribute spiciness. If you're buying a whole one, take off the casing to remove the (harmless) mold; peel it only from the portion of sausage you plan to eat, though, or the sausage will dry out.

Banger

"Banger" is British slang for sausage, but in the United States it has come to describe a specific style that is plump, soft, white, and creamy. Bangers are made from pork butt combined with crumbled rusks (dry, wheaty biscuits), so it's not surprising that they taste somewhat bready. We like to simmer bangers in water, then sear them in a skillet to bring out their naturally buttery, porky flavor.

Kielbasa

This Polish sausage tastes a bit like a coarse, garlicky hot dog. Traditionally made from all pork, most commercial kielbasa today includes beef and sometimes turkey and is seasoned with garlic, marjoram, and smoke. Kielbasa is sold fully cooked, but we like to grill it or sear it to add flavor. Some brands are much saltier than others, so always taste for seasoning when you're cooking with kielbasa (we like it in soups and stews).

Italian Sausage

Griddled or grilled, Italian sausages are popularly served either with pasta or smothered in grilled onions and frying peppers on sub rolls. They come either hot or sweet and always raw. Both sweet and hot versions are made with coarsely ground fresh (not cured or smoked) pork flavored with garlic and fennel seed. The hot variety is also seasoned with red pepper flakes. Grill or sauté whole sausages or remove the casing and crumble the meat into sauces, soups, or stews.

Pepperoni

This spicy, chewy Italian American sausage is best known for its starring role on pizza. Pork (or occasionally beef) is ground and dried; combined with black and cayenne pepper, sugar, salt, and paprika; and cured for several weeks. To prevent pepperoni slices from leaching grease over pizza, we microwave them between sheets of paper towels first, a step that degreases yet doesn't toughen the meat.

Spanish Chorizo

Spanish chorizo, which comes in links, is generally sold cured and fully cooked. It's made from chopped pork and pork fat and is seasoned with smoked paprika, garlic, and herbs. It has a jerky-like texture similar to pepperoni; its pungent smokiness and vinegary aftertaste are all its own. Eat sliced chorizo as an appetizer or add to paella or Spanish tortillas. Don't substitute it for Mexican chorizo or vice versa; they are not interchangeable. (Kielbasa and linguiça make better substitutes for Spanish chorizo.)

Mexican Chorizo

Unlike Spanish chorizo, the Mexican chorizo available in American markets is almost always sold raw, in links or bulk packs. Mexican chorizo includes paprika and garlic, but it's chili powder that provides its characteristic spicy, coffee-like flavor. The texture is crumbly, similar to ground beef. Remove chorizo from its casing, then crumble and fry it. Drain off the grease before adding cooked chorizo to soups, stews, tacos, or even scrambled eggs or omelets.

Andouille

Made in German style, given a French name (pronounced "an-DOO-ee"), and seasoned with Cajun spices, this southern Louisiana native is a proverbial melting pot. Gumbo, jambalaya, and red beans and rice wouldn't be authentic without it. Chewy, spicy andouille is made from ground pork, salt, garlic, and plenty of black pepper. It's traditionally smoked over pecan wood and sugarcane, which turns it reddish and hot and smoky. Cooking andouille isn't required, but it does improve its flavor.

Linguiça

This peppery smoked sausage from Portugal is distinctive for its tangy, heavily spiced flavor, which comes from a blend of paprika, garlic, pepper, cumin, and sometimes allspice or cinnamon. The spices are combined with pork butt and brined in vinegar and salt before smoking. Linguiça is sold primarily in areas with large Portuguese or Brazilian populations and should be cooked before serving. Try it as a pizza topping or in kale or bean soup.

Common (and Key) Prep Tips for Pork

Scoring Pork Chops

Pork chops come covered in a thin layer of fat and connective tissue (or silverskin). This layer contracts faster than the rest of the meat, causing buckling and leading to unevenly cooked chops. Cutting slits in this layer prevents the problem.

Cut 2 slits about 2 inches apart through fat and connective tissue.

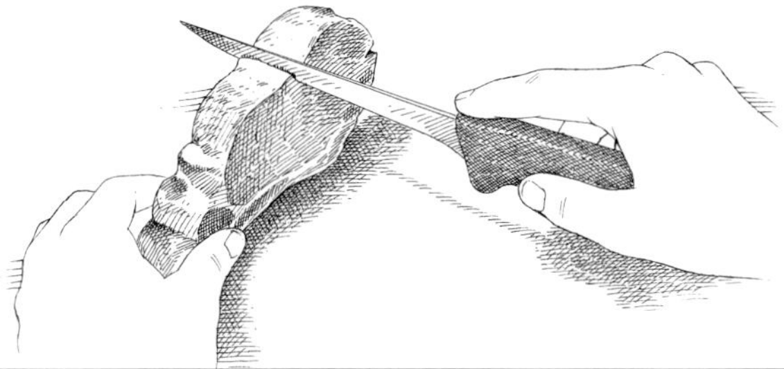

Scoring pork chops ensures they'll lie flat in the pan and cook evenly.

Trimming Silverskin from Pork Tenderloin

Silverskin, the translucent connective tissue running along the tenderloin, is chewy and unpalatable. Be sure to trim it before cooking.

Slip knife under silverskin, angle it slightly upward, and use gentle back-and-forth motion to remove it; discard skin.

Forgetting to remove the silverskin may not only make the meat difficult to chew, but it can also cause the meat to buckle, which will result in uneven cooking.

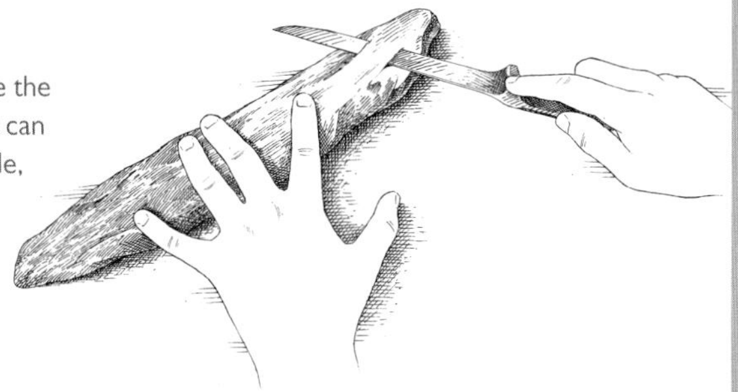

Tying a Pork Loin

No fancy knots are needed to tie a pork loin—just use double knots to secure pieces of kitchen twine at 1½-inch intervals.

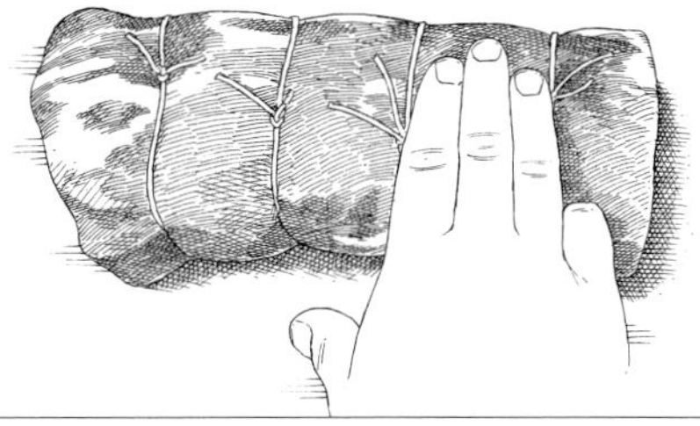

Tying a pork loin helps maintain its shape during cooking so that it cooks evenly. Spacing the ties 3 fingers apart is equal to about 1½ inches.

PORK DONENESS CHART

The chart below lists optimum internal temperatures based on maximum juiciness and flavor. For optimum safety, follow USDA guidelines: Cook whole cuts of meat to an internal temperature of at least 145 degrees and let rest for at least 3 minutes. Cook ground pork to an internal temperature of at least 160 degrees. For more information on carryover cooking and resting meat, see page 8. To determine internal temperature, insert an instant-read thermometer deep into the meat away from any bone. For small cuts, like thin pork chops, take the temperature of the meat from the side, so you can easily reach the center. For large cuts of pork, take two or three readings to make sure the entire piece of meat has reached the proper temperature.

CHOPS AND TENDERLOINS	TEMPERATURE
Medium-Well	145 degrees (150 degrees after resting)
Well-Done	160 degrees
LOIN ROASTS	
Medium-Well	140 degrees (150 degrees after resting)
Well-Done	160 degrees
GROUND PORK	
Well-Done	160 degrees

*If you do not own a food mill
or you prefer applesauce with a
coarse texture, peel the apples
before coring and cutting them
and, after cooking, mash them
against the side of the pot with
a wooden spoon or against the
bottom of the pot with a potato
masher. The applesauce can be
refrigerated for up to five days.*

1. Toss 4 pounds apples
(8 to 12 medium), preferably
Jonagold, Pink Lady, Jonathan,
or Macoun, unpeeled, cored,
and cut into rough 1½-inch
pieces, ¼ cup sugar, pinch
salt, and 1 cup water in large
Dutch oven. Cover pot and
cook apples over medium-
high heat until they begin to
break down, 15 to 20 min-
utes, checking and stirring
occasionally with wooden
spoon to break up any
large chunks.

2. Process cooked apples
through food mill fitted with
medium disk. Season with
extra sugar or add water to
adjust consistency as desired.
Serve hot, warm, at room
temperature, or chilled.
(Makes about 3½ cups.)

Easy Pork Chops

✔ WHY THIS RECIPE WORKS

For a quick, convenient dinner, throwing a few pork chops into a skillet sounds promising, but often results in dry, leathery meat. We wanted to learn how to cook pork chops right and get them on the table in just 20 minutes.

SIZE 'EM UP Boneless chops cooked up much drier than bone-in and were eliminated from contention. Average-size pork chops (1 inch or more), simply took too long, neces-sitating the use of both the stovetop and the oven to cook properly. The right thickness was ½ to ¾ inch—thin enough to keep the cooking on the stovetop yet thick enough to give the chops a fighting chance for a juicy interior.

CUT TO THE CHASE In choosing pork chops, rib chops fared best, though center-cut were a close second. We also knew from prior testing that cutting two slits in the outer layer of fat and silverskin of each chop would encourage the chops to lie flat and prevent them from buckling in the skillet.

BACK OFF THE HEAT Cooking the pork over high heat resulted in extremely dry meat; after searing, the chops were sitting in a pool of juices—which belonged in the pork. Medium heat was an improvement, but we had the best luck starting the chops in a cold pan before turning the heat to medium. After the chops had cooked for a few minutes on each side, we covered them and cooked them through over low heat. The result? Juicy, tender chops.

LOOKING GOOD, SUGAR The only drawback to our method was the color of our chops—or lack thereof. Using a little sugar in addition to salt and pepper to season them went a long way toward helping add color. We also found that instead of splitting the brown-ing time and the sugar evenly between the two sides of a chop, it was better to sugar one side and let it develop a more substantial color.

✎ AT THE MEAT COUNTER

PREFERRED CUT Bone-In Pork Rib Chops
These pork chops are also called rib cut chops or pork chops end cut (see page 180 for more information).

ALTERNATE CUT Bone-In Center-Cut Chops
Bone-in center-cut chops can be substituted for the rib chops. Because the chops contain a lean tenderloin muscle in addition to a fattier loin section, they are not as moist as a rib chop (see page 180 for more information).

EASY PORK CHOPS
SERVES 4

We prefer natural to enhanced pork (pork that has been injected with a salt solution) for this recipe. Electric burners are slower to heat up than gas burn-ers, so, if using an electric stove, begin heating the burner before seasoning the chops. Serve these sim-ple pork chops with chutney or Simple Applesauce or try one of the variations.

> 4   (6- to 8-ounce) bone-in pork rib chops, ½ to ¾ inch thick, trimmed
> 1   teaspoon vegetable oil
>   Salt and pepper
> ½   teaspoon sugar

1. Pat chops dry with paper towels. Cut 2 slits, about 2 inches apart, through outer layer of fat and silverskin on each chop. If using electric stove, turn burner to medium heat. Rub both sides of each chop with ⅛ teaspoon oil and season with salt and pepper. Sprinkle 1 side of each chop evenly with ⅛ teaspoon sugar, avoiding bone.

2. Place chops, sugared side down, in 12-inch nonstick skillet. Using your hands, press meat of each chop into pan. Set skillet over medium heat; cook until lightly browned, 4 to 9 minutes (chops should be sizzling after

2 minutes). Using tongs, flip chops. Cover skillet, reduce heat to low, and cook until each chop registers 145 degrees, 3 to 6 minutes (begin checking temperature after 2 minutes); chops will barely brown on second side. Transfer chops to platter, tent loosely with aluminum foil, and let rest for 5 minutes; do not discard liquid in skillet.

3. Add any accumulated meat juices to skillet. Set skillet over high heat and simmer vigorously until reduced to about 3 tablespoons, 30 to 90 seconds; season with salt and pepper to taste. Off heat, return pork chops to skillet, turning chops to coat with reduced juices. Serve chops, browned side up, pouring any remaining juices over them.

EASY PORK CHOPS WITH
MUSTARD-SAGE SAUCE

After transferring chops to platter, pour liquid in skillet into bowl. While chops are resting, add 1 teaspoon vegetable oil and 1 minced garlic clove to now-empty skillet; set skillet over medium heat and cook until fragrant, about 30 seconds. Add ¼ cup chicken broth; increase heat to high and simmer until reduced to about 2 tablespoons, about 3 minutes. Add pork chop juices to skillet. Off heat, whisk in 3 tablespoons cold unsalted butter, cut into 3 pieces, and 1 tablespoon Dijon mustard until combined. Stir in 1 tablespoon minced fresh sage and season with salt and pepper to taste; spoon sauce over chops and serve.

EASY PORK CHOPS WITH
BRANDY AND PRUNES

Cover ⅓ cup chopped pitted prunes with ¼ cup brandy and let stand. After transferring chops to platter, pour liquid in skillet into bowl. While chops are resting, add 1 teaspoon vegetable oil and 1 minced shallot to now-empty skillet; set skillet over medium heat and cook, stirring occasionally, until shallot is softened, about 2 minutes. Off heat, add brandy and prunes; set skillet over medium-high heat and cook until brandy is reduced to about 2 tablespoons, about 3 minutes. Add pork chop juices to skillet. Off heat, whisk in 2 tablespoons minced fresh thyme and 3 tablespoons cold unsalted butter, cut into 3 pieces, until combined. Season with salt and pepper to taste; spoon sauce over chops and serve.

Crispy Pan-Fried Pork Chops

✓ WHY THIS RECIPE WORKS

A breaded coating can be just the thing to give lean, bland pork chops a flavor boost—but not when it turns gummy and flakes off the meat. We wanted crisp chops that were fast and easy.

LOSE THE BONE To keep this dish fast and easy, we skipped bone-in pork chops and chose boneless loin chops. Shallow frying these thin chops took just a few minutes per side.

GO FOR LIGHT AND CRISPY For an ultralight, crisp coating, we started with cornstarch, which releases sticky starch as it absorbs water and forms an ultracrisp sheath when exposed to heat and fat. Scoring the chops prior to dredging helped the coating adhere.

DIP IN BUTTERMILK Instead of the typical egg wash, we used buttermilk for our liquid component. The buttermilk contributed a nice subtle tang, while a dollop of

We go through buttermilk quickly in the test kitchen, but we realize most home kitchens don't. Wondering if surplus buttermilk could be frozen, we filled ice cube trays with low-fat buttermilk. Once the cubes were frozen solid, we transferred them to plastic bags and returned them to the freezer.

Letting the frozen buttermilk defrost in the refrigerator overnight caused the whey and milky solids to separate (they are easily whisked back together with no ill effects). Microwaving the frozen cubes on medium power until melted was a faster, more efficient method of defrosting. We tested the frozen-then-thawed buttermilk against its fresh counterpart in biscuits, pancakes, and coleslaw. Tasters were hard-pressed to notice any difference between the pancakes and coleslaw made with fresh and previously frozen buttermilk. A few tasters thought the frozen buttermilk made for slightly denser biscuits, but the difference was not significant—the biscuits were perfectly acceptable. Buttermilk can be frozen for up to a month.

mustard and a little minced garlic perked up its flavor even more.

CORNFLAKES PLUS With buttermilk as our wash, bread crumbs absorbed too much liquid and lost their crunch. Instead, we used cornflakes; these crisp flakes are engineered to retain their crunch in liquid. We also added cornstarch to the cornflakes before dredging the chops. Once swollen, the starch granules worked their magic, turning the flakes even crispier in the hot fat.

REST TO SOLIDIFY BREADING We found it was important to let the pork rest after breading and before cooking. Letting the chops sit for 10 minutes before hitting the oil gave the breading a chance to solidify so it remained intact during the cooking process.

CRISPY PAN-FRIED PORK CHOPS
SERVES 4

We prefer natural to enhanced pork (pork that has been injected with a salt solution) for this recipe. Don't let the chops drain on the paper towels for longer than 30 seconds, or the heat will steam the crust and make it soggy. You can substitute ¾ cup store-bought cornflake crumbs for the whole cornflakes. If using crumbs, omit the processing step and mix the crumbs with the cornstarch, salt, and pepper.

⅔	cup cornstarch
1	cup buttermilk
2	tablespoons Dijon mustard
1	garlic clove, minced
3	cups (3 ounces) cornflakes
	Salt and pepper
8	(3- to 4-ounce) boneless pork chops, ½ to ¾ inch thick, trimmed
⅔	cup vegetable oil
	Lemon wedges

1. Place ⅓ cup cornstarch in shallow dish. In second shallow dish, whisk buttermilk, mustard, and garlic until combined. Process cornflakes, ½ teaspoon salt, ½ teaspoon pepper, and remaining ⅓ cup cornstarch in food processor until cornflakes are finely ground,

about 10 seconds. Transfer cornflake mixture to third shallow dish.

2. Adjust oven rack to middle position and heat oven to 200 degrees. Cut ¹⁄₁₆-inch-deep slits on both sides of chops, spaced ½ inch apart, in crosshatch pattern. Season chops with salt and pepper. Dredge 1 chop in cornstarch; shake off excess. Using tongs, coat with buttermilk mixture; let excess drip off. Coat with cornflake mixture; gently pat off excess. Transfer coated chop to wire rack set in rimmed baking sheet and repeat with remaining chops. Let coated chops stand for 10 minutes.

3. Heat ⅓ cup oil in 12-inch nonstick skillet over medium-high heat until shimmering. Place 4 chops in skillet and cook until golden brown and crisp, 2 to 5 minutes. Carefully flip chops and continue to cook until second side is golden brown, crisp, and chops register 145 degrees, 2 to 5 minutes longer. Transfer chops to paper towel–lined plate and let drain 30 seconds on each side. Transfer to clean wire rack set in rimmed baking sheet, then transfer to oven to keep warm. Discard oil in skillet and wipe clean with paper towels. Repeat process with remaining ⅓ cup oil and remaining pork chops. Serve with lemon wedges.

CRISPY PAN-FRIED PORK CHOPS WITH LATIN SPICE RUB

Combine 1½ teaspoons ground cumin, 1½ teaspoons chili powder, ¾ teaspoon ground coriander, ⅛ teaspoon ground cinnamon, and ⅛ teaspoon red pepper flakes in bowl. In step 2, omit pepper and coat chops with spice rub after seasoning with salt.

CRISPY PAN-FRIED PORK CHOPS WITH THREE-PEPPER RUB

Combine 1½ teaspoons pepper, 1½ teaspoons white pepper, ¾ teaspoon coriander, ¾ teaspoon ground cumin, ¼ teaspoon red pepper flakes, and ¼ teaspoon ground cinnamon in bowl. In step 2, omit pepper and coat chops with spice rub after seasoning with salt.

Pan-Seared Thick-Cut Pork Chops

✔ WHY THIS RECIPE WORKS

Because pork chops today are so lean (at least 30 percent leaner than pork sold in the 1980s), overcooking pork, even slightly, yields tough results. And the window for doneness is quite narrow—lean pork chops are best cooked to 140 to 145 degrees. Also, because pork must be cooked to a higher internal temperature than beef, heat distribution is even more inequitable. We wanted a foolproof method for producing juicy, tender pork chops.

BUY BONE-IN RIB CHOPS You can generally find four different cuts of pork chops: sirloin, blade-cut, center-cut, and rib. After comparing all four cuts, we settled on rib chops (cut from the rib section), for their meaty texture and relatively high fat content. The bone acted as an insulator and helped the chops cook gently, while the fat helped to baste the meat as it cooked.

KEEP THEM FLAT Pork often comes covered with a thin membrane called silverskin. This membrane contracts faster than the rest of the meat, causing buckling and leading to uneven cooking. Cutting two slits about 2 inches apart in the silverskin around the edges of the chops prevented this problem.

SALT FOR FLAVOR Salting the pork chops drew out moisture that, 45 minutes later, was pulled back into the meat, producing juicy, well-seasoned chops. The salt also dissolved some of the meat proteins, making them more effective at holding moisture during cooking.

ROAST, THEN SEAR Cooking the salted chops in a gentle oven and then searing them in a smoking-hot pan had a few advantages. First, chops cooked this way are supremely tender because they stay at a lower temperature for about 20 minutes longer than they do with conventional sautéing or roasting

methods. This is in part because the low oven heat helps break down collagen, helping to tenderize the meat. Second, the gentle roasting dries the exterior of the meat, creating a thin, arid layer that turns into a gratifyingly crisp crust when seared.

ACCENT THE CHOP Our pork chops are great plain but also good with traditional applesauce or an easy pan sauce. We used the fond and a little of the fat left over from cooking our chops to create two easy pan sauces. One Southeast Asian-inspired sauce features cilantro, fresh ginger, and coconut milk and the second is a French-style white wine and thyme sauce

---

PAN-SEARED THICK-CUT PORK CHOPS

SERVES 4

Pork rib chops are known as rib cut chops or pork chops end cut (see page 180 for more information). Buy chops of similar thickness so that they cook at the same rate. If the pork is enhanced (injected with a salt solution), do not salt in step 1, but season with salt in step 2. Serve the chops with a pan sauce (recipes follow) or with Simple Applesauce (page 186).

  4 (12-ounce) bone-in pork rib chops, 1½ inches thick, trimmed
      Kosher salt and pepper
1–2 tablespoons vegetable oil

1. Adjust oven rack to middle position and heat oven to 275 degrees. Pat chops dry with paper towels. Cut 2 slits, about 2 inches apart, through outer layer of fat and silverskin on each chop. Sprinkle each chop with 1 teaspoon salt. Place chops on wire rack set in rimmed

baking sheet and let stand at room temperature for 45 minutes.

2. Season chops with pepper; transfer sheet to oven. Cook until chops register 120 to 125 degrees, 30 to 45 minutes.

3. Heat 1 tablespoon oil in 12-inch skillet over high heat until just smoking. Place 2 chops in skillet and sear until well browned and crusty, 1½ to 3 minutes, lifting once halfway through to redistribute fat underneath each chop. (Reduce heat if browned bits in pan start to burn.) Using tongs, turn chops and cook until well browned on second side, 2 to 3 minutes. Transfer chops to plate and repeat with remaining 2 chops, adding 1 tablespoon oil if pan is dry.

4. Reduce heat to medium. Use tongs to stand 2 pork chops on their sides. Holding chops together with tongs, return to skillet and sear sides of chops (with exception of bone side) until browned and chops register 145 degrees, about 1½ minutes. Repeat with remaining 2 chops. Let chops rest, tented loosely with aluminum foil, for 10 minutes, then serve.

CILANTRO AND COCONUT PAN SAUCE

MAKE ABOUT ½ CUP

Regular or low-fat coconut milk can be used in this pan sauce.

    1   large shallot, minced
    1   tablespoon grated fresh ginger
    2   garlic cloves, minced
    ¾   cup canned coconut milk
    ¼   cup chicken broth
    1   teaspoon sugar
    ¼   cup chopped fresh cilantro
    2   teaspoons lime juice
    1   tablespoon unsalted butter, chilled

Pour off all but 1 teaspoon fat from pan used to cook chops and return pan to medium heat. Add shallot, ginger, and garlic and cook, stirring constantly, until softened, about 1 minute. Add coconut milk, broth, and sugar, scraping bottom of pan with wooden spoon to loosen any browned bits. Simmer until reduced to ½ cup, 6 to 7 minutes. Off heat, stir in cilantro and lime juice, then whisk in butter. Season with salt and pepper to taste, and serve with chops.

GARLIC AND THYME PAN SAUCE

MAKES ABOUT ½ CUP

A dry white wine ensures the sauce doesn't turn out too sweet.

    1   large shallot, minced
    2   garlic cloves, minced
    ¾   cup chicken broth
    ½   cup dry white wine
    1   teaspoon minced fresh thyme
    ¼   teaspoon white wine vinegar
    3   tablespoons unsalted butter, cut into
        3 pieces and chilled

Pour off all but 1 teaspoon fat from pan used to cook chops and return pan to medium heat. Add shallot and garlic and cook, stirring constantly, until softened, about 1 minute. Add broth and wine, scraping bottom of pan with wooden spoon to loosen any browned bits. Simmer until reduced to ½ cup, 6 to 7 minutes. Off heat, stir in thyme and vinegar, then whisk in butter, 1 tablespoon at a time. Season with salt and pepper to taste, and serve with chops.

SHOPPING FOR SHALLOTS

When shopping for shallots, avoid those packaged in cardboard and cellophane boxes, which prevent you from checking out each shallot. Instead, go for loose shallots or the ones packed in plastic netting. They should feel firm and heavy and have no soft spots.

Small, hard seeds like caraway, fennel, and cumin are
seemingly impossible to chop
because they scatter all over
the counter when you bear
down on them.

I. Place measured seeds in
small pile on cutting board.
Pour just enough water or oil
to moisten them.

2. Seeds can now be chopped
with chef's knife without flying
off cutting board.

Glazed Pork Chops

✓ WHY THIS RECIPE WORKS

*We wanted to combine the convenience and speed
of thin boneless pork chops with the flavor and moist,
juicy interior of their thicker, bone-in counterparts.
Additionally, we wanted our chops coated in a balanced, well-seasoned glaze.*

THIN IS IN Before searing our thin chops,
we cut through the layer of fat and silverskin
to prevent a bowing effect (especially pronounced with thin chops).

SEAR FOR FLAVOR For proper browning, we found that the chops needed an initial quick sear It was also important to use a
good-quality, heavy-bottomed skillet. Flimsy
skillets with thin bottoms can scorch and cook
food unevenly.

TRIPLE-PLAY GLAZE A sweet and sticky
glaze of cider, brown sugar, soy sauce, vinegar, and mustard went into the pan to finish cooking the chops. Not only did the sauce
give the chops rich flavor, but it also reduced
down to a nice, thick glaze.

GLAZED PORK CHOPS
SERVES 4

---

*If your chops are on the thinner side, check their
temperature after the initial sear. If they are already
at the 145-degree mark, remove them from the skillet and allow them to rest, tented loosely with aluminum foil, for 5 minutes, then add the pork juices and
glaze ingredients to the skillet and proceed with step
3. If your chops are closer to 1 inch thick, you may
need to increase the simmering time in step 2.*

½	cup distilled white vinegar or cider vinegar
⅓	cup packed light brown sugar
⅓	cup apple cider or apple juice
2	tablespoons Dijon mustard
1	tablespoon soy sauce
	Pinch cayenne pepper
4	(5- to 7-ounce) boneless pork chops, ½ to ¾ inch thick, trimmed

Salt and pepper

1 tablespoon vegetable oil

1. Combine vinegar, sugar, cider, mustard, soy sauce, and cayenne in bowl; mix
thoroughly and set aside. Pat chops dry with
paper towels. Cut 2 slits, about 2 inches apart,
through outer layer of fat and silverskin on
each chop. Season chops with salt and pepper.

2. Heat oil in 12-inch skillet over medium-
high heat until just smoking. Add chops
to skillet and cook until well browned, 4 to
6 minutes. Turn chops and cook 1 minute longer; transfer chops to plate and pour off any oil
in skillet. Return chops to skillet, browned side
up, and add glaze mixture; cook over medium
heat until chops register 145 degrees, 5 to
8 minutes. Off heat, transfer chops to clean
platter, tent loosely with aluminum foil, and
let rest for 5 minutes.

3. When chops have rested, add any accumulated juices to skillet and set over medium
heat. Simmer, whisking constantly, until glaze
is thick and color of dark caramel (heat-resistant
spatula should leave wide trail when dragged
through glaze), 2 to 6 minutes. Return chops
to skillet; turn to coat both sides with glaze.
Transfer chops back to platter, browned side up,
and spread remaining glaze over chops. Serve.

GLAZED PORK CHOPS WITH
GERMAN FLAVORS

---

*Keep a close eye on the caraway seeds; they can
burn quickly*

Toast ¾ teaspoon caraway seeds in small
dry skillet over medium heat, stirring frequently, until fragrant, 3 to 5 minutes. Chop
seeds coarse and set aside. Substitute ⅓ cup
beer for cider, reduce soy sauce to 2 teaspoons, and add 3 tablespoons whole-grain
mustard (along with Dijon mustard), 1 tablespoon minced fresh thyme, and reserved caraway seeds to glaze ingredients. Omit cayenne.

1. With paring knife positioned as shown, insert blade through center of side of chop until tip touches bone.

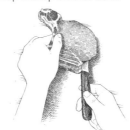

2. Holding chop firmly, carefully swing tip of blade through middle of chop to create pocket; turn knife and swing in opposite direction, being careful not to enlarge opening.

3. With your fingers, gently press stuffing mixture into pocket, without enlarging opening.

Stuffed Thick-Cut Pork Chops

✓ WHY THIS RECIPE WORKS

Stuffing a pork chop is a good idea in theory— today's lean pork needs all the help it can get— but it is rarely well executed. Most recipes insist on treating the chops like a turkey, cramming them full of bulky bread stuffing, which does little to improve the flavor or texture of the chop. We wanted a pork chop that was thick and juicy, seared crusty brown on the outside, and enhanced by a flavorful stuffing.

CHOOSE THE RIGHT CHOP Bone-in chops provide visual appeal and the bone helps the meat stay juicy, but shopping for bone-in chops can be confusing, since butchers and supermarket labels rarely agree on precisely what is called what. We found the best chop for stuffing to be the rib chop, which is cut from the rib cage and has a wide, unbroken eye of meat and a curved rib bone off to the side and out of the way.

STUFFING AND TECHNIQUE MATTERS We wanted a stuffing that would bring much-needed moisture, fat, and assertive flavor to our chops. Consistency and texture proved important too; creamy, even sticky stuffings were much easier to pack into a chop than dry, loose, crumbly ones. Butterflying the chops and then stitching them back together with toothpicks or string was ineffective and tedious; using a paring knife to cut a wide pocket with a small opening proved much more successful.

COOK THEM FAST We brined our chops to help keep them moist, then turned to high, dry heat to develop a crusty brown exterior. Searing the chops in a skillet on the stovetop, then transferring them to a preheated baking sheet in the oven to finish, ensured evenly browned, perfectly cooked chops.

STUFFED THICK-CUT PORK CHOPS
SERVES 4

Pork rib chops are also known as rib cut chops or pork chops end cut (see page 180 for more information). If the pork is enhanced (injected with a salt solution), do not brine in step 1, but season with salt in step 2. Prepare the stuffing while the chops brine. (The stuffing can also be made a day in advance, but it must be microwaved just to room temperature before being packed into the chops.) One stuffed chop makes for a very generous serving. If desired, remove the meat from the bone and cut it into ½-inch slices to serve six.

- 4 (12- to 14-ounce) bone-in pork rib chops, 1½ inches thick, trimmed
  Salt and pepper
- 3 tablespoons packed light brown sugar
- 1 recipe stuffing (recipes follow)
- 2 teaspoons vegetable oil

1. Using sharp paring knife, cut 1-inch opening into side of each chop, then cut pocket for stuffing by swinging blade through middle of chop. Dissolve 3 tablespoons salt and sugar in 1½ quarts cold water in large container. Submerge chops in brine, cover, and refrigerate for 1 hour.

2. Adjust oven rack to lower-middle position, place rimmed baking sheet on rack, and heat oven to 450 degrees. Remove chops from brine and thoroughly pat dry with paper towels. Place one-quarter of stuffing in pocket of each chop—enlarge pocket opening slightly, if necessary. Trim reserved orange (or lemon) wedges from stuffing recipe to 2-inch lengths; insert 1 orange (or lemon) wedge into each

pocket to contain stuffing. Season chops with pepper. (Chops can be stuffed and refrigerated up to 1 day ahead.)

3. Heat oil in 12-inch skillet over medium-high heat until just smoking. Arrange chops in skillet and cook without moving chops until well browned, about 3 minutes. Using tongs, flip chops and cook until well browned on second side, 2 to 3 minutes longer.

4. Using tongs, transfer chops to preheated baking sheet in oven; cook until stuffing registers 140 degrees, 15 to 20 minutes, flipping chops halfway through cooking. Transfer chops to platter, tent loosely with aluminum foil, and let rest for 10 minutes. Serve.

RED ONION JAM STUFFING WITH PORT, PECANS, AND DRIED FRUIT

MAKES ABOUT 1⅓ CUPS

1	tablespoon olive oil
1	large red onion, halved and sliced ⅛ inch thick (about 4 cups)
1	tablespoon sugar
⅓	cup chopped dates
⅓	cup dried tart cherries
¾	cup ruby port
1	orange, cut into 4 wedges
3	tablespoons white wine vinegar
2	teaspoons minced fresh thyme
	Salt and pepper
⅓	cup pecans, toasted

1. Heat oil in medium saucepan over medium heat until shimmering; add onion and sugar and cook, stirring occasionally, until beginning to color, 20 to 25 minutes. Meanwhile, combine dates, cherries, and port in bowl; cover and microwave until simmering, about 1 minute. Set aside until needed. Squeeze juice from orange wedges into small bowl; reserve juiced wedges for sealing stuffing pockets in chops.

2. When onion is soft, add dried fruit mixture, ¼ cup orange juice, 2 tablespoons vinegar, thyme, ¼ teaspoon salt, and pepper to taste; continue to cook, stirring occasionally, until mixture is jam-like, 10 to 12 minutes. Stir in remaining 1 tablespoon vinegar and pecans; transfer to bowl and let cool until just warm, about 15 minutes.

SPINACH AND FONTINA STUFFING WITH PINE NUTS

MAKES ABOUT 1⅓ CUPS

Either whole-milk or part-skim ricotta work in this recipe.

1	slice hearty white sandwich bread, torn into quarters
¼	cup pine nuts, toasted
1	tablespoon olive oil
2	garlic cloves, minced
6	ounces (6 cups) baby spinach
2	ounces Italian fontina cheese, shredded (½ cup)
¼	cup (2 ounces) ricotta cheese
1	ounce Parmesan cheese, grated (½ cup)
1	lemon, cut into 4 wedges
	Salt and pepper
	Pinch ground nutmeg

1. Pulse bread and pine nuts in food processor until evenly ground, about 10 pulses.

2. Heat oil in 12-inch skillet over medium-high heat until shimmering; add garlic and cook, stirring constantly, until fragrant, about 30 seconds. Add spinach; using tongs, turn spinach to coat with oil. Cook, stirring with tongs, until spinach is wilted, about 2 minutes. Transfer spinach to colander set in sink and gently squeeze to release excess moisture; let spinach cool until just warm.

3. Combine fontina, ricotta, and Parmesan in bowl. Add spinach and bread-crumb mixture; using spatula, mix well to break up clumps. Squeeze juice from lemon wedges into small bowl; reserve juiced wedges for sealing stuffing pockets in chops. Stir 1 tablespoon lemon juice, ¼ teaspoon salt, pepper to taste, and nutmeg into stuffing.

FITTING STUFFED PORK CHOPS INTO THE SKILLET

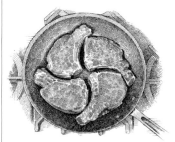

We arrange our pork chops in a pinwheel pattern so they fit easily into skillet.

Center-cut chops (boneless chops are almost always center cut) are quite lean, and left untreated they will be very dry and chewy, even when cooked to medium-well (an internal temperature of 145 degrees). The salt in the brine changes the structure of the muscle proteins and allows them to hold on to more moisture when exposed to heat. Tasters had no trouble picking out the chops that we had brined versus chops that we had left untreated.

If you're accustomed to brining a turkey for the holidays, you might think you don't have time to brine pork chops for a weeknight recipe like this. But we found that making the brine super-concentrated (with ¼ cup of table salt dissolved in 1 quart of water) gets the job done in just 30 minutes—the time it will take you to prepare the fresh bread-crumb coating. And our potent brine fits, along with four chops, in a medium container or 1-gallon zipper-lock bag. No brining bucket needed.

One exception: If you've purchased enhanced chops injected with a salt solution, don't brine them. The injected solution will make the chops moist, even spongy, and brining will make the meat way too salty. We prefer the flavor of natural chops and find that 30 minutes in a strong brine makes them plenty juicy.

Crunchy Baked Pork Chops

✓ WHY THIS RECIPE WORKS

When done right, baked breaded pork chops are the ultimate comfort food—tender cutlets surrounded by a crunchy coating that crackles apart with each bite. But use a packaged supermarket breading and you get a thin, sandy crust. Make your own breading and you have different problems: a soggy, patchy crust that won't stick to the meat. What's the secret to ultracrunchy chops?

BRINE THE CHOPS We found that the first step toward juicy, well-seasoned chops is to brine them. Although you may be tempted to skip this step, don't. Center-cut chops are quite lean, and left untreated they will be very dry and chewy, even when cooked to medium. The salt in the brine not only helps ensure juicy chops, it also seasons the meat for better flavor.

USE FRESH BREAD CRUMBS We left the dusty, stale-tasting packaged crumbs on the shelf and made our own fresh crumbs from good-quality sandwich bread. Pretoasting the crumbs ensured that they would still be plenty crunchy by the time the pork was done. Don't skip the toasting step; if you do, you must choose between a less-than-crunchy coating and overcooked pork.

MAKE A BATTER-LIKE COATING Most recipes dust the chops with flour, dip them in beaten eggs, and then coat with crumbs. The result is a soft crust that has a greater propensity to peel away when baked. (Pan frying does a better job of fusing crumbs to meat.) Our solution was to replace the beaten whole eggs with a batterlike mixture of egg whites, flour, and mustard. The fat in the yolks can make the crumbs soft, so we got rid of them. Adding flour and mustard to the egg whites turned the typically liquid-y wash into a Spackle-like paste that really stuck to the chops and held on to the crumbs.

BAKE ON A RACK Elevating the chops on a baking sheet proved essential; this allowed any moisture shed by the chops to drip harmlessly away and permitted heat to circulate around the chops, ensuring that the coated chops browned on all sides.

CRUNCHY BAKED PORK CHOPS
SERVES 4

If the pork is enhanced (injected with a salt solution), do not brine in step 1, but season with salt in step 4.

	Salt and pepper
4	(6- to 8-ounce) boneless pork chops, ¾ to 1 inch thick, trimmed
4	slices hearty white sandwich bread, torn into 1-inch pieces
2	tablespoons vegetable oil
1	small shallot, minced
3	garlic cloves, minced
2	tablespoons grated Parmesan cheese
2	tablespoons minced fresh parsley
½	teaspoon minced fresh thyme
¼	cup plus 6 tablespoons all-purpose flour
3	large egg whites
3	tablespoons Dijon mustard
	Lemon wedges

1. Adjust oven rack to middle position and heat oven to 350 degrees. Dissolve 3 tablespoons salt in 1½ quarts cold water in large container. Submerge chops in brine, cover, and refrigerate for 30 minutes to 1 hour. Remove chops from brine and thoroughly pat dry with paper towels.

2. Meanwhile, pulse bread in food processor until coarsely ground, about 8 pulses (you

should have about 3½ cups crumbs). Transfer crumbs to rimmed baking sheet and add oil, shallot, garlic, ¼ teaspoon salt, and ¼ teaspoon pepper. Toss until crumbs are evenly coated with oil. Bake until deep golden brown and dry, about 15 minutes, stirring twice during baking time. (Do not turn off oven.) Let cool to room temperature and transfer to large bowl. Add Parmesan, parsley, and thyme and stir to combine. (Bread-crumb mixture can be prepared up to 3 days in advance.)

3. Place ¼ cup flour in shallow dish. In second shallow dish, whisk egg whites and mustard until combined; add remaining 6 tablespoons flour and whisk until almost smooth, with pea-size lumps remaining.

4. Increase oven temperature to 425 degrees. Spray wire rack with vegetable oil spray and set in rimmed baking sheet. Season chops with pepper. Dredge 1 pork chop in flour; shake off excess. Using tongs, coat with egg white mixture; let excess drip off. Coat all sides of chop with bread-crumb mixture, pressing gently so that thick layer of crumbs adheres to chop. Transfer breaded chop to prepared wire rack. Repeat with remaining 3 chops.

5. Bake until chops register 145 degrees, 17 to 25 minutes. Let rest on rack for 5 minutes before serving with lemon wedges.

TO MAKE AHEAD: Breaded chops can be frozen for up to 1 week. Do not thaw before baking; simply increase cooking time in step 5 to 35 to 40 minutes.

CRUNCHY BAKED PORK CHOPS WITH PROSCIUTTO AND ASIAGO CHEESE

Omit salt added to bread-crumb mixture in step 2. Before breading, place ⅛-inch-thick slice Asiago cheese (about ½ ounce) on top of each chop. Wrap each chop with thin slice prosciutto, pressing on prosciutto so that cheese and meat adhere to one another. Proceed with recipe from step 4, being careful when handling chops so that cheese and meat do not come apart during breading.

Pork Chops with Vinegar and Sweet Peppers

✔ WHY THIS RECIPE WORKS

This Italian American dish was devised when pork chops had plenty of fat to keep them juicy; the leaner pork we have today tends to dry out and ruin it. But the thought of succulent pork with a tangy vinegar and pepper sauce spurred us to search for a way to make this dish taste the way it should.

CHOP SHOP The first step was choosing the right chop. Bone-in rib chops of medium thickness had the best flavor, and the bone helped keep the meat juicy. Brining the chops in a solution of salt and sugar added moisture and flavor, and the sugar enhanced browning.

TOGETHER IS BETTER Cooking the chops and then assembling a pan sauce of vinegar and bell peppers didn't give us the marriage of flavors the dish should have, but braising the chops in a vinegar sauce produced chalky meat. We discovered that browning the chops, removing them from the pan to build the sauce, and then finishing everything together in the oven worked best to get the flavors of the sauce into the meat.

A PACK OF PEPPERS We ditched the jarred vinegar bell peppers, which are traditional, and made our own. Roasting fresh bell peppers and marinating them in vinegar for a few hours was too fussy, but sautéing the peppers to take off the raw crunch before adding just enough vinegar to cover the peppers and letting them simmer did the trick.

VINEGAR VICTORY Most recipes call for white wine vinegar, and after testing Champagne, cider, red wine, balsamic, and plain old white vinegar, we agreed. It offered a clean, sweet taste that married perfectly with the peppers and the pork.

BUMP UP THE FLAVOR To boost the flavor of the sauce, we included some onion for sweetness, while a little garlic and anchovy added complexity. A hint of rosemary, provided simply by steeping a whole sprig in the sauce for a few minutes, was a welcome addition. To finish the sauce, we added parsley for color and butter for richness. Finally, we added a hit of vinegar just before serving.

◢ AT THE MEAT COUNTER

PREFERRED CUT Bone-In Pork Rib Chops
Pork rib chops are also known as rib cut chops or pork chops end cut (see page 180 for more information).

ALTERNATE CUT Bone-In Center-Cut Chops
Center-cut chops can be substituted for the rib chops. Note that center-cut chops contain a portion of the tenderloin and may not be as juicy as a rib chop (see page 180 for more information).

PORK CHOPS WITH VINEGAR AND SWEET PEPPERS

SERVES 4

If the pork is enhanced (injected with a salt solution), do not brine in step 1, but season with salt in step 1. To keep the chops from overcooking and becoming tough and dry, they are removed from the oven when they are just shy of fully cooked; as they sit in the hot skillet, they continue to cook with residual heat. The vinegar stirred into the sauce at the end adds a bright, fresh flavor. However, taste the sauce before you add the vinegar—you may prefer to omit it.

Salt and pepper
3 tablespoons sugar
4 (8- to 10-ounce) bone-in pork rib chops, ¾ to 1 inch thick, trimmed
2 tablespoons olive oil
1 large onion, chopped fine
1 large red bell pepper, stemmed, seeded, and cut into ¼-inch-wide strips
1 large yellow bell pepper, stemmed, seeded, and cut into ¼-inch-wide strips
2 anchovy fillets, rinsed and minced
1 sprig fresh rosemary
2 garlic cloves, minced
¾ cup water
½ cup plus 2 tablespoons white wine vinegar
2 tablespoons unsalted butter, cut into 2 pieces and chilled
2 tablespoons chopped fresh parsley

1. Dissolve 3 tablespoons salt and sugar in 1½ quarts cold water in large container. Submerge chops in brine, cover, and refrigerate for 30 minutes to 1 hour. Remove chops from brine; thoroughly pat dry with paper towels, season with ¾ teaspoon pepper, and set aside.

2. Adjust oven rack to middle position and heat oven to 400 degrees. Heat oil in 12-inch ovensafe skillet over medium-high heat until just smoking; swirl skillet to coat with oil. Place chops in skillet; cook until well browned, 3 to 4 minutes, using spoon or spatula to press down on center of chops to aid in browning. Using tongs, flip chops and brown lightly on second side, about 1 minute. Transfer chops to large plate; set aside.

3. Add onion to now-empty skillet and cook over medium-high heat, stirring occasionally, until just beginning to soften, about 2 minutes. Add bell peppers, anchovies, and rosemary sprig; cook, stirring frequently, until bell peppers just begin to soften, about 4 minutes. Add garlic and cook, stirring constantly, until fragrant, about 30 seconds. Add water and ½ cup vinegar and bring to boil, scraping bottom of pan with wooden spoon

STEMMING, SEEDING, AND SLICING BELL PEPPERS

1. Slice ¼ inch from top and bottom of pepper, then gently remove stem from top lobe.

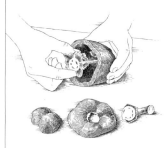

2. Pull core out of pepper.

3. Slit down 1 side of pepper, then lay it flat, skin side down, in long strip. Use sharp knife to slide along inside of pepper, removing all ribs and seeds. Slice into pieces as directed in recipe.

to loosen any browned bits. Reduce heat to medium and simmer until liquid is reduced to about ⅓ cup, 6 to 8 minutes. Off heat, discard rosemary sprig.

4. Return pork chops, browned side up, to skillet; nestle chops in bell peppers, but do not cover chops with bell peppers. Add any accumulated meat juices to skillet; transfer skillet to oven and cook until chops register 145 degrees, 8 to 12 minutes (begin checking temperature after 6 minutes). Using potholders, carefully remove skillet from oven (handle will be very hot) and cover skillet with lid or aluminum foil; let rest for 5 to 7 minutes.

Transfer chops to platter or individual plates. Swirl butter into sauce and bell peppers in skillet; stir in remaining 2 tablespoons vinegar, if using, and parsley. Season with salt and pepper to taste, then pour or spoon sauce and bell peppers over chops. Serve.

PORK CHOPS WITH BALSAMIC VINEGAR AND SWEET PEPPERS

Substitute balsamic vinegar for white wine vinegar and add 1 tablespoon chopped fresh thyme along with parsley.

Red Wine–Braised Pork Chops

✔ WHY THIS RECIPE WORKS

Pork chops are a great choice for an easy, no-frills weeknight meal; they require minimal prep and can simply be tossed into a hot skillet and on the table in minutes. But we wanted to take pork chops to a whole new level with braising—a slow, gentle approach that would not only give us flavorful, tender chops, but a rich, glossy sauce as well.

PICK THE RIGHT CHOP After brining, searing, and braising four different cuts, only one proved right for the job. Blade-cut chops contain plenty of marbling and connective tissue, which breaks down during cooking, lending the meat plenty of flavor and also preserving its juiciness.

TAP THE TRIMMINGS The only downside to our chops of choice was their tendency to buckle during searing, which prevented them from taking on much browning or developing

a good fond on the bottom of the pot. Trimming the connective tissue from the chops solved part of the problem—the chops now lay flat—but we were still missing a substantial fond. Adding the fatty trimmings back to the pot gave us such good flavor and browning that we were able to skip the step of searing the chops. Another bonus: Nestling the chops on top of the trimmings raised them above the liquid line (a combination of red wine, port, chicken broth, and red wine vinegar), keeping them in the ideal temperature range for braising. The result? Noticeably juicier meat.

LET THEM REST Resting the braised chops for 30 minutes proved key; this gave the meat juices ample time to redistribute throughout the meat.

FINAL FLOURISHES Reducing the liquid contributed body to the sauce, while a pat of butter added silky richness. A little more red wine vinegar brightened the flavor and some crushed fresh ginger and a little allspice lent a rich, spicy aroma.

RED WINE–BRAISED PORK CHOPS
SERVES 4

Look for blade-cut chops, also called pork chop end cuts, with a small eye and a large amount of marbling, as these are the most suited to braising (see page 179 for more information) The pork scraps can be removed when straining the sauce in step 4 and served alongside the chops. (They taste great.) If the pork is enhanced (injected with a salt solution), do not brine in step 1, but season with salt in step 2.

    Salt and pepper
  4 (10- to 12-ounce) bone-in blade-cut
    chops, 1 inch thick
  2 teaspoons vegetable oil
  2 onions, halved and sliced thin
  5 sprigs fresh thyme, plus ¼ teaspoon
    minced
  2 garlic cloves, peeled
  2 bay leaves
  1 (½-inch) piece ginger, peeled and
    crushed
  ⅛ teaspoon ground allspice
  ½ cup red wine
  ¼ cup ruby port
  2 tablespoons plus ½ teaspoon red
    wine vinegar
  1 cup chicken broth
  2 tablespoons unsalted butter, cut into
    2 pieces and chilled
  1 tablespoon minced fresh parsley

1. Dissolve 3 tablespoons salt in 1½ quarts cold water in large container. Submerge chops in brine, cover, and refrigerate for 1 hour.

2. Adjust oven rack to lower-middle position and heat oven to 275 degrees. Remove chops from brine and pat dry with paper towels. Trim off cartilage, meat cap, and fat opposite rib bones. Cut trimmings into 1-inch pieces. Heat oil in Dutch oven over medium-high heat until shimmering. Add trimmings and brown on all sides, 6 to 9 minutes.

3. Reduce heat to medium and add onions, thyme sprigs, garlic, bay leaves, ginger, and allspice. Cook, stirring occasionally, until onions are golden brown, 5 to 10 minutes. Stir in wine, port, and 2 tablespoons vinegar, and cook until reduced to thin syrup, 5 to 7 minutes. Add chicken broth, spread onion and pork scraps into even layer, and bring to simmer. Arrange pork chops on top of pork scraps and onions.

4. Cover, transfer to oven, and cook until meat is tender, 1¼ to 1½ hours. Remove from oven and let chops rest in pot, covered, for 30 minutes. Transfer chops to serving platter and tent with aluminum foil. Pour braising liquid through fine-mesh strainer set over large bowl; discard solids and reserve scraps, if desired. Transfer braising liquid to fat separator and let stand 5 minutes.

5. Wipe out now-empty pot with wad of paper towels. Return defatted braising liquid to pot and cook over medium-high heat until reduced to 1 cup, 3 to 7 minutes. Off heat, whisk in butter, ¼ teaspoon minced thyme, and remaining ½ teaspoon vinegar. Season with salt and pepper to taste. Pour sauce over chops, sprinkle with parsley, and serve.

Smothered Pork Chops

WHY THIS RECIPE WORKS

In the abstract, recipes for smothered pork chops sound utterly appealing: Generously season and sear pork chops, remove them from the skillet, fry lots of onions in the fat, then return the chops to the skillet to braise in the flavorful, oniony liquid. Too often the chops are dry and tough, while the "gravy" is watery and bland. We wanted a simple, straightforward recipe for juicy chops and a thick onion gravy.

CHOOSE YOUR CHOPS Bone-in chops were a must because we knew the bone would help keep the meat moist and add flavor to the sauce. Lean, meaty rib or loin chops are the standard for this dish but in test after test with this recipe, they came out dry and tough. We then turned to fattier blade-cut chops. To flavor our pork chops from the get-go, we applied a spice rub before browning them.

OVEN-BRAISE 'EM We chose to braise our chops in the gentle, even heat of the oven, rather than on the stovetop, which would have required more monitoring during the long braise.

GETTING ON THE GRAVY TRAIN Browning the onions in butter helped add richer flavor to the gravy. Chicken broth turned out a wimpy gravy but more muscular beef broth imparted hearty character. Thyme, bay leaf, and a splash of cider vinegar further boosted flavor.

DEFAT, REDUCE, AND THICKEN When the onion gravy went into the oven with the chops, it was perfectly thickened, but after the braise, it emerged thin and watery. It turned out that the chops and onions were giving up a lot of liquid during braising. The solution? After we pulled the braised chops from the pan, we defatted the liquid, measured out the amount we needed for the chops, reduced it on the stovetop, then thickened it with a broth and cornstarch slurry. Spooned over our juicy, braised chops, our onion gravy was the best yet.

SMOTHERED PORK CHOPS
SERVES 4

Blade-cut chops are also called pork chop end cuts (see page 179 for more information). Pork chops thicker than ½ inch won't be fully tender in the allotted cooking time.

1	teaspoon onion powder
½	teaspoon paprika
	Salt and pepper
¼	teaspoon cayenne pepper
4	(8- to 10-ounce) bone-in blade-cut pork chops, ½ inch thick, trimmed
1½	tablespoons vegetable oil
1	tablespoon unsalted butter
2	onions, halved and sliced ¼ inch thick
2	garlic cloves, minced
¼	teaspoon dried thyme
¾	cup plus 1 tablespoon beef broth
1	bay leaf
1	teaspoon cornstarch
1	teaspoon cider vinegar

1. Adjust oven rack to middle position and heat oven to 300 degrees. Combine onion powder, paprika, ½ teaspoon salt, ½ teaspoon pepper, and cayenne in small bowl. Pat chops dry with paper towels. Cut 2 slits, about 2 inches apart through outer layer of fat and silverskin on each chop. Rub chops with spice mixture.

2. Heat oil in 12-inch skillet over medium-high heat until just smoking. Brown chops on both sides, 6 to 8 minutes, and transfer to plate. Melt butter in now-empty skillet over medium heat. Cook onions until browned, 8 to 10 minutes. Add garlic and thyme and cook until fragrant, about 30 seconds. Stir in ¾ cup broth and bay leaf, scraping up any browned bits, and bring to boil. Return chops and any accumulated juices to skillet, cover,

and transfer to oven. Cook until chops are completely tender, about 1½ hours.

3. Transfer chops to platter and tent with aluminum foil. Discard bay leaf. Strain contents of skillet through fine-mesh strainer into large liquid measuring cup; reserve onions. Let liquid settle, then skim fat. Return 1½ cups defatted pan juices to again-empty skillet and bring to boil. Reduce heat to medium and simmer until sauce is reduced to 1 cup, about 5 minutes.

4. Whisk remaining 1 tablespoon broth and cornstarch in bowl until no lumps remain. Whisk cornstarch mixture into sauce and simmer until thickened, 1 to 2 minutes. Stir in reserved onions and vinegar. Season with salt and pepper to taste. Serve over pork chops.

Easy Grilled Pork Chops

✔ WHY THIS RECIPE WORKS

Most recipes for grilled pork chops tend to produce either beautifully charred meat that's as dry as cardboard or juicy chops that are also pale and bland. Frustrated by these half measures, we wanted to develop a recipe that paid equal attention to juiciness and browning. At the same time, we aimed to retain the speed and ease that have always made grilled pork chops such an attractive weeknight dinner in the first place.

BRINE THE CHOPS To ensure that our thin chops stayed juicy even when exposed to the high heat of the grill, we started by brining them. Adding moisture to the meat in this way allowed our chops to spend more time directly over the coals without drying out.

GIVE BROWNING A BOOST While brining provided some insurance against overcooking, our chops were still refusing to develop a good sear and rich flavor in the time it took for them to cook through. Since our chops couldn't spend any more time over the coals without drying out, we needed to find a way to treat the exterior of the chops to speed up browning. After trying everything from dry milk powder to flour, we finally landed on a mixture of anchovy paste and honey—this combination of protein and sugars gave our chops a golden, burnished crust in record time.

EASY GRILLED BONELESS PORK CHOPS

SERVES 4 TO 6

If the pork is enhanced (injected with a salt solution), do not brine in step 1. Very finely mashed anchovy fillets (rinsed and dried before mashing) can be used instead of anchovy paste. If desired, serve with Onion, Olive, and Caper Relish (recipe follows).

6	(6- to 8-ounce) boneless pork chops, ¾ to 1 inch thick, trimmed
3	tablespoons salt
1	tablespoon vegetable oil
1½	teaspoons honey
1	teaspoon anchovy paste
½	teaspoon pepper

1. Cut 2 slits, about 2 inches apart, through outer layer of fat and silverskin on each chop. Dissolve salt in 1½ quarts cold water in large container. Submerge chops in brine and let stand at room temperature for 30 minutes.

2. Whisk together oil, honey, anchovy paste, and pepper to form smooth paste. Remove chops from brine and pat dry with paper towels. Using spoon, spread half of oil mixture evenly over 1 side of each chop (about ¼ teaspoon per side).

3A. FOR A CHARCOAL GRILL: Open bottom vent completely. Light chimney starter filled with charcoal briquettes (6 quarts). When top coals are partially covered with ash, pour evenly over half of grill. Set cooking grate in place, cover, and open lid vent completely. Heat grill until hot, about 5 minutes.

3B. FOR A GAS GRILL: Turn all burners to high, cover, and heat grill until hot, about 15 minutes. Leave primary burner on high and turn off other burner(s).

4. Clean and oil cooking grate. Place chops, oiled side down, over hotter part of grill and cook, uncovered, until well browned on first side, 4 to 6 minutes. While chops are grilling, spread remaining oil mixture evenly over second side of chops. Flip chops and continue to cook until chops register 145 degrees, 4 to 6 minutes longer (if chops are well browned but register less than 145 degrees, move to cooler part of grill to finish cooking). Transfer chops to plate and let rest for 5 minutes. Serve.

ONION, OLIVE, AND CAPER RELISH
MAKES ABOUT 2 CUPS

¼	cup olive oil
2	onions, cut into ¼-inch pieces
6	garlic cloves, sliced thin
½	cup pitted kalamata olives, chopped coarse
¼	cup capers, rinsed
3	tablespoons balsamic vinegar
2	tablespoons minced fresh parsley
1	teaspoon minced fresh marjoram
1	teaspoon sugar
½	teaspoon anchovy paste
½	teaspoon pepper
¼	teaspoon salt

Heat 2 tablespoons oil in 10-inch nonstick skillet over medium heat until shimmering. Add onions and cook until softened, about 5 minutes. Stir in garlic and cook until fragrant, about 30 seconds. Transfer onion mixture to medium bowl; stir in remaining 2 tablespoons oil, olives, capers, vinegar, parsley, marjoram, sugar, anchovy paste, pepper, and salt. Serve warm or at room temperature.

CAPERS

An ideal caper has the perfect balance of saltiness, sweetness, acidity, and crunch. These sun-dried, pickled flower buds have a strong flavor that develops as they are cured, either immersed in a salty brine or packed in salt. From previous tastings we knew we preferred the compact size and slight crunch of tiny nonpareil capers, so we tasted six nationally available supermarket brands, evaluating them on their sharpness, saltiness, and overall appeal. The winner, **Reese Non Pareil Capers**, had every component of the ideal.

Grilled Bone-In Pork Chops

✓ WHY THIS RECIPE WORKS
Too many grilled chops are burnt on the outside and raw on the inside. And even if they are cooked evenly, they can still be tough and bland. We wanted great-looking and great-tasting chops with a crisp, perfectly grilled crust and juicy, flavorful meat. What's more, we wanted our chops plump and meaty, not thin and tough.

START WITH THE RIGHT CHOP Tender and flavorful bone-in rib worked best but center-cut chops were a close second. A brine significantly pumped up flavor and locked in moisture.

CHOOSE YOUR FIRE To brown the pork chops, only a really hot fire would do. But keeping them over high heat long enough to cook through dried them out. The solution was to grill the chops over a two-level fire, with one side of the grill intensely hot to sear the chops, and the other only moderately hot to allow the chops to cook through without burning the exterior.

PUMP UP THE FLAVOR Although rib chops are flavorful on their own, we wanted to boost their flavor further with a spice rub. We tried both wet and dry. The wet rubs, made with spices and a liquid, gave the chops good flavor but also caused their exteriors to turn syrupy. A dry rub worked much better: The potent combination of dried spices and sugar helped create big flavor and a crisp crust.

✎ AT THE MEAT COUNTER
PREFERRED CUT Bone-In Pork Rib Chops
Pork rib chops are also known as rib cut chops or pork chops end cut (see page 180 for more information).

ALTERNATE CUT Bone-In Center-Cut Chops
Center-cut chops can be substituted for the rib chops. Note that center-cut chops contain a portion of the tenderloin and may not be as juicy as a rib chop (see page 180 for more information).

GRILLED BONE-IN PORK CHOPS
SERVES 4

The spice rub adds a lot of flavor for very little effort, but the chops can also be seasoned with pepper alone just before grilling. If the pork is enhanced (injected with a salt solution), do not brine and add 2 teaspoons salt to the spice rub or pepper.

- 3 tablespoons salt
- 3 tablespoons sugar
- 4 (12-ounce) bone-in pork rib or center-cut chops, 1½ inches thick, trimmed
- 1 recipe Basic Spice Rub for Pork Chops (recipe follows) or 2 teaspoons pepper

1. Dissolve salt and sugar in 1½ quarts cold water in large container. Submerge chops in brine, cover, and refrigerate for 30 minutes to 1 hour. Remove chops from brine and pat dry with paper towels. Rub chops with spice rub.

2A. FOR A CHARCOAL GRILL: Open bottom vent completely. Light large chimney starter filled with charcoal briquettes (6 quarts). When top coals are partially covered with ash, pour two-thirds evenly over grill, then pour remaining coals over half of grill. Set cooking grate in place, cover, and open lid vent completely. Heat grill until hot, about 5 minutes.

2B. FOR A GAS GRILL: Turn all burners to high, cover, and heat grill until hot, about 15 minutes. Leave primary burner on high and turn off other burner(s).

3. Clean and oil cooking grate. Place chops on hotter side of grill and cook (covered if using gas) until browned on both sides, 4 to 8 minutes. Move chops to cooler side of grill, cover, and continue to cook, turning once, until meat registers 145 degrees, 7 to 9 minutes longer. Transfer chops to serving platter, tent loosely with aluminum foil, and let rest for 5 to 10 minutes. Serve.

BASIC SPICE RUB FOR PORK CHOPS
MAKES ¼ CUP

- 1 tablespoon ground cumin
- 1 tablespoon chili powder
- 1 tablespoon curry powder
- 2 teaspoons packed brown sugar
- 1 teaspoon pepper

Combine all ingredients in bowl.

Grill-Smoked Pork Chops

✔ WHY THIS RECIPE WORKS

Getting both good smoke flavor and a charred crust is an elusive grilling goal. Smokiness generally requires a lengthy exposure to a slow fire, while a charred crust requires a blast of high heat to quickly sear the exterior of the meat before the interior turns dry and leathery. We wanted chops that had it all: charred crust, rosy-pink, ultramoist meat, and true smoke flavor throughout.

PICK BIG CHOPS We found that chops at least 1½ inches thick were essential for this recipe. The larger chops meant more meat and more bone, which gave us more time on the grill to really infuse the meat with smoke before it became leathery and dry.

START LOW While many recipes start meat over higher heat to get a good sear and then move it to a cooler part of the grill to finish cooking, we reversed the order of operations. We used a double-banked fire (made by placing a disposable aluminum pan between two mounds of coals) and started our chops on the cooler center of the grill, allowing the smoke plenty of time to do its job.

SKEWER, STACK, AND SEAR As for arranging the chops on the grill, we found it best to rest each chop on its bone instead of laying it flat. To keep them from toppling over, we speared the chops together with skewers, making sure to leave a good inch between each one to allow air to circulate, then stood them upright in the center of the grill. This allowed us to keep the chops over the fire for a full 30 minutes, after which we removed the skewers, applied the glaze, and finished the chops over hot coals for a crusty char.

GRILL-SMOKED PORK CHOPS
SERVES 4

Pork rib chops are also known as rib cut chops or pork chops end cut (see page 180 for more information). Buy chops of the same thickness so they will cook uniformly. Use the large holes on a box grater to grate the onion for the sauce. If you'd like to use wood chunks instead of wood chips when using a charcoal grill, substitute two medium wood chunks, soaked in water for 1 hour, for the wood chip packet. You will need two 10-inch metal skewers for this recipe.

SAUCE
- ½ cup ketchup
- ¼ cup molasses
- 2 tablespoons grated onion
- 2 tablespoons Worcestershire sauce
- 2 tablespoons Dijon mustard
- 2 tablespoons cider vinegar
- 1 tablespoon packed light brown sugar

CHOPS
- 2 cups wood chips, soaked in water for 15 minutes and drained
- 4 (12-ounce) bone-in pork rib chops, 1½ inches thick, trimmed
- 2 teaspoons salt
- 2 teaspoons pepper
- 1 (13 by 9-inch) disposable aluminum roasting pan (if using charcoal)

1. FOR THE SAUCE: Bring all ingredients to simmer in small saucepan over medium heat and cook, stirring occasionally, until reduced to about 1 cup, 5 to 7 minutes. Transfer ½ cup sauce to small bowl and set aside remaining sauce for serving.

2. FOR THE CHOPS: Using large piece of heavy-duty aluminum foil, wrap soaked chips in foil packet and cut several vent holes in top. Pat pork chops dry with paper towels. Cut 2 slits, about 2 inches apart, through outer layer of fat and silverskin on each chop. Season each chop with ½ teaspoon salt and ½ teaspoon pepper. Place chops side by side, facing in same direction, on cutting board with curved rib bone facing down.

GRILL-SMOKING PORK CHOPS

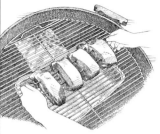

Pass 2 skewers through loin muscle of each chop to provide stability when standing on grill.

MEASURING THE INTERNAL TEMPERATURE OF A PORK CHOP

When you think a chop might be done, use a pair of tongs to hold the chop and then slide an instant-read thermometer through the edge of the chop and deep into the meat, making sure to avoid the bone.

CUTTING PORK TENDERLOIN FOR CUTLETS

Cut tenderloin in half at about 20-degree angle. Using same angle, cut each half in half again, cutting tapered tail pieces slightly thicker than middle medallions, then pound to even thickness between parchment or plastic wrap.

Pass 2 skewers through loin muscle of each chop, close to bone, about 1 inch from each end, then pull chops apart to create 1-inch space between each.

3A. FOR A CHARCOAL GRILL: Open bottom vent halfway and place disposable roasting pan in center of grill. Light large chimney starter filled with charcoal briquettes (6 quarts). When top coals are partially covered with ash, pour into 2 even piles on either side of disposable pan. Place wood chip packet on 1 pile of coals. Set cooking grate in place, cover, and open lid vent halfway. Heat grill until hot and wood chips are smoking, about 5 minutes.

3B. FOR A GAS GRILL: Place wood chip packet over primary burner. Turn all burners to high, cover, and heat grill until hot and wood chips are smoking, about 15 minutes. Turn all burners to medium-high. (Adjust burners as needed during cooking to maintain grill temperature of 300 to 325 degrees.)

4. Clean and oil cooking grate. Place skewered chops bone side down on grill (over pan if using charcoal). Cover and cook until meat registers 120 degrees, 28 to 32 minutes.

5. Remove skewers from chops, tip chops onto flat side and brush surface of each with 1 tablespoon sauce. Transfer chops, sauce side down, to hotter parts of grill (if using charcoal) or turn all burners to high (if using gas) and cook until browned on first side, 2 to 6 minutes. Brush top of each chop with 1 tablespoon sauce, flip, and continue to cook until browned on second side and meat registers 140 degrees, 2 to 6 minutes longer.

6. Transfer chops to serving platter, tent loosely with aluminum foil, and let rest for 5 to 10 minutes. Serve, passing reserved sauce separately.

Pork Schnitzel

✔ WHY THIS RECIPE WORKS

Pork schnitzel is often a soggy, greasy affair. But when done right, it features an irresistible combination of light bread-crumb coating and tender, juicy meat. Authentic schnitzel also has a puffed crust. We set out to uncover its secrets.

CHOICE CUTS Most schnitzel recipes call for boneless pork chops, pounded thin. However, pork chops have very compact muscle fibers, which means that pounding them into thin cutlets is laborious. It also means that once cooked, the pork has a dry, mealy texture. We opted for pork tenderloin instead. Pounded thin and fried, cutlets made from the tenderloin were remarkably tender with a mild flavor similar to veal.

PRECOOK THE CRUMBS Using raw homemade bread crumbs can result in a pork cutlet that is overcooked before the crumbs are crisp, with a crust that is too coarsely textured. We found that microwaving the bread cubes first on high power, then medium, and giving them a whirl in the food processor produced superfine, dry bread crumbs that fried up extra-crisp.

USE ARM POWER Wiener schnitzel's signature attribute is a wrinkled, puffy exterior. When the pan is shaken, gently but continuously, the ample hot oil heats the eggs in the coating very quickly, solidifying the proteins and creating a barrier that captures steam and begins to puff. The shaking sends the hot oil over the top of the cutlets, speeding up the setting process and enhancing the puff for perfect pork schnitzel.

BUTTERED SPAETZLE

These noodle-like dumplings are a traditional accompaniment to schnitzel and are also good with most stews. The spaetzle can be made 1 day in advance. At the end of step 2, toss dried spaetzle with 1 tablespoon oil and refrigerate in airtight container. To finish, proceed with step 3.

1. Combine 2 cups all-purpose flour, ¾ teaspoon salt, ½ teaspoon pepper, and ¼ teaspoon ground nutmeg in large bowl. Whisk ¾ cup whole milk and 3 large eggs until combined in medium bowl. Slowly whisk milk mixture into flour mixture until smooth. Cover and let rest, 15 to 30 minutes.

2. Meanwhile, set disposable aluminum pan over empty Dutch oven and poke about forty ¼-inch holes into bottom; set aside. Bring 4 quarts of water to boil in Dutch oven. Add 1 tablespoon salt to boiling water and set prepared pan on Dutch oven. Transfer half of batter to prepared pan. Use spatula to scrape batter across holes, letting it fall into water. Boil until spaetzle float, about 1 minute. Using slotted spoon, transfer spaetzle to paper towel–lined baking sheet to drain. Repeat with remaining batter. Pat dry with paper towels.

3. Heat 2 tablespoons vegetable oil in large nonstick skillet over medium-high until shimmering. Stir in 1 shallot, chopped fine, and cook until softened, about 2 minutes. Add spaetzle and cook, stirring occasionally, until golden and crisp at edges, 5 to 7 minutes. Off heat, stir in 2 tablespoons unsalted butter and season with salt and pepper. Serve. (Serves 6 to 8.)

PORK SCHNITZEL
SERVES 4

For more information on pork tenderloin, see page 182. The 2 cups of oil called for in this recipe may seem like a lot, but this amount is necessary to achieve a wrinkled texture on the finished cutlets. When properly cooked, the cutlets absorb very little oil. To ensure ample cooking space, a large Dutch oven is essential. Cutting the pork tenderloin at about a 20-degree angle will yield pounded cutlets that fit easily into the pan. In lieu of an instant-read thermometer to gauge the oil's temperature, place a fresh (not dry) bread cube in the oil and start heating; when the bread is deep golden brown, the oil is ready. Serve with Buttered Spaetzle (at left) or egg noodles.

7   slices hearty white sandwich bread, crusts removed, cut into ¾-inch cubes
½   cup all-purpose flour
2   large eggs, plus 1 large hard-cooked egg, yolk and white separated and passed separately through fine-mesh strainer (optional)
1   tablespoon plus 2 cups vegetable oil
1   (1¼-pound) pork tenderloin, trimmed and cut on angle into 4 equal pieces
    Salt and pepper
    Lemon wedges
2   tablespoons chopped fresh parsley
2   tablespoons capers, rinsed

1. Place bread cubes on large plate. Microwave for 4 minutes, stirring well halfway through microwaving. Microwave at 50 percent power until bread is dry and few pieces start to lightly brown, 3 to 5 minutes, stirring every minute. Process dry bread in food processor to very fine crumbs, about 45 seconds. Transfer bread crumbs to shallow dish (you should have about 1¼ cups crumbs). Spread flour in second shallow dish. Beat eggs with 1 tablespoon oil in third shallow dish.

2. Set wire rack in rimmed baking sheet and line plate with triple layer of paper towels. Working with one piece at a time, place pork, with 1 cut side down, between 2 sheets of parchment paper or plastic wrap and pound to even thickness between ⅛ and ¼ inch. Pat cutlets dry with paper towels and season with salt and pepper. Working with one cutlet at a time, dredge cutlets thoroughly in flour, shaking off excess; coat with egg mixture, allowing excess to drip back into dish to ensure very thin coating; and coat evenly with bread crumbs, pressing on crumbs to adhere. Place breaded cutlets in single layer on prepared wire rack; let coating dry for 5 minutes.

3. Heat remaining 2 cups oil in large Dutch oven over medium-high heat to 375 degrees. Lay 2 cutlets, without overlapping, in pot and cook, shaking pot continuously and gently, until cutlets are wrinkled and light golden brown on both sides, 1 to 2 minutes per side. Transfer cutlets to paper towel–lined plate and flip cutlets several times to blot excess oil. Repeat with remaining cutlets. Serve with lemon wedges, parsley, capers, and, if desired, hard-cooked egg.

Maple-Glazed Pork Tenderloins

✔ WHY THIS RECIPE WORKS

Pork tenderloin is quick-cooking—it can be on the table in less than 30 minutes—and when done right, nothing can match its fine-grained, buttery-smooth texture. But even when it's moist, tender, and perfectly cooked, it's still sorely lacking in flavor. We wanted to use a glaze to enhance this bland cut, but knew that getting the glaze to actually stick to the tenderloin would be a challenge.

TACKLE TECHNIQUE FIRST After testing a variety of approaches, we found that searing the tenderloins in a skillet and then transferring them to a rack set in a rimmed baking sheet to finish cooking in the oven produced well-browned meat that remained tender and juicy throughout. A relatively gentle 375-degree oven was ideal; any higher and the meat dried out, while lower temperatures simply took too long.

BALANCE THE FLAVORS Maple syrup provided a good base for the glaze, but on its own it proved to be overwhelmingly sweet for the mild tenderloin. To counter the sweetness, we replaced ¼ cup of the syrup with mildly bitter molasses and added a tablespoon of mustard. For more complex flavor, we stirred in a shot of bourbon, which brought notes of smoke and vanilla. Pinches of cinnamon, cloves, and cayenne pepper rounded out the flavors.

STICK IT TO 'EM Reducing the glaze to a syrupy consistency wasn't enough to encourage it to adhere to the tenderloins. A coating of cornstarch and sugar, however, worked wonders; mixed with cornstarch, the sugar melted and caramelized as the meat seared, creating a deep brown crust with the texture of sandpaper—perfect for holding the glaze.

AND KEEP GLAZING To achieve a truly substantial coating, we found it necessary to glaze the tenderloins repeatedly—once before going into the oven, a second time just before they finished roasting, a third when they came out of the oven, and one final glaze after the tenderloins had rested—for a beautifully burnished, flavorful exterior.

MAPLE-GLAZED PORK TENDERLOINS
SERVES 6

For more information on pork tenderloin, see page 182. If the pork is enhanced (injected with a salt solution), do not add salt to the cornstarch mixture in step 1. If your tenderloins are smaller than 1¼ pounds, reduce the cooking time in step 3. If the tenderloins don't fit in the skillet initially, let their ends curve toward each other; the meat will eventually shrink as it cooks. Make sure to cook the tenderloins until they turn deep golden brown in step 2 or they will appear pale after glazing. We prefer grade B maple syrup in this recipe. (Don't be tempted to substitute imitation maple syrup—it will be too sweet.) Be sure to pat off the cornstarch mixture thoroughly in step 1, as any excess will leave gummy spots on the tenderloins.

¾	cup maple syrup
¼	cup molasses
2	tablespoons bourbon or brandy
⅛	teaspoon ground cinnamon
	Pinch ground cloves
	Pinch cayenne pepper
¼	cup cornstarch
2	tablespoons sugar
I	tablespoon salt
2	teaspoons pepper
2	(1¼- to 1½-pound) pork tenderloins, trimmed
2	tablespoons vegetable oil
I	tablespoon whole-grain mustard

1. Adjust oven rack to middle position and heat oven to 375 degrees. Stir ½ cup maple

Grade inflation has trickled down from school to syrup: Although there are four grades of maple syrup set by the U.S. government according to color, three of them are A and the lowest is B. Vermont used to have grades A, B, and C and Fancy, but has adopted new international labeling standards. The new system eliminates the B and C grades for all syrup that is boiled down from sap, without any additives or preservatives. Instead, this pure syrup will be classified as grade A, and differentiated with labels describing color and flavor combinations such as "gold and delicate," "amber and rich," and "very dark and strong."

Keeping a maple syrup report card can obviously be very confusing.

The Federal Grades are:

Grade A Light Amber: Very light gold, with mild maple flavor; in Vermont, also known as Fancy.

Grade A Medium Amber: Slightly darker, with more maple flavor.

Grade A Dark Amber: Even darker, with a stronger maple flavor.

Grade B: Sometimes called "cooking syrup," very dark, with intense maple flavor.

syrup, molasses, bourbon, cinnamon, cloves, and cayenne together in 2-cup liquid measuring cup; set aside. Whisk cornstarch, sugar, salt, and pepper together in small bowl until combined. Transfer cornstarch mixture to rimmed baking sheet. Pat tenderloins dry with paper towels, then roll in cornstarch mixture until evenly coated on all sides. Thoroughly pat off excess cornstarch mixture.

2. Heat oil in 12-inch nonstick skillet over medium-high heat until just smoking. Reduce heat to medium and place both tenderloins in skillet, leaving at least 1 inch in between. Cook until well browned on all sides, 8 to 12 minutes. Transfer tenderloins to wire rack set in second rimmed baking sheet.

3. Pour off excess fat from skillet and return to medium heat. Add maple syrup mixture to skillet, scraping bottom of skillet with wooden spoon to loosen any browned bits, and cook until reduced to ½ cup, about 2 minutes. Transfer 2 tablespoons glaze to small bowl and set aside. Using remaining glaze, brush each tenderloin with approximately 1 tablespoon glaze. Roast until thickest part of tenderloins registers 130 degrees, 12 to 20 minutes. Brush each tenderloin with 1 tablespoon glaze and continue to roast until thickest part of tenderloins registers 145 degrees, 2 to 4 minutes

longer. Remove tenderloins from oven and brush each with remaining glaze; let rest, uncovered, 10 minutes.

4. While tenderloins rest, stir mustard and remaining ¼ cup maple syrup into reserved 2 tablespoons glaze. Brush each tenderloin with 1 tablespoon syrup-mustard glaze. Transfer meat to carving board and slice into ¼-inch-thick slices. Serve, passing remaining syrup-mustard glaze separately.

MAPLE-GLAZED PORK TENDERLOINS WITH SMOKED PAPRIKA AND GINGER

Substitute dry sherry for bourbon and ¼ teaspoon smoked paprika and 1 teaspoon grated fresh ginger for cinnamon, cloves, and cayenne. Omit mustard in step 4.

MAPLE-GLAZED PORK TENDERLOINS WITH ORANGE AND CHIPOTLE

Substitute 2 tablespoons frozen orange juice concentrate for 2 tablespoons molasses. Omit cinnamon, cloves, and cayenne and add 2 teaspoons minced canned chipotle chile plus 2 teaspoons adobo sauce to maple syrup mixture in step 1. Omit mustard in step 4.

Thick-Cut Pork Tenderloin Medallions

✓ WHY THIS RECIPE WORKS

Boneless, lean, and tender, pork tenderloin offers plenty of hope for the time-pressed weeknight cook. On the downside, this ultralean cut has an ultramild flavor that needs a major boost. Long marinades and hybrid searing-roasting techniques (the latter providing flavorful browning) help remedy such deficiencies, but they also take the home cook a long way from the realm of a no-fuss meal. We wanted a recipe that would enhance flavor and ensure juiciness, yet still be fast enough for a weeknight dinner.

BUILD FLAVOR FAST We quickly eliminated time-consuming techniques such as brining, marinating, and heating the grill or oven. For our weeknight pork tenderloin, we chose a skillet and a quick pan sauce.

FIND THE RIGHT SHAPE Slicing the meat into medallions reduced the cooking time, while keeping the pieces relatively thick—1½ inches—allowed the pork to spend enough time in the skillet to develop a well-browned exterior without overcooking the interior. The result? Incredibly flavorful, juicy meat. Standing the medallions on their sides during the searing process ensured that the entire exterior was beautifully browned. The extra browning also meant we had a great base of fond for a pan sauce.

ADD THE FINISHING TOUCH While our pork medallions briefly rested, we had just enough time to build a pan sauce starting with the flavorful fond left behind in the skillet. We developed three, each with elements of sweet, tart, and spicy that strike just the right balance of flavors.

THICK-CUT PORK TENDERLOIN MEDALLIONS

SERVES 4 TO 6

For more information on pork tenderloin, see page 182. We prefer natural to enhanced pork (pork that has been injected with a salt solution) for this recipe, though either will work. Begin checking the doneness of smaller medallions 1 or 2 minutes early; they may need to be taken out of the pan a little sooner.

2   (1- to 1¼-pound) pork tenderloins, trimmed, cut crosswise into 1½-inch pieces, and tied; thinner end pieces tied together
    Salt and pepper
2   tablespoons vegetable oil
1   recipe pan sauce (recipes follow)

Pat pork dry with paper towels and season with salt and pepper. Heat oil in 12-inch skillet over medium-high heat until shimmering. Add pork cut side down and cook, without moving pieces, until well browned, 3 to 5 minutes longer. Flip pork and brown on second

side, 3 to 5 minutes more. Reduce heat to medium. Using tongs, stand each piece on its side and cook, turning pieces as necessary, until sides are well browned and pork registers 145 degrees, 8 to 12 minutes. Transfer pork to serving platter and tent loosely with aluminum foil; let rest while making pan sauce, then serve.

BACON-WRAPPED THICK-CUT PORK TENDERLOIN MEDALLIONS

The number of bacon slices you use will depend on how many medallions you have cut. See page 214 for illustrations on securing the bacon.

Place 12 to 14 bacon slices, slightly overlapping, in pie plate and cover. Cook in microwave until slices shrink and release about ½ cup fat but are neither browned nor crisp, 1 to 3 minutes. Transfer bacon to paper towels until cool, 2 to 3 minutes. Wrap each piece of pork with 1 slice bacon and secure with 2 toothpicks where ends of bacon strip overlap, inserting toothpicks on angle and gently pushing them through to other side. Season pork with pepper (do not salt) and proceed with browning (time for searing sides may be slightly longer).

APPLE CIDER SAUCE

MAKES 1⅓ CUPS

Start the sauce before cooking the pork medallions.

1½   cups apple cider
1   cup chicken broth
2   teaspoons cider vinegar
1   cinnamon stick
4   tablespoons unsalted butter, cut into 4 pieces and chilled
2   large shallots, minced
1   Granny Smith apple, peeled, cored, and diced small
¼   cup Calvados or apple-flavored brandy
1   teaspoon minced fresh thyme
     Salt and pepper

TURNING THE TENDERLOIN END PIECE INTO A MEDALLION

After cutting the tenderloins into symmetrical 1½-inch medallions, you will inevitably have a few irregularly shaped pieces left over. The tapered end pieces of the tenderloin can be scored, folded, and tied into medallions (as shown here).

1. Score tenderloin's tapered end piece.

2. Fold in half at incision.

3. Tie medallion with kitchen twine, making sure top and bottom surfaces are flat.

TYING PORK MEDALLIONS

Thick medallions allow for more browning, but they can flop over in the pan. To prevent this, tie each piece with twine or a strip of par-cooked bacon secured with two toothpicks.

Kitchen Twine

Bacon "Twine"

HOISIN SAUCE

Hoisin is a thick reddish-brown mixture of soybeans, sugar, vinegar, garlic, chiles, and spices, the most predominant of which is five-spice powder. It is used in many classic Chinese dishes, such as Peking duck and kung pao shrimp, and we've found that it can give a variety of sauces both a sweet, tangy flavor and a rich, thick texture. Our favorite brand is **Kikkoman Hoisin Sauce**; tasters praised its initial "burn," which mellowed into a harmonious blend of sweet and savory flavors.

1. Combine cider, broth, vinegar, and cinnamon stick in medium saucepan; simmer over medium-high heat until liquid is reduced to 1 cup, 10 to 12 minutes. Discard cinnamon stick. Set sauce aside until pork is cooked.

2. Pour off any fat from skillet in which pork was cooked. Add 1 tablespoon butter and melt over medium heat. Add shallots and apple and cook, stirring occasionally, until softened and beginning to brown, 1 to 2 minutes. Remove skillet from heat and add Calvados. Return skillet to medium heat and cook about 1 minute, scraping bottom of skillet with wooden spoon to loosen any browned bits. Add reduced cider mixture, any accumulated pork juices, and thyme; increase heat to medium-high and simmer until thickened and reduced to 1¼ cups, 3 to 4 minutes. Off heat, whisk in remaining 3 tablespoons butter and season with salt and pepper to taste. Pour sauce over pork and serve.

MAPLE-MUSTARD SAUCE
MAKES 1 CUP

Whole-grain mustard is best here, though Dijon may be substituted

2	teaspoons vegetable oil
1	onion, halved and sliced thin
1	cup chicken broth
⅓	cup maple syrup
3	tablespoons balsamic vinegar
3	tablespoons whole-grain mustard
	Salt and pepper

Pour off any fat from skillet in which pork was cooked. Add oil and heat skillet over medium heat until shimmering. Add onion and cook, stirring occasionally, until softened and beginning to brown, 3 to 4 minutes. Increase heat to medium-high and add broth; bring to simmer, scraping bottom of skillet with wooden spoon to loosen any browned bits. Simmer until liquid is reduced to ⅓ cup, 3 to 4 minutes. Add maple syrup, vinegar, mustard, and any accumulated pork juices and cook until thickened and reduced to 1 cup, 3 to 4 minutes longer. Season with salt and pepper to taste, pour sauce over pork, and serve.

HOISIN-SESAME SAUCE
MAKES ¾ CUP

1	teaspoon vegetable oil
2	teaspoons grated fresh ginger
¼	cup hoisin sauce
½	cup orange juice
½	cup chicken broth
1	teaspoon toasted sesame oil
2	scallions, sliced ⅛ inch thick on bias
	Salt and pepper

Pour off any fat from skillet in which pork was cooked. Add oil and heat skillet over medium heat until shimmering. Add ginger and cook, stirring constantly, until fragrant, about 15 seconds. Add hoisin sauce, orange juice, broth, and any accumulated pork juices and bring to simmer, scraping bottom of skillet with wooden spoon to loosen any browned bits. Simmer until liquid is reduced to 1 cup, 2 to 3 minutes. Stir in sesame oil and scallions. Season with salt and pepper to taste, pour sauce over pork, and serve.

Pan-Seared Oven-Roasted Pork Tenderloins

✔ WHY THIS RECIPE WORKS

Pork tenderloin is an incredibly lean cut that is mild in flavor and prone to drying out. Yet it has its advantages, too: It's easy to prepare, cooks quickly, and has a supremely tender texture. We have found that pork tenderloin is especially suited to the grill—hot charcoal fire adds flavor. But since grilling is not a realistic year-round option for most people, our goal was to discover an indoor cooking method for cooking tenderloin that would equal results produced on the grill.

SEAR AND ROAST Roasting the tenderloins in a moderate oven produced evenly cooked meat but a pale exterior; cooking them in a skillet resulted in a beautifully browned exterior with a raw center. Combining the two approaches proved a winner. Searing the tenderloins on the stovetop and then moving them to a 400-degree oven gave us a golden crust and an evenly cooked interior.

GIVE IT A REST We removed the tenderloins from the oven when they registered 145 degrees and let them rest for 5 minutes; this brief rest allowed them to retain plenty of juices.

BUILD THE SAUCE A pan sauce is a quick way to contribute flavor to a dish, and we knew that mild pork tenderloin would certainly benefit from one. To save time, we moved the tenderloins from the skillet to a baking sheet before transferring them to the oven; while they finished cooking, we built our sauce on the stovetop starting with all the flavorful browned bits left behind in the skillet.

PAN-SEARED OVEN-ROASTED PORK TENDERLOINS

SERVES 4

For more information on pork tenderloin, see page 182. We prefer natural to enhanced pork (pork that has been injected with a salt solution) here. This recipe calls for cooking the two tenderloins at the same time in the same skillet, so be sure to buy tenderloins that are sized accordingly. If time allows, you can season the tenderloins up to 30 minutes before cooking; the seasonings will better penetrate the meat. The recipe will work in a nonstick or a traditional skillet. Make the pan sauce while the tenderloins roast; be sure to prepare all the sauce ingredients before cooking the pork.

2	(12- to 16-ounce) pork tenderloins, trimmed
1¼	teaspoons kosher salt
¾	teaspoon pepper
2	teaspoons vegetable oil
1	recipe pan sauce (recipes follow)

1. Adjust oven rack to middle position and heat oven to 400 degrees. Season tenderloins with salt and pepper; rub seasoning into meat. Heat oil in 12-inch skillet over medium-high heat until just smoking. Place both tenderloins in skillet; cook until well browned, 3 minutes. Using tongs, rotate tenderloins one-quarter turn; cook until well browned, 1 to 2 minutes. Repeat until all sides are browned. Transfer tenderloins to rimmed baking sheet and place in oven (reserve skillet for pan sauce); roast

until tenderloins register 145 degrees, 10 to 16 minutes.

2. Transfer tenderloins to carving board and tent loosely with aluminum foil; let rest for 10 minutes. Slice tenderloins crosswise into ½-inch-thick slices, arrange on serving platter or individual plates, and spoon sauce over slices; serve.

DRIED CHERRY–PORT SAUCE WITH ONION AND MARMALADE

MAKES 1½ CUPS

1 teaspoon vegetable oil
1 large onion, halved and sliced ½ inch thick
¾ cup port
¾ cup dried cherries
2 tablespoons orange marmalade
3 tablespoons unsalted butter, cut into 3 pieces and chilled
Salt and pepper

1. Immediately after placing pork in oven, add oil to still-hot skillet, swirl to coat, and set skillet over medium-high heat; add onion and cook, stirring frequently, until softened and browned around edges, 5 to 7 minutes (if drippings are browning too quickly, add 2 tablespoons water and scrape up browned bits with wooden spoon). Set skillet aside off heat.

2. While pork is resting, set skillet over medium-high heat and add port and cherries; simmer, scraping up any browned bits, until mixture is slightly thickened, 4 to 6 minutes. Add any accumulated pork juices and continue to simmer until thickened, about 2 minutes longer. Off heat, whisk in orange marmalade and butter, 1 piece at a time. Season with salt and pepper to taste.

GARLICKY LIME SAUCE WITH CILANTRO

MAKES ½ CUP

If your garlic cloves contain green sprouts or shoots, remove them before grating; their flavor is bitter and hot. The initial cooking of the garlic off heat prevents scorching.

10 garlic cloves, minced to paste (2 tablespoons)
2 tablespoons water
1 tablespoon vegetable oil
2 teaspoons packed light brown sugar
¼ teaspoon red pepper flakes
¼ cup chopped fresh cilantro
3 tablespoons lime juice (2 limes)
1 tablespoon chopped fresh chives
4 tablespoons unsalted butter, cut into 4 pieces and chilled
Salt and pepper

1. Immediately after placing pork in oven, mix garlic paste with water in small bowl. Add oil to still-hot skillet and swirl to coat; add garlic paste mixture and cook with skillet's residual heat, scraping up any browned bits, until sizzling subsides, about 2 minutes. Set skillet over low heat and continue cooking, stirring frequently, until garlic is sticky, 8 to 10 minutes; set skillet aside off heat.

2. While pork is resting, set skillet over medium heat; add sugar and pepper flakes to skillet and cook until sticky and sugar is dissolved, about 1 minute. Add cilantro, lime juice, and chives; simmer to blend flavors, 1 to 2 minutes. Add any accumulated pork juices and simmer 1 minute longer. Off heat, whisk in butter, 1 piece at a time. Season with salt and pepper to taste.

MINCING GARLIC TO A PASTE

Sprinkling minced garlic with a little salt, then mashing it, turns the garlic into a creamy paste. Why? The salt draws moisture out of the garlic cells. As the cells lose moisture, they collapse and soften. Furthermore, the grains of salt act as an abrasive, helping grind the garlic particles as you mash. Garlic that's mashed to a paste incorporates seamlessly into sauces and vinaigrettes.

1. Mince garlic, then sprinkle with salt.

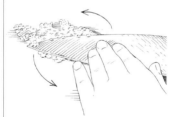

2. Drag side of chef's knife over garlic-salt mixture to form fine puree. Continue to mince and drag knife as necessary until puree is smooth.

CHOOSING PORK TENDERLOINS

Pork tenderloins are almost always sold in pairs in vacuum-sealed packages. After buying dozens of packages, we found that the average tenderloin weighs 12 to 16 ounces. However, we did find some packages with larger tenderloins (up to 1½ pounds) or with two tenderloins of dramatically different sizes. Larger loins are fine for grilling but hard to fit in a skillet. When shopping, pay attention to the total weight of the two tenderloins (which should be 1½ to 2 pounds) and squeeze the package to see if the tenderloins feel similar in size.

SHALLOT-BALSAMIC SAUCE WITH ROSEMARY AND MUSTARD

MAKES ½ CUP

4   tablespoons unsalted butter, cut into 4 pieces and chilled
2   shallots, sliced thin
2   tablespoons water
1   teaspoon packed light brown sugar
¾   cup balsamic vinegar
2   teaspoons chopped fresh rosemary
1   tablespoon Dijon mustard
    Salt and pepper

1. Immediately after placing pork in oven, add 1 tablespoon butter to still-hot skillet; when melted, stir in shallots, water, and sugar. Cook over medium-low heat, stirring frequently, until shallots are browned and caramelized, 7 to 10 minutes; set skillet aside off heat.

2. While pork is resting, set skillet over medium-low heat and add vinegar; simmer, scraping up any browned bits, until mixture is slightly thickened, 5 to 7 minutes. Add rosemary and any accumulated pork juices; continue to simmer until syrupy and reduced to about ⅓ cup, about 2 minutes longer. Off heat, whisk in mustard and remaining 3 tablespoons butter, 1 piece at a time. Season with salt and pepper to taste.

Grilled Pork Tenderloins

✔ WHY THIS RECIPE WORKS

Grilling is a terrific way to cook pork tenderloin, a sublimely tender cut of meat that benefits especially from the flavor boost provided by a live fire. But grilling a tenderloin does have its challenges. With almost no fat, the long, slender, quick-cooking tenderloin can overcook and dry out much faster than well-marbled cuts. We wanted to find a way to achieve a rich, golden, caramelized crust without destroying the texture of the delicate meat.

BUILD THE RIGHT FIRE To get both the ideal crust and a perfectly cooked interior, grilling the tenderloin over two different heat levels proved to be essential. By banking the hot coals on one half of the grill and leaving the other half empty, we could sear the meat on the hotter side before sliding it over the cooler side to gently finish cooking through.

COVER UP Once the pork was moved to the cooler side of the grill, we covered it with a disposable aluminum roasting pan to speed up the cooking time.

GIVE IT A FLAVOR BOOST Brining the tenderloins in a simple sugar-and-salt solution ensured the meat was well seasoned and juicy throughout, while a dry spice rub was quick to throw together and gave the tenderloin a fantastic, flavorful crust. (We also had success with wet rubs, which have strong flavors and give the pork a lovely, crusty, glazed effect.)

GRILLED PORK TENDERLOINS

SERVES 6 TO 8

For more information on pork tenderloin, see page 182. If the pork is enhanced (injected with a salt solution), do not brine. Pork tenderloins are often sold two to a package, each piece usually weighing 12 to 16 ounces. The cooking times below are for two average 12-ounce tenderloins; if necessary, adjust the times to suit the size of the cuts you are cooking. If you opt not to brine, bypass step 1 in the recipe and season the tenderloins generously with salt before grilling.

Salt

¼ cup sugar

2 (12- to 16-ounce) pork tenderloins, trimmed

1 recipe spice rub (recipes follow)

1. Dissolve salt and sugar in 2 quarts cold water in large container. Submerge pork tenderloins in brine, cover, and refrigerate for 30 minutes to 1 hour. Remove pork from brine and pat dry with paper towels. Coat tenderloins with spice rub.

2A. FOR A CHARCOAL GRILL: Open bottom vent completely. Light large chimney starter filled with charcoal briquettes (6 quarts). When top coals are partially covered with ash, pour evenly over half of grill. Set cooking grate in place, cover, and open lid vent completely. Heat grill until hot, about 5 minutes.

2B. FOR A GAS GRILL: Turn all burners to high, cover, and heat grill until hot, about 15 minutes. Leave all burners on high.

3. Clean and oil cooking grate. Place tenderloins on grill (hotter side if using charcoal) and cook (covered if using gas) until well browned on all sides, 10 to 12 minutes, turning as needed. Move tenderloins to cooler part of grill (if using charcoal) or turn all burners to medium-low (if using gas), cover, and continue to cook until meat registers 145 degrees, 2 to 3 minutes longer.

4. Transfer tenderloins to carving board, tent loosely with aluminum foil, and let rest for 5 to 10 minutes. Slice crosswise into 1-inch-thick pieces and serve.

FRAGRANT DRY SPICE RUB
MAKES ABOUT ¼ CUP

If using this spice rub, coat the tenderloins with 2 tablespoons vegetable oil to help the spices adhere.

1 tablespoon fennel seeds

1 tablespoon cumin seeds

1 tablespoon coriander seeds

1½ teaspoons dry mustard

1½ teaspoons packed light brown sugar

¾ teaspoon ground cinnamon

¼ teaspoon pepper

Toast fennel, cumin, and coriander seeds in small skillet over medium heat, shaking pan occasionally, until fragrant, 3 to 5 minutes. Transfer to bowl, let cool to room temperature, and grind to powder in spice grinder. Stir in mustard, sugar, cinnamon, and pepper.

ORANGE-GARLIC WET RUB
MAKES ABOUT ½ CUP

Honey can be substituted for the marmalade.

1 tablespoon grated orange zest

3 garlic cloves, minced

1 tablespoon chopped fresh sage

1 tablespoon extra-virgin olive oil

1 tablespoon orange marmalade

½ teaspoon pepper

¼ teaspoon salt

Combine all ingredients in bowl.

ASIAN BARBECUE WET RUB
MAKES ABOUT ⅓ CUP

If you don't have sambal oelek chili paste, substitute ½ teaspoon dried red pepper flakes.

2 tablespoons grated fresh ginger

2 scallions, minced

2 tablespoons packed light brown sugar

3 garlic cloves, minced

1 tablespoon hoisin sauce

1 tablespoon toasted sesame oil

1 teaspoon sambal oelek

¼ teaspoon five-spice powder

¼ teaspoon salt

Combine all ingredients in bowl.

To get around the usual
problems with grilling pork
tenderloin, we "fused" two
together and cooked them as
a single roast.

1. Scrape up flat sides of each
tenderloin with fork until surface is covered with shallow
grooves. This releases sticky
proteins that will act as "glue."

2. Arrange tenderloins with
scraped sides touching and
thick end of one nestled
against thin end of other. Tie
tenderloins together.

Grilled Glazed Pork Tenderloin Roast

✔ WHY THIS RECIPE WORKS

Pork tenderloin is wonderfully tender and versatile, it doesn't require much prep, and it's relatively inexpensive. Grilling is a great way to prepare mild meat like tenderloin (it develops a rich, meaty crust), but there are still challenges: The leanness of tenderloin makes it highly susceptible to drying out; its tapered shape makes it difficult to cook evenly; and the extreme heat and natural fluctuations in temperature during grilling make it hard to do well. We wanted to find a way to make grilled pork tenderloin a bit more foolproof—and at the same time elevate this cut above its "casual supper" status to something more special and elegant.

START BY BRINING Lean pork tenderloin needs all the help it can get; for well-seasoned, juicy meat, we found that brining was essential.

LOW HEAT FIRST, THEN HIGH Grilling pork tenderloin directly over a hot fire the entire time resulted in a well-browned exterior—but a thick band of dry, overcooked meat below its surface. A better approach was to start the tenderloin over low heat followed by searing over high heat. The initial stint on the cooler side of the grill allowed the meat's surface to warm and dry, which made for fast, efficient browning (and therefore safeguarded against overcooking) when we moved it to the hotter part of the grate.

TWO TENDERLOINS BECOME ONE The tapered end of a tenderloin inevitably overcooks by the time the rest of the roast has reached the ideal temperature. Since we needed two tenderloins anyway, we solved this problem by tying the roasts together, with the thick end of one nestled against the thin end of the other. Scraping the length of each tenderloin with a fork prior to brining and thoroughly drying them after brining

helped bond the two pieces of meat together to create one larger roast.

FINISH WITH A GLAZE Adding glutamate-rich ingredients such as mirin, hoisin, or fish sauce to a glaze significantly enhanced the savory, meaty flavor of the pork. Adding the glaze to the tenderloins over high heat allowed the glaze to char, further enhancing the rich, flavorful crust.

GRILLED GLAZED PORK TENDERLOIN ROAST

SERVES 6

For more information on pork tenderloin, see page 182. Since brining is a key step in having the two tenderloins stick together, we don't recommend using enhanced pork in this recipe.

2   (1-pound) pork tenderloins, trimmed
    Salt and pepper
    Vegetable oil
1   recipe glaze (recipes follow)

1. Lay tenderloins on cutting board, flat side (side opposite where silverskin was) up. Holding thick end of 1 tenderloin with paper towels and using dinner fork, scrape flat side lengthwise from end to end 5 times, until surface is completely covered with shallow grooves. Repeat with second tenderloin. Dissolve 3 tablespoons salt in 1½ quarts cold water in large container. Submerge tenderloins in brine and let stand at room temperature for 1 hour.

2. Remove tenderloins from brine and pat dry with paper towels. Lay 1 tenderloin, scraped side up, on cutting board and lay second tenderloin, scraped side down, on top so that thick end of 1 tenderloin matches up with thin end of other. Spray five 14-inch lengths of kitchen twine thoroughly with vegetable oil spray; evenly space twine underneath tenderloins and tie. Brush roast with vegetable oil and season with pepper. Transfer ⅓ cup glaze to bowl for grilling; reserve remaining glaze for serving.

3A. FOR A CHARCOAL GRILL: Open bottom vent completely. Light large chimney starter filled with charcoal briquettes (6 quarts). When top coals are partially covered with ash, pour into steeply banked pile against side of grill. Set cooking grate in place, cover, and open lid vent completely. Heat grill until hot, about 5 minutes.

3B. FOR A GAS GRILL: Turn all burners to high, cover, and heat grill until hot, about 15 minutes. Leave primary burner on high and turn off other burner(s).

4. Clean and oil cooking grate. Place roast on cooler side of grill, cover, and cook until meat registers 115 degrees, 22 to 28 minutes, flipping and rotating halfway through cooking.

5. Slide roast to hotter part of grill and cook until lightly browned on all sides, 4 to 6 minutes. Brush top of roast with about 1 tablespoon glaze and grill, glaze side down, until glaze begins to char, 2 to 3 minutes; repeat glazing and grilling with remaining 3 sides of roast, until meat registers 140 degrees.

6. Transfer roast to carving board, tent loosely with aluminum foil, and let rest for 10 minutes. Carefully remove twine and slice roast into ½-inch-thick slices. Serve with remaining glaze.

MISO GLAZE
MAKES ABOUT ¾ CUP

3 tablespoons sake
3 tablespoons mirin
⅓ cup white miso
¼ cup sugar
2 teaspoons Dijon mustard
1 teaspoon rice vinegar
¼ teaspoon grated fresh ginger
¼ teaspoon toasted sesame oil

Bring sake and mirin to boil in small saucepan over medium heat. Whisk in miso and sugar until smooth, about 30 seconds. Remove pan from heat and continue to whisk until sugar is dissolved, about 1 minute. Whisk in mustard, vinegar, ginger, and sesame oil until smooth.

SATAY GLAZE
MAKES ABOUT ¾ CUP

1   teaspoon vegetable oil
1   tablespoon Thai red curry paste
2   garlic cloves, minced
½   teaspoon grated fresh ginger
½   cup canned coconut milk
¼   cup packed dark brown sugar
2   tablespoons peanut butter
1   tablespoon lime juice
2½   teaspoons fish sauce

Heat oil in small saucepan over medium heat until shimmering. Add curry paste, garlic, and ginger; cook, stirring constantly, until fragrant, about 1 minute. Whisk in coconut milk and sugar and bring to simmer. Whisk in peanut butter until smooth. Remove pan from heat and whisk in lime juice and fish sauce.

SWEET AND SPICY HOISIN GLAZE
MAKES ABOUT ¾ CUP

1   teaspoon vegetable oil
3   garlic cloves, minced
1   teaspoon grated fresh ginger
½   teaspoon red pepper flakes
½   cup hoisin sauce
2   tablespoons soy sauce
1   tablespoon rice vinegar

Heat oil in small saucepan over medium heat until shimmering. Add garlic, ginger, and pepper flakes; cook until fragrant, about 30 seconds. Whisk in hoisin and soy sauce until smooth. Remove pan from heat and stir in vinegar.

MISO

An essential ingredient in the Japanese kitchen, miso paste is made by fermenting soybeans and sometimes grains (such as rice, barley, or rye) with a mold called *koji*. Packed with savory flavor, miso is used to season everything from soups and braises to dressings and sauces. Although countless variations of the salty, deep-flavored ingredient are available, three common types are white *shiro miso* (despite its name, this miso is light golden in color), red *aka*, and brownish-black *hatcho*. Flavor profiles are altered by changing the type of grain in the mix, adjusting the ratio of grain to soybeans, tweaking the amounts of salt and mold, and extending or decreasing the fermentation time, which can range from a few weeks to a few years.

We tasted the South River brand of white and red miso (available in some grocery stores, Asian markets, and online) along with an Asian brand of harder-to-find dark brown miso plain, in miso soup, and in miso-glazed salmon. The shiro miso was mild and sweet, and the hatcho miso was strong, complex, and prunelike.

Though flavor nuances will vary from brand to brand, if you're looking to keep just one type of miso on hand, moderately salty-sweet red miso is a good all-purpose choice. Miso will easily keep for up to a year in the refrigerator (some sources say it keeps indefinitely).

Even the most thin, delicate spears of asparagus still have tough, woody ends that must be removed.

To break off the ends at precisely the right point, all you need is your hands. Grip the stalk about halfway down; with the other hand, hold the stem between the thumb and index finger about an inch or so from the bottom and bend the stalk until it snaps.

Spicy Stir-Fried Pork and Asparagus

✔ WHY THIS RECIPE WORKS

A stir-fry is an ideal weeknight meal—both protein and vegetables are cooked quickly over high heat, then tossed together with a flavorful sauce and served over rice. There is nothing overly complicated about stir-fries; the key is plenty of intense heat. The pan must be hot enough to caramelize sugars, deepen flavors, and evaporate unnecessary juices all in a matter of minutes. We wanted a recipe for a quick and easy pork stir-fry, brightened by complementary vegetables and enlivened with a well-balanced sauce.

CHOOSE A LEAN CUT AND MARINATE Because pork tenderloin is so lean, it requires little prep and cooks quickly, making it an ideal choice for stir-fry. Marinating the pork in a combination of soy sauce and either sherry or fish sauce added much-needed flavor and moisture to this mild cut.

COOK IN BATCHES Cooking the pork in batches over high heat prevented overcrowding, so the meat browned instead of steamed. Similarly, we found it best to cook the vegetables in batches—both to avoid overcrowding and because different vegetables cook at different rates.

ADD AROMATICS LATER We cooked aromatics such as ginger and garlic only briefly—just long enough to develop their flavors but not long enough to burn.

TIE IT ALL TOGETHER Once the pork and vegetables were all cooked, we added them back to the pan along with the sauce to allow the flavors to meld. Chicken broth gave our sauce some backbone, and cornstarch slightly thickened it so that it lightly coated the meat and veggies.

SPICY STIR-FRIED PORK, ASPARAGUS, AND ONIONS WITH LEMON GRASS

SERVES 4

For information on pork tenderloin, see page 182. To make slicing the pork easier, freeze it for 15 minutes. Serve with Sticky Rice (page 114).

SAUCE
- ⅓ cup chicken broth
- 2 tablespoons fish sauce
- 1 tablespoon packed light brown sugar
- 2 teaspoons lime juice
- 1 teaspoon cornstarch

STIR-FRY
- 1 (12-ounce) pork tenderloin, trimmed and cut into thin strips
- 1 teaspoon fish sauce
- 1 teaspoon soy sauce
- 2 lemon grass stalks, trimmed to bottom 6 inches and minced
- 2 garlic cloves, minced
- ¾ teaspoon red pepper flakes
- 3½ tablespoons vegetable oil
- 1 pound asparagus, trimmed and cut on bias into 2-inch lengths
- 1 large onion, cut into ¼-inch wedges
- ¼ cup chopped fresh basil

1. FOR THE SAUCE: Whisk all ingredients together in small bowl and set aside.

2. FOR THE STIR-FRY: Combine pork, fish sauce, and soy sauce in small bowl. Cover with plastic wrap and refrigerate for at least 20 minutes or up to 1 hour. Meanwhile, combine lemon grass, garlic, pepper flakes, and 1 tablespoon oil in small bowl.

3. Heat 1½ teaspoons oil in 12-inch nonstick skillet over high heat until just smoking. Add half of pork, break up any clumps, and cook, stirring occasionally, until well browned, about 2 minutes. Transfer pork to medium bowl. Repeat with 1½ teaspoons oil and remaining pork.

4. Add 1 tablespoon oil to now-empty skillet. Add asparagus, and cook, stirring every 30 seconds, until browned and almost tender, 4 to 5 minutes. Transfer to bowl with pork. Add remaining 1½ teaspoons oil to skillet, add onion, and cook, stirring occasionally, until beginning to brown and soften, about 2 minutes.

5. Clear center of skillet, add lemon grass mixture, and cook, mashing mixture into pan, until fragrant, about 1 minute. Stir mixture into onion.

6. Return pork and asparagus to skillet and toss to combine. Whisk sauce to recombine, add to skillet, and cook, stirring constantly, until sauce is thickened and evenly distributed, about 30 seconds. Transfer to platter, sprinkle with basil, and serve.

STIR-FRIED PORK, GREEN BEANS, AND RED BELL PEPPER WITH GINGERY OYSTER SAUCE

SERVES 4

To make slicing the pork easier, freeze it for 15 minutes. Serve with Sticky Rice (page 114).

SAUCE
- ⅓ cup chicken broth
- 2½ tablespoons oyster sauce
- 1 tablespoon dry sherry
- 2 teaspoons toasted sesame oil
- 1 teaspoon rice vinegar
- 1 teaspoon cornstarch
- ¼ teaspoon ground white pepper

STIR-FRY
- 1 (12-ounce) pork tenderloin, trimmed and cut into thin strips
- 2 teaspoons soy sauce
- 2 teaspoons dry sherry
- 2 tablespoons grated fresh ginger
- 2 garlic cloves, minced

- 3 tablespoons vegetable oil
- 12 ounces green beans, trimmed and cut on bias into 2-inch lengths
- 1 large red bell pepper, stemmed, seeded, and cut into ¾-inch squares
- 3 scallions, sliced thin on bias

1. FOR THE SAUCE: Whisk all ingredients together in small bowl and set aside.

2. FOR THE STIR-FRY: Combine pork, soy sauce, and sherry in small bowl. Cover with plastic wrap and refrigerate for at least 20 minutes or up to 1 hour. Meanwhile, combine ginger, garlic, and 1½ teaspoons oil in small bowl.

3. Heat 1½ teaspoons vegetable oil in 12-inch nonstick skillet over high heat until just smoking. Add half of pork, break up any clumps, and cook, stirring occasionally, until well browned, about 2 minutes. Transfer pork to medium bowl. Repeat with 1½ teaspoons vegetable oil and remaining pork.

4. Add 1 tablespoon vegetable oil to now-empty skillet. Add green beans and cook, stirring occasionally, until spotty brown and crisp-tender, about 5 minutes. Transfer to bowl with pork. Add remaining 1½ teaspoons oil to skillet, add bell pepper, and cook, stirring frequently, until spotty brown, about 2 minutes.

5. Clear center of skillet, add ginger mixture, and cook, mashing mixture into pan, until fragrant, 15 to 20 seconds. Stir mixture into bell pepper.

6. Return pork and green beans to skillet and toss to combine. Whisk sauce to recombine, add to skillet, and cook, stirring constantly, until sauce is thickened and evenly distributed, about 30 seconds. Transfer to platter, sprinkle with scallions, and serve.

STIR-FRIED PORK, EGGPLANT, AND ONION WITH GARLIC AND BLACK PEPPER

SERVES 4

This take on classic Thai stir-fry is not for those with timid palates. To make slicing the pork easier, freeze it for 15 minutes. Serve with Sticky Rice (page 114).

SLICING PORK TENDERLOIN FOR STIR-FRIES

We find it helpful to freeze the meat briefly to make it firmer for slicing.

1. Place meat in freezer until just firm, about 15 minutes. With very sharp knife, cut tenderloin crosswise into ⅓-inch-thick medallions.

2. Slice each medallion into thin strips.

FISH SAUCE

Fish sauce is a salty amber-colored liquid made from fermented fish. It is used as an ingredient and condiment in certain Asian cuisines, most commonly in the foods of Southeast Asia. In small amounts, it adds a well-rounded, salty flavor to sauces, soups, and marinades. We gathered six brands of fish sauce—one from Vietnam (where fish sauce is known as *nuoc nam*), one from the Philippines (*patis*), and the rest from Thailand (*nam pla*)—from our local supermarket, natural foods store, and Asian market. Differences in the sauces were noted by tasters immediately. Color correlated with flavor; the lighter the sauce, the lighter the flavor. Tasters had preferences, but those preferences varied greatly from taster to taster. In the end, all the sauces were recommended. In fact, only one point (out of a total of 10) separated all six sauces.

With such a limited ingredient list—most of the brands contained some combination of fish extract, water, salt, and sugar—the differences between the sauces were minimal. And because fish sauce is used in such small amounts, minute flavor differences get lost among the other flavors of a dish. If you are a fan of fish sauce and use it often, you might want to make a special trip to an Asian market to buy a rich, dark sauce that is suitably pungent. But for most applications, we found that the differences were negligible. Because most supermarkets don't carry a wide selection of fish sauce, we recommend buying whatever is available.

SAUCE

- 2½ tablespoons fish sauce
- 2½ tablespoons soy sauce
- 2½ tablespoons packed light brown sugar
- 2 tablespoons chicken broth
- 2 teaspoons lime juice
- 1 teaspoon cornstarch

STIR-FRY

- 1 (12-ounce) pork tenderloin, trimmed and cut into thin strips
- 1 teaspoon fish sauce
- 1 teaspoon soy sauce
- 12 garlic cloves, minced
- 2 teaspoons pepper
- 3½ tablespoons vegetable oil
- 1 pound eggplant, cut into ¾-inch cubes
- 1 large onion, cut into ¼- to ⅜-inch wedges
- ¼ cup coarsely chopped fresh cilantro

1. FOR THE SAUCE: Whisk all ingredients together in small bowl and set aside.

2. FOR THE STIR-FRY: Combine pork, fish sauce, and soy sauce in small bowl. Cover with plastic wrap and refrigerate for at least 20 minutes or up to 1 hour. Meanwhile, combine garlic, pepper, and 1 tablespoon oil in second small bowl and set aside.

3. Heat 1½ teaspoons oil in 12-inch non-stick skillet over high heat until just smoking. Add half of pork, break up any clumps, and cook, stirring occasionally, until well browned, about 2 minutes. Transfer pork to medium bowl. Repeat with 1½ teaspoons oil and remaining pork.

4. Add 1 tablespoon oil to now-empty skillet. Add eggplant and cook, stirring every 30 seconds, until browned and no longer spongy, about 5 minutes. Transfer to bowl with pork. Add remaining 1½ teaspoons oil to skillet, add onion, and cook, stirring occasionally, until beginning to brown and soften, about 2 minutes.

5. Clear center of skillet, add garlic-pepper mixture, and cook, mashing mixture into pan, until fragrant and beginning to brown, about 1½ minutes. Stir mixture into onions.

6. Return pork and eggplant to skillet and toss to combine. Whisk sauce to recombine, add to skillet, and cook, stirring constantly, until sauce is thickened and evenly distributed, about 30 seconds. Transfer to platter, sprinkle with cilantro, and serve.

Thai Pork Lettuce Wraps

✓ WHY THIS RECIPE WORKS

Made with finely chopped, cooked meat tossed with fresh herbs and a light dressing, the Thai salad known as larb *embodies the cuisine's signature balance of sweet, sour, hot, and salty flavors. Making this light but bold-flavored Thai specialty isn't a matter of rounding up a lot of exotic ingredients. What we needed was to find a solution to a familiar problem: ensuring tender, juicy pork.*

PICK THE RIGHT PORK Preground pork from the supermarket gave us inconsistent results; for flavorful, tender pork, we used a food processor to chop the meat ourselves. Pork tenderloin was the favorite for its supreme tenderness. Briefly freezing the pork before chopping allowed the meat to process more uniformly.

USE LESS LIQUID While the pork for this dish is traditionally cooked in a large pot of boiling water, we found that it was all too easy for the meat to overcook. (Water is an excellent conductor of heat—even better than the air in an oven—so that pork cooked in boiling water quickly rises above the crucial 165-degree mark.) Using a smaller volume of liquid—a mere ¼ cup—allowed the pork to

If your Bibb lettuce comes
with the root attached, leave
the lettuce portion attached
to the root and store in the
original plastic container,
plastic produce bag, or
zipper-lock bag left slightly
open. If the lettuce is without
the root, wrap in moist paper
towels and refrigerate in a
plastic produce bag or zipper-
lock bag left slightly open.

cook much more gently. And swapping out the water for chicken broth gave the lean pork tenderloin a much-needed flavor boost.

FINESSE THE FLAVORS A ratio of 3 tablespoons lime juice to 2½ tablespoons fish sauce provided the proper balance of tart and salty flavors, while a mere ¼ teaspoon of red pepper flakes contributed just enough heat. A couple teaspoons of sugar gave our dish the requisite sweetness.

SUPERMARKET SUBSTITUTES While some recipes for larb call for hard-to-find ingredients like galangal, lemon grass, and kaffir lime leaves, we found these additions weren't worth the extra trouble. The slight pungency of thinly sliced shallots and the bright flavor of roughly chopped mint and cilantro yielded a very flavorful salad without a trip to a specialty store. Toasted ground white rice provided nutty flavor and a subtly pleasing textural contrast to the tender pork.

THAI PORK LETTUCE WRAPS
SERVES 4

For more information on pork tenderloin, see page 182. We prefer natural pork in this recipe. If using enhanced pork, skip the marinating in step 2 and reduce the amount of fish sauce to 2 tablespoons, adding it all in step 5. Don't skip the toasted rice; it's integral to the texture and flavor of the dish. Any style of white rice can be used. Toasted rice powder (kao kua) can also be found in many Asian markets; substitute 1 tablespoon rice powder for the white rice. This dish can be served with Sticky Rice (page 114) and steamed vegetables. To save time, prepare the other ingredients while the pork is in the freezer.

1	(1-pound) pork tenderloin, trimmed and cut into 1-inch chunks
2½	tablespoons fish sauce
1	tablespoon white rice
¼	cup chicken broth
2	shallots, peeled and sliced into thin rings
3	tablespoons lime juice (2 limes)
3	tablespoons roughly chopped fresh mint
3	tablespoons roughly chopped fresh cilantro
2	teaspoons sugar
¼	teaspoon red pepper flakes
1	head Bibb lettuce (8 ounces), leaves separated

1. Place pork on large plate in single layer. Freeze meat until firm and starting to harden around edges but still pliable, 15 to 20 minutes.

2. Place half of meat in food processor and pulse until coarsely chopped, 5 or 6 pulses. Transfer ground meat to medium bowl and repeat with remaining chunks. Stir 1 tablespoon fish sauce into ground meat, cover with plastic wrap, and refrigerate for 15 minutes.

3. Toast rice in 8-inch skillet over medium-high heat, stirring constantly, until deep golden brown, about 5 minutes. Transfer to small bowl and let cool for 5 minutes. Grind rice with spice grinder, mini food processor, or mortar and pestle until it resembles fine meal, 10 to 30 seconds (you should have about 1 tablespoon rice powder).

4. Bring broth to simmer in 12-inch non-stick skillet over medium-high heat. Add pork and cook, stirring frequently, until about half of pork is no longer pink, about 2 minutes. Sprinkle 1 teaspoon rice powder over pork and continue to cook, stirring constantly, until remaining pork is no longer pink, 1 to 1½ minutes longer. Transfer pork to large bowl and let cool for 10 minutes.

5. Add shallots, lime juice, mint, cilantro, sugar, pepper flakes, remaining 1½ tablespoons fish sauce, and remaining 2 teaspoons rice powder to pork and toss to combine. Serve with lettuce leaves, spooning meat into leaves at table.

Sichuan Stir-Fried Pork in Garlic Sauce

WHY THIS RECIPE WORKS

A classic Chinese stir-fry, yu xiang pork features a bold-tasting, silky sauce, tender pork, meaty mushrooms, and typically a crunchy element such as celery, bamboo shoots, or water chestnuts. The contrasting textures and salty, sweet, hot, and sour elements are irresistible. We wanted to replicate this restaurant favorite at home.

CHOOSE COUNTRY-STYLE RIBS Most recipes call for pork loin, a lean, notoriously unforgiving cut that tends to cook up dry and fibrous. Switching to country-style ribs was a big improvement; the fattier cut offered more flavor and tenderness (and it's easy to purchase in smaller quantities).

SODA SOLUTION To further enhance juiciness and tenderness, we employed the stir-fry technique of velveting, in which the meat is coated with a cornstarch slurry to provide an insulating barrier that shields the meat from the pan's high temperatures. While this helped, we found the real solution when we briefly soaked the pork in a mixture of baking soda and water. The soda raised the pH of the meat, making it incredibly tender.

STRIKE THE RIGHT BALANCE To achieve just the right balance of flavors in the sauce, we used equal parts soy sauce and sugar, along with tangy Chinese black vinegar and some rice wine. Sesame oil added a pleasing nuttiness, while fish sauce and a surprise ingredient—ketchup—substantially boosted the savory quality of our stir-fry.

SICHUAN STIR-FRIED PORK IN GARLIC SAUCE

SERVES 4 TO 6

Country-style pork ribs are also called country ribs (see page 181 for more information). If Chinese black vinegar is unavailable, substitute 2 teaspoons balsamic vinegar and 2 teaspoons rice vinegar. If Asian broad bean chili paste is unavailable, substitute 2 teaspoons Asian chili-garlic sauce or Sriracha sauce. Serve with Sticky Rice (page 114).

SAUCE

- ½ cup chicken broth
- 2 tablespoons soy sauce
- 2 tablespoons sugar
- 4 teaspoons Chinese black vinegar
- 1 tablespoon Chinese rice wine or dry sherry
- 1 tablespoon toasted sesame oil
- 2 teaspoons cornstarch
- 2 teaspoons fish sauce
- 2 teaspoons ketchup

PORK

- 12 ounces boneless country-style pork ribs, trimmed
- ½ cup water
- 1 teaspoon baking soda
- 2 teaspoons Chinese rice wine or dry sherry
- 2 teaspoons cornstarch

STIR-FRY

- 2 tablespoons Asian broad bean chili paste
- 2 scallions, white parts minced, green parts sliced thin
- 4 garlic cloves, minced
- ¼ cup vegetable oil
- 6 ounces shiitake mushrooms, stemmed and sliced thin
- 2 celery ribs, cut on bias into ¼-inch slices

1. FOR THE SAUCE: Whisk all ingredients together in bowl and set aside.

2. FOR THE PORK: Cut pork into 2-inch lengths, then cut each length into ¼-inch matchsticks. Combine pork with water and

We were among the many people who assume that there must be some kind of synthetic chemical chicanery going on in the making of "liquid smoke" flavoring. But that's not the case. Liquid smoke is made by channeling smoke from smoldering wood chips through a condenser, which quickly cools the vapors, causing them to liquefy (just like the drops that form when you breathe on a piece of cold glass). The water-soluble flavor compounds in the smoke are trapped within this liquid, while the nonsoluble, carcinogenic tars and resins are removed by a series of filters, resulting in a clean, smoke-flavored liquid.

Curious about the manufacturing process for this product, we wondered if we could bottle up some smoke for ourselves. To do this, we created a small-scale mock-up of the commercial method, involving a kettle grill, a duct fan, a siphon, and an ice-chilled glass coil condenser.

In a comparison of homemade and store-bought liquid smoke, homemade was praised for its clean, intense, smoky flavor. But we spent an entire day and $50 on materials to produce 3 tablespoons of homemade liquid smoke. Commercial liquid smoke is just fine, especially if you avoid brands with additives such as salt, vinegar, and molasses. Our top-rated brand, **Wright's Liquid Smoke**, contains nothing but smoke and water.

baking soda in bowl. Let sit at room temperature for 15 minutes.

3. Rinse pork under running water. Drain well and pat dry with paper towels. Whisk rice wine and cornstarch together in bowl. Add pork and toss to coat.

4. FOR THE STIR-FRY: Combine chili paste, scallion whites, and garlic in bowl.

5. Heat 1 tablespoon oil in 12-inch nonstick skillet over high heat until just smoking. Add mushrooms and cook, stirring frequently, until tender, 2 to 4 minutes. Add celery and continue to cook until celery is crisp-tender, 2 to 4 minutes. Transfer vegetables to separate bowl.

6. Add remaining 3 tablespoons oil to now-empty skillet and place over medium-low heat. Add garlic-scallion mixture and cook, stirring frequently, until fragrant, about 30 seconds. Transfer 1 tablespoon garlic-scallion oil to small bowl and set aside. Add pork to skillet and cook, stirring frequently, until no longer pink, 3 to 5 minutes. Whisk sauce to recombine and add to skillet. Increase heat to high and cook, stirring constantly, until sauce is thickened and pork is cooked through, 1 to 2 minutes. Return vegetables to skillet and toss to combine. Transfer to serving platter, sprinkle with scallion greens and reserved garlic-scallion oil, and serve.

Pork Lo Mein

✔ WHY THIS RECIPE WORKS

Order pork lo mein from your typical takeout joint, and the dish invariably disappoints, with greasy flavors and sodden vegetables. We wanted a dish representative of the best any good Chinese home cook could turn out: chewy noodles tossed in a salty-sweet sauce and accented with bits of smoky char siu (barbecued pork) and still-crisp cabbage.

PIN DOWN THE PORK Country-style ribs, which are meaty and naturally tender, were the ideal substitute for *char siu*, the rich and flavorful (but slow-cooking) pork shoulder traditional to the dish.

MARINATE AND STIR-FRY Marinating thin strips of the pork in a classic Chinese mixture of hoisin sauce, oyster sauce, soy sauce, toasted sesame oil, and five-spice powder and then stir-frying it over high heat resulted in tender, juicy meat with a crisp, browned exterior. While optional, a few drops of liquid smoke contributed the smoky flavor that's the hallmark of good *char siu*.

CHOOSE THE RIGHT NOODLE Fresh Chinese egg noodles can be hard to find, but the more readily available "Chinese-style" egg noodles from the supermarket have a pasty texture and inferior taste. We found that linguine made a good substitute, with a similar width and the same firm chewiness of fresh noodles.

A FRESH FINISH To round out our lo mein, we opted for the traditional choices—cabbage, scallions, and shiitake mushrooms, along with a little garlic and fresh ginger. And we found that the marinade ingredients could perform double duty as the sauce; a little chicken broth and a teaspoon of cornstarch added body.

🔪 AT THE MEAT COUNTER

PREFERRED CUT Country-Style Pork Ribs
Boneless country style pork ribs are also called country ribs (see page 181 for more information.)

ALTERNATE CUT Bone-In Country-Style Pork Ribs
1½ pounds bone-in ribs can be substituted for the boneless ribs. Pork tenderloin can also be substituted for the ribs (see page 182 for information).

PORK STIR-FRY WITH NOODLES (LO MEIN)

SERVES 4

Use a cast-iron skillet for this recipe if you have one—it will help create the best sear on the pork. When shopping for Chinese rice wine, look for one that is amber in color; if it's not available, sherry wine may be used as a substitute. If no hoisin sauce is available, substitute 1 tablespoon of sugar. If boneless pork ribs are unavailable, substitute 1½ pounds of bone-in country-style ribs, followed by the next best option, pork tenderloin. Liquid smoke provides a flavor reminiscent of traditional Chinese barbecued pork. It is important that the noodles are cooked at the last minute to avoid clumping.

3 tablespoons soy sauce

2 tablespoons oyster sauce

2 tablespoons hoisin sauce

1 tablespoon toasted sesame oil

¼ teaspoon five-spice powder

1 pound boneless country-style pork ribs, trimmed and sliced crosswise into ⅛-inch pieces

¼ teaspoon liquid smoke (optional)

½ cup chicken broth

1 teaspoon cornstarch

2 garlic cloves, minced

2 teaspoons grated fresh ginger

1½ tablespoons vegetable oil

¼ cup Chinese rice wine or dry sherry

8 ounces shiitake mushrooms, stemmed and halved if small or quartered if large

16 scallions, white parts sliced thin, green parts cut into 1-inch pieces

1 small head napa cabbage (1½ pounds), halved, cored, and sliced crosswise into ½-inch strips (4 cups)

12 ounces fresh Chinese egg noodles or 8 ounces dried linguine

1 tablespoon Asian chili-garlic sauce

1. Bring 4 quarts water to boil in Dutch oven over high heat.

2. Whisk soy sauce, oyster sauce, hoisin sauce, sesame oil, and five-spice powder together in medium bowl. Place 3 tablespoons soy sauce mixture in large zipper-lock bag; add pork and, if using, liquid smoke. Press out as much air as possible and seal bag, making sure that all pieces are coated with marinade. Refrigerate for at least 15 minutes or up to 1 hour. Whisk broth and cornstarch into remaining soy sauce mixture. In separate bowl, mix garlic and ginger with ½ teaspoon vegetable oil; set aside.

3. Heat 1 teaspoon vegetable oil in 12-inch cast-iron or nonstick skillet over high heat until just smoking. Add half of pork in single layer, breaking up clumps with wooden spoon. Cook, without stirring, for 1 minute. Continue to cook, stirring occasionally, until browned, 2 to 3 minutes. Add 2 tablespoons wine to skillet; cook, stirring constantly, until liquid is reduced and pork is well coated, 30 to 60 seconds. Transfer pork to medium bowl and repeat with 1 teaspoon vegetable oil, remaining pork, and remaining 2 tablespoons wine. Wipe skillet clean with paper towels.

4. Return now-empty skillet to high heat, add 1 teaspoon vegetable oil, and heat until just smoking. Add mushrooms and cook, stirring occasionally, until light golden brown, 4 to 6 minutes. Add scallions and continue to cook, stirring occasionally, until scallions are wilted, 2 to 3 minutes longer; transfer vegetables to bowl with pork.

5. Add remaining 1 teaspoon vegetable oil and cabbage to now-empty skillet; cook, stirring occasionally, until spotty brown, 3 to 5 minutes. Clear center of skillet; add garlic mixture and cook, mashing mixture with spoon, until fragrant, about 30 seconds. Stir garlic mixture into cabbage; return pork-vegetable mixture and broth-soy mixture to skillet; simmer until thickened and ingredients are well incorporated, 1 to 2 minutes. Remove skillet from heat.

6. While cabbage is cooking, stir noodles into boiling water. Cook, stirring occasionally, until noodles are tender, 3 to 4 minutes for fresh Chinese noodles or 10 minutes for dried linguine. Drain noodles and transfer back to Dutch oven; add cooked stir-fry mixture and chili-garlic sauce, tossing noodles constantly, until sauce coats noodles. Serve immediately.

SHIITAKE SUBSTITUTE

Can cremini mushrooms be swapped for shiitakes in cooking? They share a similar earthy flavor but do they cook at the same rate? To answer this question we first had to understand what happens when mushrooms are heated.

The goal of cooking mushrooms is to evaporate their liquid so they can brown and their flavor can intensify. Thus, to identify any difference in water weight between cremini and shiitake mushrooms that would affect cooking times, we chopped 8 ounces of each and placed them in separate pots with no liquid or oil. We covered the pots and cooked each batch for 10 minutes over medium-low heat. We then removed the mushrooms from the pans and weighed them again.

The shiitakes lost 1.1 ounces of water, or about 14 percent of their weight, while the cremini mushrooms lost 4.8 ounces, or about 60 percent of their weight. The higher water content of the creminis was confirmed when we sautéed a batch of each mushroom. The creminis took nearly 5 minutes longer than the shiitakes to release their liquid and begin to brown.

In the end, we decided that it's fine to make a substitution, keeping in mind that the creminis will have a slightly softer texture and a bit less intense flavor. Just remember to sauté or stir-fry creminis for a few extra minutes until their excess liquid completely evaporates.

1. Position roast so bones are perpendicular to cutting board. Starting from far end and working toward you, make series of small, easy strokes with boning knife between meat and bones.

2. Gradually cut along curved rib bones down to backbone until meat is free from bones.

Tuscan-Style Garlic Roast Pork Loin

✓ WHY THIS RECIPE WORKS

It's easy to fall in love with Tuscan-style roast pork; in this dish, a roast pork loin is flavored with rosemary and garlic, served boneless, and sliced thick. For such a simple roast, however, problems abound. The meat can be dry, tough, and unevenly cooked; the crust can be absent, resulting in a pale and unappealing roast; and the rosemary and garlic flavors can be either too bland or too harsh. We wanted succulent meat, a crisp crust, and balanced flavor.

USE A RIB ROAST While we tested a variety of roasts—including blade, sirloin, and loin—we ultimately selected the rib roast. With its thorough marbling and a moisturizing fat cap, the rib roast simply had the best flavor. As an added bonus, the ribs elevated the meat off the bottom of the roasting pan for better air circulation, which allowed for more even cooking.

FLAVOR INFUSION For rosemary and garlic flavor that infused—not overwhelmed—the pork, we found a multistep approach to be the most effective: We cut the meat off the bones, slathered the bones with two-thirds of a paste (a blend of garlic, rosemary, and olive oil), spread the rest on the cut in the meat, and then tied the meat back onto the bones.

SEAR, THEN ROAST For an ideal combination of well-browned exterior and moist, tender interior, searing the roast on the stovetop before finishing it in a moderate 325-degree oven was the only way to go.

TUSCAN-STYLE GARLIC-ROSEMARY ROAST PORK LOIN

SERVES 6 TO 8

Center-cut pork rib roast is also called rack of pork, pork loin rib half, center-cut roast (see page 181 for more information.) If the pork is enhanced (injected with a salt solution), do not brine in step 1, but season with salt in step 4. The roasting time is determined in part by the shape of the roast; a long, thin roast will cook faster than a roast with a large circumference. Though not traditionally served, the ribs are rich with flavor. If you'd like to serve them, increase the oven temperature to 375 degrees, untie the roast and remove the loin as directed, then scrape off the excess garlic-rosemary paste from the ribs, set them on a rimmed baking sheet, and return them to the oven for about 20 minutes, until they are brown and crisp. Slice in between the bones and serve.

PORK AND BRINE

1	(4-pound) center-cut bone-in pork rib roast, trimmed
2⅓	cups packed dark brown sugar
	Salt
10	large garlic cloves, lightly crushed and peeled
5	sprigs fresh rosemary
1	tablespoon olive oil
1	cup dry white wine
1	teaspoon pepper

GARLIC-ROSEMARY PASTE

8	garlic cloves, minced
1½	tablespoons minced fresh rosemary
1	tablespoon olive oil
1	teaspoon pepper
	Pinch salt

JUS

1	shallot, minced
1½	teaspoons minced fresh rosemary
1¾	cups chicken broth
2	tablespoons unsalted butter, cut into 4 pieces and softened

1. **FOR THE PORK AND BRINE:** Using boning knife, carefully cut meat away from rack of bones. Dissolve sugar and salt in 2 quarts cold water in large container. Stir in garlic and rosemary. Submerge pork and bones in brine, cover, and refrigerate for 1½ to 2 hours.

2. **FOR THE GARLIC-ROSEMARY PASTE:** While pork brines, mix garlic, rosemary, olive oil, pepper, and salt together in bowl to form paste; set aside.

3. Remove meat and ribs from brine and thoroughly pat dry with paper towels. Adjust oven rack to middle position and heat oven to 325 degrees. Heat oil in 12-inch skillet over medium heat until just smoking, about 4 minutes. Place roast fat side down in skillet and cook until well browned, about 8 minutes. Transfer roast browned side up to carving board and set aside to cool. Pour off fat from skillet and add wine; increase heat to high and bring to boil, scraping up any browned bits. Set skillet off heat.

4. **TO BUTTERFLY ROASTS:** Make lengthwise incision in pork loin and spread meat flat. Rub with one-third of garlic-rosemary paste, rub remaining paste on cut side of ribs, and tie meat back to ribs. Season browned side of roast with pepper and set roast rib side down in roasting pan. Pour reserved wine and browned bits from skillet into roasting pan. Roast, basting loin with pan drippings every 20 minutes, until meat registers 140 degrees, 1 hour 5 minutes to 1 hour 20 minutes. (If wine evaporates, add about ½ cup water to roasting pan to prevent scorching.) Transfer roast to clean carving board and tent loosely with aluminum foil; let rest about 15 minutes.

5. **FOR THE JUS:** While roast rests, spoon off most of fat from roasting pan and place over 2 burners at high heat. Add shallot and rosemary; scrape bottom of pan with wooden spoon to loosen any browned bits and boil until liquid is reduced by half and shallot has softened, about 2 minutes. Add broth and continue to cook, stirring occasionally, until reduced by half, about 8 minutes. Add any accumulated pork juices and cook 1 minute longer. Off heat, whisk in butter; strain jus into serving bowl.

6. Remove twine and remove meat from bones. Set meat browned side up on carving board and cut into ¼-inch-thick slices. Serve, passing jus separately.

GARLIC-ROSEMARY ROAST PORK LOIN WITH ROASTED POTATOES

Reduce wine to ¾ cup and omit jus ingredients. When pork has roasted 15 minutes, quarter 2 pounds unpeeled red potatoes. Toss with 2 tablespoons olive oil in bowl and season with salt and pepper. After pork has roasted 30 minutes, add potatoes to roasting pan; stir to coat potatoes with pan juices. After transferring roast to carving board, turn potato pieces with wide metal spatula and spread them in even layer. Increase oven temperature to 400 degrees and return potatoes to oven; continue to roast until tender and browned, 5 to 15 minutes longer. Serve potatoes with roast.

GARLIC-ROSEMARY ROAST PORK LOIN WITH FENNEL

Trim 2 fennel bulbs of stalks and fronds; finely chop 2 teaspoons fronds. Halve, core, and cut each bulb lengthwise into eighths. Toss fennel with 1 tablespoon olive oil in medium bowl and season with salt and pepper. Add 1 teaspoon finely chopped fennel seeds and chopped fennel fronds to garlic-rosemary paste. Reduce wine to ¾ cup and omit jus ingredients. Add fennel to roasting pan along with wine. After transferring roast to carving board, return fennel to oven; continue to roast until tender, 5 to 15 minutes. Serve fennel with roast.

PREPARING GARLIC ROAST PORK LOIN

1. With fat side of roast down, slice through center of entire length of meat, stopping 1 inch shy of edge. Spread meat flat.

2. Rub one-third of garlic-rosemary paste mixture in even layer on one side of cut, leaving ½ inch on each end bare.

3. Spread remaining garlic-rosemary paste mixture evenly along bones from where meat was cut, leaving ½ inch on each end bare.

4. Fold meat back together and tie meat on bones exactly from where it was cut with 7 individual lengths of kitchen twine.

Herb-Crusted Pork Roast

✔ WHY THIS RECIPE WORKS

A fresh herb crust seems like a good way to enliven a boneless pork roast—but not if the crust has little flavor and falls off. We wanted to determine how to get the crust to stay put, and also find a way to infuse the meat with bold herb presence in every bite.

PASTE PLUS BRINE We tried adding garlic and herbs to our brine, with the hope that their flavors would permeate the meat, but since the flavor compounds in herbs are oil-soluble we had little success. Instead, we found that before brining, cutting a single horizontal pocket in the roast, brining the roast, then slathering it with an herb paste gave the pork ample herb flavor. Tying the roast kept the paste in place.

BROWN AND ROAST Searing the roast on the stovetop provided a beautifully browned exterior, while transferring it to the oven at a relatively low temperature—325 degrees—allowed the roast to cook evenly and prevented the exterior from overcooking while the interior came up to temperature.

SCORE THE FAT The key to getting the crust—a combination of more herb paste and bread crumbs—to stay put was to score a crosshatch pattern into the fat cap before searing the roast. This gave the paste something to grip and helped unify the crust and meat. Parsley, thyme, and rosemary provided the herbal presence, and garlic further seasoned the paste. Some shallot and a bit of Parmesan were welcome additions to the bread crumbs, providing brightness and a nutty richness.

HERB-CRUSTED PORK ROAST

SERVES 4 TO 6

Center-cut pork loin roast is also called center-cut roast (see page 181 for more information). If the pork is enhanced (injected with a salt solution), do not brine in step 1, but season with salt in step 4. Note that you should not trim the pork of its layer of fat.

The roasting time will vary widely depending on the thickness of the meat.

1	(2½- to 3-pound) boneless center-cut pork loin roast
	Salt and pepper
¼	cup sugar
1	slice hearty white sandwich bread, torn into quarters
1	ounce Parmesan or Pecorino Romano cheese, grated (½ cup)
1	shallot, minced
¼	cup plus 2 teaspoons olive oil
⅓	cup packed fresh parsley or basil
2	tablespoons minced fresh thyme
1	teaspoon minced fresh rosemary or ½ teaspoon dried
1	large garlic clove, minced

1. Lightly score fat cap on pork, making ¼-inch crosshatch pattern. Create pocket by inserting knife ½ inch from end of roast and cutting along side of pork stopping ½ inch short of other end. Pull open roast and use gentle strokes to cut deeper pocket. Dissolve ¼ cup salt and sugar in 2 quarts cold water in large container. Submerge pork in brine, cover, and refrigerate for 1½ to 2 hours. Remove roast from brine and pat dry with paper towels.

2. Meanwhile, adjust oven rack to lower-middle position and heat oven to 325 degrees. Set wire rack in rimmed baking sheet lined with aluminum foil. Pulse bread in food processor until coarsely ground, about 16 pulses (you should have 1 cup crumbs). Transfer crumbs to medium bowl and add 2 tablespoons Parmesan, shallot, 1 tablespoon oil, ⅛ teaspoon salt, and ⅛ teaspoon pepper. Using fork, toss mixture until crumbs are evenly coated with oil.

3. Pulse parsley, thyme, rosemary, garlic, remaining 6 tablespoons Parmesan,

1. With blade parallel to counter, use knife to cut through middle of scored roast, starting ½ inch from end of roast.

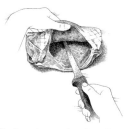

2. Cut along side of pork, stopping ½ inch short of other end. Pull open roast and use gentle strokes to cut deeper pocket.

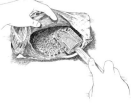

3. Spread ¼ cup herb paste evenly into pocket, using spatula and your fingers to make sure paste reaches corners of pocket.

4. Return roast to original shape and tie at even intervals along its length with 3 pieces of kitchen twine.

3 tablespoons oil, ⅛ teaspoon salt, and ⅛ teaspoon pepper in now-empty food processor until smooth, about 12 pulses. Transfer herb paste to bowl.

4. Spread ¼ cup herb paste inside roast and tie roast with 3 pieces of kitchen twine. Season roast with pepper.

5. Heat remaining 2 teaspoons oil in 12-inch skillet over medium-high heat until just smoking. Add roast, fat side down, and brown on all sides, 8 to 10 minutes, lowering heat if fat begins to smoke. Transfer roast to wire rack in prepared baking sheet.

6. Remove twine from roast. Spread remaining herb paste over roast and top with bread-crumb mixture. Transfer baking sheet with roast to oven and cook until thickest part of roast registers 140 degrees, 50 minutes to 1 hour 15 minutes. Remove roast from oven and let rest for 10 minutes. Using spatula and meat fork, transfer roast to carving board, taking care not to squeeze juices out of pocket in roast. Cut roast into ½-inch-thick slices and serve.

TO MAKE AHEAD: Roast can be brined, stuffed, and tied 1 day ahead, but don't prepare bread-crumb topping until you are ready to cook.

HERB-CRUSTED PORK ROAST WITH MUSTARD AND CARAWAY

Substitute 1 tablespoon minced garlic for shallot in bread-crumb mixture, replace rosemary with 4 teaspoons whole-grain mustard and 1 tablespoon toasted caraway seeds, and reduce oil in step 3 to 2 tablespoons.

Grill-Roasted Pork Loin

✔ WHY THIS RECIPE WORKS

Brining adds moisture to lean pork loin but proper cooking is essential, too. We wanted a foolproof recipe for cooking pork loin on the grill, a method we hoped would infuse this mild cut with deep smoky flavor.

CHOOSE YOUR CUT Butchers typically cut and merchandise a loin roast in three sections: blade end, center cut, and sirloin. After trying all three, we determined that the blade-end roast was our top choice for this recipe—the fatty pockets that separate the different muscles add moisture and flavor. We found it important to select a roast covered with a layer of fat on one side that was at least ⅛ inch thick; this helped protect the meat from drying out.

BUILD A TWO-LEVEL FIRE For this relatively large cut of meat, we found that a two-level fire worked best; we first seared the pork over the hotter side of the grill before moving it to the cooler side of the grill, where we roasted it, covered.

EMPLOY CARRYOVER COOKING While a pork loin that is properly cooked to an internal temperature of 145 degrees will still be moist, a roast cooked to an internal temperature of 160 degrees will be tough and leathery, even if it has been brined. Our solution was simple: As soon as the meat reached an internal temperature of 145 degrees, we removed it from the grill. Tenting the roast with foil and letting it rest allowed the internal temperature to gently climb to 150 degrees without any risk of overcooking the meat.

GRILL-ROASTED PORK LOIN
SERVES 4 TO 6

Boneless blade-end pork roast is also called blade roast or blade loin roast (see page 181 for more information.) Because the diameter of pork loins varies significantly, start checking the internal temperature of the loin after 30 minutes of grilling time.

If the pork is enhanced (injected with a salt solution), do not brine but add 1 tablespoon salt to the pepper or spice rub. If you'd like to use wood chunks instead of wood chips when using a charcoal grill, substitute two medium wood chunks, soaked in water for 1 hour, for the wood chip packet.

Salt
1   (2½- to 3-pound) boneless blade-end pork loin roast, trimmed and tied with kitchen twine at 1½-inch intervals
2   tablespoons olive oil
1   tablespoon pepper or 1 recipe spice rub (recipes follow)
2   cups wood chips, soaked in water for 15 minutes and drained
1   (13 by 9-inch) disposable aluminum roasting pan

1. Dissolve ¼ cup salt in 2 quarts cold water in large container. Submerge pork loin in brine, cover, and refrigerate for 1 to 1½ hours. Remove pork from brine and pat dry with paper towels. Rub pork loin with oil and coat with pepper. Let sit at room temperature for 1 hour.

2. Using large piece of heavy-duty aluminum foil, wrap soaked chips in foil packet and cut several vent holes in top.

3A. FOR A CHARCOAL GRILL: Open bottom vent halfway and place disposal pan on 1 side of grill. Light large chimney starter three-quarters filled with charcoal briquettes (4½ quarts). When top coals are partially covered with ash, pour evenly over half of grill opposite disposable pan. Place wood chip packet on coals. Set cooking grate in place, cover, and open lid vent halfway. Heat grill until hot and wood chips are smoking, about 5 minutes.

3B. FOR A GAS GRILL: Place wood chip packet directly on primary burner. Turn all burners to high, cover, and heat grill until hot and wood chips are smoking, about 15 minutes. Leave primary burner on high and turn off other burner(s). (Adjust primary burner as needed to maintain grill temperature of 300 to 325 degrees.)

4. Clean and oil cooking grate. Place pork loin on hotter side of grill, fat side up, and cook (covered if using gas) until well browned on all sides, 10 to 12 minutes, turning as needed. Move to cooler side of grill, positioning roast parallel with and as close as possible to heat. Cover (position lid vent over roast if using charcoal) and cook for 20 minutes.

5. Rotate roast 180 degrees, cover, and continue to cook until meat registers 145 degrees, 10 to 30 minutes longer, depending on thickness of roast.

6. Transfer roast to carving board, tent loosely with aluminum foil, and let rest for 15 minutes. Remove twine, cut roast into ½-inch-thick slices, and serve.

SWEET AND SAVORY SPICE RUB
MAKES ABOUT 2 TABLESPOONS

The warm spices in this rub are a perfect match with pork.

1   tablespoon cumin seeds
1½   teaspoons coriander seeds
1   teaspoon fennel seeds
½   teaspoon ground cinnamon
¼   teaspoon ground allspice

Toast cumin, coriander, and fennel seeds in small skillet over medium heat, shaking pan occasionally, until fragrant, about 2 minutes. Transfer to bowl, let cool to room temperature, and grind to powder in spice grinder. Stir in cinnamon and allspice.

CHILI-MUSTARD SPICE RUB
MAKES ABOUT 2 TABLESPOONS

This rub packs some heat, so use the lesser amount of cayenne if you want a milder rub.

2   teaspoons chili powder
2   teaspoons dry mustard
1   teaspoon ground cumin
½–1   teaspoon cayenne pepper

Combine all ingredients in bowl.

DRY-CLEAN YOUR SPICE GRINDER

The oils in spices and dried chiles can cling to a spice grinder, even after you've wiped it with a brush or cloth. Since most grinders can't be immersed in water, we developed a method to "dry-clean" ours: Add several tablespoons of raw white rice to the grinder and pulverize to a fine powder. The powder will absorb residue and oils. Discard the powder—and your grinder will be clean.

To make cider, apples are simply cored, chopped, mashed, and then pressed to extract their liquid. Most cider is pasteurized before sale, though unpasteurized cider is also available. To make apple juice, manufacturers follow the same steps used to make cider, but they also filter the extracted liquid to remove pulp and sediment. Apple juice is then pasteurized, and potassium sorbate (a preservative) is often mixed in to prevent fermentation. Finally, apple juice is sometimes sweetened with sugar or corn syrup.

We tried using unsweetened apple juice in recipes for pork chops and glazed ham that call for cider. Tasters were turned off by excessive sweetness in the dishes made with apple juice, unanimously preferring those made with cider. This made sense: The filtration process used in making juice removes some of the complex, tart, and bitter flavors that are still present in cider. (When we tested the pH level of both liquids, the cider had a lower pH than the apple juice, confirming its higher level of acidity.) The bottom line: When it comes to cooking, don't swap apple juice for cider.

Grilled Pork Loin with Apple-Cranberry Filling

✔ WHY THIS RECIPE WORKS

Pork loin has a satisfying, meaty texture, but its leanness puts it at a distinct disadvantage in the flavor department. Most grilled pork loin recipes try to compensate with some combination of brining (soaking the meat in a salt-and-sugar solution prior to cooking), rubs, sauces, or condiments. We wanted to try something different: using a stuffing to combat the dryness from the inside out.

CHOOSE CENTER-CUT While we typically favor a blade-end pork roast for grilling because of its abundant fat, we found that this asset became a liability when we tried to stuff it—as soon as we split the roast open, the meat fell apart into a lumpy mess of muscle, sinew, and fat. A center-cut loin roast proved the better choice because this solid muscle cut cleanly.

STICKY STUFFING A chutney-like filling provided deep flavor that was well suited to the pork. A combination of apples and cranberries (poached in cider and vinegar) paired well with the pork, while cayenne, allspice, and grated fresh ginger added spice and warmth. Brown sugar contributed just the right amount of sweetness, and some shallot and mustard seeds offered a pleasantly sharp contrast. Best of all, the dense, chewy consistency of our stuffing ensured it stayed put.

FLATTEN IT OUT, THEN TIE IT UP Making three or four straight, short cuts in the roast allowed us to open it up into one broad, flat piece on which we could easily spread the filling before rolling it back together. Snugly tying up the rolled roast ensured a compact shape that cooked evenly and sliced easily.

GIVE IT A ROLL Reducing the liquid leftover from preparing the filling to a thick, spreadable consistency gave us a sticky-sweet glaze that was the perfect finishing touch.

GRILLED PORK LOIN WITH APPLE-CRANBERRY FILLING

SERVES 6

Boneless center-cut pork loin roast is also called center-cut pork roast (see page 181 for more information). This recipe is best prepared with a loin that is 7 to 8 inches long and 4 to 5 inches wide and not enhanced (injected with a salt solution). To make cutting the pork easier, freeze it for 30 minutes. If mustard seeds are unavailable, stir an equal amount of whole-grain mustard into the filling after the apples have been processed. For a spicier stuffing, use the larger amount of cayenne. If you'd like to use wood chunks instead of wood chips when using a charcoal grill, substitute two medium wood chunks, soaked in water for 1 hour, for the wood chip packet. The pork loin can be stuffed and tied a day ahead of time, but don't season the exterior until you are ready to grill.

FILLING
1½	cups (4 ounces) dried apples
1	cup apple cider
¾	cup packed light brown sugar
½	cup cider vinegar
½	cup dried cranberries
1	large shallot, halved lengthwise and sliced thin crosswise
1	tablespoon grated fresh ginger
1	tablespoon yellow mustard seeds
½	teaspoon ground allspice
⅛–¼	teaspoon cayenne pepper

PORK

1 (2½-pound) boneless center-cut pork loin roast, trimmed
  Salt and pepper
2 cups wood chips, soaked in water for 15 minutes and drained

1. FOR THE FILLING: Bring all ingredients to simmer in medium saucepan over medium-high heat. Cover, reduce heat to low, and cook until apples are very soft, about 20 minutes. Pour mixture through fine-mesh strainer set over bowl, pressing with back of spoon to extract as much liquid as possible. Return liquid to saucepan and simmer over medium-high heat until reduced to ⅓ cup, about 5 minutes; reserve for glazing. Pulse apple mixture in food processor until coarsely chopped, about 15 pulses. Transfer filling to bowl and refrigerate until needed.

2. FOR THE PORK: Position roast fat side up. Insert knife ½ inch from bottom of roast and cut horizontally, stopping ½ inch before edge. Open up this flap. Cut through thicker half of roast about ½ inch from bottom, stopping about ½ inch before edge. Open up this flap. Repeat until pork is even ½-inch thickness throughout. If uneven, cover with plastic wrap and use meat pounder to even out. Season interior with salt and pepper and spread filling in even layer, leaving ½-inch border. Roll tightly and tie with kitchen twine at 1-inch intervals. Season with salt and pepper.

3. Using large piece of heavy-duty aluminum foil, wrap soaked chips in foil packet and cut several vent holes in top.

4A. FOR A CHARCOAL GRILL: Open bottom vent halfway. Light large chimney starter three-quarters filled with charcoal briquettes (4½ quarts). When top coals are partially covered with ash, pour evenly over half of grill. Place wood chip packet on coals. Set cooking grate in place, cover, and open lid vent halfway. Heat grill until hot and wood chips are smoking, about 5 minutes.

4B. FOR A GAS GRILL: Place wood chip packet directly on primary burner. Turn all burners to high, cover, and heat grill until hot and wood chips are smoking, about 15 minutes. Leave primary burner on medium-high and turn off other burner(s). (Adjust primary burner as needed to maintain grill temperature of 300 to 325 degrees.)

5. Clean and oil cooking grate. Place pork, fat side up, on cooler side of grill, cover (position lid vent over roast if using charcoal), and cook until meat registers 130 to 135 degrees, 55 minutes to 1 hour 10 minutes, flipping halfway through cooking.

6. Brush roast evenly with reserved glaze. (Reheat glaze, if necessary, to make it spreadable.) Continue to cook until glaze is glossy and meat registers 140 degrees, 5 to 10 minutes longer. Transfer to carving board, tent loosely with aluminum foil, and let rest for 15 minutes. Remove twine, cut roast into ½-inch-thick slices, and serve.

GRILLED PORK LOIN WITH APPLE-CHERRY FILLING WITH CARAWAY

Substitute dried cherries for cranberries and 1 teaspoon caraway seeds for ginger, mustard seeds, and allspice. After processing filling in food processor, transfer to bowl and stir in 2 teaspoons minced fresh thyme.

HOW TO STUFF A PORK LOIN

1. Position roast fat side up. Insert knife ½ inch from bottom of roast and cut horizontally, stopping ½ inch before edge. Open up this flap.

2. Cut through thicker half of roast about ½ inch from bottom, stopping about ½ inch before edge. Open up this flap. If necessary, repeat until loin is even ½-inch thickness. If uneven, cover with plastic wrap and use meat pounder to even out.

3. With long side of meat facing you, season meat and spread filling, leaving ½-inch border on all sides.

4. Starting from short side, roll pork loin tightly.

5. Tie roast with twine at 1-inch intervals.

Grill-Roasted Bone-In Pork Rib Roast

✓ WHY THIS RECIPE WORKS

The biggest challenge of grilling a bulky cut of meat like a pork rib roast is getting the interior cooked to the proper temperature without charring the exterior. We wanted a tender, juicy grilled roast with a thick mahogany crust and plenty of deep, rich flavor.

CHOOSE THE RIGHT CUT After testing three possible cuts from the loin section of the animal—the best cuts for a roast such as this—we determined that we liked the center-cut rib roast for its flavor and simplicity. Because the meat is a single muscle attached along one side to the bones, there is no need to tie the roast for a tidy presentation.

USE A TWO-LEVEL FIRE We figured that with such a large roast, using a two-level fire would be essential. But we were surprised to discover that we could cook the roast on the cooler side for the duration. After an hour a mahogany crust developed—no high-temperature sear needed. (It's important to position the roast away—but not too far away—from the coals or flames with the bones facing away from the fire.)

GIVE A LONG REST Letting the roast rest for a full 30 minutes after it finished on the grill allowed the meat to reabsorb some of the juices lost during cooking. Removing the roast from the heat when it registered 140 degrees ensured it reached a final temperature of 145 to 150 degrees after this resting period.

🔪 AT THE MEAT COUNTER
PREFERRED CUT Bone-In Center-Cut Pork Rib Roast
Center-cut pork roast is also called rack of pork, pork loin rib half, or center-cut roast (see page 181 for more information).

ALTERNATE CUT Blade-End Pork Roast
A blade-end roast can be substituted for the center-cut roast (see page 181 for more information), but you will need to tie it into a uniform shape with kitchen twine at 1-inch intervals; this step is unnecessary with a center-cut roast.

GRILL-ROASTED BONE-IN PORK RIB ROAST

SERVES 6 TO 8

For easier carving, ask the butcher to remove the tip of the chine bone and to cut the remainder of the chine bone between each rib. If you'd like to use wood chunks instead of wood chips when using a charcoal grill, substitute one medium wood chunk, soaked in water for 1 hour, for the wood chip packet. Serve this roast with Orange Salsa with Cuban Flavors (recipe follows), if desired.

- 1 (4- to 5-pound) center-cut bone-in pork rib roast, chine bone removed, fat trimmed to ¼ inch
- 4 teaspoons kosher salt
- 1 cup wood chips, soaked in water for 15 minutes and drained
- 1½ teaspoons pepper

1. Pat roast dry with paper towels. Cut slits in surface fat layer, spaced 1 inch apart, in crosshatch pattern, being careful not to cut into meat. Season roast with salt. Wrap with plastic wrap and refrigerate for at least 6 hours or up to 24 hours.

2. Using large piece of heavy-duty aluminum foil, wrap soaked chips in foil packet and cut several vent holes in top.

3A. FOR A CHARCOAL GRILL: Open bottom vent halfway. Light large chimney starter filled with charcoal briquettes (6 quarts).

CARVING PORK RIB ROAST

Our Grill-Roasted Bone-In Pork Rib Roast can be served on the bone in thick slabs, or the meat can be removed from the bone and sliced into thinner pieces.

For Thick Bone-In Chops

Stand roast on carving board with bones pointing up, and cut between bones into separate chops.

For Thin Boneless Slices

1. Holding tip of bones with your hand, use sharp knife to cut along rib to sever meat from bones.

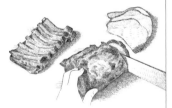

2. Set meat cut side down on carving board and slice against grain into ½-inch-thick slices.

When top coals are partially covered with ash, pour into steeply banked pile against side of grill. Place wood chip packet on coals. Set cooking grate in place, cover, and open lid vent halfway. Heat grill until hot and wood chips are smoking, about 5 minutes.

3B. FOR A GAS GRILL: Place wood chip packet directly on primary burner. Turn all burners to high, cover, and heat grill until hot and wood chips are smoking, about 15 minutes. Turn primary burner to medium-high and turn off other burner(s). (Adjust primary burner as needed during cooking to maintain grill temperature of 325 degrees.)

4. Clean and oil cooking grate. Unwrap roast and season with pepper. Place roast on grate with meat near, but not over, coals and flames and bones facing away from coals and flames. Cover (position lid vent over meat if using charcoal) and cook until meat registers 140 degrees, 1¼ to 1½ hours.

5. Transfer roast to carving board, tent loosely with aluminum foil, and let rest for 30 minutes. Carve into thick slices by cutting between ribs. Serve.

ORANGE SALSA WITH CUBAN FLAVORS

MAKES ABOUT 2½ CUPS

To make this salsa spicier, add the reserved chile seeds.

½	teaspoon grated orange zest, plus 5 oranges peeled and segmented, each segment quartered crosswise
½	cup minced red onion
1	jalapeño chile, stemmed, seeds reserved, and minced
2	tablespoons lime juice
2	tablespoons minced fresh parsley
1	tablespoon extra-virgin olive oil
2	teaspoons packed brown sugar
1½	teaspoons distilled white vinegar
1½	teaspoons minced fresh oregano
1	garlic clove, minced
½	teaspoon ground cumin
½	teaspoon salt
½	teaspoon pepper

Combine all ingredients in medium bowl.

Slow-Roasted Bone-In Pork Rib Roast

✔ WHY THIS RECIPE WORK

A center-cut pork rib roast is as close to prime rib as you can get from the pig. Treated the right way, it can be truly impressive: moist, tender, and full of rich, meaty taste. All this—and for far less money than a prime rib costs. But why doesn't it cook the same way? We were determined to find out.

GIVE IT A RUB Salting the meat and letting it rest for 6 hours ensured that the pork was well seasoned and helped it hold on to just the right amount of moisture. Removing the bones from the pork allowed us to salt the meat on all sides; we then nestled the meat back up against the bones and secured it with kitchen twine. Adding the bones back in ensured that even the interior of the meat stayed moist.

ADD SOME SUGAR The addition of some brown sugar to the salt rub provided pleasing molasses notes that paired nicely with the pork. As a bonus, it also contributed a gorgeous mahogany color, which allowed us to skip the tedious task of searing the meat. Without searing, the fat cap didn't render, but this was easily fixed by scoring deep cross-hatch marks into the fat to help it melt and baste the meat during roasting.

COOK IT LOW AND SLOW Cooking the roast in a 250-degree oven for 3 to 4 hours prevented the exterior from overcooking before the interior had a chance to reach the proper temperature, resulting in evenly cooked meat. Blasting the roast under the broiler for a couple of minutes just prior to serving ensured the fat had a chance to crisp up.

SLOW-ROASTED BONE-IN PORK RIB ROAST

SERVES 6 TO 8

Center-cut bone-in pork rib roast is also called rack of pork, pork loin rib half, or center-cut roast (see page 181 for more information). This recipe requires refrigerating the salted meat for at least 6 hours before cooking. For easier carving, ask the butcher to remove the chine bone. Monitoring the roast with an oven probe thermometer is best. If you use an instant-read thermometer, open the oven door as infrequently as possible and remove the roast from the oven while taking its temperature. The sauce may be prepared in advance or while the roast rests in step 3.

1	(4- to 5-pound) center-cut bone-in pork rib roast, chine bone removed
2	tablespoons packed dark brown sugar
1	tablespoon kosher salt
1½	teaspoons pepper
1	recipe sauce (recipes follow)

1. Using sharp knife, remove roast from bones, running knife down length of bones and following contours as closely as possible. Reserve bones. Combine sugar and salt in small bowl. Pat roast dry with paper towels. If necessary, trim thick spots of surface fat layer to about ¼-inch thickness. Using sharp knife, cut slits, spaced 1 inch apart and in crosshatch pattern, in surface fat layer, being careful not to cut into meat. Rub roast evenly with sugar mixture. Wrap roast and ribs in plastic wrap and refrigerate for at least 6 hours or up to 24 hours.

2. Adjust oven rack to lower-middle position and heat oven to 250 degrees. Sprinkle roast evenly with pepper. Place roast back on ribs so bones fit where they were cut; tie roast to bones with lengths of kitchen twine between ribs. Transfer roast, fat side up, to wire rack set in rimmed baking sheet. Roast until meat registers 145 degrees, 3 to 4 hours.

3. Remove roast from oven (leave roast on sheet), tent loosely with aluminum foil, and let rest for 30 minutes.

4. Adjust oven rack 8 inches from broiler element and heat broiler. Return roast to oven and broil until top of roast is well browned and crispy, 2 to 6 minutes.

5. Transfer roast to carving board; remove twine and remove meat from ribs. Slice meat into ¾-inch-thick slices and serve, passing sauce separately.

CIDER–GOLDEN RAISIN SAUCE

MAKES ABOUT 1¾ CUPS

2	cups apple cider
1	cup golden raisins
½	cup plus 2 teaspoons cider vinegar
4	sprigs fresh thyme, plus 2 teaspoons minced
2	shallots, minced
¼	cup heavy cream
16	tablespoons unsalted butter, cut into ½-inch pieces and chilled
1	tablespoon Calvados
1	teaspoon salt
½	teaspoon pepper

1. Combine cider and raisins in bowl and microwave until steaming, 1 to 2 minutes. Cover and let stand until plump, about 10 minutes. Strain cider through fine-mesh strainer into medium saucepan, reserving raisins.

2. Add ½ cup vinegar, thyme sprigs, and shallots to cider and bring to boil over high heat. Reduce heat to medium-high and reduce mixture until it measures ¾ cup, 14 to 16 minutes. Add cream and reduce again to ¾ cup, about 5 minutes. Discard thyme sprigs. Off

BUTCHERING PORK "PRIME RIB"

Remove the rib bones from the pork so that it can be seasoned on all sides, but don't discard them: Since bone is a poor conductor of heat, tie them back onto the roast to guard against overcooking.

1. Using sharp knife, remove roast from bones, running knife down length of bones and closely following contours.

2. Trim surface fat to ¼ inch and score with crosshatch slits; rub roast with sugar mixture and refrigerate.

3. Sprinkle roast with pepper, then place roast back on ribs; using kitchen twine, tie roast to bones between ribs

WHY ADD CREAM TO A BUTTER SAUCE?

To dress up our pork, we turned to a classic French preparation: *beurre rouge*. The beauty of this sauce, which translates as "red butter," is that at its most basic it requires just two components: butter and an acidic liquid. (Red wine and red vinegar for *beurre rouge* and white for *beurre blanc* are traditional.) The preparation is equally simple: Just whisk cold butter into the reduced acidic liquid.

The problem is that butter sauces, like any mixture of fat and water, don't always stay emulsified. That's because the butter is highly temperature-sensitive: If the sauce gets too hot (above 135 degrees), the butter—itself an emulsion of fat and water—will "break" and the butterfat will leak out. If it gets too cold (below 85 degrees), the butterfat solidifies and forms crystals that clump together and separate when the sauce is reheated.

The key to foolproofing a butter sauce is thus stabilizing the butterfat so that it doesn't separate. We do this by whisking in the butter a little bit at a time, which keeps the temperature of the sauce relatively stable. Even more important, we also add cream. Cream contains a relatively high proportion of casein proteins that surround and stabilize the butterfat droplets so that they don't separate from the emulsion. Cream is such an effective stabilizer that our sauce can be made ahead, chilled, and gently reheated before serving.

heat, whisk in butter, a few pieces at a time, until fully incorporated. Stir in Calvados, salt, pepper, raisins, remaining 2 teaspoons vinegar, and minced thyme. Cover pan and hold, off heat, until serving.

TO MAKE AHEAD: Alternatively, let sauce cool completely and refrigerate for up to 2 days. Reheat in small saucepan over medium-low heat, stirring frequently, until warm.

ORANGE-CRANBERRY SAUCE
MAKES ABOUT 1¾ CUPS

2	cups white wine
1	cup dried cranberries
1	tablespoon grated orange zest plus ½ cup juice
4	fresh sage leaves, plus 2 teaspoons minced
2	shallots, minced
¼	cup heavy cream
16	tablespoons unsalted butter, cut into ½-inch pieces and chilled
1	tablespoon Grand Marnier
1	teaspoon salt
½	teaspoon pepper

1. Combine wine and cranberries in bowl and microwave until steaming, 1 to 2 minutes. Cover and let stand until plump, about 10 minutes. Strain wine through fine-mesh strainer into medium saucepan, reserving cranberries.

2. Add orange juice, sage leaves, and shallots to wine and bring to boil over high heat. Reduce heat to medium-high and reduce mixture until it measures ¾ cup, 14 to 16 minutes. Add cream and reduce again to ¾ cup, about 5 minutes. Discard sage leaves. Off heat, whisk in butter, a few pieces at a time, until fully incorporated. Stir in Grand Marnier, salt, pepper, cranberries, orange zest, and

minced sage. Cover pan and hold, off heat, until serving.

TO MAKE AHEAD: Alternatively, let sauce cool completely and refrigerate for up to 2 days. Reheat in small saucepan over medium-low heat, stirring frequently, until warm.

PORT WINE–CHERRY SAUCE
MAKES ABOUT 1¾ CUPS

2	cups tawny port
1	cup dried cherries
½	cup balsamic vinegar
4	sprigs fresh thyme, plus 2 teaspoons minced
2	shallots, minced
¼	cup heavy cream
16	tablespoons unsalted butter, cut into ½-inch pieces and chilled
1	teaspoon salt
½	teaspoon pepper

1. Combine port and cherries in bowl and microwave until steaming, 1 to 2 minutes. Cover and let stand until plump, about 10 minutes. Strain port through fine-mesh strainer into medium saucepan, reserving cherries.

2. Add vinegar, thyme sprigs, and shallots to port and bring to boil over high heat. Reduce heat to medium-high and reduce mixture until it measures ¾ cup, 14 to 16 minutes. Add cream and reduce again to ¾ cup, about 5 minutes. Discard thyme sprigs. Off heat, whisk in butter, a few pieces at a time, until fully incorporated. Stir in salt, pepper, cherries, and minced thyme. Cover pan and hold, off heat, until serving.

TO MAKE AHEAD: Alternatively, let sauce cool completely and refrigerate for up to 2 days. Reheat in small saucepan over medium-low heat, stirring frequently, until warm.

Chinese Barbecued Pork

✔ WHY THIS RECIPE WORKS

With its ruby-red color, deeply browned and crusty edges, and sticky glazed exterior, Chinese barbecued pork (aka char siu) is irresistible and satisfying. Although these lacquered strips of pork look exotic, the meat is actually "barbecued" in the oven. We wondered if we could replicate this classic Chinese dish at home

MARINATE THE MEAT After tinkering with traditional marinade ingredients, we settled on a combination of soy sauce, dry sherry, hoisin sauce, and five-spice powder. We eliminated hard-to-find ingredients such as red bean curd, and instead boosted the flavor of the marinade with ginger, garlic, toasted sesame oil, and white pepper. Pricking the meat (pork butt) with a fork before marinating enhanced the penetration of the marinade so much that just 30 minutes was sufficient.

COVER WITH FOIL, THEN BROIL Traditional recipes call for cutting the meat into thin strips and hanging the strips on metal rods that go inside refrigerator-size ovens, which allows the heat to attack the meat from all sides and create a thick crust. To achieve similar results in a home oven, we started by cooking the strips of pork on a rack set in a baking sheet and covered with foil. We then let them cook for a while longer, uncovered, before cranking up the heat and broiling them to crisp, chewy perfection.

GET THE LACQUERED LOOK To achieve a lacquered appearance, a honey glaze is applied to *char siu* during the last few minutes of cooking. To mimic the traditional red color, we supplemented the honey with ketchup.

🔪 AT THE MEAT COUNTER

PREFERRED CUT Pork Butt Roast
Pork butt roast is also known as Boston shoulder, pork butt, or Boston butt (see page 179 for more information).

ALTERNATE CUT Boneless Country-Style Ribs
Boneless country-style ribs can be substituted for the pork butt (see page 181 for more information), but the meat will be slightly drier and less flavorful. To use ribs, reduce the uncovered cooking time in step 4 to 20 minutes and increase the broiling and glazing times in step 5 by 2 to 3 minutes per side.

CHINESE BARBECUED PORK
SERVES 6

Pork butt roast is often labeled Boston butt in the supermarket. The pork will release liquid and fat during the cooking process, so be careful when removing the pan from the oven. If you don't have a wire rack that fits in a rimmed baking sheet, you can substitute a broiler pan, although the meat may not darken as much. Pay close attention to the meat when broiling—you are looking for it to darken and caramelize, not blacken. Do not use a drawer broiler—the heat source will be too close to the meat. Instead, increase the oven temperature in step 5 to 500 degrees and cook for 8 to 12 minutes before glazing and 6 to 8 minutes once the glaze has been applied; flip the meat and repeat on the second side. This dish is best served with rice and a vegetable side dish. Leftover pork makes an excellent addition to fried rice or an Asian noodle soup.

1	(4-pound) boneless pork butt roast, halved lengthwise, each half turned on its side, cut into 8 strips, and trimmed
½	cup sugar
½	cup soy sauce
6	tablespoons hoisin sauce
¼	cup dry sherry
2	tablespoons grated fresh ginger
1	tablespoon toasted sesame oil
2	garlic cloves, minced
1	teaspoon five-spice powder
¼	teaspoon ground white pepper
⅓	cup honey
¼	cup ketchup

BUTCHERING PORK BUTT

Pork butts are usually about 4 inches thick. If using a pork butt that is thinner than 4 inches, cut it into six strips instead of eight.

1. Cut roast in half lengthwise.

2. Turn each half on cut side and slice lengthwise into 4 equal pieces.

3. Trim excess hard, waxy fat, leaving some fat to render while cooking.

Halving the pork increases its surface area, which creates more flavorful bark.

Holding your knife parallel to cutting board, press your hand against top of pork butt while cutting horizontally.

1. Using fork, prick pork 10 to 12 times on each side. Place pork in 2-gallon plastic zipper-lock bag. Combine sugar, soy sauce, hoisin, sherry, ginger, oil, garlic, five-spice powder, and pepper in medium bowl. Measure out ½ cup marinade and set aside. Pour remaining marinade into bag with pork. Press out as much air as possible; seal bag. Refrigerate for at least 30 minutes or up to 4 hours.

2. While meat marinates, combine honey and ketchup with reserved marinade in small saucepan. Cook glaze over medium heat until syrupy and reduced to 1 cup, 4 to 6 minutes.

3. Adjust oven rack to middle position and heat oven to 300 degrees. Set wire rack in aluminum foil–lined rimmed baking sheet and spray with vegetable oil spray.

4. Remove pork from marinade, letting any excess drip off, and place on prepared wire rack. Pour ¼ cup water into bottom of sheet. Cover roast with heavy-duty foil, crimping edges tightly to seal. Cook pork for 20 minutes. Remove foil and continue to cook until edges of pork begin to brown, 40 to 45 minutes longer.

5. Turn on broiler. Broil pork until evenly caramelized, 7 to 9 minutes. Remove sheet from oven and brush pork with half of glaze; broil until deep mahogany color, 3 to 5 minutes. Using tongs, flip meat and broil until other side caramelizes, 7 to 9 minutes. Brush meat with remaining glaze and continue to broil until second side is deep mahogany, 3 to 5 minutes. Let cool for at least 10 minutes, then cut into thin strips and serve.

Indoor Pulled Pork with Barbecue Sauce

✓ WHY THIS RECIPE WORKS

Here in New England, we're sometimes forced to wait for nicer weather when a craving for pulled pork strikes. We needed to find a way to bring the operation indoors.

MOISTURE IS KEY Boneless pork butt has a lot of connective tissue, which needs to break down in order for the meat to become tender. For this to happen, it needs to hold an internal temperature of around 200 degrees for at least an hour. The dry heat of the oven caused the pork to heat too slowly, which resulted in tough, leathery meat. Covering the meat with aluminum foil was an easy solution; the foil trapped steam and moisture and the temperature of the pork rose into the ideal zone much more quickly.

STRIKE THE RIGHT BALANCE At 325 degrees, 3 hours of covered cooking rendered the meat meltingly tender, while an additional hour and a half uncovered helped a nice crust to form. Splitting the pork butt in half horizontally created more surface area, which translated into even more thick crust (or bark).

ADD SOME SMOKE Adding a few tablespoons of liquid smoke to the brine infused the meat with authentic smoky flavor. We incorporated even more smokiness by adding a dry rub (which we fortified with smoked paprika) and a wet rub (mustard combined with a little more liquid smoke).

INDOOR PULLED PORK WITH SWEET AND TANGY BARBECUE SAUCE

SERVES 6 TO 8

Pork butt roast is also called Boston shoulder, pork butt, or Boston butt (see page 179 for more information). If the pork is enhanced (injected with a salt solution), do not brine in step 1. Sweet paprika may be substituted for the smoked paprika. Covering the pork with parchment paper and then aluminum foil prevents the acidic mustard from eating holes in the foil. Lexington Vinegar Barbecue Sauce or South Carolina Mustard Barbecue Sauce (recipes follow) can be substituted for the Sweet and Tangy Barbecue Sauce. Alternatively, use 2 cups of your favorite barbecue sauce thinned with ½ cup of the defatted pork cooking liquid in step 5. Serve the pork on hamburger buns with pickle chips and thinly sliced onion.

PORK

Salt and pepper

½ cup plus 2 tablespoons sugar

3 tablespoons plus 2 teaspoons liquid smoke

1 (5-pound) boneless pork butt roast, trimmed and halved lengthwise

¼ cup yellow mustard

2 tablespoons smoked paprika

1 teaspoon cayenne pepper

SWEET AND TANGY BARBECUE SAUCE

1½ cups ketchup

¼ cup molasses

2 tablespoons Worcestershire sauce

1 tablespoon hot sauce

½ teaspoon salt

½ teaspoon pepper

1. FOR THE PORK: Dissolve 1 cup salt, ½ cup sugar, and 3 tablespoons liquid smoke in 4 quarts cold water in large container. Submerge pork in brine, cover, and refrigerate for 1½ to 2 hours.

2. While pork brines, combine mustard and remaining 2 teaspoons liquid smoke in bowl; set aside. Combine paprika, cayenne, 2 teaspoons salt, 2 tablespoons pepper, and remaining 2 tablespoons sugar in second bowl; set aside.

3. Adjust oven rack to lower-middle position and heat oven to 325 degrees. Set wire rack in rimmed baking sheet lined with aluminum foil. Remove pork from brine and pat dry with paper towels. Rub mustard mixture over entire surface of each piece of pork. Sprinkle entire surface of each piece with paprika mixture. Place pork on prepared wire rack. Place piece of parchment paper over pork, then cover with sheet of foil, sealing edges to prevent moisture from escaping. Roast pork for 3 hours.

4. Remove pork from oven; remove and discard foil and parchment. Carefully pour off liquid in bottom of sheet into fat separator and reserve for sauce. Return pork to oven and cook, uncovered, until well browned and tender and meat registers 200 degrees, about 1½ hours. Transfer pork to serving dish, tent loosely with foil, and let rest for 20 minutes.

5. FOR THE BARBECUE SAUCE: While pork rests, pour ½ cup defatted cooking liquid from fat separator into medium bowl; whisk in all sauce ingredients.

6. Using 2 forks, shred pork into bite-size pieces. (Shredded and sauced pork can be cooled, tightly covered, and refrigerated for up to 2 days. Reheat gently before serving.) Toss with 1 cup sauce and season with salt and pepper to taste. Serve, passing remaining sauce separately.

LEXINGTON VINEGAR BARBECUE SAUCE

MAKES ABOUT 2½ CUPS

1 cup cider vinegar

½ cup ketchup

½ cup water

1 tablespoon sugar

¾ teaspoon salt

¾ teaspoon red pepper flakes

½ teaspoon pepper

Place all ingredients in medium bowl, add ½ cup defatted cooking liquid reserved from step 5, and whisk to combine.

YELLOW MUSTARD

Smooth and mild, yellow mustard is a North American thing. In other parts of the world, mustards are hotter, darker, and grainier. But what yellow mustard may lack in worldliness and guts, it makes up for in versatility. Yellow mustard is as much at home on a ballpark hot dog as it is on cold cuts or in potato salad, barbecue sauce, salad dressing, or marinades for chicken or pork. To determine which yellow mustard is best, we bought seven nationally available brands and tasted them plain and with steamed hot dogs.

Yellow mustard is made from white (also called yellow) mustard seed, which is flavorful but doesn't cause any of the nasal burn of brown or black mustard seed; these last two are used in Dijon, Chinese, and other spicy mustards. Our tasters wanted to actually taste the mustard seed; the two brands they judged to have the most mustard flavor both list mustard seed second in their ingredients. The other brands list it third (meaning there is proportionally less of it).

Our winner turned out to be the small organic brand, **Annie's Naturals Organic Yellow Mustard**; tasters appreciated its heat and tang as well as its relatively complex but well-balanced flavor.

And here's something else to keep in mind when you're shopping: The molecule that gives yellow mustard its assertive taste (4-hydroxybenzyl isothiocyanate, or PHBIT) dissipates over time, so note the freshness date on the jar.

SOUTH CAROLINA MUSTARD BARBECUE SAUCE

MAKES ABOUT 2½ CUPS

1	cup yellow mustard
½	cup distilled white vinegar
¼	cup packed light brown sugar
¼	cup Worcestershire sauce
2	tablespoons hot sauce
1	teaspoon salt
1	teaspoon pepper

Combine all ingredients in medium bowl with ½ cup defatted cooking liquid, reserved from step 5, and whisk to combine.

Barbecued Pulled Pork

✓ WHY THIS RECIPE WORKS

Slow-cooked pulled pork is a summertime favorite, but most recipes demand the regular attention of the cook for 8 hours or more. We wanted to find a way to make moist, fork-tender pulled pork without the marathon cooking time and constant attention to the grill.

RUB IN THE SPICES As with most every aspect of barbecuing, there is considerable controversy over what is the best combination of spices, how to combine them, and even how to apply them to the traditional pork butt. We found that keeping it simple produced great results; a blend of store-bought spices—paprika, chili powder, cumin, and oregano, along with some salt, sugar, and a trio of peppers—provided plenty of complexity and bold flavor. Simply massaging the rub into the meat was straightforward and effective.

USE THE GRILL AND THE OVEN Placing the roast in a disposable roasting pan on the grill helped protect it from the heat so there was no risk of scorching, while wood chips provided plenty of smoky flavor. We then finished the pork in the oven at a relatively low temperature for 2 hours. This method produces almost the same results as the traditional barbecue, but in considerably less time and with much less effort.

PAPER BAG IT Allowing the pork to rest for an hour inside a paper grocery sack allowed time for the flavorful juices to be reabsorbed. In addition, it produced a steaming effect that helped break down any remaining tough collagen—resulting in a much more savory and succulent roast.

BARBECUED PULLED PORK

SERVES 8

Pork butt roast is also called Boston shoulder, pork butt, or Boston butt (see page 179 for more information). Preparing pulled pork requires little effort, but lots of time. Plan on 10 hours from start to finish: 3 hours with the spice rub, 1 hour to come to room temperature, 3 hours on the grill, 2 hours in the oven, and 1 hour to rest. Hickory is the classic choice when it comes to supplying the smoke in this recipe. If you'd like to use wood chunks instead of wood chips when using a charcoal grill, substitute four medium wood chunks, soaked in water for 1 hour, for the wood chip packets. Serve on plain white bread or warmed rolls with dill pickle chips and coleslaw.

1	(6- to 8-pound) bone-in pork butt roast, trimmed
¾	cup Dry Rub for Barbecue (recipe follows)
4	cups wood chips, soaked in water for 15 minutes and drained
1	(13 by 9-inch) disposable aluminum roasting pan
2	cups barbecue sauce (recipes follow)

DIFFERENT WOOD, DIFFERENT BARBECUE

Sprinkling some soaked wood chips (or scattering a few wood chunks) over a pile of hot coals or over flames adds a great smoky flavor to grilled foods. While developing some of our grilling recipes, we found that the type of wood used can make a huge difference in the finished product.

Wood from fruit trees, such as apple, cherry, and peach, produces a slightly sweet smoke with a hint of fruitiness. Hickory and pecan woods both produce a hearty smoke that cuts through even the spiciest rubs. Maple, the traditional choice for ham, produces a mellow, sweet smoke, while oak lends a faint acidic note that many people enjoy.

Ultimately, the only wood that left tasters a bit wary was mesquite. Although the heavy, assertive flavor of mesquite smoke was enjoyable in quickly cooked meats, it had a tendency to turn bitter over long periods of cooking.

1. Pat pork dry with paper towels, then massage dry rub into meat. Wrap meat in plastic wrap and refrigerate for at least 3 hours or up to 3 days.

2. At least 1 hour prior to cooking, remove roast from refrigerator, unwrap, and let sit at room temperature. Using 2 large pieces of heavy-duty aluminum foil, wrap soaked chips in 2 foil packets and cut several vent holes in tops.

3A. FOR A CHARCOAL GRILL: Open bottom vent halfway. Light large chimney starter three-quarters filled with charcoal briquettes (4½ quarts). When top coals are partially covered with ash, pour evenly over half of grill. Place wood chip packets on coals. Set cooking grate in place, cover, and open lid vent halfway. Heat grill until hot and wood chips are smoking, about 5 minutes.

3B. FOR A GAS GRILL: Place wood chip packets directly on primary burner. Turn all burners to high, cover, and heat grill until hot and wood chips are smoking, about 15 minutes. Turn primary burner to medium-high and turn off other burner(s). (Adjust primary burner as needed to maintain grill temperature of 325 degrees.)

4. Set roast in disposable pan, place on cooler side of grill, and cook for 3 hours. During final 20 minutes of cooking, adjust oven rack to lower-middle position and heat oven to 325 degrees.

5. Wrap disposable pan with heavy-duty foil and cook in oven until meat is fork-tender, about 2 hours.

6. Carefully slide foil-wrapped pan with roast into brown paper bag. Crimp end shut and let rest for 1 hour.

7. Transfer roast to carving board and unwrap. Separate roast into muscle sections, removing fat, if desired, and tearing meat into shreds with your fingers. Place shredded meat in large bowl and toss with 1 cup barbecue sauce. Serve, passing remaining sauce separately.

DRY RUB FOR BARBECUE
MAKES ABOUT 1 CUP

You can adjust the proportions of spices in this all-purpose rub or add or subtract a spice, as you wish.

- ¼ cup paprika
- 2 tablespoons chili powder
- 2 tablespoons ground cumin
- 2 tablespoons packed dark brown sugar
- 2 tablespoons salt
- 1 tablespoon dried oregano
- 1 tablespoon granulated sugar
- 1 tablespoon pepper
- 1 tablespoon white pepper
- 1–2 teaspoons cayenne pepper

Combine all ingredients in small bowl.

EASTERN NORTH CAROLINA BARBECUE SAUCE
MAKES ABOUT 2 CUPS

This sauce can be refrigerated in an airtight container for up to four days.

- 1 cup distilled white vinegar
- 1 cup cider vinegar
- 1 tablespoon sugar
- 1 tablespoon red pepper flakes
- 1 tablespoon hot sauce
  Salt and pepper

Mix all ingredients together in bowl and season with salt and pepper to taste.

WESTERN SOUTH CAROLINA BARBECUE SAUCE
MAKES ABOUT 2 CUPS

This sauce can be refrigerated in an airtight container for up to four days.

- 1 tablespoon vegetable oil
- ½ cup finely chopped onion
- 2 garlic cloves, minced

½ cup cider vinegar

½ cup Worcestershire sauce

1 tablespoon dry mustard

1 tablespoon packed dark brown sugar

1 tablespoon paprika

1 teaspoon salt

1 teaspoon cayenne pepper

1 cup ketchup

Heat oil in small saucepan over medium heat. Add onion and cook, stirring occasionally, until softened, 5 to 7 minutes. Stir in garlic and cook until fragrant, about 30 seconds. Stir in vinegar, Worcestershire, mustard, sugar, paprika, salt, and cayenne, bring to simmer, and stir in ketchup. Cook over low heat until thickened, about 15 minutes.

MID–SOUTH CAROLINA MUSTARD SAUCE

MAKES ABOUT 2½ CUPS

This sauce can be refrigerated in an airtight container for up to four days.

1 cup cider vinegar

1 cup vegetable oil

6 tablespoons Dijon mustard

2 tablespoons maple syrup or honey

4 teaspoons Worcestershire sauce

1 teaspoon hot sauce

Salt and pepper

Mix all ingredients together in bowl and season with salt and pepper to taste.

Lexington-Style Pulled Pork

✓ WHY THIS RECIPE WORKS

Lexington-style pulled pork is so tender, so sweet, and so smoky that it seems almost unnatural. What really makes this dish distinct, though, is the sauce—thin and pungent, tart with vinegar and with a peppery kick, its acidity expertly balanced by just a hint of sugar and ketchup. But making Lexington-style pulled pork at home can be trying, because it calls for hours and hours of diligent grill tending. We wondered if this all-day recipe could be simplified without sacrificing flavor.

GRILL-START, OVEN-FINISH Slowly cooking the pork on the grill for a couple of hours allowed the meat to take on some barbecued flavor. Covering the pork and finishing it in a 325-degree oven created moist heat that melted the collagen, turning the tough pork shoulder into a savory, fork-tender piece of meat.

EKE OUT MORE SMOKE FLAVOR To intensify the smoky barbecued flavor of our meat—without more time on the grill—we coated the pork with a basic barbecue rub and doubled the amount of wood chips. With this treatment, the pork developed a deep red crust and a rich, thick smoke ring that stayed with the pork even after a couple of hours in the oven.

BALANCE THE SAUCE CAREFULLY For the sauce's characteristic sweet-and-sour components, we selected granulated sugar and cider vinegar, along with just enough ketchup to give the sauce body and a rosy color. Black pepper added a nice earthy bite, and ½ teaspoon of red pepper flakes gave the sauce a kick that matched the pungency of the vinegar.

LEXINGTON-STYLE PULLED PORK
SERVES 8

Pork butt roast is also called Boston shoulder, pork butt, or Boston butt (see page 179 for more information). If you'd like to use wood chunks instead of wood chips when using a charcoal grill, substitute four medium wood chunks, soaked in water for 1 hour, for the wood chip packets.

SPICE RUB AND PORK
- 2 tablespoons paprika
- 2 tablespoons pepper
- 2 tablespoons packed brown sugar
- 1 tablespoon salt
- 1 (4- to 5-pound) boneless pork butt roast, trimmed
- 4 cups wood chips, soaked in water for 15 minutes and drained

LEXINGTON BARBECUE SAUCE
- 1 cup water
- 1 cup cider vinegar
- ½ cup ketchup
- 1 tablespoon granulated sugar
- ¾ teaspoon salt
- ½ teaspoon pepper
- ½ teaspoon red pepper flakes

1. FOR THE SPICE RUB AND PORK: Combine paprika, pepper, sugar, and salt in bowl. Pat meat dry with paper towels and rub it evenly with spice mixture. Wrap meat in plastic wrap and let sit at room temperature for at least 1 hour or refrigerate for up to 24 hours. (If refrigerated, let sit at room temperature for 1 hour before grilling.) Using 2 large pieces of heavy-duty aluminum foil, wrap soaked chips in 2 foil packets and cut several vent holes in tops.

2A. FOR A CHARCOAL GRILL: Open bottom vent halfway. Light large chimney starter half filled with charcoal briquettes (3 quarts). When top coals are partially covered with ash, pour into steeply banked pile against 1 side of grill. Place wood chip packets on coals. Set cooking grate in place, cover, and open lid vent halfway. Heat grill until hot and wood chips are smoking, about 5 minutes.

2B. FOR A GAS GRILL: Place wood chip packets directly on primary burner. Turn all burners to high, cover, and heat grill until hot and wood chips are smoking, about 15 minutes. Turn primary burner to medium and turn off other burner(s). (Adjust primary burner as needed to maintain grill temperature of 275 degrees.)

3. Clean and oil cooking grate. Place meat on cooler side of grill. Cover (positioning lid vent over meat if using charcoal) and cook until pork has dark, rosy crust, about 2 hours. During final 20 minutes of grilling, adjust oven rack to lower-middle position and heat oven to 325 degrees.

4. Transfer pork to large roasting pan, cover pan tightly with aluminum foil, and roast pork in oven until fork slips easily into and out of meat, 2 to 3 hours. Remove pork from the oven and let rest, still covered with foil, for 30 minutes.

5. FOR THE SAUCE: Whisk all ingredients together in bowl until sugar and salt are dissolved. When cool enough to handle, unwrap pork and pull meat into thin shreds, discarding excess fat and gristle. Toss pork with ½ cup barbecue sauce, passing remaining sauce separately.

Mexican Pulled Pork (Carnitas)

✔ WHY THIS RECIPE WORKS

Spanish for "little meats," carnitas is Mexico's version of pulled pork. This taqueria staple boasts tender chunks of pork with a lightly crisped, caramelized exterior and is used as a filling in everything from tacos to burritos. Most Mexican restaurants prepare carnitas by gently frying well-marbled chunks of pork in gallons of lard or oil. We wanted a more manageable method.

SAVE THE BRAISING LIQUID While the common home technique for carnitas involves simmering the meat in a seasoned broth in the oven and then sautéing it in some of the rendered fat, we found that all that liquid dulled the pork flavor. Braising the pork in a smaller amount of liquid helped concentrate its flavor, but it wasn't enough. Rather than pour the braising liquid down the drain—and all the pork flavor with it—we reduced it to a syrupy glaze.

GLAZE AND BROIL Tossing the braised chunks of pork with the flavorful glaze and then broiling them resulted in beautifully caramelized, crisp edges. Placing the pieces of pork on a wire rack set in a baking sheet allowed excess fat to drip away as it rendered, which prevented the meat from being greasy.

REFINE THE FLAVORS With carnitas, other flavors should take a backseat to the pork. The mellow sweetness of onion worked well, while a mix of fresh lime and orange juice emulated the Mexican sour oranges used in authentic carnitas. Bay leaves and oregano gave the meat aromatic accents, and cumin brought an earthy dimension that complemented the other flavors.

MEXICAN PULLED PORK (CARNITAS)
SERVES 6

Pork butt roast is also called Boston shoulder, pork butt, or Boston butt (see page 179 for more information). We like serving carnitas spooned into small corn tortillas, taco-style, but you can also use it as a filling for tamales, enchiladas, and burritos. Pork butt roast is often labeled Boston butt in the supermarket.

PORK

- 1 (3½- to 4-pound) boneless pork butt roast, fat cap trimmed to ⅛ inch thick, cut into 2-inch pieces
- 2 cups water
- 1 onion, peeled and halved
- 2 tablespoons lime juice
- 1 teaspoon dried oregano
- 1 teaspoon ground cumin
- 2 bay leaves
  Salt and pepper
- 1 orange, halved and unpeeled

TORTILLAS AND GARNISHES

- 18 (6-inch) corn tortillas, warmed
  Lime wedges
  Minced white or red onion
  Fresh cilantro
  Thinly sliced radishes
  Sour cream

1. Adjust oven rack to lower-middle position and heat oven to 300 degrees. Combine pork, water, onion, lime juice, oregano, cumin, bay leaves, 1 teaspoon salt, and ½ teaspoon pepper in Dutch oven (liquid should just barely cover meat). Juice orange into bowl and remove any seeds (you should have about ⅓ cup juice). Add juice and spent

THE POWER OF REDUCTION

We reduce liquids all the time in recipes as a way of concentrating flavor. In our Mexican Pulled Pork recipe, we reduced the braising liquid we had used to cook the pork until it took on the thick, syrupy consistency of a glaze and its flavor deepened dramatically. As familiar as the benefits of reducing liquids are to us, the glaze's intense taste made us wonder: Was all that rich flavor derived simply from evaporating the water from the braising liquid, or was there a more complex dynamic at work?

A chat with our science editor revealed the answer: The reduction's richness is in part due to the same process that makes a seared steak taste so good—the Maillard reaction. When the proteins and sugars in meat (or most any foodstuff) are subjected to a high enough temperature (around 300 to 500 degrees), they combine, leading to browning and the creation of hundreds of new flavor compounds.

In our carnitas recipe, proteins and sugars are pulled from the pork by the braising liquid, which also contains sugars from lime and orange juices. After the meat is removed, the liquid is boiled to evaporate all the water. With the water removed, the temperature of the glaze can rise higher than water's boiling point of 212 degrees, eventually kicking off the Maillard reaction. The result: a viscous, highly concentrated glaze with exceptional depth of flavor.

orange halves to pot. Bring mixture to simmer over medium-high heat, stirring occasionally. Cover pot and transfer to oven; cook until meat is soft and falls apart when prodded with fork, about 2 hours, turning pieces of meat once during cooking.

2. Remove pot from oven and turn oven to broil. Using slotted spoon, transfer pork to bowl; remove orange halves, onion, and bay leaves from cooking liquid and discard (do not skim fat from liquid). Place pot over high heat (use caution, as handles will be very hot) and simmer liquid, stirring frequently, until thick and syrupy (heat-resistant rubber spatula should leave wide trail when dragged through glaze), 8 to 12 minutes. You should have about 1 cup reduced liquid.

3. Using 2 forks, pull each piece of pork in half. Fold in reduced liquid; season with salt and pepper to taste. Spread pork in even layer on wire rack set in rimmed baking sheet or on broiler pan (meat should cover almost entire surface of rack or broiler pan). Place sheet on lower-middle rack and broil until top of meat is well browned (but not charred) and edges are slightly crisp, 5 to 8 minutes. Using wide metal spatula, flip pieces of meat and continue to broil until tops are well browned and edges are slightly crisp, 5 to 8 minutes longer. Serve with warm tortillas and garnishes.

Pork Tinga

✔ WHY THIS RECIPE WORKS

Spicy Mexican shredded pork, known as tinga, is cooked on top of the stove and takes a fraction of the time as traditional barbecued pulled pork. The pork is sautéed after braising until it acquires deeply browned edges that stay crisp even after a quick simmer in a chipotle-infused tomato sauce. To play against its supple texture, tinga is served on crunchy tostada shells and garnished with avocado, sour cream, queso fresco, cilantro, and lime wedges. We wanted to perfect our own version.

BRAISE THE BUTT Boneless pork butt is well marbled and suited to tinga's cooking method, so it was our cut of choice. Cutting it into 1-inch pieces and simmering it in water for an hour produced tender meat, while adding some onion, garlic, and thyme to the braising liquid imparted a subtle vegetal flavor.

SHRED AND CRISP THE MEAT Shredding the pork before sautéing it created far more surface area for browning. Sautéing the meat for just 7 minutes in olive oil, along with some chopped onion and oregano, produced pork with a crisp texture all over.

GETTING SAUCY After testing several varieties of canned tomato products, we were surprised to discover that canned tomato sauce worked best, contributing a smooth texture and bright taste to our sauce. As for the smoky component, we found that canned chipotles varied too much from brand to brand; ground chipotle powder worked better, providing a consistent, deep, and complex smokiness.

SPICY MEXICAN SHREDDED PORK (TINGA) TOSTADAS

SERVES 4 TO 6

Pork butt roast is also called Boston shoulder, pork butt, or Boston butt (see page 179 for more information). The trimmed pork should weigh about 1½ pounds. Tinga is traditionally served on tostadas (crisp fried corn tortillas), but you can also use the meat in tacos and burritos or simply serve it over rice. Make sure to buy tortillas made only with corn, lime, and salt—preservatives will compromise quality. We prefer the complex flavor of chipotle powder, but two minced canned chipotle chiles can be used in its place.

BAKING TOSTADAS

Baking tortillas to create tostadas uses much less oil than frying (the traditional approach), with very comparable results. Make sure to start with corn tortillas that have no preservatives and just three ingredients: corn, lime, and salt. Serve tostadas with refried beans or other toppings, such as our Pork Tinga.

1. Arrange twelve 6-inch corn tortillas in single layer on 2 rimmed baking sheets; brush both sides of each tortilla with vegetable oil (about 2 tablespoons per tray).

2. Place wire rack upside down on top of tortillas to keep them flat. Bake on upper-middle and lower-middle racks of 450-degree oven until lightly browned and crisp, 15 to 18 minutes, switching and rotating sheets halfway through baking.

TINGA

2 pounds boneless pork butt roast, trimmed and cut into 1-inch pieces
2 onions (1 quartered, 1 chopped fine)
5 garlic cloves (3 peeled and smashed, 2 minced)
4 sprigs fresh thyme
Salt
2 tablespoons olive oil
½ teaspoon dried oregano
1 (15-ounce) can tomato sauce
1 tablespoon chipotle chile powder
2 bay leaves

TOSTADAS

¾ cup vegetable oil
12 (6-inch) corn tortillas
Salt

GARNISHES

Queso fresco or feta cheese
Fresh cilantro
Sour cream
Diced avocado
Lime wedges

1. FOR THE TINGA: Bring pork, quartered onion, smashed garlic, thyme sprigs, 1 teaspoon salt, and 6 cups water to simmer in large saucepan over medium-high heat, skimming off any foam that rises to surface. Reduce heat to medium-low, partially cover, and cook until pork is tender, 1¼ to 1½ hours. Drain pork, reserving 1 cup cooking liquid. Discard onion, garlic, and thyme sprigs. Return pork to saucepan and, using potato masher, mash until shredded into rough ½-inch pieces; set aside. (Pork can be prepared through step 1 and refrigerated for 2 days.)

2. Heat oil in 12-inch nonstick skillet over medium-high heat until shimmering. Add shredded pork, chopped onion, and oregano; cook, stirring often, until pork is well browned and crisp, 7 to 10 minutes. Add minced garlic and cook until fragrant, about 30 seconds.

3. Stir in tomato sauce, chile powder, bay leaves, and reserved pork cooking liquid; simmer until almost all liquid has evaporated, 5 to 7 minutes. Discard bay leaves and season with salt to taste.

4. FOR THE TOSTADAS: Heat oil in 8-inch skillet over medium heat to 350 degrees. Using fork, poke center of each tortilla 3 or 4 times. Place 1 tortilla in pan, holding metal potato masher in upright position on top of tortilla to keep it submerged, and fry until crisp and lightly browned, 45 to 60 seconds (no flipping is necessary). Drain on paper towel–lined plate and season with salt to taste. Repeat with remaining tortillas. (Tostadas can be made up to 1 day in advance and stored in airtight container.)

5. Spoon small amount of shredded pork onto center of each tostada and serve, passing garnishes separately.

SPICY MEXICAN SHREDDED PORK TOSTADAS WITH HOMEMADE CHORIZO

SERVES 6 TO 8

Increase amount of pork to 3 pounds (2½ pounds after trimming). Using two-thirds of pork (1½ pounds), follow recipe as directed in step 1. To make chorizo, place remaining pork pieces on large plate in single layer and freeze until firm but still pliable, about 15 minutes. Once firm, toss pork with 1 tablespoon red wine vinegar, 1¼ teaspoons chili powder, 1 small minced garlic clove, 1 teaspoon salt, ¾ teaspoon hot paprika, ¾ teaspoon chipotle chile powder, ¾ teaspoon dried oregano, ¼ teaspoon pepper, and ⅛ teaspoon ground cumin in medium bowl. Pulse half of chorizo mixture in food processor until meat is finely chopped, 8 to 10 pulses. Transfer to bowl and repeat with remaining chorizo mixture. In step 2, heat oil as directed and add chorizo mixture; cook, stirring occasionally, until slightly crisp and no longer pink, 3 to 5 minutes. Transfer meat to paper towel–lined plate, leaving rendered fat in skillet. Proceed with recipe as directed, using rendered fat to cook shredded pork and returning chorizo mixture to skillet along with tomato sauce in step 3.

French-Style Pork Stew

✔ **WHY THIS RECIPE WORKS**

In the realm of stews, beef dominates. Pork stews are harder to come by, and when you do find them, the meat often gets lost in the shadow of more assertive ingredients. One traditional French recipe claims to be robust and satisfying, with lots of pork flavor—but without a lot of heaviness. We wanted to see if this stew lived up to its promise.

MIX THE RIGHT MEATS Both pork loin and tenderloin cooked up too dry and stringy for our stew. Pork butt, cut into chunks, worked much better; with its mix of lean and fat, this cut was moist and tender, and contributed solid pork flavor to the broth. The addition of a smoked shank infused the broth with a delicate smokiness and offered plenty of shredded meat to supplement the shoulder. And kielbasa, added toward the end of cooking, provided the final meaty component.

SKIP BROWNING With so much bold, smoky flavor from the shank and sausage, we found we could save time and skip the step of browning the pork butt.

FINESSE THE BROTH Replacing some of the water with chicken broth made for a subtle flavor base that didn't compete with the pork. For even more depth, we added halved onions plus parsley, thyme, bay leaves, garlic, peppercorns, and a couple of whole cloves to the pot as the meat simmered.

VEGGIE VARIETY A mix of shredded savoy cabbage, chunks of carrots, and pieces of potatoes offered a balance of sweet, earthy flavor, substantial texture, and appealing color. Adding the vegetables to the pot later in the process helped preserve their fresh flavor.

SWITCH TO THE OVEN Typically, stews are cooked entirely on the stovetop. We found that transferring the stew to the oven after bringing it to a simmer on the stovetop ensured steady, constant, and all-encompassing heat, eliminating the need for frequent burner adjustments.

FRENCH-STYLE PORK STEW
SERVES 8 TO 10

Pork butt roast is also called Boston shoulder, pork butt, or Boston butt (see page 179 for more information). Serve this stew with crusty bread.

- 6 sprigs fresh parsley, plus ¼ cup chopped
- 3 large sprigs fresh thyme
- 5 garlic cloves, unpeeled
- 2 bay leaves
- 1 tablespoon black peppercorns
- 2 whole cloves
- 5 cups water
- 4 cups chicken broth
- 1 (3-pound) boneless pork butt roast, trimmed and cut into 1- to 1½-inch pieces
- 1 meaty smoked ham shank or 2 to 3 smoked ham hocks (1¼ pounds)
- 2 onions, halved through root end, root end left intact
- 4 carrots, peeled, narrow ends cut crosswise into ½-inch pieces, wide ends halved lengthwise and cut into ½-inch pieces
- 1 pound Yukon Gold potatoes, unpeeled, cut into ¾-inch pieces
- 12 ounces kielbasa sausage, halved lengthwise and cut into ½-inch-thick slices
- ½ head savoy cabbage, shredded (8 cups)

1. Adjust oven rack to middle position and heat oven to 325 degrees. Cut 10-inch square of triple-thickness cheesecloth. Place parsley sprigs (fold or break to fit), thyme sprigs, garlic, bay leaves, peppercorns, and cloves in center of cheesecloth and tie into bundle with kitchen twine.

2. Bring water, broth, pork, ham, onions, and herb bundle to simmer in large Dutch oven over medium-high heat, skimming off

1. Soak beans overnight in salt solution for tender texture.

2. Blanch salt pork (to remove excess salt) and sausage (to help firm up).

3. Brown sausage, remove; brown pork shoulder, carrots, and onion.

4. Return sausage and add wine. Stir in tomatoes, aromatics, salt pork, broth, and beans.

5. Bake, covered, 1½ hours, until beans are creamy and full of meaty flavor.

scum that rises to surface. Cover pot and place in oven. Cook until pork chunks are tender and skewer inserted in meat meets little resistance, 1¼ to 1½ hours.

3. Using slotted spoon, discard onions and herb bundle. Transfer ham to plate. Add carrots and potatoes to pot and stir to combine. Cover pot and return to oven. Cook until vegetables are almost tender, 20 to 25 minutes. When ham is cool enough to handle, using 2 forks, remove meat and shred into bite-size pieces; discard skin and bones.

4. Add shredded ham, kielbasa, and cabbage to pot. Stir to combine, cover, and return to oven. Cook until kielbasa is heated through and cabbage is wilted and tender, 15 to 20 minutes. Season with salt and pepper to taste, then stir in chopped parsley. Ladle into bowls and serve. (Stew can be refrigerated up to 3 days.)

French Pork and White Bean Casserole (Cassoulet)

✓ **WHY THIS RECIPE WORKS**

While debates over this classic French pork-and-bean casserole abound, two things about cassoulet are clear: This stew yields the most deeply flavorful pork and beans imaginable and, however you make it, you can count on setting aside at least a couple of days (it typically involves grinding and stuffing your own sausage and preserving duck or goose fat for confit). We were determined to find a streamlined approach using streamlined ingredients.

SKIP THE CONFIT The first component to streamline was the confit. Store-bought confit wasn't a good option, as it's expensive and inconsistent. While many variations (restaurant versions in particular) do include this deeply flavorful preserved meat, it's by no means essential. Instead, salt pork contributed plenty of richness without overpowering the dish.

PICK YOUR PORK Pork shoulder provided plenty of substance to our stew and emerged meaty and tender after the prolonged cooking. As a replacement for the homemade sausage—which should taste mainly of pork with a hint of garlic and spices—we settled on storebought Irish bangers or German bratwurst as the best substitutes.

BALANCE THE BROTH Broth made from poultry or pork is the most traditional cooking liquid, and we found that store-bought chicken broth worked just fine. The additions of tomato paste and canned diced tomatoes worked better than white wine alone in balancing the richness of the meat.

BRINE THE BEANS White beans are essential to cassoulet and while the top choice—Tarbais beans—are prohibitively expensive, we found that widely available cannellini beans worked just fine and provided a similar creaminess. Brining the beans and then cooking them with the meat saved time and allowed them to pick up plenty of meaty flavor.

THE UPPER CRUST For a crisp yet cohesive crust, we took a two-step approach to the bread crumbs: First we applied half of the bread crumbs to the casserole and baked the pot covered for 15 minutes, allowing the crumbs to slightly moisten and bind together. We then removed the cover, baked the mixture for a few more minutes, added the remaining crumbs, and let them cook until crisp.

FRENCH PORK AND WHITE BEAN CASSEROLE (CASSOULET)

SERVES 8 TO 10

Pork shoulder is also called shoulder arm picnic, picnic shoulder, fresh picnic, or picnic roast (see page 179 for more information). Instead of an overnight soak, you can quick-salt-soak the beans: In step 1, combine the salt, water, and beans in a Dutch oven and bring to a boil over high heat. Remove the pot from the heat, cover, and let stand for 1 hour. Drain and rinse the beans and proceed with the recipe. If you can't find fresh French garlic sausage, Irish bangers or bratwurst may be substituted.

	Salt and pepper
1	pound (2½ cups) dried cannellini beans, picked over and rinsed
2	celery ribs
1	bay leaf
4	sprigs fresh thyme
1½	pounds fresh French garlic sausage
4	ounces salt pork, rinsed
¼	cup vegetable oil
1½	pounds boneless pork shoulder, trimmed and cut into 1-inch chunks
1	large onion, chopped fine
2	carrots, peeled and cut into ¼-inch pieces
4	garlic cloves, minced
1	tablespoon tomato paste
½	cup dry white wine
1	(14.5-ounce) can diced tomatoes
4	cups chicken broth
4	slices hearty white sandwich bread, torn into rough pieces
½	cup chopped fresh parsley

1. Dissolve 2 tablespoons salt in 4 quarts cold water in large bowl or container. Add beans and soak at room temperature for at least 8 hours or up to 24 hours. Drain and rinse well.

2. Adjust oven rack to lower-middle position and heat oven to 300 degrees. Using kitchen twine, tie together celery, bay leaf, and thyme sprigs. Place sausage and salt pork in medium saucepan and add cold water to cover by 1 inch; bring to boil over high heat. Reduce heat to simmer and cook for 5 minutes. Transfer sausage to cutting board, let cool slightly, then cut into 1-inch pieces. Remove salt pork from water; set aside.

3. Heat 2 tablespoons oil in Dutch oven over medium-high heat until just smoking. Add sausage pieces and brown on all sides, 8 to 12 minutes. Transfer to medium bowl. Add pork shoulder and brown on all sides, 8 to 12 minutes. Add onion and carrots; cook, stirring constantly, until onion is translucent, about 2 minutes. Add garlic and tomato paste and cook, stirring constantly, until fragrant, 30 seconds. Return sausage to Dutch oven; add white wine, scraping up any browned bits. Cook until slightly reduced, about 30 seconds. Stir in tomatoes and their juice, celery bundle, and reserved salt pork.

4. Stir in broth and beans, pressing beans into even layer, adding up to 1 cup water until beans are at least partially submerged (beans may still break surface of liquid). Increase heat to high and bring to simmer. Cover pot, transfer to oven, and cook until beans are tender, about 1½ hours. Discard celery bundle and salt pork. (Alternatively, dice salt pork and return to casserole.) Using large spoon, skim fat from surface and discard. Season with salt and pepper to taste. Increase oven temperature to 350 degrees and bake, uncovered, 20 minutes.

5. Meanwhile, pulse bread and remaining 2 tablespoons oil in food processor until crumbs are no larger than ⅛ inch, 8 to 10 pulses. Transfer to medium bowl, add parsley, and toss to combine. Season with salt and pepper to taste.

6. Sprinkle ½ cup bread-crumb mixture evenly over casserole; bake, covered, 15 minutes. Remove lid and bake 15 minutes longer. Sprinkle remaining bread-crumb mixture over top of casserole and bake until topping is golden brown, about 30 minutes. Let rest for 15 minutes before serving.

Slow-Roasted Pork Shoulder with Peach Sauce

✔ WHY THIS RECIPE WORKS

When most people think of a pork roast these days, the first thing that comes to mind is pork loin; a lean cut, to be sure, but one also in need of a serious flavor boost. We wanted to explore the glories of old-fashioned, more flavorful pork. Enter the shoulder roast: It may take longer to cook, but it's also inexpensive, loaded with flavorful intramuscular fat, and crowned with a thick fat cap that renders to a bronze, bacon-like crust.

USE BONE-IN PORK BUTT Instead of the lean, center-cut loin, our choice for roasting is pork butt (also known as Boston butt). This shoulder roast packs plenty of intramuscular fat that melts and bastes the meat during cooking, and it's available with or without the bone. We prefer bone-in for two reasons: First, the bone acts as an insulator against heat. This means that the meat surrounding it stays cooler and the roast cooks at a slower, gentler pace. Second, bones have a large percentage of the meat's connective tissue attached to them, which eventually breaks down to gelatin and helps the roast retain moisture.

HERE'S THE RUB We rubbed our roast with a mixture of salt and sugar and let it rest overnight. While this may seem like a long time, the results were worth it. The salt enhanced juiciness and seasoned the meat throughout, while the sugar caramelized to create a crackling-crisp, salty-sweet crust.

GO SLOW Cooking the pork slowly (at 325 degrees for 5 to 6 hours) pushed the meat well beyond its "done" mark into the 190-degree range. In lean cuts, this would result in an incredibly dry piece of meat. But because there is so much collagen and fat in this roast, the high temperature encouraged intramuscular fat to melt, collagen to break down and tenderize the meat, and the fat cap to render and crisp.

PLACE IN A V-RACK When we cooked the pork directly in the pan, the dark layer of drippings burned quickly (thanks to its high sugar content). A V-rack and a quart of water poured into the bottom of the pan quickly remedied this problem. Once the roast was perched higher up, its fat dripped down and mixed with the water to create a significant amount of jus—with no burning.

SLOW-ROASTED PORK SHOULDER WITH PEACH SAUCE

SERVES 8 TO 12

Pork butt roast, a roast from the blade shoulder, is also called Boston shoulder, pork butt, or Boston butt. Do not confuse it with pork shoulder, which comes form the arm shoulder (see page 179 for more information on these roasts). Add more water to the roasting pan as necessary during the last hours of cooking to prevent the fond from burning. Serve the pork with the accompanying peach sauce or with cherry sauce or a sweet-tart chutney (recipes follow).

PORK ROAST

- 1 (6- to 8-pound) bone-in pork butt roast
- ⅓ cup kosher salt
- ⅓ cup packed light brown sugar
  Pepper

PEACH SAUCE

- 10 ounces frozen peaches, cut into 1-inch chunks, or 2 fresh peaches, peeled, halved, pitted, and cut into ½-inch wedges
- 2 cups dry white wine
- ½ cup granulated sugar
- 5 tablespoons unseasoned rice vinegar
- 2 sprigs fresh thyme
- 1 tablespoon whole-grain mustard

1. Cut off stalks and feathery fronds. (Fronds can be minced and used for garnish.)

2. Trim very thin slice from base and remove any tough or blemished outer layers from bulb.

3. Cut bulb in half through base. Use small, sharp knife to remove pyramid-shaped core.

4. Cut fennel halves into thin slices.

1. FOR THE PORK ROAST: Using sharp knife, cut slits 1 inch apart in crosshatch pattern in fat cap of roast, being careful not to cut into meat. Combine salt and sugar in bowl. Rub salt mixture over entire pork shoulder and into slits. Wrap roast tightly in double layer of plastic wrap, place on rimmed baking sheet, and refrigerate for 12 to 24 hours.

2. Adjust oven rack to lowest position and heat oven to 325 degrees. Unwrap roast and brush any excess salt mixture from surface. Season roast with pepper. Set V-rack in large roasting pan, spray with vegetable oil spray, and place roast on rack. Add 1 quart water to roasting pan.

3. Cook roast, basting twice during cooking, until meat is extremely tender and meat near (but not touching) bone registers 190 degrees, 5 to 6 hours. Transfer roast to carving board and let rest, tented loosely with aluminum foil, for 1 hour. Transfer liquid in roasting pan to fat separator and let stand for 5 minutes. Pour off ¼ cup jus and set aside; discard fat and reserve remaining jus for another use.

4. FOR THE SAUCE: Bring peaches, wine, sugar, ¼ cup vinegar, thyme sprigs, and ¼ cup defatted jus to simmer in small saucepan; cook, stirring occasionally, until reduced to 2 cups, about 30 minutes. Stir in mustard and remaining 1 tablespoon vinegar. Discard thyme sprigs, cover, and keep warm.

5. Using sharp paring knife, cut around inverted T-shaped bone until it can be pulled free from roast (use dish towel to grasp bone). Using serrated knife, slice roast. Serve, passing sauce separately.

SLOW-ROASTED PORK SHOULDER WITH CHERRY SAUCE

Substitute 10 ounces fresh or frozen pitted cherries for peaches, red wine for white wine, and red wine vinegar for rice vinegar, and add ¼ cup ruby port along with defatted jus. Increase granulated sugar to ¾ cup, omit thyme sprigs and mustard, and reduce mixture to 1½ cups.

FENNEL-APPLE CHUTNEY
MAKES ABOUT 2 CUPS

1 tablespoon olive oil
1 large fennel bulb, stalks discarded, bulb halved, cored, and cut into ¼-inch pieces
1 onion, chopped fine
2 Granny Smith apples, peeled, cored, and cut in ½-inch pieces
1 cup rice vinegar
¾ cup sugar
2 teaspoons grated lemon zest
1 teaspoon salt
½ teaspoon red pepper flakes

Heat oil in medium saucepan over medium heat until shimmering. Add fennel and onion and cook until softened, about 10 minutes. Add apples, vinegar, sugar, zest, salt, and pepper flakes. Bring to simmer and cook until thickened, about 20 minutes. Let cool to room temperature, about 2 hours, or refrigerate overnight.

RED BELL PEPPER CHUTNEY
MAKES ABOUT 2 CUPS

1 tablespoon olive oil
1 red onion, chopped fine
4 red bell peppers, stemmed, seeded, and cut into ½-inch pieces
1 cup white wine vinegar
½ cup plus 2 tablespoons sugar
2 garlic cloves, peeled and smashed
1 (1-inch) piece ginger, peeled, sliced into thin coins, and smashed
1 teaspoon yellow mustard seeds
1 teaspoon salt
½ teaspoon red pepper flakes

Heat oil in medium saucepan over medium heat until shimmering. Add onion and cook until softened, about 7 minutes. Add bell peppers, vinegar, sugar, garlic, ginger, mustard seeds, salt, and pepper flakes. Bring to simmer and cook until thickened, about 40 minutes. Let cool to room temperature, about 2 hours, or refrigerate overnight.

GREEN TOMATO CHUTNEY
MAKES ABOUT 2 CUPS

---

2 pounds green tomatoes, cored and cut into 1-inch pieces
¾ cup sugar
¾ cup distilled white vinegar
1 teaspoon coriander seeds
1 teaspoon salt
½ teaspoon red pepper flakes
2 teaspoons lemon juice

Bring tomatoes, sugar, vinegar, coriander seeds, salt, and pepper flakes to simmer in medium saucepan. Cook until thickened, about 40 minutes. Let cool to room temperature, about 2 hours, or refrigerate overnight. Stir in lemon juice just before serving.

Cuban-Style Grill-Roasted Pork

✔ WHY THIS RECIPE WORKS

Roast pork marinated in citrus juices, garlic, olive oil, and spices, or lechon asado, might just be the star of Cuban cuisine. Traditionally, it's a whole spit-roasted pig, but many modern versions cook a smaller cut over charcoal instead. We wanted to re-create this bold-flavored dish, with its crackling-crisp skin, tender meat, and bracing garlic-citrus sauce.

CHOOSE BONE-IN, SKIN-ON For this dish, we chose the picnic shoulder (aka pork shoulder), an inexpensive, fatty, bone-in cut that comes with a generous amount of skin attached. (The crisp skin, after all, is a hallmark of this dish.)

FIRE UP THE GRILL, THEN THE OVEN Cooking the pork entirely on the grill was tedious and time-consuming—we were constantly rotating the meat or replenishing the charcoal. Starting the pork on the grill and then moving it to the oven was the perfect solution: Filling the chimney two-thirds full allowed the pork to cook for almost 3 full hours before the coals died down, at which point we transferred the roast to a 325-degree oven. Three hours later, our pork roast was at a perfect 190 degrees with plenty of grilled flavor.

USE A FOIL SHIELD Even with our simplified method, we still had to fiddle with the roast every half-hour or so to keep the side closest to the coals from burning. A foil "shield" gave us our solution; it allowed the heat to circulate around the meat yet kept it from turning black, allowing the grill to stay closed from start to finish.

TEAM UP BOTH A MARINADE AND A PASTE We used both a hybrid brine-marinade and a wet paste to flavor our pork; the "brinerade" penetrated deep into the meat, while the paste held fast to the exterior of the pork and yielded a crisp crust.

CUBAN-STYLE GRILL-ROASTED PORK
SERVES 8 TO 10

Pork shoulder is also called shoulder arm picnic, picnic shoulder, fresh picnic, or picnic roast (see page 179 for more information). Let the meat rest

CRUSHING GARLIC

Crush garlic cloves with side of large chef's knife and discard loosened skin.

for a full hour before serving it or it will not be sufficiently tender. The pork's crisp skin should be served along with the meat. Top the meat with Mojo Sauce (recipe follows), if desired. Traditional accompaniments include black beans, rice, and fried plantains.

PORK AND BRINE

1 (7- to 8-pound) bone-in, skin-on pork shoulder
3 cups sugar
   Salt
4 cups orange juice
2 garlic heads, cloves separated, unpeeled, and crushed

GARLIC-CITRUS PASTE

12 garlic cloves, chopped coarse
2 tablespoons ground cumin
2 tablespoons dried oregano
1 tablespoon salt
1½ teaspoons pepper
6 tablespoons orange juice
2 tablespoons distilled white vinegar
2 tablespoons olive oil

1. FOR THE PORK AND BRINE: Cut 1-inch-deep slits (about 1 inch long), spaced about 2 inches apart, all over pork. Dissolve sugar and 2 cups salt in 6 quarts cold water in large container. Stir in orange juice and garlic. Submerge pork in brine, cover, and refrigerate for 18 to 24 hours. Remove pork from brine and pat dry with paper towels.

2. FOR THE GARLIC-CITRUS PASTE: Pulse garlic, cumin, oregano, salt, and pepper in food processor until coarse paste forms, about 10 pulses. With processor running, add orange juice, vinegar, and oil and process until smooth, about 20 seconds. Rub paste all over pork and into slits. Wrap pork in plastic wrap and let sit at room temperature for 1 hour.

3A. FOR A CHARCOAL GRILL: Open bottom vent halfway. Light large chimney starter two-thirds filled with charcoal briquettes (4 quarts). When top coals are partially covered with ash, pour into steeply banked pile

against side of grill. Set cooking grate in place, cover, and open lid vent halfway. Heat grill until hot, about 5 minutes.

3B. FOR A GAS GRILL: Turn all burners to high, cover, and heat grill until hot, about 15 minutes. Turn primary burner to medium-high and turn off other burner(s). (Adjust primary burner as needed to maintain grill temperature of 300 to 325 degrees.)

4. Clean and oil cooking grate. Make two ½-inch folds on long side of 18-inch length of aluminum foil to form reinforced edge. Place foil in center of cooking grate, with reinforced edge over hotter side of grill. Position pork, skin side up, over cooler side of grill so that it covers about one-third of foil. Lift and bend edges of foil to shield sides of pork, tucking in edges. Cover (position lid vent over meat if using charcoal) and cook for 2 hours. During final 20 minutes of cooking, adjust oven rack to lower-middle position and heat oven to 325 degrees.

5. Transfer pork to wire rack set in rimmed baking sheet and cook in oven until skin is browned and crisp and meat registers 190 degrees, 3 to 4 hours.

6. Transfer pork to carving board and let rest for 1 hour. Remove skin in 1 large piece. Scrape off and discard top layer of fat, then cut meat away from bone in 3 or 4 large pieces. Cut pieces of meat against grain into ¼-inch-thick slices. Scrape excess fat from underside of skin and cut skin into strips before serving

---

CUBAN-STYLE OVEN-ROASTED PORK

After rubbing pork with paste and letting it sit, wrapped in plastic for 1 hour, adjust oven rack to lower-middle position and heat oven to 325 degrees. Place paste-rubbed pork, skin side down, on wire rack set in rimmed baking sheet and cook for 3 hours. Flip pork, skin side up, and continue to cook until meat registers 190 degrees, about 3 hours longer, lightly tenting pork with aluminum foil if skin begins to get too dark.

This sauce can be refrigerated for up to 24 hours; bring to room temperature before serving.

4	garlic cloves, minced
2	teaspoons kosher salt
½	cup olive oil
½	teaspoon ground cumin
¼	cup distilled white vinegar
¼	cup orange juice
¼	teaspoon dried oregano
⅛	teaspoon pepper

1. Place garlic on cutting board and sprinkle with salt. Using flat side of chef's knife, drag garlic and salt back and forth across cutting board in small circular motions until garlic is ground into smooth paste.

2. Heat oil in medium saucepan over medium heat until shimmering. Add garlic paste and cumin and cook, stirring, until fragrant, about 30 seconds. Off heat, whisk in vinegar, orange juice, oregano, and pepper. Transfer to bowl and let cool completely. Whisk sauce to recombine before serving.

Crown Roast of Pork

✔ WHY THIS RECIPE WORKS

Consisting of two bone-in pork loin roasts tied together in a round, a crown roast offers plenty of meat for a holiday crowd and a dramatic presentation, but its unique shape presents serious challenges to even cooking. The standard method (seasoning, brushing with oil, and roasting in a moderate oven) yields roasts that are overcooked around the outer perimeter and undercooked around the inner circle of the crown.

SALT AND SEASON A crown roast is too unwieldy to brine, so we opted to salt it—6 hours was enough to get the job done. While we were at it, we decided to add seasoning to the salt—thyme, rosemary, and garlic. The seasonings not only flavored the meat, but also made for delicious pan drippings.

UPSIDE DOWN For even cooking, we turned the roast upside down and started it at a higher temperature, which allowed more air to circulate through the hard-to-cook center of the crown and better exposed the thickest part of the roast to the oven's heat. We also made sure to tie it securely, using two loops around the roast, so that it held its shape when flipped.

FLIP AND FINISH LOW After the pork cooked for an hour, we flipped it right side up and turned the heat down to finish cooking by roasting gently.

SIDELINE THE STUFFING Stuffing is a popular addition, but it was a major impediment to even cooking, so we instead roasted potatoes, shallots, and apples in the pan alongside the meat. The apples came out of the oven too soft to serve. Rather than discard them, we pureed the apples into the sauce, which gave it both a fruity flavor and a perfectly thick consistency. And the potatoes and shallots emerged from the pan bathed in the roast's flavorful juices.

A crown roast is two bone-in pork loin roasts, with the rib bones frenched and chine bones removed, that have been tied into a crown shape. This can

1. Using kitchen twine, make 2 loops around widest part of roast and tie securely to help crown hold its shape when flipped.

2. Place pork bone side down on V-rack and adjust bones to steady roast. Roast about 1 hour at 475 degrees, until meat is 110 degrees.

3. Reduce oven to 300 degrees. Using paper towels to protect your hands, flip hot roast bone side up and set it back on the V-rack to finish cooking in gentle oven.

be difficult to do, so ask your butcher to make this roast for you (see page 182 for more information on this roast). We wrap extra kitchen twine around the widest part of roast to provide more support when flipping. Use potatoes that measure 1 to 2 inches in diameter.

    Kosher salt and pepper
3   tablespoons minced fresh thyme
2   tablespoons minced fresh rosemary
5   garlic cloves, minced
1   (8- to 10-pound) pork crown roast
2   pounds small red potatoes, unpeeled
10 ounces shallots, peeled and halved
2   Golden Delicious apples, peeled, cored, and halved
8   tablespoons unsalted butter, melted
½ cup apple cider
1   cup chicken broth

    1. Combine 3 tablespoons salt, 1 tablespoon pepper, thyme, rosemary, and garlic in bowl; reserve 2 teaspoons for vegetables. Pat pork dry with paper towels and rub with remaining herb salt. Wrap kitchen twine twice around widest part of roast and tie tightly. Refrigerate roast, covered with plastic wrap, for at least 6 hours or up to 24 hours.

    2. Adjust oven rack to lower-middle position and heat oven to 475 degrees. Place V-rack inside large roasting pan. Toss potatoes, shallots, apples, 4 tablespoons melted butter, and reserved herb salt in large bowl and transfer to pan. Arrange roast bone side down in V-rack and brush with remaining 4 tablespoons melted butter. Roast until meat is well browned and registers 110 degrees, about 1 hour.

    3. Remove roast from oven and reduce oven temperature to 300 degrees. Using 2 bunches of paper towels, flip roast bone side up. Add cider to pan and return to oven, rotating pan. Roast until meat registers 140 degrees, 30 to 50 minutes. Transfer meat to carving board, tent loosely with aluminum foil, and let rest for 15 to 20 minutes.

    4. Transfer apple halves to blender and potatoes and shallots to bowl. Pour pan juices into fat separator, let liquid settle for 5 minutes, and then pour into blender. Add broth to blender with apples and pan juices and process until smooth, about 1 minute. Transfer sauce to medium saucepan and bring to simmer over medium heat. Season with salt and pepper to taste. Cover and keep warm. Remove twine from roast, slice meat between bones, and serve with vegetables and sauce.

Oven-Barbecued Spareribs

✓ WHY THIS RECIPE WORKS

When the craving for crisp-crusted, smoky ribs strikes in midwinter, we usually have two options: head to a local barbecue joint or attempt them in the oven. But most oven recipes slather on smoke-flavored sauce only to cover up the decidedly unbarbecued meat underneath. We wanted to replicate the deep, rich flavor and fork-tender texture of barbecued ribs indoors.

REMOVE THE MEMBRANE St. Louis–style spareribs are pork spareribs that have been trimmed of skirt meat and excess cartilage, making them our first choice for this recipe. Removing the thin membrane lining the concave side of the rib rack made the ribs easier to manipulate and allowed smoke to penetrate both sides of the rack directly.

MAKE YOUR OWN SMOKER Rather than crowd ribs into an indoor smoker, we created a simpler, roomier makeshift version: After spreading ground tea leaves (to replace the wood chips of a stovetop smoker) on a rimmed baking sheet, we placed a wire cooling rack on top, followed by the ribs and heavy-duty aluminum foil in order to trap the smoke. A baking stone got the tea smoking quickly.

ROAST HOT AND COLD High heat made the tea smoke quickly, but it also made for inedibly tough ribs. Freezing them quickly before cooking solved this problem: They could withstand the high heat and quickly absorb the smoke without toughening. We then lowered the temperature to 250 degrees until the ribs were fork-tender. A final pass under the high heat of the broiler turned the wet exterior into a chewy, crispy crust.

OVEN-BARBECUED SPARERIBS
SERVES 4

St. Louis–style ribs are also simply called spareribs (see page 182 for more information). To make this recipe, you will need a baking stone. It's fine if the ribs overlap slightly on the wire rack. Removing the surface fat keeps the ribs from being too greasy and removing the membrane from the ribs allows the smoke to penetrate both sides of the racks and also makes the ribs easier to eat. Note that the ribs must be coated with the rub and refrigerated at least 8 hours or up to 24 hours ahead of cooking. Be careful when opening the crimped foil to add the juice, as hot steam and smoke will billow out. Serve these ribs with barbecue sauce, if desired.

- 6 tablespoons yellow mustard
- 2 tablespoons ketchup
- 3 garlic cloves, minced
- 3 tablespoons packed brown sugar
- 1½ tablespoons kosher salt
- 1 tablespoon paprika
- 1 tablespoon chili powder
- 2 teaspoons pepper
- ½ teaspoon cayenne pepper
- 2 (2½- to 3-pound) racks St. Louis–style spareribs, trimmed, membrane removed, and each rack cut in half
- ¼ cup finely ground Lapsang souchong tea leaves (from about 10 tea bags, or ½ cup loose tea leaves ground to a powder in a spice grinder)
- ½ cup apple juice

1. Combine mustard, ketchup, and garlic in bowl; combine sugar, salt, paprika, chili powder, pepper, and cayenne in separate bowl. Spread mustard mixture in thin, even layer over both sides of ribs; coat both sides with spice mixture, then wrap ribs in plastic wrap and refrigerate for 8 to 24 hours.

2. Transfer ribs from refrigerator to freezer for 45 minutes. Adjust oven racks to lowest and upper-middle positions (at least 5 inches below broiler). Place baking stone on lower rack and heat oven to 500 degrees. Sprinkle tea evenly over bottom of rimmed baking sheet; set wire rack in baking sheet. Place ribs meat side up on rack and cover with heavy-duty aluminum foil, crimping edges tightly to seal. Place sheet on stone and roast ribs for 30 minutes, then reduce oven temperature to 250 degrees, leaving oven door open for 1 minute to cool. While oven is open, carefully open 1 corner of foil and pour apple juice into bottom of sheet; reseal foil. Continue to roast until meat is very tender and begins to pull away from bones, about 1½ hours. (Begin to check ribs after 1 hour; leave loosely covered with foil for remaining cooking time.)

3. Remove foil and carefully flip racks bone side up; place sheet on upper rack. Turn on broiler; cook ribs until well browned and crispy in spots, 5 to 10 minutes. Flip ribs meat side up and cook until second side is well browned and crispy, 5 to 7 minutes more. Let cool for at least 10 minutes before cutting into individual ribs. Serve.

REMOVING THE MEMBRANE FROM A RIB RACK

For Oven-Barbecued Spareribs, we recommend removing the thin membrane that lines the concave side of the rib rack. The ribs are easier to manipulate (and eat), and the smoke penetrates both sides of the rack directly. Insert a spoon handle between the membrane and ribs to loosen slightly. Using a paper towel, grasp the loosened membrane and pull away to remove.

Anyone who has ever grilled
a rack of sticky barbecued
ribs has had to deal with the
task of removing the sugary,
burnt-on mess that gets left
behind. The ideal time to do
this is soon after your food
comes off the grill, but, if
you're like most of us, you
close the lid and save the
mess for next time. We set
out to find a grill brush that
could make the tedious task
of cleaning a gunked-up grate
more efficient.

In the end, only two
brushes—the **Tool Wizard
BBQ Brush** and the **Grill
Wizard Grill Brush**—were
able to successfully clean the
grill grate in a reasonable
number of strokes. These
brushes have no brass bristles
to bend, break, or clog with
unwanted grease and grime.
Instead, they come equipped
with large woven mesh stainless steel "scrubbie" pads.
The pad is able to conform
to any grill grate's spacing,
size, and material, including
porcelain.

Barbecued Pork Spareribs

✓ WHY THIS RECIPE WORKS

*Authentic barbecued ribs are melt-in-your-mouth,
fall-off-the-bone tender, with a deeply smoky, meaty
flavor. But these irresistibly satisfying ribs come at a
cost: They can take a full day in the barbecue pit to
develop that deep, smoky flavor. We wanted to find
a way to make the magic happen sooner.*

SEASON WITH A RUB For bold flavor
fast, we applied a spice rub to the ribs; just
1 hour at room temperature was enough time
for the flavor of the spices to penetrate.

USE INDIRECT HEAT AND THE OVEN
We found that indirect heat was crucial to an
authentic barbecued spareribs recipe, coming closest to replicating the results of barbecue pit masters. After cooking the ribs on
the cooler side of the grill to absorb smoky
flavor, we then transferred them to the oven
and continued to cook them until they were
tender. Covering them with foil ensured they
remained moist.

DON'T FORGET THE SAUCE Barbecued
ribs need barbecue sauce, which we applied
to the ribs before they went into the oven,
reserving a portion to serve alongside the ribs.

BARBECUED PORK SPARERIBS
SERVES 4 TO 6

---

*St. Louis–style ribs are also simply called spareribs
(see page 182 for more information). If you'd like
to use wood chunks instead of wood chips when
using a charcoal grill, substitute two medium wood
chunks, soaked in water for 1 hour, for the wood
chip packet. To remove the membrane (the thin
white sheath that lines the concave side of the rack),
insert a spoon handle between the membrane and
the ribs of one rack to loosen slightly. Using a paper
towel, grasp the loosened membrane and pull away
gently to remove.*

2 (2½- to 3-pound) racks St. Louis–style
 spareribs, trimmed and membrane
 removed
¾ cup Dry Rub (recipe follows)
2 cups woods chips, soaked in water for
 15 minutes and drained
1 recipe barbecue sauce (recipes follow)

1. Rub 3 tablespoons dry rub on each side
of each rack of ribs. Let ribs sit at room temperature for 1 hour.

2. Using large piece of heavy-duty aluminum foil, wrap soaked chips in foil packet and
cut several vent holes in top.

3A. FOR A CHARCOAL GRILL: Open bottom vent halfway. Light large chimney starter
two-thirds filled with charcoal briquettes
(4 quarts). When top coals are partially covered with ash, pour evenly over half of grill.
Place wood chip packet on coals. Set cooking
grate in place, cover, and open lid vent halfway. Heat grill until hot and wood chips are
smoking, about 5 minutes.

3B. FOR A GAS GRILL: Place wood chip
packet directly on primary burner. Turn all
burners to high, cover, and heat grill until hot
and wood chips are smoking, about 15 minutes. Turn primary burner to medium-high
and turn off other burner(s). (Adjust primary burner as needed during cooking to
maintain grill temperature between 300 and
325 degrees.)

4. Clean and oil cooking grate. Place ribs
meat side down on cooler side of grill. Cover
(position lid vent over meat if using charcoal)
and cook until ribs are deep red and smoky,
about 2 hours, flipping and rotating racks halfway through cooking. During final 20 minutes
of cooking, adjust oven rack to lower-middle
position and heat oven to 325 degrees.

5. Transfer ribs to wire rack set in rimmed
baking sheet and brush evenly with ½ cup sauce.

Cover tightly with foil and cook in oven until tender, 1 to 2 hours.

6. Remove ribs from oven and let rest, still covered, for 30 minutes. Unwrap ribs, slice between bones, and serve, passing remaining sauce separately.

DRY RUB

MAKES ABOUT 1⅓ CUPS

Store leftover spice rub in an airtight container for up to three months.

- ¼ cup paprika
- 3 tablespoons celery salt
- 3 tablespoons garlic powder
- 2 tablespoons salt
- 2 tablespoons chili powder
- 2 tablespoons ground cumin
- 2 tablespoons packed dark brown sugar
- 1 tablespoon granulated sugar
- 1 tablespoon dried oregano
- 1 tablespoon white pepper
- 1 tablespoon pepper
- 2 teaspoons cayenne pepper (optional)

Combine all ingredients in bowl.

BARBECUE SAUCE

MAKES ABOUT 1 CUP

This sauce can be refrigerated for up to four days.

- 4 tablespoons unsalted butter
- 1 small onion, chopped fine
- 2 garlic cloves, minced
- 2 tablespoons lemon juice
- 1 tablespoon pepper
- 1 teaspoon paprika
- 1 teaspoon dry mustard
- ½ teaspoon hot sauce
- ½ teaspoon salt
- 1 (15-ounce) can tomato sauce
- ¼ cup cider vinegar

Heat butter in medium saucepan over medium heat. Add onion and cook, stirring occasionally, until softened, 5 to 7 minutes. Stir in garlic and cook until fragrant, about 30 seconds. Stir in lemon juice, pepper, paprika, mustard, hot sauce, and salt, bring to simmer, and cook for 5 minutes. Add tomato sauce and vinegar and continue to simmer until thickened, about 15 minutes longer.

KENTUCKY SMOKED BARBECUE SAUCE

Increase lemon juice to ¼ cup (2 lemons) and paprika to 2 teaspoons. Add ½ teaspoon liquid smoke and 2 tablespoons packed brown sugar with lemon juice.

LOUISIANA SWEET BARBECUE SAUCE

Add ¼ cup molasses, 2 tablespoons sweet sherry, and 1 tablespoon packed brown sugar with tomato sauce. Increase vinegar to 6 tablespoons.

SPICY RIO GRANDE BARBECUE SAUCE

Increase garlic to 4 cloves, lemon juice to ¼ cup (2 lemons), and hot sauce to 1 teaspoon. Add one 7-ounce can diced mild green chiles with lemon juice.

SOY SAUCE

At its most basic, soy sauce is a fermented liquid made from soybeans and wheat. Soybeans contribute a strong, pungent taste, while wheat lends sweetness. Soy sauce should add flavor and complexity to your recipes, not just make them salty. We use it not only in numerous Asian-flavored dishes, but also to enhance meaty flavor in sauces, stews, soups, and braises. Our taste test winner is **Lee Kum Kee Table Top Premium Soy Sauce**, which has a robust flavor that holds up well throughout cooking.

Memphis-Style Barbecued Spareribs

✔ WHY THIS RECIPE WORKS

Memphis pit masters pride themselves on their all-day barbecued ribs with a dark bark-like crust and distinctive chew. Up for a challenge, we decided to come up with our own version, with one change—we didn't want to tend to a grill all day.

MOP IT UP In Memphis, ribs get flavor from a spice rub and a thin, vinegary liquid—called a mop—that is basted on the ribs as they cook. For our mop, we combined apple juice and cider vinegar and brushed it on the ribs while they cooked on the grill. In addition to flavoring the ribs, this helped to cool down the meat and prevented the ribs from drying out.

RUB THE RIGHT WAY Many experts claim that the spice rub must be applied to the ribs 24 hours in advance. But the thinness of the meat on the bones means that the rub doesn't have all that far to travel. Applying the rub right before cooking gave us all the flavor we needed.

GRILL TO OVEN After failing to grill our ribs in a reasonable amount of time (less than 7 hours), we opted for a grill-to-oven approach. We piled all the coals on one half of the grill and placed a pan of water under the cooking grate on the other half of the grill. This helped maintain a stable temperature and also kept the meat moist. After cooking the ribs on the cooler side of the grill, we transferred them to the oven to finish, shaving more than 3 hours off the cooking time.

USE A THERMOMETER While wet ribs are pretty forgiving, dry-rub ribs are more exacting and have a very small window during which they are perfectly cooked. Using a thermometer allowed us to monitor the ribs and take them out of the oven when the thickest section reached 195 degrees, ensuring consistently tender meat with satisfying chew.

MEMPHIS-STYLE BARBECUED SPARERIBS

SERVES 4 TO 6

St. Louis–style ribs are also simply called spareribs (see page 182 for more information). Don't remove the membrane that runs along the bone side of the ribs; it prevents some of the fat from rendering out and is authentic to this style of ribs. If you'd like to use wood chunks instead of wood chips when using a charcoal grill, substitute one medium wood chunk, soaked in water for 1 hour, for the wood chip packet.

1	recipe Spice Rub (recipe follows)
2	(2½- to 3-pound) racks St. Louis–style spareribs, trimmed
½	cup apple juice
3	tablespoons cider vinegar
1	(13 by 9-inch) disposable aluminum roasting pan (if using charcoal) or 2 (9-inch) disposable aluminum pie plates (if using gas)
¾	cup wood chips, soaked in water for 15 minutes and drained

1. Rub 2 tablespoons spice rub on each side of each rack of ribs. Let ribs sit at room temperature while preparing grill.

2. Combine apple juice and vinegar in small bowl and set aside.

3A. FOR A CHARCOAL GRILL: Open bottom vent halfway and evenly space 15 unlit charcoal briquettes on 1 side of grill. Place disposable pan filled with 2 cups water on other side of grill. Light large chimney starter one-third filled with charcoal briquettes (2 quarts). When top coals are partially covered with ash, pour evenly over unlit coals. Sprinkle soaked wood chips over lit coals. Set cooking grate in place, cover, and open lid vent halfway. Heat grill until hot and wood chips are smoking, about 5 minutes.

3B. FOR A GAS GRILL: Place soaked wood chips in 1 pie plate with ¼ cup water and set over primary burner. Place second pie plate filled with 2 cups water on other burner(s). Turn all burners to high, cover, and heat grill until hot and wood chips are smoking, about 15 minutes. Turn primary burner to medium-high and turn off other burner(s). (Adjust primary burner as needed to maintain grill temperature of 250 to 275 degrees.)

4. Clean and oil cooking grate. Place ribs meat side down on cooler side of grill over water-filled pan. Cover (position lid vent over meat if using charcoal) and cook until ribs are deep red and smoky, about 1½ hours, brushing with apple juice mixture and flipping and rotating racks halfway through cooking. About 20 minutes before removing ribs from grill, adjust oven rack to lower-middle position and heat oven to 300 degrees.

5. Set wire rack in rimmed baking sheet and transfer ribs to rack. Brush top of each rack with 2 tablespoons apple juice mixture. Pour 1½ cups water into bottom of sheet; roast for 1 hour. Brush ribs with remaining apple juice mixture and continue to cook until meat is tender and registers 195 degrees, 1 to 2 hours. Transfer ribs to cutting board and let rest for 15 minutes. Slice ribs between bones and serve.

SPICE RUB
MAKES ABOUT ½ CUP

For less spiciness, reduce the amount of cayenne to ½ teaspoon.

2	tablespoons paprika
2	tablespoons packed light brown sugar
1	tablespoon salt
2	teaspoons chili powder
1½	teaspoons pepper
1½	teaspoons garlic powder
1½	teaspoons onion powder
1½	teaspoons cayenne pepper
½	teaspoon dried thyme

Combine all ingredients in bowl.

Chinese-Style Barbecued Spareribs

✓ WHY THIS RECIPE WORKS

Chinese sticky ribs are marinated in boldly aromatic seasonings, slow-roasted to tenderness, then glazed and broiled to caramelized perfection. Barbecued ribs, on the other hand, are rubbed with spice and smoked low and slow until they fall off the bone. We wanted to combine the best of both worlds, for tender ribs that were seasoned to the bone, kissed with smoke, and covered with a garlicky, gingery glaze.

IN THE OVEN, THEN ON THE GRILL
For ample grill flavor, we determined we'd need to finish our ribs on the grill, so we started with the oven. After several tests, we realized we could skip the marinating step and simply cook the ribs in the oven in a roasting pan with the marinade ingredients for deeply seasoned ribs. After a couple of hours, we moved them to the grill where they finished cooking over indirect heat.

USE TEA FOR SUBTLE SMOKE FLAVOR
The hickory smoke from wood chips—even just a small amount—overwhelmed the Asian

flavor of our ribs. Instead, we briefly soaked eight black tea bags in water, wrapped them in foil (so they'd burn slower and smoke longer), and set them on the coals. The mellow tea smoke permeated the meat and complemented the Asian seasonings perfectly.

GIVE IT A GLAZE Our reduced braising liquid of the marinade plus the meat juices lacked body and sheen. Adding a cup of red currant jelly ensured our glaze was sufficiently thick and sticky. Instead of applying the glaze at the end, we glazed and flipped the ribs every 30 minutes for the last 1 to 1½ hours of cooking, which ensured beautifully shellacked ribs.

CHINESE-STYLE BARBECUED SPARERIBS

SERVES 6

St. Louis–style ribs are also simply called spareribs (see page 182 for more information). To remove the membrane (the thin white sheath that lines the concave side of the rack), insert a spoon handle between the membrane and the ribs of one rack to loosen slightly. Using a paper towel, grasp the loosened membrane and pull away gently to remove. Cover the edges of the ribs loosely with foil if they begin to burn while grilling.

- 2   (2½- to 3-pound) racks St. Louis–style spareribs, trimmed, and membrane removed
- 8   bags black tea, preferably orange spice or Earl Grey
- 1½ cups ketchup
- 1   cup soy sauce
- 1   cup hoisin sauce
- 1   cup sugar
- ½   cup dry sherry
- 6   garlic cloves, minced
- 2   tablespoons grated fresh ginger
- 2   teaspoons toasted sesame oil
- 1½ teaspoons cayenne pepper
- 1   (13 by 9-inch) disposable aluminum roasting pan
- 1   cup red currant jelly

1. Cut rib racks in half. Cover tea bags with water in small bowl and soak for 5 minutes. Squeeze water from tea bags. Using large piece of heavy-duty aluminum foil, wrap soaked tea bags in foil packet and cut several vent holes in top.

2. Adjust oven rack to middle position and heat oven to 300 degrees. Whisk 1 cup ketchup, soy sauce, hoisin, sugar, sherry, garlic, ginger, sesame oil, and cayenne in large bowl; reserve ½ cup for glaze. Arrange ribs, meaty side down, in disposable pan and pour remaining ketchup mixture over ribs. Cover pan tightly with foil and cook until fat has rendered and meat begins to pull away from bones, 2 to 2½ hours. Transfer ribs to large plate. Pour pan juices into fat separator. Let liquid settle and reserve 1 cup defatted pan juices.

3. Simmer reserved pan juices in medium saucepan over medium-high heat until reduced to ½ cup, about 5 minutes. Stir in jelly, reserved ketchup mixture, and remaining ½ cup ketchup and simmer until reduced to 2 cups, 10 to 12 minutes. Reserve one-third of glaze for serving.

4A. FOR A CHARCOAL GRILL: Open bottom vent completely. Light large chimney starter filled with charcoal briquettes (6 quarts). When top coals are partially covered with ash, pour evenly over half of grill. Place tea packet on coals. Set cooking grate in place, cover, and open lid vent completely. Heat grill until hot and tea is smoking, about 5 minutes.

4B. FOR A GAS GRILL: Place tea packet directly on primary burner. Turn all burners to high, cover, and heat grill until hot and tea is smoking, about 15 minutes. Leave primary burner on high and turn off other burner(s).

5. Clean and oil cooking grate. Arrange ribs, meaty side down, on cooler side of grill and cook, covered, until ribs are smoky and edges begin to char, about 30 minutes.

6. Brush ribs with glaze, flip, rotate, and brush again. Cover and cook, brushing with glaze every 30 minutes, until ribs are fully tender and glaze is browned and sticky, 1 to 1½ hours. Transfer ribs to cutting board, tent with foil, and let rest for 10 minutes. Serve with reserved glaze.

TO MAKE AHEAD: Ribs and glaze can be prepared through step 3 up to 2 days in advance. Once ribs are cool, wrap tightly in foil and refrigerate. Transfer glaze to bowl, cover with plastic wrap, and refrigerate. Before proceeding with step 4, allow ribs to stand at room temperature for 1 hour. Before proceeding with step 6, microwave glaze until warm, about 1 minute.

Barbecued Baby Back Ribs

✔ WHY THIS RECIPE WORKS

Dry, flavorless ribs are a true culinary disaster. More often than not, baby back ribs cooked at home come out tasting like dry shoe leather on a bone. We wanted ribs that were juicy, tender, and fully seasoned, with an intense smokiness. In other words, we wanted ribs that would be well worth the time and effort.

CHOOSE THE RIGHT RIBS Meaty ribs—racks as close to 2 pounds as possible—provided substantial, satisfying portions. Leaving the skinlike membrane on the bone side of the ribs during cooking helped retain flavor and moistness and helped form a crispy crust.

BRINE AND RUB A brief stint in a standard salt-and-sugar brine ensured moist, well-seasoned ribs, while a simple spice rub of chili powder, cayenne, cumin, and brown sugar provided a good balance of sweet and spicy flavors and formed a nice, crisp crust.

ADOPT GRILL-OVEN METHOD We barbecued the ribs for a couple of hours on the cooler side of the grill with wood chips, then moved them to a baking sheet and covered them with foil to gently finish cooking, which made for moist, tender baby back ribs with an intense smoky flavor.

BARBECUED BABY BACK RIBS
SERVES 4

Baby back ribs are also called loin back ribs or riblets (see page 180 for more information). If you'd like to use wood chunks instead of wood chips when using a charcoal grill, substitute two medium wood chunks, soaked in water for 1 hour, for the wood chip packet. For information on removing the membrane from the ribs, see page 265.

½	cup sugar
	Salt
2	(1½- to 2-pound) racks baby back ribs
1	recipe Spice Rub (recipe follows)
2	cups wood chips, soaked in water for 15 minutes and drained

1. Dissolve sugar and ½ cup salt in 4 quarts cold water in large container. Submerge racks in brine, cover, and refrigerate for 1 hour. Remove pork from brine and pat dry with paper towels. Rub 1 tablespoon dry rub on each side of racks of ribs. Let ribs sit at room temperature for 1 hour.

2. Using large piece of heavy-duty aluminum foil, wrap soaked chips in foil packet and cut several vent holes in top.

3A. FOR A CHARCOAL GRILL: Open bottom vent halfway. Light large chimney starter three-quarters filled with charcoal briquettes (4½ quarts). When top coals are partially covered with ash, pour evenly over half of grill. Place wood chip packet on coals. Set cooking grate in place, cover, and open lid vent halfway. Heat grill until hot and wood chips are smoking, about 5 minutes.

3B. FOR A GAS GRILL: Place wood chip packet directly on primary burner. Turn all burners to high, cover, and heat grill until hot and wood chips are smoking, about 15 minutes. Turn primary burner to medium-high and turn off other burner(s). (Adjust primary burner as needed during cooking to maintain grill temperature of 300 to 325 degrees.)

4. Clean and oil cooking grate. Place ribs meat side down on cooler side of grill. Cover (position lid vent over meat if using charcoal) and cook until ribs are deep red and smoky, about 2 hours, flipping and rotating racks halfway through cooking. During final 20 minutes of cooking, adjust oven rack to lower-middle position and heat oven to 325 degrees.

5. Transfer ribs to wire rack set in rimmed baking sheet. Cover tightly with foil and cook in oven until tender, 1 to 2 hours.

6. Remove ribs from oven, loosen foil to release steam, and let rest for 30 minutes. Slice ribs between bones and serve.

SPICE RUB
MAKES ABOUT ¼ CUP

4	teaspoons paprika
1¾	teaspoons ground cumin
1½	teaspoons chili powder
1½	teaspoons packed dark brown sugar
1	teaspoon white pepper
¾	teaspoon dried oregano
¾	teaspoon pepper
½	teaspoon cayenne pepper

Combine all ingredients in bowl.

Weeknight Ribs

✔ WHY THIS RECIPE WORKS

Ribs on a weeknight? It's a tricky proposition. For their tough collagen to break down and the meat to turn tender, ribs must reach about 195 degrees—a process that takes several hours on the grill. The most effective shortcut is to boil the ribs before they go on the fire. Boiling brings the meat up to 195 degrees in a matter of minutes, at which point the ribs need only a quick stint over the coals to char. But boiling also dulls flavor (and risks overcooking the thinner end of the rib). We wanted grilled ribs that were reasonably tender and boasted a nice char—in short order.

RIB RULES We stocked up on baby back ribs for testing since these ribs, cut from the tender loin area, are smaller and more tender, thus more quick-cooking than ribs cut from the belly.

SIMMER IN A BRINE Cooking the ribs in a concentrated saltwater solution allowed the salt to penetrate the meat, seasoning it throughout and making up for the loss of pork flavor. Because food can never rise above the temperature of its environment, simmering the meat (at about 200 degrees) instead of boiling it (at 212 degrees) meant that

CHOOSING THE RIGHT RIBS

Butchers get three different cuts from the ribs of a pig (pigs can have anywhere from 13 to 17 sets of ribs). You can barbecue any of these cuts, but in the test kitchen, we usually reach for St. Louis–style spareribs. Because they've been trimmed of the brisket bone and surrounding meat, they fit nicely on a standard-size backyard grill and they give us consistent results. Ordinary spareribs, which come from near the pig's belly, include that brisket bone and meat; their size and irregular shape make them unwieldy on a backyard grill. Among the three, baby back ribs are smallest and leanest; they come from nearest the pig's back (and, despite the name, from an adult pig). Baby backs cook comparatively quickly, which means they tend to dry out more easily than the other cuts.

the thinner end of the rib didn't overcook as the thicker end more slowly came up to 195 degrees. The upshot: moister meat from end to end.

FINISH ON THE GRILL After simmering, the now-tender ribs needed only 15 to 20 minutes over the fire (and a few coats of glaze) to develop a nice lacquer and char flavor.

GRILLED GLAZED BABY BACK RIBS
SERVES 4 TO 6

Baby back ribs are also called loin back ribs or riblets (see page 180 for more information) Try one of the glaze recipes that follow, or use 1 cup of your favorite glaze or barbecue sauce.

> Salt
> 2 (2-pound) racks baby back ribs, trimmed, membrane removed, and each rack cut in half
> 1 recipe glaze (recipes follow)

1. Dissolve 2 tablespoons salt in 2½ quarts water in Dutch oven; place ribs in pot so they are fully submerged. Bring to simmer over high heat. Reduce heat to low, cover, and cook at bare simmer until thickest part of ribs registers 195 degrees, 15 to 25 minutes. While ribs are simmering, set up grill. (If ribs come to temperature before grill is ready, leave in pot, covered, until ready to use.)

2A. FOR A CHARCOAL GRILL: Open bottom vent halfway. Light large chimney starter filled with charcoal briquettes (6 quarts). When top coals are partially covered with ash, pour evenly over grill. Set cooking grate in place, cover, and open lid vent halfway. Heat grill until hot, about 5 minutes.

2B. FOR A GAS GRILL: Turn all burners to high, cover, and heat grill until hot, about 15 minutes. Turn all burners to medium-high.

3. Clean and oil cooking grate. Remove ribs from pot and pat dry with paper towels. Brush both sides of ribs with ⅓ cup glaze. Grill ribs, uncovered, flipping and rotating as needed, until glaze is caramelized and charred in spots, 15 to 20 minutes, brushing with another ⅓ cup glaze halfway through cooking. Transfer ribs to cutting board, brush both sides with remaining glaze, tent loosely with aluminum foil, and let rest for 10 minutes. Cut ribs between bones to separate, and serve.

SPICY MARMALADE GLAZE
MAKES ABOUT 1 CUP

> ⅔ cup orange marmalade
> ⅓ cup cider vinegar
> 2 tablespoons hot sauce
> ¾ teaspoon salt

Whisk all ingredients together in bowl.

HOISIN-COCONUT GLAZE
MAKES ABOUT 1 CUP

> ⅔ cup hoisin sauce
> ⅓ cup canned coconut milk
> 3 tablespoons rice vinegar
> ¾ teaspoon pepper

Whisk all ingredients together in bowl.

LIME GLAZE
MAKES ABOUT 1 CUP

> ⅔ cup lime juice (6 limes)
> ⅓ cup ketchup
> ¼ cup packed brown sugar
> 1 teaspoon salt

Whisk all ingredients together in bowl.

Glazed Spiral-Sliced Ham

✔ WHY THIS RECIPE WORKS

Glazed spiral-sliced ham is appealingly simple but often comes out dry and jerky-like. We wanted a top-notch glazed ham that would always be moist and tender, with a glaze that would complement, but not overwhelm, the meat.

CHOOSE THE RIGHT HAM Bone-in hams that have been spiral-sliced offered the best flavor with the least amount of carving necessary. We found it important to avoid labels that read "ham with water added" as these hams simply didn't taste as good.

GIVE THE HAM A WARM BATH For serving, you need to warm the ham to 110 to 120 degrees—a process that takes a long time if you start with a very cold roast straight from the refrigerator. Instead, we found that soaking the wrapped ham in warm water before heating it kept it moist and also cut the total roasting time by an hour. Less time in the oven meant less moisture loss.

BAKE IN AN OVEN BAG Roasting the ham in a plastic oven bag traps heat and further reduces cooking time. If you don't have an oven bag, you can achieve a similar (if slightly less effective) result by wrapping the ham in foil before it goes into the oven.

KNOW WHEN TO GLAZE We determined that it was best to apply the glaze toward the end of cooking and then again once the ham came out of the oven.

GLAZED SPIRAL-SLICED HAM
SERVES 12 TO 14

For more information on spiral-sliced ham, see page 183. If there is a tear in the ham's inner covering, wrap it in several layers of plastic wrap before soaking it. Instead of using the turkey-size plastic oven bag, the ham may be placed cut side down in the roasting pan and covered tightly with foil, but you will need to add 3 to 4 minutes per pound to the heating time. If using an oven bag, be sure to cut slits in the bag so it does not burst. We've included three optional glazes.

1 (7- to 10-pound) spiral-sliced bone-in
    half ham
1 turkey-size plastic oven bag
1 recipe glaze (recipes follow)

1. Leaving ham's inner plastic or foil covering intact, place ham in large container and cover with hot tap water; set aside for 45 minutes. Drain and cover again with hot tap water; set aside for another 45 minutes.

2. Adjust oven rack to lowest position and heat oven to 250 degrees. Unwrap ham; remove and discard plastic disk covering bone. Place ham in oven bag. Gather top of bag tightly so bag fits snugly around ham, tie bag, and trim excess plastic. Set ham cut side down in large roasting pan and cut 4 slits in top of bag with paring knife.

3. Bake ham until center registers 100 degrees, 1 to 1½ hours (about 10 minutes per pound).

4. Remove ham from oven and increase oven temperature to 350 degrees. Cut open oven bag and roll back sides to expose ham. Brush ham with one-third of glaze and roast until glaze becomes sticky, about 10 minutes (if glaze is too thick to brush, return to heat to loosen).

5. Remove ham from oven, transfer to carving board, and brush entire ham with one-third of glaze. Let ham rest, tented loosely with aluminum foil, for 15 minutes. While ham rests, heat remaining one-third of glaze with 4 to 6 tablespoons of ham juices until it forms thick but fluid sauce. Carve and serve ham, passing sauce at table.

CHERRY-PORT GLAZE
MAKES 1 CUP

½ cup ruby port
1 cup packed dark brown sugar
½ cup cherry preserves
1 teaspoon pepper

1. With tip of paring or carving knife, cut around bone to loosen attached slices.

2. Using long carving knife, slice horizontally above bone and through spiral-cut slices, toward back of ham.

3. Pull cut portion away from bone and cut between slices to separate them fully.

4. Beginning at tapered end, slice above bone to remove remaining chunk of meat. Flip ham over and repeat procedure for other side.

Simmer port in small saucepan over medium heat until reduced to 2 tablespoons, about 5 minutes. Add sugar, preserves, and pepper and cook, stirring occasionally, until sugar dissolves and mixture is thick, syrupy, and reduced to 1 cup, 5 to 10 minutes.

MAPLE-ORANGE GLAZE
MAKES 1 CUP

¾	cup maple syrup
½	cup orange marmalade
2	tablespoons unsalted butter
1	tablespoon Dijon mustard
1	teaspoon pepper
¼	teaspoon ground cinnamon

Combine all ingredients in small saucepan. Cook over medium heat, stirring occasionally, until mixture is thick, syrupy, and reduced to 1 cup, 5 to 10 minutes.

APPLE-GINGER GLAZE
MAKES 1½ CUPS

1	cup packed dark brown sugar
¾	cup apple jelly
3	tablespoons apple butter
1	tablespoon grated fresh ginger
	Pinch ground cloves

Combine all ingredients in small saucepan. Cook over medium heat, stirring occasionally, until sugar dissolves and mixture is thick, syrupy, and reduced to 1½ cups, 5 to 10 minutes.

Slow-Roasted Fresh Ham

✔ WHY THIS RECIPE WORKS

Fresh ham turns as pale as pork loin once cooked and, best of all, it has tremendous meaty flavor. But fresh hams are not easy to cook. First, they are big—usually between 8 and 10 pounds—so it's hard to season the interior, especially with a thick, tough layer of skin covering much of the meat. The fact that fresh hams are made up of different muscles (and lots of fat) that cook at different rates only compounds the problem. We wanted a foolproof method for cooking this prized roast.

CHOOSE YOUR HAM We chose a shank-end ham over a sirloin-end ham since the latter is tricky to carve.

SCORE AND SALT To prep the ham, we removed an outer layer of fat, leaving behind a ½- to ¼-inch layer to encourage fat to render. We also scored the fat to give a salt rub (bolstered with brown sugar and herbs for flavor) something to cling to. And we cut a pocket in the meaty end to help more of the rub penetrate.

BAG IT Roasting the ham in an oven bag created a moist cooking environment for evenly cooked meat.

FINISH WITH A GLAZE Toward the end of cooking we removed the ham from the bag and applied a sweet and tangy glaze made with molasses, soy sauce, and mustard. After 10 minutes, we rotated the ham, glazed it again, and finished roasting it until the meat boasted a browned, lacquered crust.

SLOW-ROASTED FRESH HAM
SERVES 12 TO 14

For more information on shank-end fresh ham, see page 183. Use a turkey-size plastic oven bag for this recipe.

1	(8- to 10-pound) bone-in, shank-end fresh ham
⅓	cup packed brown sugar

CITY HAM VERSUS COUNTRY HAM

There are three basic kinds of ham, all of which come from the hind leg of a pig: fresh ham, which is the leg in its raw state, and country and city hams, which are both cured. Country hams are dry-cured (salted, spiced, smoked, and aged for up to a year), and city hams are wet-cured by brining or injection with a saltwater solution that typically includes sugar and other seasonings, such as liquid smoke.

City hams are usually sold fully cooked and are categorized by the amount of water added to their original weight during curing. We prefer those labeled "ham" or "ham with natural juices," which contain little added water and therefore have a less spongy texture.

City hams are sold either spiral-sliced or uncut and with or without the bone. Spiral-sliced hams are easy to carve, but it's easier to put a thick glaze or crust on an uncut ham. And while bone-less hams are also easy to carve, they are compressed to a solid mass after the bone is removed, which can result in a "processed" texture. We recommend buying a bone-in ham.

⅓ cup kosher salt

3 tablespoons minced fresh rosemary

1 tablespoon minced fresh thyme

1 turkey-size plastic oven bag

2 tablespoons maple syrup

2 tablespoons molasses

1 tablespoon soy sauce

1 tablespoon Dijon mustard

1 teaspoon pepper

1. Place ham flat side down on cutting board. Using sharp knife, remove skin, leaving ½- to ¼-inch layer of fat intact. Cut 1-inch diagonal crosshatch pattern in fat, being careful not to cut into meat. Place ham on its side. Cut one 4-inch horizontal pocket about 2 inches deep in center of flat side of ham, being careful not to poke through opposite side.

2. Combine sugar, salt, rosemary, and thyme in bowl. Rub half of sugar mixture in ham pocket. Tie 1 piece of kitchen twine tightly around base of ham. Rub exterior of ham with remaining sugar mixture. Wrap ham tightly in plastic wrap and refrigerate for at least 12 hours or up to 24 hours.

3. Adjust oven rack to lowest position and heat oven to 325 degrees. Set V-rack in large roasting pan. Unwrap ham and place in oven bag flat side down. Tie top of oven bag closed with kitchen twine. Place ham, flat side down, on V-rack and cut ½-inch slit in top of oven bag. Roast until meat registers 160 degrees, 3½ to 5 hours. Remove ham from oven and let rest in oven bag on V-rack for 1 hour. Heat oven to 450 degrees.

4. Whisk maple syrup, molasses, soy sauce, mustard, and pepper together in bowl. Cut off top of oven bag and push down with tongs, allowing accumulated juices to spill into roasting pan; discard oven bag. Leave ham sitting flat side down on V-rack.

5. Brush ham with half of glaze and roast for 10 minutes. Brush ham with remaining glaze, rotate pan, and roast until deep amber color, about 10 minutes longer. Transfer ham to carving board, flat side down, and let rest for 20 minutes. Pour pan juices into fat separator. Carve ham into ¼-inch-thick slices, arrange on platter, and moisten lightly with defatted pan juices. Serve, passing remaining pan juices separately.

Glazed Picnic Ham

✓ WHY THIS RECIPE WORKS

Most supermarket ham—a lean cut from the rear leg of a pig—gets its complex salty savor from curing and smoking. But there is an even more flavorful cut, the picnic ham, that's given the same treatment. Picnic ham, which comes from the lower part of a hog's shoulder, is pleasantly smoky and salty, but the higher fat content makes it taste richer and meatier. Most of the recipes we found for picnic ham called for simmering the meat for hours, but we wanted to roast this exceptionally flavorful cut of meat.

KEEP COOKING Although picnic hams are technically fully cooked, the extra fat means they need extra cooking (not just heating through, like leg ham) to become palatable. To render the fat and avoid drying out the meat, we placed the ham on a V-rack in a roasting pan and wrapped the whole thing with foil to created a contained moist-heat environment. Cooking the ham in a relatively low oven produced moist, tender meat with much of the fat rendered out.

BALANCE THE SALT To balance the meat's salty richness, we opted for a sweet, spicy glaze. A simple mixture of brown sugar, Dijon mustard, clove, cayenne pepper, and balsamic vinegar made a perfect, slightly sticky glaze with a rich, deep color.

GLAZE AND FINISH To finish our ham and make it centerpiece-worthy, we cranked the heat to 450 degrees and slathered our flavorful glaze on the ham. A few more minutes in the oven without any foil gave the ham a perfectly caramelized exterior. Thinning out the remaining glaze with a bit of cider vinegar gave us a flavorful accompaniment to serve with the ham.

GLAZED PICNIC HAM (SMOKED SHOULDER)

SERVES 12 TO 16

Smoked picnic hams can be awkward and messy to carve, so we like to do it in the kitchen out of the sight of our guests. Hold the largest protruding bone vertically in one hand. Using a carving knife or sharp chef's knife, cut along the length of the bone to remove large sections of meat. Rotate the roast slowly as you cut. Discard any pockets of fat. Finally, carve each chunk of meat into thin slices for serving. Crimp the foil tightly around the roasting pan to keep the ham moist and help the collagen render.

1	(8- to 10-pound) bone-in smoked picnic ham
3	tablespoons dry mustard
1	teaspoon pepper
1	cup packed dark brown sugar
½	cup Dijon mustard
½	cup balsamic vinegar
¼	teaspoon cayenne pepper
⅛	teaspoon ground cloves
1	tablespoon cider vinegar or water

1. Adjust oven rack to lowest position and heat oven to 325 degrees. Line large roasting pan with aluminum foil. Remove skin from exterior of ham and trim fat to ¼-inch thickness. Score remaining fat at 1-inch intervals in crosshatch pattern. Combine 1 tablespoon mustard and pepper in small bowl. Rub ham all over with spice rub. Set ham on V-rack set inside prepared roasting pan. Cover pan tightly with foil. Bake until ham registers 140 degrees, 2 to 3 hours.

2. Meanwhile, bring sugar, Dijon mustard, balsamic vinegar, cayenne, cloves, and remaining 2 tablespoons dry mustard to boil in medium saucepan. Reduce heat to low and simmer until reduced to 1 cup, 15 to 20 minutes. (Glaze can be refrigerated in airtight container for up to 3 days. Microwave glaze until bubbling around edges before using.)

3. Remove ham from oven and let sit for 5 minutes. Increase oven temperature to 450 degrees. Discard foil and brush ham evenly with ½ cup glaze. Return ham to oven and bake until dark brown and caramelized, 25 to 30 minutes. Stir cider vinegar into remaining glaze. Transfer ham to carving board, loosely tent with foil, and let rest for 30 minutes. Carve and serve with cider-thinned glaze.

Roast Country Ham

✔ WHY THIS RECIPE WORKS

From colonial times until the advent of refrigeration, the process of packing hams in salt, smoking them, and then hanging them to dry for up to two years was a way Americans preserved meat. These days, quickly brined "city" hams have all but eclipsed this older, slower country style. Or at least they have in the North. But in the South, people still produce and eat country hams, not for preservation but because they're powerfully porky and incredibly delicious. We wanted either to learn the secrets or to uncover our own.

CHOOSE A YOUNGER HAM Because they are readily available, we chose to work with younger hams—those that are aged three to six months.

CLEAN THE HAM Mold is a natural effect of the curing and aging process, but it is easily removed with a clean brush and some cold running water.

FORGET THE SOAK Country hams are traditionally soaked in water—anywhere from 12 hours to two days—to draw out some of the salt and add back moisture. But test after test revealed to us that soaking the ham didn't make a bit of difference in either salt content or moisture levels, so we skipped this step.

SKIP THE SIMMER The ham is typically simmered on the stovetop for a few hours, after which the skin is trimmed, the fat scored, a glaze applied, and the ham baked briefly in a very hot oven to render the fat and crisp the coating. Maneuvering a large ham out of a pot of simmering water is challenging to say the least, so we wondered what would happen if we just baked it. To our surprise, this approach worked beautifully.

ADD A LITTLE WATER Pouring some water into the bottom of the roasting pan created steam and prevented scorching, all of which helped keep the meat moist as it baked. Wrapping the pan in foil prevented the water from evaporating.

ROAST COUNTRY HAM
SERVES 12 TO 15

Use hams aged six months or less for this recipe. Mold on country ham is not a sign of spoilage; it is a natural effect of the curing and aging process. Serve the ham on biscuits with Jezebel Sauce (recipe follows). Leftover ham is delicious in scrambled eggs, cheese grits, macaroni and cheese, and all manner of things.

1	(13- to 15-pound) 3- to 6-month-old bone-in country ham
½	cup packed light brown sugar
1	tablespoon dry mustard
2	teaspoons pepper

1. Adjust oven rack to middle position and heat oven to 325 degrees. Using clean, stiff-bristled brush, scrub ham under cold running water to remove any surface mold. Transfer ham to cutting board and trim off dry meat, skin, and all but ¼ inch of fat. Score fat cap in ½-inch crosshatch pattern, ¼ inch deep.

2. Transfer ham to roasting pan fat side up, add 1 quart water, and cover pan tightly with aluminum foil. Bake until thickest part of meat registers 140 degrees, 4 to 5 hours. Remove ham from oven, discard foil, and increase oven temperature to 450 degrees.

3. Combine sugar, mustard, and pepper in bowl and rub over top of ham. Return ham to oven and cook, uncovered, until glazed and lacquered, 12 to 17 minutes. Transfer ham to carving board and let rest for 20 minutes. Carve into thin slices and serve.

JEZEBEL SAUCE
MAKES ABOUT 2 CUPS

Granted, it's an odd-sounding mix of ingredients, but it's actually a surprisingly great pairing with Roast Country Ham. We like this sauce on a turkey sandwich, too. Buy refrigerated prepared horseradish, not the shelf-stable kind, which contains preservatives and additives.

⅓	cup pineapple preserves
⅓	cup apple jelly
⅓	cup yellow mustard
⅓	cup prepared horseradish
1½	teaspoons pepper
¼	teaspoon cayenne pepper

Combine all ingredients in blender and process until smooth, 20 to 30 seconds.

Grill-Roasted Ham

✔ **WHY THIS RECIPE WORKS**

Over the years, we've baked wet-cured hams in oven bags and in foil, brushed them with glazes, and rubbed them with sugar and spice, but there was one approach we had yet to explore: grilling. We resolved to take our roast outdoors and produce a ham with incredibly moist, tender meat and browned, crisp skin.

SKIP SPIRAL-SLICED When we tried to grill a spiral-sliced ham, moisture evaporated so quickly from the interior that we were left with dry meat and a tough, leathery crust. An uncut ham, with a protective layer of fat on the outside and scant exposed meat, worked much better.

USE A V-RACK While a two-level fire was ideal, fat had a tendency to drip onto the grill, setting fire to both grill and meat. Elevating the ham on a roasting V-rack solved this problem: The extra inches of protection that the rack afforded kept the ham safe from the flare-ups, and the exterior fat transformed into a crisp, pleasingly charred, flavorful crust.

MAKESHIFT ROTISSERIE Skewering the ham on either side of the bone created handles that allowed us to rotate this bulky cut safely and easily, so that it could develop a smoky charred exterior all around.

GO FOR THE RUB Sugary glazes burned on the grill, but a traditional dry barbecue rub worked great; it still had sugar, but far less than a glaze, and since it was dry, it stayed put, caramelizing nicely on the ham into a tasty, crunchy coating.

GRILL-ROASTED HAM
SERVES 16 TO 20

Do not use a spiral-sliced ham; it will dry out on the grill. You will need two 12-inch metal skewers for this recipe.

1 (7- to 10-pound) bone-in cured ham, preferably shank end, skin removed and fat trimmed to ¼ inch
¼ cup packed dark brown sugar
2 tablespoons paprika
1 teaspoon pepper
¼ teaspoon cayenne pepper

1. Score ham at 1-inch intervals in cross-hatch pattern. Combine sugar, paprika, pepper, and cayenne in small bowl. Rub spice mixture all over ham. Transfer to V-rack and let stand at room temperature 1½ hours. Thread ham with metal skewers on both sides of the bone.

2A. FOR A CHARCOAL GRILL: Open bottom vent completely. Light large chimney starter filled with charcoal briquettes (6 quarts). When top coals are partially covered with ash, pour over half of grill. Set cooking grate in place, cover, and open lid vent halfway. Heat grill until hot, about 5 minutes.

2B. FOR A GAS GRILL: Turn all burners to high, cover, and heat grill until hot, about 15 minutes. Leave primary burner on high and turn off other burner(s).

3. Clean and oil cooking grate. Arrange V-rack over cooler side of grill. Cook ham, covered, until meat registers 100 degrees, about 1½ hours.

4. For charcoal grill, light about 25 coals. When coals are covered with fine gray ash, remove grill grate and scatter over top of spent coals. (For gas grill, turn all burners to low.) Replace grill grate and position V-rack directly over coals. Grill ham until lightly charred on all sides, about 30 minutes, turning ham every 5 minutes. Transfer to carving board, tent with aluminum foil, and let rest for 15 minutes. Carve and serve.

Bacon

✔ WHY THIS RECIPE WORKS

There's no denying it: We love bacon. Maybe it's the smoky maple scent that wafts from the skillet. Or the crispy bits of fat intertwined with the chewy streaks of meat. Or the irresistible flavor it imparts to everything it comes into contact with. Bacon is just plain good. And what could be better than the store-bought stuff? Making your own. We aimed to start with a relatively inexpensive slab of pork belly and create our own personal blend of salt, sugar, and seasonings to flavor it with, for homemade bacon that would easily surpass anything we'd find at the grocery store.

REMOVE THE SKIN, LEAVE THE FAT While it is important to remove the skin, we found it essential to take time with this step to ensure you leave as much of the thick layer of fat intact as possible. Fat absorbs flavor, so once you've cured and smoked the belly, you'll be glad you left it all on there.

GIVE IT A RUBDOWN Curing the pork belly—a process that took seven to 10 days—added flavor and firmed it up. We used maple sugar as our rub's base; it gave the bacon a sweetness that perfectly complemented the meatiness. Pink salt was key as well; it contains nitrites, prevents bacterial growth, boosts flavor, and preserves the meat's red color. Flipping the pork every other day ensured the cure was evenly distributed, and a rinse under cold water prevented the bacon from being excessively salty.

IF POSSIBLE, USE A SMOKER A smoker delivered the best results because it's the ideal source for moderate, indirect heat that allows the bacon to cook slowly and evenly. (But we also found a way to make bacon using a charcoal grill—a great option if you own a charcoal grill and aren't ready to make the leap toward buying a smoker.) Placing lit coals on top of unlit charcoal allowed us to achieve the proper temperature without having to replenish the coals halfway through cooking. The water pan in the smoker also helped temper the heat.

ADD SOME SMOKE A few wood chunks placed on top of the charcoal imparted the requisite smoky flavor, and placing the pork belly fat side up to allowed the rendered fat to baste the meat.

BACON
MAKES ABOUT 3½ POUNDS

Note that it takes one week for the bacon to cure. Do not use iodized salt—we developed this recipe using Diamond Crystal kosher salt. Measurement varies among brands of kosher salt. If you use Morton kosher salt, which has larger crystals, measure out ⅓ cup for this recipe.

- 1   cup maple sugar
- ½   cup Diamond Crystal kosher salt
- 1   tablespoon peppercorns, cracked
- 2   teaspoons minced fresh thyme
- ¾   teaspoon pink salt
- 1   bay leaf, crumbled
- 1   (4-pound) pork belly, skin removed
- 4   medium hickory wood chunks, soaked in water for 1 hour

1. Combine sugar, kosher salt, peppercorns, thyme, pink salt, and bay leaf in small bowl. Place pork belly in 13 by 9-inch glass baking dish and rub all sides and edges of pork belly with dry cure mixture. Cover dish tightly with plastic wrap and refrigerate until pork feels firm yet still pliable, 7 to 10 days, flipping meat every other day.

2. Thoroughly rinse pork with cold water and pat dry with paper towels.

3. Open bottom vent of smoker completely. Arrange 1½ quarts unlit charcoal briquettes in center of smoker in even layer. Light large chimney starter three-quarters filled

Our oven-baked method allows you to cook up lots of bacon slices at once because you use a large baking sheet. If you're just cooking a few pieces of bacon, try this stovetop method. Place the bacon (in strips or cut into pieces) and just enough water to cover it in a skillet over high heat. When the water reaches a boil, lower the heat to medium. Once all of the water has simmered away, turn down the heat to medium-low and continue cooking until the bacon is crisp and well browned. When we tried this method, the meat plumped up as it cooked instead of shriveling, leaving the bacon pleasantly crisp, not tough or brittle.

The addition of water keeps the initial cooking temperature low and gentle, so the meat retains its moisture and stays tender. By the time the water reaches its boiling point (212 degrees), the bacon fat is almost completely rendered, so you're also much less likely to burn the meat while waiting for the fat to cook off.

with charcoal briquettes (4½ quarts). When top coals are partially covered with ash, pour evenly over unlit coals. Place wood chunks on coals. Assemble smoker and fill water pan with water according to manufacturer's instructions. Cover smoker and open lid vent completely. Heat smoker until hot and wood chunks are smoking, about 5 minutes.

4. Clean and oil smoking grate. Place pork belly meat side down in center of smoker. Cover (positioning lid vent over pork) and smoke until pork registers 150 degrees, 1½ to 2 hours.

5. Remove bacon from smoker and let cool to room temperature before slicing. Bacon can be wrapped tightly with plastic and refrigerated for up to 1 month or frozen for up to 2 months.

BACON ON A CHARCOAL GRILL

For step 3, open bottom vent of charcoal grill halfway and place 1 (13 by 9-inch) disposable aluminum roasting pan filled with 2 cups water on 1 side of grill. Arrange 1 quart unlit charcoal briquettes evenly over half of grill opposite roasting pan. Light large chimney starter one-third filled with charcoal briquettes (2 quarts). When top coals are partially covered with ash, pour evenly over unlit coals. Place wood chunks on coals. Set cooking grate in place, cover, and open lid vent halfway. Heat grill until hot and wood chunks are smoking, about 5 minutes. Clean and oil cooking grate. Place pork belly meat side down on cooler side of grill over water-filled pan and smoke as directed in step 4.

Oven-Fried Bacon

✓ WHY THIS RECIPE WORKS

A couple of strips of bacon are always a welcome accompaniment to a plate of eggs, but bacon requires frequent monitoring when cooked on the stovetop, and the grease can be messy. And microwaving isn't any better, producing unevenly cooked and flavorless strips. We were looking for an easier way using the oven.

USE A BAKING SHEET Because bacon renders so much fat while cooking, it was important to choose a pan that would contain it. A rimmed baking sheet worked great and also enabled us to cook more strips at the same time. Rotating the baking sheet front to back halfway through the oven time ensured even cooking.

FIND THE RIGHT TEMPERATURE After testing higher and lower temperatures, we ultimately determined that 400 degrees was ideal: The bacon was medium-well-done after 9 to 10 minutes and crisp after 11 to 12 minutes. These oven-fried strips were consistently cooked throughout, showing no raw spots and requiring no turning or flipping during cooking (which is a must with pan frying). With a texture that was more like a seared piece of meat than a brittle cracker, color that was a nice brick red, and smoky, meaty flavor, this bacon had everything we were looking for—without the mess.

OVEN-FRIED BACON
SERVES 4 TO 6

A large rimmed baking sheet is important here to contain the rendered bacon fat. If cooking more than one tray of bacon, switch their oven positions once about halfway through cooking. You can use thin- or thick-cut bacon here, though the cooking times will vary.

12   slices bacon

Adjust oven rack to middle position and heat oven to 400 degrees. Arrange bacon slices in rimmed baking sheet. Cook until fat begins to render, 5 to 6 minutes; rotate pan. Continue cooking until bacon is crisp and brown, 5 to 6 minutes for thin-cut bacon, 8 to 10 minutes for thick-cut bacon. Transfer bacon to paper towel–lined plate, drain, and serve.

Breakfast Sausage

✓ WHY THIS RECIPE WORKS

Store-bought breakfast sausage patties suffer from a multitude of sins: too sweet or too salty, too bland or too highly seasoned, too greasy. Making our own would surely taste better. But we wanted a simple recipe: no lengthy ingredients list and no complicated methods (and no grinding our own meat).

FIND THE RIGHT FLAVORS We started by flavoring ground pork with classic breakfast sausage flavors: minced garlic, dried thyme and sage, and cayenne for a touch of heat. One tablespoon of maple syrup gently sweetened the sausage and was appropriate for breakfast, as were the mild flavors. We preferred frying our sausage in butter, rather than oil, for its flavor and richness.

USE A LIGHT HAND We kneaded the meat and spices into patties with our hands, taking care not to overmix, which we found toughened the meat.

ENSURE UNIFORM PATTIES To form even patties, we greased a ¼-cup measure and quickly scooped and plopped 16 patties onto a baking sheet. We then covered the patties with plastic wrap and pressed lightly on each patty.

HOMEMADE BREAKFAST SAUSAGE
SERVES 8

Avoid lean or extra-lean ground pork; it makes the sausage dry, crumbly, and less flavorful.

2	pounds ground pork
1	tablespoon maple syrup
1	garlic clove, minced
2	teaspoons dried sage
1½	teaspoons pepper
1	teaspoon salt
½	teaspoon dried thyme
⅛	teaspoon cayenne pepper
2	tablespoons unsalted butter

1. Combine pork, maple syrup, garlic, sage, pepper, salt, thyme, and cayenne in large bowl. Gently mix with your hands until well combined. Using greased ¼-cup measure, divide mixture into 16 patties and place on rimmed baking sheet. Cover patties with plastic wrap, then gently flatten each one to ½-inch thickness.

2. Melt 1 tablespoon butter in 12-inch nonstick skillet over medium heat. Cook half of patties until well browned and cooked through, 6 to 10 minutes. Transfer to paper towel–lined plate and tent with aluminum foil. Wipe out skillet. Repeat with remaining butter and patties. Serve.

TO MAKE AHEAD: Follow recipe through step 1. Refrigerate uncooked patties for up to 1 day or freeze for up to 1 month. To serve, proceed as directed in step 2, increasing cooking time to 14 to 18 minutes.

Grilled Sausages

✓ WHY THIS RECIPE WORKS

Sausage and onions is a classic pairing that sounds tailor-made for the grill. But the reality is usually onions that are both crunchy and charred and sausages that are either dry or—even worse—catch fire. We wanted a foolproof method for grilling sausages and onions simultaneously that would produce nicely browned links with juicy interiors and tender, caramelized onions.

GIVE THE ONIONS A HEAD START Microwaving the onions—with a little thyme, salt, and pepper—for just 4 minutes jump-started the cooking process and allowed them to finish cooking evenly and thoroughly on the grill.

TAKE A CUE FROM THE BALLPARK We adapted a ballpark technique, first cooking the meat with the onions away from the direct heat and then finishing them directly over the flames. We layered the raw sausages over the hot onions in a roasting pan and wrapped it tightly in foil before setting it on the grill. Once the onions were softened and the sausages almost cooked through, we moved the sausages to the cooking grate to brown and crisp.

CARAMELIZE FOR THE FINISH Keeping the onions in the pan for an extra 5 to 10 minutes allowed the liquid to evaporate and the onions to caramelize to a deep golden brown.

GRILLED SAUSAGES WITH ONIONS
SERVES 4

This recipe will work with any raw, uncooked sausage. Serve the sausages as is or in toasted rolls.

- 2 large onions, sliced thin
- 1 teaspoon fresh thyme leaves
- ½ teaspoon salt
- ¼ teaspoon pepper
- 1 (13 by 9-inch) disposable aluminum roasting pan
- 2 pounds sweet or hot Italian sausage (8 to 12 links)

1A. FOR A CHARCOAL GRILL: Open bottom vent completely. Light large chimney starter filled with charcoal briquettes (6 quarts). When top coals are partially covered with ash, pour evenly over grill. Set cooking grate in place, cover, and open lid vent completely. Heat grill until hot, about 5 minutes.

1B. FOR A GAS GRILL: Turn all burners to high, cover, and heat grill until hot, about 15 minutes. Turn all burners to medium-high.

2. Meanwhile, microwave onions, thyme, salt, and pepper in medium bowl, covered, until onions begin to soften and tips turn slightly translucent, 4 to 6 minutes, stirring once halfway through microwaving (be careful of steam). Transfer onions to disposable pan. Place sausages in single layer over onions and wrap roasting pan tightly with aluminum foil.

3. Clean and oil cooking grate. Place roasting pan in center of grill, cover grill, and cook for 15 minutes. Move pan to one side of grill and carefully remove foil. Using tongs, place sausages on grate and cook (covered if using gas) until golden brown on all sides, 5 to 7 minutes, turning as needed.

4. Transfer sausages to serving platter and tent loosely with foil. Cover grill and continue to cook onions, stirring occasionally, until liquid evaporates and onions begin to brown, 5 to 10 minutes longer. Serve sausages, passing onions separately.

GRILLED SAUSAGES WITH PEPPERS AND ONIONS

Omit thyme and add 3 seeded and quartered red bell peppers to roasting pan with sausages. Transfer pepper pieces to cooking grate with sausages and cook until charred patches form, 5 to 7 minutes, flipping halfway through cooking.

1. Microwave onions to jump-start cooking and ensure uniformly tender texture.

2. Place sausages on top of hot onions in disposable pan so their rendered fat will flavor onions.

3. Cover pan with foil so onions will turn out tender, not crunchy.

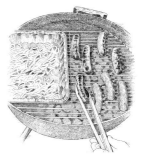

4. With most of their fat rendered, sausages can finish cooking and brown over coals with little risk of flare-ups.

Lamb and Veal

Lamb Basics

Lamb, which has traditionally been less popular than beef and pork, has been staging somewhat of a comeback—and for good reason. Lamb can be relatively inexpensive; it takes well to a variety of cooking methods, such as roasting, stewing, and grilling; and its rich flavor can't be beat. Note that most markets contain just a few of our favorite cuts, and you may need to special-order lamb. While almost all the beef and pork sold in American markets is raised domestically, you can purchase imported as well as domestic lamb. Domestic lamb is distinguished by its larger size and milder flavor, while lamb imported from Australia or New Zealand features a far gamier taste. The reason for this difference in taste boils down to diet and the chemistry of lamb fat. Imported lamb is pasture-fed on mixed grasses, while lamb raised in the United States begins on a diet of grass but finishes with grain. The switch to grain has a direct impact on the composition of the animal's fat, reducing the concentration of the medium-length branched fatty-acid chains that give lamb its characteristic "lamby" flavor—and ultimately leading to sweeter-tasting meat.

Most lamb sold in the supermarket has been slaughtered when 6 to 12 months old. (When the animal is slaughtered past the first year, the meat must be labeled mutton.) Generally, younger lamb has a milder flavor that most people prefer. The only indication of slaughter age at the supermarket is size. A whole leg of lamb weighing 9 pounds is likely to have come from an older animal than a whole leg weighing just 6 pounds. Lamb is initially divided into five primal (or major) cuts.

Primal Cuts of Lamb

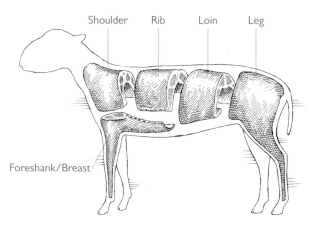

Shoulder Rib Loin Leg

Foreshank/Breast

Shoulder

This area extends from the neck through the fourth rib. Meat from this area is flavorful, although it contains a fair amount of connective tissue and can be tough. Chops, roasts, and boneless stew meat all come from the shoulder.

Rib

The rib area is directly behind the shoulder and extends from the fifth to the 12th rib. The rack (all eight ribs from this section) is cut from the rib. When cut into individual chops, the meat is called rib chops. Meat from this area has a fine, tender grain and a mild flavor.

Loin

The loin extends from the last rib down to the hip area. The loin chop is the most familiar cut from this part of the lamb. Like the rib chop, it is tender and has a mild, sweet flavor.

Leg

The leg area runs from the hip down to the hoof. It may be sold whole or broken into smaller roasts and shanks (one comes from each hind leg). These roasts may be sold with the bones in, or they may be butterflied and sold boneless.

Foreshank/Breast

The final primal cut is from the underside of the animal and is called the foreshank and breast. This area includes the two front legs (each yields a shank) as well as the breast, which is rarely sold in supermarkets.

Shopping for Lamb–Cut by Cut

Like beef, lamb has a rich red color, but the meat is generally stronger tasting. This is because the muscle itself is quite tasty and because lamb fat has a particularly strong flavor. After cooking dozens of lamb chops and roasts, we've rated selected popular cuts for flavor (★★★★ being the best) and cost ($$$$ being the most expensive).

PRIMAL CUT: SHOULDER

BLADE CHOPS

These roughly rectangular chops are cut from the shoulder area and contain a piece of the chine bone (the backbone of the animal) and a thin piece of the blade bone (the shoulder blade of the animal). Their texture is chewy but not tough and their flavor is gutsy. These chops are slightly fattier than round-bone chops.

Flavor: ★★★   **Cost:** $ $

Alternate Name: Shoulder chops

Best Cooking Method: Grilling

Recommended Recipes: Grilled Lamb Shoulder Chops (page 313), Braised Lamb Shoulder Chops (page 316), Irish Stew (page 320)

ROUND-BONE CHOPS

These oval chops are cut from the shoulder area and are leaner than blade chops. Each chop contains a cross section of the arm bone so that the chop looks a bit like a small ham steak. In addition to the arm bone, there's also a tiny line of riblets on the side of each chop. These chops have bold lamb flavor and aren't tough, despite some chewiness.

Flavor: ★★★   **Cost:** $ $

Alternate Name: Arm chops

Best Cooking Methods: Braising, grilling

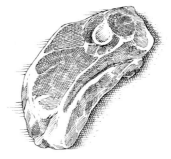

Recommended Recipes: Grilled Lamb Shoulder Chops (page 313), Braised Lamb Shoulder Chops (page 316)

PRIMAL CUT: RIB

RIB CHOPS

These chops have the most refined flavor and tender texture. The meat is mild and sweet. For best results, don't cook these lean chops past medium-rare. This cut is easily recognized by the bone that runs along one side. Rib chops often contain a lot of fat on the bone. Ask your butcher to "french" the chops by scraping away the fat from the end of the bone.

Flavor: ★★★★   **Cost:** $ $ $ $

Alternate Names: Rack chops, frenched chops

Best Cooking Methods: Grilling, pan searing

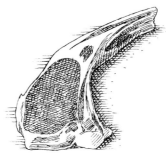

Recommended Recipes: Parmesan Breaded Lamb Chops (page 310), Tandoori Lamb Chops (page 312), Charcoal-Grilled Rib or Loin Lamb Chops (page 315)

RACK OF LAMB

The equivalent to prime rib on a cow, this cut is extremely flavorful and tender. It's also very expensive. This roast contains either eight or nine rib bones, depending on how the meat has been butchered.

Flavor: ★★★★   **Cost:** $ $ $ $

Alternate Names: Rack roast, rib roast

Best Cooking Methods: Roasting, grilling

Recommended Recipes: Simple Roasted Rack of Lamb (page 306), Grilled Rack of Lamb (page 308)

PRIMAL CUT: LOIN

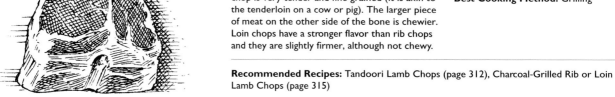

LOIN CHOPS

Like a T-bone steak, this chop has meat on either side of the bone running down the center. The small piece on the right side of the bone on this chop is very tender and fine-grained (it is akin to the tenderloin on a cow or pig). The larger piece of meat on the other side of the bone is chewier. Loin chops have a stronger flavor than rib chops and they are slightly firmer, although not chewy.

Flavor: ★★★★   **Cost:** $ $ $ $

Alternate Name: None

Best Cooking Method: Grilling

Recommended Recipes: Tandoori Lamb Chops (page 312), Charcoal-Grilled Rib or Loin Lamb Chops (page 315)

PRIMAL CUT: LEG

LEG OF LAMB

The whole leg generally weighs 6 to 10 pounds (although smaller legs are available from younger lambs) and includes both the wider sirloin end and the narrower shank end. An entire leg of lamb consists of three main parts: Up near the hip is the butt end (which includes the sirloin, or hip meat); below that is the shank end, with the shank (or ankle) at the very bottom. We prefer the shank end, which is easier to work with and yields more meat. Make sure the butcher has removed the hip bone and aitchbone or carving will be very difficult.

A leg of lamb is so big and so tricky to cook that we generally opt for a boneless leg, which is usually butterflied into a single piece of varying thickness. This cut can be grilled as is (the thicker parts will provide rare or medium-rare meat for those who like it) or stuffed, rolled, and tied.

Flavor: ★★★   **Cost:** $ $ $

Alternate Names: Whole leg, sirloin-on leg

Best Cooking Methods: Roasting, grilling

Recommended Recipes: Garlic-Roasted Leg of Lamb (page 296), Roast Boneless Crusted Leg of Lamb (page 297), Roast Butterflied Leg of Lamb (page 301), Grilled Lamb Kebabs (page 303), Indian Lamb Curry with Whole Spices (page 305)

Veal Basics

Veal can be controversial. Many people are opposed to milk-fed veal because the calves are confined to small stalls before being butchered. "Natural" is the term used to inform the consumer that the calves are allowed to move freely, without the confines of the stalls. Natural veal is also generally raised on grass (the calves can forage) and without hormones or antibiotics.

Moral issues aside, the differences in how the calves are raised create differences in the texture and flavor of the veal. Natural veal is darker, meatier, and more like beef. Milk-fed veal is paler in color, more tender, and milder in flavor. When we grilled both types of veal chops in the test kitchen, each had its supporters.

Several tasters preferred the meatier, more intense flavor of the natural veal. They thought the milk-fed veal seemed bland in comparison. Other tasters preferred the softer texture and milder flavor of the milk-fed veal. They felt that the natural veal tasted like "wimpy" beef and that the milk-fed chops had the mild, sweet flavor they expected from veal.

Both natural and milk-fed veal chops grill well, so the choice is really a personal one. Milk-fed veal is sold in most grocery stores, while natural veal is available at butcher shops, specialty markets, and natural foods stores. When shopping, read labels and check the color of the meat. If the meat is red (rather than pale pink), it most likely came from an animal raised on grass rather than milk.

Primal Cuts of Veal

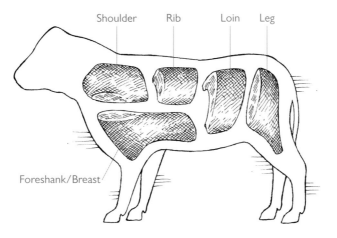

Shoulder

This area includes the front of the animal and runs from the neck through the fifth rib. Cuts from the shoulder are moderately tough and better suited to stewing than grilling. Many markets sell cutlets cut from the shoulder but they will buckle in the pan and are not recommended.

Rib

Our favorite chops come from this prime area of the calf, which includes ribs 6 through 12 along the top half of the animal. Expensive rib chops are ideal candidates for grilling.

Loin

Farther back from the rib, the loin section runs along the top half of the animal and extends from the 13th rib back to the hip bone. Meat from this area is tender and lean. It is also very expensive and best suited to grilling.

Leg

The section includes both the sirloin (the hip) and the actual leg. Cuts from this section often contain multiple muscles and connective tissue. Veal cutlets, known as scaloppini, come from this portion of the animal.

Foreshank/Breast

The underside of the animal yields various cuts, most of which require prolonged cooking to make tender. Veal shanks, also known as osso buco, come from this area, which is also home to the breast roast.

Shopping for Veal–Cut by Cut

Veal is cow in miniature. The primal cuts are the same as on a cow, with the exception that the underside of the animal is grouped into one primal cut rather than three and the back half of the animal (the sirloin and leg) is combined into one primal cut. Veal cuts are generally more tender than their beef counterparts and have a milder (some might say blander) flavor. Based on our kitchen tests, we've rated selected popular cuts for flavor (★★★★ being the best) and cost ($$$$ being the most expensive).

PRIMAL CUT: SHOULDER

SHOULDER ROAST
This boneless roast is usually sold in netting at the market. It is our favorite choice for stews since the roast is meaty and does not contain too much gristle or fat.

Flavor: ★★
Cost: $ $ $

Alternate Name: Rolled veal roast

Best Cooking Method: Braising

Recommended Recipe: Italian Veal Stew (page 339)

SHOULDER CHOPS
These tough, sinewy chops are not suitable for grilling (our preferred method for cooking chops). Although their texture improves when braised, their flavor does not.

Flavor: ★★
Cost: $ $

Alternate Names: Round-bone chops, shoulder arm chops

Best Cooking Method: Braising

PRIMAL CUT: RIB

RIB CHOPS
Our favorite chops because they are especially juicy and flavorful. To identify this cut, look for the bone running down the edge of the chop, with all the meat on one side.

Flavor: ★★★★
Cost: $ $ $ $

Alternate Name: None

Best Cooking Methods: Grilling, pan searing

Recommended Recipes: Pan-Seared Veal Chops (page 335), Breaded Veal Chops (page 336), Grilled Rib Veal Chops (page 337)

PRIMAL CUT: LOIN

LOIN CHOPS
A good choice but a tad leaner and less flavorful than rib chops. Looks like a small T-bone steak with the bone running down the center and meat on either side.

Flavor: ★★★
Cost: $ $ $ $

Alternate Name: None

Best Cooking Methods: Grilling, pan searing

Recommended Recipe: Grilled Rib Veal Chops (page 337)

PRIMAL CUT: LEG

TOP ROUND ROAST

This lean, tender roast is the source for true scaloppini. Good butchers will hand-slice scaloppini from this cut but most supermarkets will not. Unless you trust your butcher, buy this boneless roast and trim cutlets yourself.

Flavor: ★★

Cost: $ $ $

Alternate Name: Leg round roast

Best Cooking Method: Roasting, pan searing

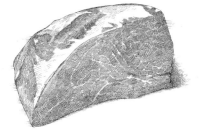

Recommended Recipe: Breaded Veal Cutlets (page 329), Veal Scaloppini (page 330), Sautéed Veal Cutlets with Prosciutto and Sage (page 333)

PRIMAL CUT: FORESHANK/BREAST

VEAL BREAST ROAST

The boneless roast is usually sold tied at the market. This cut is lean and takes well to being stuffed and roasted. It also works well in a boiled dinner.

Flavor: ★★

Cost: $ $ $

Alternate Name: None

Best Cooking Method: Roasting

VEAL SHANKS

Cut crosswise from the front legs, the shanks contain both meat and bone. Depending on the butcher, shanks can vary in thickness and diameter, so shop carefully. Although sometimes sold boneless, you want shanks with the marrow-packed bone, which adds flavor to the braising medium.

Flavor: ★★★

Cost: $ $ $

Alternate Name: Osso Buco

Best Cooking Method: Braising

Recommended Recipe: Osso Buco (page 340)

LAMB AND VEAL DONENESS CHART

The chart below lists optimum internal temperatures based on maximum juiciness and flavor. For optimum safety, follow U.S. Department of Agriculture guidelines: Cook whole cuts of meat to an internal temperature of at least 145 degrees and let rest for at least 3 minutes. Cook ground lamb and veal to an internal temperature of at least 160 degrees. For more information on carryover cooking and resting meat, see page 8.

To determine internal temperature, insert an instant-read thermometer deep into the meat away from any bone—and take two or three readings to make sure the entire piece of meat has reached the proper temperature. For small cuts, like chops, take the temperature of the meat from the side.

CHOPS, CUTLETS, AND ROASTS	TEMPERATURE
Rare	115 to 120 degrees (120 to 125 degrees after resting)
Medium-Rare	120 to 125 degrees (125 to 130 degrees after resting)
Medium	130 to 135 degrees (135 to 140 degrees after resting)
Medium-Well	140 to 145 degrees (145 to 150 degrees after resting)
Well-Done	150 to 155 degrees (155 to 160 degrees after resting)
GROUND LAMB AND VEAL	
Medium-Rare	125 to 130 degrees
Medium	135 to 140 degrees
Medium-Well	145 to 160 degrees
Well-Done	160 degrees and up

1. Following natural seams (delineated by lines of fat), separate into 3 smaller roasts, using sharp boning knife as needed.

2. Trim visible fat and gristle from roasts. Make small cuts to remove interior pockets of gristle, fat, and silverskin. (Roasts will open up and flatten slightly.) Reserve loose meaty scraps for Roasted Garlic Jus.

3. Lightly score inside of each roast, making ¼-inch-deep cuts spaced 1 inch apart in crosshatch pattern.

4. Rub surface of brined lamb with garlic-parsley paste, working paste into grooves.

5. Roll into compact roast, tucking in flaps, to form log shape. Tie with kitchen twine at 1-inch intervals.

Garlic-Roasted Leg of Lamb

✔ WHY THIS RECIPE WORKS

Few roasts make as grand an entrance as roasted leg of lamb, but its charm quickly fades upon carving—copious amounts of sinew and fat make serving this roast a challenge, especially since lamb fat is a key source of the musky flavor that even adventurous eaters can find off-putting. We wanted a roasted leg of lamb without the gristle or gaminess.

LOSE THE BONE We started with a meaty, boneless shank-end roast for best flavor and easy carving.

DIVIDE AND CONQUER We then separated the meaty lobes to create three tidy mini roasts from which we could easily trim away all visible fat and gristle, thus eliminating gamy flavor.

SPIKE THE BRINE We wanted garlic flavor through and through. To that end, we seasoned our brine with garlic. Finally, we added even more garlic flavor by rubbing a roasted garlic and parsley paste onto one side of each mini roast before rolling and tying them up.

GARLIC-ROASTED LEG OF LAMB
SERVES 8 TO 10

Look for rolled, boneless leg of lamb wrapped in netting, not butterflied and wrapped on a tray. The desirable cut is the shank end, which is the whole boneless leg without the sirloin muscle attached. If only bone-in or semiboneless leg is available, ask your butcher to remove the bones for you. Plan on spending about 30 minutes trimming the lamb of fat and silverskin. This advance work is well worth the effort; your roasts will present elegantly and have a much cleaner flavor. If you opt for the 30-minute trim, you will have enough meat scraps left over to make the Roasted Garlic Jus (recipe follows).

LAMB AND BRINE

¼ cup sugar

12 garlic cloves, lightly crushed and peeled

1 (5- to 7-pound) boneless leg of domestic lamb, preferably shank end, with sirloin muscle removed, separated into 3 smaller roasts, trimmed, and scored

GARLIC-PARSLEY PASTE

2 garlic heads, outer papery skins removed and top third of head cut off and discarded

1 tablespoon olive oil

2 tablespoons minced fresh parsley
Salt and pepper

3 tablespoons vegetable oil

1. FOR THE LAMB AND BRINE: Dissolve sugar and 2 tablespoons salt in 2 quarts cold water in large container; stir in crushed garlic. Submerge lamb in brine, cover, and refrigerate for 2 hours.

2. FOR THE PASTE: While lamb brines, adjust oven rack to middle position and heat oven to 400 degrees. Place garlic heads cut side up on sheet of aluminum foil and drizzle with olive oil. Wrap foil tightly around garlic; place on baking sheet and roast until cloves are very soft and golden brown, 40 to 45 minutes. When cool enough to handle, squeeze garlic head to remove cloves from skins. Mash cloves into paste with side of chef's knife. Combine 2 tablespoons garlic paste and parsley in small bowl. (Reserve remaining paste for Roasted Garlic Jus, if desired.)

3. Remove lamb from brine and pat dry with paper towels. Rub surface of each roast with garlic paste, then roll and tie with kitchen twine at 1-inch intervals. Season each roast with salt and pepper.

4. Heat vegetable oil in 12-inch ovensafe skillet over medium-high heat until shimmering. Place lamb roasts in skillet and cook until well browned on all sides, about 12 minutes total. Place skillet in oven and roast until each roast registers 120 to 125 degrees (for medium-rare) or 130 to 135 degrees (for medium). (Roasting time will range from 8 to 25 minutes depending on size of roasts; begin checking after 7 minutes and transfer each roast to platter as it reaches desired temperature.) Let lamb rest, tented loosely with foil, about 15 minutes. Snip off twine, cut into ¼-inch slices, and serve.

TO MAKE AHEAD: Lamb can be trimmed, brined, rubbed with paste, and tied, then stored overnight in refrigerator (do not season meat). Let lamb stand at room temperature for 30 minutes before proceeding with recipe.

ROASTED GARLIC JUS
MAKES ABOUT 2 CUPS

Trimming the lamb into three roasts will yield a few large, meaty scraps, which we recommend using to make this accompanying jus. (Discard smaller pieces of fat and silverskin.) Start the jus while the lamb is in the oven, and finish simmering it while the lamb rests. Keep it warm in a small saucepan and return to a simmer just before serving.

1	tablespoon vegetable oil
1–1½	cups meaty lamb scraps, trimmed of fat and cut into 1-inch pieces
1	onion, chopped
½	cup dry white wine
4	cups chicken broth
2	tablespoons garlic paste reserved from Garlic-Roasted Leg of Lamb
1	teaspoon red wine vinegar

Heat oil in Dutch oven over medium-high heat until shimmering; add lamb scraps and onion and cook, stirring occasionally, until lamb is well browned and onion is soft and golden, about 8 minutes (reduce heat to medium if fond becomes very dark). Add wine and simmer until reduced by half, about 1 minute, scraping bottom of pot with wooden spoon to loosen any browned bits. Add broth and garlic paste; simmer until reduced by half, 15 to 20 minutes. Add any accumulated lamb juices from platter. Strain jus through fine-mesh strainer into small saucepan; add vinegar and serve with sliced lamb, or keep warm until needed.

Roast Boneless Crusted Leg of Lamb

✔ WHY THIS RECIPE WORKS

Boneless leg of lamb would seem to be an easy supper; after all, it already comes boned, rolled, and tied. But it's not as simple as seasoning the lamb, throwing it in the oven, and then checking on it occasionally—the meat can emerge brown and rubbery and the outer layer of fat is prone to smoking, which can result in an offensive gamy flavor. We wanted a foolproof method for achieving a crisp crust and perfectly cooked interior every time.

SELECT A HALF LEG Whole boneless legs are great for a crowd, but impractical for a small, elegant dinner; we determined that a half leg was just the right amount to serve four to six people.

1. Cover lamb with plastic wrap and pound to uniform ¾-inch thickness. Season meat with salt and pepper.

2. Spread herb mixture over meat, leaving 1-inch border around edge. Roll meat lengthwise, around filling, into a roast.

3. Tie roast with kitchen twine to secure.

4. To brown ends of roast, hold roast upright with tongs.

5. When lamb is almost midway through cooking, remove it from oven and carefully remove twine. Coat lamb with mustard and herb and bread-crumb mixture, pressing it on well to ensure that it sticks.

SEAR, THEN ROAST Searing the roast on the stovetop jump-started the cooking process and ensured a golden brown crust, while finishing it in a 375-degree oven allowed the meat to cook through at an even rate, guaranteeing a juicy and tender interior.

ADD THE CRUST MIDWAY THROUGH COOKING A savory crumb crust—flavored with fresh herbs, garlic, and some Parmesan—was a welcome addition to our roast. To prevent the crust from falling apart once the twine was cut, we cut the twine halfway through cooking, after the lamb had roasted long enough to hold its shape, and then applied the crust to the lamb.

ROAST BONELESS LEG OF LAMB WITH GARLIC, HERB, AND BREAD-CRUMB CRUST

SERVES 4 TO 6

We prefer the sirloin end rather than the shank end for this recipe, though either will work well.

1	slice hearty white sandwich bread
¼	cup olive oil
¼	cup minced fresh parsley
3	tablespoons minced fresh rosemary
2	tablespoons minced fresh thyme
3	garlic cloves, peeled
1	ounce Parmesan cheese, grated (½ cup)
1	(3½- to 4-pound) boneless half leg of lamb, untied, trimmed, and pounded to even ¾-inch thickness
	Salt and pepper
1	tablespoon Dijon mustard

1. Adjust oven rack to lower-middle position and heat oven to 375 degrees. Pulse bread in food processor until coarsely ground, about 10 pulses (you should have about 1 cup crumbs). Transfer to bowl and set aside. In now-empty processor, process 1 teaspoon oil, parsley, rosemary, thyme, and garlic until minced, scraping down sides of bowl as needed, about 1 minute. Transfer 1½ tablespoons herb

mixture to bowl and reserve. Scrape remaining mixture into bowl of bread crumbs; stir in Parmesan and 1 tablespoon oil and set aside.

2. Lay lamb with rough interior side (which was against bone) facing up; rub with 2 teaspoons oil and season with salt and pepper. Spread reserved herb mixture evenly over meat, leaving 1-inch border around edge. Roll and tie roast with kitchen twine at 1-inch intervals. Season roast with salt and pepper, then rub with 1 tablespoon oil.

3. Set wire rack in rimmed baking sheet. Heat remaining 1 tablespoon oil in 12-inch skillet over medium-high heat until just smoking, about 3 minutes. Sear lamb until well browned on all sides, about 8 minutes. Using tongs, stand roast on each end to sear, about 30 seconds per end. Transfer to rack and roast until meat registers 120 degrees, 30 to 35 minutes. Transfer lamb to carving board; remove and discard twine. Brush lamb exterior with mustard, then carefully press bread-crumb mixture onto top and sides of roast with your hands, pressing firmly to form solid, even coating that adheres to meat. Return coated roast to rack; roast until meat registers 120 to 125 degrees (for medium-rare) or 130 to 135 degrees (for medium), 15 to 25 minutes longer. Transfer meat to carving board, tent loosely with aluminum foil, and let rest for 10 to 15 minutes. Cut into ½-inch-thick slices and serve.

INDIAN-SPICED ROAST BONELESS LEG OF LAMB WITH HERBED ALMOND-RAISIN CRUST

SERVES 4 TO 6

¼	cup fresh mint leaves
¼	cup fresh cilantro leaves
3	tablespoons olive oil
1	(1-inch) piece fresh ginger, peeled and quartered
3	garlic cloves, peeled
1	teaspoon garam masala

¼ teaspoon ground coriander

¼ teaspoon ground cumin

¼ cup slivered almonds

¼ cup raisins

1 tablespoon plain yogurt

1 (3½- to 4-pound) boneless half leg of lamb, untied, trimmed, and pounded to even ¾-inch thickness
   Salt and pepper

1. Adjust oven rack to lower-middle position and heat oven to 375 degrees. Process mint, cilantro, 1 teaspoon oil, ginger, garlic, ½ teaspoon garam masala, ⅛ teaspoon coriander, and ⅛ teaspoon cumin in food processor until herbs are minced, scraping down sides of bowl with rubber spatula as necessary, about 1 minute. Transfer 1½ tablespoons herb mixture to bowl and reserve. Add almonds and raisins to food processor; continue processing until finely ground, about 45 seconds, and transfer to another bowl. Combine yogurt with remaining ½ teaspoon garam masala, ⅛ teaspoon coriander, and ⅛ teaspoon cumin; set aside.

2. Lay lamb with rough interior side (which was against bone) facing up; rub with 2 teaspoons oil and season with salt and pepper. Spread reserved herb mixture evenly over meat, leaving 1-inch border around edge. Roll and tie roast with kitchen twine at 1-inch intervals. Season roast with salt and pepper, then rub with 1 tablespoon oil.

3. Set wire rack in rimmed baking sheet. Heat remaining 1 tablespoon oil in 12-inch skillet over medium-high heat until just smoking, about 3 minutes. Sear lamb until well browned on all sides, about 8 minutes. Using tongs, stand roast on each end to sear, about 30 seconds per end. Transfer to rack and roast until meat registers 120 degrees, 30 to 35 minutes. Transfer lamb to carving board; remove and discard twine. Brush lamb exterior with yogurt mixture, then carefully press almond-raisin mixture onto top and sides of roast with your hands, pressing firmly to form solid, even coating that adheres to meat. Return coated

roast to rack; roast until meat registers 120 to 125 degrees (for medium-rare) or 130 to 135 degrees (for medium), 15 to 25 minutes longer. Transfer meat to carving board, tent loosely with aluminum foil, and let rest for 10 to 15 minutes. Cut into ½-inch-thick slices and serve.

MOROCCAN-SPICED ROAST BONELESS LEG OF LAMB

SERVES 6

Reserve the pan drippings to pour over the sliced lamb before serving—they are extremely flavorful.

1 cup chicken broth

½ cup fresh cilantro leaves

5 garlic cloves, minced

2 teaspoons dried thyme

2 teaspoons paprika

2 teaspoons ground cumin
   Salt and pepper

8 tablespoons unsalted butter, softened

1 (3½- to 4-pound) boneless half leg of lamb, untied, trimmed, and pounded to ¾-inch thickness

1 tablespoon olive oil

1. Adjust oven rack to lower-middle position and heat oven to 375 degrees. Set rack inside large roasting pan, add broth to pan, and set aside. Process cilantro, garlic, thyme, paprika, cumin, 1 teaspoon salt, and ½ teaspoon pepper in food processor until finely chopped, about 10 seconds. Add butter and process until smooth, about 20 seconds.

2. Lay lamb with rough interior side (which was against bone) facing up; rub half of butter mixture evenly over meat, leaving 1-inch border around edge. Roll and tie roast with kitchen twine at 1-inch intervals. Pat roast dry with paper towels and season with salt and pepper.

3. Heat oil in 12-inch skillet over medium-high heat until just smoking, about 3 minutes. Sear lamb until well browned on all sides, about 8 minutes. Using tongs, stand roast on

each end to sear, about 30 seconds per end. Melt remaining butter mixture in small saucepan over low heat or in microwave at 50 percent power for 1 minute; set aside.

4. Transfer browned roast to rack in roasting pan and roast until thickest part registers 120 to 125 degrees (for medium-rare) or 130 to 135 degrees (for medium), 45 to 55 minutes, basting with reserved melted butter mixture every 10 minutes. Transfer meat to carving board, tent with aluminum foil, and let rest for 10 to 15 minutes. Cut into ½-inch slices, pour pan drippings over lamb, and serve.

Roast Butterflied Leg of Lamb

✔ WHY THIS RECIPE WORKS

Lamb has a richness of flavor unmatched by beef or pork, with a meaty texture that can be as supple as that of tenderloin. It pairs well with a wide range of robust spices, and one of our favorite cuts, the leg, can single-handedly elevate a holiday meal from ordinary to refined. But roasting a bone-in leg of lamb can be difficult—it cooks unevenly and is hard both to flavor and to carve. Choosing the boneless version alleviates some of these issues—the meat cooks more evenly and carving is simplified—but it has its own problems: a poor ratio of well-browned crust to tender meat and pockets of sinew and fat that hide among the mosaic of muscles. We wanted a roast leg of lamb with a good ratio of crispy crust to evenly cooked meat and one that was dead simple to carve and serve, all the while providing us with a ready-made sauce.

BUTTERFLIED IS BEST We decided to forgo bone-in and tied boneless roasts in favor of a butterflied leg of lamb. Essentially a boneless leg in which the thicker portions have been sliced and opened up, this cut has several benefits: a uniform thickness for even cooking; easy access to big pockets of chewy intermuscular fat and connective tissue (making removal of these portions easy); and the ability to season the roast thoroughly and efficiently.

SALT INSTEAD OF BRINE While many people brine lamb, we found that generously seasoning the leg with salt worked better; as with a brine, salting the lamb resulted in well-seasoned, juicy, and tender meat. Unlike brining, however, salting left the lamb with a relatively dry surface—one that browned and crisped far better during roasting. Scoring the fat cap in a crosshatch pattern ensured that the salt penetrated the meat thoroughly.

START LOW, FINISH HIGH With a roast too large for stovetop searing, we knew we'd have to sear it in the oven. Finishing with the sear—rather than the typical approach of starting with it—produced the best results. After slowly roasting our lamb at 250 degrees, we finished it under the broiler, for juicy, tender roasted lamb with a burnished, crisp crust.

SPICE INFUSION We tried a standard spice rub to flavor our lamb, but it scorched under the intense heat of the broiler, so we ditched it in favor of a spice-infused oil. The oil seasoned the lamb during cooking and then became a quick sauce for serving alongside the juicy, boldly spiced lamb.

ROAST BUTTERFLIED LEG OF LAMB WITH CORIANDER, CUMIN, AND MUSTARD SEEDS

SERVES 8 TO 10

We prefer the subtler flavor and larger size of lamb labeled "domestic" or "American" for this recipe. The amount of salt (2 tablespoons) in step 1 is for a 6-pound leg. If using a larger leg (7 to 8 pounds), add an additional teaspoon of salt for every pound.

LAMB

- 1 (6- to 8-pound) butterflied leg of lamb
   Kosher salt
- ⅓ cup vegetable oil
- 3 shallots, sliced thin
- 4 garlic cloves, peeled and smashed
- 1 (1-inch) piece ginger, peeled, sliced into ½-inch-thick rounds, and smashed
- 1 tablespoon coriander seeds
- 1 tablespoon cumin seeds
- 1 tablespoon mustard seeds
- 3 bay leaves
- 2 (2-inch) strips lemon zest

SAUCE

- ⅓ cup chopped fresh mint
- ⅓ cup chopped fresh cilantro
- 1 shallot, minced
- 2 tablespoons lemon juice
   Salt and pepper

1. FOR THE LAMB: Place lamb on cutting board with fat cap facing down. Using sharp knife, trim any pockets of fat and connective tissue from underside of lamb. Flip lamb over, trim fat cap to between ⅛ and ¼ inch thick, and pound roast to even 1-inch thickness. Cut slits, spaced ½ inch apart, in fat cap in cross-hatch pattern, being careful to cut down to but not into meat. Rub 2 tablespoons salt over entire roast and into slits. Let stand, uncovered, at room temperature for 1 hour.

2. Meanwhile, adjust an oven rack to lower-middle position and second rack 4 to 5 inches from broiler element and heat oven to 250 degrees. Stir together oil, shallots, garlic, ginger, coriander seeds, cumin seeds, mustard seeds, bay leaves, and lemon zest on rimmed baking sheet and bake on lower rack until spices are softened and fragrant and shallots and garlic turn golden, about 1 hour. Remove sheet from oven and discard bay leaves.

3. Pat lamb dry with paper towels and transfer, fat side up, to sheet (directly on top of spices). Roast on lower rack until lamb registers 120 degrees, 30 to 40 minutes. Remove sheet from oven and heat broiler. Broil lamb on upper rack until surface is well browned and charred in spots and lamb registers 125 degrees (for medium-rare), or 130 to 135 degrees (for medium), 3 to 8 minutes.

4. Remove sheet from oven and, using 2 pairs of tongs, transfer lamb to carving board (some spices will cling to bottom of roast); tent loosely with aluminum foil and let rest for 20 minutes.

5. FOR THE SAUCE: Meanwhile, carefully pour pan juices through fine-mesh strainer into medium bowl, pressing on solids to extract as much liquid as possible; discard solids. Stir in mint, cilantro, shallot, and lemon juice. Add any accumulated lamb juices to sauce and season with salt and pepper to taste.

6. With long side facing you, slice lamb with grain into 3 equal pieces. Turn each piece and slice against grain into ¼-inch-thick slices. Serve with sauce. (Briefly warm sauce in microwave if it has cooled and thickened.)

ROAST BUTTERFLIED LEG OF LAMB WITH CORIANDER, ROSEMARY, AND RED PEPPER FLAKES

Omit cumin and mustard seeds. Toss 6 sprigs fresh rosemary and ½ teaspoon red pepper flakes with oil mixture in step 2. Substitute parsley for cilantro in sauce.

Grilled Lamb Kebabs

✓ WHY THIS RECIPE WORKS

Shish kebab—skewers of lamb and vegetables—is perhaps the greatest "barbecue" dish from Turkey and the Middle East. When done right, the lamb is well browned and the vegetables are crisp and tender. Everything is perfumed with the flavor of smoke. But shish kebab has its challenges: The components cook at different rates, and if the grill temperature isn't just right you get charred meat or no crust at all. We wanted a foolproof method for grilling shish kebab that would give us perfectly cooked vegetables and meat every time.

USE BONELESS LEG OF LAMB For tender, flavorful kebabs that wouldn't break the bank, we opted to use the shank end of a boneless leg of lamb: It's inexpensive, requires little trimming, and yields the perfect amount of meat for six people. Cutting the meat into 1-inch pieces preserved the supple, chewy texture of the lamb.

SELECT THE RIGHT VEGETABLES Many vegetables either don't cook through or have a tendency to fall apart by the time the lamb reaches the right temperature. After extensive testing, we found two that worked well: red onions and bell peppers. They have a similar texture and cook through at about the same rate; when cut fairly small, these two vegetables were the perfect accompaniments to the lamb, adding flavor and color to the kebabs without demanding any special attention.

MARINATE FOR FLAVOR Marinating the meat added a layer of moisture that kept the kebabs from drying out on the grill while their flavors penetrated the meat. Two hours in the marinade was sufficient time to achieve some flavor, but it took a good 8 hours for these flavors to really sink in. Marinating for 12 hours, or overnight, was even better.

GRILLED LAMB KEBABS
SERVES 6

You will need twelve 12-inch metal skewers for this recipe.

1	recipe marinade (recipes follow)
2¼	pounds boneless leg of lamb (shank end), trimmed and cut into 1-inch pieces
3	bell peppers (1 red, 1 yellow, and 1 orange), stemmed, seeded, and cut into twenty-four 1-inch pieces each
1	large red onion, cut into thirty-six ¾-inch pieces
	Lemon or lime wedges (optional)

1. Toss marinade and lamb in 1-gallon zipper-lock plastic bag or large bowl; seal bag, pressing out as much air as possible, or cover bowl and refrigerate until fully seasoned, at least 2 hours or up to 24 hours.

2A. FOR A CHARCOAL GRILL: Open bottom vent completely. Light large chimney starter filled with charcoal briquettes (6 quarts). When top coals are partially covered with ash, pour evenly over grill, then spread additional 6 quarts unlit briquettes over lit coals. Set cooking grate in place, cover, and open lid vent completely. Heat grill until hot, about 5 minutes.

2B. FOR A GAS GRILL: Turn all burners to high, cover, and heat grill until hot, about 15 minutes. Leave all burners on high.

3. Clean and oil cooking grate. Starting and ending with meat, thread 4 pieces meat, 3 pieces onion (three 3-layer stacks), and 6 pieces bell pepper in mixed order on each of 12 metal skewers.

4. Grill kebabs (covered if using gas), turning each kebab one-quarter turn every 1½ to 2 minutes to brown all sides. Remove kebabs from grill when meat is well browned all over, grill-marked, and registers 120 to 125 degrees

1. Trim off stem and root ends and cut onion into quarters. Peel 3 outer layers of onion away from core.

2. Working with outer layers only, cut each quarter in lengthwise into 3 equal strips.

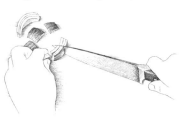

3. Cut each of 12 strips crosswise into 3 pieces. You should have thirty-six 3-layer stacks of separate pieces of onion.

(for medium-rare), about 7 minutes, or 130 to 135 degrees (for medium), about 8 minutes. Transfer kebabs to serving platter; squeeze lemon wedges over kebabs, if using; and serve.

WARM SPICED PARSLEY MARINADE WITH GINGER

MAKES ABOUT 1 CUP

½	cup olive oil
½	cup fresh parsley leaves
1	jalapeño chile, stemmed, seeded, and chopped coarse
2	tablespoons grated fresh ginger
3	garlic cloves, peeled
1	teaspoon ground cumin
1	teaspoon ground cardamom
1	teaspoon ground cinnamon
1	teaspoon salt
⅛	teaspoon pepper

Process all ingredients in food processor until smooth, about 1 minute.

SWEET CURRY MARINADE WITH BUTTERMILK

MAKES ABOUT ¾ CUP

¾	cup buttermilk
1	tablespoon lemon juice
3	garlic cloves, minced
1	tablespoon packed brown sugar
1	tablespoon curry powder
1	teaspoon red pepper flakes
1	teaspoon ground coriander
1	teaspoon chili powder
1	teaspoon salt
⅛	teaspoon pepper

Combine all ingredients in 1-gallon zipper-lock plastic bag or large bowl.

GARLIC AND CILANTRO MARINADE WITH GARAM MASALA

MAKES ABOUT ¾ CUP

Garam masala is a warm spice blend that typically contains black pepper, dried chiles, cinnamon, cardamom, and coriander.

½	cup olive oil
½	cup fresh cilantro leaves
¼	cup raisins
1½	tablespoons lemon juice
3	garlic cloves, peeled
1	teaspoon salt
½	teaspoon garam masala
⅛	teaspoon pepper

Process all ingredients in food processor until smooth, about 1 minute.

ROSEMARY-MINT MARINADE WITH GARLIC AND LEMON

MAKES ABOUT ¾ CUP

Be sure to use fresh rosemary—dried rosemary will give the marinade a wan flavor.

½	cup olive oil
10	fresh mint leaves
1½	teaspoons chopped fresh rosemary
1½	teaspoons grated lemon zest plus 2 tablespoons juice
3	garlic cloves, peeled
1	teaspoon salt
⅛	teaspoon pepper

Process all ingredients in food processor until smooth, about 1 minute.

Indian Lamb Curry with Whole Spices

✓ WHY THIS RECIPE WORKS

Indian curries can be intimidating to make at home, with complicated processes and unfamiliar ingredients. And too often, all that work produces overly heavy curries with dull, murky flavors. We wanted a complex but not heavy-flavored Indian curry that wouldn't take all day to prepare.

USE WHOLE AND GROUND SPICES Toasting a fragrant combination of whole spices in oil infused the cooking oil with flavor and provided the authentic, intense flavor we were after, while ground spices added later provided an aromatic backbone to the dish. Garlic, onion, and ginger further deepened the flavor, while jalapeño offered subtle spice.

SKIP THE BROWNING Instead of browning the meat, we simply stirred it into the pot along with crushed tomatoes and cooked the mixture until the liquid evaporated and the oil separated. This classic Indian technique allowed the spices to further release and develop their flavors in the oil, which was then absorbed by the meat. We then added water and simmered the mixture until the meat was tender.

FINISH SIMPLY Adding potatoes at the end of cooking lent heartiness and appealing contrasting texture, and a little cilantro provided a fresh finish.

INDIAN LAMB CURRY WITH WHOLE SPICES

SERVES 4 TO 6

You may substitute a scant ½ teaspoon of cayenne pepper for the jalapeño, adding it to the skillet with the other ground dried spices. Feel free to increase the aromatics (garlic, ginger, jalapeños, and onions) or dry spice quantities. For a creamier curry, use yogurt rather than the crushed tomatoes. Serve with Basmati Rice Pilaf.

WHOLE SPICE BLEND

1½	cinnamon sticks
4	whole cloves
4	green cardamom pods
8	black peppercorns
1	bay leaf

CURRY

¼	cup vegetable oil
1	onion, sliced thin
1½	pounds boneless leg of lamb, trimmed and cut into ¾-inch cubes
⅔	cup canned crushed tomatoes
4	large garlic cloves, minced
1	tablespoon grated fresh ginger
2	teaspoons ground cumin
2	teaspoons ground coriander
1	teaspoon ground turmeric
	Salt
2	cups water
1	jalapeño chile, stemmed, halved, and seeded
4	medium red potatoes, peeled and cut into ¾-inch cubes
¼	cup chopped fresh cilantro

1. FOR THE SPICE BLEND: Combine ingredients in small bowl.

2. FOR THE CURRY: Heat oil in Dutch oven over medium-high heat until shimmering. Add spice blend and cook, stirring with wooden spoon until cinnamon sticks unfurl and cloves pop, about 5 seconds. Add onion and cook until softened, 3 to 4 minutes.

3. Stir in lamb, tomatoes, garlic, ginger, cumin, coriander, turmeric, and ½ teaspoon salt and cook, stirring frequently, until liquid evaporates, oil separates and turns orange, and spices begin to fry, 5 to 7 minutes. Continue

ON THE SIDE
BASMATI RICE PILAF

Heat 1 tablespoon canola oil, vegetable oil, or corn oil in medium saucepan over high heat until almost smoking. Add 1 cinnamon stick, halved; 2 green cardamom pods; and 2 whole cloves and cook, stirring until they pop. Add ¼ cup thinly sliced onion and cook, stirring until translucent, about 2 minutes. Stir in 1 cup basmati rice and cook, stirring until fragrant, about 1 minute. Add 1½ cups water and 1 teaspoon salt; bring to boil. Reduce heat, cover tightly, and simmer until all water has been absorbed, about 17 minutes. Let stand, covered, at least 10 minutes, fluff with fork, and serve. (Serves 4.)

1. Place racks in hot pan with meat in center and ribs facing outward.

2. After meat is browned, stand racks up in pan and lean them against each other to brown bottoms.

to cook, stirring constantly, until spices are very fragrant, about 30 seconds longer.

4. Add water and jalapeño. Bring to simmer, then reduce heat to low, cover, and simmer until meat is tender, 30 to 40 minutes.

5. Add potatoes and cook until tender, about 15 minutes. Stir in cilantro, simmer for 3 minutes, season with salt to taste, and serve.

LAMB CURRY WITH FIGS AND FENUGREEK

Omit Whole Spice Blend and potatoes. Add ½ teaspoon fenugreek along with cumin, coriander, and turmeric in step 3 and ¼ cup dried figs, chopped coarse, along with water in step 4.

Simple Roasted Rack of Lamb

✔ WHY THIS RECIPE WORKS

The word "mouthwatering" must have been coined to describe rack of lamb. The meat is ultratender and more refined in flavor than almost any other cut of lamb. And like other simple but fabulous dishes, there's nothing to cooking it except that there's no disguising imperfection. You want the meat to be perfectly pink and juicy, the outside to be intensely browned to boost flavor and provide contrasting texture, and the fat to be well enough rendered to encase the meat in a thin, crisp, brittle shell. With all of this in mind, we set out to find a foolproof way to roast this extravagant cut.

TRIM WELL We found it necessary to trim the cap—a thin piece of meat separating layers of fat—in order to remove some of the internal fat and avoid a greasy finished dish. Removing the silverskin (a pearlescent membrane found on certain cuts of meat) was also key; it is very tough and caused the meat to curl up.

GET A GOOD SEAR Searing the racks of lamb on the stovetop was the way to go for a solid, well-caramelized crust. In order to brown the strip of eye meat that lies below the bones on the bony side of the rack, we leaned two racks upright against each other in the pan; this allowed us to brown all parts of the meat.

ROAST IN THE OVEN Roasting the lamb at 425 degrees proved ideal; racks of lamb cooked at this temperature tasted at least as good as (if not better than) racks cooked at a lower temperature, and there was more room for error than when they cooked at a higher heat.

FINISH WITH A SAUCE To streamline our recipe as much as possible, we transferred the racks to a second pan after browning on top of the stove; this allowed us to make a pan sauce in the skillet while the lamb roasted.

SIMPLE ROASTED RACK OF LAMB
SERVES 4 TO 6

Have your butcher french the racks for you; inevitably, the ribs will need some cleaning up, but at least the bulk of the work will be done. Should you choose to make an accompanying pan sauce (recipes follow), have all the ingredients ready before browning the lamb and begin the sauce just as the lamb goes into the oven. This way, the sauce will be ready with the meat.

2 (1½- to 1¾-pound) racks of lamb (8 ribs each), frenched and trimmed
   Salt and pepper
2 tablespoons vegetable oil

1. Adjust oven rack to lower-middle position, place rimmed baking sheet on oven rack, and heat oven to 425 degrees.

2. Season lamb with salt and pepper. Heat oil in 12-inch skillet over high heat until shimmering. Place racks of lamb in skillet, meat side down in center of pan, with ribs facing outward; cook until well browned and nice crust has formed on surface, about 4 minutes. Using tongs, stand racks up in skillet, leaning them against each other to brown bottoms; cook until bottom sides have browned, about 2 minutes longer.

3. Transfer lamb to preheated sheet. Roast until center of each rack registers about 120 to 125 degrees (for medium-rare) or 130 to 135 degrees (for medium), 12 to 15 minutes. Tent loosely with aluminum foil and let rest about 10 minutes. Carve, slicing between each rib, into individual chops. Season with salt and pepper and serve.

RED WINE PAN SAUCE WITH ROSEMARY

MAKES ABOUT ¾ CUP

2 shallots, minced
1 cup dry red wine
2½ teaspoons minced fresh rosemary
1 cup chicken broth
2 tablespoons unsalted butter, softened
   Salt and pepper

Pour off all but 1½ tablespoons fat from skillet used to brown lamb; place skillet over medium heat. Add shallots and cook until softened, about 1 minute. Add red wine and rosemary, scrape bottom of pan with wooden spoon to loosen any browned bits, and increase heat to medium-high and simmer until dark and syrupy, about 7 minutes. Add broth and simmer until reduced to about ¾ cup, about 5 minutes longer. Off heat, swirl in butter, season with salt and pepper to taste, and serve with lamb.

ORANGE PAN SAUCE WITH MIDDLE EASTERN SPICES

MAKES ABOUT ¾ CUP

2 shallots, minced
2 teaspoons sugar
1 teaspoon ground cumin
¼ teaspoon pepper
¼ teaspoon ground cinnamon
¼ teaspoon ground cardamom
⅛ teaspoon cayenne pepper
3 tablespoons red wine vinegar
¼ cup orange juice
1½ cups chicken broth
1 tablespoon minced fresh cilantro
   Salt

Pour off all but 1½ tablespoons fat from skillet used to brown lamb; place skillet over medium heat. Add shallots and cook until softened, about 1 minute. Stir in sugar, cumin, pepper, cinnamon, cardamom, and cayenne; cook until fragrant, about 1 minute. Stir in vinegar, scraping bottom of pan with wooden spoon to loosen any browned bits. Add orange juice, increase heat to medium-high, and simmer until very thick and syrupy, about 2 minutes. Add broth and simmer until slightly thickened and reduced to about ¾ cup, 8 to 10 minutes. Off heat, stir in cilantro, season with salt to taste, and serve with lamb.

EASIER CITRUS JUICING

A citrus press can be a handy tool, but using one to press the juice from multiple oranges or lemons can be a pain. Try cutting the fruit into quarters rather than halves. Juicing a quarter is not only easier than juicing a half, but it also yields more juice.

1. If rack has fat cap, peel back thick outer layer of fat from racks, along with thin flap of meat underneath it. Use boning knife to cut any tissue connecting fat cap to rack.

2. Using boning or paring knife, trim remaining thin layer of fat that covers loin, leaving strip of fat that separates the loin and small eye of meat directly above it.

3. Make straight cut along top side of bones, 1 inch up from small eye of meat.

4. Remove any fat above this line and scrape any remaining meat or fat from exposed bones.

Grilled Rack of Lamb

✔ WHY THIS RECIPE WORKS

Lamb and the grill have great chemistry. The intense heat of the coals produces a great crust and melts away the meat's abundance of fat, distributing flavor throughout, while imparting a smokiness that's the perfect complement to lamb's rich, gamy flavor. Rack of lamb can seem intimidating—we wanted to find a foolproof way to grill this impressive cut.

TRIM THE FAT The key to lamb's unique flavor and tenderness is its high proportion of fat, most of which covers one side of the rack like a cap. We know from experience that leaving on the fat leads to aggressive flare-ups over hot coals. We didn't want to remove all the fat because this would leave us with a dry rack with little flavor, though. Therefore, we left a thin layer of fat over the loin and removed most of the fat between the bones.

BUILD A SPLIT FIRE In order to avoid charring the meat and causing way too many fat flare-ups, we built a split fire with no coals (or lit burners) in part of the grill. In a charcoal grill, we did this by piling the coals on either side of the grill and placing an aluminum pan directly between the two mounds. This way, the outer edges of the grill were the hottest, and we were able to cook the lamb more gently and evenly in the center. For a gas grill, we found that it was possible to leave just one burner on high and turn the others off. Cooking the lamb over the pan (in a charcoal grill) or over the turned-off burners (in a gas grill), eliminated the chance of flare-ups.

REVERSE THE COOKING ORDER Traditionally, we sear lamb over high heat to develop flavor and browning and then finish cooking it over gentler heat to promote tenderness and juiciness. Here, however, we found that searing first caused the ample fat to flare up on the grill. What to do? We reversed the order. Cooking lamb on the cooler part of the grill first allowed the fat to render. Once that fat was sufficiently rendered, we moved the racks to direct heat to brown the exterior.

The result was a rack of lamb that was pink and juicy, with a well-browned crust that contrasted nicely with the lush, ultratender exterior. (And no towering inferno.)

USE A WET RUB Our goal in seasoning the lamb was to enhance its already-wonderful flavor without overwhelming it. We tried a number of things, including a marinade and a dry rub, but we found that the best option was a wet rub consisting of garlic and a couple of robust herbs (rosemary and thyme) mixed with a little oil (just enough to adhere the flavorings to the lamb without causing flare-ups). Brushed on the racks as they browned over the direct heat, the wet rub added just the right note to the perfectly cooked meat.

GRILLED RACK OF LAMB
SERVES 4 TO 6

While most lamb is sold frenched (meaning part of each rib bone is exposed), chances are there will still be some extra fat between the bones. Remove the majority of this fat, leaving an inch at the top of the small eye of meat. See the illustrations at left for more information on frenching the rib bones. Also, make sure that the chine bone (along the bottom of the rack) has been removed to ensure that it will be easy to cut between the ribs after cooking. Ask the butcher to do it; it's very hard to cut off at home.

 1   (13 by 9-inch) disposable aluminum pan (if using charcoal)
 4   teaspoons olive oil
 4   teaspoons chopped fresh rosemary
 2   teaspoons chopped fresh thyme
 2   garlic cloves, minced
 2   (1½- to 1¾-pound) racks of lamb (8 ribs each), frenched and trimmed
    Salt and pepper

1A. FOR A CHARCOAL GRILL: Open bottom vent completely and place disposable pan in center of grill. Light large chimney starter

filled with charcoal briquettes (6 quarts). When top coals are partially covered with ash, pour into 2 even piles on either side of disposable pan. Set cooking grate in place, cover, and open lid vent completely. Heat grill until hot, about 5 minutes.

1B. FOR A GAS GRILL: Turn all burners to high, cover, and heat grill until hot, about 15 minutes. Leave primary burner on high, turning off other burner(s).

2. Clean and oil cooking grate. Combine 1 tablespoon oil, rosemary, thyme, and garlic in bowl. Pat lamb dry with paper towels, rub with remaining 1 teaspoon oil, and season with salt and pepper. Place racks bone side up on cooler part of grill with meaty side of racks very close to, but not quite over, hot coals or lit burner. Cover and cook until meat is lightly browned, faint grill marks appear, and fat has begun to render, 8 to 10 minutes.

3. Flip racks over, bone side down, and move to hotter parts of grill. Cook until well browned, 3 to 4 minutes. Brush racks with herb mixture. Flip racks bone side up and continue to cook until well browned, 3 to 4 minutes longer. Stand racks up and lean them against each other; continue to cook (over hotter side of grill if using charcoal) until bottom is well browned and meat registers 120 to 125 degrees (for medium-rare) or 130 to 135 degrees (for medium), 3 to 8 minutes longer.

4. Transfer lamb to carving board, tent loosely with aluminum foil, and let rest for 15 minutes. Cut between ribs to separate chops and serve.

GRILLED RACK OF LAMB WITH SWEET MUSTARD GLAZE

Omit rosemary and add 3 tablespoons Dijon mustard, 2 tablespoons honey, and ½ teaspoon grated lemon zest to oil, thyme, and garlic. Reserve 2 tablespoons glaze, then brush racks as directed in step 3 and brush with reserved glaze after meat rests.

Parmesan Breaded Lamb Chops

✔ WHY THIS RECIPE WORKS

An emblematic dish savored throughout Italy, Parmesan breaded lamb chops is an ideal choice for an elegant meal. The execution is relatively simple: Take some lamb chops, lightly coat them with Parmesan cheese and bread crumbs, and sauté the breaded chops to golden-brown perfection. But because lamb chops can be quite expensive, we wanted a foolproof recipe to avoid costly mistakes.

CHOOSE YOUR CHOPS We found it important to purchase the youngest and smallest loin or rib chops we could find, and to ensure that they were all of the same thickness; ¾ to 1 inch thick worked best. When we bought chops of different sizes, we ended up with some perfectly cooked chops and some that were either overcooked or undercooked.

REPLACE FLOUR WITH PARMESAN While these chops are prepared in the classic breading style (dredged in flour, dipped in egg, and finally coated with bread crumbs), we substituted Parmesan for the flour. Grating the cheese by hand produced the best texture.

DITCH THE STORE-BOUGHT CRUMBS Dried bread crumbs simply did not do justice to this delicate, elegant piece of meat; fresh bread crumbs were a must. Toasting the bread crumbs was unnecessary since they would be coming into direct contact with the hot pan when we sautéed the lamb chops; however, we found that the addition of some fresh rosemary and mint provided a welcome flavor boost.

LET THE CHOPS REST It was essential to let the chops rest after being breaded; this ensured that the crust adhered to the chops.

COOK QUICKLY Cooking the chops in a generous amount of oil over medium-high heat worked best, and getting the oil super-hot before we added the chops was also key: This meant the chops could achieve a golden-brown crust quickly, ensuring a perfectly rosy, medium-rare interior.

PARMESAN BREADED LAMB CHOPS
SERVES 4

Make sure the oil is good and hot before adding the chops. You want them to brown quickly because these thin chops will overcook if left in the pan too long.

2	slices hearty white sandwich bread
1	teaspoon minced fresh rosemary
2	teaspoons minced fresh mint
1	ounce Parmesan cheese, grated fine (½ cup)
2	large eggs
1	tablespoon plus ½ cup extra-virgin olive oil
12	(4-ounce) lamb rib or loin chops, ¾ to 1 inch thick, trimmed
½	teaspoon salt
¼	teaspoon pepper
	Lemon wedges

1. Pulse bread in food processor to coarse crumbs, about 10 pulses; place crumbs in shallow dish and combine with rosemary and mint. Place Parmesan in second shallow dish. Beat eggs and 1 tablespoon oil in third shallow dish. Sprinkle chops with salt and pepper.

2. Working with 1 chop at a time, dredge chops in Parmesan, patting them to make cheese adhere. Using tongs, dip both sides of chops in egg mixture, coating thoroughly and allowing excess to drip back into dish. Dip both sides of chops in bread-crumb mixture, pressing crumbs with your fingers to form even, cohesive coat. Place breaded chops in single layer on wire rack set in rimmed baking sheet and refrigerate for at least 30 minutes or up to 4 hours.

3. Adjust oven rack to lower-middle position, set large heatproof platter on rack, and heat oven to 200 degrees.

4. Heat ¼ cup oil in nonstick 12-inch skillet over medium-high heat until shimmering but not quite smoking. Add 6 chops (oil should go halfway up sides) and cook, turning once, until well browned on both sides and medium-rare in center (chops should register 120 to 125 degrees), about 5 minutes. Line heated platter with paper towels, transfer chops to platter, and return to oven.

5. Discard used oil. Wipe skillet clean using tongs and large wad of paper towels. Repeat with remaining ¼ cup oil and remaining 6 chops. Blot second batch of chops with paper towels. Remove platter from oven, remove paper towels, add just-cooked chops, and serve immediately with lemon wedges.

STORING PARMESAN CHEESE

After conducting a number of tests to find the best storage method for Parmesan wedges, we found that the best way to preserve its flavor and texture is to wrap it in parchment paper, then aluminum foil. However, if you're hanging on to just a small piece of cheese, tossing it in a zipper-lock bag works almost as well; just be sure to squeeze out as much air as possible before fastening the seal. Note these methods also work for Pecorino Romano.

Tandoori Lamb Chops

✔ WHY THIS RECIPE WORKS

To most people, tandoori conjures images of unnaturally red dyed meat from local Indian restaurants. What they often don't realize is that the red dye has taken the place of a fiery coating of red pepper and that tandoori is not really a dish at all, but a cooking method. A tandoor oven is a beehive-shaped structure that cooks both meats and breads at a very high temperature—in excess of 900 degrees—in a very short time. Meat is skewered on long metal stakes and the heat circulates freely around the roasting meat. We wanted to find a way to mimic the tandoor's searing heat and coal-roasted flavor at home, while infusing the meat (in this case, lamb chops, a popular tandoori meat) with a flavorful marinade and some serious spice.

USE A REALLY HOT OVEN While grilling or broiling seemed like the best bet for replicating the intense heat of a tandoor, both approaches resulted in dry, charred meat. Starting the lamb chops in a 500-degree oven before cranking up the broiler worked best. Chops cooked this way had a perfect, medium-rare interior with slightly charred edges and the crispy crust we wanted.

TAKE OUT YOUR BLENDER Most tandoori marinades use yogurt for its tang and also as a cool background for the pungent aromatics and spices. To the yogurt we added a generous amount of minced aromatics, but the pieces of garlic, ginger, and onion seemed to just float in the marinade without contributing much flavor. Pureeing all the marinade ingredients in a blender easily solved this problem. This simple step allowed for maximum flavor extraction from the aromatics, creating an intensely flavorful marinade.

ADD OIL Adding vegetable oil to the marinade served several functions. First, since spices are oil-soluble, the oil in the marinade allowed them to bloom when heated. Next, the oil enriched the yogurt. And finally, the oil helped the exterior of the meat to crisp and brown. A marinating time of at least 4 hours and up to 24 hours was ideal. (Going longer than 24 hours didn't increase the flavor any, but did turn the texture of the meat a bit mushy.)

SPICE IT UP Coriander, cumin, garam masala, cloves, nutmeg, cinnamon, and pepper contributed a warm fragrance, while some tomato paste and extra garlic added depth and rounded out the flavor of our marinade.

TANDOORI LAMB CHOPS
SERVES 4

Whole-milk, low-fat, and nonfat yogurt all work equally well here. Since the lamb chops cook so quickly, it is necessary to broil them for the last few minutes to achieve the traditional charred flavor and appearance. We think lamb chops taste best when cooked to medium-rare; to cook them to a medium doneness, roast the chops to 105 to 110 degrees in step 2 (the chops should register 135 to 140 degrees after broiling).

SPICE MIXTURE
1   tablespoon ground coriander
1   tablespoon ground cumin
1   tablespoon garam masala
½   teaspoon ground cloves
½   teaspoon ground nutmeg
½   teaspoon ground cinnamon
¼   teaspoon pepper

LAMB AND MARINADE
1   cup plain yogurt
¼   cup vegetable oil
1   onion, chopped coarse
10   garlic cloves, peeled
1   (2-inch) piece fresh ginger, peeled and chopped coarse
3   tablespoons tomato paste
2   teaspoons salt
8   (4-ounce) lamb rib or loin chops, ¾ to 1 inch thick, trimmed

1. Puree spices, yogurt, oil, onion, garlic, ginger, tomato paste, and salt in blender or food processor until smooth, about 30 seconds. Transfer ¼ cup marinade to small bowl and refrigerate. Combine remaining marinade with lamb in 1-gallon zipper-lock bag. Press out as much air as possible and seal the bag. Refrigerate for at least 4 hours or up to 24 hours, flipping occasionally to ensure that lamb marinates evenly.

2. Adjust 1 oven rack to middle position and second rack 4½ inches from broiler element and heat oven to 500 degrees. Line rimmed baking sheet with aluminum foil and set wire rack in sheet. Remove lamb chops from marinade and place on wire rack. Roast until thickest part of lamb chops registers 100 degrees, about 10 minutes.

3. Remove lamb from oven and turn oven to broil. Flip lamb chops over, spread reserved marinade evenly over top, and broil until spotty brown and chops register 120 to 125 degrees (for medium-rare) or 130 to 135 (for medium), about 5 minutes. Let rest for 5 minutes before serving.

Grilled Lamb Shoulder Chops

✓ WHY THIS RECIPE WORKS

When done right, lamb chops are juicy and tender, with just a touch of gamy richness. But preparing them well, especially when grilling, is easier said than done. The high heat of a hot fire can scorch the meat or generate flare-ups as rendered fat splatters on the coals beneath. We wanted a recipe that would get it right, every time.

CHOOSE A CHOP The first step to grilling great-tasting chops is choosing the right cut, and we tested all three styles—loin, rib, and shoulder. Inexpensive shoulder chops, with a gutsier flavor than the others (they actually taste like lamb) and a satisfyingly chewy texture, were our top choice. We also found them to be the most versatile of the bunch, holding up in both taste and texture when cooked to varying degrees of doneness.

THICKNESS MATTERS Thin chops went from rare to well-done in a flash. Chops between ¾ and 1 inch thick, on the other hand, provided a more generous margin. More time on the grill also meant better grilled flavor and a thicker crust.

BUILD A TWO-LEVEL FIRE Because shoulder chops contain a fair amount of fat, they are particularly prone to flare-ups on the grill. To avoid a charred exterior, we built a two-level fire to cook our chops: a pile of coals on one side of the grill and a single layer on the other. Starting the chops on the hotter side gave them a well-browned crust, and sliding them to the cooler side to finish cooking through reduced the risk of flare-ups.

GRILLED LAMB SHOULDER CHOPS
SERVES 4

See page 291 for information on lamb shoulder chops. Try to purchase lamb shoulder chops that are at least ¾ inch thick, since they are less likely to overcook. If you can only find chops that are ½ inch thick, reduce the cooking time on the cooler side of the grill by about 30 seconds on each side. If you prefer your lamb medium-well (140 to 145 degrees), it will take about 9 minutes total to finish cooking on the cooler side of the grill.

4 (8- to 12-ounce) lamb shoulder chops (blade or round bone), ¾ to 1 inch thick, trimmed

2 tablespoons extra-virgin olive oil
Salt and pepper

1A. FOR A CHARCOAL GRILL: Open bottom vent completely. Light large chimney starter filled with charcoal briquettes (6 quarts). When top coals are partially covered with ash, pour two-thirds evenly over half of grill, then pour remaining coals over other half of grill. Set cooking grate in place, cover, and open lid vent completely. Heat grill until hot, about 5 minutes.

1B. FOR A GAS GRILL: Turn all burners to high, cover, and heat grill until hot, about 15 minutes. Leave primary burner on high and turn other burner(s) to medium.

2. Clean and oil cooking grate. Rub chops with oil and season with salt and pepper. Place chops on hotter side of grill and cook (covered if using gas) until well browned, about 2 minutes per side. Slide chops to cooler side of grill and continue to cook until meat registers 120 to 125 degrees (for medium-rare) or 130 to 135 degrees (for medium), 2 to 4 minutes per side. Transfer chops to large platter, tent loosely with aluminum foil, and let rest for 5 minutes before serving.

GRILLED LAMB SHOULDER CHOPS WITH NEAR EAST RED PEPPER PASTE

SERVES 4

Spicy and sweet, this paste both encourages browning and lends an interesting flavor to the lamb chops.

3 tablespoons extra-virgin olive oil

½ red bell pepper, chopped coarse

½ serrano or jalapeño chile, chopped coarse

2 teaspoons lemon juice

1½ teaspoons chopped fresh mint

1 garlic clove, minced

½ teaspoon ground cumin

½ teaspoon dried summer savory

¼ teaspoon ground cinnamon

4 (8- to 12-ounce) lamb shoulder chops (blade or round bone), ¾ to 1 inch thick, trimmed
Salt and pepper

1. Heat 1 tablespoon oil in 8-inch skillet over medium-high heat until shimmering. Add bell pepper and serrano and cook, stirring frequently, until just beginning to soften, about 2 minutes. Reduce heat to medium-low and continue to cook until softened, about 5 minutes.

2. Transfer bell pepper mixture to food processor. Add lemon juice, mint, garlic, cumin, savory, cinnamon, and remaining 2 tablespoons oil and process until almost smooth (some chunky pieces of bell pepper will remain), about 20 seconds.

3. Rub chops with pepper paste. Transfer chops to 13 by 9-inch baking dish, cover with plastic wrap, and refrigerate for at least 20 minutes or up to 24 hours.

4A. FOR A CHARCOAL GRILL: Open bottom vent completely. Light large chimney starter filled with charcoal briquettes (6 quarts). When top coals are partially covered with ash, pour two-thirds evenly over half of grill, then pour remaining coals over other half of grill. Set cooking grate in place, cover, and open lid vent completely. Heat grill until hot, about 5 minutes.

4B. FOR A GAS GRILL: Turn all burners to high, cover, and heat grill until hot, about 15 minutes. Leave primary burner on high and turn other burner(s) to medium.

5. Clean and oil cooking grate. Season chops with salt and pepper. Place chops on hotter side of grill and cook (covered if using gas) until well browned, about 2 minutes per side. Slide chops to cooler side of grill and continue to cook until meat registers 120 to 125 degrees (for medium-rare) or 130 to 135 degrees (for medium), 2 to 4 minutes per side. Transfer chops to large platter, tent loosely with aluminum foil, and let rest for 5 minutes before serving.

GRILLED LAMB SHOULDER CHOPS
WITH GARLIC-ROSEMARY MARINADE

Combine 2 tablespoons extra-virgin olive oil, 1 tablespoon minced fresh rosemary, 2 minced large garlic cloves, and pinch cayenne pepper in small bowl and substitute for pepper paste.

GRILLED LAMB SHOULDER CHOPS
WITH SOY-SHALLOT MARINADE

Combine ¼ cup minced shallot or scallion, 3 tablespoons lemon juice, 2 tablespoons canola oil, 2 tablespoons minced fresh thyme, 2 tablespoons minced fresh parsley, and 2 tablespoons soy sauce in bowl; season with pepper to taste, and transfer to zipper-lock bag. Place chops in bag with marinade and toss to coat; press out as much air as possible and seal bag. Refrigerate chops for at least 20 minutes or up to 1 hour. Omit pepper paste in step 3 and salt and pepper in step 5.

Charcoal-Grilled Rib or Loin Lamb Chops

✓ WHY THIS RECIPE WORKS

Lamb and the grill have great chemistry. The intense heat of the coals produces a great crust and melts away the meat's abundance of fat, distributing flavor. While we love the bold flavor and pleasantly chewy texture of lamb shoulder chops, sometimes we want something a bit more refined. Chops from the rib and loin have a milder, sweeter flavor and a more tender texture than shoulder chops—but at $12 or more a pound, they aren't cheap. If we were going to splurge on these pricey, elegant chops, we wanted to make sure we had a foolproof technique for grilling them.

CHOOSE THICK CHOPS Chops 1¼ to 1½ inches thick were ideal; these chops were substantial and could spend enough time on the grill to develop plenty of smoky flavor.

BUILD A TWO-LEVEL FIRE A two-level fire was essential; it allowed us to sear the chops over the hotter portion and then move them to the cooler side to gently finish cooking through. This dual-heat fire also made sense because lamb tends to cause flare-ups due to its high fat content; we could simply move the chops to the cooler part of the grill to allow the flames to die down (though it's still a good idea to have a squirt bottle filled with water on hand).

DON'T COOK PAST MEDIUM Unlike shoulder chops, rib or loin chops are best cooked to medium-rare in order to retain their delicate flavor and tender texture; chops cooked past medium were dry and less flavorful and juicy.

CHARCOAL-GRILLED RIB OR
LOIN LAMB CHOPS
SERVES 4

While loin and rib chops are especially tender cuts of lamb, they tend to dry out if cooked past medium since they have less intramuscular fat than shoulder chops. To make these chops worth their high price tag, keep an eye on the grill to make sure the meat does not overcook. These chops are smaller than shoulder chops, so you will need two for each serving. *Their flavor is more delicate and refined, so season lightly with just salt and pepper, or perhaps herbs (as in the variation that follows). Aggressive spices don't make sense with these rarefied chops.*

> 8 (4-ounce) lamb rib or loin chops, 1¼ to 1½ inches thick, trimmed
> 2 tablespoons extra-virgin olive oil
> Salt and pepper

1A. FOR A CHARCOAL GRILL: Open bottom vent completely. Light large chimney starter filled with charcoal briquettes (6 quarts). When top coals are partially covered with ash, pour two-thirds evenly over half of grill, then pour remaining coals over other half of grill. Set cooking grate in place, cover, and open lid vent completely. Heat grill until hot, about 5 minutes.

1B. FOR A GAS GRILL: Turn all burners to high, cover, and heat grill until hot, about 15 minutes. Leave primary burner on high and turn other burner(s) to medium.

2. Clean and oil cooking grate. Rub chops with oil and season with salt and pepper. Place chops on hotter side of grill and cook (covered if using gas) until well browned, about 2 minutes per side. Slide chops to cooler side of grill and continue to cook until meat registers 120 to 125 degrees (for medium-rare) or 130 to 135 degrees (for medium), 2 to 4 minutes per side. Transfer chops to large platter, tent loosely with aluminum foil, and let rest for 5 minutes before serving.

GRILLED RIB OR LOIN LAMB CHOPS WITH MEDITERRANEAN HERB AND GARLIC PASTE

The delicate flavor of loin or rib lamb chops is enhanced—not overwhelmed—by this spirited Mediterranean-inspired paste.

Combine ¼ cup extra-virgin olive oil, 3 minced garlic cloves, 1 tablespoon chopped fresh parsley leaves, and 2 teaspoons each chopped fresh sage, thyme, rosemary, and oregano in small bowl. Rub chops with herb paste and refrigerate for at least 20 minutes or up to 24 hours. Omit oil, season chops with salt and pepper, and then grill as directed.

Braised Lamb Shoulder Chops

✓ WHY THIS RECIPE WORKS
When buying lamb, many people turn to the tried and true—and expensive—rib or loin chop. The oddly shaped, much less expensive shoulder chop rarely gets a second look, which is unfortunate because it is less exacting to cook and a few chops make for an easy weeknight supper. Their assertive flavor and somewhat chewy texture are particularly well suited to braising; we wanted a recipe for braised shoulder chops that would yield tender meat and a rich, flavorful sauce.

KEEP IT BRIEF Because shoulder chops aren't a tough cut of meat, we found that they don't need to cook for a long time to become tender. A relatively quick stovetop braise of just 15 to 20 minutes was all it took for these chops to cook.

MAKE IT BOLD The robust flavor of shoulder chops stands up well to an equally bold sauce. After sautéing some onion and garlic, we deglazed the pan with red wine. Tomatoes balanced out the acidity of the wine, and parsley added a hit of freshness.

BRAISED LAMB SHOULDER CHOPS WITH TOMATOES AND RED WINE

SERVES 4

Because they are generally leaner, round-bone chops, also called arm chops, are preferable for this braise. If available, however, lean blade chops also braise nicely. See page 291 for information on lamb shoulder chops.

4	(8- to 12-ounce) lamb shoulder chops (round bone or blade), about ¾ inch thick, trimmed
	Salt and pepper
2	tablespoons olive oil
1	small onion, chopped fine
2	small garlic cloves, minced
⅓	cup dry red wine
1	cup canned whole peeled tomatoes, chopped
2	tablespoons minced fresh parsley

1. Season chops with salt and pepper. Heat 1 tablespoon oil in 12-inch skillet over medium-high heat until shimmering. Brown chops, in batches if necessary, on both sides, 4 to 5 minutes. Set aside.

2. Pour off fat from skillet. Add remaining 1 tablespoon oil and heat over medium heat until shimmering. Add onion and cook until softened, about 4 minutes. Add garlic and cook until fragrant, about 30 seconds longer. Add wine and simmer until reduced by half, scraping up browned bits from bottom of pan, 2 to 3 minutes. Stir in tomatoes, then return chops to pan. Reduce heat to low and cover and simmer until chops are cooked through and tender, 15 to 20 minutes.

3. Transfer chops to individual plates. Stir parsley into sauce and simmer until sauce thickens, 2 to 3 minutes. Season with salt and pepper to taste, spoon sauce over each chop, and serve.

BRAISED LAMB SHOULDER CHOPS WITH CAPERS, BALSAMIC VINEGAR. AND RED PEPPER

Add 1 diced red bell pepper with onion and stir in 2 tablespoons rinsed capers and 2 tablespoons balsamic vinegar with parsley.

BRAISED LAMB SHOULDER CHOPS WITH FIGS AND NORTH AFRICAN SPICES

Soak ⅓ cup dried figs in ⅓ cup warm water for 30 minutes. Drain and reserve liquid and cut figs into quarters. Add 1 teaspoon ground coriander, ½ teaspoon ground cumin, ½ teaspoon cinnamon, and ⅛ teaspoon cayenne pepper with garlic. Omit red wine and replace with ⅓ cup soaking water from figs. Add 2 tablespoons honey with tomatoes. Stir figs in with parsley.

Braised Lamb Shanks

✓ WHY THIS RECIPE WORKS

One of the great pleasures of cooking is turning a relatively tough cut of meat into a meltingly tender one. Among the most richly flavored of these cuts is the lamb shank, and braising is the ideal cooking method for it; this long, slow, moist cooking method causes the connective tissue to disintegrate and renders the fat without drying out the meat. But lamb shanks have a high fat content, and all too often the result is a greasy sauce. We wanted to find a way to lose the fat without sacrificing flavor.

TRIM WELL Even a long, slow braise will not successfully render all the exterior fat on a lamb shank. If your butcher has not already done so, it is essential to take the time to carefully trim the lamb shanks of the excess fat that encases the meat.

CANNED WHOLE TOMATOES

San Marzano tomatoes are often praised as being the best canned tomatoes—bright, sweet, and tangy, with meat that's plush and soft but doesn't dissolve in long-simmered sauce—so we held a taste-off: San Marzanos versus everything else. We sampled 10 brands—three labeled San Marzano and the remaining seven a mix of Italian, Canadian, and American products—plain, in a quick-cooked tomato sauce, and in a slow-simmered version.

Overall, tasters liked tomatoes that had higher levels of sugar balanced by a lot of acidity. Surprisingly, the San Marzano tomatoes were either not sweet enough or too sweet and lacking the acidity necessary to counter the sweetness. When it came to texture, we liked tomatoes with a firm yet tender bite, even after a lengthy simmer. Tomatoes that were rubbery or broke down completely and became mushy scored poorly. Again, the San Marzano tomatoes fell behind, with domestic brands performing better and retaining a firmer texture due to being treated with calcium chloride; the imported brands did not use this additive.

In the end, our favorite brand was domestic. **Muir Glen Organic Whole Peeled Tomatoes** won tasters over with their bold acidity, appealing sweetness, and firm bite. These tomatoes were "sweet in a natural way," "vibrant," and had a "nice firm texture" that held up even after hours of simmering.

If you can't find herbes de Provence, you can make your own by combining 2 teaspoons dried marjoram, 2 teaspoons dried thyme, 1 teaspoon dried basil, 1 teaspoon dried rosemary (crumbled), 1 teaspoon dried sage, and ⅛ teaspoon ground fennel.

ON THE SIDE
RAS EL HANOUT

This North African seasoning blend contains a host of warm spices. The blend can be stored for up to 6 months before it loses its punch.

In spice grinder, grind the following to fine powder: 15 black peppercorns, 8 allspice berries, 8 cardamom pods, ½ inch cinnamon stick, 1 tablespoon ground ginger, 1 teaspoon coriander seeds, 1 teaspoon fennel seeds, 1 teaspoon ground nutmeg, ½ teaspoon anise seeds, ½ teaspoon cumin seeds, ⅛ teaspoon mace, and ⅛ teaspoon red pepper flakes. Transfer to small bowl. (Makes about ½ cup)

BROWN THE SHANKS We found that browning the shanks served two important functions: It helped render some of the exterior fat, and it also provided a great deal of flavor to the dish. (Be sure to drain the fat from the pan after browning.)

DEFAT THE LIQUID The final step to avoiding a greasy finished product was to defat the braising liquid after the shanks had cooked—either by skimming it from the surface using a ladle, or by refrigerating the braising liquid, then lifting off the solidified fat from the top.

USE PLENTY OF LIQUID A combination of wine and chicken broth provided a well-balanced braising liquid that complemented the flavor of the lamb. We found that using a generous amount of liquid—more than is called for in most braises—guaranteed that plenty would remain in the pot, resulting in moist, tender meat.

BRAISED LAMB SHANKS IN RED WINE WITH HERBES DE PROVENCE

SERVES 6

If you're using smaller shanks than the ones called for in this recipe, reduce the braising time by up to 30 minutes. Serve with Creamy Parmesan Polenta (page 339) or Classic Mashed Potatoes (page 99). Côtes du Rhône works particularly well here.

6	(12- to 16-ounce) lamb shanks, trimmed
	Salt and pepper
2	tablespoons vegetable oil
3	carrots, peeled and cut into 2-inch pieces
2	onions, sliced thick
2	celery ribs, cut into 2-inch pieces
2	tablespoons tomato paste
4	garlic cloves, minced
1	tablespoon herbes de Provence
2	cups dry red wine
3	cups chicken broth

1. Adjust oven rack to middle position and heat oven to 350 degrees. Pat lamb shanks dry and season with salt. Heat 1 tablespoon oil in

Dutch oven over medium-high heat until just smoking. Brown 3 shanks on all sides, 7 to 10 minutes. Transfer shanks to large plate and repeat with remaining 1 tablespoon oil and remaining 3 lamb shanks.

2. Drain all but 2 tablespoons fat from pot. Add carrots, onions, celery, tomato paste, garlic, herbes de Provence, and pinch of salt and cook until vegetables are just starting to soften, 3 to 4 minutes. Stir in wine, then broth, scraping up browned bits on bottom of pan, and bring to simmer. Nestle shanks, along with any accumulated juices, into pot.

3. Return to simmer, cover pot, transfer to oven, and cook for 1½ hours. Uncover and continue to cook until tops of shanks are browned, about 30 minutes. Flip shanks and continue to cook until remaining sides are browned and fork slips easily in and out of shanks, 15 to 30 minutes longer.

4. Remove pot from oven and let rest for 15 minutes. Using tongs, transfer shanks and vegetables to large plate and tent with aluminum foil. Skim fat from braising liquid and season with salt and pepper to taste. Return shanks to braising liquid to warm through before serving.

BRAISED LAMB SHANKS WITH LEMON AND MINT

Add 1 quartered lemon to braising liquid. Substitute 1 tablespoon minced fresh mint for herbes de Provence and substitute dry white wine for red wine. After skimming fat from braising liquid, stir in 1 tablespoon grated lemon zest and 1 tablespoon more minced fresh mint.

BRAISED LAMB SHANKS WITH NORTH AFRICAN SPICES

Serve with Simple Couscous (page 395) and one or more of the following: sautéed onion, lemon zest, parsley, mint, toasted almonds, and additional ras el hanout (at left).

Substitute 2 tablespoons ras el hanout for herbes de Provence. Add 2 minced ancho chile peppers (or 2 or 3 minced jalapeños) to onions, carrots, and celery.

Irish Stew

✔ WHY THIS RECIPE WORKS

At its most traditional, Irish stew is made with just lamb, onions, potatoes, and water. There's no browning or precooking; the raw ingredients are layered in the pot and cooked until tender. Nutritious and sustaining, perhaps, but satisfying and memorable? Only if you like bland food. We wanted a rich, deeply flavored stew as delicious as it was filling—the sort of dish for cold winter nights and snowbound days.

CHOOSE CHOPS Because it's a collagen-rich cut, we figured leg of lamb would be ideal for stew, but it lacked the subtly gamy flavor we expect of lamb. Shoulder chops, with their robust flavor, were a much better choice.

BROWNING AND BONES We knew that browning the chops would be important for flavor, but we were surprised to discover how essential the bones were for a complex, meaty broth. While unusual for stew, adding the bones provided an unparalleled richness and velvety texture. We found it worked best to cut the meat off the bones before browning and then add the bones to the pot after the liquid.

KEEP THE FLAVORS SIMPLE Onions are an important part of this stew, and thoroughly browning them resulted in a sweet, caramelized flavor base. Chicken broth muted the flavor of the lamb, so we stuck with water for the liquid component.

STARCHY STUFF While we typically prefer low-starch red potatoes in stews because they hold their shape well, broken-down potatoes serve as a thickener in Irish stew in conjunction with a bit of flour cooked with the onions. After trying batches of the stew with starchier russets and Yukon Golds, we favored the latter for their buttery, rich flavor as well as the soft, creamy texture they contributed to the stew.

IRISH STEW
SERVES 6

Try to buy the shoulder chops from the butcher. In most supermarkets, lamb shoulder chops are thin, often about ½ inch thick. At this thickness, the stew meat is too insubstantial. We like chops cut 1½ inches thick, but 1-inch chops will suffice.

4½	pounds lamb shoulder chops (blade or round bone), 1 to 1½ inches thick, trimmed
	Salt and pepper
3	tablespoons vegetable oil
3	large onions, chopped
¼	cup all-purpose flour
3	cups water
1	teaspoon dried thyme
2	pounds Yukon Gold potatoes, peeled and cut into 1-inch cubes
¼	cup minced fresh parsley

1. Adjust oven rack to lower-middle position and heat oven to 300 degrees. Cut meat from bones and reserve bones. Trim meat of excess fat and cut into 1½-inch cubes. Season meat generously with salt and pepper.

2. Heat 1 tablespoon oil in large Dutch oven over medium-high heat until shimmering, about 2 minutes. Add half of meat to pot so that individual pieces are close together but not touching. Cook, without moving, until sides touching pot are well browned, 2 to 3 minutes. Using tongs, turn each piece and continue cooking until most sides are well browned, about 5 minutes longer. Transfer meat to medium bowl, add 1 tablespoon oil to pot, and swirl to coat pan bottom. Brown remaining lamb; transfer meat to bowl and set aside.

3. Reduce heat to medium and add remaining 1 tablespoon oil to now-empty pot. Add onions and ¼ teaspoon salt and cook, stirring frequently, scraping bottom of pot with wooden spoon to loosen browned bits, until onions have browned, about 8 minutes. Add flour and stir until onions are evenly coated, 1 to 2 minutes.

4. Stir in 1½ cups water, scraping bottom and edges of pot with wooden spoon to loosen any browned bits. Gradually add remaining 1½ cups water, stirring constantly and scraping pot edges to dissolve flour. Add thyme and 1 teaspoon salt and bring to simmer. Add reserved bones and then meat and any accumulated juices. Return to simmer, cover, and place in oven. Cook for 1 hour.

5. Remove pot from oven and place potatoes on top of meat and bones. Cover and return pot to oven and cook until meat is tender, about 1 hour. If serving immediately, stir potatoes into liquid, wait 5 minutes, and spoon off any fat that rises to top. (Stew can be covered and refrigerated for up to 3 days. Spoon off congealed fat and bring back to simmer over medium-low heat.)

6. Stir in parsley and season with salt and pepper to taste. Remove bones if desired. Serve immediately.

Moussaka

✓ WHY THIS RECIPE WORKS

Moussaka, a rich casserole of roasted eggplant, tomato sauce enriched with meat (usually ground lamb), and creamy béchamel, is a cornerstone of Greek cuisine. It is similar to lasagna in that it is a layered casserole, with sheets of eggplant instead of noodles sandwiching the filling and sauce. The problem, we find, is that often the eggplant is loaded with oil and the filling and sauce are cloyingly rich yet disappointingly bland—nothing like the delicate, nuanced casserole that it should be. We wanted to make a version that was as close to authentic as we could get, and worth all of the effort.

ROAST THE EGGPLANT Frying the eggplant for our moussaka made for a greasy finished dish. Roasting improved matters greatly—the eggplant required a minimum amount of oil to brown, and it had a superior texture and flavor. The high heat of the oven effectively caramelized the eggplant, magnifying its sweetness and tempering its bitterness.

SHAPE MATTERS Cutting the eggplants into chunks—rather than slicing them into broad planks—was a bit unconventional, but proved to be a real timesaver. It allowed us to fit more eggplant on the baking sheets, which meant we could roast it all in one batch.

BROWN AND DRAIN THE LAMB Ground lamb is almost always fatty. We quickly realized that the meat needed to be browned and the excess fat drained off before we could add the filling's other ingredients.

FLAVOR THE FILLING A generous amount of onions and garlic provided sweetness and piquancy, lending the filling a solid base of flavor. Pureed canned tomatoes reduced to a thick, jammy consistency, and a little tomato paste and sugar complemented the tomatoes' fruity sweetness. Red wine contributed welcome acidity, oregano brought freshness, and a modest amount of cinnamon provided a warm, spicy note.

Ground cinnamon and dried oregano are key flavorings in the filling for moussaka, and we found that the flavor of the finished dish was greatly affected by the freshness of the cinnamon and oregano we used. We go through spices pretty quickly in the test kitchen, but that isn't always the case in home kitchens, where ground spices and dried herbs can linger in the cabinet for months, if not years. Rancid or stale spices impart a muddy, dull taste to foods, whereas fresh spices and dried herbs strengthen a dish's fragrant aroma and taste.

In most cases, purchasing whole spices and grinding them is preferable to buying ground spices, but since most home cooks opt for the convenience of ground spices and dried herbs, it's good to know how best to store them. When storing ground spices and dried herbs, the biggest mistake cooks make is keeping them close to the stove. Heat, moisture, air, and light quickly shorten the shelf life of spices, leaving them dull; keep spices in a cool, dark, dry place, in a well-sealed container.

EGGPLANT VARIETIES

Four of the most common varieties of eggplant found in the supermarket are large globe, small Italian, slender Chinese, and apple-shaped Thai. Can they all be used interchangeably in recipes? To find out, we prepared each type in five dishes calling for different cooking methods: roasted and pureed in baba ghanoush, sautéed in *pasta alla norma*, baked in eggplant Parmesan, stewed in Thai curry, and stir-fried with Asian sweet chili sauce. Only the generously sized globe eggplant was a true multi-tasker, suitable for all dishes and responding well to all cooking methods. The smaller varieties were prevented by their size from being good choices in eggplant Parmesan, and their excessive amount of seeds made for overly coarse baba ghanoush. The Thai eggplant, with its crisp, apple-like texture, was notable for tasting bright, grassy, and appealing simply eaten raw.

THICKEN THE BÉCHAMEL The béchamel needed to be quite thick in order to form a generous blanket over the top of the casserole and seal in the filling. Increasing the flour and adding a healthy dose of Parmesan (similar in flavor to *myzithra*, a Greek cheese used in classic recipes) did the trick.

MOUSSAKA

SERVES 6 TO 8

When buying eggplants, look for those that are glossy, feel firm, and are heavy for their size. Do not substitute low-fat or skim milk in the sauce.

- 4 pounds eggplant, peeled and cut into ¾-inch cubes
- 3 tablespoons olive oil
- Salt and pepper
- 2 pounds ground lamb
- 1 onion, chopped fine
- 4 garlic cloves, minced
- ¾ teaspoon ground cinnamon
- 2 tablespoons tomato paste
- 1 (28-ounce) can tomato puree
- ½ cup dry red wine
- 1 tablespoon minced fresh oregano or 1 teaspoon dried
- 1 teaspoon sugar
- 3 tablespoons unsalted butter
- ¼ cup all-purpose flour
- 2 cups whole milk
- 2 ounces Parmesan cheese, grated (1 cup)
- Pinch ground nutmeg

1. Adjust oven racks to lower-middle and upper-middle positions and heat oven to 450 degrees. Line 2 rimmed baking sheets with aluminum foil and spray with vegetable oil spray. Toss eggplant with oil, 1 teaspoon salt, and ¼ teaspoon pepper. Spread eggplant evenly over prepared sheets and bake until light golden brown, 40 to 50 minutes, switching and rotating sheets halfway though roasting time. Set aside to cool.

2. Meanwhile, cook lamb in large Dutch oven over medium-high heat, breaking meat into small pieces with wooden spoon, until meat is no longer pink and fat has rendered, about 5 minutes. Drain lamb in fine-mesh strainer, reserving drippings.

3. Return 2 tablespoons of reserved lamb drippings to now-empty pot and set it over medium heat until shimmering. Add onion and 1 teaspoon salt and cook until softened and lightly browned, 5 to 7 minutes. Stir in garlic and cinnamon and cook until fragrant, about 30 seconds. Stir in tomato paste and cook for 30 seconds. Stir in drained lamb, tomato puree, wine, oregano, and sugar. Bring to simmer, reduce heat to low, cover partially, and cook, stirring occasionally, until juices have evaporated and filling has thickened, 25 to 30 minutes. Season with salt and pepper to taste. Reduce oven to 400 degrees.

4. While lamb filling simmers, melt butter in medium saucepan over medium-high heat. Add flour and cook, stirring constantly, for 1 minute. Gradually whisk in milk. Bring to simmer and cook, whisking often, until béchamel thickens and no longer tastes of flour, about 5 minutes. Off heat, whisk in Parmesan and nutmeg and season with salt and pepper to taste; cover and set aside.

5. Spread roasted eggplant evenly into 13 by 9-inch baking dish. Spread lamb filling over eggplant, then pour béchamel evenly over top.

6. Bake until top of casserole is light golden brown, 25 to 35 minutes. Serve.

TO MAKE AHEAD: Wrap dish tightly with plastic wrap that has been sprayed with oil spray, then wrap with foil and refrigerate for up to 2 days or freeze for up 1 month. (If frozen, casserole must be thawed completely in refrigerator, about 24 hours, before baking.) Unwrap dish and cover tightly with foil that has been sprayed with oil spray. Bake until casserole is heated through, 20 to 40 minutes. Remove foil and continue to bake until top is light golden brown, 15 to 20 minutes longer.

Pastitsio

✓ WHY THIS RECIPE WORKS

Literally translated from the Greek as "made from pasta," pastitsio is a layered, baked casserole of pasta, creamy béchamel sauce, ground meat and tomato sauce, and cheese. It can be quite good—sustaining comfort food at its best—but that's rarely true for home-cooked versions. Most are a messy assemblage of soggy, bloated pasta, gluey béchamel, and overly seasoned, greasy meat sauce. We wanted to make a stellar version in which the components worked together in harmony.

GO FOR RICH, NOT GREASY While lamb's high fat content can make for a greasy sauce, browning the lamb and then draining off all the rendered fat made our sauce too lean. Reserving 2 tablespoons of fat to add back to the sauce provided just the right amount of richness.

BE SELECTIVE WITH YOUR SPICES While plenty of onion and garlic was a welcome addition, an abundance of spices was not. We liked a simple combination of oregano, cinnamon, and nutmeg, all of which served to complement the flavors of the lamb and tomato without overwhelming them.

TOMATO TIMES TWO Crushed tomatoes worked well in this dish, marrying with the other sauce ingredients, but weren't quite bold enough on their own; the addition of ¼ cup of tomato paste lent depth and sweetness. A little Pecorino Romano (a close substitute for the Greek cheese *kefalotyri*) further enriched the sauce, while sharpening the flavor of the lamb.

USE PLENTY OF BÉCHAMEL Adding an egg to our béchamel (milk thickened with a roux of flour and butter) helped it cling to the pasta, and using a generous 6 cups of béchamel ensured a casserole with a rich, creamy texture.

PICK A SMALL PASTA SHAPE We preferred small macaroni nestled into tight, compact layers so that each bite contained even amounts of all three casserole components.

PASTITSIO (PASTA AND GROUND LAMB CASSEROLE)

SERVES 6 TO 8

The baking dish is full when it goes into the oven, so bake it on an aluminum foil–lined rimmed baking sheet. Do not substitute low-fat or skim milk in the sauce.

2	pounds ground lamb
2	onions, chopped fine
	Salt and pepper
¼	cup tomato paste
9	garlic cloves, minced
I	tablespoon minced fresh oregano or I teaspoon dried
I	teaspoon ground cinnamon
½	teaspoon ground nutmeg
I	(28-ounce) can crushed tomatoes
3	ounces Pecorino Romano cheese, grated (1½ cups)
12	ounces (3 cups) elbow macaroni
4	tablespoons unsalted butter
⅓	cup all-purpose flour
6	cups whole milk
I	large egg

1. Adjust oven rack to middle position and heat oven to 400 degrees. Cook lamb in 12-inch skillet over medium-high heat, breaking meat into small pieces with wooden spoon, until no longer pink and fat has rendered, about 5 minutes. Drain lamb in fine-mesh strainer, reserving drippings.

2. Return 2 tablespoons reserved lamb drippings to now-empty skillet, add half of chopped onions and ½ teaspoon salt, and cook over medium heat until softened, 5 to 7 minutes. Stir in tomato paste, 2 tablespoons garlic, oregano, cinnamon, and ¼ teaspoon nutmeg and cook until fragrant, about 30 seconds. Stir in drained lamb and crushed tomatoes. Bring to simmer and cook over medium-low heat until sauce has thickened, about 5 minutes. Off

Whisking constantly, trickle the hot béchamel mixture into the beaten egg with a ladle.

heat, stir in ½ cup Pecorino and season with salt and pepper to taste; set aside.

3. Meanwhile, bring 4 quarts water to boil in Dutch oven. Add macaroni and 1 tablespoon salt and cook, stirring often, until almost al dente, about 5 minutes. Drain pasta, rinse under cool water until cold, and leave in colander.

4. Wipe out Dutch oven, add butter, and return to medium heat until melted. Add remaining onion and ½ teaspoon salt and cook until softened, 5 to 7 minutes. Stir in remaining garlic and cook until fragrant, about 30 seconds. Stir in flour and cook, stirring constantly, 1 minute. Gradually whisk in milk. Bring to simmer and cook, whisking often, until sauce thickens and no longer tastes of flour, about 10 minutes.

5. Off heat, whisk in ½ cup Pecorino and remaining ¼ teaspoon nutmeg. Season with salt and pepper to taste. Crack egg into small bowl. Whisk ½ cup béchamel into egg to temper, then slowly whisk egg mixture back into sauce. Stir in macaroni until evenly coated with sauce.

6. Spread half of macaroni into 13 by 9-inch baking dish, then spread lamb mixture evenly over top. Spread remaining macaroni evenly over lamb and sprinkle with remaining ½ cup Pecorino.

7. Place baking dish on aluminum foil–lined rimmed baking sheet and bake until edges are bubbling and top is lightly golden, about 30 minutes. Let stand about 10 minutes before serving.

TO MAKE AHEAD: After step 6, casserole can be wrapped in plastic and refrigerated for up to 2 days. To reheat, remove plastic, cover dish with foil, and bake for 30 to 40 minutes, then uncover and continue to bake for 15 to 20 minutes.

Greek-Style Lamb Pita Sandwiches

✔ WHY THIS RECIPE WORKS

What's not to love about gyros, sandwiches of seasoned, marinated lamb, tomato, lettuce, and cucumber-yogurt tzatziki sauce stuffed inside a soft pita? The traditional method for cooking the meat employs an electric vertical rotisserie, on which layers of sliced and marinated leg of lamb are stacked. After cooking for hours, the meat is shaved with a long slicing knife, revealing pieces with crisp exteriors and moist interiors infused with garlic and oregano. We wanted to translate this recipe for the home kitchen.

USE GROUND LAMB Surprising though it seems, using ground lamb—which we formed into patties and pan-fried—was easy and came close to reproducing the texture of rotisserie lamb.

ADD SOME PITA Flavoring the patties with traditional marinade ingredients—oregano, finely chopped onion, and minced garlic—was a given, but the texture of the patties was dense and dry. Adding a modified panade of pita bread crumbs, lemon juice, and garlic gave our patties a sturdier structure and fuller, more savory flavor.

COOK ON THE STOVETOP To achieve the meat's traditional duality of texture—crisp outside, moist inside—we cooked the patties in a large oiled skillet over medium-high heat.

DON'T FORGET THE TZATZIKI

The cooling combination of yogurt, garlic, cucumber, mint or dill, and lemon juice is more than just a condiment; it's a necessity. Plain full-fat yogurt, drained for 30 minutes to achieve a thick texture, worked great and salting the cucumber reduced excess moisture.

GREEK-STYLE LAMB PITA SANDWICHES

SERVES 4

Since the yogurt and cucumbers in the Tzatziki Sauce (recipe follows) need to drain for 30 minutes, start making the sauce before the patties. For the patties, we prefer the flavor of fresh oregano, but 1 teaspoon of dried can be substituted. The skillet may appear crowded when you begin cooking the patties, but they will shrink slightly as they cook. If using pocketless pitas, heat them in a single layer on a baking sheet in a 350-degree oven for 5 minutes. When cooking the patties, use a splatter screen to keep the mess to a minimum.

LAMB PATTIES

- 4 (8-inch) pita breads
- ½ onion, chopped coarse
- 1 tablespoon minced fresh oregano
- 4 teaspoons lemon juice
- 2 garlic cloves, minced
- ½ teaspoon salt
- ¼ teaspoon pepper
- 1 pound ground lamb
- 2 teaspoons vegetable oil

ACCOMPANIMENTS

- 1 recipe Tzatziki Sauce (recipe follows)
- 1 large tomato, cored and sliced thin
- 2 cups shredded iceberg lettuce
- 2 ounces feta cheese, crumbled (½ cup)

1. FOR THE LAMB PATTIES: Adjust oven rack to middle position and heat oven to 350 degrees. Cut top quarter off each pita bread. Tear quarters into 1-inch pieces. (You should have ¾ cup pita pieces.) Stack pitas and tightly wrap with aluminum foil. Process pita bread pieces, onion, oregano, lemon juice, garlic, salt, and pepper in food processor until smooth paste forms, about 30 seconds. Transfer bread mixture to large bowl; add lamb and gently mix with your hands until thoroughly combined. Divide mixture into 12 equal pieces and roll into balls. Gently flatten balls into round disks about ½ inch thick and 2½ inches in diameter. (Patties can be refrigerated for up to 1 day or frozen before cooking as directed in step 2. Frozen patties should be thawed in refrigerator prior to cooking.)

2. Place foil-wrapped pitas directly on oven rack and heat for 10 minutes. Meanwhile, heat oil in 12-inch nonstick skillet over medium-high heat until just smoking. Add patties and cook until well browned and crust forms, 3 to 4 minutes. Flip patties, reduce heat to medium, and cook until well browned and crust forms on second side, about 5 minutes longer. Transfer patties to paper towel–lined plate.

3. Using soupspoon, spread ¼ cup Tzatziki Sauce inside each pita. Divide patties evenly among pitas; fill each sandwich with tomato slices, ½ cup shredded lettuce, and 2 tablespoons feta. Serve immediately.

GREEK-STYLE BEEF PITA SANDWICHES

Decrease lemon juice to 1 tablespoon, increase oregano to 2 tablespoons, increase garlic to 3 cloves, and increase oil to 1 tablespoon. Substitute 1 pound 80 percent lean ground chuck for lamb.

GRILLED GREEK-STYLE LAMB PITA SANDWICHES

The grill imparts a smoky flavor to the meat and pitas in this variation.

1A. FOR A CHARCOAL GRILL: Open bottom vent completely. Light large chimney starter three-quarters filled with charcoal (4½ quarts). When top coals are partially covered with ash, pour evenly over half of grill. Set cooking grate in place, cover, and open vent completely. Heat grill until hot, about 5 minutes.

IB. FOR A GAS GRILL: Turn all burners to high, cover, and heat grill until hot, about 15 minutes. Leave primary burner on high and turn other burner(s) to medium-high.

2. Clean and oil cooking grate. Place patties on hotter side of grill, cover (if using gas), and cook, turning once, until well browned and crust forms on each side, 8 to 12 minutes. Transfer patties to plate. Place pitas in single layer on hotter side of grill. Cook, turning once, until each pita is thoroughly warmed and faint grill marks appear, 30 to 40 seconds. Remove pitas from grill and wrap tightly with aluminum foil until ready to assemble sandwiches.

TZATZIKI SAUCE
MAKES ABOUT ⅔ CUP

Although we prefer the richness of plain whole-milk yogurt, low-fat yogurt can be substituted. Greek yogurt can also be substituted, but use ½ cup and skip the step of draining. While we didn't like the flavor of dried mint, ½ teaspoon dried dill may be used in place of fresh dill.

1	cup plain whole-milk yogurt
½	cucumber, peeled, halved lengthwise, seeded, and chopped fine
1	tablespoon lemon juice
⅜	teaspoon salt
1	tablespoon finely chopped fresh mint or dill
1	small garlic clove, minced

1. Line fine-mesh strainer set over deep container or bowl with coffee filter. Spoon yogurt into lined strainer, cover, and refrigerate for 1 hour.

2. Meanwhile, combine cucumber, lemon juice, and ⅛ teaspoon salt in colander set over bowl and let stand 30 minutes.

3. Discard drained liquid from yogurt. Combine thickened yogurt, drained cucumber, remaining ¼ teaspoon salt, mint, and garlic in clean, dry bowl.

WHOLE-MILK YOGURT

For recipes like our Tzatziki Sauce, we prefer to use plain whole-milk yogurt, which can have about three times more fat than low-fat versions—and far more flavor. Our favorite brand of plain whole-milk yogurt is **Brown Cow Cream Top Plain Yogurt**.

Grilled Lamb Kofte

✔ WHY THIS RECIPE WORKS
In the Middle East, kebabs called kofte *feature ground meat, not chunks, mixed with lots of spices and fresh herbs. These ground lamb patties are typically grilled over high heat on long metal skewers, making them tender and juicy on the inside and encasing them in a smoky, crunchy coating of char. We wanted to get their sausage-like texture just right.*

BUY GROUND LAMB While kofte is traditionally made by mincing the meat by hand with a cleaver, we wanted to make our recipe as streamlined as possible, so we decided to use ground lamb from the grocery.

USE A LITTLE GELATIN We typically use a panade made from soaked bread or bread crumbs to keep ground meat patties moist when cooked through, since their starches help hold on to moisture released by the meat as it cooks. But a panade gave our kofte an unwelcome pastiness. Instead, we found that a small amount of gelatin helped the meat firm up and hold fast to the skewer, resulting in tender, juicy kofte.

ADD SOME PINE NUTS Kneading the kofte was necessary to help keep them together on the grill, but it also made the patties overly springy and less tender once cooked. Adding ground pine nuts to the mixture solved the problem, preventing toughness and adding their own pleasant texture and a noticeable boost in richness.

SPICE IT UP Hot smoked paprika, cumin, coriander, cloves, cinnamon, and nutmeg contributed warm spice notes, while parsley and mint offered bright, grassy flavors. Adding a little tahini to the sauce—traditionally a mixture of crushed garlic, lemon juice, and yogurt—gave it more complexity.

HACK A KOFTE GRILL To mimic the concentrated heat of a traditional kofte grill, we pile charcoal into a disposable aluminum roasting pan and set it on the kettle.

GRILLED LAMB KOFTE

SERVES 4 TO 6

Serve with rice pilaf or make sandwiches with warm pita bread, sliced red onion, and chopped fresh mint. You will need eight 12-inch metal skewers for this recipe. Grate the onion on the large holes of a box grater.

YOGURT-GARLIC SAUCE

1	cup plain whole-milk yogurt
2	tablespoons lemon juice
2	tablespoons tahini
1	garlic clove, minced
½	teaspoon salt

KOFTE

½	cup pine nuts
4	garlic cloves, peeled
1½	teaspoons hot smoked paprika
1	teaspoon salt
1	teaspoon ground cumin
½	teaspoon pepper
¼	teaspoon ground coriander
¼	teaspoon ground cloves
⅛	teaspoon ground nutmeg
⅛	teaspoon ground cinnamon
1½	pounds ground lamb
½	cup grated onion, drained
⅓	cup minced fresh parsley
⅓	cup minced fresh mint
1½	teaspoons unflavored gelatin
1	disposable aluminum roasting pan (if using charcoal)

1. FOR THE YOGURT-GARLIC SAUCE: Whisk all ingredients together in bowl. Set aside.

2. FOR THE KOFTE: Process pine nuts, garlic, paprika, salt, cumin, pepper, coriander, cloves, nutmeg, and cinnamon in food processor until coarse paste forms, 30 to 45 seconds. Transfer mixture to large bowl. Add lamb, onion, parsley, mint, and gelatin; knead with your hands until thoroughly combined and mixture feels slightly sticky, about 2 minutes. Divide mixture into 8 equal portions. Shape each portion into 5-inch-long cylinder about 1 inch in diameter. Using 8 (12-inch) metal skewers, thread 1 cylinder onto each skewer, pressing gently to adhere. Transfer skewers to lightly greased baking sheet, cover with plastic wrap, and refrigerate for at least 1 hour or up to 24 hours.

3A. FOR A CHARCOAL GRILL: Using skewer, poke 12 holes in bottom of disposable pan. Open bottom vent completely and place disposable pan in center of grill. Light large chimney starter two-thirds filled with charcoal briquettes (4 quarts). When top coals are partially covered with ash, pour into disposable pan. Set cooking grate in place, cover, and open lid vent completely. Heat grill until hot, about 5 minutes.

3B. FOR A GAS GRILL: Turn all burners to high, cover, and heat grill until hot, about 15 minutes. Leave all burners on high.

4. Clean and oil cooking grate. Place skewers on grill (directly over coals if using charcoal) at 45-degree angle to grate. Cook (covered if using gas) until browned and meat easily releases from grill, 4 to 7 minutes. Flip skewers and continue to cook until browned on second side and meat registers 160 degrees, about 6 minutes longer. Transfer skewers to platter and serve, passing yogurt-garlic sauce separately.

Breaded Veal Cutlets

✔ WHY THIS RECIPE WORKS

Veal cutlets pan-fried with a cloak of mild-flavored crumbs have universal appeal. Almost every cuisine has such a dish. In Italy, grated Parmesan is added to the coating, and the dish is called veal Milanese; in Austria, the cutlets are often cooked in butter and the dish is called Wiener schnitzel. Though simple, this dish can fall prey to a host of problems. The veal itself may be rubbery and tasteless, and the coating (called a bound breading and arguably the best part of the dish) often ends up uneven, greasy, pale, or even burnt. We wanted a breading that was mild and comforting but not dull and certainly not greasy.

FRESH CRUMBS ARE BEST Dry bread crumbs had an unmistakably stale flavor. Fresh bread crumbs—made from fresh sliced white sandwich bread ground fine in the food processor—were the undisputed favorite, with a mild, subtly sweet flavor and a light, crisp texture.

DRY THE CUTLETS THOROUGHLY If the cutlets were even slightly moist, the breading peeled off the finished cutlets in sheets. Drying the cutlets well and coating them with flour before adding the egg wash and crumbs ensured the breading stayed put.

PRESS AND REST Pressing the crumbs onto the cutlets ensured an even, thorough cover, and letting the breaded cutlets rest for about 5 minutes before frying them also helped bind the breading to the meat.

ADD A LITTLE OIL Beaten eggs are thick and viscous, and have a tendency to form too heavy a layer on the meat, giving the breading a thick, indelicate quality. Thinning the egg with a little oil solved this problem; as a bonus, the addition of oil helped the breading brown a little more deeply.

BREADED VEAL CUTLETS
SERVES 4

Six cutlets is a realistic number to serve four people. (Allow one cutlet per person, then halve the remaining two cutlets after cooking to yield four smaller additional servings.) Panko can be substituted for the fresh bread crumbs. The veal is cooked in two batches because the crust is noticeably crisper if the pan is not overcrowded.

½ cup all-purpose flour
2 large eggs
1 tablespoon plus 1 cup vegetable oil
2 cups fresh bread crumbs (page 336)
6 (4-ounce) veal cutlets, about ½ inch thick
   Salt and pepper
   Lemon wedges

1. Adjust oven rack to lower-middle position, set large ovensafe plate on rack, and heat oven to 200 degrees. Set wire rack in rimmed baking sheet. Spread flour in shallow dish. Beat eggs with 1 tablespoon oil in second shallow dish. Spread bread crumbs in third shallow dish.

2. Cover cutlets with plastic wrap and pound to even ¼-inch thickness with meat pounder. Pat cutlets dry and season with salt and pepper.

3. Working with 1 cutlet at a time, dredge in flour, shaking off excess, then coat with egg mixture, allowing excess to drip off. Coat all sides with bread crumbs, pressing gently so crumbs adhere. Place breaded cutlets in single layer on prepared rack and let coating dry for 5 minutes.

4. Meanwhile, heat ½ cup oil in nonstick 12-inch skillet over medium-high heat until shimmering but not smoking. Lay 3 cutlets

BUYING VEAL CUTLETS

Veal cutlets should be cut from the top round. Most supermarkets use the leg or sirloin and do not butcher the meat properly, cutting it with the grain, not across the grain, as is best. When shopping, look for cutlets in which no linear striation is evident. The linear striation in the top cutlet is an indication that the veal has been cut with the grain and will be tough. Instead, the cutlet should have a smooth surface, like the cutlet on the bottom, in which no lines are evident. If your market doesn't offer cutlets that look this, consider cutting your own cutlets from a piece of top round, following the illustrations below.

CUTTING VEAL CUTLETS

1. With boning knife, remove silverskin from piece of veal top round roast.

2. Once silverskin has been removed, use long slicing knife to cut slices on bias and against grain that are between ¼ and ½ inch thick.

in skillet. Fry until deep golden brown and crisp on first side, about 2½ minutes. Using tongs, flip cutlets, reduce heat to medium, and continue to cook until second side is deep golden brown, again checking browning partway through, about 2½ minutes longer. Line warmed plate with double layer of paper towels and set cutlets on top; return plate to oven. Discard oil in skillet and wipe skillet clean using tongs and a large wad of paper towels.

5. Repeat step 4 using remaining ½ cup oil and clean skillet to cook remaining 3 cutlets. Serve immediately with lemon wedges.

VEAL MILANESE

Replace some of the bread crumbs with grated Parmesan cheese and you have veal Milanese.

Reduce bread crumbs to 1½ cups and mix ½ cup grated Parmesan cheese with crumbs.

Veal Scaloppini

✓ WHY THIS RECIPE WORKS

Thinly sliced veal cutlets are remarkably easy to prepare: Gently pound the cutlets, sauté them quickly, and serve with a basic pan sauce. With its tender meat and delicate flavor, veal should be a natural choice for this preparation. But veal at the supermarket is typically from the shoulder or the leg, the two toughest parts of the calf, and quite unlike the veal scaloppini from the rib or loin served by top chefs. We wanted to re-create restaurant-quality veal scaloppini using supermarket-quality cutlets, which meant we'd need to find a way to transform them from tough to tender.

USE A MEAT TENDERIZER We quickly eliminated the idea of slicing our own cutlets from a loin roast or rib chop; it was just too much work for what we wanted to be a simple recipe. For incredibly tender chops, we found our solution in a surprise, old-fashioned ingredient: meat tenderizer. Just a sprinkling of this (decidedly unglamorous) product turned reasonably priced supermarket cutlets into cutlets every bit as tender as those found in restaurants.

FLOUR ONLY ONE SIDE Dredging the seasoned cutlets in flour helped to develop a well-browned crust, but browning both sides led to overcooked meat. Browning just one side solved the problem, but then the other, quickly cooked side was pasty. Flouring just the side of the cutlet that would be browned gave us everything we wanted: a rich, golden-brown exterior with no trace of gumminess.

MAKE THE PAN SAUCE FIRST To ensure streamline our recipe even further, we reversed the usual process and made the pan sauce in a separate saucepan before cooking the veal. Once the last batch was done, we poured the almost-finished sauce into the skillet and scraped the pan to incorporate the fond into our sauce.

VEAL SCALOPPINI
SERVES 4

Cook the veal in batches to avoid overcrowding the skillet; because the size of packaged cutlets varies, each batch may contain as few as three cutlets or as many as six. Start preparing the sauce before cooking the cutlets, then finish in the skillet used to brown the cutlets. Because meat tenderizer contains sodium, it is unnecessary to salt the cutlets.

1½	pounds veal cutlets, about ¼ inch thick
¾	teaspoon meat tenderizer
⅛	teaspoon pepper
½	cup all-purpose flour
3	tablespoons vegetable oil
1	recipe sauce (recipes follow)

1. If cutlets are thicker than ¼ inch, place plastic wrap over cutlets and pound to even ¼-inch thickness with skillet or meat pounder. If some cutlets are thinner than ¼ inch, pound to even ⅛-inch thickness, then fold in half. Pat cutlets dry with paper towels. Sprinkle tenderizer and pepper evenly over both sides of cutlets.

2. Place flour in rimmed baking sheet and spread to thin, even layer. Heat 1 tablespoon oil in 12-inch nonstick skillet over high heat until just smoking. Dredge first batch of cutlets in flour on 1 side only, shake off excess, and place in skillet, floured side down, making sure cutlets do not overlap. Cook, without moving cutlets, until well browned, 1 to 1½ minutes. Flip with tongs and cook until second sides are no longer pink and cutlets feel firm when pressed, about 30 seconds. Transfer cutlets to platter and tent loosely with aluminum foil. Repeat with remaining 2 tablespoons oil and remaining cutlets, in 2 batches. (If skillet becomes too dark after cooking second batch, rinse before continuing.) Return pan to medium heat, finish pan sauce, pour over cutlets, and serve.

LEMON-PARSLEY SAUCE
MAKES ABOUT ¾ CUP

---

 2 teaspoons vegetable oil
 2 shallots, minced
 1½ cups chicken broth
 2 tablespoons minced fresh parsley
 2 tablespoons unsalted butter, cut into
    4 pieces and chilled
    Salt and pepper
 1–2 tablespoons lemon juice

1. Heat oil in medium saucepan over medium-high heat until shimmering. Add shallots and cook until beginning to soften, about 1 minute. Add broth and increase heat to high; simmer rapidly until liquid is reduced to ¾ cup, about 8 minutes. Set aside.

2. After transferring last batch of cutlets to platter, pour sauce into now-empty skillet and bring to simmer over medium heat, scraping bottom of skillet with wooden spoon to loosen any browned bits. Off heat, whisk in parsley and butter and season with salt, pepper, and lemon juice to taste. Pour sauce over cutlets and serve.

PORCINI-MARSALA PAN SAUCE
MAKES ABOUT 1 CUP

 ⅓ ounce dried porcini mushrooms, rinsed
 2 teaspoons vegetable oil
 2 shallots, minced
 1 cup dry Marsala
 1½ cups chicken broth
 2 tablespoons unsalted butter, cut into
    4 pieces and chilled
 1 tablespoon minced fresh chives
    Salt and pepper

1. Microwave ½ cup water and porcini mushrooms in covered bowl until steaming, about 1 minute. Let sit until softened, about 5 minutes. Drain mushrooms in fine-mesh strainer lined with coffee filter, reserve liquid, and chop mushrooms into ¼-inch pieces. Set mushrooms and liquid aside.

2. Heat oil in medium saucepan over medium-high heat until shimmering. Add shallots and cook until beginning to soften, about 1 minute. Off heat, add Marsala. Return pan to high heat and simmer rapidly until liquid is reduced to ½ cup, about 4 minutes. Add mushrooms and strained soaking liquid and simmer until liquid in pan is again reduced to ½ cup, about 4 minutes. Add broth and simmer until liquid is reduced to 1 cup, about 8 minutes. Set aside.

3. After transferring last batch of cutlets to platter, pour sauce into now-empty skillet and bring to simmer over medium heat, scraping bottom of skillet with wooden spoon to loosen any browned bits. Off heat, whisk in butter

and chives and season with salt and pepper to taste. Pour sauce over cutlets and serve.

TARRAGON-SHERRY CREAM SAUCE
MAKES ¾ CUP

2	teaspoons vegetable oil
2	shallots, minced
¾	cup dry sherry
½	cup chicken broth
¾	cup heavy cream
2	tablespoons minced fresh tarragon
½	teaspoon lemon juice
	Salt and pepper

I. Heat oil in 10-inch skillet over medium-high heat until shimmering. Add shallots and cook until beginning to soften, about 1 minute. Add sherry and increase heat to high; simmer rapidly until liquid is reduced to ½ cup, about 2 minutes. Add broth and simmer until liquid is again reduced to ½ cup, about 4 minutes. Add cream and set aside.

2. After transferring last batch of cutlets to platter, pour sauce into now-empty skillet and bring to simmer over medium heat, scraping bottom of pan with wooden spoon to loosen any browned bits. Pour sauce through fine-mesh strainer into bowl, pressing on any solids in strainer with spatula to extract liquid. Wipe pan clean with paper towels; add strained sauce and set pan over medium-high heat. Simmer until sauce is reduced to ¾ cup, about 5 minutes. Stir in tarragon and lemon juice and season with salt and pepper to taste. Pour sauce over cutlets and serve.

Sautéed Veal Cutlets with Prosciutto and Sage

✔ **WHY THIS RECIPE WORKS**

Its name literally meaning "jump in the mouth," saltimbocca is a variation on a basic veal scaloppini. Thinly sliced pieces of prosciutto and leaves of sage are pressed into veal cutlets and secured with a toothpick before the cutlets are quickly sautéed and served with a light pan sauce. The combination of these three flavors is so good that the cutlets jump into your mouth. Though simple, this dish is not without its pitfalls—the thin cutlets are prone to overcooking before they have a chance develop a browned crust, and the cutlets have a tendency to turn tough and buckle as they cook. We aimed to solve these problems.

PREPARE YOUR OWN CUTLETS Proper veal scaloppini should be cut from the top round, the upper portion of the leg, which is lean and has no muscle separation. Cutting our own was easy enough, and pounding the cutlets further ensured a delicate texture and uniform thinness.

FLOUR THE CUTLETS Because these thin cutlets cook so quickly, we had trouble getting a good crust without overcooking them. Flouring the cutlets helped the exterior brown and crisp, and the flour (along with the prosciutto) acted as a barrier that helped protect the delicate meat as it cooked.

HANDLE THE PROSCIUTTO AND SAGE GENTLY While many recipes call for pounding the prosciutto and sage into the cutlets, we found this didn't work very well; the pounding tore the thin prosciutto and fragile sage to shaggy pieces. Instead, we simply pressed

the tacky prosciutto into the already pounded cutlet with our hands. We then placed a sage leaf on top of the prosciutto and secured the trio with a toothpick.

FINISH WITH THE SAUCE Since thin cutlets cool off fast, we found it best to hold the cooked cutlets in a warm oven while preparing the sauce. With the fond left in the skillet as our base, we made a straightforward pan sauce using shallot, lemon juice, parsley, butter, and broth. A little white wine helped to round out the other flavors.

SAUTÉED VEAL CUTLETS WITH PROSCIUTTO AND SAGE (SALTIMBOCCA ALLA ROMANA)

SERVES 4

Be sure to use large cutlets that will each serve one person (about 6 ounces each). If the cutlets are on the small side, consider serving two cutlets per person; you will need to cook them in additional batches with extra oil in step 1.

- 4 (6-ounce) veal cutlets, about ½ inch thick
- 4 thin slices prosciutto (about 3 ounces)
- 4 large fresh sage leaves
  Salt and pepper
- ⅓ cup all-purpose flour
- 3 tablespoons extra-virgin olive oil
- 1 large shallot, minced
- ¾ cup chicken broth
- ½ cup dry white wine
- 3 tablespoons unsalted butter, cut into 2 pieces
- 1 tablespoon minced fresh parsley
- 1 teaspoon lemon juice

1. Adjust oven rack to middle position and heat oven to 200 degrees.

2. Cover cutlets with plastic wrap and pound to even ¼-inch thickness with meat pounder. Pat cutlets dry.

3. Place 1 slice prosciutto on top of each cutlet and lay 1 sage leaf in center, pressing them into veal. Use toothpick, set at diagonal, to secure prosciutto and sage to cutlet. Season cutlets with salt and pepper. Place flour in shallow dish. Working with 1 cutlet at a time, dredge in flour, shaking off excess,

4. Heat 1 tablespoon oil in 12-inch skillet over medium-high heat until just shimmering but not smoking. Lay 2 cutlets, prosciutto side down, in skillet, making sure they do not overlap, and cook without moving until lightly browned, about 1 minute. Flip cutlets over and continue to cook until meat feels firm when pressed, 30 to 60 seconds. Transfer cutlets to ovenproof plate, cover with aluminum foil, and transfer to warm oven. Repeat with 1 tablespoon oil and remaining 2 cutlets; transfer to plate in oven.

5. Add remaining 1 tablespoon oil and shallot to now-empty skillet, return to medium heat, and cook until softened, about 2 minutes. Stir in broth and wine and cook, scraping up browned bits, until slightly thickened, about 8 minutes. Reduce heat to low, stir in any accumulated juices from cutlets, then whisk in butter, 1 piece at a time. Off heat, stir in parsley and lemon juice and season with salt and pepper to taste. Arrange cutlets, prosciutto side up, on large platter or individual plates and pour sauce over cutlets. Serve.

Pan-Seared Veal Chops

✔ WHY THIS RECIPE WORKS

Tossing pricey veal chops into a smoking-hot pan takes a bit of courage on the part of the cook. Without precise timing and a properly heated pan, a lot can go wrong in a hurry. But a perfectly pan-seared veal chop, with a thick, brown crust yielding to a juicy, tender interior, is well worth the careful stove-side attention it requires.

CHOOSE THE RIGHT CHOP Loin chops tasted good, but tended to cook unevenly; rib chops were a better option, possessing full flavor and tender meat. Cooked to medium, these chops remained juicy, with a tender texture and just a faint trace of pink at the center.

THICKNESS MATTERS Lean veal can quickly cross the line between undercooked and overcooked, so determining the ideal size and thickness of the chops was key. A weight of 8 to 12 ounces and a thickness of 1 to 1½ inches were ideal; chops in this size range could be nicely seared and then cooked to the proper doneness by adjusting the cooking time in the pan.

LOOK FOR A LITTLE SMOKE The best indication of a pan ready to sear meat is smoking vegetable oil. A thin slick of oil across the skillet bottom is all that's necessary; once smoke is wafting from the surface, the pan is ready. If the chops are added too early, the meat will take too long to form a crust and is liable to overcook—something not worth risking with meat this expensive.

DON'T MOVE THE CHOPS Once the chops were in the pan, we found it crucial to let them sit undisturbed for at least 4 minutes; otherwise, the meat stuck to the pan, which marred its surface. Once we flipped the chops, we reduced the temperature to medium to allow the veal to finish cooking through without drying out or charring the exterior.

PAN-SEARED VEAL CHOPS
SERVES 4

Make sure to let the cooked chops rest, tented with aluminum foil, for 5 minutes before serving.

- 4 (8- to 12-ounce) bone-in veal rib chops, 1 to 1½ inches thick, trimmed
  Salt and pepper
- 2 teaspoons vegetable oil
  Lemon wedges

1. Pat chops dry with paper towels and season with salt and pepper. Heat oil in 12-inch skillet over medium-high heat until smoking. Lay chops in pan and cook without moving until well browned, 4 to 5 minutes. Using tongs, flip chops. Reduce heat to medium, and continue to cook until chops register 130 degrees, 8 to 12 minutes.

2. Transfer chops to large plate, tent with aluminum foil, and let rest for 5 minutes. Serve immediately with lemon wedges.

PAN-SEARED VEAL CHOPS WITH WILTED SPINACH AND GREMOLATA

Make gremolata, a classic Italian garnish of garlic, lemon zest, and parsley, before searing the chops. Then, while the chops rest, you can wilt spinach in the skillet used for the chops. You will need three bunches of flat-leaf spinach, each weighing about 10 ounces, washed, dried, and torn into pieces (about 4 quarts).

Combine 2 tablespoons extra-virgin olive oil, 1 teaspoon grated lemon zest, 1 minced garlic clove, and 2 tablespoons minced fresh parsley leaves in a small bowl. Set gremolata aside. While chops rest, heat 1 tablespoon extra-virgin olive oil in now-empty skillet over

You can turn almost any
plain white bread (baguette
or rustic country-style) into
crumbs, but we prefer the
sweetness of high-quality
white sandwich bread. To
make homemade bread
crumbs, tear the bread into
pieces and grind them in a
food processor until evenly
textured, 20 to 30 seconds.
One slice of sandwich bread
yields about ¾ cup crumbs.

medium-high heat. Add 4 quarts washed, dried, and torn flat-leaf spinach leaves, a handful at a time. Use tongs to stir and coat spinach with oil. Continue stirring with tongs until spinach is uniformly wilted, about 2 minutes.

Sprinkle spinach with 2 teaspoons lemon juice and season with salt and pepper to taste. Divide spinach among 4 plates, top each with chop, and top each chop with spoonful of gremolata. Serve immediately.

Breaded Veal Chops

✓ WHY THIS RECIPE WORKS

We love the delicate flavor and texture of veal chops, but that delicate flavor could use help. Breading the chops before pan-frying them, as cooks do in Milan, adds flavor and texture as well as a protective coating that shields the delicate meat. We wanted to find a way to keep the breading from becoming soggy and falling off the meat.

CHOOSE THE RIGHT CHOP We favored rib chops over shoulder chops, which were tough and chewy, and loin chops, which had a bone in the middle and two smaller portions of meat on either side. Medium-thick chops (roughly 1 inch thick) fried up best; thinner chops overcooked before the bread crumbs had a chance to brown, while thicker chops were simply too bulky and took too long to cook through.

USE FRESH BREAD CRUMBS We preferred the flavor of homemade bread crumbs for our chops. Letting the breaded chops rest in the refrigerator for at least 30 minutes before cooking helped the coating adhere.

BE GENEROUS WITH THE OIL For a uniformly crisp, golden brown crust, it is essential that the oil reach halfway up the chops as they cook. We also found it necessary to use fresh oil when frying the second batch; when we didn't change the oil, small crumbs fell off the chops in the first batch, burned, then stuck to the coating of the second batch, making them taste scorched.

CRANK UP THE HEAT Heating the oil over high heat for a couple of minutes before adding the chops ensured that the coating would brown and crisp in the time it took for the chops to reach a perfect medium-rare to medium.

BREADED VEAL CHOPS
SERVES 4 TO 6

Good sliced sandwich bread works best for making the crumbs for this recipe.

- ½   cup all-purpose flour
- 2   large eggs
- I   tablespoon plus I cup vegetable oil
- 3   cups fresh bread crumbs
- 4   (8-ounce) bone-in rib veal chops, I inch thick, trimmed
       Salt and pepper
       Lemon wedges

I. Spread flour in a shallow dish. Beat eggs with 1 tablespoon oil in second shallow dish. Spread bread crumbs in third shallow dish.

2. Pat chops dry with paper towels and season with salt and pepper. Working with 1 chop at a time, dredge in flour, shaking off excess. Using tongs, dip both sides of chops in egg mixture, allowing excess to drip back into dish. Dip both sides of chops in bread crumbs, pressing crumbs with your fingers to form even, cohesive coat. Place breaded chops in single layer on wire rack set in rimmed baking sheet and refrigerate for at least 30 minutes or up to 4 hours.

3. Adjust oven rack to lower-middle position, set large ovensafe plate on rack, and heat oven to 200 degrees.

4. Heat ½ cup oil in nonstick 12-inch skillet over medium-high heat until shimmering. Place 2 chops in skillet and fry until crisp and deep golden brown on first side, gently pressing down on them with wide metal spatula to help ensure even browning and checking partway through, about 3 minutes. Using tongs, flip chops and reduce heat to medium. Continue to cook until meat feels firm when pressed gently and second side is deep golden brown and crisp, again checking partway through, 2 to 3 minutes longer. Line warmed plate with double layer of paper towels and set chops on top; return plate to oven.

5. Discard used oil and wipe skillet clean using tongs and large wad of paper towels. Repeat step 4, using remaining ½ cup oil and the now-clean skillet and preheating oil 2 minutes to cook remaining 2 chops. Blot second batch of chops with paper towels. Remove plate from oven, remove paper towels, add just-cooked chops, and serve immediately with lemon wedges.

Grilled Veal Chops

✔ WHY THIS RECIPE WORKS

When done right, grilled veal chops are utterly irresistible: deeply browned, meaty, rich, and juicy, they require little adornment. But simple doesn't always mean easy, and charred, dried-out veal chops are an expensive disappointment. We wanted to guarantee perfect results every time.

CHOOSE THE RIGHT CHOP Veal chops are cut from the shoulder, loin, and rib. Shoulder chops proved to be tough and chewy and better suited to slow, low-temperature cooking methods like braising. Both the rib and loin chops, though expensive, were tender and flavorful when cooked relatively quickly, making them ideal choices for the grill.

NOT TOO THICK, NOT TOO THIN Chops that were of medium thickness—about 1¼ inches—worked best; these chops could spend enough time on the grill to develop a golden crust without drying out.

LESS IS MORE Unlike a steak, which can be enjoyed at a range of temperatures, the flavor and texture of veal are optimized between medium-rare and medium; this meant we needed to build our fire carefully. A two-level fire worked best, allowing us to sear the chops on the hotter side to develop a rich-tasting crust, then finish them over the cooler coals until perfectly pink inside. Flipping the chops while on the cooler side ensured both sides cooked evenly.

GRILLED RIB VEAL CHOPS
SERVES 6

Be sure to trim the veal chops of excess fat to prevent flare-ups. Keep a squirt bottle filled with water on hand to spray flare-ups that may still occur.

> 6 bone-in rib or loin veal chops, about
>   1¼ inches thick, trimmed
>   Salt and pepper

1A. FOR A CHARCOAL GRILL: Open bottom vent completely. Light large chimney starter filled with charcoal briquettes (6 quarts). When top coals are partially covered with ash, pour two-thirds evenly over half of grill, then pour remaining coals over other half of grill. Set cooking grate in place, cover, and open lid vent completely. Heat grill until hot, about 5 minutes.

1B. FOR A GAS GRILL: Turn all burners to high, cover, and heat grill until hot, about

DOUSING FLAMES ON THE GRILL

No one wants an uncontrolled fire that chars food on the grill, especially pricey veal chops. To avoid this, keep a squirt bottle or plant mister filled with water near the grill. At the first sign of flames, try to pull foods to a cooler part of the grill and douse the flames with water.

15 minutes. Leave primary burner on high and turn other burner(s) to medium.

2. Clean and oil cooking grate. Season chops evenly with salt and pepper.

3. Grill chops (covered if using gas) over hotter side of grill until browned, about 2 minutes on each side. (If flare-ups occur, slide chops briefly to cooler side of grill and, if necessary, extinguish flames with squirt bottle.) Move chops to cooler side of grill. Continue grilling, turning once, until meat is still rosy pink at center and registers 130 to 135 degrees (for medium), 10 to 11 minutes.

4. Remove chops from grill and let rest for 5 minutes before serving.

GRILLED VEAL CHOPS WITH MEDITERRANEAN HERB PASTE

If you don't have all the herbs in the recipe, feel free to use additional amounts of what you do have to make up the difference.

¼ cup plus 2 tablespoons extra-virgin olive oil
5 garlic cloves, minced (5 teaspoons)
2 tablespoons minced fresh parsley
1 tablespoon minced fresh sage
1 tablespoon minced fresh thyme
1 tablespoon minced fresh rosemary
1 tablespoon minced fresh oregano
Salt and pepper
6 bone-in rib or loin veal chops, about 1¼ inches thick, trimmed
1 lemon, cut into wedges, for serving

Mix oil, garlic, and herbs together in small bowl. Season with salt and pepper to taste. Rub herb paste over chops. Grill as directed and serve with lemon wedges.

PORCINI-RUBBED GRILLED VEAL CHOPS

Grind ¾ ounce dried porcini mushrooms to powder in spice grinder. Mix ground mushrooms with 9 tablespoons extra-virgin olive oil, 3 minced garlic cloves, 1½ teaspoons salt, and ½ teaspoon pepper in small bowl. Rub chops with mushroom paste. Do not season chops with salt and pepper before grilling. Grill as directed.

GRILLED VEAL CHOPS ON A BED OF ARUGULA

Note: The heat of the chops wilts the arugula, rendering it just slightly soft.

6 bone-in rib or loin veal chops, about 1¼ inches thick, trimmed
7 tablespoons plus 2 teaspoons extra-virgin olive oil
5 teaspoons balsamic vinegar
1 garlic clove, minced
Salt and pepper
12 ounces (12 cups) baby arugula

While chops are grilling, whisk together oil, vinegar, and garlic in small bowl. Season with salt and pepper to taste. Toss arugula and dressing in large bowl. Transfer arugula to platter or divide among individual plates. As soon as chops are done, arrange on arugula. Let rest 5 minutes, then serve.

Italian Veal Stew

✓ **WHY THIS RECIPE WORKS**

Osso buco, also known as braised veal shanks, is one of northern Italy's most renowned dishes. And there is good reason for that: The ultratender braised shanks are richly flavored and perfectly balanced by a wine-laced broth and a clarifying garnish of gremolata (fresh-chopped parsley, garlic, and lemon zest). Ladled over creamy polenta or saffron risotto, it's as good as braised meat gets. But this special-occasion dish takes the better part of a day to prepare, and veal shanks are both expensive and enormous. We wondered if we could capture the essence of osso buco into a streamlined stew without the unwieldy veal shanks and an entire afternoon spent in the kitchen.

COOK OVER MEDIUM-HIGH HEAT AND STIR THE MEAT Since shanks were out, a shoulder roast seemed like the next best option for braising. Cutting the meat into bite-size pieces and cooking it in two batches over medium-high heat helped the juices from this boneless cut reduce and caramelize. Stirring the meat—typically discouraged during browning—further aided evaporation. While the pieces of meat didn't brown or achieve a crisp crust, they did become coated with a uniform, golden-brown glaze that tasted great.

SIMMER IN A MODERATE OVEN We knew our cubed meat would cook faster than veal shanks, and after experimenting with varying times and temperatures, we determined that 1½ to 1¾ hours at 300 degrees rendered ideal results: fork-tender, flavorful meat.

THICKEN THE BROTH To compensate for the lack of gelatin from the shanks, we needed to find another way to thicken the broth of our stew. After testing a variety of thickeners—from flour and cornstarch to tapioca and powdered gelatin—we decided that flour worked just fine, making the broth suitably viscous without drawing attention to itself.

ITALIAN VEAL STEW
SERVES 6

Serve this stew over *Creamy Parmesan Polenta, Saffron Risotto (page 340), Classic Mashed Potatoes (page 99),* or buttered noodles.

2   pounds boneless veal shoulder roast, trimmed and cut into 1-inch pieces
    Salt and pepper
3   tablespoons olive oil
2   onions, cut into ½-inch dice
2   carrots, peeled and cut into ½-inch dice
2   celery ribs, cut into ½-inch dice
6   garlic cloves, minced
2   tablespoons all-purpose flour
¾   cup dry white wine
1½ cups chicken broth
1   (14.5-ounce) can diced tomatoes, drained
2   bay leaves
1   recipe Gremolata (page 341)

1. Adjust oven rack to middle position and heat oven to 300 degrees.

2. Season veal with salt and pepper. Heat 1 tablespoon oil in Dutch oven over medium-high heat until just smoking. Add half of veal and cook, stirring frequently, until it has released juices and is lightly browned, 4 to 6 minutes. Transfer veal to plate and set aside. Repeat with 1 tablespoon oil and remaining veal.

3. Add remaining 1 tablespoon oil to pot and heat over medium heat until shimmering. Add onions, carrots, and celery and cook, scraping bottom of pot occasionally with wooden spoon, until onions are soft and lightly browned, 6 to 10 minutes. Add garlic and cook until fragrant, 10 to 30 seconds. Add

ON THE SIDE
CREAMY PARMESAN POLENTA

Do not use instant or quick-cooking polenta here. Coarse-ground degerminated cornmeal such as yellow grits (with uniform grains the size of couscous) will work, but do not use whole-grain, stone-ground, or regular cornmeal. Do not omit the baking soda—it reduces the cooking time and makes for a creamier polenta. Using a high-quality Parmesan is crucial in this simple side dish.

1. Bring 9½ cups water to boil in large saucepan over medium-high heat. Stir in 2 teaspoons salt and pinch baking soda. Slowly add 2 cups polenta while whisking constantly in circular motion to prevent clumping. Bring to simmer, stirring constantly, about 1 minute. Reduce heat to lowest possible setting and cover.

2. Cook for 5 minutes, then whisk polenta to smooth out lumps, about 15 seconds. Cover and continue to cook, without stirring, until grains of polenta are tender but slightly al dente, about 30 minutes longer. (Polenta should be loose and barely hold its shape but will continue to thicken as it cools.)

3. Off heat, stir in 2½ cups grated Parmesan and 3 tablespoons unsalted butter and season with salt and pepper to taste. Let polenta sit, covered, for 5 minutes. Serve, passing additional Parmesan separately.

flour and cook for 20 seconds. Add wine, scraping up any bits on bottom of pot, and simmer until thickened. Increase heat to high and add broth, stirring constantly and scraping pan edges. Add tomatoes, bay leaves, and veal along with any accumulated juices and bring to simmer. Cover and place pot in oven. Cook until veal is tender and easily pierced with paring knife, 1½ to 1¾ hours. (Stew can be covered and refrigerated for up to 3 days; reheat over medium-low heat.)

4. Remove pot from oven and stir in gremolata. Let stand, covered, for 5 minutes. Season with salt and pepper to taste, and serve.

Osso Buco

✓ WHY THIS RECIPE WORKS

This well-known Italian classic is made from simple ingredients, but it's plagued by complex problems. For this special occasion—worthy meal, we wanted to make sure our pricey veal shanks cooked evenly and developed deep flavor throughout. We also wanted a rich, flavorful braising liquid that would provide a savory backbone for the veal without making the dish soupy.

BUY SAME-SIZE SHANKS Part of the appeal of osso buco is that each diner receives their own veal shank, but if the shanks are too large or simply butchered unevenly, cooking and serving become much more difficult. To ensure perfect serving sizes, we found that careful shopping was key. Look for shanks that are about 1½ inches thick and weigh about 8 ounces, with two nicely cut, flat sides to facilitate browning.

SKIP THE FLOUR Many traditional recipes call for dredging the shanks in flour to promote browning, but we found this merely gave us browned flour (not browned meat) and a gummy coating that sometimes peeled off during braising. To develop deep flavor, we opted to season the shanks simply with salt and pepper and then brown them in two batches. This allowed us to deglaze the pan twice, thereby doubly enriching the braising liquid.

SIMPLIFY YOUR SAUCE The braising liquid for osso buco traditionally begins with meat stock. But few cooks have homemade veal stock on hand, and store-bought beef broth made a poor substitute. Two cups of chicken broth, along with generous amounts of softened garlic, onion, carrot, and celery, made a flavorful base for our braising liquid. The white wine we used to deglaze the pan where we seared the veal shanks along with some additional fresh wine rounded out the liquid's flavor nicely. Thoroughly drained canned diced tomatoes provided just the right amount of tomato flavor without overwhelming the other flavors. The liquid reduced to a perfect quantity and thickness during its stay in the oven.

DOUBLE UP ON GREMOLATA In some recipes, the gremolata—a mixture of minced garlic, parsley, and lemon zest—is sprinkled on at the end, while in others it is stirred in just before serving. We opted to take both approaches, stirring half of the gremolata right into the braise, then garnishing each serving with an additional dollop for a final hit of fresh flavor.

OSSO BUCO
SERVES 6

Use a Dutch oven that holds 6 quarts or more for this recipe. To keep the meat attached to the shank bone during the long simmering process, many recipes—ours included—call for tying a piece of kitchen twine around the thickest portion of each shank before it is browned. Osso buco is traditionally served with Saffron Risotto (page 340). Classic Mashed Potatoes (page 99) and Creamy Parmesan Polenta (page 339) are good side dish options as well.

OSSO BUCO

6	tablespoons vegetable oil
6	(8- to 10-ounce) veal shanks, 1½ inches thick, trimmed and tied around equator
	Salt and pepper
2½	cups dry white wine
2	onions, chopped
2	carrots, peeled and chopped
2	celery ribs, chopped
6	garlic cloves, minced
2	cups chicken broth
1	(14.5-ounce) can diced tomatoes, drained
2	bay leaves

GREMOLATA

¼	cup minced fresh parsley
3	garlic cloves, minced
2	teaspoons grated lemon zest

1. FOR THE OSSO BUCO: Adjust oven rack to lower-middle position and heat oven to 325 degrees.

2. Heat 2 tablespoons oil in Dutch oven over medium-high heat until shimmering. Pat shanks dry with paper towels, then season generously with salt and pepper. Place 3 shanks in single layer in pot and brown until golden, about 5 minutes per side. Transfer shanks to bowl and set aside. Off heat, add ½ cup wine to pot, scraping up any browned bits. Pour liquid into bowl with browned shanks. Return pot to medium-high heat, add 2 tablespoons oil, and heat until shimmering. Brown remaining 3 shanks. Transfer shanks to bowl with other shanks. Off heat, add 1 cup wine to pot, scraping up any browned bits. Pour liquid into bowl with shanks.

3. Set pot over medium heat. Add remaining 2 tablespoons oil to pot and heat until shimmering. Add onions, carrots, and celery and cook, stirring occasionally, until vegetables are soft and lightly browned, about 9 minutes. Add garlic and cook until lightly browned, about 1 minute longer.

4. Increase heat to high and stir in broth, tomatoes, bay leaves, accumulated juices from shanks, and remaining 1 cup wine. Add shanks to pot (liquid should just barely cover shanks). Cover pot, bring liquid to simmer, adjust lid of pot so it is slightly ajar, and place pot in oven. Cook shanks until fork slips easily in and out of meat but meat is not falling off bone, about 2 hours.

5. FOR THE GREMOLATA: Combine parsley, garlic, and lemon zest in small bowl.

6. Stir half of gremolata into pot, reserving rest for garnish. Season with salt and pepper to taste. Let osso buco stand, uncovered, for 5 minutes.

7. Remove shanks from pot. Remove kitchen twine and place 1 shank in each serving bowl. Discard bay leaves. Ladle some braising liquid over each shank and sprinkle each shank with portion of remaining gremolata. Serve immediately.

TO MAKE AHEAD: Osso buco may be prepared through step 3 and refrigerated for up to 3 days. Before serving, scrape chilled fat off top and bring osso buco to simmer over medium-low heat in covered Dutch oven; adjust consistency with broth or water as needed. Gremolata should be prepared just before serving.

TYING VEAL SHANKS

To ensure even cooking and to prevent the meat from falling off the bone, the veal shanks should be bound around the middle with kitchen twine.

Poultry

(CONTINUED)

Poultry Basics

Owing in large part to its relatively low cost and fat content, poultry has become America's favorite meat. But problems with shopping, preparing, and cooking chicken and turkey at home abound—mostly because there are so many conflicting theories about how to handle it and cook it. Here's what you need to know.

LABELING

Many claims cited on poultry packaging have no government regulation, while those that do are often poorly enforced. Here's how to evaluate which claims are meaningful—and which are full of loopholes or empty hype.

Air-Chilled

"Air-chilled" means that chickens (or turkeys) were not water-chilled en masse in a chlorinated bath and the meat did not absorb any water during processing. (Water-chilled birds can retain up to 14 percent water—which must be printed on the label—diluting flavor and inflating cost.) Instead, individual chickens hang from a conveyor belt and circulate around a cold room.

USDA Organic

The seal "USDA Organic" is considered the gold standard for organic labeling. This label ensures that poultry eat organic feed that doesn't contain animal byproducts, are raised without antibiotics, and have access to the outdoors (how much access, however, isn't regulated).

Raised Without Antibiotics

"Raised without antibiotics" and other claims regarding antibiotic use are important; too bad they're not strictly enforced. (The only rigorous enforcement is when the claim is subject to the USDA Organic seal.) Loopholes seem rife, like injecting the eggs—not the chickens—with antibiotics or feeding them feather meal laced with residual antibiotics from treated birds.

Natural and All Natural

Beware the ubiquitous "natural" and "all natural" food labels. In actuality, the USDA has defined the term just for fresh meat, stipulating only that no synthetic substances have been added to the cut. Producers may thus raise their chickens under the most unnatural circumstances on the most unnatural diets, inject birds with broth during processing, and still put the claim on their packaging.

Hormone-Free

When used with poultry (and pork) "hormone-free" is an empty reassurance, since the USDA does not allow the use of hormones or steroids in the production of either poultry or pork.

Vegetarian-Fed and Vegetarian Diet

"Vegetarian-fed" and "vegetarian diet" sound healthy, but are they? Since such terms aren't regulated by the government, you're relying on the producer's notion of the claim, which may mean feeding chickens cheap "vegetarian" bakery leftovers. The winners of our whole chicken tasting assured us that their definitions mean a diet consisting of corn and soy.

SHOPPING FOR CHICKEN

Compared to beef and pork, which possess myriad cuts, often with alternate names, chicken can be less confusing to shop for at the market. That said, there are particular considerations you should be aware of when shopping for chicken.

Whole: Broilers, Fryers, and Roasters

Whole chickens come in various sizes. Broilers and fryers are younger chickens that weigh 2½ to 4½ pounds. A roaster (or oven-stuffer roaster) is an older chicken and usually weighs between 5 and 7 pounds.

Our tasting and research proved processing is the major player in texture and flavor. We found that specimens that are "water-chilled" (see above) or "enhanced" (injected with broth and flavoring) are unnaturally spongy and are best avoided. Labeling law says water gain must be shown on the product label, so these should be easily identifiable. When buying a whole bird, look for those that are labeled "air-chilled" (in the test kitchen, we like **Mary's Free Range Air Chilled Chicken** or **Bell & Evans Air Chilled Premium Fresh Chicken**). Without the excess water weight, we found these chickens to be less spongy in texture (but still plenty juicy) and to taste more chicken-y.

Bone-In Parts

You can buy a whole cut-up chicken or chicken parts at your supermarket, but sometimes it's hard to tell by looking at the package if it's been properly butchered. If you have a few minutes of extra time, consider buying a whole chicken and butchering it yourself. (See "How to Cut Up a Whole Chicken" on page 348 for more details.)

Boneless, Skinless Breasts and Cutlets

If you're buying boneless, skinless breasts, you should be aware that breasts of different sizes are often packaged together, which is a problem since they won't cook through at the same rate. Try to pick a package with breasts of similar size, and pound them to an even thickness. We prefer **Bell & Evans Air Chilled Boneless, Skinless Chicken Breasts**.

You can buy cutlets ready to go at the grocery store, but we don't recommend it. These cutlets are usually ragged and of various sizes; it's better to cut your own cutlets from breasts. (See "How to Make Chicken Cutlets" on page 349 for more details.)

Ground

Ground chicken is typically sold one of two ways: prepackaged or ground to order. The prepackaged variety is made from either dark or white meat. Higher-end markets and specialty markets grind their chicken to order, and therefore the choice of meat is yours. When it comes to flavor, however, our tasters were unanimous—dark meat is far superior. In most of our testing, we found ground white meat chicken to be exceedingly dry and almost void of flavor. The dark meat was more flavorful and juicy due to its higher fat content.

SHOPPING FOR TURKEY

Most of us purchase a whole turkey just a few times a year, but typically it's for a special occasion so it's key to shop wisely. There are also turkey breasts and ground meat to consider.

Whole

Modern commercial turkeys don't contain much fat, yet, as we all know, fat is what provides meat with juiciness and flavor. To make up for it, some birds are "prebasted" (injected with a solution), but our tasters found that these birds can have a "wet" texture. Pasture-raised, organic turkeys promise a flavor improvement because of their diverse diet, but we didn't find that to be the case; plus, the meat was slightly stringier and tougher (you will need to brine these birds if you buy them). Heritage turkeys are directly descended from wild turkeys, and they nearly disappeared in the mid-20th century as commercial Broad-Breasted Whites were bred by the poultry industry. Over the years, some heritage turkeys have found favor with consumers, but given the range of taster opinion about flavor, from "outstanding" to "funky," we aren't sure the high price tag and the effort it takes to track one down are worth it.

We like turkeys that have been koshered (covered in kosher salt, then rinsed multiple times). Koshering works to season the meat, improve its texture, and help it retain moisture—if you buy a kosher turkey there's no need to brine or salt it. However, kosher turkeys aren't always easy to find, so we typically call for "all-natural" turkeys. These turkeys have been fed a vegetarian diet and are free to roam. These turkeys also tend to contain less fat, which translates to a drier bird, so we always recommend brining them.

Bone-In Breasts

Most supermarkets offer two slightly different styles of whole bone-in turkey breast: regular (aka true cut) and hotel (aka country-style). Regular-cut turkey breast includes the whole bone-in breast with ribs, a portion of the wing meat, and a portion of the back and neck skin. The hotel-cut turkey breast is essentially the same cut, though it comes with its wings, neck, and giblets, important if you intend to make a gravy or sauce. These tend to cost a little more and are almost always sold fresh, not frozen.

Whichever style you purchase, try to avoid turkey breasts that have been injected with a saline solution (a brine of sorts)—these are often called "self-basters." We found that the solution masks the natural flavor of the turkey. (If the only bird you can find is a self-baster, do not brine it, as the meat will already be quite salty.) Also, ignore the pop-up timer that comes with some turkey breasts; the meat will be long overcooked before the popper pops. If your turkey has a pop-up timer, leave it in and gauge doneness according to an instant-read thermometer. Don't remove the timer until the meat is done; it will leave a gaping hole from which juices will flow.

Ground

The guidelines for buying ground turkey are the same as those for buying ground chicken. Ground dark meat has more flavor than white, so make sure you buy ground turkey that is a mix of the two; do not buy ground turkey breast (also labeled 99 percent fat-free).

Principles of Poultry Cookery

A number of cooking methods work well when preparing poultry. But whether you are roasting a whole turkey, grilling chicken parts, or sautéing cutlets, there are a few basic cooking principles that you should always keep in mind.

Brine or Salt to Increase Juiciness

In the same way that you prepare beef or pork for cooking, brining poultry in a saltwater solution boosts the flavor and juiciness of the meat. However, there's a drawback to brining skin on poultry: Because it's soaking up liquid, achieving perfectly crisp skin is more difficult. In these cases, make sure to pat the skin as dry as possible prior to cooking. Alternatively, for some cuts you might opt to salt the poultry. See page 347 for more general information about how brining and salting work and for details on salting and brining specific cuts of poultry.

Cook White Meat Less Than Dark Meat

Dark meat (thighs and drumsticks) cooks more slowly than white breast meat. This is mainly a result of the fact that dark meat is denser because it has more fat and proteins. To account for this difference when cooking a whole bird, we've found it best to shield the breast meat to protect it from the heat by starting the bird either breast side down or with the breast to the side, and then finishing breast side up. When cooking chicken pieces, things are a little bit easier because you can remove pieces as they are done, if necessary. We cook white meat to 160 degrees and dark meat to 175 degrees.

Crisp the Skin or Lose the Skin

For many of us, the crispy skin on a piece of poultry is the best part. But flabby chicken or turkey skin isn't appetizing or visually appealing, so make sure the skin is crispy or remove it. The key to crisp skin is rendering all the fat that is between the skin and the meat. We typically brown skin-on chicken pieces in a hot skillet, then finish cooking the chicken at a lower temperature or in the even heat of the oven (this also creates flavorful fond in the skillet, great for making a pan sauce). If you're roasting a whole bird but you don't want to serve the skin, you can still keep it on while cooking to protect the delicate breast meat; discard it before serving. For stews and braises, if you don't crisp the skin and render the fat, you should typically discard the skin before cooking, or your dish will be overly greasy.

Let It Rest

As poultry cooks, the juices are driven toward the center of the cut, so a resting period after cooking is essential to allow those juices time to redistribute evenly throughout. Logically, the larger the piece of poultry, the longer the resting time required. A big turkey needs 40 minutes, a whole chicken 10 to 20 minutes, and chicken parts 5 to 10 minutes. For more information about resting, see page 8.

SALTING POULTRY

Salting poultry in advance is one way to season the meat and keep it juicy. When salt is applied to raw poultry, juices inside are drawn to the surface. The salt then dissolves in the exuded liquid, forming a brine that is eventually reabsorbed by the poultry. The salt changes the structure of the muscle proteins, allowing them to hold on to more of their own natural juices. Salting requires time, but it won't thwart the goal of crispy skin. We prefer to use kosher salt for salting because it's easier to distribute the salt evenly. The chart below lists the poultry items that we typically salt, along with notes on timing and method. We use Diamond Crystal Kosher Salt; if using Morton Kosher Salt, reduce the amounts listed by 33 percent (e.g. use ⅔ teaspoon Morton Kosher Salt in place of 1 teaspoon Diamond Crystal).

SALTING POULTRY

CUTS	TIME	KOSHER SALT	METHOD
Whole Chicken	At least 6 hours or up to 24 hours	1 teaspoon per pound	Apply salt evenly inside cavity and under skin of breasts and legs and let rest in refrigerator on wire rack set in rimmed baking sheet. (Wrap with plastic wrap if salting for longer than 12 hours.)
Bone-In Chicken Pieces; Boneless or Bone-In Turkey Breast	At least 6 hours or up to 24 hours	¾ teaspoon per pound	If poultry is skin-on, apply salt evenly between skin and meat, leaving skin attached, and let rest in refrigerator on wire rack set in rimmed baking sheet. (Wrap with plastic wrap if salting for longer than 12 hours.)
Whole Turkey	24 to 48 hours	1 teaspoon per pound	Apply salt evenly inside cavity and under skin of breasts and legs, wrap tightly with plastic wrap, and let rest in refrigerator.

BRINING POULTRY

Brining works in much the same way as salting. Salt in the brine seasons the poultry and promotes a change in its protein structure, reducing its overall toughness and creating gaps that fill up with water and keep the meat juicy and flavorful. Brining works faster than salting and can also result in juicier lean cuts since it adds, versus merely retains, moisture. But note that brining inhibits browning, and it requires fitting a brining container in the fridge. We prefer to use table salt for brining since it dissolves quickly in the water. The chart below lists the poultry items that we typically brine, along with notes on timing and the amount of water needed.

BRINING POULTRY

CHICKEN	TIME	COLD WATER	TABLE SALT
1 whole chicken (3½ to 4 pounds)	½ to 1 hour	2 quarts	½ cup
2 whole chickens (3½ to 4 pounds each)	½ to 1 hour	3 quarts	¾ cup
4 pounds bone-in chicken pieces (whole breasts, split breasts, leg quarters, thighs, and/or drumsticks)	½ to 1 hour	2 quarts	½ cup
4 boneless, skinless chicken breasts	½ to 1 hour	2 quarts	¼ cup
TURKEY			
1 whole turkey (12 to 17 pounds)	6 to 12 hours	2 gallons	1 cup
1 whole turkey (18 to 24 pounds)	6 to 12 hours	3 gallons	1½ cups
1 bone-in turkey breast (6 to 8 pounds)	3 to 6 hours	1 gallon	½ cup

HOW MUCH SODIUM IS IN BRINED FOOD?

We've often wondered just how much sodium ends up in brined food. To find out, we sent cooked samples of boneless, skinless chicken breasts and boneless center-cut pork chops that we brined for our standard recommended times to an independent lab for sodium analysis. We also analyzed plain water–soaked samples so that we could subtract any naturally occurring sodium. Here's how much sodium brining adds to each food. (Note: The Dietary Guidelines for Americans recommend less than 2,300 milligrams daily for people under 51 and less than 1,500 milligrams for those 51 and older.)

SODIUM LEVELS IN BRINED MEAT

CHICKEN	BRINING FORMULA	ADDED SODIUM	SALT EQUIVALENT
6 ounces cooked boneless, skinless chicken breast	2 quarts water, ¼ cup salt, 1 hour	270 milligrams	Less than ⅛ teaspoon

DON'T BRINE WATER-CHILLED CHICKEN

When we brined both air-chilled and water-chilled boneless skinless chicken breasts, we found that the air-chilled chicken absorbed 3½ times as much brine as the water-chilled chicken did. After cooking, the air-chilled samples were notably juicier and better seasoned than water-chilled samples.

Why? Since the chicken with retained water is limited in its ability to take up brine, it is also unable to absorb much of the brine's salt, which not only seasons the meat but keeps it moist during cooking, too. The water absorbed during processing simply drains off during cooking, leaving the meat almost as dry and unseasoned as chicken that isn't brined at all. But you aren't out of luck if only water-chilled breasts are available: Opt to salt rather than brine—treat water-chilled chicken breasts with kosher salt (1½ teaspoons per pound) for 1 hour.

Common (and Key) Prep Tips for Poultry

How to Cut Up a Whole Chicken

Cutting up a whole chicken may seem like an intimidating process, but it's a handy technique to learn. For one thing, cutting up a chicken yourself is economical since you aren't paying for the labor to have someone cut up the chicken for you. If a recipe calls for four split breasts, you can simply butcher two whole chickens and save the thighs, wings, and drumsticks for another recipe. Second, butchering your own chicken ensures that the parts are the right size and properly butchered, which is not always the case with the prepackaged pieces you buy at the supermarket.

1. Start cutting where leg attaches to breast. Pop leg joint out of its socket with your hands, then continue cutting through to detach leg from body.

2. Cut each leg into 2 pieces—drumstick and thigh—by slicing through joint, marked by thin line of fat.

3. Flip chicken over and remove wings by slicing through each wing joint. Then cut through cartilage around wingtip to remove and discard.

4. Turn chicken on its side and, using kitchen shears, remove back.

5. Flip breast skin side down and, using chef's knife, cut in half through breast plate, which is marked by thin white line of cartilage.

6. Flip each breast piece over and cut in half crosswise.

Cutting off the somewhat awkward leg quarters first makes it easier to butcher the rest of the chicken properly.

Some recipes may use whole leg quarters, but most often you'll want to separate drumsticks and thighs.

Most recipes calling for a whole butchered chicken don't utilize the wings since they're far smaller and less meaty than the other pieces, but you can freeze and use them for making stock or Oven-Fried Chicken Wings (page 403).

The back of a chicken has almost no meat, and the bone only gets in the way of butchering the breast. However, the backbone, like the wings, is good to use when making stock.

Split breasts are perhaps the most common cut of chicken. Using a good chef's knife is key for this step.

Whole split breasts are fairly large, so cutting each split breast in half crosswise speeds up the cooking time. You'll need to do this for recipes that call for a whole chicken cut into eight pieces (like fried chicken).

How to Split and Trim Breasts

We typically buy breasts already split, but more than once we've gotten back to the kitchen only to discover that they aren't similar in size. That leads to uneven cooking and uneven portions. Buying one whole breast from the butcher and splitting it yourself offers an advantage: You are guaranteed evenly sized pieces. If you plan to buy chicken breasts that have already been split, inspect the package and make sure they are of similar size.

Whether you buy them split or split your own, you should always trim off the rib section from each split breast prior to cooking. This allows you to fit more chicken breasts in the pan or pot and ensures even cooking. We also trim excess fat and skin to prevent greasiness.

1. With whole breast skin side down on cutting board, center knife on breastbone, then apply pressure to cut through and separate breast into 2 halves.

2. Using kitchen shears, trim off rib section from each breast, following vertical line of fat from tapered end of breast up to socket where wing was attached.

3. Using chef's knife or kitchen shears, trim excess fat and skin from chicken breasts prior to cooking, so your dish doesn't turn out greasy.

To cut the whole breast in half, it's easiest to see where to cut if it's skin side down. You'll see a thin white line of cartilage where you should cut. It's critical to have a good chef's knife for this step.

Because there isn't a lot of meat on the rib section, we always trim it off to allow more room in the pan for the chicken breasts. Removing it also allows for more even cooking since the breasts can lay flat in the pot or skillet.

How to Make Chicken Cutlets

A cutlet is simply a thin piece of meat. In the case of chicken, cutlets are typically made by cutting a chicken breast in half horizontally. Sure, you can find chicken cutlets ready to go in the supermarket. But shortcutting this prep step is one we wouldn't recommend; store-bought cutlets are often ragged and they vary widely in size and thickness. Instead, buy boneless, skinless chicken breasts and make the cutlets yourself. You'll not only guarantee your cutlets are of equal size but also save a little money in the process.

1. Remove tenderloin from 6- to 8-ounce boneless, skinless chicken breast.

2. Lay chicken breast flat on cutting board, smooth side facing up. Rest your hand on top of chicken and, using chef's knife, slice chicken in half horizontally.

3. Place cutlets, smooth side down, on large sheet of plastic wrap. Cover with second sheet of plastic and pound gently to even thickness.

Sometimes a thin strip of meat, the tenderloin, is attached to the breast. This loose strip is likely to come off during cooking, so we always remove it.

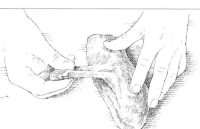

Holding the breast steady as you cut will help ensure you cut on a level plane. If you have time, you can freeze the chicken breasts for 15 minutes first to make the slicing easier. Each cutlet should be about ½ inch thick.

Chicken breasts are always thicker on one end; pounding the meat so that it is even from end to end helps ensure even cooking. Often we pound cutlets thinner, to ¼ inch. Pounding between plastic wrap is an easy way to keep the counter and the meat pounder clean.

Common (and Key) Prep Tips for Poultry

How to Butterfly a Whole Chicken

Butterflying a chicken involves removing the backbone and then opening and flattening the bird. Butterflying offers two advantages: First, it allows for more even cooking by giving the thighs greater exposure to the heat so that they cook at the same rate as the more delicate white breast meat. Second, butterflying allows you to cook a whole chicken in less time. And because the backbone has been removed, it's easy to add flavor under the skin with a spice rub or compound butter. You can use this same method to butterfly a turkey. Because of a turkey's larger size, using the handle of a wooden spoon to gently loosen the skin works well.

1. Place chicken on cutting board breast side down and cut along each side of backbone to remove it.

2. Flip chicken breast side up, then use heel of your hand to flatten chicken.

3. The thin, small wingtips easily burn, so it's important to tuck them behind the back of the chicken.

4. Slip your fingers between skin and breast, loosening membrane. If using compound butter, a spoon makes the process easier: Scoop butter onto spoon, slide under breast skin, and push it off with your fingers. Gently press on skin to distribute butter evenly.

Removing the backbone is what will allow you to flatten the chicken. This isn't a job you want to do with a knife; using shears makes the task fast, simple, and safe.

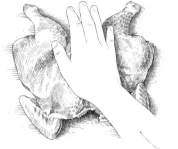

The chicken will easily flatten with just a little pressure applied with the heel of your hand. You will actually hear a crack when you've done it correctly. Some recipes may also call for pounding the chicken with a mallet or meat pounder once you've flattened it by hand to ensure an even thickness.

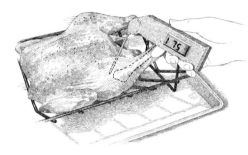

The skin is attached to the meat with a thin membrane. The skin should stretch easily to allow you to season the chicken—whether with a compound butter or simply salt and pepper. Work carefully so you don't poke a hole in the skin.

Gauging Doneness of Poultry

Taking a chicken or turkey's temperature is trickier than taking the temperature of other meat like steaks and chops because breast meat cooks faster than thigh meat and, unlike a dense pork loin, a whole bird contains a large cavity. To gauge doneness, you should take the temperature of both thigh and breast meat when cooking poultry. When doing so, try to avoid hitting bones, cavities, or the surface of the pan, as this will result in an inaccurate reading. When temping a whole chicken, use the following methods:

A. For thigh meat: Insert thermometer at angle into area between drumstick and breast, taking care not to hit bone. It should register 175 degrees.

B. For breast meat: Insert thermometer from neck end, holding thermometer parallel to bird. It should register 160 degrees.

If cooking chicken or turkey pieces, use same technique described above, while lifting piece with tongs and inserting thermometer sideways into thickest part of the meat, taking care to avoid bones.

Avoid hitting the bone when testing for doneness. Take one reading from the thigh.

Take a second reading from the breast.

HOW TO CARVE A WHOLE CHICKEN

After brining and roasting the perfect bird, you still have one task left before bringing it to the table: carving it. And while carving isn't difficult, there is definitely a way to approach it that will yield nicely portioned chicken parts and slices of boneless breast. You want portions that look attractive on the platter and are easy to serve. Before you start, make sure that you've let the chicken rest for 10 to 20 minutes. The resting time not only allows the juices to redistribute, but it also makes carving easier. While you might think a carving knife is the proper tool for this task given its name, a chef's knife is, in fact, the better choice because of the maneuvering carving requires—it's something you just can't do with the long blade of a carving knife.

1. START WITH LEG QUARTER
Cut chicken where leg meets breast.

2. SEPARATE LEG JOINT Pull leg quarter away from carcass. Separate joint by gently pressing leg out to side and pushing up on joint.

3. REMOVE LEG Carefully cut through joint to remove leg quarter. Repeat steps 1–3 on chicken's other side.

4. SEPARATE DRUMSTICK AND THIGH Cut through joint that connects drumstick to thigh.

5. REMOVE BREAST Cut down along 1 side of breastbone, pulling breast meat away from breastbone as you cut.

6. SLICE BREAST MEAT Remove wing from breast by cutting through wing joint. Slice breast crosswise on bias into slices. Repeat steps 4–6 with other side.

HOW MUCH MEAT IS ON A WHOLE CHICKEN?

We roasted 3-, 4-, and 5-pound chickens and then picked them clean to find out how much meat we could get per pound. The birds averaged about 1 cup of cooked picked chicken per pound of raw chicken (the 3-pound raw chicken yielded about 3 cups cooked chicken), and the proportion of white meat to dark was about 2 to 1. Handy information if you need cooked chicken for a recipe.

HOW TO CARVE BUTTERFLIED CHICKEN

A chicken that has been flattened and butterflied can be carved in just a couple of steps.

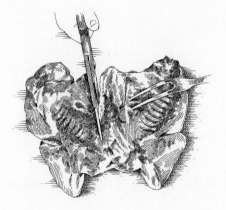

1. SPLIT BREAST Place chicken skin-side down and use kitchen shears to cut through breastbone. (Since breastbone is broken and meat is flattened during pounding, this should be easy.)

2. SEPARATE LEG AND THIGH Once breast has been split, only skin is holding portions together. Separate each leg and thigh from each breast and wing. Proceed to carve breast following illustration below and separate drumstick from the thigh.

HOW TO CARVE BONE-IN CHICKEN BREASTS

Follow this simple technique for carving breasts when an attractive presentation is important.

1. SEPARATE BONE To remove meat, cut straight down along 1 side of breastbone.

2. REMOVE MEAT Run knife down along rib cage to remove entire breast half.

3. SLICE BREAST Slice each breast half crosswise on bias, making thin slices.

HOW TO CARVE A TURKEY

Rather than carving the Thanksgiving bird tableside, we recommend tackling this messy job in the kitchen. As with carving a chicken, a chef's knife is the best tool for carving this bird. Make sure to rest the bird for about 40 minutes before carving so it is cool enough to handle and its juices have time to redistribute.

1. START WITH LEG Remove any twine used to truss bird. Start by slicing skin between meat of breast and leg.

2. REMOVE LEG Continue to cut down to joint, using fork to pull leg away from bird while tip of knife severs joint between leg and breast.

3. SEPARATE DRUMSTICK AND THIGH Cut through joint between thigh and leg. (This should be easy since you are not cutting through bone.)

4. SLICE LEG MEAT Slice medallions from leg, turning it so you can cut off all meat.

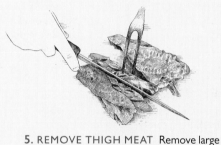

5. REMOVE THIGH MEAT Remove large pieces of meat from either side of thighbone.

6. SLICE THIGH MEAT Slice these large thigh pieces, leaving a bit of skin attached to each slice.

7. SEPARATE WING Use fork to pull wing away from body. Cut through joint between wing and breast to separate wing from bird.

8. HALVE WING Cut wing in half for easier eating.

9. SEPARATE BREAST With tip of knife, cut along length of breastbone.

10. REMOVE BREAST Angle blade of knife, and slice along line of rib cage to remove entire breast half. Use fork to pull breast half away from cage in single piece.

11. SLICE BREAST Cut thin slices from breast, slicing against grain of meat.

Perfect Poached Chicken

✔ WHY THIS RECIPE WORKS

All too often, boneless, skinless chicken breasts are dry and stringy. Sure, they're lean and mild, but the way we treat them doesn't help: We throw them onto white-hot grills, sear them hard in a skillet, and even toss them under the broiler—all potential paths to leathery flesh. Poaching is one way to ensure tender, moist chicken, but this finicky technique rarely gets any attention these days. We wanted to take away some of the fussiness and figure out how to use this method to boost flavor, for meat that's exceptionally moist, succulent, and anything but bland.

BRINE FIRST Brining is a surefire way to ensure well-seasoned breast meat, and we found that this held true even when poaching. To our typical saltwater brine we added a little sugar, as well as a couple of unusual ingredients: soy sauce, which contributed meatiness and depth, and several smashed garlic cloves, for a complex, sweet background flavor.

LET THE BRINE DOUBLE AS THE POACHING LIQUID Rather than toss out our flavor-packed brine, we used it as our poaching liquid as well. And with the chicken breasts and poaching liquid combined from the beginning, we had a much more hands-free poaching method: We simply heated the pot over medium heat until the water temperature reached 175 degrees; we then removed the pot from the heat and allow it to sit, covered, until the breasts were cooked through.

USE PLENTY OF WATER Using 4 quarts of water meant we had a larger reserve of heat and thus better assurance that the breasts would hit the desired internal temperature of 160 degrees.

EMPLOY A STEAMER BASKET AND A MALLET Raising the breasts off the bottom of the pot with a steamer basket eliminated the risk of one side cooking faster, and lightly pounding the thicker end of the breasts further promoted more even cooking.

PERFECT POACHED CHICKEN BREASTS
SERVES 4

To ensure that the chicken cooks through, don't use breasts that weigh more than 8 ounces each. If desired, serve the chicken with one of our sauces (recipes follow) or in a salad or sandwiches.

4	(6- to 8-ounce) boneless, skinless chicken breasts, trimmed
½	cup soy sauce
¼	cup salt
2	tablespoons sugar
6	garlic cloves, peeled and smashed

1. Cover chicken breasts with plastic wrap and pound thick ends gently with meat pounder until ¾ inch thick. Whisk 4 quarts water, soy sauce, salt, sugar, and garlic in Dutch oven until salt and sugar are dissolved. Arrange breasts, skinned side up, in steamer basket, making sure not to overlap them. Submerge steamer basket in brine and let sit at room temperature for 30 minutes.

2. Heat pot over medium heat, stirring liquid occasionally to even out hot spots, until water registers 175 degrees, 15 to 20 minutes. Turn off heat, cover pot, remove from burner, and let stand until meat registers 160 degrees, 17 to 22 minutes.

3. Transfer breasts to carving board, cover tightly with aluminum foil, and let rest for 5 minutes. Slice each breast on bias into ¼-inch-thick slices, transfer to serving platter or individual plates, and serve.

WHY DO WE EAT RARE BEEF BUT NOT RARE CHICKEN?

Whether or not it's safe to eat rare meat has to do with the bacteria associated with the meat. A temperature of 165 degrees is considered a safety point for killing all harmful bacteria. We don't eat raw or rare chicken or turkey because it has an unpleasant texture, but also because it can be infected by the bacteria salmonella, which can live inside the muscle tissue. For beef, the problem isn't the inside of muscle (which is sterile) but the outside, as *Escherichia coli* (or *E. coli*) can reside there. So steaks can safely be cooked rare (burgers are most safely cooked to well-done, as *E. coli* can be mixed into the meat during grinding). The bottom line? Poultry is safe to eat when it reaches 165 degrees. You can stop cooking it at 160 degrees, as residual heat will take it the final 5 degrees. (Dark meat is best cooked to 175.)

Individually halving cherry tomatoes can be time-consuming. Here's a way to speed things along.

1. Place medium-size plastic lid, such as cottage cheese container lid, on counter with lip side up. Place single layer of tomatoes in lid. Place second lid, lip side down, over tomatoes.

2. With 1 hand gently but firmly holding top lid and other hand holding sharp chef's or serrated knife, slice horizontally between lids, cutting tomatoes in half.

CUMIN-CILANTRO YOGURT SAUCE
MAKES ABOUT 1 CUP

Mint may be substituted for the cilantro. This sauce is prone to curdling and thus does not reheat well; prepare it just before serving.

- 2 tablespoons extra-virgin olive oil
- 1 shallot, minced
- 1 garlic clove, minced
- 1 teaspoon ground cumin
- ⅛ teaspoon red pepper flakes
- ½ cup plain whole-milk yogurt
- ⅓ cup water
- 1 teaspoon lime juice
  Salt and pepper
- 2 tablespoons chopped fresh cilantro

Heat 1 tablespoon oil in 8-inch skillet over medium heat until shimmering. Add shallot and cook until softened, about 2 minutes. Stir in garlic, cumin, and pepper flakes and cook until fragrant, about 30 seconds. Remove from heat and whisk in yogurt, water, lime juice, and remaining 1 tablespoon oil. Season with salt and pepper to taste, and cover to keep warm. Stir in cilantro just before serving.

WARM TOMATO-GINGER VINAIGRETTE
MAKES ABOUT 2 CUPS

Parsley may be substituted for the cilantro.

- ¼ cup extra-virgin olive oil
- 1 shallot, minced
- 1½ teaspoons grated fresh ginger
- ⅛ teaspoon ground cumin
- ⅛ teaspoon ground fennel
- 12 ounces cherry tomatoes, halved
  Salt and pepper
- 1 tablespoon red wine vinegar
- 1 teaspoon packed light brown sugar
- 2 tablespoons chopped fresh cilantro

Heat 2 tablespoons oil in 10-inch nonstick skillet over medium heat until shimmering. Add shallot, ginger, cumin, and fennel and cook until fragrant, about 15 seconds. Stir in tomatoes and ¼ teaspoon salt and cook, stirring frequently, until tomatoes have softened, 3 to 5 minutes. Off heat, stir in vinegar and sugar and season with salt and pepper to taste; cover to keep warm. Stir in cilantro and remaining 2 tablespoons oil just before serving.

Sautéed Chicken Cutlets

✔ WHY THIS RECIPE WORKS

French pan sauces are built around the fond (intensely flavorful bits of browned protein) left in the skillet after you have cooked meat or poultry. These sauces are quick, reliable, and easy, but classic recipes require an awful lot of butter, usually about 1 tablespoon per serving. Newer sauces based on chutneys, relishes, and salsas have less fat, but they generally don't take advantage of the savory fond. We wanted to create a simple sautéed chicken cutlet recipe with lower-fat versions of classic French pan sauces—sauces that might be a bit lighter but, don't skip on flavor.

ADD A LITTLE FLOUR Pan sauces typically begin with an empty pan covered with fond. Aromatics are then added, followed by a liquid—usually broth and/or wine—for deglazing. Finally, the sauce is enriched with a generous amount of cold butter. Simply reducing the amount of butter left our sauces thin and brothy, but adding just a teaspoon of flour with the aromatics helped to thicken the sauce, allowing us to reduce the butter to just 1 tablespoon.

ADD SOME ACIDITY While using less butter had the benefit of amplifying the other flavors, we also found that adding an acidic ingredient to the finished sauce (we had good luck with lemon juice, sherry, mustard, and brandy) provided a final blast of flavor.

SAUTÉED CHICKEN CUTLETS WITH LEMON-CAPER PAN SAUCE
SERVES 4

To make slicing the chicken easier, freeze it for 20 minutes. More pan sauce recipes follow.

CHICKEN

4   (6- to 8-ounce) boneless, skinless chicken breasts, tenderloins removed, trimmed
     Salt and pepper
2   tablespoons vegetable oil

LEMON-CAPER PAN SAUCE

2   teaspoons vegetable oil
1   shallot, minced
1   teaspoon all-purpose flour
¾   cup chicken broth
1   tablespoon capers, rinsed and chopped
1   tablespoon chopped fresh parsley
1   tablespoon unsalted butter, chilled
2   teaspoons lemon juice
     Salt and pepper

1. FOR THE CHICKEN: Adjust oven rack to middle position and heat oven to 200 degrees. Halve chicken horizontally, then cover chicken halves with plastic wrap and pound to even ¼-inch thickness with meat pounder. Pat chicken dry with paper towels and season with salt and pepper.

2. Heat 1 tablespoon oil in 12-inch skillet over medium-high heat until just smoking. Place 4 cutlets in skillet and cook until browned on first side, about 2 minutes. Flip cutlets and continue to cook until second side is opaque, 15 to 20 seconds; transfer to large ovensafe platter. Repeat with remaining 1 tablespoon oil and remaining 4 cutlets; transfer to platter. Tent loosely with aluminum foil and transfer to oven to keep warm while preparing sauce.

3. FOR THE PAN SAUCE: Heat oil in now-empty skillet over low heat until shimmering. Add shallot and cook, stirring often, until softened, about 2 minutes. Add flour and cook, stirring constantly, for 30 seconds. Slowly whisk in broth, scraping up any browned bits. Bring to simmer and cook until reduced to ½ cup, 2 to 3 minutes. Stir in any accumulated chicken juices; return to simmer and cook for 30 seconds. Off heat, whisk in capers, parsley, butter, and lemon juice. Season with salt and pepper to taste. Pour sauce over chicken and serve immediately.

VERMOUTH, LEEK, AND TARRAGON PAN SAUCE
MAKES ABOUT 1 CUP

2   teaspoons vegetable oil
1   leek, white and light green parts only, halved lengthwise, sliced ¼ inch thick, and washed thoroughly
1   teaspoon all-purpose flour
¾   cup chicken broth
½   cup dry vermouth or dry white wine
1   tablespoon unsalted butter, chilled
2   teaspoons chopped fresh tarragon
1   teaspoon whole-grain mustard
     Salt and pepper

Heat oil in now-empty skillet over medium heat until shimmering. Add leek and cook, stirring often, until softened and lightly browned, about 5 minutes. Add flour and cook, stirring constantly, for 30 seconds. Slowly whisk in broth and vermouth, scraping up any browned bits. Bring to simmer and cook until reduced to ¾ cup, 3 to 5 minutes. Stir in any accumulated chicken juices; return to simmer and cook for 30 seconds. Off heat, whisk in butter, tarragon, and mustard. Season with salt and pepper to taste. Pour sauce over chicken and serve immediately.

THE BEST CHICKEN BROTH

Store-bought chicken broth is a real timesaver, but is any brand a worthy stand-in for homemade? We discovered that finding a broth with two important characteristics was key: less than 700 milligrams of sodium per serving (some contain up to 1,350 milligrams per serving) and a short ingredient list that includes vegetables such as carrots, celery, and onions. Our favorite broth, **Swanson Certified Organic Free Range Chicken Broth**, won tasters over with its "very chicken-y flavor" and "hints of roastiness."

You can certainly roast your
own peppers at home, but
jarred peppers are especially
convenient. We tasted eight
supermarket brands. Our
tasters preferred firmer,
smokier, sweeter-tasting
peppers in strong yet simple
brines of salt and water.
Peppers packed in brines
that contained garlic, vinegar,
olive oil, and grape must—
characteristic of most of the
European peppers—rated
second. The extra ingredients
provided "interesting" and
"lively" flavor profiles, but
the vinegar often masked the
authentic red pepper flavor
and smoky notes that tasters preferred. The blandest
peppers, which were also the
slimiest ones, rated dead last.
Our winner? The domestically
produced **Dunbars Sweet
Roasted Peppers**, which
lists only red bell peppers,
water, salt, and citric acid on
its ingredient list.

SHERRY, RED PEPPER, AND TOASTED GARLIC PAN SAUCE

MAKES ABOUT I CUP

2   teaspoons vegetable oil
3   garlic cloves, minced
I   teaspoon all-purpose flour
¼   teaspoon paprika
¾   cup chicken broth
½   cup plus I teaspoon dry sherry
¼   cup jarred roasted red peppers, patted
    dry and cut into ¼-inch pieces
I   tablespoon unsalted butter, chilled
½   teaspoon chopped fresh thyme
    Salt and pepper

Heat oil and garlic in now-empty skillet over
low heat. Cook, stirring often, until garlic
turns golden but not brown, about 1 minute. Add flour and paprika and cook, stirring constantly, for 30 seconds. Slowly whisk
in broth and ½ cup sherry, scraping up any
browned bits. Bring to simmer and cook
until reduced to ¾ cup, 3 to 5 minutes. Stir
in any accumulated chicken juices; return to
simmer and cook for 30 seconds. Off heat,
whisk in peppers, butter, thyme, and remaining 1 teaspoon sherry. Season with salt and
pepper to taste. Pour sauce over chicken and
serve immediately.

BRANDY, CREAM, AND CHIVE PAN SAUCE

MAKES ABOUT ¾ CUP

*Be sure to add the broth to the skillet before adding
the brandy.*

2   teaspoons vegetable oil
I   shallot, minced
I   teaspoon all-purpose flour
¾   cup chicken broth
5   tablespoons brandy
2   tablespoons heavy cream
2   tablespoons chopped fresh chives
2   teaspoons lemon juice
I   teaspoon Dijon mustard
    Salt and pepper

Heat oil in now-empty skillet over low heat
until shimmering. Add shallot and cook,
stirring often, until softened, about 2 minutes. Add flour and cook, stirring constantly,
for 30 seconds. Slowly whisk in broth, then
¼ cup brandy, scraping up any browned bits.
Bring to simmer and cook until reduced to
½ cup, 2 to 3 minutes. Stir in cream and any
accumulated chicken juices; return to simmer
and cook until thickened, about 1 minute. Off
heat, whisk in chives, lemon juice, mustard,
and remaining 1 tablespoon brandy. Season
with salt and pepper to taste. Pour sauce over
chicken and serve immediately.

Chicken Saltimbocca

✔ WHY THIS RECIPE WORKS

*Chicken seems like it would offer a fresh spin on an
old Italian classic, Veal Saltimbocca (Sauteed Veal
Cutlets with Prosciutto and Sage, page 333). But
most chicken adaptations of this dish take it too far
from its roots, wrapping the cutlet around stuffing or
adding unnecessary breading or cheese. We wanted
to avoid the temptation to overcomplicate this dish.*

FLOUR THE CUTLETS FIRST Flouring
the cutlets before adding the sage and prosciutto—rather than after, as many recipes
call for—allowed the ham to crisp and the
chicken to brown evenly while eliminating any
uncooked, gummy spots.

SIZING UP PROSCIUTTO Prosciutto
that was too thick overwhelmed the flavor

of everything else, while ham that was ultra-thin fell apart too easily. The ideal slice was just thick enough to hold its shape, and trimming the prosciutto to fit the cutlet in a single layer provided just the right balance of ham to chicken.

BOOST THE SAGE FLAVOR For an even distribution of herbal flavor, we minced the sage leaves and sprinkled them over the floured cutlets before adding the ham. Frying whole sage leaves to place on the cooked cutlets, while not essential, provided an elegant (and traditional) finishing touch.

SKIP THE TOOTHPICK Once the prosciutto hit the hot oil, it practically sealed to the chicken, making the step of securing it with a toothpick unnecessary.

CHICKEN SALTIMBOCCA
SERVES 4

Make sure to buy prosciutto that is thinly sliced, not shaved; also avoid slices that are too thick, as they won't stick to the chicken. The prosciutto slices should be large enough to fully cover one side of each cutlet. To make slicing the chicken easier, freeze it for 15 minutes. Although whole sage leaves make a beautiful presentation, they are optional and can be left out of step 3.

- 4 (6- to 8-ounce) boneless, skinless chicken breasts, tenderloins removed, trimmed
- ½ cup all-purpose flour
  Salt and pepper
- 1 tablespoon minced fresh sage, plus 8 large fresh leaves (optional)
- 8 thin slices prosciutto (3 ounces)
- ¼ cup olive oil
- 1¼ cups dry vermouth or dry white wine
- 2 teaspoons lemon juice
- 4 tablespoons unsalted butter, cut into 4 pieces and chilled
- 1 tablespoon minced fresh parsley

1. Halve chicken horizontally, then cover chicken halves with plastic wrap and pound to even ¼-inch thickness with meat pounder. Combine flour and 1 teaspoon pepper in shallow dish.

2. Pat chicken dry with paper towels. Working with 1 cutlet at a time, dredge in flour mixture, shaking off excess, and transfer to work surface. Sprinkle cutlets evenly with minced sage. Place 1 prosciutto slice on top of each cutlet, covering sage, and press lightly to help it adhere.

3. Heat 2 tablespoons oil in 12-inch skillet over medium-high heat until shimmering. Add sage leaves, if using, and cook until leaves begin to change color and are fragrant, about 15 to 20 seconds. Remove sage leaves with slotted spoon and transfer to paper towel–lined plate; set aside.

4. Place 4 cutlets in now-empty skillet, prosciutto side down, and cook over medium-high heat until golden brown on first side, about 3 minutes. Flip cutlets, reduce heat to medium, and continue to cook until no longer pink and lightly browned on second side, about 2 minutes longer. Transfer cutlets to large platter. Wipe out skillet with paper towels. Repeat with remaining 2 tablespoons oil and remaining 4 cutlets; transfer to platter. Tent loosely with aluminum foil and set aside while preparing sauce.

5. Pour off all fat left in skillet. Add vermouth, scraping up any browned bits. Bring to simmer and cook until reduced to ⅓ cup, 5 to 7 minutes. Stir in lemon juice. Reduce heat to low and whisk in butter, 1 tablespoon at a time. Off heat, stir in parsley and season with salt and pepper to taste. Pour sauce over chicken, place sage leaf on top of each cutlet, if using, and serve immediately.

SIMPLIFYING SALTIMBOCCA

1. No need to flour prosciutto before sautéing, just chicken.

2. Sprinkling cutlets with sage and topping with prosciutto distributes flavor evenly.

3. Searing cutlets prosciutto side down helps ham stick.

4. Stir vermouth into pan, reduce, and finish with butter. Spoon over cutlets.

Crispy-Skinned Chicken Breasts

✓ WHY THIS RECIPE WORKS

Pollo alla diavola *is an impressive and unbelievably flavorful dish featuring tender chicken with gorgeously bronzed and shatteringly crisp skin, served with a spicy pickled cherry pepper sauce. But restaurant versions serve half a chicken per person, removing all but the wing bones from the meat before searing it. This flattens out the bird so that its entire surface makes direct, even contact with the pan—a must for producing thoroughly rendered, deeply crisped skin. We wanted to keep the incredibly crisp skin but eliminate most of the knife work, making this a dish we could easily prepare at home.*

TRADE IN THE BIRD FOR BREASTS By opting to use only breast meat, we eliminated more than half of the butchering; removing the breastbones required just a few quick strokes of a sharp knife.

SALT FOR MOISTER MEAT, DRIER SKIN Salting the chicken breasts prior to searing them not only seasoned the meat and helped it retain moisture as it cooked, but salting also assisted in drying out the skin, an important step toward crispness. Poking holes in both the skin and meat with a sharp knife prior to salting further encouraged these results.

POUND AND WEIGH IT DOWN Pounding the chicken created breasts of even thickness, which promoted evenly cooked meat, while weighing down the breasts with a Dutch oven for a portion of the cooking time ensured that more of the skin would remain in contact with the pan for consistent, even browning.

START WITH A COLD PAN While pounding the chicken and weighing it down promoted more even cooking, it wasn't enough; the lean meat was still drying out in the time it took for the skin to crisp. The solution was to start the breasts in a cold pan. Putting the meat skin side down in the oiled pan before turning on the heat allowed more time for the skin to render its fat before the temperature of the meat reached its doneness point.

FINISH WITH A TANGY SAUCE A reduction of pickled-pepper vinegar and chicken broth, thickened with a little flour and butter and garnished with a few chopped pickled peppers, finished our dish; the tanginess of the sauce made it the perfect accompaniment to the skin's ultrameaty flavor.

CRISPY-SKINNED CHICKEN BREASTS WITH VINEGAR-PEPPER PAN SAUCE

SERVES 2

This recipe requires refrigerating the salted meat for at least 1 hour before cooking. Two 10- to 12-ounce chicken breasts are ideal, but three smaller ones can fit in the same pan; the skin will be slightly less crispy. A boning knife or sharp paring knife works best to remove the bones from the breasts. To maintain the crispy skin, spoon the sauce around, not over, the breasts when serving.

CHICKEN

2 (10- to 12-ounce) bone-in split chicken breasts
Kosher salt and pepper
2 tablespoons vegetable oil

PAN SAUCE

1 shallot, minced
1 teaspoon all-purpose flour
½ cup chicken broth
¼ cup chopped jarred hot cherry peppers, plus ¼ cup brine
1 tablespoon unsalted butter, chilled
1 teaspoon minced fresh thyme
Salt and pepper

BONING A SPLIT CHICKEN BREAST

Removing the bones allows the entire surface of the breast meat to lie flat and even against the pan—a must for perfectly crispy skin.

1. With chicken breast skin side down, run tip of boning or sharp paring knife between breastbone and meat, working from thick end of breast toward thin end.

2. Angling blade slightly toward rib cage, repeat cutting motion several times to free breast from rib cage.

3. Holding rib cage, run tip of knife around remnant of wishbone along top edge of breast to remove it.

1. FOR THE CHICKEN: Place 1 chicken breast, skin side down, on cutting board, with ribs facing away from knife hand. Run tip of knife between breastbone and meat, working from thick end of breast toward thin end. Angling blade slightly and following rib cage, repeat cutting motion several times to remove ribs and breastbone from breast. Find short remnant of wishbone along top edge of breast and run tip of knife along both sides of bone to separate it from meat. Remove tenderloin (reserve for another use) and trim excess fat, taking care not to cut into skin. Repeat with second breast.

2. Using tip of paring knife, poke skin on each breast evenly 30 to 40 times. Turn breasts over and poke thickest half of each breast 5 or 6 times. Cover breasts with plastic wrap and pound thick ends gently with meat pounder until ½ inch thick. Evenly sprinkle each breast with ½ teaspoon kosher salt. Place breasts, skin side up, on wire rack set in rimmed baking sheet, cover loosely with plastic, and refrigerate for 1 hour or up to 8 hours.

3. Pat breasts dry with paper towels and sprinkle each breast with ¼ teaspoon pepper. Pour oil in 12-inch skillet and swirl to coat. Place breasts, skin side down, in oil and place skillet over medium heat. Place heavy skillet or Dutch oven on top of breasts. Cook breasts until skin is beginning to brown and meat is beginning to turn opaque along edges, 7 to 9 minutes.

4. Remove weight and continue to cook until skin is well browned and very crispy, 6 to 8 minutes. Flip breasts, reduce heat to medium-low, and cook until second side is lightly browned and meat registers 160 degrees, 2 to 3 minutes. Transfer breasts to individual plates and let rest while preparing pan sauce.

5. FOR THE PAN SAUCE: Pour off all but 2 teaspoons oil from skillet. Return skillet to medium heat and add shallot; cook, stirring occasionally, until shallot is softened, about 2 minutes. Add flour and cook, stirring constantly, for 30 seconds. Increase heat to medium-high, add broth and brine, and bring to simmer, scraping up any browned bits. Simmer until thickened, 2 to 3 minutes. Stir in any accumulated chicken juices; return to simmer and cook for 30 seconds. Remove skillet from heat and whisk in butter, thyme, and cherry peppers; season with salt and pepper to taste. Spoon sauce around breasts and serve.

CRISPY-SKINNED CHICKEN BREASTS WITH LEMON-ROSEMARY PAN SAUCE

In step 5, increase broth to ¾ cup and substitute 2 tablespoons lemon juice for brine. Omit peppers and substitute rosemary for thyme.

CRISPY-SKINNED CHICKEN BREASTS WITH MAPLE–SHERRY VINEGAR PAN SAUCE

In step 5, substitute 2 tablespoons sherry vinegar for brine, 1 tablespoon maple syrup for peppers, and sage for thyme.

Crisp Breaded Chicken Cutlets

✔ WHY THIS RECIPE WORKS

Breaded cutlets, for all their apparent simplicity, can be problematic. Too often, they end up with either an underdone or burnt coating, which falls off the tasteless, rubbery chicken underneath. We wanted chicken cutlets with flavorful meat and a crunchy crust that would adhere nicely to the meat.

POUND FOR EVEN THICKNESS To ensure even cooking, we flattened the chicken breasts to ½ inch thick; thin enough to cook evenly, but thick enough to make a hearty, crisp cutlet.

ADD OIL TO THE EGG WASH Beaten egg alone formed a heavy a layer on the meat, making the breading too thick. Adding a little oil thinned out the egg, resulting in a more delicate coat. The small amount of oil also helped the breading brown a bit more deeply.

GIVE IT A REST Letting the chicken rest for just 5 minutes after breading helped everything to solidify, ensuring that the breading stayed put.

USE PLENTY OF OIL AND COOK IN BATCHES A generous amount of vegetable oil—enough to reach one-third to one-half of the way up the sides of the cutlets—was essential for even browning. Cooking the cutlets two at a time was equally important; crowding the pan resulted in too much steam, which inhibited the formation of a crisp, golden brown crust.

CRISP BREADED CHICKEN CUTLETS
SERVES 4

If you'd rather not prepare fresh bread crumbs, use 1½ cups panko, the extra-crisp Japanese bread crumbs. The chicken is cooked in batches of two because the crust is noticeably more crisp if the pan is not overcrowded.

4 (6- to 8-ounce) boneless, skinless chicken breasts, tenderloins removed, trimmed
   Salt and pepper
3 slices hearty white sandwich bread, torn into quarters
¾ cup all-purpose flour
2 large eggs
1 tablespoon plus ¾ cup vegetable oil
   Lemon wedges

1. Cover chicken breasts with plastic wrap and pound to even ½-inch thickness with meat pounder. Pat chicken dry with paper towels and season with salt and pepper.

2. Adjust oven rack to middle position and heat oven to 200 degrees. Set wire rack in rimmed baking sheet. Pulse bread in food processor to coarse crumbs, about 10 pulses; transfer to shallow dish. Spread flour in second shallow dish. Beat eggs and 1 tablespoon oil together in third shallow dish.

3. Working with 1 cutlet at a time, dredge in flour, shaking off excess, then coat with egg mixture, allowing excess to drip off. Coat all sides of cutlet with bread crumbs, pressing gently so that crumbs adhere; transfer to prepared wire rack and let sit for 5 minutes.

4. Heat 6 tablespoons oil in 10-inch nonstick skillet over medium-high heat until shimmering. Place 2 cutlets in skillet and cook until deep golden brown and crisp on first side, about 3 minutes. Flip cutlets, reduce heat to medium, and continue to cook until deep golden brown and crisp on second side and meat feels firm when pressed gently, about 3 minutes longer. Drain cutlets briefly on paper towel–lined plate, then transfer to clean dry wire rack set in rimmed baking sheet and keep warm in oven. Pour off all oil left in skillet

BREADING CHICKEN CUTLETS

1. Dredge cutlets lightly but thoroughly in flour mixture, shaking off excess.

2. Using tongs, dip both sides of cutlets in egg mixture, taking care to coat them thoroughly and allowing excess to drip back into dish to ensure a very thin coating. Tongs keep egg from coating your fingers.

3. Dredge both sides of cutlets in bread crumbs, pressing crumbs in place with your fingers to form even, cohesive coat.

4. Place breaded cutlets in single layer on wire rack set over baking sheet and allow coating to dry for about 5 minutes. This drying time stabilizes breading so that it can be sautéed without sticking to skillet or falling off.

and wipe out with paper towels. Repeat with remaining 6 tablespoons oil and remaining 2 cutlets. Serve with lemon wedges.

DEVILED CRISP BREADED CHICKEN CUTLETS

Rub each breast with generous pinch cayenne before dredging in flour. Lightly beat 3 tablespoons Dijon mustard, 1 tablespoon Worcestershire sauce, and 2 teaspoons minced fresh thyme into eggs along with oil.

CRISP BREADED CHICKEN CUTLETS WITH GARLIC AND OREGANO

Lightly beat 3 tablespoons minced fresh oregano and 8 garlic cloves, minced to paste, into eggs along with oil.

CRUSHED TOMATOES

The coarse consistency of crushed tomatoes provides great body and flavor for tomato sauces. We prefer chunky and fresh-tasting **Tuttorosso Crushed Tomatoes in Thick Puree with Basil**. Muir Glen Organic Crushed Tomatoes with Basil came in a close second in our testing.

Best Chicken Parmesan

✔ WHY THIS RECIPE WORKS

In traditional recipes for chicken Parmesan, boneless, skinless chicken breasts are pounded until thin and then coated in breading and fried until crispy and golden. But then those fully cooked cutlets are blanketed with tomato sauce and cheeses and baked in the oven—during which time the sauce saturates and softens the crust, the chicken overcooks, and the cheeses meld into a thick, tough mass. We wanted a method for preparing chicken Parmesan that would give us juicy chicken, a crisp crust, and rich, cheesy flavor offset by a zippy tomato sauce.

PREVENT OVERCOOKED CUTLETS Cutlets that were pounded too thin inevitably overcooked; halving two large breasts horizontally and pounding only the thick end of each piece to achieve a consistent ½-inch thickness from end to end worked best. Salting the cutlets for 20 minutes further ensured perfectly cooked cutlets; the salt helped the meat hold on to more of its moisture.

KEEP THE CRUST CRISP Replacing half of the bread crumbs—which readily absorb liquid and become soft—with grated Parmesan not only made the crust more moisture-proof, but it also contributed a nutty richness to the coating, giving our cutlets a major flavor boost.

TWO-STEP BREADING We found that we could eliminate the tedious and messy three-step breading process by combining the flour and eggs.

ADD FONTINA FOR CREAMINESS Replacing a portion of the mozzarella with creamy fontina prevented the cheese from forming a leathery layer atop our cutlets.

CHEESE COMES BEFORE SAUCE Placing the cheese between the breaded cutlets and the sauce provided a protective barrier and prevented a soggy crust. Broiling the assembled dish allowed the cheese to melt and brown quickly; this further ensured a crisp crust, since the cheese and sauce spent less time on top of the breaded cutlets.

BEST CHICKEN PARMESAN
SERVES 4

This recipe makes enough sauce to top the cutlets as well as four servings of pasta. Serve with pasta and a simple green salad.

SAUCE

2	tablespoons extra-virgin olive oil
2	garlic cloves, minced
	Kosher salt and pepper
¼	teaspoon dried oregano
	Pinch red pepper flakes
1	(28-ounce) can crushed tomatoes
¼	teaspoon sugar
2	tablespoons coarsely chopped fresh basil

To prevent cheese from clogging the holes of your box grater and to make cleanup a breeze, lightly coat the coarse side with vegetable oil spray and then shred the cheese as usual.

CHICKEN

2   (6- to 8-ounce) boneless, skinless chicken breasts, tenderloins removed, trimmed, halved horizontally, and pounded ½ inch thick
1   teaspoon kosher salt
2   ounces whole-milk mozzarella cheese, shredded (½ cup)
2   ounces fontina cheese, shredded (½ cup)
1   large egg
1   tablespoon all-purpose flour
1½ ounces Parmesan cheese, grated (¾ cup)
½   cup panko bread crumbs
½   teaspoon garlic powder
¼   teaspoon dried oregano
¼   teaspoon pepper
⅓   cup vegetable oil
¼   cup torn fresh basil

1. FOR THE SAUCE: Heat 1 tablespoon oil in medium saucepan over medium heat until just shimmering. Add garlic, ¾ teaspoon salt, oregano, and pepper flakes; cook, stirring occasionally, until fragrant, about 30 seconds. Stir in tomatoes and sugar; increase heat to high and bring to simmer. Reduce heat to medium-low and simmer until thickened, about 20 minutes. Off heat, stir in basil and remaining 1 tablespoon oil; season with salt and pepper to taste. Cover and keep warm.

2. FOR THE CHICKEN: Sprinkle each side of each cutlet with ⅛ teaspoon salt and let stand at room temperature for 20 minutes. Combine mozzarella and fontina in bowl; set aside.

3. Adjust oven rack 4 inches from broiler element and heat broiler. Whisk egg and flour together in shallow dish until smooth. Combine Parmesan, panko, garlic powder, oregano, and pepper in second shallow dish. Pat chicken dry with paper towels. Working with 1 cutlet at a time, dredge cutlet in egg mixture, allowing excess to drip off. Coat all sides in Parmesan mixture, pressing gently so crumbs adhere. Transfer cutlet to large plate and repeat with remaining cutlets.

4. Heat oil in 10-inch nonstick skillet over medium-high heat until shimmering. Carefully place 2 cutlets in skillet and cook without moving them until bottoms are crispy and deep golden brown, 1½ to 2 minutes. Using tongs, carefully flip cutlets and cook on second side until deep golden brown, 1½ to 2 minutes. Transfer cutlets to paper towel–lined plate and repeat with remaining cutlets.

5. Place cutlets on rimmed baking sheet and sprinkle cheese mixture evenly over cutlets, covering as much surface area as possible. Broil until cheese is melted and beginning to brown, 2 to 4 minutes. Transfer chicken to serving platter and top each cutlet with 2 tablespoons sauce. Sprinkle with basil and serve immediately, passing remaining sauce separately.

Skillet Chicken Fajitas

✓ WHY THIS RECIPE WORKS

While fajitas are traditionally a simple affair, with the focus on the meat, vegetables, and lightly charred tortillas, today's fajitas are lost under a blanket of heavy toppings. We wanted to create indoor chicken fajitas that didn't require a slew of compensatory ingredients to be tasty.

BRINERATE THE CHICKEN Marinating the boneless, skinless chicken breasts in a brinerade—a concentrated liquid with the salt content of a brine plus the acid and seasonings of a marinade—seasoned the chicken and helped keep it moist. Salt, lime juice, garlic, cumin, cayenne, and a little oil formed the base of our brinerade, while a little sugar

helped the chicken brown faster and a touch of smoked paprika alluded to the smoky heat of a grill.

SEAR ONE SIDE, THEN FINISH IN THE OVEN By searing just one side of the chicken over high heat in a skillet and then moving it to a low oven to finish cooking, we got both flavorful char and tender, moist chicken.

REVAMP THE VEGETABLES We nixed the usual bland mix of bell pepper and onion in favor of our take on *rajas con crema*, strips of roasted chile and onion cooked down with tangy Mexican cultured cream. We charred poblano chiles and onion for maximum flavor and substituted heavy cream, with a splash of lime for tang, for the crema.

SKILLET CHICKEN FAJITAS
SERVES 4

We like to serve these fajitas with crumbled queso fresco or feta in addition to the other garnishes listed.

CHICKEN

¼	cup vegetable oil
2	tablespoons lime juice
4	garlic cloves, peeled and smashed
1½	teaspoons smoked paprika
1	teaspoon sugar
1	teaspoon salt
½	teaspoon ground cumin
½	teaspoon pepper
¼	teaspoon cayenne pepper
1½	pounds boneless, skinless chicken breasts, trimmed and pounded to ½-inch thickness

RAJAS CON CREMA

1	pound (3 to 4) poblano chiles, stemmed, halved, and seeded
1	tablespoon vegetable oil
1	onion, halved and sliced ¼ inch thick
2	garlic cloves, minced
¼	teaspoon dried thyme
¼	teaspoon dried oregano
½	cup heavy cream
1	tablespoon lime juice
½	teaspoon salt
¼	teaspoon pepper

8–12	(6-inch) flour tortillas, warmed
¼	cup minced fresh cilantro
	Spicy Pickled Radishes (recipe follows)
	Lime wedges

1. FOR THE CHICKEN: Whisk 3 tablespoons oil, lime juice, garlic, paprika, sugar, salt, cumin, pepper, and cayenne together in bowl. Add chicken and toss to coat. Cover and let stand at room temperature for 30 minutes to 1 hour.

2. FOR THE RAJAS CON CREMA: Meanwhile, adjust oven rack 4 inches from broiler element and heat broiler. Arrange poblanos, skin side up, on aluminum foil–lined rimmed baking sheet and press to flatten. Broil until skin is charred and puffed, 4 to 10 minutes, rotating sheet halfway through cooking. Transfer poblanos to bowl, cover, and let steam for 10 minutes. Rub majority of skin from poblanos and discard (preserve some skin for flavor); slice into ¼-inch-thick strips. Adjust oven racks to middle and lowest positions and heat oven to 200 degrees.

3. Heat oil in 12-inch nonstick skillet over high heat until just smoking. Add onion and cook until charred and just softened, about 3 minutes. Add garlic, thyme, and oregano and cook until fragrant, about 15 seconds. Add cream and cook, stirring frequently, until reduced and cream lightly coats onion, 1 to 2 minutes. Add poblano strips, lime juice, salt, and pepper and toss to coat. Transfer vegetables to bowl, cover with foil, and place on middle oven rack. Wipe out skillet with paper towels.

4. Remove chicken from marinade and wipe off excess. Heat remaining 1 tablespoon oil in now-empty skillet over high heat until just smoking. Add chicken and cook without moving it until bottom side is well charred, about 4 minutes. Flip chicken; transfer skillet to lower oven rack. Bake until chicken registers 160 degrees, 7 to 10 minutes. Transfer to cutting board and let rest for 5 minutes; do not wash out skillet.

5. Slice chicken crosswise into ¼-inch-thick strips. Return chicken strips to skillet and toss to coat with pan juices. To serve, spoon few pieces of chicken into center of warmed tortilla and top with spoonful of vegetable mixture, cilantro, and Spicy Pickled Radishes. Serve with lime wedges.

SPICY PICKLED RADISHES
MAKES ABOUT 1¾ CUPS

10	radishes, trimmed and sliced thin
½	cup lime juice (4 limes)
½	jalapeño chile, sliced thin
1	teaspoon sugar
¼	teaspoon salt

Combine all ingredients in bowl. Cover and let stand at room temperature for 30 minutes, or refrigerate for up to 24 hours.

SIMPLER SLICING

It can be difficult to slice radishes thinly and evenly with a chef's knife. Instead, try using a vegetable peeler. The sharp blade makes it easy to cut wafer-thin slices.

Pan-Roasted Chicken Breasts

✔ WHY THIS RECIPE WORKS

Bone-in, skin-on chicken breasts offer more flavor than their boneless, skinless counterparts, but getting the skin to crisp without overcooking the delicate breast meat can be a challenge. We wanted to use pan roasting—a common restaurant technique—to produce crisp skin, moist meat, and a quick, flavorful pan sauce.

BRINE THE CHICKEN Brining the chicken breasts ensured that the meat was well seasoned and remained moist.

START SKIN SIDE DOWN Starting the chicken in the pan skin side down allowed much of the fat to be rendered and jump-started the browning process. Once the skin was browned, we flipped the chicken and seared it lightly on the second side.

KEEP THE OVEN HOT We flipped the chicken skin side down once more before transferring the skillet to a 450-degree oven; keeping the skin in direct contact with the hot skillet ensured crackling-crisp skin.

DEGLAZE FOR A QUICK SAUCE After removing the chicken from the hot pan and setting it aside to rest, we built a quick sauce starting with the flavorful fond left in the skillet. After sautéing a little shallot, we deglazed the pan with a combination of chicken broth and vermouth. We then added sage for an herbal note before finishing the sauce with some butter for richness and sheen.

PAN-ROASTED CHICKEN BREASTS WITH SAGE-VERMOUTH SAUCE
SERVES 4

We prefer to split whole chicken breasts ourselves because store-bought split chicken breasts are often sloppily butchered. However, if you prefer to purchase split chicken breasts, try to choose 10- to 12-ounce pieces with the skin intact. If the split breasts are of different sizes, check the smaller ones a few minutes early to see if they are cooking more quickly. If using kosher chicken, do not brine in step 1, but season with salt as well as pepper.

CHICKEN

Salt and pepper

2 (1½-pound) whole bone-in chicken breasts, split through breastbone and trimmed

1 tablespoon vegetable oil

SAUCE

1 large shallot, minced

¾ cup chicken broth

½ cup dry vermouth

4 fresh sage leaves, each leaf torn in half

3 tablespoons unsalted butter, cut into 3 pieces and chilled

Salt and pepper

1. FOR THE CHICKEN: Dissolve ½ cup salt in 2 quarts cold water in large container. Submerge chicken in brine, cover, and refrigerate for 30 minutes. Remove chicken from brine and pat dry with paper towels. Season chicken with pepper.

2. Adjust oven rack to lowest position and heat oven to 450 degrees. Heat oil in 12-inch ovensafe skillet over medium-high heat until just smoking. Place chicken breasts skin side down in skillet and cook until well browned, 6 to 8 minutes, reducing heat if chicken begins to scorch. Flip chicken skin side up and continue to cook until lightly browned on second side, about 3 minutes.

3. Flip chicken skin side down and transfer skillet to oven. Roast until chicken registers 160 degrees, 15 to 18 minutes.

4. Using potholders (skillet handle will be hot) remove skillet from oven. Transfer chicken to serving platter and let rest while making sauce (if not making sauce, let chicken rest for 5 minutes before serving).

5. FOR THE SAUCE: Being careful of hot skillet handle, pour off all but 1 teaspoon fat left in skillet, add shallot, and cook over medium-high heat until softened, about 2 minutes. Stir in broth, vermouth, and sage leaves, scraping up any browned bits. Bring to simmer and cook until thickened and measures

¾ cup, about 5 minutes. Stir in any accumulated chicken juices; return to simmer and cook for 30 seconds.

6. Off heat, discard sage leaves and whisk in butter 1 piece at a time. Season with salt and pepper to taste. Pour sauce over chicken and serve immediately.

PAN-ROASTED CHICKEN BREASTS WITH GARLIC-SHERRY SAUCE

Substitute 7 sliced garlic cloves for shallot and cook, stirring often, until garlic turns golden but not brown, about 1½ minutes. Substitute dry sherry for dry vermouth and 2 sprigs fresh thyme for sage. Stir ½ teaspoon lemon juice into sauce before seasoning with salt and pepper.

PAN-ROASTED CHICKEN BREASTS WITH ONION AND ALE SAUCE

Brown ale gives this sauce a nutty, toasty, bittersweet flavor. Newcastle Brown Ale and Samuel Smith Nut Brown Ale are good choices.

Substitute ½ onion, sliced very thin, for shallot and cook until onion is softened, about 5 minutes. Substitute brown ale for dry vermouth and 1 sprig fresh thyme for sage. Stir 1 bay leaf and 1 tablespoon packed brown sugar into skillet along with broth. Discard bay leaf with thyme sprig and stir ½ teaspoon cider vinegar into sauce before seasoning with salt and pepper.

PAN-ROASTED CHICKEN BREASTS WITH SWEET-TART RED WINE SAUCE

This sauce is a variation on the Italian sweet-sour flavor combination called agrodolce.

Substitute ¼ cup red wine and ¼ cup red wine vinegar for dry vermouth and 1 bay leaf for sage. Stir 1 tablespoon sugar and ¼ teaspoon pepper into skillet with broth.

Chicken Enchiladas with Red Chili Sauce

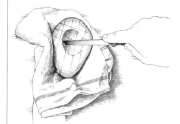

✓ WHY THIS RECIPE WORKS

Chicken enchiladas are a complete meal that offers a rich and complex combination of flavors, textures, and ingredients. The problem with preparing enchiladas at home is that traditional cooking methods require a whole day of preparation. We wanted a recipe for a simplified version of chicken enchiladas that could be made in 90 minutes from start to finish.

GO FOR CORN TORTILLAS Corn tortillas have a substantial flavor and small size that provided the best proportion of tortilla to filling to sauce, and they fit neatly into a 9-inch-wide baking dish.

SKIP THE TEDIOUS, MESSY PREP Rather than follow the traditional approach of dipping each tortilla in hot oil and then in sauce prior to assembly, we created pliable tortillas by simply spraying them with vegetable oil spray and warming them on a baking sheet in the oven.

POACH THE CHICKEN RIGHT IN THE SAUCE We created a quick chili sauce with onion, garlic, spices, and tomato sauce, and to further enhance the sauce's flavor, we poached the chicken right in the sauce. This step also made for moist, flavorful meat. Some cheddar spiked with jarred jalapeños and fresh cilantro rounded out our rich, flavorful filling.

FILL AND ROLL ON AN ASSEMBLY LINE Spreading the oil-sprayed, oven-warmed tortillas on the counter and placing a portion of the filling down the center of each before rolling and placing them in a baking dish was fast and simple.

CHICKEN ENCHILADAS WITH RED CHILI SAUCE

SERVES 4 TO 5

If you prefer, Monterey Jack can be used instead of cheddar or, for a mellower flavor and creamier texture, try substituting an equal amount of farmer's cheese. Be sure to cool the chicken filling before stuffing the tortillas; otherwise, the hot filling will make the enchiladas soggy.

SAUCE AND FILLING

1½	tablespoons vegetable oil
1	onion, chopped fine
3	tablespoons chili powder
3	garlic cloves, minced
2	teaspoons ground coriander
2	teaspoons ground cumin
2	teaspoons sugar
½	teaspoon salt
12	ounces boneless, skinless chicken thighs, trimmed and cut into ¼-inch-wide strips
2	(8-ounce) cans tomato sauce
¾	cup water
11	ounces sharp cheddar cheese, shredded (2¾ cups)
½	cup chopped fresh cilantro
¼	cup chopped jarred jalapeños, chopped

TORTILLAS

10	(6-inch) corn tortillas
	Vegetable oil spray

GARNISHES

¾	cup sour cream
1	avocado, halved, pitted, and cut into ½-inch pieces
5	romaine lettuce leaves, shredded
	Lime wedges

2. Separate diced flesh from skin using spoon inserted between skin and flesh and gently scoop out avocado cubes.

1. FOR THE SAUCE AND FILLING: Heat oil in medium saucepan over medium-high heat until shimmering. Add onion and cook, stirring occasionally, until softened and lightly browned, 5 to 7 minutes. Stir in chili powder, garlic, coriander, cumin, sugar, and salt and cook, stirring constantly, until fragrant, about 30 seconds. Add chicken and cook, stirring constantly, until coated with spices, about 30 seconds. Add tomato sauce and water, bring to simmer, and cook, stirring occasionally, until chicken is cooked through and flavors have melded, about 8 minutes. Strain mixture through fine-mesh strainer into bowl, pressing on chicken and onion to extract as much sauce as possible; set chili sauce aside. Transfer chicken mixture to plate; place in refrigerator to cool, about 20 minutes, then combine with 2 cups cheddar, cilantro, and jalapeños in bowl and set aside.

2. Adjust oven racks to upper-middle and lower-middle positions and heat oven to 350 degrees.

3. FOR THE TORTILLAS: Spread ¾ cup reserved chili sauce evenly over bottom of 13 by 9-inch baking dish. Place tortillas in single layer on 2 baking sheets. Spray both sides of tortillas lightly with oil spray. Bake until tortillas are soft and pliable, 2 to 4 minutes.

4. Increase oven temperature to 400 degrees. Place warm tortillas on counter and spread ⅓ cup chicken filling down center of each tortilla. Roll each tortilla tightly and place in baking dish, seam side down. Pour remaining chili sauce over top of enchiladas and spread into even layer so that it coats top of each tortilla. Sprinkle remaining ¾ cup cheddar down center of enchiladas and cover tightly with aluminum foil.

5. Bake enchiladas on lower rack until heated through and cheddar is melted, 20 to 25 minutes. Uncover and serve immediately, passing sour cream, avocado, lettuce, and lime wedges separately.

Enchiladas Verdes

✓ WHY THIS RECIPE WORKS

In Mexico, enchiladas come in myriad forms, but for us, enchiladas topped by green sauce—enchiladas verdes—are as perfect a comfort food as any we know, especially when they include moist, tender pieces of chicken. But enchiladas verdes with chicken can be hard to re-create at home. The sauce is often too watery and thin, the tortillas mushy, and the filling marred by bland, dried-out chicken overpowered by cheese. We wanted to get this Mexican restaurant classic right.

GO GREEN Broad, dark green poblano chiles have a mild to moderate heat and a deep herbal flavor that made them an ideal choice for this sauce; fresh tomatillos are increasingly available year-round and offered a tangy flavor that just wasn't found in canned versions.

BROIL AWAY Traditional recipes dry-roast whole tomatillos and poblanos on the stovetop using a flat cast-iron vessel known as a *comal*; this step imparts smokiness and concentrates flavor, all the while wicking away excess moisture that makes for a watery sauce. Broiling the vegetables gave us similar results, tempering the tartness of the tomatillos and bringing a near-sweet richness to the poblanos.

GET THE TEXTURE JUST RIGHT For a coarse, rustic texture, we pulsed the tomatillos and poblanos in the food processor; the addition of a little broth lent a subtle richness and thinned the sauce while maintaining its body.

POACH THE CHICKEN To keep our recipe both streamlined and flavorful, we poached the chicken in a broth spiked with sautéed onion, garlic, and cumin.

ADD SOME RICHNESS Shredded pepper Jack added a mildly spicy kick to our filling and contributed a gooey richness that had been missing.

ENCHILADAS VERDES
SERVES 4 TO 6

You can substitute three 11-ounce cans tomatillos, drained and rinsed, for the fresh ones in this recipe. Halve large tomatillos (more than 2 inches in diameter) and place them skin side up for broiling in step 2 to ensure even cooking and charring. If you can't find poblanos, substitute 4 large jalapeño chiles (with seeds and ribs removed). To increase the spiciness of the sauce, reserve some of the chiles' ribs and seeds and add them to the food processor in step 4. Be sure to cool the chicken filling before stuffing the tortillas; hot filling will make the enchiladas soggy.

4	teaspoons vegetable oil
1	onion, chopped
½	teaspoon ground cumin
3	garlic cloves, minced
1½	cups chicken broth
1	pound boneless, skinless chicken breasts, trimmed
1½	pounds tomatillos (16 to 20 medium), husks and stems removed, rinsed well and dried
3	poblano chiles, halved lengthwise, stemmed, and seeded
1–2½	teaspoons sugar
	Salt and pepper
½	cup chopped fresh cilantro
8	ounces pepper Jack or Monterey Jack cheese, shredded (2 cups)
12	(6-inch) corn tortillas
	Vegetable oil spray

GARNISHES

2	scallions, sliced thin
	Thinly sliced radishes
	Sour cream

1. Adjust 1 oven rack to middle position and second rack 6 inches from broiler element and heat broiler. Heat 2 teaspoons oil in medium saucepan over medium heat until shimmering. Add onion and cook, stirring often, until softened and lightly browned, 5 to 7 minutes. Stir in cumin and two-thirds of garlic and cook, stirring often, until fragrant, about 30 seconds. Decrease heat to low and stir in broth. Add chicken, cover, and simmer until it registers 160 degrees, 15 to 20 minutes, flipping chicken halfway through cooking. Transfer chicken to large bowl; place in refrigerator to cool, about 20 minutes. Measure out and reserve ¼ cup broth and set aside; discard remaining liquid.

2. Meanwhile, toss tomatillos and poblanos with remaining 2 teaspoons oil. Arrange tomatillos cut side down and poblanos skin side up on aluminum foil–lined rimmed baking sheet. Broil on upper rack until vegetables blacken and start to soften, 5 to 10 minutes, rotating baking sheet halfway through broiling.

3. Remove tomatillos and poblanos from oven, let cool slightly, then remove skins from poblanos (leave tomatillo skins intact). Reduce oven temperature to 350 degrees. Discard foil from baking sheet and set baking sheet aside for warming tortillas.

4. Transfer vegetables, along with any accumulated juices, to food processor. Add 1 teaspoon sugar, 1 teaspoon salt, remaining garlic, and reserved broth to food processor and pulse until sauce is somewhat chunky, about 8 pulses. Season with salt and pepper to taste, and adjust tartness by stirring in remaining sugar to taste, ½ teaspoon at a time; set aside.

5. When chicken is cool, use 2 forks to shred into bite-size pieces. Combine chicken with cilantro and 1½ cups pepper Jack; season with salt to taste.

6. Spread ¾ cup tomatillo sauce evenly over bottom of 13 by 9-inch baking dish. Place tortillas in single layer on 2 baking sheets. Spray both sides of tortillas lightly with vegetable oil spray. Bake until tortillas are soft and pliable, 2 to 4 minutes. Increase oven

TOMATILLOS

Called tomates verdes (green tomatoes) in much of Mexico, tomatillos have a tangier, more citrusy flavor than true green tomatoes. When choosing tomatillos, look for pale-green orbs with firm flesh that fills and splits open the fruit's outer papery husk, which must be removed before cooking. The flavor of canned tomatillos is less bright but they make a fine substitute when fresh are not available.

temperature to 450 degrees. Place warm tortillas on counter and spread ⅓ cup chicken filling down center of each tortilla. Roll each tortilla tightly and place in baking dish, seam side down. Pour remaining tomatillo sauce over top of enchiladas and spread into even layer so that it coats top of each tortilla.

Sprinkle with remaining ½ cup pepper Jack and cover tightly with foil.

7. Bake enchiladas on lower rack until heated through and cheese is melted, 15 to 20 minutes. Uncover, sprinkle with scallions, and serve immediately, passing radishes and sour cream separately.

Chicken Tikka Masala

✔ WHY THIS RECIPE WORKS

Most recipes for chicken tikka masala—a staple in Indian restaurants—call for marinating chicken breast chunks in yogurt, often for 24 hours, then skewering them, kebab-style, for cooking. The tandoor oven is replaced with a broiler or grill, and the masala sauce is quick and easy to prepare. But all too often the result is dry or mushy chicken and an unbearably rich, overspiced sauce. We wanted tender, moist pieces of chicken napped with a lightly spiced tomato cream sauce.

USE THE BROILER We wanted a four-season dish, so we opted to use the broiler rather than the grill.

COOK THE CHICKEN BREASTS WHOLE Broiling the boneless chicken breasts whole and cutting them into pieces only after they were cooked prevented the meat from drying out and got rid of the fussy step of skewering raw, slippery chicken.

SKIP THE MARINADE Marinating the chicken in yogurt made the meat mushy; instead, we rubbed the breasts with a salt-spice mixture—featuring coriander, cumin, and cayenne—and let them sit for 30 minutes, then dipped them in yogurt right before cooking. Adding a little oil to the yogurt encouraged gentle charring, while some minced garlic and freshly grated ginger contributed an aromatic presence.

STREAMLINE THE SAUCE Rather than pile on an extensive combination of spices, we settled on using garam masala, which blends warm spices such as cardamom, black pepper, cinnamon, and coriander all in one jar. Crushed tomatoes and cream formed the base of our sauce, while tomato paste helped it retain an attractive hue.

CHICKEN TIKKA MASALA
SERVES 4 TO 6

This dish is best when prepared with whole-milk yogurt, but low-fat yogurt can be substituted. For a spicier dish, do not remove the ribs and seeds from the chile. Serve with Basmati Rice Pilaf (page 305).

CHICKEN

1	teaspoon salt
½	teaspoon ground cumin
½	teaspoon ground coriander
¼	teaspoon cayenne pepper
2	pounds boneless, skinless chicken breasts, trimmed
1	cup plain whole-milk yogurt
2	tablespoons vegetable oil
1	tablespoon grated fresh ginger
2	garlic cloves, minced

SAUCE

3	tablespoons vegetable oil
1	onion, chopped fine
2	garlic cloves, minced
2	teaspoons grated fresh ginger
1	serrano chile, stemmed, seeded, and minced

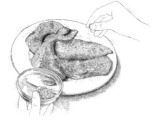

1. Coat chicken in salt and
spice mixture and refrigerate.

2. Prepare creamy tomato-
masala sauce.

3. Dunk chicken in protective
coating of yogurt and oil.

4. Broil chicken, then allow
to rest.

5. Cut chicken into chunks
and add to sauce.

1 tablespoon tomato paste
1 tablespoon garam masala
1 (28-ounce) can crushed tomatoes
2 teaspoons sugar
  Salt
⅔ cup heavy cream
¼ cup chopped fresh cilantro

1. FOR THE CHICKEN: Combine salt, cumin, coriander, and cayenne in small bowl. Sprinkle both sides of chicken with spice mixture, pressing gently so mixture adheres. Place chicken on plate, cover with plastic wrap, and refrigerate for 30 minutes to 1 hour. Meanwhile, whisk yogurt, oil, ginger, and garlic together in large bowl and set aside.

2. FOR THE SAUCE: Heat oil in Dutch oven over medium heat until shimmering. Add onion and cook, stirring frequently, until light golden, 8 to 10 minutes. Add garlic, ginger, serrano, tomato paste, and garam masala and cook, stirring frequently, until fragrant, about 3 minutes. Add crushed tomatoes, sugar, and ½ teaspoon salt and bring to boil. Reduce heat to medium-low, cover, and simmer for 15 minutes, stirring occasionally. Stir in cream and return to simmer. Remove pan from heat and cover to keep warm.

3. TO COOK THE CHICKEN: While sauce simmers, adjust oven rack 6 inches from heating element and heat broiler. Set wire rack in rimmed baking sheet lined with aluminum foil (or line broiler pan with foil). Using tongs, dip chicken into yogurt mixture (chicken should be coated with thick layer of yogurt) and arrange on prepared rack. Discard excess yogurt mixture. Broil chicken until thickest part registers 160 degrees and exterior is lightly charred in spots, 10 to 18 minutes, flipping chicken halfway through cooking.

4. Let chicken rest for 5 minutes, then cut into 1-inch chunks and stir into warm sauce (do not simmer chicken in sauce). Stir in cilantro, season with salt to taste, and serve. (Sauce can be made ahead, refrigerated for up to 4 days and gently reheated before adding hot chicken.)

Stir-Fried Chicken and Vegetables

✔ WHY THIS RECIPE WORKS

While a stir-fry should be an easy weeknight meal, making a stir-fry with chicken presents one big challenge: The lean meat inevitably becomes dry and stringy when cooked over high heat. We were after a stir-fry that featured tender, juicy, bite-size pieces of chicken paired with just the right combination of vegetables in a simple yet complex-flavored sauce. And because this was a stir-fry, it had to be fairly quick.

COMBINE THE BRINE AND MARINADE While brining certainly added moisture to lean chicken breasts, it also took a fair amount of time; since we wanted to add more flavor with a marinade anyway, we decided to combine the two, using soy sauce to provide the high level of salt in our brine.

COAT WITH CORNSTARCH For tender, supple chicken we turned to a traditional Chinese technique known as velveting. Coating our chicken pieces with a mixture of cornstarch, flour, and oil protected them from the high heat of the skillet, ensuring that they remained tender and juicy.

DON'T STIR THE CHICKEN Though it seems counterintuitive for a stir-fry, we found that cooking the strips of chicken without stirring them resulted in better browning.

FINISH WITH A SAUCE Chicken broth provided a good base for our sauce, while ingredients like soy sauce, hoisin, dry sherry, and orange juice worked nicely as flavoring ingredients. A small amount of cornstarch ensured that the sauce thickened slightly and clung to the meat.

SWEET, SOUR, AND SPICY ORANGE CHICKEN AND BROCCOLI WITH CASHEWS

SERVES 4

To make slicing the chicken easier, freeze it for 15 minutes. Serve with Sticky Rice (page 114).

SAUCE
¼	cup chicken broth
¼	cup orange juice
¼	cup white vinegar
2	teaspoons soy sauce
2	teaspoons hoisin sauce
1	teaspoon cornstarch
1	tablespoon sugar
½	teaspoon red pepper flakes

STIR-FRY
3	tablespoons plus 1 teaspoon vegetable oil
2	garlic cloves, minced
1	teaspoon grated fresh ginger
1¼	cups water
¼	cup soy sauce
¼	cup dry sherry
1	pound boneless, skinless chicken breasts, trimmed and sliced thin
2	tablespoons toasted sesame oil
1	tablespoon cornstarch
1	tablespoon all-purpose flour
1½	pounds broccoli, florets cut into 1-inch pieces, stalks peeled and sliced ¼ inch thick on bias
1	cup toasted cashews
4	scallions, sliced ¼ inch thick on bias

1. FOR THE SAUCE: Whisk ingredients together in small bowl and set aside.

2. FOR THE STIR-FRY: Combine 1 tablespoon vegetable oil, garlic, and ginger in small bowl and set aside. Combine 1 cup water, soy sauce, and sherry in medium bowl. Add chicken and stir to break up clumps. Cover with plastic wrap and refrigerate for at least 20 minutes or up to 1 hour. Pour off excess liquid from chicken.

3. Mix sesame oil, cornstarch, and flour in medium bowl until smooth. Toss chicken in cornstarch mixture until evenly coated.

4. Heat 2 teaspoons vegetable oil in 12-inch nonstick skillet over high heat until smoking. Add half of chicken in even layer and cook, without stirring, until golden brown on first side, about 1 minute. Flip chicken pieces over and cook until lightly browned on second side, about 30 seconds. Transfer chicken to clean bowl. Repeat with 2 teaspoons vegetable oil and remaining chicken.

5. Add remaining 1 tablespoon vegetable oil to skillet and heat until just smoking. Add broccoli and cook 30 seconds. Add remaining ¼ cup water, cover, and lower heat to medium-low. Cook broccoli until crisp-tender, about 3 minutes, then transfer to paper towel–lined plate. Add garlic mixture to skillet, increase heat to medium-high, and cook, mashing mixture into pan, until fragrant and golden brown, 15 to 20 seconds.

6. Return chicken to skillet and toss to combine. Whisk sauce to recombine, add to skillet, and cook, stirring constantly, until sauce is thickened and evenly distributed, about 1 minute. Off heat, add broccoli and cashews and stir to combine. Transfer to platter, sprinkle with scallions, and serve immediately.

PREPARING CHICKEN FOR A STIR-FRY

1. Freeze breasts for 15 minutes to make slicing easier. Then, separate tenderloin from breast. Starting at thick end, cut into ¼-inch slices. Stop slicing when you reach tapered triangle end.

2. With flat side of knife, press each slice to even ¼-inch thickness and then cut slices into 1-inch squares.

3. Use same technique for tenderloin, flattening it with side of knife and then cutting into 1-inch pieces.

GINGERY STIR-FRIED CHICKEN AND BOK CHOY

SERVES 4

To make slicing the chicken easier, freeze it for 15 minutes. Serve with Sticky Rice (page 114).

SAUCE

- ¼ cup chicken broth
- 2 tablespoons dry sherry
- 1 tablespoon soy sauce
- 1 tablespoon oyster sauce
- 2 teaspoons grated fresh ginger
- ½ teaspoon toasted sesame oil
- 1 teaspoon cornstarch
- 1 teaspoon sugar
- ¼ teaspoon red pepper flakes

STIR-FRY

- 2 tablespoons plus 2 teaspoons vegetable oil
- 2 teaspoons grated fresh ginger
- 1 garlic clove, minced
- 1 cup water
- ¼ cup soy sauce
- ¼ cup dry sherry
- 1 pound boneless, skinless chicken breasts, trimmed and sliced thin
- 2 tablespoons toasted sesame oil
- 1 tablespoon cornstarch
- 1 tablespoon all-purpose flour
- 1 pound bok choy, stalks sliced ¼ inch thick on bias and greens cut into ½-inch strips
- 1 small red bell pepper, stemmed, seeded, and cut into ¼-inch-wide strips

1. FOR THE SAUCE: Whisk all ingredients together in small bowl and set aside.

2. FOR THE STIR-FRY: Combine 1 teaspoon vegetable oil, ginger, and garlic in small bowl and set aside. Combine water, soy sauce, and sherry in medium bowl. Add chicken and stir to break up clumps. Cover with plastic wrap and refrigerate for at least 20 minutes or up to 1 hour. Pour off excess liquid from chicken.

3. Mix sesame oil, cornstarch, and flour in medium bowl until smooth. Toss chicken in cornstarch mixture until evenly coated.

4. Heat 2 teaspoons vegetable oil in 12-inch nonstick skillet over high heat until smoking. Add half of chicken to skillet in single layer and cook, without stirring, until golden brown on first side, about 1 minute. Flip chicken pieces over and cook until lightly browned on second side, about 30 seconds. Transfer chicken to clean bowl. Repeat with 2 teaspoons vegetable oil and remaining chicken.

5. Add remaining 1 tablespoon vegetable oil to skillet and heat over high heat until just smoking. Add bok choy stalks and bell pepper and cook, stirring, until beginning to brown, about 1 minute. Clear center of skillet, add ginger mixture, and cook, mashing mixture into pan, until fragrant, 15 to 20 seconds. Stir mixture into vegetables and continue to cook until stalks are crisp-tender, about 30 seconds longer. Stir in bok choy greens and cook until beginning to wilt, about 30 seconds.

6. Return chicken to skillet. Whisk sauce to recombine, add to skillet, reduce heat to medium, and cook, stirring constantly, until sauce is thickened and chicken is cooked through, about 30 seconds. Transfer to platter and serve immediately.

PREPPING BOK CHOY

1. Trim bottom inch from head of bok choy. Wash and dry leaves and stalks. Cut leafy green portion away from either side of white stalk.

2. Stack leafy greens and then slice them crosswise into ½-inch-wide strips.

3. Cut each stalk in half lengthwise and then crosswise into ¼-inch-wide pieces.

Thai-Style Stir-Fried Noodles with Chicken

✔ WHY THIS RECIPE WORKS

The street food of Thailand is amazingly varied and inventive; one of our favorite offerings is pad see ew, which is a soft tangle of chewy, lightly charred rice noodles studded with tender slices of meat, crisp Chinese broccoli, and moist egg, all very lightly coated with a beautifully balanced sweet and salty soy-based sauce. We wanted to find substitutions for some of the more exotic ingredients—fresh wide rice noodles, sweet Thai soy sauce, and leafy Chinese broccoli—for a deliciously simple dish we could make right at home, any night of the week.

PRECISION COUNTS Since authentic fresh rice noodles can be hard to find, we substituted flat, ¼-inch-wide dried noodles known as rice sticks. To shorten our prep time, we opted to soak them in boiling water, but this meant our timing had to be precise; an 8-minute soak was exactly right—otherwise, the noodles could turn mushy

ADD A LITTLE BAKING SODA Soaking the chicken breasts briefly in a baking soda and water solution helped keep the lean meat tender.

KEEP IT CONVENIENT Broccolini was an accessible substitute for Chinese broccoli; unbeaten eggs gave our dish the dense, variegated curds that usually feature in Asian stir-fries; and we replicated the sweet, salty sauce by mixing up ingredients we already had on hand: oyster sauce, brown sugar, molasses, fish sauce, garlic, and—of course—soy sauce.

GO NONSTICK AND COOK IN BATCHES A nonstick skillet allowed us to cook our stir-fry over high heat without the need for an overload of oil, and cooking the components in batches prevented an overcrowded skillet, which meant we could maximize the heat.

DON'T STIR Surprisingly, the key to this stir-fry was to not stir at all—at least at the end. Once all the ingredients were added back to the skillet for a final warm-through, we let everything sit over high heat until the ideal char developed.

THAI-STYLE STIR-FRIED NOODLES WITH CHICKEN AND BROCCOLINI

SERVES 4

The flat pad thai–style rice noodles that are used in this recipe can be found in the Asian foods section of most supermarkets. If you can't find broccolini, you can substitute an equal amount of conventional broccoli, but be sure to trim and peel the stalks before cutting.

CHILE VINEGAR

- ⅓ cup distilled white vinegar
- 1 serrano chile, stemmed and sliced into thin rings

STIR-FRY

- 12 ounces boneless, skinless chicken breasts, trimmed and cut against grain into ¼-inch-thick slices
- 1 teaspoon baking soda
- 8 ounces (¼-inch-wide) rice noodles
- ¼ cup vegetable oil
- ¼ cup oyster sauce
- 2 tablespoons packed dark brown sugar
- 5 teaspoons soy sauce
- 1 tablespoon distilled white vinegar
- 1 teaspoon molasses
- 1 teaspoon fish sauce
- 3 garlic cloves, sliced thin
- 3 large eggs
- 10 ounces broccolini, florets cut into 1-inch pieces, stalks cut on bias into ½-inch pieces (5 cups)

1. **FOR THE CHILE VINEGAR:** Combine vinegar and serrano in bowl. Let stand at room temperature for at least 15 minutes.

2. **FOR THE STIR-FRY:** Combine chicken with 2 tablespoons water and baking soda in bowl. Let sit at room temperature for 15 minutes. Rinse chicken in cold water and drain well.

3. Bring 6 cups water to boil. Place noodles in large bowl. Pour boiling water over noodles. Stir, then soak until noodles are almost tender, about 8 minutes, stirring once halfway through soak. Drain and rinse with cold water. Drain well and toss with 2 teaspoons oil.

4. Whisk oyster sauce, sugar, soy sauce, vinegar, molasses, and fish sauce together in bowl.

5. Heat 2 teaspoons oil and garlic in 12-inch nonstick skillet over high heat, stirring occasionally, until garlic is deep golden brown, 1 to 2 minutes. Add chicken and 2 tablespoons sauce mixture, toss to coat, and spread chicken into even layer. Cook, without stirring, until chicken begins to brown, 1 to 1½ minutes. Using tongs, flip chicken and cook, without stirring, until second side begins to brown, 1 to 1½ minutes. Push chicken to 1 side of skillet. Add 2 teaspoons oil to cleared side of skillet. Add eggs to clearing. Using rubber spatula, stir eggs gently and cook until set but still wet. Stir eggs into chicken and continue to cook, breaking up large pieces of egg, until eggs are fully cooked, 30 to 60 seconds. Transfer chicken mixture to bowl.

6. Heat 2 teaspoons oil in now-empty skillet until smoking. Add broccolini and 2 tablespoons sauce and toss to coat. Cover skillet and cook for 2 minutes, stirring once halfway through cooking. Remove lid and continue to cook until broccolini is crisp and very brown in spots, 2 to 3 minutes, stirring once halfway through cooking. Transfer broccolini to bowl with chicken mixture.

7. Heat 2 teaspoons oil in again-empty skillet until smoking. Add half of noodles and 2 tablespoons sauce and toss to coat. Cook until noodles are starting to brown in spots, about 2 minutes, stirring halfway through cooking. Transfer noodles to bowl with chicken mixture. Repeat with remaining 2 teaspoons oil and remaining noodles and sauce. When second batch of noodles is cooked, add contents of bowl back to skillet and toss to combine. Cook, without stirring, until everything is warmed through, 1 to 1½ minutes. Transfer to platter and serve immediately, passing chile vinegar separately.

Thai-Style Chicken with Basil

✔ **WHY THIS RECIPE WORKS**
Unlike a high-heat stir-fry (common in Chinese cooking), in which the aromatics are added at the end to prevent scorching, Thai stir-fries use a lower-temperature method in which the aromatics are sautéed at the very beginning. The flavor of the aromatics infuses the oil they're cooked in, which in turn coats the protein, giving the dish deep, complex flavor. We wanted to try our hand at this approach to create one of our favorite Thai street dishes: gai pad krapow, or chicken with hot basil.

START WITH A COLD SKILLET For aromatics cooked to a perfect, even shade of golden brown, we started them in a cold skillet with a couple tablespoons of oil; this allowed them to cook slowly and evenly, with no chance of burning.

BASIL STEMS VERSUS LEAVES

We have found that cilantro stems have the same fresh flavors as their leaves and can be used as long as their crunchier texture is acceptable. To see if basil stems could also be put to use, we first got our bearings by asking tasters to sample basil leaves as well as various portions of the stems raw. All agreed that the tender, thinner, younger stems tasted clean and sweet, comparable to the leaves. However, as tasters reached thicker, older portions of stem, particularly the lower portion of the central stem, bitter flavors began to dominate.

With that in mind, we made two batches of a classic basil pesto in our food processor, one with leaves that had been stemmed and another with equal volumes of both leaves and tender stems. Tasters were unable to tell one batch from the other.

The bottom line? While we don't recommend using the thicker stems from a bunch of basil, it's perfectly fine to make the most of your basil bunch and put the younger, more tender stems to use.

BALANCE SPICY AND SWEET To tone down the heat for an American audience, we reduced the amount of chiles by half; this also meant we needed to cut the sugar by half to avoid a cloyingly sweet dish.

PUT THE FOOD PROCESSOR TO WORK Chopping chicken by hand (the traditional method) was enormously time-consuming. Fortunately, we found that chopping tender breast meat in the food processor yielded a coarse texture similar to that of hand-chopped. Using the processor to chop the garlic and chiles further streamlined the dish.

COOK THE CHICKEN IN ONE BATCH Because the aromatic oil and sauce provide so much complexity, we could skip the high heat sear essential to flavorful browning and cook the chicken in a single batch.

BRIGHTEN THE SAUCE A teaspoon of white vinegar balanced the heaviness of the oyster sauce while a spoonful of the raw garlic-chile mixture, added to the sauce at the end of cooking, brightened the dish substantially.

ADD A DOUBLE DOSE OF BASIL Unlike hot basil, which has a robust texture that can stand up to prolonged cooking, sweet Italian basil simply wilts under heat—but simply adding it at the end doesn't add nearly enough flavor. The solution? Chopping a cup of basil to cook with the chiles and aromatics, then stirring in an additional cup of whole basil leaves right before serving.

THAI-STYLE CHICKEN WITH BASIL
SERVES 4

Since tolerance for spiciness can vary, we've kept our recipe relatively mild. Sweetness without sufficient heat can become cloying, so we also cut back the sugar. For a very mild version of the dish, remove the seeds and ribs from the chiles. If fresh Thai chiles are unavailable, substitute two serranos or one medium jalapeño. In Thailand, red pepper flakes and sugar are passed at the table, along with extra fish sauce and white vinegar, so the dish can be adjusted to suit individual tastes. Serve with steamed rice and vegetables, if desired.

2 cups fresh basil leaves

3 garlic cloves, peeled

6 green or red Thai chiles, stemmed

2 tablespoons fish sauce, plus extra for serving

1 tablespoon oyster sauce

1 tablespoon sugar, plus extra for serving

1 teaspoon distilled white vinegar, plus extra for serving

1 pound boneless, skinless chicken breasts, trimmed and cut into 2-inch pieces

3 shallots, sliced thin

2 tablespoons vegetable oil
Red pepper flakes, for serving

1. Pulse 1 cup basil, garlic, and Thai chiles in food processor until finely chopped, 6 to 10 pulses, scraping down sides of bowl once during processing. Transfer 1 tablespoon basil mixture to small bowl and stir in 1 tablespoon fish sauce, oyster sauce, sugar, and vinegar; set aside. Transfer remaining basil mixture to 12-inch nonstick skillet.

2. Pulse chicken and 1 tablespoon fish sauce in now-empty food processor until meat is chopped into approximate ¼-inch pieces, 6 to 8 pulses. Transfer to medium bowl and refrigerate for 15 minutes.

3. Stir shallots and oil into basil mixture in skillet. Heat over medium-low heat (mixture should start to sizzle after about 1½ minutes; if it doesn't, adjust heat accordingly), stirring constantly, until garlic and shallots are golden brown, 5 to 8 minutes.

4. Add chicken, increase heat to medium, and cook, stirring and breaking up chicken with potato masher or rubber spatula, until only traces of pink remain, 2 to 4 minutes. Add reserved basil–fish sauce mixture and continue to cook, stirring constantly, until chicken is no longer pink, about 1 minute. Stir in remaining 1 cup basil and cook, stirring constantly, until basil is wilted, 30 to 60 seconds. Serve immediately, passing extra fish sauce, sugar, vinegar, and pepper flakes separately.

Grilled Lemon-Parsley Chicken Breasts

✔ **WHY THIS RECIPE WORKS**

Because they have no skin and little fat, plain bone-less chicken breasts invariably turn out dry and leathery when grilled. A common solution, marinating them in bottled salad dressing—which is usually laden with artificial ingredients—often imparts off-flavors. We wanted grilled chicken breasts that would come off the grill juicy and flavorful, and we wanted to look beyond bottled salad dressing to get there.

MAKE A TWO-LEVEL FIRE Cooked over a hot, single-level fire, the outer layers of chicken breasts burn before the inside is cooked through. Using a two-level fire and cooking the chicken, covered, over the cooler side of the grill until almost done and finishing with a quick sear solved this problem, and we were rewarded with perfectly cooked breasts.

MAKE YOUR OWN MARINADE A simple combination of olive oil, lemon juice, garlic, salt, pepper, and a bit of sugar was easy to prepare and tasted worlds better than any store-bought option.

ACID TO FINISH Adding too much acid to the marinade caused the exterior of the chicken breasts to turn white and made the meat mushy. Reducing the amount of lemon juice in the marinade and supplementing it with a complementary vinaigrette after cooking amped up the flavors.

GRILLED LEMON-PARSLEY CHICKEN BREASTS

SERVES 4

The chicken should be marinated for no less than 30 minutes and no more than 1 hour. Serve with a simply prepared vegetable or use in sandwiches or salad.

6 tablespoons olive oil
2 tablespoons lemon juice
1 tablespoon minced fresh parsley
1¼ teaspoons sugar
1 teaspoon Dijon mustard
   Salt and pepper
2 tablespoons water
3 garlic cloves, minced
4 (6- to 8-ounce) boneless, skinless chicken breasts, trimmed

1. Whisk 3 tablespoons oil, 1 tablespoon lemon juice, parsley, ¼ teaspoon sugar, mustard, ¼ teaspoon salt, and ¼ teaspoon pepper together in bowl and set aside for serving.

2. Whisk water, garlic, remaining 3 tablespoons oil, remaining 1 tablespoon lemon juice, remaining 1 teaspoon sugar, 1½ teaspoons salt, and ½ teaspoon pepper together in bowl. Place marinade and chicken in 1-gallon zipper-lock bag and toss to coat; press out as much air as possible and seal bag. Refrigerate for at least 30 minutes or up to 1 hour, flipping bag every 15 minutes.

3A. FOR A CHARCOAL GRILL: Open bottom vent completely. Light large chimney starter filled with charcoal briquettes (6 quarts). When top coals are partially covered with ash, pour evenly over half of grill. Set cooking grate in place, cover, and open lid vent completely. Heat grill until hot, about 5 minutes.

3B. FOR A GAS GRILL: Turn all burners to high, cover, and heat grill until hot, about 15 minutes. Leave primary burner on high and turn off other burner(s).

4. Clean and oil cooking grate. Remove chicken from bag, allowing excess marinade to drip off. Place chicken on cooler side of grill, smooth side down, with thicker sides facing coals and flames. Cover and cook until bottom of chicken just begins to develop light grill marks and is no longer translucent, 6 to 9 minutes.

5. Flip chicken and rotate so that thinner sides face coals and flames. Cover and continue to cook until chicken is opaque and firm to touch and registers 140 degrees, 6 to 9 minutes longer.

6. Move chicken to hotter side of grill and cook until dark grill marks appear on both sides and chicken registers 160 degrees, 2 to 6 minutes longer.

7. Transfer chicken to carving board, tent loosely with aluminum foil, and let rest for 5 to 10 minutes. Slice each breast on bias into ¼-inch-thick slices and transfer to individual plates. Drizzle with reserved sauce and serve.

GRILLED CHIPOTLE-LIME CHICKEN BREASTS

Substitute lime juice for lemon juice and use an extra teaspoon juice in reserved sauce. Substitute 1 teaspoon minced canned chipotle chile in adobo sauce for mustard and cilantro for parsley.

GRILLED ORANGE-TARRAGON CHICKEN BREASTS

Substitute orange juice for lemon juice and tarragon for parsley. Add ¼ teaspoon grated orange zest to reserved sauce.

Grilled Glazed Bone-In Chicken Breasts

✓ WHY THIS RECIPE WORKS

There's a lot to admire about a perfectly grilled chicken breast. Cooked bone-in with the skin on for extra flavor and juiciness, the smoke-infused meat should be tender and succulent and the skin golden and crisp. But don't let the everyday nature of this grill favorite fool you: This dish isn't that easy to get right. Burnt, limp skin and sooty, parched meat are too often the reality. To help inject as much precision as possible into the process, we knew every detail would have to count.

INDIRECT HEAT IS ESSENTIAL Having a cooler side of the grill—a portion with no coals—allowed the chicken to cook through gently and evenly through indirect heat, with no risk of flare-ups.

POSITION MATTERS Arranging the chicken breasts so that thicker sides faced the fire promoted even cooking.

USE A FOIL SHIELD To get all the breasts to cook at a similar rate, we placed a sheet of aluminum foil over them before closing the grill lid. When cooked on the cooler side of the grill this way, the foil trapped a layer of heat against the meat that maintained a consistent temperature.

START HIGH, FINISH HIGH An initial brief stint over the hotter part of the grill helped the skin crisp. Moving the breasts back to the hotter side for the final few minutes of cooking resulted in an even deeper golden hue—and because most of the fat had already been rendered, there was little risk of flare-ups.

GRILLED GLAZED BONE-IN CHICKEN BREASTS

SERVES 4

If using kosher chicken, do not brine in step 1, but season with salt as well as pepper. Remember to reserve half of the glaze for serving.

Salt
4 (10- to 12-ounce) bone-in split chicken breasts, trimmed
Pepper
1 recipe glaze (recipes follow)

1. Dissolve ½ cup salt in 2 quarts cold water in large container. Submerge chicken breasts in brine, cover, and refrigerate for 30 minutes to 1 hour. Remove chicken from brine and pat dry with paper towels. Season chicken with pepper.

2A. FOR A CHARCOAL GRILL: Open bottom vent completely. Light large chimney starter filled with charcoal briquettes (6 quarts). When top coals are partially covered with ash, pour evenly over half of grill. Set cooking grate in place, cover, and open lid vent completely. Heat grill until hot, about 5 minutes.

2B. FOR A GAS GRILL: Turn all burners to high, cover, and heat grill until hot, about 15 minutes. Leave primary burner on high and turn off other burner(s). (Adjust primary burner as needed to maintain grill temperature of 350 degrees.)

3. Clean and oil cooking grate. Place chicken on hotter side of grill, skin side up, and cook (covered if using gas) until lightly browned on both sides, 6 to 8 minutes, flipping halfway through cooking. Move chicken, skin side down, to cooler side of grill, with thicker end of breasts facing coals and flames. Cover and continue to cook until chicken registers 150 degrees, 15 to 20 minutes longer.

4. Brush bone side of chicken generously with half of glaze, move to hotter side of grill, and cook until browned, 5 to 10 minutes. Brush skin side of chicken with remaining glaze, flip chicken, and continue to cook until chicken registers 160 degrees, 2 to 3 minutes longer.

5. Transfer chicken to serving platter, tent loosely with aluminum foil, and let rest for 5 to 10 minutes before serving, passing reserved glaze separately.

ORANGE-CHIPOTLE GLAZE

MAKES ABOUT ¾ CUP

For a spicier glaze, use the greater amount of chipotle chiles.

1 teaspoon grated orange zest plus ⅔ cup juice (2 oranges)
1–2 tablespoons minced canned chipotle chile in adobo sauce
1 small shallot, minced
2 teaspoons minced fresh thyme
1 tablespoon molasses
¾ teaspoon cornstarch
Salt

Combine orange zest and juice, chipotle, shallot, and thyme in small saucepan. Whisk in molasses and cornstarch, bring to simmer, and cook over medium heat until thickened, about 5 minutes. Season with salt to taste. Reserve half of glaze for serving and use remaining glaze to brush on chicken.

SOY-GINGER GLAZE

MAKES ABOUT ¾ CUP

Reduce the amount of salt in the brine to ¼ cup when using this glaze.

⅓ cup water
¼ cup soy sauce
2 tablespoons mirin
1 tablespoon grated fresh ginger
2 garlic cloves, minced
3 tablespoons sugar
¾ teaspoon cornstarch
2 scallions, minced

Combine water, soy sauce, mirin, ginger, and garlic in small saucepan, then whisk in sugar and cornstarch. Bring to simmer over medium

---

MAKING CHIPOTLES IN ADOBO SAUCE LAST

Because a little bit of chipotle chile goes a long way, it can be difficult to use up an entire can once it is opened. Rather than let the remaining chipotles go bad in the refrigerator, we like to portion out the chipotles and freeze them for later use.

1. Spoon out chipotles, each with a couple of teaspoons of adobo sauce, onto different areas of baking sheet lined with parchment paper, then place in freezer.

2. Transfer frozen chiles to zipper-lock freezer bag, store in freezer, and use as needed.

heat and cook until thickened, about 5 minutes; stir in scallions. Reserve half of glaze for serving and use remaining glaze to brush on chicken.

CURRY-YOGURT GLAZE
MAKES ABOUT ¾ CUP

- ¾ cup plain whole-milk yogurt
- 2 garlic cloves, minced
- 2 teaspoons grated fresh ginger
- 2 teaspoons minced fresh cilantro
- 1½ teaspoons curry powder
- ½ teaspoon grated lemon zest
- ½ teaspoon sugar
  Salt and pepper

Whisk all ingredients together in bowl and season with salt and pepper to taste. Reserve half of glaze for serving and use remaining glaze to brush on chicken.

Grilled Glazed Boneless Chicken Breasts

✔ WHY THIS RECIPE WORKS

Throwing a few boneless, skinless chicken breasts on the grill and painting them with a glaze always sounds like a good idea, at least in theory. But if you wait to apply the glaze until the meat is browned well, the meat is usually dry and leathery by the time you've lacquered on a few layers. If you apply the glaze too soon, however, you don't give the chicken a chance to brown, and the sugary glaze is prone to burning before the chicken cooks through. We wanted tender, juicy chicken with the smoky taste of the grill, glistening with a thick coating of glaze.

CREATE A BALANCED GLAZE We created a variety of glazes featuring thick—but not sweet—base ingredients such as coconut milk, mustard, and hoisin. For balance and complexity, we introduced acidity in the form of citrus juice or vinegar, as well as a healthy dose of spices and aromatics.

MAKE IT STICKY AND THICK Corn syrup gave the glazes just the right amount of stickiness while keeping the sweetness in check, and a small amount of cornstarch thickened them to just the right consistency.

SPEED UP BROWNING Browning the chicken faster meant more time to build a thick glaze that would add even more flavor. To achieve this goal we turned to an unusual ingredient: dry milk powder. Just ½ teaspoon per breast helped the chicken brown twice as fast; it also created a thin, tacky surface that was perfect for holding on to the glaze.

APPLY MULTIPLE COATS With faster browning accomplished, we had time to lacquer our chicken with four solid coats of glaze before it finished cooking. And applying the glaze immediately after the chicken was flipped meant less glaze stuck to the grill; it also meant the glaze applied to the top of the chicken had time to dry out and cling, for a thick, lacquered coating.

GRILLED GLAZED BONELESS, SKINLESS CHICKEN BREASTS

SERVES 4

Don't skip the milk powder—it's essential to this recipe.

- ¼ cup salt
- ¼ cup sugar
- 4 (6- to 8-ounce) boneless, skinless chicken breasts, trimmed
- 2 teaspoons nonfat dry milk powder
- ¼ teaspoon pepper
  Vegetable oil spray
- 1 recipe glaze (recipes follow)

1. Dissolve salt and sugar in 1½ quarts cold water. Submerge chicken in brine, cover, and refrigerate for at least 30 minutes or up to 1 hour. Remove chicken from brine and pat dry with paper towels. Combine milk powder and pepper in bowl.

2A. FOR A CHARCOAL GRILL: Open bottom vent completely. Light large chimney starter mounded with charcoal briquettes (7 quarts). When top coals are partially covered with ash, pour two-thirds evenly over half of grill, then pour remaining coals over other half of grill. Set cooking grate in place, cover, and open lid vent completely. Heat grill until hot, about 5 minutes.

2B. FOR A GAS GRILL: Turn all burners to high, cover, and heat grill until hot, about 15 minutes. Leave primary burner on high and turn other burner(s) to medium-high.

3. Clean and oil cooking grate. Sprinkle half of milk powder mixture over 1 side of chicken. Lightly spray coated side of chicken with oil spray until milk powder is moistened. Flip chicken and sprinkle remaining milk powder mixture over second side. Lightly spray with oil spray.

4. Place chicken, skinned side down, over hotter part of grill and cook until browned on first side, 2 to 2½ minutes. Flip chicken, brush with 2 tablespoons glaze, and cook until browned on second side, 2 to 2½ minutes. Flip chicken, move to cooler side of grill, brush with 2 tablespoons glaze, and cook for 2 minutes. Repeat flipping and brushing 2 more times, cooking for 2 minutes on each side. Flip chicken, brush with remaining glaze, and cook until chicken registers 160 degrees, 1 to 3 minutes. Transfer chicken to plate and let rest for 5 minutes before serving.

COCONUT CURRY GLAZE

MAKES ABOUT ⅔ CUP

- 2 tablespoons lime juice
- 1½ teaspoons cornstarch
- ⅓ cup canned coconut milk
- 3 tablespoons corn syrup
- 1 tablespoon fish sauce
- 1 tablespoon Thai red curry paste
- 1 teaspoon grated fresh ginger
- ¼ teaspoon ground coriander

Whisk lime juice and cornstarch together in small saucepan until cornstarch has dissolved. Whisk in coconut milk, corn syrup, fish sauce, curry paste, ginger, and coriander. Bring mixture to boil over high heat. Cook, stirring constantly, until thickened, about 1 minute. Transfer glaze to bowl.

HONEY MUSTARD GLAZE

MAKES ABOUT ⅔ CUP

- 2 tablespoons cider vinegar
- 1 teaspoon cornstarch
- 3 tablespoons Dijon mustard
- 3 tablespoons honey
- 2 tablespoons corn syrup
- 1 garlic clove, minced
- ¼ teaspoon ground fennel seeds

Whisk vinegar and cornstarch together in small saucepan until cornstarch has dissolved. Whisk in mustard, honey, corn syrup, garlic, and fennel seeds. Bring mixture to boil over high heat. Cook, stirring constantly, until thickened, about 1 minute. Transfer glaze to bowl.

SPICY HOISIN GLAZE
MAKES ABOUT ⅔ CUP

For a spicier glaze, use the larger amount of Sriracha sauce.

- 2 tablespoons rice vinegar
- 1 teaspoon cornstarch
- ⅓ cup hoisin sauce
- 2 tablespoons corn syrup
- 1–2 tablespoons Sriracha sauce
- 1 teaspoon grated fresh ginger
- ¼ teaspoon five-spice powder

Whisk vinegar and cornstarch together in small saucepan until cornstarch has dissolved. Whisk in hoisin, corn syrup, Sriracha, ginger, and five-spice powder. Bring mixture to boil over high heat. Cook, stirring constantly, until thickened, about 1 minute. Transfer glaze to bowl.

MISO SESAME GLAZE
MAKES ABOUT ⅔ CUP

- 3 tablespoons rice vinegar
- 1 teaspoon cornstarch
- 3 tablespoons white miso
- 2 tablespoons corn syrup
- 1 tablespoon toasted sesame oil
- 2 teaspoons grated fresh ginger
- ¼ teaspoon ground coriander

Whisk vinegar and cornstarch together in small saucepan until cornstarch has dissolved. Whisk in miso, corn syrup, oil, ginger, and coriander. Bring mixture to boil over high heat. Cook, stirring constantly, until thickened, about 1 minute. Transfer glaze to bowl.

Grilled Chicken Souvlaki

✔ WHY THIS RECIPE WORKS

In modern Greece, souvlaki is usually made with pork, but at Greek restaurants here in the United States, boneless, skinless chicken breast is common. The chunks of white meat are marinated in a tangy mixture of lemon juice, olive oil, oregano, parsley, and sometimes garlic before being skewered and grilled until nicely charred. The chicken is placed on a lightly grilled pita, slathered with a yogurt-based tzatziki sauce, and eaten out of hand. We wanted to perfect this dish.

MARINADE MATTERS Traditional long-soaking marinades made the chicken mushy. Plus, the marinade's flavor only penetrated the surface of the meat. Instead we brined the chicken briefly and then tossed the chicken with a flavorful mixture of olive oil, lemon juice, herbs, black pepper, and honey before grilling, which gave the chicken a flavorful crust. Reserving some of our marinade to mix in with the cooked chicken gave it a boost of brightness.

EAT YOUR VEGETABLES We did find that the chicken on the ends of the skewers cooked faster than the pieces in the middle. To solve this problem, we strung chunks of bell pepper and red onion on the ends of each skewer. The vegetables functioned as shields, protecting the end pieces of chicken from the heat so they cooked at the same rate as the middle pieces.

GET SAUCY We tempered the raw garlic flavor in our tzatziki sauce by mincing the garlic and briefly steeping it in lemon juice. For the perfect drizzling consistency, we mixed the yogurt and unsalted cucumbers together and let the sauce rest, allowing the salt in the sauce to draw out the water from the cucumbers.

THAT'S A WRAP Traditionally, souvlaki is wrapped in soft pocketless pitas, which are hard to find at regular supermarkets. Instead, we moistened the tops and bottoms of regular pocketed pitas and wrapped them in foil before putting them on the cooler side of the grill. The gently steamed pitas were soft, warm, and floppy—perfect for wrapping.

GRILLED CHICKEN SOUVLAKI
SERVES 4

This tzatziki is fairly mild; if you like a more assertive flavor, double the garlic. A rasp-style grater makes quick work of turning the garlic into a paste. We like the chicken as a wrap, but you may skip the pita and serve the chicken, vegetables, and tzatziki with rice. You will need four 12-inch metal skewers.

TZATZIKI SAUCE
- 1 tablespoon lemon juice
- 1 small garlic clove, minced to paste
- ¾ cup plain Greek yogurt
- ½ cucumber, peeled, halved lengthwise, seeded, and diced fine (½ cup)
- 3 tablespoons minced fresh mint
- 1 tablespoon minced fresh parsley
- ⅜ teaspoon salt

CHICKEN
- Salt and pepper
- 1½ pounds boneless, skinless chicken breasts, trimmed and cut into 1-inch pieces
- ⅓ cup extra-virgin olive oil
- 2 tablespoons minced fresh parsley
- 1 teaspoon grated lemon zest plus ¼ cup juice (2 lemons)
- 1 teaspoon honey
- 1 teaspoon dried oregano
- 1 green bell pepper, stemmed, seeded, and quartered, each quarter cut into 4 pieces
- 1 small red onion, ends trimmed, peeled, halved lengthwise, each half cut into 4 chunks
- 4 (8-inch) pita breads

1. FOR THE TZATZIKI SAUCE: Whisk lemon juice and garlic together in small bowl. Let stand for 10 minutes. Stir in yogurt, cucumber, mint, parsley, and salt. Cover and set aside.

2. FOR THE CHICKEN: Dissolve 2 tablespoons salt in 1 quart cold water in large container. Submerge chicken in brine, cover, and refrigerate for 30 minutes. While chicken is brining, combine oil, parsley, lemon zest and juice, honey, oregano, and ½ teaspoon pepper in medium bowl. Transfer ¼ cup oil mixture to large bowl and set aside to toss with cooked chicken.

3. Remove chicken from brine and pat dry with paper towels. Toss chicken with remaining oil mixture. Thread 4 pieces of bell pepper, concave side up, onto one 12-inch metal skewer. Thread one-quarter of chicken onto skewer. Thread 2 chunks of onion onto skewer, and place skewer on plate. Repeat skewering remaining chicken and vegetables on 3 more skewers. Lightly moisten 2 pita breads with water. Sandwich 2 unmoistened pita breads between moistened pita breads and wrap stack tightly in lightly greased heavy-duty aluminum foil.

4A. FOR A CHARCOAL GRILL: Open bottom vent completely. Light large chimney starter mounded with charcoal briquettes (7 quarts). When top coals are partially covered with ash, pour evenly over half of grill. Set cooking grate in place, cover, and open lid vent completely. Heat grill until hot, about 5 minutes.

4B. FOR A GAS GRILL: Turn all burners to high, cover, and heat grill until hot, about 15 minutes. Leave primary burner on high and turn off other burner(s).

5. Clean and oil cooking grate. Place skewers on hotter side of grill and cook, turning occasionally, until chicken and vegetables are well browned on all sides and chicken registers 160 degrees, 15 to 20 minutes. Using fork, push chicken and vegetables off skewers into bowl of reserved oil mixture. Stir gently,

DICING CUCUMBERS

1. Cut ¾-inch section off both ends of cucumbers. Halve cucumbers lengthwise and scoop out seeds with dinner spoon. Cut each seeded half lengthwise into ¼-inch strips.

2. Turn strips 90 degrees and cut into even ¼-inch pieces.

breaking up onion chunks; cover with foil and let sit for 5 minutes.

6. Meanwhile, place packet of pitas on cooler side of grill. Flip occasionally to heat, about 5 minutes.

7. Lay each warm pita on 12-inch square of foil. Spread each pita with 2 tablespoons tzatziki. Place one-quarter of chicken and vegetables in middle of each pita. Roll into cylindrical shape and serve.

Filipino Chicken Adobo

✓ WHY THIS RECIPE WORKS

Adobo may be considered the national dish of the Philippines but, thanks to the country's melting pot ancestry, the formula for making it is remarkably varied. The core concept is meat marinated and braised in vinegar and soy sauce, with lots of garlic, bay leaves, and black pepper. Everything from that point on, however, is open to interpretation, including the types of meat, vinegar, and additional ingredients you use. We wanted to come up with a foolproof version of this classic dish that stayed true to its Filipino heritage but worked perfectly in American kitchen.

PREMARINATE IN SOY SAUCE Starting the chicken in a quick soy sauce-only marinade helped tenderize and flavor the meat—the salt in the soy sauce penetrated the surface of the meat without toughening it up or making it mushy.

BALANCE THE MARINADE To even out the sharp saltiness of the traditional vinegar and soy sauce braising liquid, we took a cue from a regional variation and added a can of coconut milk. The thick, rich milk mellowed the harsh flavors while still allowing plenty of tanginess.

START WITH A COLD PAN To render the gummy fat layer in the chicken skin and crisp its surface, we started the meat in a room-temperature nonstick skillet and then turned up the heat. As the pan gradually got hotter, the fat had time to melt before the exterior burned. We then dumped the excess fat in the skillet, which kept our braise from turning greasy.

FLIP 'EM We didn't want to go to all the trouble of rendering the fat only to have the skin turn flabby in the braising liquid, so to preserve as much crispness as possible, we placed the chicken pieces skin side up in the braising liquid—this gave the skin a chance to dry out a little before serving.

FILIPINO CHICKEN ADOBO
SERVES 4

Light coconut milk can be substituted for the regular coconut milk. Serve this dish over rice.

- 8 (5- to 7-ounce) bone-in chicken thighs, trimmed
- ⅓ cup soy sauce
- 1 (13.5-ounce) can coconut milk
- ¾ cup cider vinegar
- 8 garlic cloves, peeled
- 4 bay leaves
- 2 teaspoons pepper
- 1 scallion, sliced thin

1. Toss chicken with soy sauce in large bowl. Refrigerate for at least 30 minutes or up to 1 hour.

2. Remove chicken from soy sauce, allowing excess to drip back into bowl. Transfer chicken, skin side down, to 12-inch nonstick skillet; set aside soy sauce.

3. Place skillet over medium-high heat and cook until chicken skin is browned, 7 to 10 minutes. While chicken is browning, whisk

HOMEMADE COCONUT MILK

Homemade coconut milk is noticeably thinner than store-bought. Without the stabilizers of the canned coconut milk, the homemade version does tend to curdle if heated to a simmer, but we found a quick fix: Add ¼ teaspoon baking soda for every 1¾ cups of coconut milk (whisk the baking soda into the milk before adding it to the pot). You can skip the baking soda if you are using just a small amount and the clumps won't be noticed.

Combine 1¾ cups unsweetened shredded coconut and 1¾ cups water just off the boil (between 200 and 205 degrees) in blender and blend for 2 minutes. Transfer to fine-mesh strainer set over large liquid measuring cup and press to extract as much liquid as possible; let cool for 15 minutes. Transfer shredded coconut to dish towel in large bowl. Gather sides of dish towel around coconut and squeeze out remaining milk. (Makes 1¾ cups, the equivalent of 1 [13.5-ounce] can coconut milk.)

coconut milk, vinegar, garlic, bay leaves, and pepper into soy sauce.

4. Transfer chicken to plate and discard fat in skillet. Return chicken to skillet skin side down, add coconut milk mixture, and bring to boil. Reduce heat to medium-low and simmer, uncovered, for 20 minutes. Flip chicken skin side up and continue to cook, uncovered, until chicken registers 175 degrees, about 15 minutes. Transfer chicken to platter and tent loosely with aluminum foil.

5. Discard bay leaves and skim any fat off surface of sauce. Return skillet to medium-high heat and cook until sauce is thickened, 5 to 7 minutes. Pour sauce over chicken, sprinkle with scallion, and serve.

Moroccan Chicken with Olives and Lemon

✓ WHY THIS RECIPE WORKS

Tagines are exotically spiced, assertively flavored stews slow-cooked in earthenware vessels of the same name. They can include all manner of meats, vegetables, and fruit, though our hands-down favorite combines chicken with briny olives and tart lemon. But time-consuming techniques and esoteric ingredients make cooking authentic Moroccan chicken a daunting proposition. We wanted a recipe that was ready in an hour and relied on supermarket staples.

ARRANGE THE MEAT RIGHT Raising the white meat above the simmering liquid by placing it on top of large pieces of carrot allowed it to cook gently, while giving the dark meat a 5-minute head start and simmering it directly in the liquid meant all the chicken was ready at the same time.

REMOVE THE SKIN While leaving the skin on the meat to brown it gave the braising liquid a deep flavor, pulling it off before simmering kept the dish free of rubbery skin.

BE SELECTIVE ABOUT SPICES The spice blend for tagines can contain upward of 30 spices; we experimented with a broad range until we landed on a blend that was short on ingredients but long on flavor. Cumin and

ginger lent depth, cinnamon brought warmth that tempered a little cayenne heat, and citrusy coriander boosted the stew's lemon flavor. Paprika added sweetness and colored the broth a deep, attractive red.

FIND THE RIGHT OLIVES We replaced the hard-to-find big, meaty, green Moroccan olives with Greek "cracked" olives, which tasted great and were readily available. Adding them just before serving helped them retain their piquant flavor and firm texture.

DITCH THE PRESERVED LEMON The lemon flavor in authentic tagines comes from preserved lemon, a long-cured Moroccan condiment that can be hard to find. Rather than try to imitate this unique flavor, we added a few broad ribbons of lemon zest and some juice for a rich citrus back note.

MOROCCAN CHICKEN WITH OLIVES AND LEMON

SERVES 4

Bone-in chicken parts can be substituted for the whole chicken. For the best results, use four chicken thighs and two chicken breasts, each breast split in half; the dark meat contributes valuable flavor to the broth and should not be omitted. Use a vegetable peeler to remove wide strips of zest from the lemon before juicing it. Make sure to trim any white pith from the zest, as it can impart a bitter flavor. If the olives are particularly salty, give them a rinse. Serve with couscous.

1¼	teaspoons paprika
½	teaspoon ground cumin
½	teaspoon ground ginger
¼	teaspoon cayenne pepper
¼	teaspoon ground coriander
¼	teaspoon ground cinnamon
3	(2-inch) strips lemon zest
5	garlic cloves, minced (5 teaspoons)
1	(3½- to 4-pound) whole chicken, giblets discarded, cut into 8 pieces (4 breast pieces, 2 thighs, 2 drumsticks), trimmed, wings discarded
	Salt and pepper
1	tablespoon olive oil
1	large onion, halved and sliced ¼ inch thick
1¾	cups chicken broth
1	tablespoon honey
2	carrots, peeled and cut crosswise into ½-inch-thick rounds, very large pieces cut into half-moons
1	cup cracked green olives, pitted and halved
3	tablespoons lemon juice
2	tablespoons chopped fresh cilantro

1. Combine paprika, cumin, ginger, cayenne, coriander, and cinnamon in small bowl and set aside. Mince 1 strip lemon zest, then combine with 1 teaspoon minced garlic and mince together until reduced to fine paste; set aside.

2. Season both sides of chicken pieces with salt and pepper. Heat oil in Dutch oven over medium-high heat until beginning to smoke. Working in batches, add chicken pieces, skin side down, and cook without moving until skin is deep golden, about 5 minutes. Using tongs, flip chicken pieces and brown on second side, about 4 minutes longer. Transfer chicken to large plate; when cool enough to handle, discard skin. Pour off all but 1 tablespoon fat from pot.

3. Add onion and 2 remaining lemon zest strips to pot and cook, stirring occasionally, until onion slices have browned at edges but still retain their shape, 5 to 7 minutes (add 1 tablespoon water if pan gets too dark). Add remaining 4 teaspoons garlic and cook, stirring, until fragrant, about 30 seconds. Add spices and cook, stirring constantly, until darkened and very fragrant, 45 to 60 seconds. Stir in broth and honey, scraping up any browned bits. Add thighs and drumsticks, reduce heat to medium, and simmer for 5 minutes.

4. Add carrots and breast pieces with any accumulated juices to pot, arranging breast pieces in single layer on top of carrots. Cover, reduce heat to medium-low, and simmer until breast pieces register 160 degrees, 10 to 15 minutes.

5. Transfer chicken to plate and tent with aluminum foil. Add olives to pot; increase heat to medium-high and simmer until liquid has thickened slightly and carrots are tender, 4 to 6 minutes. Return chicken to pot and stir in garlic mixture, lemon juice, and cilantro; season with salt and pepper to taste. Serve immediately.

MOROCCAN CHICKEN WITH CHICKPEAS AND APRICOTS

Replace 1 carrot with 1 cup dried apricots, halved, and replace olives with 1 (15-ounce) can chickpeas, rinsed.

ON THE SIDE
SIMPLE COUSCOUS

We use a pilaf-style method to make fluffy, flavorful couscous.

Heat 2 tablespoons unsalted butter in medium saucepan over medium-high heat. When foaming subsides, add 2 cups couscous and cook, stirring frequently, until grains are just beginning to brown, about 5 minutes. Add 1 cup water, 1 cup chicken broth, and 1 teaspoon salt; stir briefly to combine, cover, and remove pan from heat. Let stand until grains are tender, about 7 minutes. Uncover and fluff grains with fork. Season with pepper to taste, and serve. (Serves 4 to 6.)

Tandoori Chicken

✔ WHY THIS RECIPE WORKS

This traditional dish features tender chicken marinated in a spiced yogurt mixture and cooked in the fierce heat of a tandoor oven, resulting in moist, smoky, flavorful meat. We weren't going to let a 24-hour marinade or the lack of a 900-degree oven keep us from turning this great Indian classic into an easy weeknight dinner. We set out to reinvent tandoori chicken as a recipe that could be made year-round in the oven.

CONVENTIONAL OVEN, NOT TANDOOR Trying to replicate the intense heat of a tandoor oven by cranking our home oven as high as it would go produced dry, overcooked chicken—and using only the broiler was no better. For nicely charred yet still juicy meat, we had the best results starting the chicken in a moderate oven and then finishing it under the broiler.

DITCH THE LONG MARINADE Yogurt contains acid, which caused the proteins in the chicken to break down if left to soak for too long in the marinade, resulting in mushy meat. Giving the chicken just a quick dip in the marinade eliminated this problem.

ADD A SPICE RUB Without a lengthy soak in the yogurt marinade, the chicken didn't have a chance to soak up much flavor. We easily solved this problem by creating a salt-spice rub for the meat. Featuring the same spices we used in the marinade— garam masala, ground cumin, and a little chili powder—as well as some ginger, garlic, and lime, the flavors of our spice rub penetrated deep into the meat, for chicken that was well seasoned throughout.

TANDOORI CHICKEN
SERVES 4

We prefer this dish with whole-milk yogurt, but low-fat yogurt can be substituted. Serve with Basmati Rice Pilaf (page 305) and a few chutneys or relishes.

If using large chicken breasts (about 1 pound each), cut each breast into three pieces. If using smaller breasts (10 to 12 ounces each), cut each breast into two pieces. Serve with Raita (recipe follows).

2   tablespoons vegetable oil
6   garlic cloves, minced
2   tablespoons grated fresh ginger
1   tablespoon garam masala
2   teaspoons ground cumin
2   teaspoons chili powder
1   cup plain whole-milk yogurt
¼   cup lime juice (2 limes), plus lime wedges for serving
2   teaspoons salt
3   pounds bone-in chicken pieces (split breasts cut in half, drumsticks, and/or thighs), trimmed

1. Heat oil in 10-inch skillet over medium heat until shimmering. Add garlic and ginger and cook until fragrant, about 30 seconds. Stir in garam masala, cumin, and chili powder and continue to cook until fragrant, 30 seconds longer. Transfer half of garlic mixture to medium bowl, stir in yogurt and 2 tablespoons lime juice, and set aside. In large bowl, combine remaining garlic mixture, remaining 2 tablespoons lime juice, and salt.

2. Using sharp knife, make 2 or 3 short slashes into skin of each piece of chicken, taking care not to cut into meat. Transfer chicken to large bowl and gently rub with salt-spice mixture until all pieces are evenly coated. Let sit at room temperature for 30 minutes.

3. Adjust oven rack to upper-middle position and heat oven to 325 degrees. Set wire rack in aluminum foil–lined rimmed baking sheet. Pour yogurt mixture over chicken and toss until chicken is evenly coated with thick layer. Arrange chicken pieces, scored side down, on prepared wire rack. Discard excess yogurt mixture. Roast chicken until breast pieces register 125 degrees and thighs and/or drumsticks register 130 degrees, 15 to 25 minutes. (Smaller pieces may cook faster than larger pieces. Remove pieces from oven as they reach correct temperature.)

4. Adjust oven rack 6 inches from broiler element and heat broiler. Return chicken to prepared wire rack, scored side up, and broil until chicken is lightly charred in spots and breast pieces register 160 degrees and thighs and/or drumsticks register 175 degrees, 8 to 15 minutes. Transfer chicken to serving plate, tent loosely with foil, and let rest for 5 minutes. Serve with lime wedges.

RAITA
MAKES ABOUT 1 CUP

The raita is best made with whole-milk yogurt, although low-fat yogurt can be used. Do not use non-fat yogurt; the sauce will taste hollow and bland.

- 1 cup plain whole-milk yogurt
- 2 tablespoons minced fresh cilantro
- 1 garlic clove, minced
   Salt
   Cayenne pepper

Mix all ingredients together and season with salt and cayenne to taste. Cover and refrigerate until needed.

ON THE SIDE
CILANTRO-MINT CHUTNEY

The chutney can be refrigerated for one day.

Process 2 cups fresh cilantro leaves, 1 cup fresh mint leaves, ¼ cup onion, finely chopped, ½ teaspoon ground cumin, ¼ teaspoon salt, 1½ teaspoons sugar, 1 tablespoon fresh lime juice, and ⅓ cup plain yogurt in food processor until smooth, about 20 seconds, scraping down sides of bowl with rubber spatula after 10 seconds. (Makes about 1 cup.)

Chicken Paprikash

✓ WHY THIS RECIPE WORKS

Chicken paprikash should be an easy-to-make braise with succulent chicken, a balance of heat, spice, and aromatics, and a rich, flavorful sauce with paprika at center stage. Our goal was to pare down the usual mile-long ingredient list.

DITCH THE SKIN Removing the skin after browning prevented the accumulation of excess fat and a greasy sauce.

THE TYPE OF PAPRIKA MATTERS The brilliant red powder we call "paprika" comes from the dried pods (fruit) of a family of peppers that ranges from sweet bells to the very hottest chiles. Several varieties are used to produce paprika and as a result there are many different kinds of paprika. We found that chicken paprikash is best flavored with Hungarian sweet paprika. (Other sweet paprikas can deliver good results, but don't use hot paprika in this dish.)

GIVE IT A DOUBLE DOSE For bold paprika flavor, we added it to our recipe twice: once while sautéing the vegetables to let its

flavor bloom, then once again when adding sour cream to finish the dish.

TEMPER THE SAUCE Adding sour cream directly to the pot caused it to curdle, so we found it essential to temper the sour cream by stirring a few tablespoons of the hot liquid from the stew pot together with the sour cream in a small bowl, then adding the warmed mixture to the pot.

CHICKEN PAPRIKASH
SERVES 4

Rice, mashed potatoes, and buttered egg noodles all make good accompaniments.

- 8 (5- to 7-ounce) bone-in chicken thighs, trimmed
   Salt and pepper
- 1 teaspoon vegetable oil
- 1 large onion, halved and sliced thin
- 1 large red bell pepper, stemmed, seeded, halved widthwise, and cut into ¼-inch-wide strips

1   large green bell pepper, stemmed,
     seeded, halved widthwise, and cut into
     ¼-inch-wide strips
3½   tablespoons paprika
1   tablespoon all-purpose flour
¼   teaspoon dried marjoram
½   cup dry white wine
1   (14.5-ounce) can diced tomatoes,
     drained
⅓   cup sour cream
2   tablespoons chopped fresh parsley

1. Adjust oven rack to lower-middle position and heat oven to 300 degrees. Season both sides of chicken with salt and pepper. Heat oil in Dutch oven over medium-high heat until shimmering. Add 4 chicken thighs, skin side down, and cook without moving until skin is crisp and well browned, about 5 minutes. Using tongs, flip chicken and brown on second side, about 5 minutes longer; transfer to large plate. Repeat with remaining 4 chicken thighs and transfer to plate; set aside. When chicken is cool enough to handle, discard skin. Pour off all but 1 tablespoon fat from pot.

2. Add onion to pot and cook, stirring occasionally, over medium heat until softened, 5 to 7 minutes. Add bell peppers and cook, stirring occasionally, until onion is browned and peppers are softened, about 3 minutes. Stir in 3 tablespoons paprika, flour, and marjoram and cook, stirring constantly, until fragrant, about 1 minute. Add wine, scraping up browned bits. Stir in tomatoes and 1 teaspoon salt. Add chicken and any accumulated juices, submerging them in vegetables; bring to a simmer, then cover transfer pot to oven. Cook until chicken is no longer pink when cut into with paring knife, about 30 minutes. (At this point, stew can be cooled to room temperature, then refrigerated for up to 3 days. Bring to simmer over medium-low heat before proceeding.)

3. Combine sour cream and remaining 1½ teaspoons paprika in small bowl. Transfer chicken to individual plates. Stir a few tablespoons of hot sauce into sour cream to temper, then stir mixture back into sauce in pot. Spoon sauce and peppers over chicken, sprinkle with parsley, and serve immediately.

Pan-Roasted Chicken with Shallot-Vermouth Sauce

✔ WHY THIS RECIPE WORKS

To make a good basic roast chicken, some planning is required, and even then it can be a challenge to cook. For a moist, well-seasoned bird, you brine it; for the crispiest skin, you air-dry it; to coordinate the doneness of the thigh and breast, you flip the bird as it roasts. We hoped to use pan roasting to deliver superior skin, shorter preparation time, and a rich, savory pan sauce.

CUT UP THE CHICKEN Breaking down the chicken into parts and discarding the wings meant all the pieces could fit in a 12-inch skillet.

SHORTEN THE BRINING TIME Brining the chicken parts ensured moist, well-seasoned meat; because the pieces were relatively small, just 30 minutes did the trick.

LIGHTLY COAT THE SKILLET Just a tablespoon of oil—enough to barely coat the skillet's surface—promoted even browning.

SKIN SIDE DOWN FOR THE OVEN After browning the parts on all sides on the stovetop, we arranged the pieces skin side down for their stint in a 450-degree oven: The contact between the chicken skin and the hot pan produced a crackling crisp, russet-toned skin.

BUILD THE SAUCE RIGHT IN THE SKILLET Once the chicken was removed from the skillet, the fond was crusty and plentiful, so we needed only a handful of ingredients to turn it into a sauce. Sautéed shallot, chicken broth, vermouth, and thyme struck just the right notes. Simmering the liquid to half its original volume concentrated all the flavors.

PAN-ROASTED CHICKEN PARTS WITH SHALLOT-VERMOUTH SAUCE

SERVES 4

If using kosher chicken, do not brine in step 1, but season with salt as well as pepper.

CHICKEN
Salt and pepper
1 (3½- to 4-pound) whole chicken, cut into 8 pieces (4 breast pieces, 2 drumsticks, 2 thighs), wings and giblets discarded
1 tablespoon vegetable oil

SAUCE
1 large shallot, minced
¾ cup chicken broth
½ cup dry vermouth
2 sprigs fresh thyme
3 tablespoons unsalted butter, cut into 3 pieces and chilled
Salt and pepper

1. FOR THE CHICKEN: Dissolve ½ cup salt in 2 quarts cold water in large container. Submerge chicken in brine, cover, and refrigerate for 30 minutes to 1 hour. Remove chicken from brine and pat dry with paper towels. Season chicken with pepper.

2. Adjust oven rack to lowest position and heat oven to 450 degrees. Heat oil in 12-inch ovensafe skillet over medium-high heat until just smoking. Place chicken skin side down in skillet and cook until well browned, 6 to 8 minutes, reducing heat if pan begins to scorch. Flip chicken skin side up and continue to cook until lightly browned on second side, about 3 minutes.

3. Flip chicken skin side down and transfer skillet to oven. Roast chicken until breasts register 160 degrees and thighs and drumsticks register 175 degrees, about 10 minutes longer.

4. Using potholders (skillet handle will be hot), remove skillet from oven. Transfer chicken to serving platter and let rest while making sauce (if not making sauce, let chicken rest for 5 minutes before serving).

5. FOR THE SAUCE: Being careful of hot skillet handle, pour off all but 1 teaspoon fat left in skillet, add shallot, and cook over medium-high heat until softened, about 2 minutes. Stir in broth, vermouth, and thyme sprigs, scraping up any browned bits. Bring to simmer and cook until thickened and measures ⅔ cup, about 6 minutes Stir in any accumulated chicken juices; return to simmer and cook for 30 seconds. Off heat, discard thyme sprigs and whisk in butter, 1 piece at a time. Season with salt and pepper to taste. Pour sauce over chicken and serve immediately.

PAN-ROASTED CHICKEN WITH SHERRY-ROSEMARY SAUCE

Substitute dry sherry for dry vermouth and 2 fresh rosemary sprigs for thyme sprigs.

PAN-ROASTED CHICKEN WITH COGNAC-MUSTARD SAUCE

Be sure to add the broth to the skillet before adding the wine and cognac.

Substitute ¼ cup white wine and ¼ cup cognac or brandy for dry vermouth and 1 tablespoon Dijon mustard for 1 tablespoon butter.

Oven-Roasted Chicken Thighs

✓ **WHY THIS RECIPE WORKS**

When we need a chicken dinner on the fly, chicken thighs are what we turn to most. They're more flavorful than lean breasts, meatier than drumsticks, and, thanks to their uniform size and thickness, less prone to overcooking, which eliminates any need for brining or salting. The only catch? The fat underneath the skin that helps keep the meat moist during cooking often leads to flabby skin. We wanted to come up with a quick recipe for thighs sheathed in crackling skin—without sacrificing the succulent, tender meat.

POKE HOLES IN THE SKIN Puncturing about a dozen holes in the skin of each thigh with a skewer allowed the fat under the skin to render more quickly.

ROAST ON A PREHEATED BAKING SHEET Roasting the thighs skin side down on a preheated baking sheet brought the skin into contact with concentrated heat; this helped the fat to render sufficiently and also protected the meat from drying out.

FINISH UNDER THE BROILER While roasting the chicken skin side down on a hot baking sheet fixed most of our problems, it also created a new one: The thighs were now sitting in rendered fat and juices, which prevented the skin from fully crisping. Flipping them skin side up for a final stint under the broiler did the trick—the meat emerged succulent and juicy under a layer of crackly, deeply browned skin.

or chutney (recipes follow). If making one of the accompanying salsas or chutney, cook the foil packet while the chicken cooks and finish preparing the recipe while the chicken rests.

8 (6- to 8-ounce) bone-in chicken thighs, trimmed
1¼ teaspoons salt
    Pepper
    Vegetable oil spray

1. Adjust oven racks to middle and lowest positions, place rimmed baking sheet on lower rack, and heat oven to 450 degrees.

2. Using metal skewer, poke skin side of chicken thighs 10 to 12 times. Season both sides of thighs with salt and pepper; spray skin lightly with vegetable oil spray. Place thighs skin side down on preheated sheet. Return sheet to lower rack.

3. Roast chicken until skin side is beginning to brown and meat registers 160 degrees, 20 to 25 minutes, rotating sheet halfway through cooking. Remove chicken from oven and heat broiler.

4. While broiler heats, flip chicken skin side up. Broil chicken on upper rack until skin is crisp and well browned and meat registers 175 degrees, about 5 minutes, rotating sheet as needed for even browning. Transfer chicken to platter and let rest for 5 minutes. Serve.

OVEN-ROASTED CHICKEN THIGHS
SERVES 4

For best results, trim all visible fat from the thighs. Use a heavy-duty baking sheet and fully preheat the oven and baking sheet before adding the chicken. The chicken can be served plain or with a salsa

---

ROASTED GARLIC SALSA VERDE
MAKES ABOUT ½ CUP

1 garlic head, cloves separated and unpeeled
5 tablespoons olive oil

2 tablespoons lemon juice
1 cup fresh parsley leaves
2 anchovy fillets, rinsed and patted dry
2 tablespoons capers, rinsed
¼ teaspoon salt
¼ teaspoon red pepper flakes

1. While oven preheats, toss garlic cloves and 1 tablespoon oil in bowl. Cover bowl and microwave until garlic is softened, 2 to 5 minutes, stirring once halfway through microwaving. Place garlic in center of 12-inch square of aluminum foil. Cover with second 12-inch square of foil; fold edges together to create packet about 7 inches square. Place packet on upper rack and roast for 10 minutes.

2. Squeeze garlic cloves out of skins. While chicken is resting, process garlic, lemon juice, parsley, anchovies, capers, and salt in food processor until coarsely chopped, about 5 seconds. Add remaining ¼ cup oil and pepper flakes; pulse until combined, scraping bowl as necessary. Serve.

ROASTED SHALLOT AND MINT CHUTNEY

MAKES ABOUT ½ CUP

---

3 shallots, sliced thin
4 tablespoons vegetable oil
1 cup fresh mint leaves
½ cup fresh cilantro leaves
1 jalapeño chile, stemmed, seeded, and chopped
1 tablespoon lime juice
½ teaspoon sugar
¼ teaspoon salt

1. While oven preheats, toss shallots and 1 tablespoon oil in bowl. Cover bowl and microwave until shallots have softened, 2 to 5 minutes, stirring once halfway through microwaving. Place shallots in center of 12-inch square of aluminum foil. Cover with second 12-inch square of foil; fold edges together to create packet about 7 inches square. Place packet on upper rack and roast for 10 minutes.

2. While chicken is resting, process shallots, mint, cilantro, jalapeño, lime juice, sugar, and salt in food processor until finely chopped, about 5 seconds. With food processor running, slowly add remaining 3 tablespoons oil in steady stream until smooth, scraping down bowl as necessary. Serve.

ROASTED POBLANO-CILANTRO SALSA

MAKES ABOUT ½ CUP

---

2 medium poblano chile peppers
1 bunch cilantro, washed, stems trimmed, and roughly chopped (about 2 cups)
½ cup pumpkin seeds, lightly toasted
1 garlic clove, peeled
3 tablespoons lime juice (2 limes)
½ teaspoon sugar
1 teaspoon salt
½ cup water

1. While oven preheats, place poblanos in bowl. Cover bowl and microwave until poblanos are slightly softened, 2 to 5 minutes, stirring once halfway through microwaving. Place poblanos in center of 12-inch square of aluminum foil. Cover with second 12-inch square of foil; fold edges together to create packet about 7 inches square. Place packet on upper rack and roast for 10 minutes.

2. While chicken is resting, peel, core, and seed poblanos. Process poblanos, cilantro, pepitas, garlic, lime juice, sugar, and salt until finely chopped, about 5 seconds. With food processor running, slowly add water in steady stream until sauce is smooth, scraping down bowl as necessary. Serve.

Oven-Fried Chicken Wings

✔ WHY THIS RECIPE WORKS

Most of us enjoy wings only in bars and restaurants because frying them at home can be a lot of work and too much mess. But what if we could figure out a way to make truly crispy wings in the oven?

COAT THE SKIN FOR CRISPINESS Tossing the wings with baking powder and salt helped break down the proteins within the skin, as well as aiding in browning. This gave our wings a dry skin that crisped up nicely in the oven.

START LOW We started the wings at 250 degrees on a baking sheet set on a rack in the lower-middle part of the oven to ensure that the fat was rendered before the meat had a chance to get overcooked. This kept them from getting rubbery.

FINISH HIGH We then turned the oven up to 425 degrees to finish roasting the wings and crisp the skin. We also moved the pan toward the top of the oven to capitalize on the reflected heat and maximize browning.

TOSS WITH SAUCE Letting the wings stand for 5 minutes before tossing them with the sauce helps preserve the crispy skin.

OVEN-FRIED CHICKEN WINGS
SERVES 4 TO 6

If you buy chicken wings that are already split, with the tips removed, you will need only 3½ pounds.

- 4 pounds chicken wings, cut at joints, wingtips discarded
- 2 tablespoons baking powder
- ¾ teaspoon salt
- 1 recipe wing sauce (recipes follow)

1. Adjust oven racks to upper-middle and lower-middle positions and heat oven to 250 degrees. Set wire rack in aluminum foil–lined rimmed baking sheet. Pat wings dry with paper towels and transfer to 1-gallon zipper-lock bag. Combine baking powder and salt, add to wings, seal bag, and toss to evenly coat.

2. Arrange wings, skin side up, in single layer on prepared wire rack. Bake wings on lower rack for 30 minutes. Move wings to upper rack, increase oven temperature to 425 degrees, and roast until wings are golden brown and crispy, 40 to 50 minutes longer, rotating sheet halfway through baking. Remove sheet from oven and let stand for 5 minutes. Transfer wings to bowl with wing sauce, toss to coat, and serve.

BUFFALO WING SAUCE
MAKES ABOUT ¾ CUP

Classic Buffalo sauce is made with Frank's RedHot Original Cayenne Pepper Sauce.

- ½ cup hot sauce
- 4 tablespoons unsalted butter, melted
- 1 tablespoon molasses

Combine all ingredients in large bowl.

SMOKY BARBECUE WING SAUCE
MAKES ABOUT ¾ CUP

- ¼ cup chicken broth
- ¼ cup ketchup
- 1 tablespoon molasses
- 1 tablespoon cider vinegar
- 1 tablespoon minced canned chipotle chile in adobo sauce
- ¼ teaspoon liquid smoke

Combine all ingredients in large bowl.

CUTTING UP CHICKEN WINGS

1. With chef's knife, cut into skin between larger sections of wing until you hit joint.

2. Bend back 2 sections to pop and break joint.

3. Cut through skin and flesh to completely separate 2 meaty portions.

4. Hack off wingtip and discard.

It's easy enough to know when regular milk has gone bad—it will simply smell bad. But what about buttermilk? Our experience has shown that refrigerated buttermilk won't turn truly bad (signified by the growth of blue-green mold) until at least three weeks after opening. That it can last this long is not surprising, since buttermilk is high in lactic acid, which is hostile to the growth of harmful bacteria. That said, the flavor of buttermilk changes the longer it's stored, losing its buttery flavor and becoming bland.

Here's why: The bacteria in buttermilk produce lactic acid and diacetyl, a flavor compound that gives buttermilk its characteristic buttery aroma and taste (diacetyl is also the dominant flavor compound in butter). As time passes, the buttermilk continues to ferment and becomes more acidic. The abundance of acid kills off virtually all the bacteria that produce the buttery-tasting diacetyl. So three-week-old buttermilk will retain its tartness (from lactic acid) but lose much of its signature buttery taste, giving it less dimension. The good news is that there is a way to prolong the shelf life and preserve the flavor of buttermilk: Freeze it.

Extra-Crunchy Fried Chicken

✓ WHY THIS RECIPE WORKS

Preparing homemade fried chicken is a notoriously messy, labor-intensive ordeal that rarely yields the satisfying crunch you would expect from fast-food restaurants. We wanted to find a mess-free way to re-create that crispy coating without overcooking the chicken in the process.

SEASON DOWN TO THE BONE We noticed that the fried coating on fast-food varieties often masked bland, overcooked chicken—so that's where we started. In order to keep the chicken moist, we soaked it in a buttermilk and salt solution—the result was juicy, well-seasoned meat.

THE IDEAL CRUNCH Dredging in flour alone won't yield the crispy skin you expect from fried chicken, and other recipes dip the chicken in egg or buttermilk before coating it in flour. Chicken fried this way is reasonably crunchy, but we wanted colonel-style crunch. As odd is it sounded, we found a few recipes that used pancake mix, which is essentially a combination of flour, baking powder, and buttermilk. A fluid "pancake" mixture didn't do the trick, but dredging the chicken in flour and baking powder just moistened with buttermilk delivered what we were after: a coating that clung to the chicken and fried up into a sturdy, craggy crust.

MINIMIZE THE MESS For many home cooks, the splattered chaos that comes with frying chicken is a dealbreaker. We contained the mess by swapping a skillet for a Dutch oven and keeping the pot covered during the first half of the frying time. The cover captured escaping steam and made the chicken even more moist, giving us the ultimate fried chicken—made in our own home kitchen, instead of from a bucket.

EXTRA-CRUNCHY FRIED CHICKEN
SERVES 4

Keeping the oil at the correct temperature is essential to producing crunchy fried chicken that is neither too brown nor too greasy. You will need at least a 6-quart Dutch oven for this recipe. If you want to produce a slightly lighter version of this recipe, you can remove the skin from the chicken before soaking it in the buttermilk. The chicken will be slightly less crunchy.

2	tablespoons salt
2	cups plus 6 tablespoons buttermilk
1	(3½-pound) whole chicken, cut into 8 pieces (4 breast pieces, 2 drumsticks, 2 thighs), wings and giblets discarded
3	cups all-purpose flour
2	teaspoons baking powder
¾	teaspoon dried thyme
½	teaspoon pepper
¼	teaspoon garlic powder
1	quart peanut or vegetable oil

1. Dissolve salt in 2 cups buttermilk in large container. Submerge chicken in brine, cover, and refrigerate for 1 hour.

2. Whisk flour, baking powder, thyme, pepper, and garlic powder together in large bowl. Add remaining 6 tablespoons buttermilk; with your fingers rub flour and buttermilk together until buttermilk is evenly incorporated into flour and mixture resembles coarse, wet sand. Set wire rack in rimmed baking sheet.

3. Remove chicken form buttermilk and pat dry with paper towels. Dredge chicken pieces in flour mixture and turn to coat thoroughly, gently pressing flour mixture onto

chicken. Shake excess flour from each piece of chicken and transfer to prepared wire rack.

4. Line platter with triple layer of paper towels. Add oil to large Dutch oven until it measures about ¾ inch deep and heat over medium-high heat to 375 degrees. Place chicken pieces skin side down in oil, cover, and fry until deep golden brown, 8 to 10 minutes. Remove lid after 4 minutes and lift chicken pieces to check for even browning; rearrange if some pieces are browning faster than others. Adjust burner, if necessary, to maintain oil temperature between 300 and 315 degrees. Turn chicken pieces over and continue to fry, uncovered, until chicken pieces are deep golden brown on second side and breasts register 160 degrees and thighs and drumsticks register 175 degrees, 6 to 8 minutes. Using tongs, transfer chicken to prepared platter; let stand for 5 minutes. Serve.

Honey Fried Chicken

✔ WHY THIS RECIPE WORKS

The concept of drizzling fried chicken with honey was popularized in the 1930s, but over the years, the pairing has mostly vanished. And no wonder— the recipes we found turned out dry, chalky chicken whose crispy coating had been made soggy with a heavy honey glaze. We set out to bring this traditional favorite back to life.

BRINE FIRST To keep the chicken moist and flavorful all the way through the cooking process, we brined it in the tried-and-true test kitchen combination of water, salt, and sugar.

FRY TWICE To solve the problem of the soggy coating, we turned to a popular method for Korean fried chicken: double frying. This method—in which the chicken is fried until just beginning to crisp, removed from the oil and rested, then returned to the oil again—is particularly effective at evaporating the moisture in chicken skin. Before frying, we dusted the chicken with cornstarch, which helped our simple cornstarch-water batter stick to the chicken.

HEAT YOUR HONEY Straight out the jar, thick honey coated the chicken inconsistently. To thin it out, we heated it in the microwave until it was pourable. A couple of tablespoons of hot sauce balanced the sweetness and gave our glaze a kick. A quick dunk in the glaze and a drip-dry on a baking rack gave our chicken an irresistibly sticky, sweet-spicy coating.

HONEY FRIED CHICKEN
SERVES 4

You will need at least a 6-quart Dutch oven for this recipe.

BRINE
- ½ cup salt
- ½ cup sugar
- 3 pounds bone-in chicken pieces (split breasts cut in half, drumsticks, and/or thighs), trimmed

BATTER
- 1½ cups cornstarch
- ¾ cup water
- 2 teaspoons pepper
- 1 teaspoon salt
- 3 quarts peanut or vegetable oil

HONEY GLAZE
- ¾ cup honey
- 2 tablespoons hot sauce

DISPOSING OF OIL NEATLY

Deep-fried foods, such as fried chicken, are a real treat, but cleaning up after frying is not. Disposing of the spent oil neatly and safely is a particular challenge. Here's how we do it. First we allow the oil to cool completely. Then we make a quadruple- or quintuple-layered bag using four or five leftover plastic grocery bags. With someone holding the layered bags open over a sink or in an outdoor area, we carefully pour the cooled frying oil from the pot into the innermost bag. We tie the bag handles shut and dispose of the oil in the garbage.

1. FOR THE BRINE: Dissolve ½ cup salt and sugar in 2 quarts cold water in large container. Submerge chicken in brine, cover, and refrigerate for 30 minutes to 1 hour.

2. FOR THE BATTER: Whisk 1 cup cornstarch, water, pepper, and salt together in bowl until smooth. Refrigerate batter while chicken is brining.

3. Sift remaining ½ cup cornstarch into medium bowl. Remove chicken from brine and pat dry with paper towels. Working with 1 piece at a time, coat chicken thoroughly with cornstarch, shaking to remove excess; transfer to platter.

4. Set wire rack in rimmed baking sheet. Add oil to large Dutch oven until it measures about 2 inches deep and heat over medium-high heat to 350 degrees. Whisk batter to recombine. Transfer half of chicken to batter and turn to coat. Remove chicken from batter, allowing excess to drip back into bowl, and add chicken to hot oil. Adjust burner, if necessary, to maintain oil temperature between 325 and 350 degrees. Fry chicken, stirring to prevent pieces from sticking together, until slightly golden and just beginning to crisp, 5 to 7 minutes. (Chicken will not be cooked through at this point.) Transfer parcooked chicken to platter. Return oil to 350 degrees and repeat with remaining raw chicken and batter. Let each batch of chicken rest for 5 to 7 minutes.

5. Return oil to 350 degrees. Return first batch of chicken to oil and fry until breasts register 160 degrees and thighs and drumsticks register 175 degrees, 5 to 7 minutes. Using tongs, transfer to prepared wire rack. Return oil to 350 degrees and repeat with remaining chicken.

6. FOR THE HONEY GLAZE: Combine honey and hot sauce in large bowl and microwave until hot, about 1½ minutes. Add chicken pieces one at a time to honey mixture and turn to coat; return to wire rack, skin side up, to drain. Serve

Sweet and Tangy Barbecued Chicken

✔ WHY THIS RECIPE WORKS

While most of us have happy memories of eating barbecued chicken during childhood summers, it's clearly nostalgia that makes us look back with fondness. In reality, barbecued chicken falls victim to numerous pitfalls: The chicken cooks unevenly, frequent flare-ups cause the skin to blacken, and the sauce is usually cloyingly thick and sweet. We knew it could be better, and we set out to foolproof this American classic.

GIVE IT A RUB For chicken that was well seasoned all the way to the bone, we applied a rub: Salt, onion and garlic powders, paprika, a touch of cayenne, and some brown sugar maintained a bold presence even after grilling.

ADD A PAN OF WATER Placing a disposable aluminum pan opposite the coals and filling it partially with water lowered the temperature inside the grill by about 50 degrees (both the pan and the water absorb heat); this ensured that all the chicken pieces cooked at a slow, steady rate.

SHARPEN THE SAUCE We smartened the typical ketchup-based sauce with molasses, while cider vinegar, Worcestershire sauce, and Dijon mustard kept the sweetness in check. Grated onion, minced garlic, chili powder, cayenne, and pepper rounded out the flavors.

HOLD OFF ON THE SAUCE Waiting to apply the barbecue sauce until after searing

Some leg quarters come with the backbone still attached. Here's an easy way to remove it.

Holding the leg quarter skin side down, grasp the backbone and bend it back to pop the thigh bone out of its socket. Place the leg on a cutting board and cut through the joint and any attached skin.

prevented the sauce from burning and gave the skin a chance to develop color first. Applying it in stages, rather than all at once, ensured that its bright tanginess wasn't lost.

SWEET AND TANGY BARBECUED CHICKEN

SERVES 6 TO 8

When browning the chicken over the hotter side of the grill, move it away from any flare-ups. Use the large holes of a box grater to grate the onion for the sauce.

CHICKEN

2	tablespoons packed dark brown sugar
1½	tablespoons kosher salt
1½	teaspoons onion powder
1½	teaspoons garlic powder
1½	teaspoons paprika
¼	teaspoon cayenne pepper
6	pounds bone-in chicken pieces (split breasts and/or leg quarters), trimmed

SAUCE

1	cup ketchup
5	tablespoons molasses
3	tablespoons cider vinegar
2	tablespoons Worcestershire sauce
2	tablespoons Dijon mustard
¼	teaspoon pepper
2	tablespoons vegetable oil
⅓	cup grated onion
1	garlic clove, minced
1	teaspoon chili powder
¼	teaspoon cayenne pepper

1	large disposable aluminum roasting pan (if using charcoal) or 2 disposable aluminum pie plates (if using gas)

1. FOR THE CHICKEN: Combine sugar, salt, onion powder, garlic powder, paprika, and cayenne in bowl. Arrange chicken on rimmed baking sheet and sprinkle both sides evenly with spice rub. Cover with plastic wrap and refrigerate for at least 6 hours or up to 24 hours.

2. FOR THE SAUCE: Whisk ketchup, molasses, vinegar, Worcestershire, mustard, and pepper together in bowl. Heat oil in medium saucepan over medium heat until shimmering. Add onion and garlic; cook until onion is softened, 2 to 4 minutes. Add chili powder and cayenne and cook until fragrant, about 30 seconds. Whisk in ketchup mixture and bring to boil. Reduce heat to medium-low and simmer gently for 5 minutes. Set aside ⅔ cup sauce to baste chicken and reserve remaining sauce for serving. (Sauce can be refrigerated for up to 1 week.)

3A. FOR A CHARCOAL GRILL: Open bottom vent halfway and place disposable pan filled with 3 cups water on 1 side of grill. Light large chimney starter filled with charcoal briquettes (6 quarts). When top coals are partially covered with ash, pour evenly over other half of grill (opposite disposable pan). Set cooking grate in place, cover, and open lid vent halfway. Heat grill until hot, about 5 minutes.

3B. FOR A GAS GRILL: Place 2 disposable pie plates, each filled with 1½ cups water, directly on 1 burner of gas grill (opposite primary burner). Turn all burners to high, cover, and heat grill until hot, about 15 minutes. Turn primary burner to medium-high and turn off other burner(s). (Adjust primary burner as needed to maintain grill temperature of 325 to 350 degrees.)

4. Clean and oil cooking grate. Place chicken, skin side down, over hotter part of grill and cook until browned and blistered in spots, 2 to 5 minutes. Flip chicken and cook until second side is browned, 4 to 6 minutes. Move chicken to cooler part and brush both sides with ⅓ cup sauce. Arrange chicken, skin side up, with leg quarters closest to fire and breasts farthest away. Cover (positioning lid vent over chicken if using charcoal) and cook for 25 minutes.

5. Brush both sides of chicken with remaining ⅓ cup sauce and continue to cook, covered, until breasts register 160 degrees and leg quarters register 175 degrees, 25 to 35 minutes longer.

6. Transfer chicken to serving platter, tent loosely with aluminum foil, and let rest for 10 minutes. Serve, passing reserved sauce separately.

Smoked Chicken

✓ WHY THIS RECIPE WORKS

Unlike hot and fast cooking methods, smoking is a gentle process in which a low fire burns slowly to keep pieces of wood smoldering, allowing chicken to cook gradually. When done right, the meat is juicy, tender, and imbued throughout with insistent yet balanced smokiness. The skin is well rendered, but instead of being crackly-crisp, it's moist, supple, and stained a deep brown. But getting the heat just right is a challenge, and the smoke flavor can be fickle—sometimes barely there, other times harsh and bitter. We wanted to nail down a fire setup and a specific window of smoking time that would produce tender, juicy meat with clean, full-bodied smoke flavor.

BRINE, DON'T SALT While brining and salting both season meat and help it retain juices, brining plumps up the chicken with additional moisture—key in a recipe in which the meat is prone to drying out.

CHOOSE CHICKEN PARTS By using chicken parts rather than a whole bird, the white meat could sit as far from the heat as possible, and the smoke could evenly surround the smaller individual pieces. Pieces also cooked faster than a whole bird, and were more space-efficient, which meant we could fit another half chicken's worth of pieces on the grill.

CREATE A SLOW BURN Covering a small pile of unlit coals with a batch of lit coals allowed the heat from the lit briquettes to trickle down and lights the cold coals—a technique that extended the life of the fire without the need for opening the grill to refuel and allowing precious heat to escape.

ADD SOME WATER A pan of water under the chicken on the cooler side of the grill provided humidity, which helped stabilize the temperature of the grill and prevented the delicate breast meat from drying out.

SMOKE FOR ONLY HALF THE TIME When we smoked the chicken for the entire cooking time the smoke flavor was harsh and overpowering. Adding wood chunks just once at the beginning of cooking—and not refueling once they had burned out—gave us fresh, clean-tasting smoke flavor.

SMOKED CHICKEN
SERVES 6 TO 8

If using kosher chicken, do not brine in step 1. If you'd like to use wood chunks instead of wood chips when using a charcoal grill, substitute two medium wood chunks, soaked in water for 1 hour, for the wood chip packets.

    Salt
1   cup sugar
6   pounds bone-in chicken pieces (split breasts, drumsticks and/or thighs), trimmed

---

SMOKING CHICKEN IN A CHARCOAL KETTLE

To produce tender, juicy, smoky chicken, we devised a three-part fire setup in our charcoal kettle. It mimics the slow, steady, indirect heat that pit masters get from a dedicated smoker; plus, it avoids sooty flavors.

Two Quarts of Unlit Coals banked to one side of the grill with 3 quarts of lit coals piled on top kept the fire going without it being necessary to open the lid.

Two Soaked Wood Chunks placed on top of the coals smoldered for about 45 minutes—just long enough to infuse the chicken with smoky (not sooty) flavor.

A Water Pan placed underneath the grill grate opposite the coals created steam, which helped stabilize the temperature and keep the meat moist.

If you are questioning the age
and freshness of an already-
opened jar, crumble a small
amount between your fingers
and take a whiff. If it releases
a lively aroma, it's good to
use. If it doesn't, it's best to
get a new jar. If the fragrance
is present but relatively mild,
consider using more than you
normally would.

3 tablespoons vegetable oil
   Pepper
3 cups wood chips, 1½ cups soaked in
   water for 15 minutes and drained, plus
   1½ cups wood chips unsoaked
1 (16 by 12-inch) disposable aluminum
   roasting pan (if using charcoal) or
   disposable aluminum pie plate (if
   using gas)

1. Dissolve 1 cup salt and sugar in 4 quarts cold water in large container. Submerge chicken pieces in brine, cover, and refrigerate for 30 minutes to 1 hour. Remove chicken from brine and pat dry with paper towels. Brush chicken evenly with oil and season with pepper.

2. Using large piece of heavy-duty aluminum foil, wrap soaked chips in foil packet and cut several vent holes in top. Repeat with another sheet of foil and unsoaked wood chips.

3A. FOR A CHARCOAL GRILL: Open bottom vent halfway. Arrange 2 quarts unlit charcoal banked against 1 side of grill and disposable pan filled with 2 cups water on empty side of grill. Light large chimney starter half filled with charcoal briquettes (3 quarts). When top coals are partially covered with ash, pour on top of unlit charcoal, to cover one-third of grill with coals steeply banked against side of grill. Place wood chip packets on top of coals. Set cooking grate in place, cover, and open lid vent halfway. Heat grill until hot and wood chips begin to smoke, about 5 minutes.

3B. FOR A GAS GRILL: Place wood chip packets directly on primary burner. Place disposable pie plate filled with 2 cups water on other burner(s). Turn all burners to high, cover, and heat grill until hot and wood chips begin to smoke, about 15 minutes. Turn primary burner to medium-high and turn off other burner(s). (Adjust primary burner as needed to maintain grill temperature of 325 degrees.)

4. Clean and oil cooking grate. Place chicken on cooler side of grill, skin side up, as far away from heat as possible with thighs closest to heat and breasts farthest away. Cover (positioning lid vents over chicken if using charcoal) and cook until breasts register 160 degrees and thighs and drumsticks register 175 degrees, 1¼ to 1½ hours.

5. Transfer chicken to serving platter, tent loosely with foil, and let rest for 5 to 10 minutes. Serve.

Jerk Chicken

✔ WHY THIS RECIPE WORKS
Modern-day jerk chicken recipes call for marinating the meat with an intensely flavorful liquid paste of allspice berries, fiery Scotch bonnet chiles, herbs, and spices and then smoking it over pimento wood. When done well, the chicken emerges aromatic, woodsy, spicy, and sweet, with a clean, lingering burn from the fresh chiles. But most recipes are rife with pitfalls: dense, thick spice pastes are tricky to spread evenly and tend to burn, while thinner concoctions run right off the chicken and into the fire. We wanted a marinade that struck the ideal aromatic-sweet-spicy balance, and we needed to find a replacement for the traditional pimento wood.

INCLUDE ALL THE FLAVOR ELEMENTS
For authentic jerk flavor we settled on a bold and complex list of ingredients: Spices and chiles were definites, as were scallions for their grassy freshness, and plenty of garlic and salt. A mixture of dried thyme, basil, and rosemary added woodsy depth; ground nutmeg and ginger, plus a touch of brown sugar, provided warmth and sweetness; a good amount of grated lime zest and yellow mustard offered brightness; and soy sauce contributed a savory boost.

START COOL Starting the chicken pieces on the cooler side of the grill gave the marinade a chance to dry out and set on the skin, which prevented the pieces from sticking to the grate.

FINISH HOT To ensure that the hotter side was still plenty hot for a good sear at the end of cooking, we placed a pile of unlit coals underneath the lit ones; this approach extended the life of the fire significantly.

ADD HERBS WITH WOOD CHIPS To mimic pimento wood's fresh, sweet, herbal smoke flavor, we looked to our spice cabinet: Smoking allspice berries, thyme, and rosemary along with the hickory chips gave our chicken authentic jerk flavor.

JERK CHICKEN
SERVES 4

For a milder dish, use one seeded chile. If you prefer your food very hot, use up to three chiles including their seeds and ribs. Scotch bonnet chiles can be used in place of the habaneros. Wear gloves when working with the chiles.

JERK MARINADE

1½	tablespoons coriander seeds
1	tablespoon allspice berries
1	tablespoon black peppercorns
1–3	habanero chiles, stemmed, seeds and ribs reserved (optional), and quartered
8	scallions, chopped
6	garlic cloves, peeled
3	tablespoons vegetable oil
2	tablespoons soy sauce
2	tablespoons grated lime zest (3 limes), plus lime wedges for serving
2	tablespoons yellow mustard
1	tablespoon dried thyme
1	tablespoon ground ginger
1	tablespoon packed brown sugar
2¼	teaspoons salt
2	teaspoons dried basil
½	teaspoon dried rosemary
½	teaspoon ground nutmeg

CHICKEN

3	pounds bone-in chicken pieces (split breasts cut in half, drumsticks, and/or thighs), trimmed
2	tablespoons allspice berries
2	tablespoons dried thyme
2	tablespoons dried rosemary
2	tablespoons water
1	cup wood chips, soaked in water for 15 minutes and drained

1. FOR THE JERK MARINADE: Grind coriander seeds, allspice berries, and peppercorns in spice grinder or mortar and pestle until coarsely ground. Transfer spices to blender jar. Add habanero(s), seeds and ribs (if using), scallions, garlic, oil, soy sauce, lime zest, mustard, thyme, ginger, brown sugar, salt, basil, rosemary, and nutmeg and process until smooth paste forms, 1 to 3 minutes, scraping down sides of blender jar as necessary. Transfer marinade to 1-gallon zipper-lock bag.

2. FOR THE CHICKEN: Place chicken pieces in bag with marinade and toss to coat; press out as much air as possible and seal bag. Let stand at room temperature for 30 minutes while preparing grill, flipping bag after 15 minutes. (Marinated chicken can be refrigerated for up to 24 hours.)

3. Combine allspice berries, thyme, rosemary, and water in bowl and set aside to moisten for 15 minutes. Using large piece of heavy-duty aluminum foil, wrap soaked chips and moistened allspice mixture in foil packet and cut several vent holes in top.

4A. FOR A CHARCOAL GRILL: Open bottom vent halfway. Arrange 1 quart unlit charcoal briquettes in single layer over half of grill. Light large chimney starter one-third filled with charcoal briquettes (2 quarts). When top coals are partially covered with ash, pour on top of unlit charcoal, keeping coals arranged over half of grill. Place wood chip packet on top of coals. Set cooking grate in place, cover, and open lid vent halfway. Heat grill until hot and wood chips are smoking, about 5 minutes.

4B. FOR A GAS GRILL: Place wood chip packet directly on primary burner. Turn all

burners to high, cover, and heat grill until hot and wood chips are smoking, 15 to 25 minutes. Turn primary burner to medium and turn off other burner(s).

5. Clean and oil cooking grate. Place chicken on cooler side of grill, with marinade clinging and skin side up, as far away from fire as possible, with thighs closest to heat and breasts farthest away. Cover (positioning lid vent over chicken if using charcoal) and cook for 30 minutes.

6. Move chicken, skin side down, to hotter side of grill; cook until browned and skin renders, 3 to 6 minutes. Using tongs, flip chicken pieces and cook until browned on second side and breasts register 160 degrees and thighs and drumsticks register 175 degrees, 5 to 12 minutes longer.

7. Transfer chicken to serving platter, tent loosely with foil, and let rest for 5 to 10 minutes. Serve warm or at room temperature with lime wedges.

Chicken Stew

✓ WHY THIS RECIPE WORKS

Living in a nation of chicken lovers, we're always surprised at how rarely we find chicken stew on a menu or in a cookbook. The few versions that do exist are either too fussy or too fancy, or seem more soup than stew, with none of the complexity and depth we expect from the latter. We wanted a recipe for a simple, hearty chicken stew that would satisfy like the beef kind—one with succulent bites of chicken, tender vegetables, and a truly robust gravy.

START WITH WINGS Because boneless, skinless thighs have very little connective tissue, chicken stew tends to lack richness and body. For a full-flavored gravy, we seared (and then discarded) a pound of wings; the collagen and flavor they contributed to the stew resulted in a velvety texture and rich flavor.

BOOST FLAVOR A few strips of bacon, crisped in the pot before we browned the wings in the rendered fat, lent porky depth and just a hint of smoke. And while they may sound like strange additions to an all-American chicken stew, soy sauce and anchovy paste were essential flavor components as well, boosting the meaty, savory flavor of our stew substantially.

REDUCE TWO WAYS After sautéing the aromatics, we concentrated flavor by reducing a portion of the broth—along with wine and soy sauce—until fully evaporated. Cooking the stew uncovered for part of the time once the thighs were added further enhanced the rich flavor of this soul-satisfying stew.

BEST CHICKEN STEW
SERVES 6 TO 8

Mashed anchovy fillets (rinsed and dried before mashing) can be used instead of anchovy paste. Use small red potatoes measuring 1½ inches in diameter.

2	pounds boneless, skinless chicken thighs, halved crosswise and trimmed
	Kosher salt and pepper
3	slices bacon, chopped
1	pound chicken wings, cut at joint
1	onion, chopped fine
1	celery rib, minced
2	garlic cloves, minced
2	teaspoons anchovy paste
1	teaspoon minced fresh thyme
5	cups chicken broth
1	cup dry white wine, plus extra for seasoning
1	tablespoon soy sauce
3	tablespoons unsalted butter, cut into 3 pieces

⅓ cup all-purpose flour

1 pound small red potatoes, unpeeled, quartered

4 carrots, peeled and cut into ½-inch pieces

2 tablespoons chopped fresh parsley

1. Adjust oven rack to lower-middle position and heat oven to 325 degrees. Arrange chicken thighs on baking sheet and lightly season both sides with salt and pepper; cover with plastic wrap and set aside.

2. Cook bacon in Dutch oven over medium-low heat, stirring occasionally, until fat renders and bacon browns, 6 to 8 minutes. Using slotted spoon, transfer bacon to medium bowl. Add chicken wings to pot, increase heat to medium, and cook until well browned on both sides, 10 to 12 minutes; transfer wings to bowl with bacon.

3. Add onion, celery, garlic, anchovy paste, and thyme to pot; cook, stirring occasionally, until dark fond forms on pan bottom, 2 to 4 minutes. Increase heat to high; stir in 1 cup broth, wine, and soy sauce, scraping up any browned bits; and bring to boil. Cook, stirring occasionally, until liquid evaporates and vegetables begin to sizzle again, 12 to 15 minutes. Add butter and stir to melt; sprinkle flour over vegetables and stir to combine. Gradually whisk in remaining 4 cups broth until smooth. Stir in wings and bacon, potatoes, and carrots; bring to simmer. Transfer to oven and cook, uncovered, for 30 minutes, stirring once halfway through cooking.

4. Remove pot from oven. Use wooden spoon to draw gravy up sides of pot and scrape browned fond into stew. Place over high heat, add thighs, and bring to simmer. Return pot to oven, uncovered, and continue to cook, stirring occasionally, until chicken offers no resistance when poked with fork and vegetables are tender, about 45 minutes longer. (Stew can be refrigerated for up to 2 days.)

5. Discard wings and season stew with up to 2 tablespoons wine. Season with salt and pepper to taste, sprinkle with parsley, and serve.

Quick Chicken Fricassee

✓ WHY THIS RECIPE WORKS

Classic recipes for chicken fricassee poach chicken pieces, mushrooms, and pearl onions in stock and sauce them with a cream-enriched reduction of the cooking liquid. While this dish captures both richness and clean chicken flavor all on one platter, it's also fussy and time-consuming. We wanted a stream-lined technique that would give this classic French braise weeknight potential and a brighter, more complex sauce.

OPT FOR BONELESS Thick bone-in chicken parts took up too much room to brown in a single batch and required nearly 30 minutes of poaching. Boneless, skinless breasts and thighs fit nicely into a 12-inch skillet and were mostly cooked through after an initial sear.

ADD RICHNESS Browning the meat in a combination of butter and oil provided much-needed richness and flavor that was lost when we eliminated bone-in, skin-on parts.

CARAMELIZE THE VEGETABLES To build up savory flavor even more, we swapped the pearl onions for a regular chopped onion, which provided more surface area for browning and caramelization. We also upped the amount of mushrooms to a full pound, significantly boosting the meaty flavor.

FINISH THE SAUCE Sour cream added body and a pleasant tang to our dish, while the addition of an egg yolk (a technique popular in many early fricassee recipes) resulted in an incredibly silky sauce.

QUICK CHICKEN FRICASSEE

SERVES 4 TO 6

Two tablespoons of chopped fresh parsley may be substituted for the tarragon in this recipe.

2 pounds boneless, skinless chicken breasts and/or thighs, trimmed
Salt and pepper
1 tablespoon unsalted butter
1 tablespoon olive oil
1 pound cremini mushrooms, trimmed and sliced ¼ inch thick
1 onion, chopped fine
¼ cup dry white wine
1 tablespoon all-purpose flour
1 garlic clove, minced
1½ cups chicken broth
⅓ cup sour cream
1 large egg yolk
2 teaspoons lemon juice
2 teaspoons minced fresh tarragon
½ teaspoon ground nutmeg

1. Pat chicken dry with paper towels and sprinkle with 1 teaspoon salt and ½ teaspoon pepper. Heat butter and oil in 12-inch skillet over medium-high heat until butter is melted. Place chicken in skillet and cook until browned, about 4 minutes. Using tongs, flip chicken and cook until browned on second side, about 4 minutes longer. Transfer chicken to large plate.

2. Add mushrooms, onion, and wine to now-empty skillet and cook, stirring occasionally, until liquid has evaporated and mushrooms are browned, 8 to 10 minutes. Add flour and garlic; cook, stirring constantly, for 1 minute. Add broth and bring mixture to boil, scraping up any browned bits from bottom of pan. Add chicken and any accumulated juices to skillet. Reduce heat to medium-low, cover, and simmer until breasts register 160 degrees and thighs register 175 degrees, 5 to 10 minutes.

3. Transfer chicken to platter and tent loosely with aluminum foil. Whisk sour cream and egg yolk together in medium bowl. Whisking constantly, slowly stir ½ cup hot sauce into sour cream mixture to temper. Stirring constantly, slowly pour sour cream mixture into simmering sauce. Stir in lemon juice, tarragon and nutmeg; return to simmer. Season with salt and pepper to taste, pour sauce over chicken, and serve.

Old-Fashioned Chicken Pot Pie

✔ WHY THIS RECIPE WORKS

Most everyone loves a good chicken pot pie, but like a lot of satisfying dishes, traditional pot pie takes time. Before the pie even makes it to the oven, the cook must poach a chicken; take the meat off the bone and cut it up; strain the broth; prepare and blanch vegetables; make a sauce; and mix and roll out biscuit or pie dough. Our goal was to make the best pot pie as quickly as possible.

POACH IT IN BROTH Poaching boneless, skinless chicken parts in broth was simple and produced moist, tender chicken.

PREVENT OVERCOOKED VEGETABLES Sautéed vegetables retained their color and flavor better than parboiled ones (and vegetables that went into the pie raw didn't fully cook through).

ARRANGING DOUGH ON POT PIE

1. Roll dough loosely over rolling pin and unroll evenly over baking dish.

2. Lay rectangle of dough over pot-pie filling, trimming dough to within ½ inch of pan lip.

3. For fluted edge, tuck overhanging dough back under itself so folded edge is flush with lip of pan.

4. Holding dough with your thumb and index finger, push dough with index finger of your other hand to form a pleated edge. Repeat all around edge.

SKIP THE BOTTOM CRUST Using a single crust for our pot pie served three purposes: It kept the pie from becoming overly rich; it streamlined the recipe; and it allowed for a shorter cooking time, which provided further insurance against limp, overcooked vegetables.

TRADE CREAM FOR MILK To our surprise, a sauce enriched with milk rather than cream was actually better; using a fairly large quantity (1½ cups) kept the sauce creamy in both color and flavor. A little flour thickened the sauce to the proper consistency, while a few tablespoons of sherry gave our sauce a flavor boost without dulling the vegetables.

OLD-FASHIONED CHICKEN POT PIE
SERVES 6

Mushrooms can be sautéed along with the celery and carrots, and blanched pearl onions can stand in for the onion.

DOUGH

1½	cups (7½ ounces) all-purpose flour
½	teaspoon salt
4	tablespoons vegetable shortening, cut into ¼-inch pieces and chilled
8	tablespoons unsalted butter, cut into ¼-inch pieces and chilled
3–4	tablespoons ice water

FILLING

1½	pounds boneless, skinless chicken breasts and/or thighs, trimmed
2	cups chicken broth
1½	tablespoons vegetable oil
1	large onion, chopped fine
3	carrots, peeled and sliced ¼ inch thick
2	small celery ribs, sliced ¼ inch thick
	Salt and pepper
4	tablespoons unsalted butter
½	cup all-purpose flour
1½	cups whole milk
½	teaspoon dried thyme
¾	cup frozen peas, thawed
3	tablespoons dry sherry
3	tablespoons minced fresh parsley

1. FOR THE PIE DOUGH: Process flour and salt in food processor until combined, about 5 seconds. Scatter shortening over top and pulse until mixture resembles coarse cornmeal, about 10 pulses. Scatter butter over top and pulse mixture until it resembles coarse crumbs, about 10 pulses; transfer to large bowl.

2. Sprinkle 3 tablespoons ice water over flour mixture. Stir and press dough together, using stiff rubber spatula, until dough sticks together. If dough does not come together, stir in remaining 1 tablespoon ice water.

3. Turn dough onto sheet of plastic wrap and flatten into 4-inch disk. Wrap dough tightly in plastic and refrigerate for at least 1 hour. Before rolling out dough, let it sit on counter to soften slightly, about 10 minutes.

4. FOR THE FILLING: Bring chicken and broth to simmer in covered Dutch oven and cook until chicken is tender and cooked through, 8 to 10 minutes. Transfer chicken to large bowl. Pour broth through fine-mesh strainer into liquid measuring cup and reserve. Meanwhile, adjust oven rack to lower-middle position and heat oven to 400 degrees.

5. Heat oil in now-empty pot over medium heat until shimmering. Add onion, carrots, celery, ¼ teaspoon salt, and ¼ teaspoon pepper and cook until softened, about 5 minutes. While vegetables are cooking, use 2 forks to shred chicken into bite-size pieces. Transfer vegetables to bowl with chicken; set aside.

6. Melt butter in again-empty pot over medium heat. Add flour and cook, stirring constantly, for 1 minute. Slowly whisk in reserved broth, milk, any accumulated chicken juices, and thyme. Bring to simmer and cook until sauce thickens, about 1 minute. Off heat, stir in chicken-vegetable mixture, peas, sherry, and parsley and season with salt and pepper to taste.

7. Pour chicken mixture into 13 by 9-inch baking dish. Roll dough out to 15 by 11-inch rectangle, about ⅛ inch thick, on lightly floured counter. Loosely roll dough around rolling pin and gently unroll it over filling. Trim, fold, and crimp edges and cut 4 vent holes in top.

8. Place pot pie on aluminum foil–lined rimmed baking sheet and bake until filling is bubbling on sides and crust is golden brown, about 30 minutes. Let cool for 10 minutes before serving.

TO MAKE AHEAD: Dough can be wrapped and refrigerated for up to 2 days or frozen for up to 1 month. If frozen, let dough thaw completely in refrigerator before rolling out. Chicken filling can be cooled and refrigerated overnight. Reheat filling before transferring to baking dish and proceeding with recipe.

Chicken Pot Pie with Savory Crumble Topping

✓ WHY THIS RECIPE WORKS

As homey as traditional chicken pot pie is, it can be a production. We wanted a streamlined version of this comforting favorite full of tender, juicy chicken and bright vegetables that could be on the table in 90 minutes.

GO BONELESS Cooking, cooling, and dismantling a whole chicken, or even bone-in parts, took a long time. But we found that by poaching boneless, skinless breasts and thighs in chicken broth, we could cook the meat in about 10 minutes. With the skin and bones already removed, the meat was easy to handle and shredded nicely into bite-size morsels. The poaching liquid could then double as a flavorful base for a velvety, full-bodied sauce that didn't need reducing.

COOK THE VEGGIES SEPARATELY Although it was tempting to cook the chicken and veggies together (we chose a traditional medley of onions, carrots, celery, and peas), poaching the vegetables sapped their flavor and made them mushy. To make sure they maintained their distinct flavors and textures in the pie, we sautéed them in oil before adding them to the baking dish. A squirt of fresh lemon juice ensured that the filling stayed bright.

SUPPLEMENT THE SAVORY FLAVOR A butter-and-flour roux mixed with the chicken poaching liquid and milk tasted clean and nicely chicken-y, but without the benefit of a fond from dark, caramelized bits of roasted chicken or the deeply concentrated jus of a pot-roasted bird, it lacked savory depth. To enhance the sauce, we added sautéed mushrooms along with some soy sauce and tomato paste. These glutamate-rich ingredients deepened the savory flavor without giving themselves away.

MAKE A CRUMBLE Traditional pie crust was too time-consuming for our streamlined recipe, and biscuits didn't provide the textural contrast we were looking for. For a crisp, buttery top to our pie, we made a savory crumble topping by rubbing butter into a mixture of flour, salt, pepper, baking powder, and a bit of cayenne. Parmesan cheese gave our crumble a savory tang, and cream added richness. We prebaked the crumble so that our pie filling wouldn't overbake.

CHICKEN POT PIE WITH SAVORY CRUMBLE TOPPING

SERVES 6

This recipe relies on two unusual ingredients: soy sauce and tomato paste. Do not omit them. They don't convey their distinctive tastes but greatly deepen the savory flavor of the filling. When making the topping, do not substitute milk or half-and-half for the heavy cream.

ENSURING A CRISPY CRUMBLE TOPPING

We swapped the traditional labor-intensive crust for a simpler savory crumble topping. Prebaking the crumble before sprinkling it over the pie guarantees that it stays crisp. This also allows us to limit the time that the assembled casserole spends in the oven, so the chicken won't dry out and the vegetables stay tender yet firm.

FILLING

- 1½ pounds boneless, skinless chicken breasts and/or thighs, trimmed
- 3 cups chicken broth
- 2 tablespoons vegetable oil
- 1 onion, chopped fine
- 3 carrots, peeled and sliced ¼ inch thick
- 2 small celery ribs, minced
  Salt and pepper
- 10 ounces cremini mushrooms, trimmed and sliced thin
- 1 teaspoon soy sauce
- 1 teaspoon tomato paste
- 4 tablespoons unsalted butter
- ½ cup all-purpose flour
- 1 cup whole milk
- 2 teaspoons lemon juice
- 3 tablespoons minced fresh parsley
- ¾ cup frozen peas

CRUMBLE TOPPING

- 2 cups (10 ounces) all-purpose flour
- 2 teaspoons baking powder
- ¾ teaspoon salt
- ½ teaspoon pepper
- ⅛ teaspoon cayenne pepper
- 6 tablespoons unsalted butter, cut into ½-inch pieces and chilled
- 1 ounce Parmesan cheese, grated fine (½ cup)
- ¾ cup plus 2 tablespoons heavy cream

1. FOR THE FILLING: Bring chicken and broth to simmer in covered Dutch oven and cook until chicken is tender and cooked through, 8 to 10 minutes. Transfer chicken to large bowl. Pour broth through fine-mesh strainer into liquid measuring cup and reserve. Meanwhile, adjust oven rack to upper-middle position and heat oven to 450 degrees.

2. FOR THE TOPPING: Combine flour, baking powder, salt, pepper, and cayenne in large bowl. Sprinkle butter pieces over top of flour. Using fingers, rub butter into flour mixture until it resembles coarse cornmeal. Stir in Parmesan. Add cream and stir until just combined. Crumble mixture into irregularly shaped pieces ranging from ½ to ¾ inch each onto parchment paper–lined rimmed baking sheet. Bake until fragrant and starting to brown, 10 to 13 minutes. Set aside.

3. Heat 1 tablespoon oil in now-empty pot over medium heat until shimmering. Add onion, carrots, celery, ¼ teaspoon salt, and ¼ teaspoon pepper; cover and cook, stirring occasionally, until just tender, 5 to 7 minutes. While vegetables are cooking, use 2 forks to shred chicken into bite-size pieces. Transfer vegetables to bowl with chicken; set aside.

4. Heat remaining 1 tablespoon oil in again-empty pot over medium heat until shimmering. Add mushrooms; cover and cook, stirring occasionally, until mushrooms have released their liquid, about 5 minutes. Remove cover and stir in soy sauce and tomato paste. Increase heat to medium-high and cook, stirring often, until liquid has evaporated, mushrooms are well browned, and dark fond begins to form on surface of pan, about 5 minutes. Transfer mushrooms to bowl with chicken and vegetables. Set aside.

5. Melt butter in again-empty pot over medium heat. Add flour and cook, stirring constantly, for 1 minute. Slowly whisk in reserved broth and milk. Bring to simmer, scraping up any browned bits, and cook until sauce thickens, about 1 minute. Off heat, stir in lemon juice and 2 tablespoons parsley, then stir chicken mixture and peas into sauce. Season with salt and pepper to taste.

6. Pour chicken mixture into 13 by 9-inch baking dish. Scatter crumble topping evenly over filling. Place pot pie on aluminum foil–lined rimmed baking sheet and bake until filling is bubbling and topping is well browned, 12 to 15 minutes. Sprinkle with remaining 1 tablespoon parsley and serve.

Thai Chicken Curry

✔ WHY THIS RECIPE WORKS

There are many interpretations of Thai curries, but one of our favorites is a less well-known variety called massaman. *Unlike many Thai dishes that feature hot, sour, salty, and sweet elements, massaman curry trades on a warm, faintly sweet, and not overly spicy profile, thanks to a mix of warm spices, roasted dried chiles and aromatics like shallots, garlic, and fresh galangal (a sweet-spicy cousin of ginger). A last-minute addition of either shrimp paste or fish sauce and a few teaspoons of tangy tamarind balance the rich sauce, which is typically paired with chicken (or beef), potato chunks, and roasted peanuts. We wanted to tackle massaman curry and make it accessible to the home cook by eliminating the hard-to-find ingredients and much of the tedious prep work.*

GO FOR THIGHS Boneless, skinless chicken thighs were a must; their rich flavor stood up well to the other substantial elements of this dish.

ROAST THE CHILES AND AROMATICS After sampling curry pastes made with both raw and roasted chiles and aromatics, we quickly determined that roasting was an essential step. Not only was the roasted version richer-tasting, with rounder, more complex flavor, we also discovered that there was a textural advantage to precooking: The heat had softened the vegetables, making them easier to blend into a uniform paste.

SAVE TIME WITH PREGROUND SPICES While we couldn't take a shortcut with the chiles and aromatics, we had great success substituting preground spices for the traditional whole spices, which are ground and toasted. Blooming the spices in oil deepened their flavor.

ADD A LITTLE LIME JUICE For a bit of brightness, we replaced some of the water in the paste with a spoonful of lime juice, which served as a fairly good substitute for the tamarind. Finishing the curry with lime zest and cilantro freshened it up even more.

THAI CHICKEN CURRY WITH POTATOES AND PEANUTS

SERVES 4 TO 6

The ingredients for the curry paste can be doubled to make extra for future use. Refrigerate the paste for up to one week or freeze it for up to two months. It will be easier to zest the lime before juicing it. Serve the curry with jasmine rice.

CURRY PASTE

6	dried New Mexican chiles
4	shallots, unpeeled
7	garlic cloves, unpeeled
½	cup chopped fresh ginger
¼	cup water
1½	tablespoons lime juice
1½	tablespoons vegetable oil
1	tablespoon fish sauce
1	teaspoon five-spice powder
½	teaspoon ground cumin
½	teaspoon pepper

CURRY

1	teaspoon vegetable oil
1¼	cups chicken broth
1	(13.5-ounce) can coconut milk
1	pound Yukon Gold potatoes, unpeeled, cut into ¾-inch pieces
1	onion, cut into ¾-inch pieces
⅓	cup dry-roasted peanuts
¾	teaspoon salt
1	pound boneless, skinless chicken thighs, trimmed and cut into 1-inch pieces
2	teaspoons grated lime zest
¼	cup chopped fresh cilantro

1. FOR THE CURRY PASTE: Adjust oven rack to middle position and heat oven to 350 degrees. Line rimmed baking sheet with aluminum foil. Arrange New Mexican chiles on prepared sheet and toast until puffed

---

CRACKING COCONUT CREAM

Traditional Thai curry recipes call for frying the spice paste in coconut cream that's been "cracked"—that is, simmered until its oil separates out. Simmering the coconut cream forces water to evaporate, making for a slightly more concentrated curry. We skip this step in our Thai Chicken Curry with Potatoes and Peanuts and fry the paste in vegetable oil to keep things simple, but if you want to achieve a slightly richer-tasting curry, follow the steps below and then proceed with step 4 of the recipe, adding the curry paste to the saucepan and omitting the oil. (Add the remaining coconut milk with the broth.) In step 5, add up to ¾ cup water to ensure that the chicken pieces are just submerged in the liquid.

In our testing, we found that **Thai Kitchen Coconut Milk** worked best in this application.

1. Skim solid layer of cream from can of coconut milk to yield roughly ¾ cup.

2. Simmer cream over medium heat, stirring constantly, until cream is texture of yogurt and sizzles at edges, 7 to 12 minutes.

and fragrant, 4 to 6 minutes. Transfer New Mexican chiles to large plate. Heat broiler.

2. Place shallots and garlic on foil-lined sheet and broil until softened and skin is charred, 6 to 9 minutes.

3. When cool enough to handle, stem and seed chiles and tear into 1½-inch pieces. Process chiles in blender until finely ground, about 1 minute. Peel shallots and garlic. Add shallots, garlic, ginger, water, lime juice, oil, fish sauce, five-spice powder, cumin, and pepper to blender. Process to smooth paste, scraping down sides of blender jar as needed, 2 to 3 minutes. You should have 1 cup paste.

4. FOR THE CURRY: Heat oil in large saucepan over medium heat until shimmering. Add curry paste and cook, stirring constantly, until paste begins to brown, 2½ to 3 minutes. Stir in broth, coconut milk, potatoes, onion, peanuts, and salt, scraping up any browned bits. Bring to simmer and cook until potatoes are just tender, 12 to 14 minutes.

5. Stir in chicken and continue to simmer until chicken is cooked through, 10 to 12 minutes. Off heat, stir in lime zest. Serve, passing cilantro separately.

Barbecued Chicken Kebabs

✓ WHY THIS RECIPE WORKS

In theory, barbecued chicken kebabs sound pretty great: char-streaked chunks of juicy meat lacquered with sweet and tangy barbecue sauce. But without an insulating layer of skin, even the fattiest thigh meat can dry out and toughen when exposed to the blazing heat of the grill—and forget about ultralean skinless breast meat. Simply slathering on barbecue does little to address this fundamental problem. Our goal was simple: juicy, tender chicken with plenty of sticky-sweet, smoke-tinged flavor.

CHOOSE SUBSTANTIAL CHUNKS OF MEAT After tinkering with a variety of sizes, we determined that 1-inch chunks were ideal; they cooked through relatively quickly yet required enough time on the grill to pick up smoky flavor.

RUB WITH SALT Brining is one common way to safeguard against dry meat, but in this case the brine made the meat so slick that the barbecue sauce refused to stick. A salt rub worked much better; the rub crisped up on the chicken's exterior as it cooked, forming a craggy surface that the sauce could really cling to.

GIVE IT A BACON INFUSION For incredible depth of flavor as well as juicy meat, we turned to an unusual technique: grinding bacon to a paste and applying it to the salted meat. Combined with both sweet and smoked paprika and a little sugar, our bacony rub created chicken that was juicy, tender, and full-flavored, with a smoky depth that complemented the barbecue sauce.

BARBECUED CHICKEN KEBABS
SERVES 6

Use the large holes of a box grater to grate the onion for the sauce. We prefer flavorful dark thigh meat for these kebabs, but white meat can be used. Whichever you choose, don't mix white and dark meat on the same skewer, since they cook at different rates. If you have thin pieces of chicken, cut them larger than 1 inch and roll or fold them into approximate 1-inch cubes. Turbinado sugar is commonly sold as Sugar in the Raw. Demerara sugar can be substituted. You will need four 12-inch metal skewers for this recipe.

SAUCE

- ½ cup ketchup
- ¼ cup molasses
- 2 tablespoons grated onion
- 2 tablespoons Worcestershire sauce
- 2 tablespoons Dijon mustard
- 2 tablespoons cider vinegar
- 1 tablespoon packed light brown sugar

CHICKEN

- 2 tablespoons paprika
- 4 teaspoons turbinado sugar
- 2 teaspoons kosher salt
- 2 teaspoons smoked paprika
- 2 slices bacon, cut into ½-inch pieces
- 2 pounds boneless, skinless chicken thighs or breasts, trimmed, cut into 1-inch chunks

1. FOR THE SAUCE: Bring all ingredients to simmer in small saucepan over medium heat and cook, stirring occasionally, until reduced to about 1 cup, 5 to 7 minutes. Transfer ½ cup sauce to small bowl and set remaining sauce aside for serving.

2. FOR THE CHICKEN: Combine paprika, sugar, salt, and smoked paprika in large bowl. Process bacon in food processor until smooth paste forms, 30 to 45 seconds, scraping down sides of bowl as needed. Add bacon paste and chicken to spice mixture and mix with hands or rubber spatula until ingredients are thoroughly blended and chicken is completely coated. Cover with plastic wrap and refrigerate for 1 hour. Thread chicken tightly onto four 12-inch metal skewers.

3A. FOR A CHARCOAL GRILL: Open bottom vent completely. Light large chimney starter three-quarters filled with charcoal briquettes (4½ quarts). When top coals are partially covered with ash, pour evenly over half of grill. Set cooking grate in place, cover, and open lid vent completely. Heat grill until hot, about 5 minutes.

3B. FOR A GAS GRILL: Turn all burners to high, cover, and heat grill until hot, about 15 minutes. Turn all burners to medium-high.

4. Clean and oil cooking grate. Place skewers on hotter part of grill (if using charcoal), and cook (covered if using gas), turning kebabs every 2 to 2½ minutes, until well browned and slightly charred, 8 to 10 minutes. Brush top surface of skewers with ¼ cup sauce, flip, and cook until sauce is sizzling and browning in spots, about 1 minute. Brush second side with remaining ¼ cup sauce, flip, and continue to cook until sizzling and browning in spots, about 1 minute longer.

5. Transfer skewers to serving platter, tent loosely with aluminum foil, and let rest for 5 to 10 minutes. Serve, passing reserved sauce separately.

Classic Roast Chicken

✓ WHY THIS RECIPE WORKS

Roasting chicken should be a simple affair, but getting the white and dark meat to cook at the same rate while also developing crisp, golden skin is often a challenge. Brining the bird helps the white meat stay moist, but it can make the skin soggy, slowing browning and crisping. We wanted a foolproof technique for roasting a whole chicken—and we wanted it to be simple.

BLOT DRY Since excess moisture can cause the skin to steam and become flabby, we made sure to thoroughly dry the bird after brining. Adding a little sugar to our brine also encouraged browning.

BUTTER THE MEAT, NOT SKIN Because a chicken cooks so fast, brushing the bird with melted butter isn't a good idea. The moisture in the butter can soften poultry skin and there isn't enough time for it to crisp up. Instead, we put the butter where it does the most good—directly on top of the lean breast meat.

OIL THE EXTERIOR To help the skin crisp, we rubbed a little oil all over the bird.

ELEVATE AND FLIP To promote even cooking, we found it was essential to roast the chicken on a V-rack, which allowed heat to circulate around the bird. Placing the V-rack in a preheated roasting pan jump-started the browning of the skin, while turning the bird two times as it cooked helped protect the white meat from overcooking and crisped the entire exterior of the bird.

CLASSIC ROAST CHICKEN
SERVES 2 OR 3

If using kosher chicken, do not brine in step 1, but season with salt as well as pepper in step 3. We recommend using a V-rack to roast the chicken. If you don't have a V-rack, set the bird on a regular roasting rack and use balls of aluminum foil to keep the roasting chicken propped up on its side.

Salt and pepper
½ cup sugar
1 (3-pound) whole chicken, giblets discarded
2 tablespoons unsalted butter, softened
1 tablespoon olive oil

1. Dissolve ½ cup salt and sugar in 2 quarts cold water in large container. Submerge chicken in brine, cover, and refrigerate for 1 hour. Remove chicken from brine and pat dry with paper towels.

2. Adjust oven rack to lower-middle position, place roasting pan on rack, and heat oven to 400 degrees. Coat V-rack with vegetable oil spray and set aside.

3. Using your fingers, gently loosen chicken skin covering each side of breast. Place softened butter under skin, directly on meat in center of each side of breast. Gently press on skin to distribute butter over meat. Tuck wings behind back. Rub skin with oil, season with pepper, and place chicken, wing side up, on prepared V-rack. Place V-rack in preheated roasting pan and roast for 15 minutes.

4. Remove roasting pan from oven and, using 2 large wads of paper towels, rotate chicken so that opposite wing side is facing up. Return roasting pan to oven and roast for another 15 minutes.

5. Using 2 large wads of paper towels, rotate chicken again so that breast side is facing up and continue to roast until breast registers 160 degrees and thighs register 175 degrees, 20 to 25 minutes longer. Transfer chicken to carving board and let rest for 10 minutes. Carve and serve.

STABILIZING A V-RACK

If your V-rack and your roasting pan are not well matched in size, or if you have a nonstick roasting pan, the V-rack and its heavy contents can slide around the pan and create a dangerous situation. Here's how to stabilize a slippery rack.

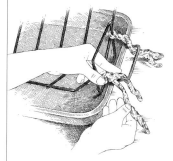

Make 4 ropes of twisted aluminum foil and twist two onto each end of V-rack base. Feed free ends of ropes through pan handles and twist to fasten them around handles.

Weeknight Roast Chicken

WHY THIS RECIPE WORKS

Roast chicken should be a simple dish, but the actual process of preparing and roasting a chicken is anything but simple; recipes often call for complicated trussing techniques and rotating the bird multiple times during cooking. And while brining or salting the bird is a step that ensures juiciness and well-seasoned meat, it is time-consuming. We wanted to find a way to get roast chicken on the table in just an hour without sacrificing flavor.

SKIP THE COMPLICATED TRUSSING We quickly realized that trussing was not necessary; we could simply tie the legs together and tuck the wings underneath.

PREHEAT THE PAN We found we could eliminate the V-rack—typically used to allow for even cooking and to prevent the chicken from sitting in juices, which prevents the skin from crisping—by placing the chicken breast side up in a preheated pan. This gave the thighs a jump start on cooking and it also meant we could eliminate flipping the chicken, since placing the breast directly against the pan's hot surface for part of the cooking time dried it out.

TURN THE OVEN OFF Starting the chicken in a 450-degree oven and then turning the oven off while the chicken finished cooking slowed the evaporation of juices, ensuring moist, tender meat.

USE A SKILLET Since the higher oven temperature forced more of the juices to evaporate, we had less juices left for a pan sauce. Switching to a skillet solved the problem: The juices pooled in the smaller space and didn't evaporate as quickly. (Plus, its long handle and less cumbersome shape made shuffling the chicken in and out of the oven easier.)

WEEKNIGHT ROAST CHICKEN
SERVES 4

We prefer to use a 3½- to 4-pound chicken for this recipe. If roasting a larger bird, increase the time when the oven is on in step 2 to 35 to 40 minutes. Cooking the chicken in a preheated skillet will ensure that the breast and thigh meat finish cooking at the same time. Serve with Tarragon-Lemon Pan Sauce, if desired (recipe follows). If making the sauce, be sure to save 1 tablespoon of the pan drippings.

- 1 tablespoon kosher salt
- ½ teaspoon pepper
- 1 (3½- to 4-pound) whole chicken, giblets discarded
- 1 tablespoon olive oil

1. Adjust oven rack to middle position, place 12-inch ovensafe skillet on rack, and heat oven to 450 degrees. Combine salt and pepper in bowl. Pat chicken dry with paper towels. Rub entire surface with oil. Sprinkle salt mixture evenly over surface of chicken, then rub in mixture with your hands to coat evenly. Tie legs together with kitchen twine and tuck wing tips behind back.

2. Transfer chicken, breast side up, to preheated skillet in oven. Roast chicken until breast registers 120 degrees and thighs register 135 degrees, 25 to 35 minutes. Turn oven off and leave chicken in oven until breast registers 160 degrees and thighs register 175 degrees, 25 to 35 minutes.

3. Using potholders (skillet handle will be hot), transfer chicken to carving board and let rest for 20 minutes. Carve and serve.

1   shallot, minced
1   cup chicken broth
2   teaspoons Dijon mustard
2   tablespoons unsalted butter
2   teaspoons minced fresh tarragon
2   teaspoons lemon juice
    Pepper

While chicken rests, remove all but 1 tablespoon fat from skillet (handle will be very hot) using large spoon, leaving any browned bits and jus in skillet. Place skillet over medium-high heat, add shallot, and cook until softened, about 2 minutes. Stir in broth and mustard, scraping up any browned bits. Simmer until reduced to ¾ cup, about 3 minutes. Off heat, whisk in butter, tarragon, and lemon juice. Season with pepper to taste; cover and keep warm.

Crisp Roast Chicken

✓ WHY THIS RECIPE WORKS

During roasting, juices and rendered fat can accumulate beneath the chicken skin and turn it wet and flabby. We wanted a juicy roasted chicken with skin that would crackle against our teeth with every bite.

ADD BAKING SODA TO THE SALT RUB A little baking soda made a big difference: It helped dehydrate the skin and also reacted with the proteins and fat in the chicken skin to produce a crunchier texture.

PUNCH HOLES Soggy chicken skin is often caused by poorly rendered fat, which accumulates under the skin with nowhere to go. We poked holes in the fat deposits of the breast and thighs to provide an escape route.

LOOSEN THE SKIN Sometimes holes aren't enough: To allow fat to flow freely from the roasting chicken, we separated the skin from the meat over much of the bird. Cutting a few holes near the back of the chicken provided extra-large channels for the rendering fat to drip down and escape.

USE A HOT OVEN Cooking the bird in a really hot oven was key; we found that roasting the chicken at 450 degrees for the majority of the time and then at 500 for the last few minutes really crisped the skin. Starting the chicken breast side down and flipping it midway through cooking protected the meat and cooked it gently enough to keep it tender and juicy.

PROTECT WITH A FOIL SHIELD The high heat had a tendency to cause the escaped juices to burn, creating clouds of smoke; for an easy fix, we placed a sheet of aluminum foil with holes punched in it under the chicken to shield the rendered fat from the direct oven heat.

CRISP ROAST CHICKEN
SERVES 3 TO 4

Do not brine the bird; it will prohibit the skin from becoming crisp. The sheet of foil between the roasting pan and V-rack will keep drippings from burning and smoking.

1   (3½- to 4-pound) whole chicken,
    giblets discarded
1½ teaspoons salt
1   teaspoon baking powder
½   teaspoon pepper

1. Place chicken breast side down on cutting board. Insert tip of sharp knife to make four 1-inch incisions along back of chicken.

Using your fingers, gently loosen skin covering breast and thighs. Using metal skewer, poke 15 to 20 holes in fat deposits on top of breast and thighs. Tuck wings behind back.

2. Combine salt, baking powder, and pepper in bowl. Pat chicken dry with paper towels and sprinkle evenly all over with salt mixture. Rub in mixture with your hands, coating entire surface evenly. Set chicken breast side up in V-rack set on rimmed baking sheet and refrigerate, uncovered, for 12 to 24 hours.

3. Adjust oven rack to lowest position and heat oven to 450 degrees. Using paring knife, poke 20 holes about 1½ inches apart in 16 by 12-inch piece of aluminum foil. Place foil loosely in roasting pan. Flip chicken breast side down and set V-rack in prepared pan on top of foil. Roast chicken for 25 minutes.

4. Remove pan from oven. Using 2 large wads of paper towels, rotate chicken breast side up. Continue to roast until breast registers 135 degrees, 15 to 25 minutes.

5. Increase oven temperature to 500 degrees. Continue to roast chicken until skin is golden brown and crisp, breast registers 160 degrees, and thighs register 175 degrees, 10 to 20 minutes. Transfer chicken to carving board and let rest for 20 minutes. Carve and serve.

Herbed Roast Chicken

✔ WHY THIS RECIPE WORKS

Adding herb flavor to roast chicken sounds easy enough—even downright simple. The reality is that this is one of the hardest culinary tasks to get right. The delicate flavor of herbs does not easily penetrate deep into the bird, while the heat of the oven tends to wilt fresh herbs, dulling their flavor. The most common approach—spreading herb butter under the skin of the breast—only succeeds in flavoring the chicken weakly at best. We wanted the entire bird—not just the breast—seasoned with herbs throughout.

DOUBLE UP ON HERB BUTTER We determined that an herb butter was part of the flavor equation, but rather than just applying it under the skin of the breast, we spread more of the paste—a combination of butter, scallions, tarragon, thyme, and garlic—over the entire chicken halfway through cooking.

SLASH AND BUTTERFLY THE BIRD Making shallow cuts in the dark meat created pockets to trap the herb paste on the thighs, while butterflying the chicken allowed the bird to lie flat in the pan, helping the herbs to stay put once the butter was slathered on.

START ON THE STOVETOP Because the moisture in both the herbs and the butter was slowing down the melting of fat in the skin, we decided to start the chicken on the stovetop in a skillet; boosted by the browning, the rendering process was well under way as the chicken entered the oven.

FINISH WITH A PAN SAUCE FOR EVEN MORE HERB FLAVOR Just to make sure that every bite of chicken was bursting with herb flavor, we made a quick pan sauce using the drippings in the skillet, finishing it off with a couple tablespoons of extra herb butter and a few drops of lemon juice.

HERBED ROAST CHICKEN
SERVES 4

You can substitute an equal amount of basil for the tarragon and replace the thyme with rosemary, oregano, or sage. Do not use dried herbs, which will turn the dish gritty. If using a kosher chicken, do not brine in step 1. The chicken should not exceed 5 pounds or it won't fit in the skillet. The chicken may slightly overhang the skillet at first, but once browned it will fit.

1. To help herbs stay put, flatten bird, first removing backbone.

2. Use heel of your hand to press firmly on breastbone so chicken will lie flat, helping herbs stay on top.

3. Make shallow cuts on legs and thighs to create pockets that can trap herbs.

CHICKEN

- 1 (5-pound) whole chicken, giblets discarded

  Salt and pepper
- 6 scallions, green parts only, sliced thin
- ¼ cup fresh tarragon leaves
- 1 tablespoon fresh thyme leaves
- 1 garlic clove, minced
- 6 tablespoons unsalted butter, softened
- 1 tablespoon vegetable oil

SAUCE

- 1–1½ cups chicken broth
- 2 teaspoons all-purpose flour
- 1 teaspoon lemon juice

  Salt and pepper

1. FOR THE CHICKEN: Using kitchen shears, cut along both sides of chicken's backbone to remove it. Flatten breastbone and tuck wings underneath. Using sharp knife, lightly score skin of thighs and legs, making 2 slashes on each part about ⅛ inch into meat and about ¾ inch apart. Dissolve ½ cup salt in 2 quarts cold water in large container. Submerge chicken in brine, cover, and refrigerate for 1 hour.

2. Meanwhile, adjust oven rack to middle position and heat oven to 450 degrees. Place scallions, tarragon, thyme, garlic, ¼ teaspoon salt, and ¼ teaspoon pepper on cutting board; mince to fine paste. Transfer herb paste to medium bowl, add butter, and mix until combined. Transfer 2 tablespoons herb butter to small bowl and refrigerate; set aside remainder at room temperature.

3. Remove chicken from brine and pat dry with paper towels. Using your fingers, gently loosen skin covering each side of breast; place 1 tablespoon softened herb butter under skin, directly on meat in center of each side of breast. Gently press on skin to distribute butter over meat. Season with pepper.

4. Heat oil in 12-inch ovensafe skillet over medium-high heat until just smoking. Place chicken skin side down in skillet and reduce heat to medium. Cook until lightly browned, 8 to 10 minutes. Transfer skillet to oven and roast chicken for 25 minutes. Using 2 large wads of paper towels, flip chicken skin side up. Using spoon or spatula, evenly coat chicken skin with remaining softened herb butter and return to oven. Roast chicken until skin is golden brown, breast registers 160 degrees, and thighs register 175 degrees, 15 to 20 minutes. Transfer chicken to carving board and let rest for 20 minutes.

5. FOR THE SAUCE: While chicken rests, use potholder (skillet will be hot) to pour pan juices into fat separator; allow liquid to settle for 5 minutes. Pour juices into 2-cup liquid measuring cup and add enough broth to measure 1½ cups. Heat 2 teaspoons fat from fat separator in now-empty skillet over medium heat until shimmering. Add flour and cook, stirring constantly, until golden, about 1 minute. Slowly whisk in broth, scraping up any browned bits. Bring to rapid simmer and cook until reduced to 1 cup, 5 to 7 minutes. Stir in any accumulated juices from carving board; return to simmer and cook for 30 seconds. Off heat, whisk in cold herb butter and lemon juice; season with salt and pepper to taste. Carve chicken and serve, passing sauce separately.

Peruvian Roast Chicken with Garlic and Lime

✔ WHY THIS RECIPE WORKS

Peruvian chicken joints have recently developed something of a cult following in the United States, and for good reason. The rotisserie bird that they serve, known as pollo a la brasa, *is deeply bronzed from its slow rotation in a wood-fired oven and impressively seasoned with garlic, spices, lime juice, chiles, and a paste made with* huacatay, *or black mint. Off the spit, the chicken is carved and served with a garlicky, faintly spicy, mayonnaise-like sauce. We wanted to replicate this robustly flavored dish using an oven and supermarket staples.*

SEASON THOROUGHLY Applying a paste of salt, garlic, oil, lime juice, and cumin directly to the meat (underneath the skin) as well as to the exterior of the bird seasoned the chicken thoroughly from skin to bone.

CHOOSE SMART SUBSTITUTES To our basic paste we added fresh mint (the best replacement for the earthy black mint paste), some dried oregano, grated lime zest (for more citrus flavor without too much acidity), black pepper, sugar, and just a teaspoon of minced habanero chile. Finally, a little smoked paprika subtly approximated the smoky rotisserie flavor.

USE A VERTICAL ROASTER Cooking the bird on a vertical roaster—a tall cone which allows the chicken to stand upright—allowed heat to circulate freely around the bird for evenly cooked results. It also enabled fat to drip freely out of the bird, resulting in rendered and beautifully browned skin.

USE TWO HEAT LEVELS Starting the chicken at 325 degrees prevented the delicate white meat from drying out; letting the chicken rest briefly at room temperature before finishing at 500 degrees gave it a crisp, golden brown exterior.

FINISH WITH A SAUCE The ideal texture of the sauce for this dish is thinner than traditional mayonnaise; with that in mind, we whipped a whole egg and vegetable oil in the food processor with a little water, onion, lime juice, cilantro, yellow mustard, and garlic. Finally, jarred jalapeños contributed the punch traditionally provided by the elusive aji chiles.

PERUVIAN ROAST CHICKEN WITH GARLIC AND LIME

SERVES 3 TO 4

If habanero chiles are unavailable, 1 tablespoon of minced serrano chile can be substituted. Wear gloves when working with hot chiles. This recipe calls for a vertical poultry roaster. If you don't have one, substitute a 12-ounce can of beer. Open the beer and pour out (or drink) about half of the liquid. Spray the can lightly with vegetable oil spray and proceed with the recipe. Serve with Spicy Mayonnaise (recipe follows).

¼	cup fresh mint leaves
3	tablespoons extra-virgin olive oil
6	garlic cloves, chopped coarse
1	tablespoon salt
1	tablespoon pepper
1	tablespoon ground cumin
1	tablespoon sugar
2	teaspoons smoked paprika
2	teaspoons dried oregano
2	teaspoons grated lime zest plus ¼ cup juice (2 limes)
1	teaspoon minced habanero chile
1	(3½- to 4-pound) whole chicken, giblets discarded

1. Process mint, oil, garlic, salt, pepper, cumin, sugar, paprika, oregano, lime zest and juice, and habanero in blender until smooth paste forms, 10 to 20 seconds. Use your fingers

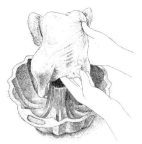

While we like vertical roasters because they let poultry cook evenly and get the skin crisp all over, many cooks don't own one. A 12-ounce beer can is a suitable substitute, but you can also use a Bundt pan. Once the chicken has been seasoned, slide it onto the center post of the pan, legs facing down, so the chicken stands upright.

to gently loosen skin covering breast and thighs; place half of paste under skin, directly on meat of breast and thighs. Gently press on skin to distribute paste over meat. Spread entire exterior surface of chicken with remaining paste. Tuck wings behind back. Place chicken in 1-gallon zipper-lock bag and refrigerate for at least 6 hours or up to 24 hours.

2. Adjust oven rack to lowest position and heat oven to 325 degrees. Place vertical roaster on rimmed baking sheet. Slide chicken onto vertical roaster so drumsticks reach down to bottom of roaster, chicken stands upright, and breast is perpendicular to bottom of pan. Roast chicken until skin just begins to turn golden and breast registers 140 degrees, 45 to 55 minutes. Carefully remove chicken and pan from oven and increase oven temperature to 500 degrees.

3. Once oven has come to temperature, place 1 cup water in bottom of baking sheet and continue to roast until entire chicken skin is browned and crisp, breast registers 160 degrees, and thighs register 175 degrees, about 20 minutes, rotating baking sheet halfway through roasting. Check chicken halfway through roasting; if top is becoming too dark, place 7-inch square piece of aluminum foil over neck and wingtips of chicken and continue to roast. (If pan begins to smoke and sizzle, add additional water to pan.)

4. Carefully remove chicken from oven and let rest, still on vertical roaster, for 20 minutes. Using 2 large wads of paper towels, carefully lift chicken off vertical roaster and onto carving board to rest. Carve and serve.

SPICY MAYONNAISE
MAKES ABOUT 1 CUP

If you have concerns about consuming raw eggs, ¼ cup of an egg substitute can be used in place of the egg.

1	large egg
2	tablespoons water
1	tablespoon finely chopped onion
1	tablespoon lime juice
1	tablespoon minced fresh cilantro
1	tablespoon minced jarred jalapeños
1	garlic clove, minced
1	teaspoon yellow mustard
½	teaspoon kosher salt
1	cup vegetable oil

Process egg, water, onion, lime juice, cilantro, jalapeños, garlic, mustard, and salt in food processor until finely chopped, about 5 seconds. With processor running, slowly drizzle in oil in steady stream until mixture reaches mayonnaise-like consistency, scraping down sides of bowl as needed.

French Chicken in a Pot

✔ WHY THIS RECIPE WORKS

Poulet en cocotte *(chicken in a pot) is a classic French specialty. The method is simple: Place a seasoned chicken in a pot, brown it, scatter in some vegetables, cover, and bake. When done right, this dish forgoes crispy skin for unbelievably tender, succulent meat and deep flavor. But too much moisture in the pot (which washes out flavor) and overcooking are* common pitfalls. *We wanted chicken in a pot that delivered moist meat and rich, concentrated flavor.*

BROWN FIRST While browning the chicken isn't essential for this dish, since the emphasis is on the meat rather than the skin, we found that lightly searing the chicken was still important because it contributed rich flavor to the jus.

COVER WITH FOIL Placing a sheet of aluminum foil over the pot before covering it with the lid helped create the tightest seal possible and prevented any steam from escaping from the pot as the chicken cooked.

COOK BREAST SIDE UP Arranging the chicken breast side up in the pot allowed the dark meat to rest on the bottom of the pot, where heat transfer is best; this enabled it to cook faster than the white meat, so that both reached the proper temperature at about the same time.

STRAIN THE SAUCE After transferring the chicken to a carving board and tenting it with foil to rest, we strained the chicken juices from the pot through a fine-mesh strainer; this not only created a smooth sauce, but also made for a more intensely flavored jus.

FRENCH CHICKEN IN A POT

SERVES 4

You will need at least a 6-quart Dutch oven with a tight-fitting lid for this recipe. If you choose not to serve the skin with the chicken, simply remove it before carving. The amount of jus will vary depending on the size of the chicken; season it with about ¼ teaspoon lemon juice for every ¼ cup.

1	(4½- to 5-pound) whole chicken, giblets discarded
	Salt and pepper
1	tablespoon olive oil
1	small onion, chopped
1	small celery rib, chopped
6	garlic cloves, peeled
1	bay leaf
1	sprig fresh rosemary (optional)
½–1	teaspoon lemon juice

1. Adjust oven rack to lowest position and heat oven to 250 degrees. Pat chicken dry with paper towels, tuck wings behind back, and season with salt and pepper. Heat oil in Dutch oven over medium heat until just smoking. Add chicken breast side down and scatter onion, celery, garlic, bay leaf, and rosemary sprig, if using, around chicken. Cook until breast is lightly browned, about 5 minutes. Using wooden spoon inserted into cavity of chicken, flip chicken breast side up and cook until chicken and vegetables are well browned, 6 to 8 minutes.

2. Off heat, place large sheet of aluminum foil over pot and cover tightly with lid. Transfer pot to oven and cook chicken until breast registers 160 degrees and thighs register 175 degrees, 1 hour 20 minutes to 1 hour 50 minutes.

3. Transfer chicken to carving board, tent loosely with foil, and let rest for 20 minutes. Meanwhile, strain chicken juices from pot through fine-mesh strainer into fat separator, pressing on solids to extract liquid; discard solids. Let juices settle for 5 minutes, then pour into small saucepan and set over low heat. Carve chicken, adding any accumulated juices to saucepan. Season sauce with lemon juice, salt, and pepper to taste. Serve chicken, passing sauce separately.

Grill-Roasted Beer Can Chicken

✔ WHY THIS RECIPE WORKS

While it may sound like a gimmick, beer can chicken is the real deal: The bird is rubbed with spices, then an open, partially filled beer can is inserted in the chicken's cavity and the bird is grill-roasted upright. The beer simmers and turns to steam as the chicken roasts, which makes the meat remarkably juicy and rich-textured, similar to braised chicken. And the dry heat crisps the skin and renders the fat away. It's a near-perfect way to cook a chicken—if you can get the details just right.

INDIRECT HEAT IS KEY Banking the coals on either side of the grill allowed for a cooler spot in the middle where the chicken could cook through evenly and gently.

MAINTAIN THE PROPER TEMPERATURE Filling a chimney starter two-thirds full provided just enough coals to maintain the grill at the proper temperature for the entire time it took to cook the bird.

ADD SOME SMOKE A few wood chips was all it took to contribute a pleasing smoky flavor that didn't overwhelm the chicken.

KEEP THE SPICES SIMPLE A simple but flavorful blend of pantry staples such as garlic powder, dried thyme, celery seeds, and cayenne provided a rub that was rich and a little bit spicy, the perfect complement to the smokiness imparted by the fire.

GRILL-ROASTED BEER CAN CHICKEN

SERVES 4

If you'd like to use wood chunks instead of wood chips when using a charcoal grill, substitute two medium wood chunks, soaked in water for 1 hour, for the wood chip packets. If you prefer, use lemonade instead of beer; fill an empty 12-ounce soda or beer can with 10 ounces (1¼ cups) of lemonade and proceed as directed.

1 (12-ounce) can beer
2 bay leaves
1 (3½- to 4-pound) whole chicken, giblets discarded
3 tablespoons spice rub (recipe follows)
2 cups wood chips, soaked in water for 15 minutes and drained
1 (13 by 9-inch) disposable aluminum roasting pan (if using charcoal)

1. Open beer can and pour out (or drink) about ¼ cup. With church key can opener, punch 2 more large holes in top of can (for total of 3 holes). Crumble bay leaves into beer.

2. Pat chicken dry with paper towels. Rub chicken evenly, inside and out, with spice rub, lifting up skin over breast and rubbing spice rub directly onto meat. Using skewer, poke skin all over. Slide chicken over beer can so that drumsticks reach down to bottom of can and chicken stands upright; set aside at room temperature.

3. Using large piece of heavy-duty aluminum foil, wrap soaked chips in foil packet and cut several vent holes in top.

4A. FOR A CHARCOAL GRILL: Open bottom vent halfway and place disposable pan in center of grill. Light large chimney starter two-thirds filled with charcoal briquettes (4 quarts). When top coals are partially covered with ash, pour into 2 even piles on either side of disposable pan. Place wood chip packet on 1 pile of coals. Set cooking grate in place, cover, and open lid vent halfway. Heat grill until hot and wood chips are smoking, about 5 minutes.

4B. FOR A GAS GRILL: Place wood chip packet directly on primary burner. Turn all burners to high, cover, and heat grill until hot and wood chips are smoking, about 15 minutes. Turn all burners to medium. (Adjust

SETTING UP BEER CAN CHICKEN

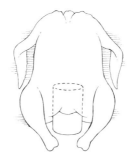

With the legs pointing down, slide the chicken over the open beer can. The two legs and the beer can form a tripod that steadies the chicken on the grill.

burners as needed to maintain grill temperature of 325 degrees.)

5. Clean and oil cooking grate. Place chicken (with can) in center of grill (over roasting pan if using charcoal), using drumsticks to help steady bird. Cover (position lid vent over chicken if using charcoal) and cook until breast registers 160 degrees and thighs register 175 degrees, 1 to 1½ hours.

6. Using large wad of paper towels, carefully transfer chicken (with can) to tray, making sure to keep can upright. Tent loosely with foil and let rest for 15 minutes. Carefully lift chicken off can and onto carving board. Discard remaining beer and can. Carve chicken and serve.

SPICE RUB
MAKES 1 CUP

Store leftover spice rub in an airtight container for up to 3 months.

½	cup paprika
2	tablespoons kosher salt
2	tablespoons garlic powder
1	tablespoon dried thyme
2	teaspoons ground celery seeds
2	teaspoons pepper
2	teaspoons cayenne pepper

Combine all ingredients in bowl.

Grilled Wine-and-Herb Marinated Chicken

✔ WHY THIS RECIPE WORKS

Wine is a natural fit with chicken. The bold acidity and fruity, complex flavors of both red and white wines pair beautifully with mild chicken—think of the classic French braised coq au vin or a wine-based sauce spooned over roasted chicken. Yet many of those classics are more suited to cold weather. We wanted to develop a recipe for winey, herby grilled chicken that could be enjoyed in the warmer months. Making the wine flavor shine in our summery grilled take on this pairing required a few simple tricks.

USE DRY WHITE WINE Dry wines, such as Sauvignon Blanc (as opposed to the oftentimes sweeter types such as Riesling or Gewürztraminer), imparted a more distinct flavor to the meat. Price, however, did not matter—an inexpensive wine will work just fine in this recipe. Pick a wine that is good enough to drink on its own.

BLEND THE MARINADE Whizzing the marinade mixture in a blender rather than simply stirring it together broke down the herbs for optimal flavor and distribution.

BUTTERFLY THE BIRD Butterflying the bird increased the meat's exposure to heat, allowing it to cook more evenly and more quickly. Less time on the grill meant that the chicken had less time to dry out. A butterflied chicken was also easier to manipulate on the grill than a whole bird or parts.

ENCOURAGE GREAT MARINATING Poking holes in the chicken with a skewer helped the flavors of the marinade penetrate the bird with no appreciable loss of juices in the meat. We also found that the chicken had the best flavor if marinated for at least two hours.

GRILL INDIRECTLY We started the chicken over the cooler part of the grill with the skin side down until the meat was almost done before flipping and finishing directly above the fire with the bone side down, which ensured evenly cooked meat with a crisp skin.

USE A MOP In the barbecue world, a mop is a thin basting sauce used to add complexity and freshness to grilled meat. Reserving a quarter cup of the marinade (minus the salt) to brush on the chicken near the end of cooking reinforced the bright, winey flavor.

GRILLED WINE-AND-HERB MARINATED CHICKEN

SERVES 4

Use a dry white wine, such as Sauvignon Blanc, for this recipe.

2   cups dry white wine
3   tablespoons lemon juice
3   tablespoons extra-virgin olive oil
2   tablespoons chopped fresh parsley
2   tablespoons chopped fresh thyme
2   tablespoons packed light brown sugar
4   garlic cloves, minced
1   teaspoon pepper
2   tablespoons salt
1   (4-pound) whole chicken, giblets discarded

1. Process wine, lemon juice, oil, parsley, thyme, sugar, garlic, and pepper in blender until emulsified, about 40 seconds. Reserve ¼ cup marinade. Add salt to remaining mixture in blender and process to dissolve, about 20 seconds.

2. Using kitchen shears, cut along both sides of chicken's backbone to remove it. Flatten breastbone and tuck wings underneath.

Use your hands or handle of wooden spoon to loosen skin over breast and thighs and remove any excess fat.

3. Poke holes all over chicken with skewer. Place chicken in large zipper-lock bag, pour in salted marinade, seal bag, and turn to coat. Set bag in baking dish, breast side down, and refrigerate for 2 to 3 hours.

4A. FOR A CHARCOAL GRILL: Open bottom vent completely. Light large chimney starter filled with charcoal briquettes (6 quarts). When top coals are partially covered with ash, pour evenly over half of grill. Set cooking grate in place, cover, and open lid vent completely. Heat grill until hot, about 5 minutes.

4B. FOR A GAS GRILL: Turn all burners to high, cover, and heat grill until hot, about 15 minutes. Turn secondary burner(s) to low and primary burner to medium. (Adjust primary burner as needed to maintain grill temperature of 350 to 375 degrees.)

5. Remove chicken from marinade and pat dry with paper towels. Discard used marinade. Clean and oil cooking grate. Place chicken skin side down over cooler part of grill (over secondary burner(s) for gas), with legs closest to hotter side of grill. Cover and cook until chicken is well browned and thigh meat registers 160 degrees, 50 to 65 minutes. Brush chicken with half of reserved marinade. Flip chicken, move it to hotter side of grill (over primary burner for gas), and brush with remaining reserved marinade. Cook, covered, until breasts register 160 degrees and thighs register 175 degrees, 10 to 15 minutes longer.

6. Transfer chicken to carving board, tent loosely with aluminum foil, and let rest for 15 minutes. Carve and serve.

Grilled Lemon Chicken with Rosemary

✔ WHY THIS RECIPE WORKS

Grilling a whole chicken can be challenging: The fat in the skin melts and rains onto the coals, sending up flames that carbonize the exterior before the interior is cooked. For this reason, most grilled chicken recipes call for variable heat: low and slow first—to gently render fat and initiate cooking—and then high heat to finish cooking, crisp the skin, and get an enticing char. But these recipes took so long that the coals had nearly burned out by the time we moved the chicken to the hotter side of the grill, and the chicken tasted more roasted than grilled, with dry, chalky white meat. We wanted all the smoky flavor of the grill with tender, moist chicken—and we wanted it in under an hour.

BRINE AND BUTTERFLY Brining the chicken in a sugar and saltwater solution helped to keep even the delicate breast meat moist, and the sugar in the brine promoted browning on the grill. Butterflying the bird increased the meat's exposure to heat, allowing it to cook more evenly and more quickly. Less time on the grill also meant that the chicken had less time to dry out.

REMOVE THE SKIN Taking a cue from tandoori chicken, we removed the skin from the chicken. This solved several problems at once: It eliminated the risk of flare-ups since there was no dripping fat, sped up cooking time, and allowed our flavorful rub to penetrate deep into the meat. Securing the legs with a couple of skewers ensured that the bird stayed together.

SLASH FOR FLAVOR To ensure that our rub of lemon juice, rosemary, mustard, and pepper flavored the chicken all the way through, we cut slashes in the meat before brining, then massaged the rub deep into the knife cuts. We also mixed our rub ingredients into some melted butter to make a basting sauce. For a smoky, fresh finish, we grilled

lemon wedges and then spritzed the chicken with the charred lemon.

GRILLED LEMON CHICKEN WITH ROSEMARY

SERVES 4

For a better grip, use a paper towel to grasp the skin when removing it from the chicken.

- 1 (3½- to 4-pound) whole chicken, giblets discarded
- ¾ cup sugar
  Salt and pepper
- 2 lemons
- 1 tablespoon vegetable oil
- 2 teaspoons minced fresh rosemary
- 1½ teaspoons Dijon mustard
- 2 tablespoons unsalted butter

1. With chicken breast side down, using kitchen shears, cut through bones on either side of backbone; discard backbone. Flip chicken over and press on breastbone to flatten. Using fingers and shears, peel skin off chicken, leaving skin on wings.

2. Tuck wings behind back. Turn legs so drumsticks face inward toward breasts. Using chef's knife, cut ½-inch-deep slits, spaced ½ inch apart, in breasts and legs. Insert skewer through thigh of 1 leg, into bottom of breast, and through thigh of second leg. Insert second skewer, about 1 inch lower, through thigh and drumstick of 1 leg and then through thigh and drumstick of second leg.

3. Dissolve sugar and ¾ cup salt in 3 quarts cold water in large, wide container. Submerge chicken in brine, cover, and refrigerate for at least 30 minutes or up to 1 hour.

4. Zest lemons (you should have 2 tablespoons grated zest). Juice 1 lemon (you should

ZESTING CITRUS

To quickly and easily make finely grated zest, rub fruit against holes of rasp-style grater, grating over same area of fruit only once or twice to avoid grating bitter white pith beneath skin.

1. Cut through bones on either side of backbone; discard.

2. Flip chicken and crack and flatten its breastbone for fast, even grilling.

3. Fat rendering from the skin can cause flare-ups. We take it off.

4. Skewers inserted through thighs and legs provide stability.

5. Deep cuts in the meat allow seasonings to penetrate to the bone.

have 3 tablespoons juice) and quarter remaining lemon lengthwise. Combine zest, oil, 1½ teaspoons rosemary, 1 teaspoon mustard, and ½ teaspoon pepper in small bowl; set aside. Heat butter, remaining ½ teaspoon rosemary, remaining ½ teaspoon mustard, and ½ teaspoon pepper in small saucepan over low heat, stirring occasionally, until butter is melted and ingredients are combined. Remove pan from heat and stir in lemon juice; leave mixture in saucepan.

5. Remove chicken from brine and pat dry with paper towels. With chicken skinned side down, rub ½ teaspoon zest mixture over surface of legs. Flip chicken over and rub remaining zest mixture evenly over entire surface, making sure to work mixture into slits.

6A. FOR A CHARCOAL GRILL: Open bottom vent completely. Light large chimney starter mounded with charcoal briquettes (7 quarts). When top coals are partially covered with ash, pour evenly over half of grill. Set cooking grate in place, cover, and open lid vent completely. Heat grill until hot, about 5 minutes.

6B. FOR A GAS GRILL: Turn all burners to high, cover, and heat grill until hot, about

15 minutes. Leave primary burner on high and turn off other burner(s).

7. Clean and oil cooking grate. Place chicken, skinned side down, and lemon quarters over hotter part of grill. Cover and cook until chicken and lemon quarters are well browned, 8 to 10 minutes. Transfer lemon quarters to bowl and set aside. Flip chicken over and brush with one-third of butter mixture (place saucepan over cooler side of grill if mixture has solidified). Cover chicken loosely with aluminum foil. Continue to cook, covered, until chicken is well browned on second side, 8 to 10 minutes.

8. Remove foil and slide chicken to cooler side of grill. Brush with half of remaining butter mixture, and re-cover with foil. Continue to cook, covered, until breasts register 160 degrees and thighs and drumsticks register 175 degrees, 8 to 10 minutes longer.

9. Transfer chicken to carving board, brush with remaining butter mixture, tent loosely with foil, and let rest for 5 to 10 minutes. Carve into pieces and serve with reserved lemon quarters.

Roast Brined Turkey

✔ WHY THIS RECIPE WORKS

With variables too numerous to count, uncovering the secrets of a perfectly roasted turkey can be an elusive goal. But that didn't stop us from trying. We wanted to give everything a shot—from oven roasting to grill roasting to high roasting, as well as brining, air drying, basting, and trussing—to come up with a surefire approach to roasting a turkey.

BRINE FOR THE RIGHT AMOUNT OF TIME While brining a bird for an hour or two longer than called for doesn't make a significant difference, brining for much beyond that resulted in an overly salty bird.

(And brining for too little time didn't provide enough of the benefits.)

USE A V-RACK A V-rack held the turkey in position during roasting and kept it from rolling to one side or the other. It also elevated the meat above the bottom of the roasting pan, allowing air to circulate and promoting even cooking and browning.

BASTE THE BIRD AT THE OUTSET While brushing the turkey with butter before roasting contributed to browning and added a mild buttery flavor, we found that basting during roasting is an unnecessary extra step and can turn the crisp skin soft.

KEEP THE TEMPERATURE STEADY
After testing every possible temperature combination, we were happy to discover that roasting the bird at 400 degrees for the entire cooking time was simple and produced evenly cooked meat.

LET IT REST Resting the turkey once it reached the desired temperature allowed for the redistribution and reabsorption of the juices in the meat. This not only made for ultramoist, flavorful meat, but it also gave the bird a chance to cool for easier carving.

ROAST BRINED TURKEY
SERVES 10 TO 12

If using a self-basting turkey or kosher turkey, do not brine in step 1, but season with salt after brushing with melted butter in step 5. Resist the temptation to tent the roasted turkey with foil while it rests on the carving board. Covering the bird will make the skin soggy. See page 353 for information on carving.

1   cup salt
1   (12- to 14-pound) turkey, neck, giblets, and tailpiece removed and reserved for gravy
6   sprigs fresh thyme
2   onions, chopped coarse
2   carrots, peeled and chopped coarse
2   celery ribs, chopped coarse
3   tablespoons unsalted butter, melted
1   cup water, plus extra as needed
1   recipe Giblet Pan Gravy (recipe follows)

1. Dissolve salt in 2 gallons cold water in large container. Submerge turkey in brine, cover, and refrigerate or store in very cool spot (40 degrees or less) for 6 to 12 hours.

2. Set wire rack in rimmed baking sheet. Remove turkey from brine and pat dry, inside and out, with paper towels. Place turkey on prepared wire rack. Refrigerate, uncovered, for at least 8 hours or overnight.

3. Adjust oven rack to lowest position and heat oven to 400 degrees. Line V-rack with heavy-duty aluminum foil and poke several holes in foil. Set V-rack in roasting pan and spray foil with vegetable oil spray.

4. Toss thyme sprigs and half of vegetables with 1 tablespoon melted butter in bowl and place inside turkey. Tie legs together with kitchen twine and tuck wings behind back. Scatter remaining vegetables in pan.

5. Pour water over vegetable mixture in pan. Brush turkey breast with 1 tablespoon melted butter, then place turkey breast side down on V-rack. Brush with remaining 1 tablespoon butter.

6. Roast turkey for 45 minutes. Remove pan from oven. Using 2 large wads of paper towels, turn turkey breast side up. If liquid in pan has totally evaporated, add another ½ cup water. Return turkey to oven and roast until breast registers 160 degrees and thighs register 175 degrees, 50 to 60 minutes.

7. Remove turkey from oven. Gently tip turkey so that any accumulated juices in cavity run into pan. Transfer turkey to carving board and let rest, uncovered, for 30 minutes. Carve turkey and serve with gravy.

GIBLET PAN GRAVY
MAKES ABOUT 6 CUPS

Complete step 1 up to a day ahead, if desired. Begin step 3 once the bird has been removed from the oven and is resting on a carving board.

1   tablespoon vegetable oil
    Reserved turkey neck, giblets, and tailpiece
1   onion, chopped
4   cups chicken broth
2   cups water
2   sprigs fresh thyme
8   sprigs fresh parsley
3   tablespoons unsalted butter
¼   cup all-purpose flour
1   cup dry white wine
    Salt and pepper

1. Heat oil in Dutch oven over medium heat until shimmering. Add neck, giblets, and tailpiece and cook until golden and fragrant,

FLIPPING THE TURKEY

With large wads of paper towels in each hand, grasp the turkey and flip it over, placing it breast side up on the rack.

To keep gravy warm at the table, as well as easy to pour, use an insulated coffee carafe. It cuts down on spills and keeps gravy hot throughout the meal.

about 5 minutes. Stir in onion and cook until softened, about 5 minutes. Reduce heat to low, cover, and cook until turkey parts and onion release their juices, about 15 minutes. Stir in broth, water, thyme sprigs, and parsley sprigs, bring to boil over medium heat, and adjust heat to low. Simmer, uncovered, skimming any impurities that may rise to surface, until broth is rich and flavorful, about 30 minutes longer. Strain broth into large container and reserve giblets. When cool enough to handle, chop giblets. Refrigerate giblets and broth until ready to use. (Broth can be stored in refrigerator for up to 1 day.)

2. While turkey is roasting, return reserved turkey broth to simmer in saucepan. Melt butter in separate large saucepan over medium-low heat. Add flour and cook, whisking constantly (mixture will froth and then thin out again), until nutty brown and fragrant,

10 to 15 minutes. Vigorously whisk all but 1 cup of hot broth into flour mixture. Bring to boil over medium heat, then continue to simmer, stirring occasionally, until gravy is lightly thickened and very flavorful, about 30 minutes longer. Set aside until turkey is done.

3. When turkey has been transferred to carving board to rest, spoon out and discard as much fat as possible from pan, leaving caramelized herbs and vegetables. Place pan over 2 burners set on medium-high heat. Return gravy to simmer. Add wine to pan of caramelized vegetables, scraping up any browned bits. Bring to boil and cook until reduced by half, about 5 minutes. Add remaining 1 cup turkey broth, bring to simmer, and cook for 15 minutes; strain pan juices into gravy, pressing as much juice as possible out of vegetables. Stir reserved giblets into gravy and return to boil. Season with salt and pepper to taste, and serve.

Old-Fashioned Stuffed Turkey

✓ WHY THIS RECIPE WORKS

We know that even the best recipes for roasted turkey involve compromise. Cook a turkey long enough to get the skin immaculately burnished and the white meat is usually dry as sawdust. Brining adds moisture to the meat, but can turn skin soggy. Salting solves the crisping woes, but the drippings get too seasoned to make a proper gravy. Stuffing the cavity compounds the headaches, slowing the roasting time to a crawl and upping the chance for uneven cooking. We were determined to have everything in one package: juicy meat, crisply burnished skin, rich-flavored stuffing that cooked inside the bird, and drippings suitable for gravy.

START WITH SALT Unwilling to compromise on skin, we opted for salting over brining; using 3 tablespoons was enough

to season the bird, but not so much that the drippings became overbearingly salty.

GO IN REVERSE Rather than the usual technique of starting meat at a high temperature and finishing at a lower one, we reversed the order. By cooking the bird at 325 degrees for a couple of hours and then cranking up the heat to 450 for a final blast of heat, we got both moist, tender meat and beautifully browned, crisp skin.

RUB WITH BAKING POWDER To take the skin from crisp to crunchy, we brought out a secret weapon: massaging the skin with a baking powder and salt rub. The baking powder had a twofold effect: It helped the skin dehydrate more readily and raised its pH, making it more conducive to browning.

FINISH THE STUFFING WHILE THE TURKEY RESTS Instead of letting the turkey roast until the stuffing reached a safe temperature—at which point the breast meat would be bone-dry—we removed the stuffing while the turkey rested and combined it with a batch of uncooked stuffing, then put it all in the oven to finish. This ensured plenty of richly flavored stuffing to feed a crowd.

ADD SOME SALT PORK Our final touch was draping the bird with salt pork before it went into the oven; the salt pork contributed an intense meaty flavor that enhanced the mild turkey without overwhelming it.

OLD-FASHIONED STUFFED TURKEY

SERVES 10 TO 12

If using a self-basting turkey or kosher turkey, do not salt in step 1. Table salt is not recommended for this recipe because it is too fine. Look for salt pork that is roughly equal parts fat and lean meat. Note that you can complete step 1 of the gravy recipe up to a day ahead, if desired. Begin step 3 once the bird has been removed from the oven and is resting on a carving board. The bread can be toasted up to one day in advance. See page 353 for information on carving.

TURKEY

- 1 (12- to 14-pound) turkey, neck, giblets, and tailpiece removed and reserved for gravy
- 3 tablespoons plus 2 teaspoons kosher salt
- 2 teaspoons baking powder
- 1 (36-inch) square cheesecloth, folded in quarters

CLASSIC HERB STUFFING

- 1½ pounds hearty white sandwich bread, cut into ½-inch cubes (12 cups)
- 4 tablespoons unsalted butter
- 1 onion, chopped fine
- 2 celery ribs, minced
- 1 teaspoon table salt
- 1 teaspoon pepper
- 2 tablespoons minced fresh thyme
- 1 tablespoon minced fresh marjoram

- 1 tablespoon minced fresh sage
- 1½ cups chicken broth
- 2 large eggs

- 12 ounces salt pork, cut into ¼-inch-thick slices and rinsed
- 1 recipe Giblet Pan Gravy (page 439)

1. FOR THE TURKEY: Use your fingers or thin wooden spoon handle to gently loosen skin covering breast, thighs, drumsticks, and back; avoid breaking skin. Rub 1 tablespoon salt evenly inside cavity of turkey, 1½ teaspoons salt under skin of each side of breast, and 1½ teaspoons salt under skin of each leg. Wrap turkey tightly with plastic wrap and refrigerate for at least 24 hours or up to 48 hours.

2. FOR THE STUFFING: Adjust oven rack to lowest position and heat oven to 250 degrees. Spread bread cubes in single layer on rimmed baking sheet; bake until edges have dried but centers are slightly moist (cubes should yield to pressure), about 45 minutes, stirring several times during baking. (Bread can be toasted up to 1 day in advance.) Transfer dried bread to large bowl.

3. While bread dries, melt butter in 12-inch skillet over medium-high heat. Add onion, celery, salt, and pepper and cook, stirring occasionally, until vegetables are softened and lightly browned, 5 to 7 minutes. Stir in thyme, marjoram, and sage and cook until fragrant, about 1 minute. Add vegetable mixture to bowl with dried bread; add 1 cup broth and toss until evenly moistened (you should have about 12 cups stuffing).

4. Remove turkey from refrigerator and pat dry, inside and out, with paper towels. Using metal skewer, poke 15 to 20 holes in fat deposits on top of breast halves and thighs, 4 or 5 holes in each deposit. Tuck wings behind back.

5. Increase oven temperature to 325 degrees. Combine remaining 2 teaspoons kosher salt and baking powder in bowl. Sprinkle surface of turkey with salt mixture and rub in mixture with your hands, coating entire surface evenly. Line turkey cavity with

SECRETS TO OLD-FASHIONED STUFFED TURKEY

1. Salting the turkey for 24 to 48 hours seasons the meat and keeps moisture inside.

2. Poking holes in the fatty deposits speeds up the fat-rendering process. Rubbing the skin with baking powder and salt just before roasting encourages browning.

3. Draping strips of salt pork on the turkey enriches it with deep flavor as it roasts.

4. Mixing stuffing cooked inside the bird with uncooked stuffing, then baking, yields the best flavor.

1. Cut off stalks and feathery fronds. (Fronds can be minced and used for garnish.)

2. Trim very thin slice from base and remove any tough or blemished outer layers from bulb.

3. Cut bulb in half through base. Use small, sharp knife to remove pyramid-shaped core.

4. Cut fennel halves into thin slices.

cheesecloth, pack with 4 to 5 cups stuffing, and tie ends of cheesecloth together. Cover remaining stuffing with plastic wrap and refrigerate. Using kitchen twine, loosely tie turkey legs together. Place turkey breast side down in V-rack set in roasting pan and drape salt pork slices over back.

6. Roast turkey until breast registers 130 degrees, 2 to 2½ hours. Remove pan from oven (close oven door to retain oven heat) and increase oven temperature to 450 degrees. Transfer turkey in V-rack to rimmed baking sheet. Remove and discard salt pork. Using 2 large wads of paper towels, rotate turkey breast side up. Cut twine binding legs and remove stuffing bag; empty into reserved stuffing in bowl. Pour drippings from roasting pan into fat separator and reserve for gravy, if making.

7. Once oven has come to temperature, return turkey in V-rack to roasting pan and roast until skin is golden brown and crisp, breast registers 160 degrees, and thighs register 175 degrees, about 45 minutes, rotating pan halfway through roasting. Transfer turkey to carving board and let rest, uncovered, for 30 minutes.

8. While turkey rests, reduce oven temperature to 400 degrees. Whisk eggs and remaining ½ cup broth from stuffing recipe together in bowl. Pour egg mixture over stuffing and toss to combine, breaking up any large chunks; spread stuffing into buttered 13 by 9-inch baking dish. Bake until stuffing registers 165 degrees and top is golden brown, about 15 minutes. Carve turkey and serve with stuffing and gravy.

DRIED FRUIT AND NUT STUFFING
MAKES ABOUT 12 CUPS

Dried cranberries can be substituted for the raisins.

1½	pounds hearty white sandwich bread, cut into ½-inch cubes (12 cups)
4	tablespoons unsalted butter
1	onion, chopped fine
2	celery ribs, minced
1	teaspoon salt
1	teaspoon pepper
2	tablespoons minced fresh thyme
1	tablespoon minced fresh marjoram
1	tablespoon minced fresh sage
1	cup raisins
1	cup dried apples, chopped fine
1	cup walnuts, chopped coarse
1½	cups chicken broth
3	large eggs

1. Adjust oven rack to lowest position and heat oven to 250 degrees. Spread bread cubes in single layer on rimmed baking sheet; bake until edges have dried but centers are slightly moist (cubes should yield to pressure), about 45 minutes, stirring several times during baking. (Bread can be toasted up to 1 day in advance.) Transfer dried bread to large bowl and increase oven temperature to 325 degrees.

2. While bread dries, melt butter in 12-inch skillet over medium-high heat. Add onion, celery, salt, and pepper and cook, stirring occasionally, until vegetables are softened and lightly browned, 5 to 7 minutes. Stir in thyme, marjoram, and sage and cook until fragrant, about 1 minute. Add vegetable mixture, raisins, dried apples, and walnuts to bowl with dried bread; add 1 cup broth and toss until evenly moistened (you should have about 12 cups stuffing).

3. Use stuffing as directed in Old-Fashioned Stuffed Turkey (page 440), adding eggs and remaining ½ cup broth in step 6.

SAUSAGE AND FENNEL STUFFING
MAKES ABOUT 12 CUPS

1½	pounds hearty white sandwich bread, cut into ½-inch cubes (12 cups)
1	teaspoon vegetable oil
8	ounces bulk pork sausage
4	tablespoons unsalted butter
1	onion, chopped fine
1	fennel bulb, stalks discarded, bulb halved, cored, and chopped fine
1	teaspoon salt
1	teaspoon pepper
2	tablespoons minced fresh sage

1 tablespoon minced fresh marjoram
1 tablespoon minced fresh thyme
1½ cups chicken broth
3 large eggs

1. Adjust oven rack to lowest position and heat oven to 250 degrees. Spread bread cubes in single layer on rimmed baking sheet; bake until edges have dried but centers are slightly moist (cubes should yield to pressure), about 45 minutes, stirring several times during baking. (Bread can be toasted up to 1 day in advance.) Transfer dried bread to large bowl and increase oven temperature to 325 degrees.

2. While bread dries, heat oil in 12-inch nonstick skillet over medium-high heat until shimmering. Add sausage and cook, breaking it up into small pieces with wooden spoon, until browned, 5 to 7 minutes. Remove sausage with slotted spoon and transfer to paper towel–lined plate.

3. Melt butter in fat left in skillet over medium-high heat. Add onion, fennel, salt, and pepper and cook, stirring occasionally, until vegetables are softened and lightly browned, 5 to 7 minutes. Stir in sage, marjoram, and thyme and cook until fragrant, about 1 minute. Add vegetable mixture and sausage to bowl with dried bread; add 1 cup broth and toss until evenly moistened (you should have about 12 cups stuffing).

4. Use stuffing as directed in Old-Fashioned Stuffed Turkey (page 440), adding eggs and remaining ½ cup broth in step 6.

MAKESHIFT CARVING BOARD

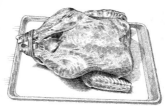

Good carving boards—we prefer the Williams-Sonoma Medium Maple Reversible Carving Board—come with a well in the center and a moat around the edges to capture juices that would otherwise drip onto the countertop and floor. But when we have to carve multiple roasts at once during testing, we often run out of proper boards. Our solution is to substitute a flat cutting board placed inside a rimmed baking sheet; the raised sides keep the juices from leaking out as we carve.

Turkey for a Crowd

✓ WHY THIS RECIPE WORKS

Unless you have access to multiple ovens, only a very large turkey will do when you've got a crowd coming to dinner. But finding a container large enough to brine a gargantuan bird can be tricky. And turning the bird in the oven, our usual method for evenly cooking meat, can be hot, heavy, and dangerous. For crowd-pleasing roast turkey, we wanted a Norman Rockwell picture of perfection: crisp, mahogany skin wrapped around tender, moist meat. And it had to be easy to prepare in a real home kitchen.

CHOOSE THE RIGHT BIRD We opted to go with either a Butterball or a kosher turkey. Both of these have been, in essence, brined—the Butterball is injected with a saltwater solution and the kosher bird is packed in salt during koshering.

START HIGH, FINISH LOW A combination of high and low heat gave our turkey a crisp skin but kept the bird tender and juicy without drying it out. Be careful to dry the skin thoroughly before brushing the bird with butter; otherwise, it will have spotty brown skin.

PUMP UP FLAVOR We made the meat and pan drippings more flavorful with the addition of onion, carrot, and celery. A quartered lemon added bright, clean flavor.

REST UNCOVERED After roasting, we allowed the turkey to rest so the juices would redistribute, but didn't tent it with foil so the skin wouldn't become soggy. This recipe should give you enough time while the turkey rests to prepare plenty of gravy to go around.

TURKEY FOR A CROWD
SERVES ABOUT 20

Rotating the bird helps produce moist, evenly cooked meat, but for the sake of ease, you may opt not to rotate it. In that case, skip the step of lining the V-rack with foil and roast the bird breast side up for the entire cooking time. Because we do not brine the bird, we had the best results with a frozen Butterball turkey (injected with salt and water) or a kosher bird (soaked in salt water during processing). See page 353 for information on carving.

3	onions, chopped coarse
3	carrots, peeled and chopped coarse
3	celery ribs, chopped coarse
1	lemon, quartered
6	sprigs fresh thyme
5	tablespoons unsalted butter, melted
1	(18- to 22-pound) frozen Butterball or kosher turkey, neck, giblets, and tailpiece removed and reserved for gravy
1	cup water, plus extra as needed
	Salt and pepper
1	recipe Giblet Pan Gravy for a Crowd (recipe follows)

1. Adjust oven rack to lowest position and heat oven to 425 degrees. Line V-rack with heavy-duty aluminum foil and poke several holes in foil. Set V-rack in flameproof roasting pan and spray foil with vegetable oil spray.

2. Toss half of vegetables, half of lemon, and thyme sprigs with 1 tablespoon melted butter in bowl and place inside turkey. Tie legs together with kitchen twine and tuck wings behind back. Scatter remaining vegetables in pan.

3. Pour water over vegetable mixture in pan. Brush turkey breast with 2 tablespoons melted butter, then sprinkle with ½ teaspoon salt and ½ teaspoon pepper. Place turkey, breast side down, on prepared V-rack. Brush with remaining 2 tablespoons melted butter and sprinkle with ½ teaspoon salt and ½ teaspoon pepper.

4. Roast turkey for 1 hour. Baste turkey with juices from pan. Using 2 large wads of paper towels, turn turkey breast side up. If liquid in pan has totally evaporated, add another ½ cup water. Reduce oven temperature to 325 degrees. Continue to roast until breast registers 160 degrees and thighs register 175 degrees on, about 2 hours longer.

5. Remove turkey from oven. Gently tip turkey up so that any accumulated juices in cavity run into pan. Transfer turkey to carving board. Let rest, uncovered, for 35 to 40 minutes. Carve turkey and serve with gravy.

WHAT'S IN THAT BAG?

That little bag that comes inside the turkey cavity contains the makings of a flavorful gravy. The turkey neck and the "giblets," or internal organs, are mechanically separated, washed, and then repackaged during turkey processing precisely for the purpose of making gravy. Here's what's in the bag:

Neck
The neck is the large, elongated muscle with a bone through the center. It contains some very flavorful meat. Cut it into several pieces for easy browning, then simmer it in the broth. Discard after straining the broth.

Neck

Giblets (Heart, Gizzard, and Liver)
The heart is the small, oblong, dark-colored organ. Brown it along with the neck and gizzard, then simmer it in the broth. Reserve after straining the broth, then dice and return to the gravy before serving.

The gizzard is the reddish, spherical organ. It is a grinding organ from the bird's digestive tract, recognizable by a butterfly-shaped strip of connective tissue. Cut the gizzard in half, brown it along with the heart and neck, then reserve it after straining the broth. Dice the gizzard and return it to the gravy along with the heart.

The liver is the soft, brownish, flat organ. Because the liver tends to impart a characteristically strong flavor, we don't recommend using it to make gravy.

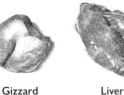

Heart   Gizzard   Liver

GIBLET PAN GRAVY FOR A CROWD
MAKES ABOUT 8 CUPS

Complete step 1 up to a day ahead, if desired. Begin step 3 once the bird has been removed from the oven and is resting on a carving board.

1	tablespoon vegetable oil
	Reserved turkey neck, giblets, and tailpiece
1	onion, unpeeled and chopped
6	cups chicken broth
3	cups water
2	sprigs fresh thyme
8	sprigs fresh parsley
5	tablespoons unsalted butter
¼	cup plus 2 tablespoons all-purpose flour
1½	cups dry white wine
	Salt and pepper

1. Heat oil in Dutch oven over medium heat until shimmering. Add neck, giblets, and tailpiece and cook until golden and fragrant, about 5 minutes. Stir in onion and cook until softened, about 5 minutes. Reduce heat to low, cover, and cook until turkey parts and onion release their juices, about 15 minutes. Stir in broth, water, and herbs, bring to boil over medium heat, and adjust heat to low. Simmer, uncovered, skimming any impurities that may rise to surface, until broth is rich and flavorful, about 30 minutes longer. Strain broth into large container and reserve giblets. When cool enough to handle, chop giblets. Refrigerate giblets and broth until ready to use. (Broth can be stored in refrigerator for up to 1 day.)

2. While turkey is roasting, return reserved turkey broth to simmer in medium saucepan. Melt butter in large saucepan over medium-low heat. Add flour and cook, whisking constantly (the mixture will froth and then thin out again), until nutty brown and fragrant, 10 to 15 minutes. Vigorously whisk all but 2 cups of hot broth into flour mixture. Bring to boil, then continue to simmer, stirring occasionally, until gravy is lightly thickened and very flavorful, about 35 minutes longer. Set aside until turkey is done.

3. When turkey has been transferred to carving board to rest, spoon out and discard as much fat as possible from roasting pan, leaving caramelized thyme sprigs and vegetables. Place pan over 2 burners set on medium-high heat. Return gravy to simmer. Add wine to pan of caramelized vegetables, scraping up any browned bits. Bring to boil and cook until reduced by half, about 7 minutes. Add remaining 2 cups turkey broth, bring to simmer, and cook for 15 minutes; strain pan juices into gravy, pressing as much juice as possible out of vegetables. Stir reserved giblets into gravy and return to boil. Season with salt and pepper to taste, and serve.

Butterflied Turkey with Cranberry-Molasses Glaze

✓ WHY THIS RECIPE WORKS

A gorgeously bronzed turkey coated in a dark mahogany glaze is a familiar magazine-cover shot during the holidays; and while it seems as though the execution would be straightforward, glazing a whole turkey is a lot trickier than it looks. Most glazes slide right off, no matter how diligently they're painted on the bird's skin. What's more, glazing poultry sets two objectives at odds: You want the skin to dry out so that it can thoroughly render its fat and crisp, but applying a glaze means adding moisture to the equation, thereby thwarting any skin-crisping efforts. We wanted to figure out a way to have it all—juicy, flavorful meat and paper-thin, crackly skin with a tangy-sweet glaze.

DEHYDRATE THE SKIN Rubbing salt on the skin helped dry it out, while baking powder promoted browning and helped break down proteins to produce a crunchier texture.

COOK, REST, AND COOK AGAIN For evenly cooked meat with a nicely browned exterior, we roasted the turkey at 275 degrees until it was almost done, then let it rest for a half-hour before returning the bird to a much hotter (450-degree) oven to finish.

START WITH MOLASSES We selected molasses for our sticky glaze component; its slightly bitter, smoky edge lent the glaze complexity, and its dark complexion helped color

Sticky ingredients like molasses and honey take their time flowing out of a measuring cup and require a spoon to scrape out the remaining bits. If you don't own an adjustable measuring cup (a cup pushes ingredients up and out from the bottom), try this method.

Spray measuring cup with vegetable oil spray before filling it. When emptied, liquid should slide right out of cup.

the turkey a rich shade of brown. Apple cider and cider vinegar complemented the flavor of the molasses and helped thin it out.

CONSISTENCY IS KEY Reducing our glaze ingredients intensified their flavors and got the glaze to a workable consistency, but it was the addition of some cranberries—with their ample pectin—that really thickened our glaze enough to make it cling to the skin.

WAIT TO GLAZE Applying the glaze toward the end of cooking—rather than at the beginning—prevented the skin from turning flabby.

FLATTEN THE BIRD Butterflying the turkey so that it lay flat ensured that the glaze stayed on the skin.

BUTTERFLIED TURKEY WITH CRANBERRY-MOLASSES GLAZE

SERVES 10 TO 12

If using a self-basting turkey or kosher turkey, do not salt in step 1. Table salt is not recommended for this recipe because it is too fine. If you have a V-rack that, when inverted, still fits into your roasting pan, place the turkey on that rather than on the onions. Butterflying a whole turkey is similar to butterflying a whole chicken; see page 350 for more information.

TURKEY

- 1 (12- to 14-pound) turkey, neck, giblets, and tailpiece discarded
  Kosher salt and pepper
- 2 teaspoons baking powder
- 2 large onions, halved

GLAZE

- 3 cups apple cider
- 4 ounces (1 cup) frozen or fresh cranberries
- ½ cup molasses
- ½ cup cider vinegar
- 1 tablespoon Dijon mustard
- 1 tablespoon grated fresh ginger
- 2 tablespoons unsalted butter, cut into 2 pieces and chilled

1. FOR THE TURKEY: Using kitchen shears, cut along both sides of backbone to remove it. Flatten breastbone and tuck wings underneath. Using your fingers, gently loosen skin covering breast and thighs. Using metal skewer, poke 15 to 20 holes in fat deposits on top of breast and thighs, 4 or 5 holes in each deposit. Rub bone side of turkey evenly with 2 teaspoons salt and 1 teaspoon pepper. Flip turkey skin side up and rub 1 tablespoon salt evenly under skin. Tuck wings under turkey. Push legs up to rest on lower portion of breast and tie legs together with kitchen twine.

2. Combine 1 tablespoon salt, 1 teaspoon pepper, and baking powder in bowl. Pat skin side of turkey dry with paper towels. Sprinkle surface of turkey with salt mixture and rub in mixture with your hands, coating entire surface evenly. Transfer turkey to roasting pan, skin side up. Place 1 onion half under each breast and thigh to elevate turkey off bottom of roasting pan. Let turkey stand at room temperature for 1 hour.

3. Adjust oven rack to lower-middle position and heat oven to 275 degrees. Roast turkey until breast registers 160 degrees and thighs register 175 degrees, 2½ to 3 hours. Remove pan from oven and let turkey rest in pan for at least 30 minutes or up to 1½ hours. Thirty minutes before returning turkey to oven, increase oven temperature to 450 degrees.

4. FOR THE GLAZE: While turkey rests, bring cider, cranberries, molasses, vinegar, mustard, and ginger to boil in medium saucepan. Cook, stirring occasionally, until reduced to 1½ cups, about 30 minutes. Strain mixture through fine-mesh strainer into 2-cup liquid measuring cup, pressing on solids to extract as much liquid as possible. Discard solids (you should have about 1¼ cups glaze). Transfer ½ cup glaze to small saucepan and set aside.

5. Brush turkey with one-third of glaze in measuring cup, transfer to oven, and roast for 7 minutes. Brush on half of remaining glaze in measuring cup and roast additional 7 minutes. Brush on remaining glaze in measuring

1. Using kitchen shears, cut through bones on either side of backbone, staying as close as possible to backbone, then remove and discard it.

2. Flip turkey over and press down firmly with heels of your hands to flatten breastbone.

cup and roast until skin is evenly browned and crisp, 7 to 10 minutes. Transfer turkey to carving board and let rest for 20 minutes.

6. While turkey rests, remove onions from pan and discard. Strain liquid from pan into fat separator (you should have about 2 cups liquid). Allow liquid to settle for 5 minutes, then pour into saucepan with reserved glaze, discarding any remaining fat. Bring mixture to boil and cook until slightly syrupy, about 10 minutes. Remove pan from heat and whisk in butter. Carve turkey and serve, passing sauce separately.

BUTTERFLIED TURKEY WITH
APPLE-MAPLE GLAZE

Substitute ½ cup dried apples for cranberries and ½ cup maple syrup for molasses.

Roast Salted Turkey

✔ WHY THIS RECIPE WORKS

Brining is the best way to guarantee a moist turkey, but it isn't always the most practical way, especially if you have limited refrigerator space. We wanted to develop an alternative method that would both season the meat and keep it moist.

SALT IT Instead of brining, we turned to salting, which is in essence a dry brine—salting seasons the meat, but no space-hogging bucket of liquid brine is required. We wanted to make sure the salt penetrated the meat, but we didn't want to tear the skin. We found that either chopsticks or the handle of a wooden spoon worked well to help us gently separate the skin from the meat before applying the salt.

ICE THE TURKEY To ensure moist breast meat, we chilled the breast by placing a small bag of ice inside the cavity against the breast and setting the turkey, breast side down, on ice for an hour. This trick brought down the temperature of the breast, thus allowing it to cook through over a longer period in the oven (more in line with the cooking time of the dark meat) without drying out.

DRY, THEN ROAST Wiping away any excess salt and drying the bird with paper towels before roasting kept the meat from getting too salty and ensured that the roasted bird emerged from the oven crisp and brown, and very nearly as moist and flavorful as a brined turkey.

ROAST SALTED TURKEY
SERVES 10 TO 12

If using a self-basting turkey or kosher turkey, do not salt in step 1, but season with salt after brushing with melted butter in step 5. Don't use table salt for this recipe; it is too fine. Note that you can complete step 1 of the gravy recipe up to a day ahead, if desired. Begin step 3 once the bird has been removed from the oven and is resting on a carving board. See page 353 for information on carving.

1   (12- to 14-pound) turkey, neck, giblets, and tailpiece removed and reserved for gravy
    Kosher salt
1   (5-pound) bag ice cubes
4   tablespoons unsalted butter, melted
3   onions, chopped coarse
2   carrots, peeled and chopped coarse
2   celery ribs, chopped coarse
6   sprigs fresh thyme
1   cup water
1   recipe Giblet Pan Gravy (page 439)

1. Use your fingers or thin wooden spoon handle to gently loosen skin covering breast, thighs, drumsticks, and back of turkey; avoid breaking skin. Rub 1 tablespoon salt evenly inside cavity of turkey, 1 tablespoon salt under skin of each side of breast, and 1 teaspoon salt under skin of each leg. Wrap turkey tightly with plastic wrap and refrigerate for at least 24 hours or up to 48 hours.

2. Add ice to two 1-gallon zipper-lock bags until each is half full. Place bags in roasting pan and lay turkey breast side down on top of ice. Add ice to two 1-quart zipper-lock bags until each is one-third full; place 1 bag of ice in large cavity of turkey and other bag in neck cavity. (Make sure that ice touches breast only, not thighs or legs.) Keep turkey on ice for 1 hour (pan should remain on counter).

3. Meanwhile, adjust oven rack to lowest position and heat oven to 425 degrees. Line V-rack with heavy-duty aluminum foil, poke several holes in foil, and spray foil with vegetable oil spray.

4. Remove turkey from ice and pat dry with paper towels (discard ice). Tuck tips of drumsticks into skin at tail to secure and tuck wings behind back. Brush turkey breast with 2 tablespoons melted butter.

5. Set V-rack in pan, then scatter vegetables and thyme sprigs in pan and pour water over vegetable mixture. Place turkey, breast side down, on V-rack. Brush turkey with remaining 2 tablespoons melted butter.

6. Roast turkey for 45 minutes. Remove pan from oven and reduce oven temperature to 325 degrees. Using 2 large wads of paper towels, rotate turkey breast side up; continue to roast until breast registers 160 degrees and thighs register 175 degrees, 1 to 1½ hours longer. Transfer turkey to carving board and let rest, uncovered, for 30 minutes. Carve turkey and serve with gravy.

Herbed Roast Turkey

✔ WHY THIS RECIPE WORKS

Throwing a bunch of herbs into the cavity of a turkey or rubbing the outside of the bird with a savory paste only flirts with great herb flavor. We wanted an intensely herby turkey, one with a powerful, aromatic flavor that was more than skin-deep.

MAKE AN HERB POCKET We made a vertical slit in the breast meat and, using a paring knife, created an expansive pocket by sweeping the blade back and forth.

FOUR WAYS WITH HERBS In addition to the innovation of the pocket technique, we incorporated three other herbal applications—underneath the skin, inside the cavity, and over the skin—which gave every bite of turkey formidable herb flavor.

BALANCE THE FLAVORS The herb paste itself, balanced with small amounts of pungent herbs (sage and rosemary) and greater amounts of softer herbs (thyme and parsley), also included lemon zest for a fresh, bright note and olive oil and Dijon mustard to make it spreadable. The final product was a moist roast turkey packed with bright herb flavor.

HERBED ROAST TURKEY

SERVES 10 TO 12

If using a self-basting turkey or kosher turkey, do not brine in step 1. If you have the time and the refrigerator space, air drying produces extremely crisp skin and is worth the effort. After brining and patting the turkey dry, place the turkey breast side up on a wire rack set in a rimmed baking sheet and refrigerate, uncovered, for 8 to 24 hours. Proceed with the recipe. See page 353 for information on carving.

See page 353 for information on carving.

PINK TURKEY MEAT

Having prepared thousands of turkeys in the test kitchen, we have experienced the occasional slice of pink turkey meat, even when the bird is fully cooked. (We always rely on an instant-read thermometer to ascertain doneness when roasting poultry. In the case of turkey, look for 165 degrees in the thickest portion of the breast and 170 to 175 degrees in the thickest part of the thigh.)

Just because a slice of turkey has a pinkish tint doesn't necessarily mean it is underdone. In general, the red or pink color in meat is due to the red protein pigment called myoglobin in the muscle cells that store oxygen. Because the areas that tend to get the most exercise—the legs and thighs—require more oxygen, they contain more myoglobin (and are therefore darker in color) than the breasts. When oxygen is attached to myoglobin in the cells, it is bright red. As turkey (or chicken) roasts in the oven, the oxygen attached to the myoglobin is released, and the meat becomes lighter and browner in color. However, if there are trace amounts of other gases formed in a hot oven or grill, they may react to the myoglobin to produce a pink color, even if the turkey is fully cooked.

ACHIEVING HERB FLAVOR

1. Carefully separate skin from meat on breast, thigh, and drumstick areas.

2. Rub herb paste under skin and directly onto the flesh, distributing it evenly.

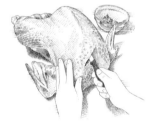

3. Make 1-inch slit in each breast. Swing knife tip through breast to create large pocket.

4. Place thin layer of paste inside each pocket.

5. Rub remaining paste inside turkey and on skin.

TURKEY AND BRINE

1   cup salt
1   (12- to 14-pound) turkey, neck, giblets, and tailpiece discarded
1   recipe All-Purpose Gravy (recipe follows)

HERB PASTE

1¼   cups chopped fresh parsley
4   teaspoons minced fresh thyme
2   teaspoons chopped fresh sage
1½   teaspoons minced fresh rosemary
1   shallot, minced
2   garlic cloves, minced
1   teaspoon pepper
¾   teaspoon grated lemon zest
¾   teaspoon salt
¼   cup olive oil
1   teaspoon Dijon mustard

1. FOR THE TURKEY AND BRINE: Dissolve salt in 2 gallons cold water in large container. Submerge turkey in brine, cover, and refrigerate or store in very cool spot (40 degrees or less) for 6 to 12 hours.

2. Remove turkey from brine and pat dry, inside and out, with paper towels. Place turkey, breast side up, on wire rack set in rimmed baking sheet or roasting pan and refrigerate, uncovered, for 30 minutes.

3. FOR THE HERB PASTE: Pulse parsley, thyme, sage, rosemary, shallot, garlic, pepper, lemon zest, and salt together in food processor until coarse paste is formed, 10 pulses. Add oil and mustard; continue to pulse until mixture forms smooth paste, 10 to 12 pulses; scrape down sides of bowl with rubber spatula after 5 pulses. Transfer mixture to bowl.

4. TO PREPARE THE TURKEY: Adjust oven rack to lowest position and heat oven to 400 degrees. Line V-rack with heavy-duty aluminum foil and poke several holes in foil. Set V-rack in roasting pan and spray foil with vegetable oil spray. Remove turkey from refrigerator and wipe away any water collected in baking sheet; set turkey breast side up on sheet.

5. Using your fingers, gently loosen skin covering breast, thighs, and drumsticks. Place 1½ tablespoons paste under skin on each side of breast. Gently press on skin to distribute paste over breast, thigh, and drumstick meat.

6. Using sharp paring knife, cut 1½-inch vertical slit into thickest part of each side of breast. Starting from top of incision, swing knife tip down to create 4- to 5-inch pocket within flesh. Place 1 tablespoon paste in pocket of each side of breast; using your fingers, rub paste in thin, even layer.

7. Rub 1 tablespoon paste inside turkey cavity. Rotate turkey breast side down; apply half of remaining herb paste to turkey skin; flip turkey breast side up and apply remaining herb paste to skin, pressing and patting to make paste adhere; reapply herb paste that falls onto baking sheet. Tuck tips of drumsticks into skin at tail to secure, and tuck wings behind back.

8. TO ROAST THE TURKEY: Place turkey breast side down on prepared V-rack. Roast turkey for 45 minutes.

9. Remove pan from oven. Using 2 large wads of paper towels, rotate turkey breast side up. Continue to roast until breast registers 160 degrees and thighs register 175 degrees, 50 minutes to 1 hour longer. Transfer turkey to carving board and let rest, uncovered, for 30 minutes. Carve turkey and serve with gravy.

ALL-PURPOSE GRAVY
MAKES 2 CUPS

This gravy can be served with almost any type of poultry or meat or with mashed potatoes. If you would like to double the recipe, use a Dutch oven to give the vegetables ample space for browning and increase the cooking times by roughly 50 percent.

1   small carrot, peeled and chopped
1   small celery rib, chopped
1   small onion, chopped
3   tablespoons unsalted butter
¼   cup all-purpose flour
2   cups chicken broth
2   cups beef broth

1 bay leaf
¼ teaspoon dried thyme
5 whole black peppercorns
Salt and pepper

1. Pulse carrot in food processor until broken into rough ¼-inch pieces, about 5 pulses. Add celery and onion; pulse until all vegetables are broken into ⅛-inch pieces, about 5 pulses.

2. Melt butter in large saucepan over medium-high heat. Add vegetables and cook, stirring often, until softened and well browned, about 7 minutes. Reduce heat to medium; add flour and cook, stirring constantly, until thoroughly browned and fragrant, about 5 minutes. Slowly whisk in chicken broth and beef broth; bring to boil, skimming off any foam that forms on surface. Add bay leaf, thyme, and peppercorns, reduce to simmer, and cook, stirring occasionally, until thickened and measures 3 cups, 20 to 25 minutes.

3. Strain gravy into clean gravy boat or pitcher, pressing on solids to extract as much liquid as possible; discard solids. Season with salt and pepper to taste and serve.

TO MAKE AHEAD: Gravy can be frozen for up to 1 month. To thaw either single or double recipe, place gravy and 1 tablespoon water in saucepan over low heat and bring slowly to simmer. Gravy may appear broken or curdled as it thaws, but vigorous whisking will recombine it.

Braised Turkey with Gravy

✓ **WHY THIS RECIPE WORKS**

While less common than roasting or grilling, braising is a terrific way to cook turkey. Since the temperature in the pot can never rise above the boiling point of water (212 degrees), the method is inherently gentle, minimizing the risk of drying out the breast. On top of that, the simmering broth produces a rich, ready-made gravy. But if cooked too long or at the wrong temperature, braised meat can dry out just as readily as roasted meat. We wanted to find the optimal cooking time and oven temperature and just the right ingredients to add deeper complexity to the meat.

USE A ROASTING PAN Arranging bone-in, skin-on breasts, drumsticks, and thighs in a roasting pan—rather than a Dutch oven—allowed us to fit plenty of parts in one layer.

SEAR FIRST Cranking the oven to 500 degrees initially—before adding the braising liquid—allowed the parts to develop good color, which contributed rich, roasted flavor to the broth.

FIND A HAPPY MEDIUM Braising the parts at a moderate 325 degrees proved to be ideal; cooked at this temperature, the turkey cooked relatively quickly yet for long enough that the collagen in the thighs had a chance to break down, and the breasts remained moist.

BUILD SOME FLAVOR Browning some aromatics with the turkey parts—along with pepper, bay leaves, thyme, parsley, and a handful of ultrasavory dried porcini mushrooms—boosted the flavor of our braising liquid dramatically, creating a rich base for a glossy gravy.

BRAISED TURKEY WITH GRAVY
SERVES 10 TO 12

Instead of drumsticks and thighs, you may use two whole leg quarters, 1½ to 2 pounds each. The recipe will also work with turkey breast alone; in step 1, reduce the salt and sugar to ½ cup each and the

water to 4 quarts. If you are braising kosher or self-basting turkey parts, skip the brining step and instead season the turkey parts with 1½ teaspoons of salt. See page 353 for information on carving.

TURKEY

Salt and pepper

1 cup sugar

1 (5- to 7-pound) whole bone-in turkey breast, trimmed

4 pounds turkey drumsticks and thighs, trimmed

3 onions, chopped

3 celery ribs, chopped

2 carrots, peeled and chopped

6 garlic cloves, peeled and smashed

2 bay leaves

6 sprigs fresh thyme

6 sprigs fresh parsley

½ ounce dried porcini mushrooms, rinsed

4 tablespoons unsalted butter, melted

4 cups chicken broth

1 cup dry white wine

GRAVY

3 tablespoons all-purpose flour

Salt and pepper

1. FOR THE TURKEY: Dissolve 1 cup salt and sugar in 2 gallons cold water in large container. Submerge turkey pieces in brine, cover, and refrigerate or store in very cool spot (40 degrees or less) for 3 to 6 hours.

2. Adjust oven rack to lower-middle position and heat oven to 500 degrees. Remove turkey pieces from brine and pat dry with paper towels. Toss onions, celery, carrots, garlic, bay leaves, thyme sprigs, parsley sprigs, porcini, and 2 tablespoons melted butter in large roasting pan; arrange in even layer. Brush turkey pieces with remaining 2 tablespoons butter and season with pepper. Place turkey pieces, skin side up, over vegetables, leaving at least ¼ inch between pieces. Roast until skin is lightly browned, about 20 minutes.

3. Remove pan from oven and reduce temperature to 325 degrees. Pour broth and wine around turkey pieces (it should come about three-quarters of way up legs and thighs). Place 12 by 16-inch piece of parchment paper over turkey pieces. Cover roasting pan tightly with aluminum foil. Return covered roasting pan to oven and cook until breasts register 160 degrees and thighs register 175 degrees, 1¾ to 2¼ hours. Transfer turkey to carving board, tent loosely with foil, and let rest for 20 minutes.

4. FOR THE GRAVY: Strain vegetables and liquid from roasting pan through fine-mesh strainer set over large bowl. Press solids with back of spatula to extract as much liquid as possible. Discard solids. Transfer liquid to fat separator; allow to settle, about 5 minutes. Reserve 3 tablespoons fat and measure out 3 cups braising liquid (reserve any remaining broth for another use).

5. Heat reserved fat in medium saucepan over medium-high heat. Add flour and cook, stirring constantly, until flour is dark golden brown and fragrant, about 5 minutes. Whisk in 3 cups braising liquid and bring to boil. Reduce heat to medium-low and simmer, stirring occasionally, until gravy is thick and reduced to 2 cups, 15 to 20 minutes. Season with salt and pepper to taste.

6. Carve turkey and serve, passing gravy separately.

SMOOTHING OUT LUMPY GRAVY

Trying to thicken gravy by sprinkling in flour can result in unsightly lumps and a consistency that is still too thin because the starch has not dispersed. This simple technique can help. (This does not work with mushroom or giblet gravy.)

1. Fill blender no more than half full with lumpy gravy and process until gravy is smooth, about 30 seconds.

2. To thicken gravy, pour it back into saucepan and bring it to simmer. Strain out any remaining small lumps with fine-mesh strainer.

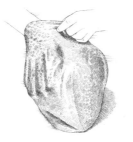

1. Using your hands, separate skin from meat, taking care to not tear membrane around breast; release skin on either side of breastbone.

2. Using spoon, work half of softened butter under skin on 1 side of breast. Repeat with remaining butter on other side of breast.

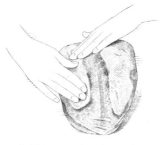

3. Using your hands, gently rub turkey skin to evenly distribute butter over entire breast.

Easy Roast Turkey Breast

✔ WHY THIS RECIPE WORKS

Roasting a whole turkey breast should be easy. The biggest challenge with the holiday bird is that the dark meat takes longer to cook than the white meat; this is neatly avoided by the all-white breast. But the reality is that the results are inconsistent: Sometimes the meat is moist and juicy, but more often than not the lean white meat comes out chalky and dry. The layers closest to the skin get especially parched, and the skin is never as crisp as we'd like. We wanted a foolproof technique for roasting a turkey breast.

START WITH A BRINE Salt changes the protein structure in meat and helps it hold on to moisture, so brining our turkey breast was a must for juicy meat.

BUTTER MAKES IT BETTER Rubbing the meat with softened butter had several benefits: Loosening the skin helped it to lift and separate from the meat, which promoted even browning and created crisper skin, and the fat in the butter helped keep the breast meat moist and added much-needed flavor.

USE TWO TEMPERATURES Starting the turkey breast at 425 degrees provided an initial blast of heat that kick-started browning, while lowering the temperature to a more moderate 325 degrees for the last half of cooking allowed the meat to cook gently and stay moist and tender.

ADD A LITTLE WATER Just a cup of water added to the roasting pan prevented the drippings from smoking.

EASY ROAST TURKEY BREAST
SERVES 8 TO 10

Supermarkets sell "hotel-style" turkey breasts. Try to avoid these if you can, as they still have the wings and rib cage attached. If this is the only type of breast you can find, you will need to remove the wings and cut away the rib cage with kitchen shears before proceeding with the recipe. If using a self-basting turkey or kosher turkey, do not brine in step 1. See page 353 for information on carving.

Salt
1 (6- to 7-pound) bone-in whole turkey breast, trimmed
4 tablespoons unsalted butter, softened
¼ teaspoon pepper

1. Dissolve ½ cup salt in 1 gallon cold water in large container. Submerge turkey in brine, cover, and refrigerate for 3 to 6 hours.

2. Adjust oven rack to middle position and heat oven to 425 degrees. Set V-rack inside roasting pan and spray with vegetable oil spray. Combine butter and pepper in bowl.

3. Remove turkey from brine and pat dry with paper towels. Using your fingers, gently loosen skin covering each side of breast. Place butter mixture under skin, directly on meat in center of each side of breast. Gently press on skin to distribute butter mixture over meat. Place turkey skin side up on prepared V-rack and add 1 cup water to pan.

4. Roast turkey for 30 minutes. Reduce oven temperature to 325 degrees and continue to roast until turkey registers 160 degrees, about 1 hour longer. Transfer turkey to carving board and let rest for 20 minutes. Carve turkey and serve.

EASY ROAST TURKEY BREAST WITH LEMON AND THYME

Add 3 minced garlic cloves, 2 tablespoons minced fresh thyme, and 1 teaspoon grated lemon zest to butter mixture.

EASY ROAST TURKEY BREAST WITH ORANGE AND ROSEMARY

Add 3 minced garlic cloves, 1 tablespoon minced fresh rosemary, 1 teaspoon grated orange zest, and ¼ teaspoon red pepper flakes to butter mixture.

Grill-Roasted Boneless Turkey Breast

✔ WHY THIS RECIPE WORKS

Introducing a mild-mannered turkey breast to the smoky fire of a grill is a surefire way to add great flavor. The problem is that unlike fatty pork butt or brisket, ultralean turkey breast easily dries out; plus its irregular shape can lead to uneven cooking. We were determined to get around these issues with a recipe that would deliver a grill-roasted breast with all the richness and juiciness we associate with thighs and legs, along with crisp, well-rendered skin and meat that was moist all the way through.

SUREFIRE SOLUTION We started with a bone-in whole breast, removed the skin and bones, then salted the meat to help season the turkey and add moisture. Next we stacked the breasts on top of one another, draped them with the turkey skin, and tied the "roast" together. The skin helps protect the meat from the fire and the stacked breasts ensure the meat cooks more slowly on the grill. Salting a whole turkey breast kept the meat moist as it cooked and was a good first step in improving the meat's flavor and texture.

LOW HEAT FOR EVEN COOKING Because low heat helps meat cook evenly, we started the turkey breast on the cooler side of the grill. Once its internal temperature reached 150 degrees, the meat was still moist and most of the fat from the skin had rendered; a quick sear on the hotter side of the grill took care of the skin, and after resting, the breast had reached the ideal serving temperature of 165 degrees.

POSITION MATTERS Despite our solid technique, the tapered ends of the breast were still overcooked and dry; removing the breast halves from the bone and arranging them so that the thick end of one was pressed against the tapered end of the other created an even thickness throughout.

1. Starting at 1 side of breast and using your fingers to separate skin from meat, peel skin off breast meat and reserve. Using tip of knife, cut along rib cage to remove each breast half completely.

2. Arrange 1 breast half cut side up; top with second breast half, cut side down, thick end over tapered end. Drape skin over breast halves and tuck ends under.

GIVE IT A FLAVOR BOOST Sprinkling wood chips over the hot coals while the turkey roasted lent a touch of smokiness and a variation with fresh herb butter provided welcome richness.

GRILL-ROASTED BONELESS TURKEY BREAST

SERVES 6 TO 8

We prefer either a natural (unbrined) or kosher turkey breast for this recipe. Using a kosher turkey breast (rubbed with salt and rinsed during processing) or self-basting turkey breast (injected with salt and water) eliminates the need for salting in step 1. If the breast has a pop-up timer, remove it before cooking. If you'd like to use wood chunks instead of wood chips when using a charcoal grill, substitute one small wood chunk, soaked in water for 1 hour, for the wood chip packet.

- ½ cup wood chips, soaked in water for 15 minutes and drained (optional)
- 1 (5- to 7-pound) bone-in whole turkey breast, trimmed
  Salt and pepper
- 1 teaspoon vegetable oil

1. Remove skin from breast meat and then cut along rib cage to remove breast halves (discard bones or save for stock). Pat turkey breast halves dry with paper towels and season with 2 teaspoons salt. Stack breast halves on top of one another with cut sides facing each other, and alternating thick and tapered ends. Stretch skin over exposed meat and tuck in ends. Tie kitchen twine lengthwise around roast. Then tie 5 to 7 pieces of twine at 1-inch intervals crosswise along roast. Transfer roast

3. Tie one 36-inch piece of kitchen twine lengthwise around roast.

4. Tie 5 to 7 pieces of twine at 1-inch intervals crosswise along roast, starting at its center, then at either end, and then filling in the rest.

GRAVY FOR SIMPLE GRILL-ROASTED TURKEY

MAKES 6 CUPS

1 tablespoon vegetable oil
  Reserved turkey neck,
  cut into 1-inch pieces,
  and giblets
1 pound onions,
  chopped coarse
4 cups low-sodium
  chicken broth
4 cups beef broth
2 small carrots, peeled
  and chopped coarse
2 small celery ribs,
  chopped coarse
6 tablespoons unsalted
  butter
½ cup all-purpose flour
2 bay leaves
½ teaspoon dried thyme
10 whole black peppercorns
  Salt and pepper

1. Heat oil in Dutch oven over medium-high heat until shimmering. Add turkey neck and giblets; cook, stirring occasionally, until browned, about 5 minutes. Add half of onions and cook, stirring occasionally, until softened, about 3 minutes. Reduce heat to low; cover and cook, stirring occasionally, until turkey parts and onions release their juices, about 20 minutes.

2. Add chicken and beef broths; increase heat to high and bring to boil. Reduce heat to low and simmer, covered, skimming any foam that rises to surface, until broth

CONTINUED NEXT PAGE

to wire rack set in rimmed baking sheet and refrigerate for 1 hour.

2. Using large piece of heavy-duty aluminum foil, wrap soaked chips in foil packet and cut several vent holes in top.

3A. FOR A CHARCOAL GRILL: Open bottom vent halfway. Light large chimney starter filled with charcoal briquettes (6 quarts). When top coals are partially covered with ash, pour evenly over half of grill. Place wood chip packet, if using, on coals. Set cooking grate in place, cover, and open lid vent halfway. Heat grill until hot and wood chips are smoking, about 5 minutes.

3B. FOR A GAS GRILL: Place wood chip packet, if using, directly on primary burner. Turn all burners to high, cover, and heat grill until hot and wood chips are smoking, about 15 minutes. Turn all burners to medium-low. (Adjust burner(s) as needed during cooking to maintain grill temperature of 300 degrees.)

4. Clean and oil cooking grate. Rub surface of roast with oil and season with pepper. Place roast on grill (cooler side if using charcoal). Cover (position lid vents over meat if using charcoal) and cook until roast registers 150 degrees, 40 to 60 minutes, turning 180 degrees halfway through cooking.

5. Slide roast to hotter side of grill (if using charcoal) or turn all burners to medium-high

(if using gas). Cook until roast is browned and skin is crisp on all sides, 8 to 10 minutes, rotating every 2 minutes.

6. Transfer roast to carving board, tent loosely with foil, and let rest for 15 minutes. Cut into ½-inch-thick slices, removing twine as you cut. Serve.

GRILL-ROASTED BONELESS TURKEY BREAST WITH HERB BUTTER

Mince ¼ cup fresh tarragon leaves, 1 tablespoon fresh thyme leaves, 2 minced garlic cloves, and ¼ teaspoon pepper to fine paste. Combine herb paste and 4 tablespoons softened unsalted butter. Spread butter evenly over cut side of each turkey breast half before assembling roast.

GRILL-ROASTED BONELESS TURKEY BREAST WITH OLIVES AND SUN-DRIED TOMATOES

Combine ¼ cup finely chopped kalamata olives, 3 tablespoons finely chopped sun-dried tomatoes, 1 minced garlic clove, 1 teaspoon minced fresh thyme, ½ teaspoon anchovy paste, and ½ teaspoon red pepper flakes in bowl. Spread olive mixture evenly over cut side of each turkey breast half before assembling roast.

Grill-Roasted Turkey

✔ WHY THIS RECIPE WORKS

Roasting a large turkey monopolizes both your oven and your time; you need to constantly monitor the bird to ensure perfectly juicy, tender results. Moving the turkey out to the grill could help and might be even better than the oven since it could eliminate a perennial turkey-roasting problem: unevenly cooked meat. However, we wanted to make sure we could find a way to grill-roast the bird so it emerged tasting pretty much as if it had been roasted in the oven— meaning no smoky or sooty flavors.

KEEP IT SIMPLE We started by salting the turkey. Salting, essentially a dry brine, is easier than traditional brining: You simply apply salt to the bird rather than immersing it in a big bucket of brine, which can be a challenge to fit in the fridge. As for the grill, the simplest charcoal cooking setup is a split fire, with heat on both sides of the bird, which eliminates the need for rotating. We used a long-lasting fire built in part from unlit coals so that we could leave the lid on for the whole cooking time. On the gas grill, we mimicked the split fire by only lighting one burner and rotating the turkey just once during cooking.

LOWER THE HEAT To roast the bird more gently, eliminating the flare-ups and soot that can give grilled meat a smoky taste, we placed a disposable pan partially filled with water between the heat and the meat. The pan of water absorbed heat, decreasing the overall temperature of the grill and keeping the meat tasting clean and traditional.

CRISP SKIN SECRETS In order to get crisp, golden-brown skin to match the perfectly roasted meat, we cut slits along the backbone to speed up the rendering of excess fat, patted the skin dry with paper towels, and rubbed the skin with salt, pepper, and baking powder which helped break down its proteins. This produced a beautifully bronzed, crisp-skinned turkey that looked and tasted every bit as though it had emerged from the oven, rather than coming off the grill.

SIMPLE GRILL-ROASTED TURKEY
SERVES 10 TO 12

Don't use table salt for this recipe; it is too fine. If using a self-basting turkey (such as a frozen Butterball) or a kosher turkey, don't salt in step 1, but do season with salt in step 2. Check the wings halfway through roasting; if they are getting too dark, slide a small piece of foil between the wing and the cooking grate to shield the wings from the flame. As an accompaniment, try our All-Purpose Gravy (page 450). See page 353 for information on carving.

 | (12- to 14-pound) turkey, neck, giblets, and tailpiece discarded
   Kosher salt and pepper
 | teaspoon baking powder
 | tablespoon vegetable oil
   Large disposable aluminum roasting pan (if using charcoal) or 2 disposable aluminum pie plates (if using gas)

1. Place turkey, breast side down, on work surface. Make two 2-inch incisions below each thigh and breast along back of turkey (4 incisions total). Using fingers or handle of wooden spoon, carefully separate skin from thighs and breast. Rub 4 teaspoons salt evenly inside cavity of turkey, 1 tablespoon salt under skin of each breast, and 1 teaspoon salt under skin of each leg.

2. Combine 1 teaspoon salt, 1 teaspoon pepper, and baking powder in small bowl. Pat turkey dry with paper towels and evenly sprinkle baking powder mixture all over. Rub in mixture with hands, coating entire surface evenly. Wrap turkey tightly with plastic wrap; refrigerate for 24 to 48 hours.

3. Remove turkey from refrigerator and discard plastic. Tuck wings underneath turkey. Using hands, rub oil evenly over entire surface.

4A. FOR A CHARCOAL GRILL: Open bottom vent halfway and place disposable pan filled with 3 cups water in center of grill. Arrange 1½ quarts unlit charcoal briquettes on either side of pan (3 quarts total) in even layer. Light large chimney starter two-thirds filled with charcoal briquettes (4 quarts). When top coals are partially covered with ash, pour 2 quarts of lit coals on top of each pile of unlit coals. Set cooking grate in place, cover, and open lid vent halfway. Heat grill until hot, about 5 minutes.

4B. FOR A GAS GRILL: Place 2 disposable pie plates with 2 cups water in each directly on 1 burner over which turkey will be cooked. Turn all burners to high, cover, and heat grill until hot, about 15 minutes. Turn primary burner (burner opposite pie plates) to medium and turn off other burner(s). (Adjust primary burner as needed to maintain grill temperature of 325 degrees.)

5. Clean and oil cooking grate. Place turkey, breast side up, in center of charcoal grill or on cooler side of gas grill, making sure bird is over disposable pans and not over flame. Cover (placing vents over turkey on charcoal grill) and cook until breasts register 160 degrees and thighs and drumsticks register 175 degrees, 2½ to 3 hours, rotating turkey after 1¼ hours if using gas grill.

6. Transfer turkey to carving board and let rest for 45 minutes. Carve turkey and serve.

CONTINUED FROM PREVIOUS PAGE

is rich and flavorful, about 30 minutes. Strain broth into large bowl (you should have about 8 cups), reserving giblets, if desired; discard neck. Reserve broth. If using giblets, when cool enough to handle, remove gristle from giblets, dice, and set aside. (Broth can be refrigerated for up to 2 days.)

3. Pulse carrots in food processor until broken into rough ¼-inch pieces, about 5 pulses. Add celery and remaining onions; pulse until all vegetables are broken into ⅛-inch pieces, about 5 pulses.

4. Melt butter in now-empty Dutch oven over medium-high heat. Add vegetables and cook, stirring frequently, until softened and well browned, about 10 minutes. Reduce heat to medium; stir in flour and cook, stirring constantly, until thoroughly browned and fragrant, 5 to 7 minutes. Whisking constantly, gradually add reserved broth; bring to boil, skimming off any foam that forms on surface. Reduce heat to medium-low and add bay leaves, thyme, and peppercorns; simmer, stirring occasionally, until thickened and reduced to 6 cups, 30 to 35 minutes.

5. Strain gravy through fine-mesh strainer into clean saucepan, pressing on solids to extract as much liquid as possible; discard solids. Stir in diced giblets, if using. Season with salt and pepper to taste.

Juicy Grilled Turkey Burgers

✓ WHY THIS RECIPE WORKS

What accounts for turkey's appeal as a healthier alternative to beef in a burger—its relative lack of fat—is also what makes these patties cook up dry, chalky, and bland. We wanted to work toward a turkey burger that delivered everything we look for in a beef version—that is, tender, juicy, and flavorful meat without the distraction of extraneous spices or other superficial fixes. And if we could throw them over a hot grill to give the meat some smoky char, all the better.

GRIND YOUR OWN TURKEY Preground turkey meat may be a timesaver, but it's typically ultralean—an immediate setback when you're going for flavor and juiciness. Grinding our own meat allowed us to control both the cut of meat (thighs provided the best flavor) and the size of the grind (coarsely chopped meat gave us tender, loose-textured burgers).

MAKE THE MEAT AS MOIST AS POSSIBLE For incredibly juicy burgers with a satisfying texture, we employed some unusual ingredients and techniques. A pinch of baking soda mixed in with the ground turkey helped tenderize its muscle fibers and gave it a looser structure; some gelatin helped the meat hold on to water; and finally, pureeing a portion of the ground turkey trapped copious amounts of moisture and fat.

KEEP IT LOOSE To prevent our turkey emulsion from binding the meat together too tightly, we added some raw white mushrooms; as a bonus, their high level of glutamates helped boost meatiness, as did a last-minute addition of soy sauce.

JUICY GRILLED TURKEY BURGERS
SERVES 6

To ensure the best texture, don't let the burgers stand for more than an hour before cooking. Serve the burgers with Malt Vinegar–Molasses Burger Sauce (recipe follows) or your favorite toppings.

1	(2-pound) bone-in turkey thigh, skinned, boned, trimmed, and cut into ½-inch pieces
1	tablespoon unflavored gelatin
3	tablespoons chicken broth
6	ounces white mushrooms, trimmed
1	tablespoon soy sauce
	Pinch baking soda
2	tablespoons vegetable oil, plus extra for brushing
	Kosher salt and pepper
6	large hamburger buns

1. Place turkey pieces on large plate in single layer. Freeze meat until very firm and hardened around edges, 35 to 45 minutes. Meanwhile, sprinkle gelatin over chicken broth in small bowl and let sit until gelatin softens, about 5 minutes. Pulse mushrooms in food processor until coarsely chopped, about 7 pulses, stopping and redistributing mushrooms around bowl as needed to ensure even grinding. Set mushrooms aside.

2. Pulse one-third of turkey in now-empty food processor until coarsely chopped into ⅛-inch pieces, 18 to 22 pulses, stopping and redistributing turkey around bowl as needed to ensure even grinding. Transfer meat to large bowl and repeat two more times with remaining turkey.

3. Return ½ cup (about 3 ounces) ground turkey to bowl of again-empty food processor along with softened gelatin, soy sauce,

and baking soda. Process until smooth, about 2 minutes, scraping down bowl as needed. With processor running, slowly drizzle in oil, about 10 seconds; leave paste in food processor. Return mushrooms to food processor and pulse to combine with paste, 3 to 5 pulses, stopping and redistributing mixture as needed to ensure even mixing. Transfer mushroom mixture to bowl with ground turkey and use your hands to evenly combine.

4. With lightly greased hands, divide meat mixture into 6 balls. Flatten into ¾-inch-thick patties about 4 inches in diameter; press shallow indentation into center of each burger to ensure even cooking. (Shaped patties can be frozen for up to 1 month. Frozen patties can be cooked straight from freezer.)

5A. FOR A CHARCOAL GRILL: Open bottom vent completely. Light large chimney starter filled with charcoal briquettes (6 quarts). When top coals are partially covered with ash, pour evenly over half of grill. Set cooking grate in place, cover, and open lid vent completely. Heat grill until hot, about 5 minutes.

5B. FOR A GAS GRILL: Turn all burners to high, cover, and heat grill until hot, about 15 minutes. Leave primary burner on high and turn off other burner(s).

6. Clean and oil cooking grate. Brush 1 side of patties with oil and season with salt and pepper. Using spatula, flip patties, brush with oil, and season second side. Place burgers over hotter part of grill and cook until burgers are well browned on both sides and register 160 degrees, 4 to 7 minutes per side. (If cooking frozen burgers: After burgers are browned on both sides, transfer to cool side of grill, cover, and continue to cook until burgers register 160 degrees.)

7. Transfer burgers to plate and let rest for 5 minutes. While burgers rest, grill buns over hotter side of grill. Transfer burgers to buns, add desired toppings, and serve.

MALT VINEGAR–MOLASSES BURGER SAUCE

MAKES ABOUT 1 CUP

¾ cup mayonnaise
4 teaspoons malt vinegar
½ teaspoon molasses
¼ teaspoon Worcestershire sauce
¼ teaspoon salt
¼ teaspoon pepper

Whisk all ingredients together in bowl.

GETTING CORNISH GAME HENS TO CRISP QUICKLY AND EVENLY

Because the meat on Cornish game hens finishes cooking long before their skin crisps, we devised a few tricks to accelerate the skin's progress.

1. For each bird, cut through the bones on either side of the backbone; discard the backbone.

2. Cutting through the center of the breast makes two halves that lie flat for better browning.

3. Loosening and poking holes in the skin allows the fat to drain during cooking, aiding crisping. Rubbing the birds with salt and baking powder and then chilling them evaporates moisture.

4. Starting the birds skin side down on a preheated baking sheet effectively (and efficiently) crisps their skin.

Oven-Roasted Cornish Game Hens

✔ WHY THIS RECIPE WORKS

Since they first appeared on American tables in the 1950s, Cornish game hens have typically been more of a special-occasion meal than a weeknight family dinner. But these petite birds have attributes that make them appealing to serve any night of the week: They cook quickly; the breasts are less prone to drying out before the interiors cook through, a perennial hurdle when roasting regular chickens; and they have a high skin-to-meat ratio, which makes them both forgiving and flavorful. But because Cornish hens cook so quickly, the skin usually isn't crisp. We wanted to change that.

HELP THE FAT TO RENDER Loosening the skin and poking holes in the thick pockets of fat created channels through which the fat could drain.

CORNISH GAME HENS

Cornish game hens are neither from Cornwall nor wild game, and they can be hens or roosters. They were reportedly first bred in the 1950s by a Connecticut couple, Jacques and Alphonsine Makowsky, who crossed breeds of domestic chickens with a Cornish gamecock and sold the hybrid when it was very young. As a result, Cornish game hens typically weigh less than 2 pounds, so they cook faster than larger chickens and look nice on a plate—traits that make them popular with consumers. They also feature small breasts and a high ratio of fatty skin to meat. The fatty underside bastes the meat as it cooks, which might explain why we found both their white and dark portions more tender, juicy, and flavorful than those on regular chickens. We prefer **Bell and Evans Cornish Game Hens**.

ELIMINATE MOISTURE Rubbing the skin with a mixture of salt and baking powder helped dry out the skin and promote crisping and browning, while air-drying the chickens further evaporated moisture from the skin.

BUTTERFLY AND SPLIT Removing the hens' backbones allowed them to lie flat, ensuring that the skin would have even more exposure to the heating element for uniform browning. Splitting them in half made them more manageable to serve.

ROAST ON A PREHEATED SHEET Starting the hens on a hot baking sheet jump-started the browning process.

USE HIGH HEAT Because Cornish hens contain a good amount of fat and moisture, they can withstand fairly intense heat without drying out; an initial stint at 500 degrees followed by a turn under the broiler gave us hens with juicy meat and beautifully burnished skin.

OVEN-ROASTED CORNISH GAME HENS

SERVES 4

This recipe requires refrigerating the salted meat for at least 4 hours and up to 24 hours before cooking.

4	(1¼- to 1½-pound) whole Cornish game hens, giblets discarded
	Kosher salt and pepper
¼	teaspoon vegetable oil
1	teaspoon baking powder
	Vegetable oil spray

1. Use kitchen shears to cut along both sides of backbone to remove it. Flatten hens and lay breast side up on counter. Using sharp chef's knife, cut through center of breast to make 2 halves.

2. Using your fingers, carefully separate skin from thighs and breast. Using metal skewer or tip of paring knife, poke 10 to 15 holes in fat deposits on top of breast halves and thighs. Tuck wing tips underneath hen. Pat hens dry with paper towels.

3. Sprinkle 1 tablespoon salt on underside (bone side) of hens. Combine 1 tablespoon salt and oil in small bowl and stir until salt is evenly coated with oil. Add baking powder and stir until well combined. Turn hens skin side up and rub salt mixture evenly over surface. Transfer hens, skin side up, to wire rack set in rimmed baking sheet, and refrigerate, uncovered, for at least 4 hours or up to 24 hours.

4. Adjust oven racks to upper-middle and lower positions, place rimmed baking sheet on lower rack, and heat oven to 500 degrees.

5. Once oven is fully heated, spray skin side of hens with oil spray and season with pepper to taste. Carefully transfer hens, skin side down, to baking sheet and cook for 10 minutes.

6. Remove hens from oven and heat broiler. Flip hens skin side up. Transfer baking sheet with hens to upper rack and broil until well browned and breasts register 160 degrees and thighs register 175 degrees, about 5 minutes, rotating as necessary to promote even browning. Transfer to platter or individual plates and serve.

HERB-ROASTED CORNISH GAME HENS

In step 3, combine 2 tablespoons kosher salt with 1 teaspoon dried thyme, 1 teaspoon dried marjoram, and 1 teaspoon dried crushed rosemary. Sprinkle half of salt mixture on underside of hens; stir oil into remaining salt-herb mixture until mixture is evenly coated with oil. Add baking powder to oil-salt mixture and proceed with recipe.

OREGANO-ANISE ROASTED CORNISH GAME HENS

In step 3, combine 2 tablespoons kosher salt with 1 teaspoon dried oregano, ½ teaspoon anise seeds, and ½ teaspoon hot smoked paprika. Sprinkle half of salt mixture on underside of hens; stir oil into remaining salt mixture until mixture is evenly coated with oil. Add baking powder to oil-salt mixture and proceed with recipe.

Grill-Roasted Cornish Game Hens

✓ WHY THIS RECIPE WORKS

Grilling has the potential to add smoky flavor and deliver really crisp skin on Cornish game hens, but it's not without its problems: Rendered fat from the skin can cause flare-ups, and getting the skin crisp without overcooking the delicate breast meat is tricky. We wanted great grilled game hens.

USE A DRIP PAN Placing a disposable roasting pan in the middle of the grill allowed us to bank coals on either side and also provided a place for the rendered fat to drip without causing flare-ups.

BUTTERFLY THE BIRDS Butterflying the hens had two benefits: It made each bird a uniform thickness, which promoted even cooking, and it also put all of the skin on one side, which could face the coals and crisp more quickly.

SECURE THE LEGS To keep our Cornish game hens intact once butterflied, we skewered them; this helped secure the legs to the body and prevented the skin from tearing.

SPICE IT UP To emphasize the smoky flavor of our birds, we used a spice rub. As a bonus, the rub helped crisp the skin even further, giving it a gorgeous mahogany hue.

GRILL-ROASTED CORNISH GAME HENS

SERVES 4

To add smoke flavor to the hens, use the optional wood chips. If you'd like to use wood chunks instead of wood chips when using a charcoal grill, substitute four medium wood chunks, soaked in water for 1 hour, for the wood chip packets. You will need four 8- to 10-inch flat metal skewers for this recipe. If desired, serve with Barbecue Glaze or Asian Barbecue Glaze (recipes follow).

Salt

4 (1¼- to 1½-pound) whole Cornish game hens, giblets discarded

2 tablespoons packed brown sugar

1 tablespoon paprika

2 teaspoons garlic powder

2 teaspoons chili powder

1 teaspoon pepper

1 teaspoon ground coriander

⅛ teaspoon cayenne pepper

4 cups wood chips, soaked in water for 15 minutes and drained (optional)

1 (16 by 12-inch) disposable aluminum roasting pan

1. TO BUTTERFLY GAME HENS: Use kitchen shears to cut along both sides of backbone to remove it. With skin side down, make ¼-inch cut into bone separating breast halves. Lightly press on ribs to flatten hen. Fold wing tips behind bird to secure them.

2. Dissolve ½ cup salt in 4 quarts cold water in large container. Submerge hens in brine, cover, and refrigerate for 30 minutes to 1 hour.

3. Combine sugar, paprika, garlic powder, chili powder, pepper, coriander, and cayenne in bowl. Remove hens from brine and pat dry with paper towels.

4. TO SKEWER HENS: Insert flat metal skewer ½ inch from end of drumstick through skin and meat and out other side. Turn leg so that end of drumstick faces wing, then insert tip of skewer into meaty section of thigh under bone. Press skewer all the way through breast and second thigh. Fold end of drumstick toward wing and insert skewer ½ inch from end. Press skewer so that blunt end rests against bird and stretches skin tight over legs, thighs, and breast halves. Rub hens evenly with spice mixture and refrigerate while preparing grill.

5. Using 2 large pieces of heavy-duty aluminum foil, wrap soaked chips, if using, in 2 foil packets and cut several vent holes in tops.

6A. FOR A CHARCOAL GRILL: Open bottom vent completely and place disposable pan in center of grill. Light large chimney starter filled with charcoal briquettes (6 quarts). When top coals are partially covered with ash, pour into 2 even piles on either side of disposable pan. Place 1 wood chip packet, if using, on each pile of coals. Set cooking grate in place, cover, and open lid vent completely. Heat grill until hot and wood chips are smoking, about 5 minutes.

6B. FOR A GAS GRILL: Place wood chip packets, if using, directly on primary burner. Turn all burners to high, cover, and heat grill until hot and wood chips are smoking, about 15 minutes. Turn all burners to medium. (Adjust burners as needed during cooking to maintain grill temperature of 325 degrees.)

7. Clean and oil cooking grate. Place hens in center of grill (over disposable pan if using charcoal), skin side down. Cover (position lid vent over birds if using charcoal) and cook until thighs register 160 degrees, 20 to 30 minutes.

8. Using tongs, move the birds to the hot sides of the grill (if using charcoal; 2 hens per side), keeping them skin side down, or turn all burners to high (if using gas). Cover and continue to cook until browned, about 5 minutes. Brush the birds with half of glaze, flip, and cook for 2 minutes. Brush remaining glaze

over hens, flip, and continue to cook until breasts register 160 degrees and thighs register 175 degrees, 1 to 3 minutes longer.

9. Transfer hens to carving board, tent loosely with foil, and let rest for 5 to 10 minutes. Cut hens in half through breastbone and serve.

BARBECUE GLAZE
MAKES ABOUT ½ CUP

½ cup ketchup
2 tablespoons packed brown sugar
1 tablespoon soy sauce
1 tablespoon distilled white vinegar
1 tablespoon yellow mustard
1 garlic clove, minced

Combine all ingredients in small saucepan, bring to simmer, and cook, stirring occasionally, until thickened, about 5 minutes.

ASIAN BARBECUE GLAZE
MAKES ABOUT ½ CUP

¼ cup ketchup
¼ cup hoisin sauce
2 tablespoons rice vinegar
1 tablespoon soy sauce
1 tablespoon toasted sesame oil
1 tablespoon grated fresh ginger

Combine all ingredients in small saucepan, bring to simmer, and cook, stirring occasionally, until thickened, about 5 minutes.

SECURING THE LEGS

To ensure even cooking and the crispiest skin, we butterflied the Cornish game hens using a process similar to butterflying a regular chicken (see page 438). Then, we skewered the legs to keep the birds intact on the grill.

1. Insert flat metal skewer ½ inch from end of drumstick through skin and meat and out other side.

2. Turn leg so that end of drumstick faces wing, then insert tip of skewer into meaty section of thigh under bone.

3. Press skewer all the way through breast and second thigh. Fold end of drumstick toward wing and insert skewer ½ inch from end.

4. Press skewer so that blunt end rests against bird and stretch skin tight over legs, thighs, and breast halves.

A Note on Conversions

Some say cooking is a science and an art. We would say that geography has a hand in it, too. Flour milled in the United Kingdom and elsewhere will feel and taste different from flour milled in the United States. So, while we cannot promise that the loaf of bread you bake in Canada or England will taste the same as a loaf baked in the States, we can offer guidelines for converting weights and measures. We also recommend that you rely on your instincts when making our recipes. Refer to the visual cues provided. If the bread dough hasn't "come together in a ball," as described, you may need to add more flour—even if the recipe doesn't tell you so. You be the judge.

The recipes in this book were developed using standard U.S. measures following U.S. government guidelines. The charts below offer equivalents for U.S., metric, and Imperial (U.K.) measures. All conversions are approximate and have been rounded up or down to the nearest whole number. For example:

1 teaspoon = 4.929 milliliters, rounded up to 5 milliliters
1 ounce = 28.349 grams, rounded down to 28 grams

VOLUME CONVERSIONS

U.S.	METRIC
1 teaspoon	5 milliliters
2 teaspoons	10 milliliters
1 tablespoon	15 milliliters
2 tablespoons	30 milliliters
¼ cup	59 milliliters
⅓ cup	79 milliliters
½ cup	118 milliliters
¾ cup	177 milliliters
1 cup	237 milliliters
1¼ cups	296 milliliters
1½ cups	355 milliliters
2 cups	473 milliliters
2½ cups	592 milliliters
3 cups	710 milliliters
4 cups (1 quart)	0.946 liter
1.06 quarts	1 liter
4 quarts (1 gallon)	3.8 liters

WEIGHT CONVERSIONS

OUNCES	GRAMS
½	14
¾	21
1	28
1½	43
2	57
2½	71
3	85
3½	99
4	113
4½	128
5	142
6	170
7	198
8	227
9	255
10	283
12	340
16 (1 pound)	454

CONVERSIONS FOR INGREDIENTS COMMONLY USED IN BAKING

Baking is an exacting science. Because measuring by weight is far more accurate than measuring by volume, and thus more likely to achieve reliable results, in our recipes we provide ounce measures in addition to cup measures for many ingredients. Refer to the chart below to convert these measures into grams.

INGREDIENT	OUNCES	GRAMS
Flour		
I cup all-purpose flour*	5	142
I cup cake flour	4	113
I cup whole wheat flour	5½	156
Sugar		
I cup granulated (white) sugar	7	198
I cup packed brown sugar (light or dark)	7	198
I cup confectioners' sugar	4	113
Cocoa Powder		
I cup cocoa powder	3	85
Butter†		
4 tablespoons (½ stick, or ¼ cup)	2	57
8 tablespoons (I stick, or ½ cup)	4	113
16 tablespoons (2 sticks, or I cup)	8	227

* U.S. all-purpose flour, the most frequently used flour in this book, does not contain leaveners, as some European flours do. These leavened flours are called self-rising or self-raising. If you are using self-rising flour, take this into consideration before adding leavening to a recipe.

† In the United States, butter is sold both salted and unsalted. We generally recommend unsalted butter. If you are using salted butter, take this into consideration before adding salt to a recipe.

OVEN TEMPERATURES

FAHRENHEIT	CELSIUS	GAS MARK (IMPERIAL)
225	105	¼
250	120	½
275	130	1
300	150	2
325	165	3
350	180	4
375	190	5
400	200	6
425	220	7
450	230	8
475	245	9

CONVERTING TEMPERATURES FROM AN INSTANT-READ THERMOMETER

We include doneness temperatures in many of our recipes, such as those for poultry, meat, and bread. We recommend an instant-read thermometer for the job. Refer to the table above to convert Fahrenheit degrees to Celsius. Or, for temperatures not represented in the chart, use this simple formula:

Subtract 32 degrees from the Fahrenheit reading, then divide the result by 1.8 to find the Celsius reading.

EXAMPLE:
"Roast until chicken thighs register 175 degrees."
To convert:

175° F − 32 = 143°
143° ÷ 1.8 = 79.44°C, rounded down to 79°C

Index

A

All-Purpose Gravy, 450–51

Almond(s)

Picada, 140

-Raisin Crust, Herbed, Indian-Spiced Roast Boneless Leg of Lamb
with, 298–99

Romesco Sauce, 104

Anchovies

fillets compared with paste, 204

Roasted Garlic Salsa Verde, 400–402

Andouille, about, 184

Anise-Oregano Roasted Cornish Game Hens, 460

Apple Cider

compared with apple juice, 236

–Golden Raisin Sauce, 241–42

Sauce, 213–14

Apple(s)

-Cherry Filling with Caraway, Grilled Pork Loin with, 237

-Cranberry Filling, Grilled Pork Loin with, 236–37

Dried Fruit and Nut Stuffing, 442

-Fennel Chutney, 260

-Ginger Glaze, 277

juice, compared with apple cider, 236

-Maple Glaze, Butterflied Turkey with, 448

Simple Applesauce, 186

Applesauce, Simple, 186

Apricots and Chickpeas, Moroccan Chicken with, 395

Arugula

a Bed of, Grilled Veal Chops on, 338

Salsa Verde with, 104

Asiago Cheese

about, 198

and Prosciutto, Crunchy Baked Pork Chops with, 198

Asian Barbecue Glaze, 463

Asian Barbecue Wet Rub, 219

Asparagus

Pork, and Onions, Spicy Stir-Fried, with Lemon Grass, 222–23

trimming tough ends, 222

Avocados

Chicken Enchiladas with Red Chili Sauce, 371–72

dicing, 371

Ground Beef Tacos, 150–51

B

Bacon

and Black Beans, Beef Chili with, 145

on a Charcoal Grill, 284

-Cheeseburgers, Well-Done, 158

cooking a few pieces on stovetop, 284

cured and smoked, about, 178

homemade, recipe for, 283–84

nitrites and nitrates in, 178

Oven-Fried, 284–86, *285*

-Wrapped Meatloaf with Brown Sugar–Ketchup Glaze, 165–66

-Wrapped Thick-Cut Pork Tenderloin Medallions, 213

Baking sheets, rimmed, ratings of, 26

Balsamic (Vinegar)

Capers, and Red Pepper, Braised Lamb Shoulder Chops with, 317

-Shallot Sauce with Rosemary and Mustard, 218

and Sweet Peppers, Pork Chops with, 200

Baltimore Pit Beef, *108*, 109–10

Bangers, about, 184

Barbecue, Dry Rub for, 248

Barbecued, Oven- , Spareribs, 264–65

Barbecued Baby Back Ribs, 272–73

Barbecued Beef Brisket, 116–17

Barbecued Beef Ribs, Texas, 110–11

Barbecued Chicken, Sweet and Tangy, *406*, 407–8

Barbecued Chicken Kebabs, *420*, 421–22

Barbecued Pork, Chinese, 243–44

Barbecued Pork Spareribs, 266–67

Barbecued Pulled Pork, 246–48, *247*

Barbecued Spareribs, Chinese-Style, 270–72

Barbecued Spareribs, Memphis-Style, *268*, 269–70

Barbecued Tri-Tip, California, *84*, 85–86

Barbecue Glaze, 463

D

Dairy, curdle-free, 63
Deep frying, note about, 75
Deep-frying oil, disposing of, 405
Deviled Crisp Breaded Chicken Cutlets, 365
Digital thermometers, ratings of, 25
Dried Cherry–Port Sauce with Onion and Marmalade, 217
Dried Fruit and Nut Stuffing, 442
Dry aging meat, 7
Dry Rub for Barbecue, 248
Dry Rub for Spareribs, 267
Dutch ovens, ratings of, 27

E

Eastern North Carolina Barbecue Sauce, 248
Easy Grilled Boneless Pork Chops, 204–5
Easy Pork Chops, 186–87
    with Brandy and Prunes, 187
    with Mustard-Sage Sauce, 187
Easy Roast Turkey Breast, 454
    with Lemon and Thyme, 454
    with Orange and Rosemary, 454
Eggplant
    Moussaka, 321–22
    Pork, and Onion, Stir-Fried, with Garlic and Black Pepper, 223–24
    Stir-Fried Red Curry Beef with, 71–72
    varieties of, 71, 322
Empanadas, Beef, 169–72, *170*
Enchiladas
    Chicken, with Red Chili Sauce, 371–72
    Verdes, 372–74
Equipment, for cooking meat, 24–27
Equipment, ratings of
    carving boards, 25
    carving forks, 24
    charcoal grills, 27
    cutting boards, 25
    Dutch ovens, 27
    fat separators, 25
    food processors, 25
    garlic press, 27
    gas grills, 27
    grill brushes, 266
    kitchen shears, 25
    knives, boning, 24
    knives, chef's, 24

Equipment, ratings of (cont.)
    knives, paring, 24
    knives, slicing, 24
    knives, steak, 24, 60
    measuring cups, 26
    measuring spoons, 26
    meat cleavers, 24
    meat pounders, 24
    meat tenderizers, hand-held, 24
    pepper mills, 27, 101
    rimmed baking sheets, 26
    roasting pans, 27
    saucepans, 27
    skillets, 26
    thermometers, digital, 25
    thermometers, oven, 26
    thermometers, remote, 25
    tongs, 26
    twine, 25
    V-racks, 27
Extra-Crunchy Fried Chicken, 404–5

F

Fajitas, Classic Beef, 88–89
Fajitas, Skillet Chicken, 366–69, *367*
Fat, skimming, methods for, 136
Fatback, about, 178
Fat separators
    alternatives to, 136
    ratings of, 25
Fennel
    -Apple Chutney, 260
    Garlic-Rosemary Roast Pork Loin with, 231
    preparing, 260, 442
    and Sausage Stuffing, 442–43
Fenugreek and Figs, Lamb Curry with, 306
Feta cheese
    Greek-Style Beef Pita Sandwiches, 326
    Greek-Style Lamb Pita Sandwiches, *324*, 325–26
    Grilled Greek-Style Lamb Pita Sandwiches, 326–27
    taste tests on, 326
Figs
    and Fenugreek, Lamb Curry with, 306
    and North African Spices, Braised Lamb Shoulder Chops with, 317
Filipino Chicken Adobo, 392–94, *393*
Fish sauce, about, 224

L

Lamb (about)

chops, salting, 5
domestic, flavor of, 290
doneness temperatures, 8, 295
foreshank/breast, about, 290
imported, flavor of, 290
leg
  about, 290
  shopping for, 292
loin
  about, 290
  shopping for, 292
primal cuts, 290
ribs
  about, 290
  rack of, trimming and frenching, 308
  shopping for, 291–92
shoulder
  about, 290
  shopping for, 291
young, flavor of, 290

Lamb (recipes)

Chops
  Parmesan Breaded, 310–11
  Rib or Loin, Charcoal-Grilled, 315–16
  Rib or Loin, Charcoal-Grilled, with Mediterranean Herb and
    Garlic Paste, 316
  Tandoori, 312–13
Chops, Shoulder
  Braised, with Capers, Balsamic Vinegar, and Red Pepper, 317
  Braised, with Figs and North African Spices, 317
  Braised, with Tomatoes and Red Wine, 316–17
  Grilled, 313–14
  Grilled, with Garlic-Rosemary Marinade, 315
  Grilled, with Near East Red Pepper Paste, 314
  Grilled, with Soy-Shallot Marinade, 315
Curry
  with Figs and Fenugreek, 306
  Indian, with Whole Spices, 305–6
Grilled Shish Kebab, 303–4
Ground, and Pasta Casserole (Pastitsio), 323–25
Irish Stew, 320–21
Kofte, Grilled, 327–28
Leg of
  Garlic-Roasted, 296–97
  Roast Boneless, Indian-Spiced, with Herbed Almond-Raisin Crust,
    298–99

Lamb (recipes), Leg of (cont.)

Roast Boneless, Moroccan-Spiced, 299–301
Roast Boneless, with Garlic, Herb, and Bread-Crumb Crust, 297–98
Roast Butterflied, with Coriander, Cumin, and Mustard Seeds,
  300, 301–2
Roast Butterflied, with Coriander, Rosemary, and Red Pepper, 302
Moussaka, 321–22
Pita Sandwiches
  Greek-Style, *324,* 325–26
  Grilled Greek-Style, 326–27
Rack of
  Grilled, 308–10, *309*
  Grilled, with Sweet Mustard Glaze, 310
  Simple Roasted, 306–7
Shanks
  Braised in Red Wine with Herbes de Provence, 317–18, *319*
  Braised with Lemon and Mint, 318
  Braised with North African Spices, 318

Latin Spice Rub, Crispy Pan-Fried Pork Chops with, 188

Leek, Vermouth, and Tarragon Pan Sauce, 357

Lemon Grass

preparing, 90
Spicy Stir-Fried Pork, Asparagus, and Onions with, 222–23

Lemon(s)

-Basil Salsa Verde, 104
-Caper Pan Sauce, Sautéed Chicken Cutlets with, 356–57
Chicken with Rosemary, Grilled, *436,* 437–38
and Garlic, Rosemary-Mint Marinade with, 304
Gremolata, 341
juicing, tip for, 307
and Mint, Lamb Shanks Braised with, 318
and Olive Oil, Grilled Tuscan Steaks with, 52–54, *53*
and Olives, Moroccan Chicken with, 394–95
-Parsley Chicken Breasts, Grilled, 383–84
-Parsley Sauce, 331
and Rosemary Marinade, Grilled Beef Kebabs with, 92–93
-Rosemary Pan Sauce, Crispy-Skinned Chicken Breasts with, 362
-Tarragon Pan Sauce, 426
and Thyme, Easy Roast Turkey Breast with, 454
zested, keeping juicy, 92
zesting, 437

Lettuce

Bibb, storing, 226
Chicken Enchiladas with Red Chili Sauce, 371–72
Greek-Style Beef Pita Sandwiches, 326
Greek-Style Lamb Pita Sandwiches, *324,* 325–26
Grilled Greek-Style Lamb Pita Sandwiches, 326–27
Ground Beef Tacos, 150–51
Wraps, Thai Pork, 224–26, *225*

M

U

V